Lincoln Christian College

Less Than Conquerors
How Evangelicals Entered the Twentieth Century

Douglas Frank

William B. Eerdmans Publishing Company
Grand Rapids, Michigan

To my father and mother,
Walter and Ethel,
who first taught me the difference
between being religious and hearing the good news

Library of Congress Cataloging-in-Publication Data:

Frank, Douglas, 1941-
Less than conquerors.

Bibliography: p. 299
1. Evangelicalism—United States—History—19th
century. 2. Evangelicalism—United States—History—20th
century. 3. United States—Church history—19th century.
4. United States—Church history—20th century.
I. Title
BR1642.U5F73   1986   277.3'081   86-24355

ISBN 0-8028-0228-1

Contents

Preface   vii

I. Harder for a Rich Man   1

II. I Will Die in My Nest   30

III. I Am Doing a Work in Your Days   60

IV. Bear Fruit That Befits Repentance   103

V. They Have Healed My People Lightly   167

VI. Put No Confidence in the Flesh   232

Epilogue   271

Notes   279

Bibliography   299

Index   305

Scripture Index   309

To point out the sins, faults, and weaknesses of the scholastics and the mystics, Reformers and Papists, Lutherans and Reformed, rationalists and pietists, orthodox and liberal—even though these failings certainly dare not be overlooked or left unmentioned—cannot become a more urgent task than seeing and understanding them all in the light of the forgiveness of sins that is necessary and promised to us all.

—KARL BARTH

Preface

I once read about certain primitive tribespeople who, when asked how they had come to live on their particular spot of earth, informed the inquisitive anthropologist that their ancestors had descended from the heavens on a vine. I grew up thinking something very similar about where evangelicals had come from. We were simply the current manifestation of the first-century church, as modified very slightly, after a long period of Roman darkness, by the Protestant Reformation. But exactly how we had gotten here from there was shrouded in a mystery that no one seemed interested in exploring. That the particulars of our journey through history, over many centuries and in many lands, and especially in this American land, might have something to do with our present beliefs and practices, did not seem to occur to anybody. This left us fairly naive and un-self-critical at best. At worst it tempted us to self-righteousness, as if we had escaped the ravages of history by our own merits, and thus embodied the only faithful remnant still in evidence.

This book is a kind of report on my own journey toward what I think is a more honest historical consciousness. It began by surprise, despite my professional training in historical study. When I presented the sabbatical committee at Trinity College with the rough outline of a book I hoped to write, my concern was to investigate the evangelical community in American society today. Background reading, especially in George Marsden's book *Fundamentalism and American Culture*, gradually drew me into the late nineteenth and early twentieth centuries, where the most significant clues to explain our current situation seemed to lay hidden. A projected introductory chapter, intended as a brief summary of evangelicalism's recent history, kept growing, and when a year of study found me still nosing around in the nineteenth century, I knew I had a very different book to write.

The focus of my study, then, is on my evangelical forebears at the turn of the last century. At one level, the parameters seem narrow. I have confined my study to several theological, devotional, and evangelistic currents that achieved popularity during the period from 1850 to 1920, which, I will try to show, was a traumatic period for American evangelicals. The currents I have chosen are (1) dispensational premillennialism, a unique interpretation of world history that looked enthusiastically to the

vii

imminent second coming of Jesus Christ; (2) the Victorious Life theology, which offered Christians a mechanism whereby they might live (or, better, Christ might live through them) a life of perfect obedience and emotional calm; and (3) the evangelistic revivalism of Billy Sunday, whose buffoonery masked his role as the most significant and revealing champion of the Lord in his day. These three ingredients in the emerging twentieth-century evangelical consensus found their adherents most commonly among white, northern, middle-class Christians who had been strongly influenced by Calvinist theology—in other words, Baptists and Presbyterians. My study thus ignores a major portion of the evangelical Christian community, from the "evangelical liberals" on the one end of the spectrum to the Pentecostal groups on the other, not to mention the black evangelicals and the evangelical community in the South. All these deserve closer attention in their own right. My narrower focus is accounted for less by the historical importance of the groups I chose—although I do believe they represent a kind of mainstream evangelicalism and encompass many of the theological emphases of these other groups—than by sheer personal interest. They are my people, and thus to know them is to know myself.

So what follows is a very personal document. It is not an autobiography, and thus the first few pages may be misleading. It is a study of evangelical theology at a crucial point in American history, a time of difficulty for all Americans, and particularly evangelicals. But the theology that evolved during those years has helped define evangelicalism throughout the twentieth century, continuing to do so as that century draws to its close. It has helped define me, my closest friends and family, the churches of which I have been a part, the colleges I have been associated with as student and teacher, and the books I have read. It has fashioned the lenses through which, until very recently, I read the Bible, lenses on the whole more powerful because I did not know I wore them. Recognizing and evaluating those lenses is very much what this book is about, and that, I hope, is what may recommend it to a lay evangelical audience and not just historians or theologians. I hope you will read it to find yourself in it, as I have written it to find myself.

More important than finding myself, however, has been the opportunity this study has afforded me of hearing the gospel. I am not sure the two can be disentangled, but I do know that the really good news in my life these last several years has had to do with Jesus Christ, not self-discovery. My experience as an "evangelical by coercion"—the very gentle, caring coercion of an evangelical family upbringing—was that the gospel was boring. Familiarity bred *ennui*, if not contempt. If I am hard on an earlier generation of evangelicals in this book, it is because I believe that they are unwittingly and in part (but only in part) responsible for this boredom. They hid the gospel behind a wall of doctrinal certainties, theo-

logical catchwords, devotional prescriptions, and obvious self-justifica-
tions, all of which informed the reader of exactly what he or she would
find in the pages of the Bible before the book was even opened, making it
much less probable that the Word might be a surprise. They did so with a
reason, as I hope to show, although a reason of the heart, not one they
ever articulated. Moreover, their true intentions in handling the gospel
were often very subtly in conflict with that gospel, again in a way quite
hidden from themselves. All this simply confirms what the Bible has long
known and proclaimed concerning the human condition: that the heart is
deceitful beyond understanding and that we are lost in a thick darkness.
It is thus a certainty that my own hidden intentions and self-deceits will
get in the way of my articulation of the gospel, and so I offer my study
with a certain fear and trembling. God has always taken the risk,
however, of placing his Word into unfaithful human hands, and seems to
have a means of giving that Word a penetrating and a comforting power
in the most unpromising of circumstances. I trust he will do so for the
readers of this book.

I have been told by trusted, friendly critics that the tone of my pages is
negative. This surprised me at first, since I have understood my purpose
from the very beginning to be a constructive one. I yearn for a fresh
visitation by the Word, and for the gospel to be spoken and heard by
American Christians. My hope is that by examining evangelicalism in the
presence of the biblical text, and in reference to my own self-deceptions
and those of the community of evangelicals to which I belong, I might
contribute to the clearing of the ground for such a visitation. I now see
that such ground-clearing might be perceived as unrelentingly negative. I
confess that I have not found a way to relieve the reader of that spirit. It is
my sincere hope, however, that the bad news that covers many of these
pages will not dim but rather cause to shine ever more brightly the good
news of salvation in Jesus Christ.

My largest debt incurred in the writing of this book is to a good friend
and colleague, John Linton. John has conducted a running seminar in
biblical exegesis for me ever since our first acquaintance a decade ago. His
reading of the biblical text has set me back on my heels time and again and
has frequently been the occasion for my stubborn ears at last to hear the
good news in all its stunning and joyful immediacy. The biblical themes
utilized in the following chapters were almost entirely at John's suggestion, and in working out those themes I have followed his exegetical
formulations in almost every detail. John is a few steps ahead of me in
understanding the gospel, and so I suspect that my phrasing and elaboration are not always exactly as he would have written them. But I present
them to him as a kind of midterm examination, and I know that he will be
as generous in grading me as he has been with others of his students
through the years.

Much of my dialogue with John has taken place at the Oregon Extension of Trinity College. Our small mountain community of Lincoln, in southern Oregon, hosts about thirty undergraduate students every fall for an intensive, biblically oriented, interdisciplinary liberal arts study program. A very rich and stimulating conversation has been conducted there since its inception over a decade ago, and it has been primarily in the course of that conversation that I have thought most fruitfully about evangelicalism in its historic and contemporary forms and in its relations to the wider currents in American society. My faculty colleagues and very dear friends Jim Titus and Sam Alvord have consistently been vital participants in that conversation from its inception in late-night campfire ramblings, and it is under their prodding and in their presence that I have experienced most of my intellectual as well as spiritual development. Both of them also helped prepare this manuscript in specific, sacrificial ways. I thank them for their contributions to my thought as well as to my life.

Of the many others to whom I am indebted, I name only a few: Pat Alvord, Steve and Maurine Bridges, Nancy Linton, Angelika Titus, Anne Foley, Dave and Kate Willis, Howard and Esther Claassen, Larry Nyberg, and Steve Cory for their unique contributions to life in the Lincoln community; Bobby Sloan for his serious and sensitive friendship, for his eagerness for the gospel, and for encouraging me to listen to my intuitions; Mark Noll for reading an early draft and emboldening me with his enthusiasm; Joel Carpenter, Kenn Inskeep, David Schlafer, Ken Shipps, Kevin and Carole Cragg, Bill Moulder, Doris Roethlisberger, Will Graddy, Ed Hakes, Jacqueline Bell, and Dawn Ward for participating in my education in the faculty lounge at Trinity College; Bob Baptista for consistent support and a timely sabbatical; Loren and Mary Ruth Wilkinson for challenging my ideas but still inviting me to Regent College to hone them at their expense; Gary Lee, Jon Pott, and Charles Van Hof for making publication possible and pleasurable; Loren Peterson and Linda Buturain for hours spent at the word processor on my behalf; Stacy Sheagley, for conscientious proofreading; my neighbors in the Lincoln Christian Church for studying the Bible diligently with me; and my students over the years for sharing with me their experiences of "growing up evangelical" and for asking me the right questions. I thank, also, two whom I know primarily through their books: George Marsden for writing a work to which mine is largely an edifying footnote, and Jacques Ellul for setting a standard in biblically based social critique that is as generally unrecognized as it is unparalleled.

As is customary, I come at the end of all acknowledgments to the mention of those who are beyond acknowledgment. My wife is Marjorie and my daughter is Sara. A simple "thank you" seems an insufficient response to their love. But it will have to do, for now.

Chapter I

Harder for a Rich Man

I

I grew up in the 1940s and 1950s in a world I knew was shrinking. As a child of fundamentalist parents, I carried with me a sense of my own strangeness in an increasingly strange land. I knew my faith was shared by only a few—and those few not, on the whole, among the mighty of the land. Certainly, we could point to the successful businessman who shared our humble pew; but the rarity of such an exception and the attention paid him served only to prove the rule. Occasionally we remarked gratefully on a successful revival meeting—these were the days of the young evangelist Billy Graham—but we knew that even conversions by the thousands were barely making a dent on the empire of unbelief America had become. Jesus' words about the congestion on the broad road to destruction seemed confirmed in our own neighborhood, and his description of the relative unpopularity of the narrow road helped form our consciousness of ourselves and our place in a secular society.

It came as something of a surprise to me, therefore, to see what amounted to an evangelical cultural resurgence beginning to take shape in the decade of the 1970s. Who would have predicted the election of an evangelical as president of the United States, or the popularity of television evangelists and Christian recording stars, or the apparent revival of conservative moral standards along with the development of a political organization powerful enough to turn them into campaign issues? Who could have expected the revival of a frank supernaturalism in the midst of an urban, technological, media-soaked, scientifically oriented environment? We knew, of course, that there had been a time when the nation had been called "Christian"—when people much like ourselves, we thought, had actually shaped the society to reflect biblical norms. But the memory of that time was very faint. Our clearest historical examples of a Christian cultural dominance seemed to come from the very first days of our nation's colonial history, when Pilgrims and Puritans and Quakers had set out with good intentions to build a "city on a hill." Even a

1

modicum of historical understanding seemed to indicate that the Christian consensus had only lasted a few years, perhaps decades at best, and that by the eighteenth century the Enlightenment and the first thrusts of pluralism had pretty much done the city on the hill to death. The notion that now, after two or three centuries, and at the very brink of the last times, America might actually turn to God was a bit hard to swallow.

But there was, indeed, some evidence that America was turning to God, or at least that God was receiving a somewhat better press than usual. This meant a kind of identity crisis for many evangelicals. Woven firmly into our self-image, by at least a century of cultural backpedaling, was the defensiveness of an embattled minority. The possibility of real social, or even political, power threw us off balance and raised questions that we had not taken seriously for several generations. Is there such a thing as a Christian nation? Is the great tribulation perhaps not so near at hand as we thought? Is evangelism too narrow a scope for Christian action in the world? Should we join the struggle for political influence in our nation? Might Christian moral values once again bring the unruly American people under rein? Such questions, arising out of the widespread confusion of the 1960s and 1970s, fomented new theological ruminations and also sent many of us scurrying through the pages of history in search of a guiding precedent.

As it happened, there was just such a precedent waiting to be rediscovered by a new generation of Christian historians, themselves examples of the rising cultural respectability of evangelicalism and the awakening of interest in evangelical roots. That precedent was a period in the mid-nineteenth century when, it could be said, evangelical Christians "ran the show" in the United States.[1] During the decades roughly bounded by 1820 and 1860, it seems, the spirit and the language, the concerns and the aspirations of evangelicals dominated the national consciousness and set the national agenda. Dissenting, unbelieving, and even scoffing voices were present, of course, and greatly to be deplored. But they were muted—enough so, at least, that they offered no real challenge to the commonplace assumption of America's status as a "Christian nation."[2] Pulpits and religious periodicals across the land rang with the rhetoric of patriotic self-congratulation. The Second Great Awakening, a decades-long spiritual revival of national scope, had shaped an American citizenry that professed a Christian experience growing out of a personal meeting with God. The newly converted aspired to exacting moral standards. They put in a hard day's work at the office, factory, or farm, professed to do business with honesty, integrity, and the hope of fair monetary gain, and faithfully attended to civic duties. All this contributed to the widespread expectation that the kingdom of God was at hand in America, an expectation not the least dampened by the bloody Civil War. In 1865 the churchman Edward Beecher could exult: "Now that God has smitten slavery unto death, he has opened the way for the redemption of our whole social system."[3]

Leading twentieth-century American historians had noted this mid-nineteenth-century evangelical hegemony for at least several decades before evangelicals became interested in looking more closely at the period.[4] The study of history, it appears, is not a disinterested exploration of an arbitrarily selected portion of the past so much as a very selective ransacking of that past for clues to our identity and information that might be useful in accomplishing our goals. For the better part of a century, since the demise of the celebrated mid-nineteenth-century Christian consensus, evangelicals had not been terribly interested in their own history. A shrinking and defensive minority does not find it fruitful or comforting to remember when it was "running the show," particularly if those days seem gone forever. They might keep alive a hazy kind of nostalgia for "the good old days," but they have little to gain by scholarly concentration on the times of their lost dominance. This is especially true if their adjustment to the loss of dominance has led them to a new vision of history as an ineluctable downward spiral leading to the apostasy and wickedness of the very last times before the supernatural return of Christ. There is no reason for an interest in history when we believe that our imminent rescue will come from beyond history and will put history to an end.

So twentieth-century evangelicalism evinced little interest in its own history—for understandable reasons. Until recently, that is, when evangelicalism once again began to look like a going concern. Two evangelical factions in particular, each with a growing self-confidence and aspirations toward influence in American society, discovered a useful past in mid-nineteenth-century evangelicalism. The first of these was a group of social activists of a dissenting spirit that coalesced out of the protests against racism and the Vietnam War in the late 1960s and achieved self-definition in the formation of Evangelicals for Social Action in 1973. The past these Christian activists of the left discovered was the one in which evangelicals of many denominations had marched out into the political arena to champion the rights of black slaves, women, the poor, the illiterate, and other suffering minorities. An early favorite in chronicling the last century's period of evangelical political and social activism was Timothy L. Smith's book *Revivalism and Social Reform,* published in 1957; but the most celebrated and useful recent statement has been Donald Dayton's *Discovering an Evangelical Heritage* (1976). Its obvious delight in the crusading spirit of the evangelicals of a century past was echoed by a younger generation of

Christians, who read *Sojourners* and *The Other Side* magazines and joined the battle against racism, nuclearism, and the oppression of peoples here in America and around the world. The message of these books and magazines, often implicit, seemed unmistakable: "We did it before, and we can do it again."

Much the same message emerged in the 1970s from the evangelical right, though to "do it again" naturally meant something quite different. These evangelicals, led by the successful television preacher Jerry Falwell and inspired by the ideas of Francis Schaeffer, turned to the same mid-nineteenth-century epoch for an example of a time when Americans were truly "one nation under God" and shared a single outlook on life—and particularly on moral issues. In the America of a century ago, the original "moral majority" had found such things as abortion, homosexuality, divorce, sexual promiscuity, and pornography utterly distasteful. The sensibilities of the nation, it was said, were rooted in a Christian dogma faithful to the Bible, even though each citizen who shared them was not necessarily a fervent, or even professed, Christian. To the evangelical right wing in the 1970s, the growth of their numbers gave promise of returning to that time of moral consensus, and thus of turning around the century-long drift—greatly accelerated during the 1960s—toward secularism and "humanism" and the kind of moral laxity that made good people fear for their children. The vision of a nation dominated by evangelicals in the nineteenth century meant comfort and hope for those evangelicals striving for hegemony in the twentieth.

I find it interesting that these two manifestations of the evangelical resurgence should have found useful precedents in the very same historical era. Their use of these precedents appears essentially self-serving, and yet what an ideological difference seems to exist between the selves being served! The Christian activists of the left are, on the whole, alienated from the capitalistic economic system, as they are from American economic and military policies around the world. They are critical of America's role in the arms race, and they tend to recommend some version of unilateral action to freeze or diminish the number of bombs and missiles in the world. They are aware of the powerful opiate represented by the affluent lifestyle of middle-class America, and their concern is to identify with its victims, the poor. They are sympathetic to the demands of women for equal treatment, and they seem interested in fashioning Christians into communities at the same time that they act to strengthen the traditional family. Those who style themselves a "moral majority," on the other hand, seem patriotically committed both to the capitalist system and to American dominance around the world. They tend to support the building of a strong nuclear deterrent force and are more comfortable with military action than are their fellow Christians on the left. They are conservative on social issues such as women's liberation, and they focus on the nuclear family as the backbone of a God-fearing country. In most ways, the American way of life is not offensive to them, although they are sincere in rejecting "materialism." There are very few social or political issues on which these two evangelical factions see eye to eye, and yet both seem to draw inspiration from the very same era in American history. Perhaps their ideological differences hide a deeper similarity.

I would suggest that they do. What they both seem to find attractive about the nineteenth-century evangelical consensus is precisely that it "ran the show." Both the left and the right in evangelicalism today would, I suspect, like to run the show. Each believes it knows what the country needs, and each craves the influence to implement its vision. The rapid and highly visible emergence of evangelicalism during the 1970s and '80s gives each faction the hope that perhaps this influence is within its grasp. It is significant, I think, that the *Sojourners* community moved from Chicago to Washington, D.C., the seat of national power, and that the Moral Majority has aligned itself with the leading nonreligious but conservative political action groups, whose financial and technological resources are directed toward victory at the polls. The evangelicals of the left and the evangelicals of the right may not share political platforms, but they do seem to share a desire to remake America according to their own version of Christian principles, and they like the fact that at one time in our history evangelicals had the opportunity to do exactly that.

From a commonsense point of view, all this is quite normal. Power is a reality in human society, and someone will possess it. In a democratic society this power is meant to be most accessible to the people who organize or sway the largest number of their fellow citizens. Evil forces can exercise power by this means, as can good forces. And in this sense it appears that power is neutral, available to all comers and with a potential to effect any cause, noble or destructive. Why should not Christians grasp this power when they have the chance and wield it for the cause of Christ? Is not power more to be trusted in the hands of Christians than in those of unbelievers? Will not Christians ultimately rule in people's best interests? If Christians refuse to exercise power, the field is left to the enemy, and all mankind suffers as a result. No one who truly loves his or her neighbor would wish this on the world.

So goes the argument from common sense. It is an appealing argument, if only because the alternative seems so uncharitable and ultimately unacceptable. It is a troublesome argument, however, because it seems in one very important respect to run against a central biblical understanding. Those characters to whom God spoke in the Bible—and who had ears to hear—were not much impressed with their own success or power in this realm. On the contrary, they were aware of themselves as downtrodden, as empty, as failures by worldly standards, as foolish in the cause of the gospel. They pointed not to the possibilities of their own power but to the power of God that, in human terms, appears to be weakness. They seem to have heard Jesus' warning that they went out as sheep among wolves, and they did not expect that the tables would be turned in this life so that they might enjoy exercising the power of the wolves. They did not long for the day when they would once again be in the driver's seat, but they longed for the Driver to come. They did not admire worldly influence but gloried in their sufferings.

Those who hear the Word of God and hear it truly are those to whom Jesus refers as the "poor in spirit." The psalmist is this poor one when he writes:

> But thou, O God my Lord,
>   deal on my behalf for thy name's sake;
>   because thy steadfast love is good, deliver me!
> For I am poor and needy,
>   and my heart is stricken within me.
> I am gone, like a shadow at evening;
>   I am shaken off like a locust.
> My knees are weak through fasting;
>   my body has become gaunt.
> I am an object of scorn to my accusers;
>   when they see me, they wag their heads.
> Help me, O Lord my God!
>   Save me according to thy steadfast love!
>   (Ps. 109:21-26)

The writer of this psalm is clearly aware of his lostness, not of his success. He knows that, even as king, his hope is not in his exercise of power but in the gracious deliverance of the Lord. He is not looking backward to a time of his own ascendancy, but forward to God's salvation; and it is to this God, not his own conquering armies, that his praise is lifted. The psalmist knows he is bereft. The Bible presents him as poor and recommends to us his poverty.

The Bible also knows quite another sort of person, one who points confidently to his or her own assets as signs of worth and guarantees of security. It calls this person rich, and "woe to the rich" is its refrain. We are used to hearing this refrain directed solely against those who possess great material wealth. I find this convenient, because it lets me off the hook in most respects; but I also find it quite natural, living as I do in a money-soaked society where economic values dominate our private lives as well as our public policy decisions. Unfortunately, the evangelical left has often helped muddy the waters by framing the Bible's understanding of the rich person in narrow economic terms—and thus losing the deeper spiritual import of richness. The disciples, however, give us a hint of this deeper level in their reaction to Jesus' words, "How hard it will be for those who have riches to enter the kingdom of God!" (Mk. 10:23ff.). In their astonishment they asked: "Then who can be saved?" Why were they astonished? Perhaps because it dawned on them that, even though they had "left everything" to follow Jesus, they were somehow still potentially included in the category of those having riches. Perhaps they were beginning to understand that riches include more than houses and lands.

I would suggest that, in biblical terms, to be rich means to see oneself not as poor and needy but as quite adequately prepared to meet life's challenges, and thus as needless of the grace of God. The rich are those whose "wealth"—whether it be actual money and goods, or perhaps talent, connections, future prospects, morality, power, success, reputation, or any other personal resources—permits them to believe that they are somehow insulated from disaster by what they possess. These spiritually rich take a certain comfort in their circumstances. They congratulate themselves on their good fortune and derive from it a feeling of invulnerability. On the basis of past successes they predict even brighter futures. If they speak of God, it is only lip service, because they have no need of anyone but themselves. In all these ways they assert their independence and self-sufficiency—in the manner of the character in Jesus' parable:

> The land of a rich man brought forth plentifully; and he thought to himself, "What shall I do, for I have nowhere to store my crops?" And he said, "I will do this: I will pull down my barns, and build larger ones; and there I will store all my grain and my goods. And I will say to my soul, Soul, you have ample goods laid up for many years; take your ease, eat, drink, be merry." But God said to him, "Fool! This night your soul is required of you; and the things you have prepared, whose will they be?" So is he who lays up treasure for himself, and is not rich toward God.
>
> (Lk. 12:16b-21)

If the rich of the Bible are really as we have described them, and if the disciples themselves had to awaken to their own richness, then it is safe to surmise that to be rich is simply to be human. Perhaps all who enter the kingdom of God enter as camels. Who of us does not strive for the kind of success that can calm our fears and offer a kind of invulnerability? For what one of us does the taste of success not become addicting? How often has good fortune not left us standing just a little taller, a little less "poor in spirit" before God, not tempted us to feel somewhat more self-sufficient despite our ritual use of pious language? If we are dealing here with a situation confronting us all, then we should not be surprised if the new prominence enjoyed by evangelicals in our own day tempts them to a certain self-righteous quest for power, causes them to be quite pleased with themselves and optimistic about their prospects. Nor should we be surprised when their search for historical parallels lands them in that period of American history when evangelicals, along with their countrymen in general, felt very complacent, very rich indeed.

II

As American evangelicals surveyed their world in the mid-nineteenth century, they found themselves perched atop one of history's great success stories. They and their fellow citizens comprised the ragtag and restless castoffs of a culturally advanced and settled European continent, many arriving penniless and illiterate on these shores. Much of their new homeland was less than a lifetime away from uninhabited forest and was peopled by foreboding natives. By the skin of their teeth, and the luck of distracting hostilities elsewhere, they had won their independence, only to confront their own geographical, class, political, and religious quarrels that bade fair to tear them into thirteen separate entities. They had chosen a system of government that no one predicted could work. They had inherited an economy tuned to the needs of the British Empire and not to the requirements of balance and independence. But here they were, as the middle decades of the nineteenth century approached, thriving in almost every respect, proudly putting the "old world" to shame, mocking the predictions of their hasty demise, astounding foreign visitors with their energy and the return they were enjoying on investments of labor and hope.

The most apparent example of their success—and one related to our theme of richness—was the working of the American economy. Free-enterprise capitalism was turning out to be tailor-made for the opportunities of a raw but bountiful land. It offered the promise that a little money and a measure of skill, when combined with frugality, hard work, and foresight, would pay handsome dividends in material comfort. Recent studies have tended to show that "rags to riches" was not entirely a myth in the middle decades of the nineteenth century.[5] A farmer's son, an apprentice machinist, an initially unskilled factory worker, an immigrant craftsman—each one could save his money for a time, open a modest workshop, eventually own a sizable factory, and live in a style his parents most certainly would have considered princely beyond their dreams. In Paterson, New Jersey, for example, in the 1850s, "so many successful manufacturers who had begun as workers walked the streets of that city . . . that it is not hard to believe that others less successful or just starting out on the lower rungs of the occupational mobility ladder could be convinced by personal knowledge that 'hard work' resulted in spectacular material and social improvement."[6] In his thorough study of the manufacturing villages surrounding Rockdale, Pennsylvania, Anthony F. C. Wallace demonstrates the very same pattern during these decades. Humble cotton-mill employees developed their skills, worked long hours, and saved money even at low wages, then invested in a small business or farm (often farther west) and became respected members of the middle class. Their examples reinforced the common understanding of America as a place where anybody who really wanted to could make it, if not to the very top, at least to a position of surprising comfort and security.[7]

The American economy experienced unusual growth in the period from 1840 to 1860. American population almost doubled, fed in part by the rapidly increasing rate of immigration from Great Britain and Western Europe. In 1854, a record year, over half a million immigrants arrived on American shores. This influx contributed to the most rapid urbanization in American history. In 1840 only forty-four cities could boast populations of 8,000 or more; by 1860, 141 cities had reached that size. During these two decades New York City increased its population from about 300,000 to over 1.1 million and became the financial and commercial hub of the expanding nation. Health and sanitary conditions may have worsened somewhat during these years, as municipalities grew faster than did the technologies to make them livable. Most larger cities were only beginning to solve the problems of water supply, adequate street lighting, sewage disposal, transportation, and public safety before the Civil War.

Meanwhile, these cities played a most important part in the rapidly advancing industrialization of the United States. They supplied both labor and markets as the factory system invaded one industry after another, making the "American system of manufacturing"—involving standardization, interchangeable parts, extensive use of machine tools—the envy of Western nations and an object of imitation even in such an advanced nation as Great Britain. British visitors estimated that in the 1850s "American levels of mechanization and standardization led the world when it came to woodwork, shoes, plows and mowing machines, files, nuts, bolts, screws, nails, locks, clocks, watches, pistols, typewriters, sewing machines, and railroad locomotives."[8] Between 1840 and 1860 the aggregate value of American manufactured goods quadrupled. During the

1850s output soared, especially in textiles. Economic interchange was made possible first by a system of roads and canals, and then by the railroads, which first appeared as a practical reality in 1830 but had grown to a network of 30,000 miles by 1860. The railroad not only moved people and goods; it also represented a constant demand for iron (later steel) and coal, key industries in the widening economic transformation.

The spirit of innovation seemed to be affecting every area of economic life in the mid-nineteenth century. Patents increased 1,000 percent between 1840 and 1860; more than 25,000 were registered during the 1850s alone. These decades saw the invention of the Morse telegraph, the McCormick harvester, Goodyear's process for vulcanizing rubber, Elias Howe's sewing machine—to name only the most prominent. Nowhere did the newly invented machines have more of a transforming effect than in American agriculture. The antebellum period was "the brightest in American agricultural history," in the words of one historian, "an era of confident expansion in which the future looked secure."[9] As the Census of 1860 reported:

> By the improved plow, labor equivalent to that of one horse in three is saved. By means of drills two bushels of seed will go as far as three bushels scattered broadcast, while the yield is increased six to eight bushels per acre. . . . The reaping machine is a saving of more than one-third the labor when it cuts and rakes. . . . The threshing machine is a saving of two-thirds on the old hand flail mode. . . . The saving in the labor of handling hay in the field and barn by means of horserakes and horsehayforks is equal to one-half.[10]

Agricultural productivity and the export of staple crops grew rapidly, and rising farm income made possible many of the comforts of life to the average farm family.

> Drafty log houses, with their crude interiors, were being abandoned for frame structures with decorative fireplaces, sturdy stoves with provisions for heating water, sufficient bedrooms to provide for the growing family, and a well-shuttered parlor for the entertainment of visiting clergymen, politicians, and relatives. Emphasis upon self-sufficiency was declining, spinning and weaving were moving into the new factories, cheese-making was just beginning to be centered in modern establishments, and increasing dependence was being placed on store goods. New and tighter barns, with great mows overhanging the stalls, and with rope and pulley devices for unloading hay, were lightening the work load. . . .[11]

From the vantage point of the farmer in the 1850s, "everything seemed to be going his way."[12]

The benefits of industrialization were not limited to farmers, of course.

While conditions among the poorer working classes of the eastern cities were often appalling, the middle classes enjoyed substantial increases in per capita incomes and thus also in material benefits during these years. Machine-produced objects now made their appearance in daily life: safety pins, cotton textiles, window glass, floor carpeting.

> In good but not lavish homes of the 1860s, there were cast-iron stoves, spring mattresses, roller shades at the windows, flush toilets, wallpaper, gaslights, "patent" furniture, silver-plated tableware, a daguerreotype on the wall. Perhaps the most important change, in terms of quality of life, was the invention of chloroform, the first effective anesthetic.[13]

Such standard, home-produced items as clothing, soap, beer, flour, and tools could now be "store-bought." Cheap watches, vulcanized rainwear, factory-sewn shoes, and railroad travel all helped reduce the differences between upper- and middle-class lifestyles. Although we now see that the period of greatest industrial transformation was still in the future, to the Americans of the 1840s and 1850s, "the momentum of change was unmistakable," and the sense of economic well-being unprecedented.[14]

Certainly such economic successes, and the fact that evangelicals participated fully in their fruits, must have contributed to the sense of self-satisfaction one hears in the testimony of mid-nineteenth-century Americans. But evangelicals were interested in more than quantitative indexes of material well-being. They were interested in the advancement of the kingdom of God, and the figures looked bright in that department as well. To Americans, as well as to foreign travelers, the nation seemed swept by a religious interest.[15] Between 1832 and 1854, the number of evangelical clergy increased at a rate more than double the population growth. The immigrant Lutheran churchman Philip Schaff noted that New York City had about five times as many churches per capita as the city of Berlin. About twice as many American citizens, proportionately, claimed membership in a Protestant congregation as had at the turn of the century, and this at a time when, particularly in evangelical groups, such membership was "a strenuous affair."[16] Schaff declared: "There are in America probably more awakened souls and more individual self-sacrifice for religious purposes, proportionately, than in any other country in the world, Scotland alone, perhaps, excepted."[17]

The most common and successful means of "awakening" American souls, and the clearest evidence of the triumph of the faith, was the revival. In America, the revival was a fact of religious life—a means of recruiting new church members, revitalizing old ones, and raising the general moral tone of society. During a revival the Spirit of the Lord was said to visit a people, to call them to repent of their sins, and to offer them

cleansing. Often the medium of revival was a particularly dynamic pastor
or evangelist who spoke with power and directness to the hearts of men
and women, and whose presence virtually guaranteed a fresh outpouring
of the Spirit. Sure marks of a revival were certain dramatic emotional
exhibits on the part of the conscience-stricken and a new dedication to
upright behavior and energetic personal evangelism on the part of the
newly converted. By the mid-1850s these patterns were familiar to most
Americans, even to those who were personally unenthusiastic about the
revival tradition. Since the First Great Awakening in the colonies in the
1730s and 1740s, and particularly since a fresh wave at the turn of the
nineteenth century, revivals had become a staple on the American religious scene. Some of the most recognizable American names were leading figures in the revival tradition: Jonathan Edwards, George Whitefield,
Timothy Dwight, Lyman Beecher, and Charles Finney, to name only the
best known. None of the major Protestant denominations could stand
aloof from revivalism; even the Boston Unitarians tried it, to the amusement of the local evangelicals.[18] Revivalism spawned new denominations, fractured old ones, founded colleges, and fomented interminable
theological controversies. It was responsible for much of the shape of
evangelical religious experience by the middle of the century. Perry Miller
called it "the one clearly given truth" of American culture.[19]

To the evangelical eye in the 1850s, such recurring outpourings of the
Spirit signified a vital quality to American religious experience that could
not be found elsewhere. Revivalism seemed to be part of the remarkable
American success story. And the fruits of revivalism were more remarkable still. Scores of voluntary associations dotted the landscape,
organized for evangelism, Bible and tract publication and distribution,
education, and foreign missions. These comprised, in the words of one
observer, "an unsuspected though powerful assault upon the man of
sin."[20] Crusades were launched against intemperance, Sabbath-breaking, profanity, gambling; shelters were built for orphans, unwed mothers, the handicapped, the poor; sermons were preached against slave-
owning, political corruption, and child labor abuses. Evangelicals came to
national prominence as reformers: Arthur and Lewis Tappan, Orange
Scott, Theodore Weld, Angelina and Sarah Grimke, among others. Home
missionary societies established Sunday schools to educate unchurched
children, and they distributed clothing, food, and money to the needy.[21]
All these enterprises, as well as the sheer volume of evangelical energy
involved in them, contributed to the impression that a mighty reform of
individual and social life was underway in America at mid-century. Already in 1840 a Presbyterian assembly observed that, "with the general
progress of religion in the church, the standard of morality in the world
appears to be rising."[22]

All of this added up to a social climate in which, I believe, it would have been very difficult for evangelicals to feel poor and needy; the temptation to luxuriate in their own richness must have been overwhelming. If we listen to their own testimony, we can hear clearly the notes of self-congratulation and self-sufficiency between the lines. Here is Robert J. Breckinridge boasting about the growth of Old School Presbyterianism:

> As it regards the *power* with which the Church has acted since 1838 . . . and the manifestations of her rapidly increasing efforts, in every good and every great enterprise—the indications are such as ought to fill our hearts with joy. How many Churches have been built—how many souls converted— what a vast increase in numbers—what a prodigious extension of her borders—what immense sums collected to endow schools, colleges, and seminaries—to print books—to educate ministers—to spread the Gospel through the earth![23]

Listen to Samuel H. Cox, a New School Presbyterian, regaling his English audience with the favored status of his native land:

> Allow me to say that, in America, the state of society is without parallel in universal history. With all our mixtures, there is a leaven of heaven; there is goodness there; there is excellent principle there. I really believe that God has got America within anchorage, and that upon that arena, He intends to display His prodigies for the millennium.[24]

A Union Seminary professor, speaking without a note of modesty, said: "But we are Americans. We are here by the ordering of Providence, in charge of the final theatre and the final problems of history."[25] One could cite such examples indefinitely; the literature of the time is full of them. The evangelicals of the mid-nineteenth century, according to A. F. C. Wallace, "lived in what they felt was historical time. Their lives spanned the coming of the industrial age to America; they saw themselves as participants in a grand process of development that was bringing technological progress and material prosperity to all mankind, and with it . . . salvation and even the millennium. . . ."[26] This is the self-portrait of Christian people who felt themselves to be very rich indeed.

III

Let us take a closer look at what it means to be rich—in a spiritual sense. Doing so may not only throw the nature of nineteenth century evangelicalism into sharper relief but may also open our minds to the dangers inherent in our own richness in the twentieth century. It will also prepare us to understand the trauma of sudden poverty that evangelicals living in the generation around 1900 were forced to endure.

The first and perhaps most basic thing we notice about the rich is their confidence and self-assurance. They have determined that their good fortune is largely a product of their own capabilities and hard work, and it is virtually impossible for them to imagine that they do not merit their favored position. In moments of false modesty they may attribute their success to the whims of chance or the unmerited favor of God, but they cannot avoid feeling that in some respect, even a small one, they have deserved their good harvest. They find it convenient and natural to think of themselves as "self-made," as having freely grasped their opportunities and advanced themselves above their fellows. This makes them feel optimistic about human capacities, particularly their own, and contributes to their sense that they can trust themselves to know and to do what is right.

If the rich count themselves Christian, they will certainly want to provide for themselves a theology that supports this sense of self-trust. For our evangelical forebears of the nineteenth century, this meant a major theological renovation.[27] As it had been from the earliest days of the colonial experience, Calvinism was the reigning dogma, and Calvinism was not particularly sanguine about human nature. The great Reformation figure John Calvin had infused his theology with "the free grace of God and the sovereignty of the freely gracious God as the beginning of all Christian truth and of all Christian apprehension of truth."[28] This emphasis had caused him to take very seriously the biblical description of humans as fallen—radically fallen—creatures. Calvin's God was majestic, holy, and free in his utter transcendence, and he remained mysterious enough to discourage humans from thinking they could lay hold of him by the exercise of their own common sense. Human beings, in Calvin's opinion, were utterly depraved, enslaved to their own reckless and base appetites, and incapable of seeing or knowing the truth without the gracious enlightenment of the Holy Spirit. This Spirit came to people wholly independently of their own wishes or powers, and only to those whom God had, without consulting individual merits, elected for the gift of salvation.

Now all this, while impressive as a theological structure and routinely subscribed to by many generations of Christians in the Reformed tradition, made less and less sense as the nineteenth century progressed. It did not seem to do justice to what evangelicals were experiencing. To the mind of the successful and prospering Christian, the ways of God seemed not mysterious but very plain indeed. The capabilities of mankind were obvious—and most impressive. The notion that religious conversion was purely God's doing seemed controverted by the evidence offered daily that dynamic Christian evangelists, by rational persuasion and emotional techniques, could guarantee the gathering-in of converts. The eternal selectiveness of this inscrutable God did not seem properly democratic, nor was it useful in confirming the superiority of an American system in which every person had an equal chance at temporal salvation, with the prizes going to the worthiest.[29]

So while Calvinism was not, as Max Weber has pointed out, completely without its consolations for the successful of the world, it did seem out of harmony with the particular form of richness being enjoyed by nineteenth-century Americans. The historian William L. McLoughlin has put it well: the Calvinists' "insistence on man's total dependence upon God and total unworthiness in the sight of God, and particularly their claim that absolutely nothing a sinner can do is pleasing in the sight of God, caused intense frustration. . . . Warning men constantly against the sin of pride and the hopelessness of human effort just at the moment when the new nation needed all the confidence it could muster brought anger and quiet desperation to pious men."[30] Pious, perhaps, but we must ask whether it was not misled piety, given its anger at hearing of its own potential for pride. The rich, of course, do not want to hear that they are proud; rather, they want to hear that they are right, that they are free and capable, that they can trust their own powers, and that God is on their side when they do so. All this meant that Calvinism needed an overhaul if it was to be serviceable to those who were feeling rich. It is not surprising, then, that a number of prominent nineteenth-century theologians rose to the challenge and left mid-century evangelicalism a somewhat more suitable theological container for its self-sufficiency.

Close at hand for this task of renovation was a philosophical point of view in America that made a good bit more of human capacities than Calvin ever had: the "Scottish" philosophy, or Common Sense Realism. As an offspring of the Enlightenment, it looked with confidence on the possibilities of human nature, and particularly of the human mind. But it did not share the antireligious bias of the French philosophers or the epistemological skepticism of David Hume, whose ruminations seemed to remove any sure basis for human knowledge. Instead, it found its inspiration in the calm and unreflective empirical method of Sir Francis Bacon, who touted inductive research as the only reliable path to truth. Thomas Reid, the most prominent spokesman for the Common Sense school, posited an innately human intuitive "judgment" to validate the existence of the external world and the reliability of the mind to know it accurately, thus neatly sidestepping what may have been the biggest epistemological problem of the century. His message, translated into the vernacular, was simple: you can trust your senses to lead you to the truth. In the opinion of virtually every scholar who has examined the period, this message and its optimistic implications became the closest thing to an official philosophy that can be found in nineteenth-century America.[31]

Obviously, it pleased the rich to think this way. As Henry F. May writes, "it was never anti-scientific nor obscurantist, never cynical, and it opened no doors to intellectual or moral chaos." Instead, it promised an "intuitive certainty" for the findings of common sense.[32] Does the cosmos appear to be an orderly, law-abiding affair, knowable and predictable to human intelligence? Does this world seem to have been constructed by an all-powerful Mind whose creative and intelligent processes seem mirrored in the human mind? Are there identifiable moral laws in this universe, laws imprinted on the human conscience, that allow us all to know good and evil with certainty? Do all persons, upon introspection, know that they are essentially free to use their reasoning powers, arrive at truth, and incorporate that truth into daily life? Of course! All humanity knows these things, and thus they are to be trusted. Common sense dictates that the world is as it appears to be, and men and women can have confidence that, in knowing it and dealing with it rationally, they will not be led astray.

These comforting sentiments went a long way toward relieving the self-doubt inherent in a Calvinist point of view and the anger of the pious in response to it. When used as a starting point for theological reconstruction, they tended to lead toward the discovery that the Bible is really a book of simple common sense, not essentially in disagreement with what one discovers about God and human nature in honest introspection. A leading New School Presbyterian minister, Albert Barnes, asserted, "The teachings of the Bible *commend themselves* to man's reason."[33] While he did not exactly say it, the implication is that God's ways are man's ways, and his thoughts man's thoughts. What God appeared to be saying about human beings, according to this new, more rational view of the Bible's content, was that they are not such bad fellows after all.

It was at Yale, beginning in the 1820s, under the rubric "New Haven Theology" and the leadership of Nathaniel W. Taylor, that these matters were most clearly and systematically spelled out for the evangelical community. Taylor thought pragmatically—before the word was coined—and pragmatism, tuned as it is to the practical consequences of an idea, is of special use to the spiritually rich. Taylor was alarmed by Calvin's implication that human depravity so blinds the mind and the will that the exhortations of revivalists cannot be considered a certain and predictable means of bringing the sinner to God. Calvinism in this respect appeared both unproductive and untrue to experience. It needed a good dose of common sense, which was readily available since, as a leading evangelical authority points out, "Taylor frankly accepted reason as on a par with revelation." In Taylor's own words, "The clear, unperverted deductions of reason are as binding in their authority and not less truly to be relied on, than the Word of God; and . . . the former can never contradict the latter."[34] This gave Taylor an epistemological and exegetical basis for a somewhat more upbeat assessment of the human situation than Calvin could provide.

Taylor started with God. In his hands, God's judgment and his love were opposed to one another, and he took the former much less seriously than he did the latter. A loving God would offer salvation to all who would accept, not solely to the fortunate "elect." A reasonable God would not condemn an individual for the sin of Adam, but only for the individual's own specific acts of disobedience. And naturally, a reasonable God would deal reasonably with humanity, which meant one might trust one's common sense as a basis for personal responsibility, personal freedom, and the achievement of righteousness. This also implied that, if God expected people to choose the good, he would have to have given them the ability to freely choose the good. If we consult our common sense, we find this to be true, Taylor thought: "Let a man look into his own breast, and he cannot but perceive inward freedom—*inward freedom*—for if freedom be not in the mind it is nowhere. And liberty in the mind implies self-determination."[35] The fact that one *can* do good, of course, did not mean to Taylor that the human being *will* do good. Protesting his loyalty to the Calvinist notion of depravity, Taylor agreed that each person's nature still leads him or her unfailingly to sin. But human freedom allowed evangelists to place full responsibility for human sin on human choice, while also urging the person to choose differently for the sake of the soul's salvation. The Holy Spirit, of course, was an influence on the heart of the unbeliever but in no way compelled him or her. "Whatever that influence may be, the sinner, under its operation, chooses and acts just as voluntarily, as when he yields in any case to the solicitations of a friend."[36]

Once Taylor had established a relatively tame and friendly God and a free, responsible human being, he could dispense with the old Calvinist view that, in justification, Christ's righteousness is imputed to sinners in satisfaction of God's justice. Rather, Christ came to sacrifice himself as a sign of his love for mankind. This voluntary act of self-sacrifice served as a stimulus for reasonable people to sacrifice their own interests for the good of their neighbors.[37] Christ's death, therefore, showed God to be a "benevolent moral governor" who wished to promote benevolent moral action in all men.[38] The morality of God and the morality of humanity are essentially the same, even as God's reason and human reason mesh nicely in this most orderly of cosmic systems.

In the hands of theologians like Taylor, nineteenth-century Christianity lost a good deal of its epistemological and metaphysical bite. Thomas Reid's "reasonable and predictable God," who was "closer to the deity of Jefferson or Paine than to that of [Jonathan] Edwards," became the God of many evangelicals.[39] Richard F. Lovelace calls this "an increasingly kindly, fatherly and thoroughly comprehensible God," who was, in effect, "the projection of grandmotherly kindness mixed with the gentleness and winsomeness of a Jesus who hardly needed to die for our sins. Many American congregations were in effect paying their ministers to protect them from the real God."[40] Doubtless, these same congregations were being protected from the traditional Christian truths about human nature. The most striking change seems to have been a trivialization of the understanding of "sin." This biblical concept, which in the writings of the apostle Paul is laden with deep spiritual meaning and is thick with psychological subtlety, became in evangelicalism a description of certain human acts that, if one pursues the logic of Common Sense philosophy, are rooted in nothing much more serious than erroneous reasoning.

The evangelical consensus, by mid-century, seems to have lost the dark vision of human nature that the Reformers had felt and expressed with such shattering force. To the likes of Luther and Calvin, it would have been unthinkable that mere unreasonableness or discrete acts of disobedience separated us from God. They held that radical human unbelief, a spirit of rebellion, distorts all our faculties, bringing even the best use of human reason and the highest of human purposes to their service.[41] Thus, a fallen reason can be trusted only to build a network of lies, to substitute "agreeable false portraits of God" and of humans for the truth.[42] Christian theology had to come quite a distance from John Calvin's view that human beings are held in bondage to their own corrupt natures to Nathaniel Taylor's confidence that men and women are free agents, attested by nothing more empirical than self-examination. In truth, as one observer puts it, the evangelical theological innovators of the nineteenth century had twisted Calvinism "almost beyond recognition."[43]

They did this, I would suggest, because Calvinism in its traditional formulation did not offer the consolations that the spiritually rich evangelicals of the nineteenth century desired. Their misstep, I believe, was not in criticizing Calvinism. Certainly that theological system is itself a product of human reasoning, although in some ways of a brand of reasoning more humble than the Enlightenment-soaked mind we have been examining. It is right and good to scrutinize Calvinism—and every other theological construction. But when one's agenda calls for self-justification and self-congratulation, and when one's explicit commitment is to that culturally bound entity called common sense, one can expect to arrive at a theology whose convenience is more to be valued than its honesty to Scripture or its dedication to the truth. In a time of national prosperity and exuberant optimism, in the flush of revivalistic enthusiasm, one can expect a theology for the rich. One will not hear the psalmist's plaintive cry: "As for me, I am poor and needy; but the Lord takes thought for me" (Ps. 40:17).

IV

In the Bible, to be poor and needy is usually to be waiting for God. Elijah sat in the cave at Horeb feeling forsaken, "and the word of the Lord came to him. . ." (I Kings 9:19). Jeremiah, lamenting the catastrophe befalling Jerusalem, remembered that "the Lord is good to those who wait for him" (Lam. 3:25). Jonah, buried in the belly of the fish, "called to the Lord, out of my distress, and he answered me" (Jon. 2:2). Habakkuk, helpless to stem the tide of violence in his city, stationed himself in the tower, waiting—"and the Lord answered me" (Hab. 2:1-2). Saul of Tarsus, sitting blinded in Damascus, waited to "be told all that is appointed for you to do" (Acts 22:10). In each case, the collapse of a "rich man's" plans opened the way to a humble expression of neediness. Each could repeat the words of the psalmist: "This poor man cried, and the Lord heard him, and saved him out of all his troubles" (Ps. 34:6).

I believe we can say that those who are rich do not wait for God. Why wait for a deliverer when your deliverance is within your own grasp, or already assured? The plan the rich have for their lives is in every way intact and moving forward splendidly; their successes have made optimists of them. Their own efforts have been responsible for whatever happy situation they find themselves in, and they have no reason to believe that this will not continue to be the case. Everything depends, of course, on their own energy and skill, and they are anxious to apply these without stint. Thus rich people are often quite confident in the efficacy of their own actions. They are not so much waiting for God as aware that God is waiting for them. They do not wish to let this God down but to demonstrate that his trust in them is well founded. They operate under a commonsense maxim: God helps those who help themselves.

Spiritually, this means that the central Christian truth of God's grace is at risk in the hands of the rich: the proclamation of grace is an affront to those who are pleased with their riches. Perhaps I need forgiveness for my moral slip-ups, the rich say, but certainly not for the very person I am.

Perhaps at conversion I need God's rescue, but once his moral reformation of me is well underway, I am no longer on a sinking ship, and he may apply his grace elsewhere. The Christian rich experience God's grace as a kind of medical application, administered one time, something that sets them on their feet but thereafter, except for minor lapses, is unnecessary. The rich, in being impressed with their own actions and assuming that God feels the same, are always flirting with the doctrine of salvation by works. Their dedication to their own programs of action are given a certain urgency by their belief that they really matter to God in some ultimate sense. Their attempt to generate and control similar actions in others encourages them to identify their own ends with God's ends, and to impress these upon their neighbors as God's will for them as well. The rich are thus rich in their own moralism and, if they do not encounter the grace of God afresh, soon settle into a comfortable legalism.

The evangelicals about whom we have been speaking do not seem to have been feeling bereft, and one finds little evidence that they were waiting for God. Rather, they were caught up in a flurry of activity, confident of God's approval of their plans. They were racing madly ahead with schemes for personal piety, for church growth, for social improvement and moral reform, for missionary enterprise—ultimately for the inauguration of the millennium in America. In their intoxication with human action, they were simply mirroring the spirit of the age. In 1854 a magazine editor described Common Sense Realism as the reigning system of thought among Anglo-Saxons, and he attributed to this philosophy the "great development . . . of enterprise and activity in every direction, temporal and religious." A few years earlier, a leading church spokesperson, Absalom Peters, had pronounced the keynote of his time: "The present is an age not of light and knowledge, but of benevolent actions."[44] This is a strangely transparent statement. It hints at the essential pragmatism of Christians and non-Christians alike, the impatience with knowledge that did not lead to action, with light that was not readily translatable into heat. For mid-century Americans the age of enterprise was in full swing. The possibility that God might be judging the righteous works of his people as filthy rags did not seem to occur to the evangelical mind of the time. Timothy Smith, perhaps somewhat too approvingly, characterizes the evangelicals of mid-century America as trusting in "divine grace to supplement human efforts."[45] When divine grace becomes a booster system for human action rather than God's caution to our easy identification of our ends with his ends, one wonders whether it is still the grace of Jesus Christ. Perhaps it is simply a theological cloak for our unending attempts to save ourselves by our own efforts.

This note comes through in a critique of the old Calvinism by Presbyterian Albert Barnes: "It contains dogmas so abhorrent to the obvious teachings of the Bible; so repellant to the common sense of mankind; so at variance with what are found to be just principles of philosophy; so fitted to retard a work of grace; and so utterly contradictory to what a man is constrained to preach . . . that he cannot preach them." Barnes and other evangelical activists were enthusiastic about the doctrinal innovations of the New Haven Theology because they made of the gospel a more practical and effective instrument than had been available under the older Calvinism. "We place ourselves in the pulpit," Barnes confessed, "and ask what may be preached so as to answer the ends of preaching—so that men will perceive it to be true, and so that they will be converted to God."[46] Behind this statement lurks the assumption that the ends justify the means, that if our listeners find the gospel we preach foolish and unacceptable, we ought to change our message to something they can believe. Sidney Ahlstrom, a leading American historian of religion, describes Nathaniel Taylor as consciously setting out to create a "plausibly rationalistic 'revival theology'" for nineteenth-century evangelicalism.[47]

We have seen how Taylor's theology better suited the demands of common sense, particularly in the way it gave human nature a somewhat higher evaluation than did the more traditional Calvinism. But it is no accident that these same commonsense conclusions were more consistent with demands for human efficacy than was the older theology. Martin Marty observes: "A new and 'higher' view of human nature . . . came into prominence just in time to be used for the transformation of the environment in the century of enterprise."[48] For evangelicals, revival was the central means to the transformation of the environment. A revival theology called for an emphasis on human freedom, on one's capacity to choose aright and one's sole responsibility for his own life. A person must know that his actions count if he is to act. If the preacher was to be effective in dramatizing the sorry state of the sinners, as congregations demanded, he had to be able to show that the sinner alone is responsible for sinfulness, and that sins are specific acts that are avoidable. Taylor's theology put a powerful weapon in the hands of ambitious revivalists and, as George Marsden has pointed out, this was exactly the result he intended to produce.[49] It was a theology stripped for action.

If Nathaniel Taylor is the key theologian for an era rich in enterprise, Charles Finney stands eminently as the man of action. Finney was the most popular and successful revivalist of the first half of the nineteenth century. Ordained a Presbyterian, he eventually made a break from that denomination, admitting honestly that he had left the old Calvinism far behind. Finney's God was not only the "grandmother" of Lovelace's description but also a holy and powerful hater of sin. Yet Finney wielded him as if God were the revivalist's personal weapon against an easily identifiable class of recalcitrant sinners and thus one of his useful, entirely manageable revivalist techniques. The human beings to whom these techniques were applied were, in Finney's appraisal, free moral agents who lay under God's call to "change their own hearts," in the words of one of Finney's sermon titles. God's role was to persuade—but so gently and lovingly that the choice of the sinner was still made in freedom. A Christianity that did not include such freedom for mankind, Finney thought, was to be rejected as "contrary to right reason." Finney assured his listeners that "as, therefore, God requires men to make themselves a new heart on pain of eternal death, it is the strongest possible evidence that they are able to do it."[50]

Charles Finney made it his business to bring about the conversion of these free moral agents by whatever means possible. Calvinists in the tradition of Jonathan Edwards had known that "God's grace could not be forced; heaven could not be taken by storm. Men must pray and wait for conversion."[51] Finney knew otherwise, from personal experience. Conversion, he declared, "is not a miracle or dependent on a miracle in any sense. . . . It is purely a philosophical result of the right use of constituted means. . . . The connection between the right use of means for a revival and a revival is as philosophically sure as between the right use of means to raise grain and a crop of wheat."[52] In this spirit Finney pioneered a series of "new measures" designed to ensure a visitation of grace. He used harsh, sensationalistic, forceful, and sentimental language to "excite" his listeners; he spoke directly to individuals in his audience, naming sinners' names. He carefully planned and promoted his gatherings, profiting from the latest publicity techniques to rivet an entire city's attention on his "protracted meetings."[53]

> He recruited lay workers in cooperating churches and organized prayer meetings in advance of his arrival; his lay workers posted placards, advertised in newspapers, and distributed notices of his meetings from door to door or to passersby in the streets. He trained the ministers and laity to work with awakened sinners after his sermons and to invite converts to join their churches. . . . He practiced house to house visitation and even hired a special musical assistant to direct the singing at his meetings, and his wife led special meetings for women.[54]

These were new techniques in the revival business. They reflected Finney's own understanding of revival as a human enterprise, and they benefited from—as well as were directed toward—the rising civilization of the city in America. These techniques, combined with his dynamic personality, made Finney the most popular and effective revivalist of his era and a model for preachers everywhere. When opponents criticized his use of such methods, Finney replied: "The results justify my methods. Show me the fruits of your ministry, and if they so far exceed mine as to give me evidence that you have found a more excellent way, I will adopt your views."[55] There is no record that either Finney or his admiring listeners put Jesus' ministry to this test. Rather, this pragmatic approach became very popular among evangelical churches, which were known to pray fervently, "Lord send us a man like Finney." The local pastor who could not periodically produce a successful revival campaign was not in high demand among the action-oriented evangelicals of the nineteenth century.[56]

Finney had discovered what so many modern revivalists after him have discovered: it is possible by organizational, publicity, and oratorical techniques to widen the straight and narrow gate and keep the turnstyle revolving at ever greater speed. But he was not content to leave his converts in the lurch after having seen to their conversion. Finney offered the new Christians a disciplined life of zeal and good works. As his message placed full responsibility on the individual to choose salvation, it also obligated the new believer to work toward moral perfection in this life—a possibility Finney believed to be sanctioned by Scripture. Although he identified this achievable state of holiness, or sanctification, with a subjective state of complete and selfless love of God, he never doubted that such perfection would issue in identifiable external acts of personal morality and the promotion of the morality of others. The struggle to be holy was not meant for weaklings, in Finney's view. He would have agreed with a contemporary Presbyterian educator who wrote that "the very essence of virtue is a manly struggle against inordinate appetite, and a valorous beating down of the flesh to serve the behest of the spirit."[57] Finney's perfectionism was thus of a piece with his revivalism in its reliance on human capabilities. "In effect," writes Lovelace, "he taught justification by sanctification and not by faith, and sanctification by will power more than by grace."[58]

As with all works-oriented theologies, Finney's perfectionism drifted inevitably into a kind of legalism. Oberlin College, founded by Finney and permeated by his aura, exuded a self-righteous and moralistic air, and it encouraged a separatism based on a confident labeling of sin and sinners. Finney himself offered a model of the regimented lifestyle, prohibiting himself even the delights of coffee and tea. Other Oberlin taboos included tobacco, all stimulants, pepper, mustard, oil, and vinegar.[59] Even the rather staid Princeton theologian B. B. Warfield saw in Finney's perfectionism a religion of works rather than dependence on God. "Ev-

erywhere and always," he said, "the initiative belongs to man; everywhere and always God's action is suspended upon man's will."[60] Warfield's comment demonstrates that one need not be impious to see in
Finney's perfectionism an overturning of the heart of the gospel. And yet
it was by means of this perfectionism, as well as by other similar confusions of human action with God's will, that a Christian church drunk on
its own possibilities could find theological affirmation in the age of
enterprise.

Evangelicals like Finney were not content to direct their energetic and
confident actions toward personal reformation alone. As Edward Beecher
put it, "an elevated state of personal holiness" is simply the beginning of a
larger Christian task: "To re-organize human society in accordance with
the laws of God. To abolish all corruptions in religion and all abuses in the
social system and, so far as it has been erected on false principles, to take it
down and erect it anew."[61] Charles Finney added his voice to the call for
Christian social action:

> Now the great business of the church is to reform the world—to put away
> every kind of sin. The church of Christ was originally organized to be a body
> of reformers . . . to reform individuals, communities, and governments,
> and never rest until the kingdom and the greatness of the kingdom under
> the whole heaven shall be given to the people of the saints of the most high
> God—until every form of iniquity shall be driven from the earth.[62]

Finney never really lost his belief that evangelism, and not social or political programs, was primary in bringing in the kingdom. He particularly
accentuated his own identity as a revivalist and not a political agitator or
legislator. But he used millennial imagery quite flagrantly, and he seemed
to have his hopes set on a society gradually brought to perfection in this
realm and in the not-too-distant future. He was certain that genuine
Christian conversion and the process of sanctification would naturally
result in a Christianizing of society.

The embrace by Finney and most evangelicals of his day of a
postmillennial eschatology was reminiscent of Nathaniel Taylor's interest
in a theology whose potential for results he could calculate. This point of
view, on the American scene at least since the days of Jonathan Edwards,
foresaw a thousand years of peace with Christ reigning in people's hearts,
along with correspondingly beneficent results in the wider social sphere.
This millennium was to be ushered in quite soon, as the American people
gradually turned themselves and their social institutions over to God.
Finney felt that this postmillennial position was not only true to Scripture
but also practical in inspiring benevolent Christian action. George T.
Ladd was explicit in his embrace of postmillennialism on pragmatic
grounds. When premillennialism, with its pessimism about the efficacy

of human action in bringing in the kingdom, began to make forays into the evangelical mind, Ladd predicted that it would tend to "let down the tone of the Christian life and to discourage ministers from feeling that they are working 'for the Ages,' and 'for the race.' "[63] His criticism pointed to a feeling that was common among many evangelicals of his day, that fine points of theology might have to be settled on the basis of whether they furthered or hindered what Christians had decided was God's program of action on this earth.

Armed with their human-centered and works-oriented theologies, and caught up in the reformist spirit of the age, evangelicals rushed into action against a wide variety of personal and social evils. Both Donald Dayton and Timothy Smith have told these stories, providing detailed and often inspiring examples of sacrificial actions by devoted Christian people. Evangelicals spoke out against the brutal treatment of children and the mentally ill; they defended the rights of women to an education and to be heard on the important issues of the day; they fought against the abuse of alcohol and gave themselves in service to the poor; and they led the fight against the curse of black slavery in America. We must not belittle their contribution to the relief of suffering and injustice in their day. It bespeaks genuine compassion and a remarkable determination to act concretely on what they understood to be a biblical standard of righteousness.

But neither can we help but notice, in reading their stories, the shrill and self-righteous tone that pervades much of their language. We must ask whether they did not, to some extent, do these things as those who are spiritually rich. Was there not a note of arrogance in the assertion of a Wesleyan Methodist minister that to preach the gospel is "to attack and condemn all wrong, and to assert and defend all righteousness"?[64] Do we hear self-satisfaction in the evangelical claim to be returning the nation "to those habits of industry, temperance, moderation, economy and general virtue which our common Christianity inculcates"? Can we not sense the aspirations to power in Charles Finney's warning that the friends of strong drink would "never yield, until the friends of God and man can form a public sentiment so strong as to crush the character of every man who will not give it up"?[65] Where do we hear the word of grace in the Oberlin church's resolution that "as Slavery is a Sin, no person shall be invited to preach or Minister to this church, or any Brother be invited to commune who is a slaveholder"?[66] And must we not understand the tragedy of the Civil War, at least in some small way, as the fruit of a Christian activism that promoted self-righteousness rather than humility and moralism rather than compassion and forgiveness?

After the city of Richmond fell to the Union troops, Rev. Phillips Brooks of Massachusetts prayed this prayer: "We thank Thee, O God, . . . for the triumph of right over wrong. We thank Thee for the loyal soldiers planted in the streets of wickedness."[67] Brooks's prayer gave evidence of the spirit of Christian activism that emerged out of fatness instead of forgiveness. His self-assurance—and that which evangelicals generally felt about the parameters of right and wrong, along with their sense of being destined to prepare the nation for its entry into the millennial kingdom—may cause us to take a closer look at their moral and social reform activities. We may ask whether they carried out those activities as people who knew they were poor in spirit, or as people who knew they were right.

V

The rich are builders. Proverbs identifies them as such: "A rich man's wealth is his strong city" (Prov. 10:15). Cain, the brother of Abel, set the precedent in the first pages of the Bible, and we have repeated it ever since. Banishing him to the life of a wanderer, a still merciful God promised Cain that he would protect his life. Cain, it is implied, rejected the offer by rejecting the penalty: instead of wandering, he settled down in the land of Nod and built a city. As Jacques Ellul has shown in *The Meaning of the City*, the Bible sees the city as a human attempt to fashion a secure home on earth, where the creature can become the creator, where the powerless can take control of their lives, where God is not welcome because he is not needed. Spiritually speaking, the city is humanity's alternative to trusting in the Lord.

This explains God's condemnation of the rich man who, in Jesus' story, thought to tear down his barns and build larger ones. By building and filling new and better barns, the rich think they have secured themselves against the ravages of life. They suppose they are protected—without recourse to God. They ready themselves for a life of ease. But "woe to those who are at ease in Zion," God says to the rich (Amos 6:1). God calls the builder of barns a "fool" for trusting in his own treasures and for not being "rich toward God" (Lk. 12:21). To be "rich toward God," as the Sermon on the Mount makes clear, is to acknowledge that one really is poor.

The Old Testament sees those who trust in themselves not only as gatherers of wealth and founders of cities but also as builders of fortresses and towers. In each case their motivation is their pride and their intention is autonomy. In Amos, those who trust in their own strength build "strongholds" and feel secure.(1:4, 7, 10, etc.). Others build "houses of hewn stone" (5:11). Much earlier, in the land of Shinar, the people gathered together and said: "Come, let us build ourselves a city, and a tower with its top in the heavens, and let us make a name for ourselves . . ." (Gen. 11:4). These are the rich of the world—confident, optimistic, active—and their product is inevitably a monument to their own achievements and a provision for their continuing victory. Who of us is not one with them in being builders on this earth?

In our perusal of mid-nineteenth-century evangelicalism we have been examining what amounts to a spiritual tower of Babel. It is disconcerting—but not unexpected within a biblical framework—to see that it is those who claim to be the church of Jesus Christ who are putting stone upon stone. The posture of humility and the message of grace are fleeting realities, momentary breaks in the routines of business as usual for the inveterate builders we seem to be. The cross of Christ tells us that we will always be poor and needy, but we have become adept at transforming spiritual poverty into spiritual wealth by coating our building projects with a thin layer of what we call God's grace or blessing. This simply means, I believe, that we are in constant need of hearing the word of mercy and forgiveness afresh. But that word comes to us first of all as one of rejection and judgment—judgment of our noblest plans and our most moral actions. It destroys the foundations of our fortresses and dissolves the optimism that has been animating our frenzied activity and our good works. It cuts to the very heart of our confident religiosity and leaves us knowing, once again, that we are poor and needy.

In the documents that survive from the mid-nineteenth century it is quite difficult to hear this note of poverty. One senses that our evangelical forebears—perhaps much like ourselves—were not attuned to the word of God's judgment pronounced over the best of their works. Rather, one hears words that connote self-satisfaction and an easy identification of God's ways with the ways of his fallen creatures. Such words as "progress," "universal," "perfect," "righteous," "moral," and "power" punctuate the evangelical speech of the time in a bizarre mixture of Enlightenment idealism and traditional theological language. A certain cosmic hyperbole prevailed: "conquest of the whole world for Christ," or "*all* is Progress," or "regenerate the nation," or "the conversion and sanctifying of the world."[68] Behind these words one hears a people drunk on their own power—and confusing it with the power of God. Listen to a Methodist minister speaking of "the great central idea of the whole book of God . . . *the holiness of the human soul, heart, mind, and will.*" He continues: "It may be called fanaticism, but that, dear friend, is our mission. If we keep to that, the next century is ours. Our work is a moral work; that is to say, the work of making man holy. . . . There is our mission. There is our glory. There is our power, and there shall be our triumph."[69]

Of course, the next century was not "ours"—at least not in a sense that this exuberant evangelical would have recognized. As we shall see, these lines were spoken not at the inauguration of a long millennial reign but at the beginning of the end for American evangelical dominance. This might lead us to speculate—though very carefully and with a tentative spirit— about the meaning of the evangelical decline. Was that decline an evidence of the power of evil or unbelieving men and women to thwart the purposes of God and, by their cunning, delay the expected reign of Christ? Or was it the manifestation of the strange mercy of God, who found the evangelical construction site so filled with the din of clinking trowels and banging hammers that he could not be heard except in judgment? Did God find it necessary to dismantle an imposing evangelical structure so that his people, once again poor and needy, might know the difference between themselves and their Deliverer?

We must admit that we are on slippery ground in asking such questions about the working of God in history. We must acknowledge, with Paul the apostle, that his judgments are unsearchable and his ways inscrutable (Rom. 11:33). But we might want to consider what happens in Scripture to the rich whom God confronts. God tends to attract the attention of the rich in ways that, at first glance, appear harsh and unloving. Here is what Jesus says to the angel of the church at Laodicea: "For you say, I am rich, I have prospered, and I need nothing; not knowing that you are wretched, pitiable, poor, blind, and naked." To these deluded Christians Jesus says, "I will spew you out of my mouth." But he goes on to announce his purpose and his care: "Those whom I love, I reprove and chasten; so be zealous and repent. Behold, I stand at the door and knock . . ." (Rev. 3:16-20). God's love comes, as it often must to ourselves as rich, first of all as a word of judgment, so that losing our towers and our fortresses and seeing once again our true condition of nakedness and poverty and blindness, we will hear the word of forgiveness. Forgiveness cannot be heard except as caricature where riches and the cultural buildings that hold them remain intact. One cannot really gain perspective until one loses one's tower.

Perhaps this is why God presents himself in Amos as the one who destroys fortresses and strongholds and who breaks great and small houses into fragments (5:8-9; 6:11). Or why, in Isaiah 25, he is the one who "hast made the city a heap, the fortified city a ruin." His purpose in Isaiah seems clear: "Therefore strong peoples will glorify thee; cities of ruthless nations will fear thee" (25:2-3). God crushes strongholds—even religious strongholds on which we ask his blessing—because they are ultimately built for human glorification. If we are to glorify him, we must leave our cities and barns and towers behind and perhaps meet him in the wilderness, where we have nothing to lean on but him. Then we will know the further message of Isaiah 25: "For thou hast been a stronghold to the poor, a stronghold to the needy in his distress . . ." (v. 4). Amos points to the same action by God in describing his judgment on the rich and the strong: "'Flight shall perish from the swift, and the strong shall not retain his strength, nor shall the mighty save his life . . . and he who is stout of heart among the mighty shall flee away naked in that day,' says the Lord" (2:14, 16).

By 1900 the evangelicals of America knew the next century was not theirs. They had come a long way since the triumphant days of mid-century. Their strong city had been taken from them. Perhaps they felt naked. If so, they could rest in the knowledge that Jesus came, himself naked and poor, to preach good news to the poor. He who was rich in ways that perhaps we who are rich would not recognize or want to recognize became poor for our sake, that we by his poverty might become rich (Lk. 4:18; II Cor. 8:9). Perhaps it is ultimately not such a bad thing to be naked, hungry, and poor. As Mary said in the Magnificat, "He has shown strength with his arm, he has scattered the proud in the imagination of their hearts, he has put down the mighty from their thrones, and exalted those of low degree; he has filled the hungry with good things, and the rich he has sent empty away" (Lk. 1:51-53).

We still may not have reached the end of the story. He has sent the rich away empty. But if they go away sorrowful, as did the rich young man after hearing Jesus' command to sell all his goods, then perhaps they go away with a new hunger, a new nakedness. Perhaps then they are ready to be filled. This may be the meaning behind Jesus' answer to his disciples, who asked that question: "Then who can be saved?" "Jesus looked at them and said, 'With men it is impossible, but not with God; for all things are possible with God'" (Mk. 10:26-27).

Chapter II

I Will Die in My Nest

I

The rich do not often attract sympathy. Whether we speak in the traditional sense of the rich as those who have great material wealth and comfort, or in the spiritual sense we have been using, as those who boast of their success and think themselves in some way secure, we are referring to people who are difficult to pity. We pay attention to them; we may admire and emulate them; and perhaps we envy them. With all that, however, many of us also resent them, particularly if their good fortunes contrast with our needier state. Occasionally we hope for their demise, and if their demise occurs by some unforeseen circumstance, we do not lose much sleep over their fate. We may be secretly happy that they received "justice" or "equal treatment" and relieved that by their example we will no longer be made to feel like failures.

In the first chapter we dealt rather harshly with the spiritually rich evangelicals of the mid-nineteenth century. In this chapter we shall look in on their demise. It would be tempting perhaps to applaud their fate, especially if their proud triumphalism has grated on our ears. However, by too quickly adopting the view that their misfortunes were God's doing, we may mistakenly embrace an attitude of judgmentalism and perhaps even superiority toward them. This would both arrogate to ourselves knowledge of God's mind, which we surely do not have, and falsify the very attitude God himself seems to take toward those he judges. It would be to forget that when God comes in judgment it is as a God of love who suffers for and with his people. It would also signify our unwillingness to admit that we are the rich as much as were our brothers and sisters of a century past.

The Bible paints the picture of a particular rich man whose story may help educate our feelings as we observe the evangelical decline of the late nineteenth century. The man is Job, who is said to have been upright and blameless: he feared God and turned away from evil. Does this mean he was more righteous than the mid-nineteenth century evangelicals we have been describing? That is difficult to say. In religious observance, moralism, and energy for good works, the evangelicals would be difficult to better. But in examining them we have focused on a deep ambivalence in the human breast, one that can give expression to a pride and self-sufficiency at the very moment of the most sincere feelings of faithfulness to God. Has any human being, even Job, not shared this ambivalence—a sign of the fact that there is *none* righteous, not even one? In describing Job as blameless and upright, was God exempting Job from the number of those for whom Christ died and thus from the company of the un-righteous? Perhaps Job was indeed upright in the finest sense possible to humans; and perhaps this was the very same sense in which the nine-teenth-century evangelicals were upright. Perhaps Job did not himself know the compromises he was making in his heart, even as he turned piously and obediently away from evil.

We cannot know these things for sure. But we can know that Satan questioned Job's integrity, asking God: "Does Job fear God for nothing?" Satan's suspicion was that things were going too well for Job, that his good fortune was the foundation of a faith that was too easy. Satan challenged God to test this faith: "Hast thou not put a hedge about him and his house and all that he has, on every side? Thou hast blessed the work of his hands, and his possessions have increased in the land. But put forth thy hand now, and touch all that he has, and he will curse thee to thy face" (Job 1:10-11). So God let Satan loose to deprive Job of every-thing he had. Without family, without material wealth, and without health, perhaps Job would turn against God, giving Satan the satisfaction of knowing that Job did not indeed love God for nothing. Perhaps God was interested in answering the same question.

So Job lost it all. In the chapters that tell his story we listen as he bemoans his fate, puzzles over the ways of God, struggles to justify himself and yet to retain his humility before God. We sense his faith being tried in a crucible of personal suffering, and we feel pity for him, if not anger at his fate. He seems so innocent, so undeserving of his fate. We share his failure to comprehend and the anguish of his soul. Somehow the fact that he was a rich man does not prevent our feeling for a fellow man.

It will help us to see the demise of evangelicalism through Job's eyes. When we hear his plaintive cry, "Let the day perish wherein I was born," we do not think of him as a rich man getting just what he deserves but as an upright man being cruelly oppressed. When we hear his "groanings . . . poured out like water," we do not think of one who simply desires the return of his material comfort but of one who seeks to understand his plight and the God who seems to stand behind it. Perhaps there is a place

within us where his words echo: "I am not at ease, nor am I quiet; I have
no rest; but trouble comes" (Job 3:26). Let us remember that inner place as
we explore the plight of our brothers and sisters a century ago.

II

By 1900 the evangelicals of America were not on the whole "at ease in
Zion." Less than a half-century earlier, they had been at the helm of the
American enterprise, and they imagined themselves on the cutting edge
of world history. Now, in the space of a person's lifetime, their Zion lay in
ruins. Like Job, they knew trouble had come. Their plight found expression in the words of their hero of the moment, the revivalist Dwight L.
Moody: "I look on this world as a wrecked vessel."[1] In these few words he
measured the distance evangelicals had come since their halcyon days.

Moody himself had grown up during the era of Charles Finney's greatest influence. His conversion had come at the height of evangelical optimism, in the mid-1850s, and both his short-lived but promising business
career and his beginnings as an evangelist on the streets of Chicago had
brimmed with the entrepreneurial energy and confidence of the age.
Although he seems to have been constitutionally incapable of despair or
cynicism and remained remarkably free of the fearful defensiveness of so
many of his fellow Christians until his death in the fading moments of the
nineteenth century, his self-conscious break with the giddy millennial
dreams of Finney's crowd was a significant sign of the times. Even among
those evangelicals who were not prepared to adopt his premillennial
stance, those whose social ethics took them far beyond his simple revivalism in treating the ills of the day, or those who faulted his biblicism in light
of the findings of the new higher criticism, Moody found respect and
support. He knew that this world suffered from a terminal disease, and
even where his prescriptions were not embraced, his perception of the
symptoms rang true. Americans, particularly Christians, flocked to his
revival meetings. Most of them, it seems, already knew the way of salvation. What may have attracted them was the hope that the evangelist
would tell them what was wrong, what was wrecking the vessels of their
own lives. Perhaps this evangelical hero could help them make sense of
their inner uneasiness.

The uneasiness evangelicals were feeling was not unique to people of
deep religious conviction. Late nineteenth-century America was making
its way—sometimes steering but usually drifting before strong currents—
through the stormy passage we now call modernization. As we look back
on it, we recognize that it was the inevitable and complex coming of age of

industrial capitalism in America. Much of the Western world was in the throes of the same transition: some, like England and Germany, were a bit ahead of the United States, and others, like Russia, quite a ways behind. We can now see how the early stages of this process were already underway during the time of Finney and Taylor, how the forces of change were gathering momentum even as the evangelicals declared their ascendancy and proclaimed their control—in God's name—of the dynamics of history. From our present vantage, the Civil War serves as a turning point. After that bloody crusade, the industrial development that had virtually assured the Union forces of victory assumed unchallenged leadership, North and South, and the transformation of America proceeded apace. Economic development accelerated exponentially. Forces not readily susceptible to rational human control took America out of the hands of the evangelicals—in fact, it soon appeared, out of virtually everyone's hands. Americans as a whole, and evangelicals among them, were caught up both in the exhilaration and the bewilderment of rapid, unforeseen change.

The Americans who lived through this period had few reliable charts to help steer them through the shoals. They could observe the British experience with a modicum of distance and objectivity; but the shortness of their historical perspective, the relative infancy of the social sciences, and their own conviction that America would break the mold contributed to their essential myopia. As is always true of historical change, the participants in the drama did not easily attain the disinterestedness necessary to a penetrating assessment of their situation. And even when they pinpointed the problem within the economic arena, they could not admit at that early date what only the most advanced thinkers on the continent were beginning to see: that men and women of good will could create, quite unwittingly, a giant and unrelenting economic mechanism that would meet its requirements for continued growth and health by its own historical logic and with blatant disregard for human sentiment. Thus even those who knew that economic forces were becoming oppressive often could not advance to the truth of the matter: that things in America were very much out of control.

To a large degree, of course, the sense of control enjoyed by pre–Civil War Americans had been illusory. In its early stages industrial capitalism had not so much destroyed as utilized, and for some enriched, the possibilities of small-town life—the life most Americans enjoyed. On the other hand, there were those who knew already in the eighteenth century that the economic mechanism had a life of its own. In fact, the early proponents of free-enterprise capitalism in Great Britain defended it *as* a mechanism that would work best if it were relieved of the misguided tinkering of political authority. Adam Smith, the leading economic theorist of the time, advanced a model of economics that operated somewhat on the order of God's sovereignty. He imagined an "invisible hand" that would guarantee that the selfish concerns of millions of citizens, each an acquisitive economic unit, would automatically redound to the health of the larger economic society—whether world or nation—and the greatest good for the greatest number. Just let the system follow its own logic, said the classical economists, and while you may not have paradise, you will do about as well as you can expect to in providing for the material needs and physical comforts of the human race.

The people of the United States never fully embraced this model, unsure that an impersonal system, particularly one fueled by self-interest, could be trusted to guard a "Christian" civilization. In the early nineteenth century it would have been difficult for Americans to admit that personal morality or altruistic activism were irrelevant to the economic and spiritual health of a people. Already in the years following the Revolution, Americans had begun to debate the desirability of industrialization. Machines, if used according to the precepts of free enterprise, did seem to offer material prosperity and economic independence for the new nation. But they also contributed to a love of luxury among the fortunate, which led inevitably to "effeminacy intoxication extravagance Vice and folly [sic]," not to mention sensuality and sloth. And of course, as anyone who had traveled in England could see, they created a class of permanently degraded and poverty-stricken men, women, and children of the working class—a class obviously out of step with the high republican hopes of the American nation, particularly since so many of that nation's populace located true virtue in the tilling of the soil rather than in the manipulation of a machine.[2]

The national debate over the merits of industrialization seems to have ended with an agreement that things would have to be different here. The love of luxury would have to become a spur to the virtues of persistent hard work. The selfishness of the successful would have to be transmuted into the stewardship of one's wealth for the good of others. The threat of a vicious industrial working class would have to be relieved by the limitless opportunities for mobility, both social and geographical, in the new continent; but also by the personal virtues both of employer and employee in partnership with one another for the common good. Lyman Beecher and other revivalists assured Americans that the moral purity following a religious conversion would guarantee that the fires of free enterprise and industrial progress would not eventually consume the American people. Morally renewed American industrialists were to wield the powerful weapon of the machine in responsible ways, assuring an industrial order in which all would profit. By means of a kindly Christian paternalism, the free enterprise system would be humanized, the worst excesses of economic greed minimized, and all without sacrificing the technological progress so entrancing to America in the nineteenth century.[3]

For a long while it looked as though this American variety of free enterprise was working relatively well. Employers, by investing wisely, created factories full of machines. The spectacular productive capacity of these machines enabled working-class families to purchase for everyday use what had previously been considered luxury items. Employees, many of them recent immigrants, earned a wage that, in time, might allow them to move up to a more satisfying status of property ownership and self-employment. Meanwhile, they worked in factories often small enough to offer personal contact with employers, and they lived in neighborhoods where the geographical proximity of poor and rich encouraged a certain community feeling across class lines. In small mill towns, owner and worker worshiped together in the same churches, called on one another in times of disaster, and carried out their lives within the same orbit. Criticisms of the factory as an inherently oppressive institution could be countered by citing popular industrial experiments like the one in Lowell, Massachusetts, where employers looked after the spiritual as well as economic well-being of the thousands of young women employed in the mills. Intermittent economic downswings could be blamed on the machinations of foreign powers or on a few atypically evil Americans. Unequal distribution of wealth appeared offensive only to the degree that the rich refused to exercise Christian stewardship. Poverty was treated as a temporary condition, a spur to personal industry that would sooner or later be transcended by all but the stupid or lazy. The fact that Americans, whether rich or poor, generally shared these values and, to a large degree, the benefits of the system permitted the nineteenth-century economist Henry C. Carey to characterize this system as a "harmony of interests" in which all classes came up winners.[4]

This may explain why most evangelicals did not include in their reformist platforms any serious overhaul of the capitalist economic order. Sidney Mead has pointed out how evangelicals typically mixed the rhetoric of social renovation with an essentially conservative belief that rational persuasion and Christian evangelism would eventually right society's wrongs. To those familiar with a Marxist critique of the underlying class relationships in society, or even to those simply aware of the workings of pressure groups and power politics in a twentieth-century democracy, the reform enthusiasms of these nineteenth-century evangelicals may sound sentimental and naive.[5] One is especially struck by the absence of any serious critique of the free enterprise system as a whole. It was not too

early for evangelicals to see the tragic human results of child labor, ma-
chine-related accidents or illness, starvation wages, and periodic unem-
ployment. Yet it was assumed that the evils of capitalism were side
effects, not systemic and inherent in the very operation of the economy.
They would be remedied by the same voluntary and essentially pater-
nalistic processes—by employers being fair and solicitous of their workers' welfare, by workers being patient during hard times, by the rich
channeling their excess wealth to worthy programs of charity for the
poor.

John P. Crozier, the successful entrepreneur of the 1840s and 1850s
sensitively portrayed in Wallace's *Rockdale,* represents both the possibilities and the limits of the principle of voluntarism. This Baptist lay-
man drove a hard bargain in the cotton industry, fired workers who
reacted to cruel wage cuts by daring to organize strikes, and delayed
implementing Pennsylvania's new ten-hour law for his mill hands because it would give out-of-state mills an unfair competitive advantage.
Yet he "devoted much of his time to religious causes and regarded himself
as God's steward, managing his mills and mill hands and his wealth for
the advancement of the community. He kept a diary in which he carefully
recorded the spiritual transformation he was experiencing as the love of
victory and the desire for gold were transmuted into a longing to be of
service to his Savior."[6] It seems that this service did not imply any relax-
ing, in business life, of his dedication to the "bottom line." But within the
strict limits of profitability he showed solicitude for his workers' interests,
invited their personal trust, visited them in sickness and bereavement,
and by a taut factory regimen exhibited his concern for their morals. In
later life he devoted his energy to divesting himself of the great wealth he
had accumulated through his business acumen; most of it went to religious and educational causes, especially the training of Baptist ministers. In his own church he always insisted that pastors "confine
themselves to strictly biblical themes, and to the achievement of distinctly
spiritual results," for he maintained that evangelism was ultimately the
only answer to this world's ills.[7]

Crozier, and the many others like him, support the observation of
George Marsden, American evangelicalism's premier historian, that by
the end of the Civil War era "evangelical Protestantism . . . was fast
becoming synonymous with the middle class *status quo.*"[8] As the rich of
their day, evangelicals shared with most Americans the belief that their
economic system was beneficent, and susceptible to the guidance and
correction of good Christian people. In retrospect, of course, we can see
that the serious social problems that became endemic in the twentieth
century were already beginning to surface in the 1840s and 1850s. In

particular, urbanization was fashioning its peculiar combination of lavish wealth and abject poverty side-by-side. The symbiotic development of material productivity and economic decay had already presaged the dual role of industrialization as symbol of hope and betrayer of human aspiration. Immigrants were crowding into filthy tenements, their children uneducated and exploited, their most basic needs all but ignored by the baffled or the calloused among the city fathers. But no framework as yet existed in the mass mind to allow for these matters to become meaningful data. It was still possible to believe that, although progress had a price and a few would get hurt in the betterment of the many, the system itself had no long-term disabilities that good-hearted people could not overcome.

By the 1880s and 1890s Americans were losing some of that optimistic mid-century naiveté. It is likely that many first sensed their new malaise as a loss of control. The most obvious and concrete symbol of this loss was the labor unrest, complete with revolutionary language and mob violence, that sprinkled the last three decades of the century. To many minds such turmoil raised the specter of the huddled masses of the tenement districts, recently augmented by the much less familiar immigrants from southern and eastern Europe, spilling out of the cities to wreak havoc on an old-stock American populace that still believed in playing by the rules. At the same time, while their sympathies were still for the owners of property against whom these working classes did battle, middle-class Americans were beginning to sense the dangers that lay in the emerging group of super-rich and their corporate entities. Highly visible entrepreneurs with names like Gould and Rockefeller and Vanderbilt seemed capable of riding roughshod over the welfare of countless small businessmen. Despite their claims, it was becoming evident that they were no more enamored of the rules of the free enterprise game than were their working-class foes. The neat world of middle-class (usually Christian) professionals and businessmen, as orderly in its workings as the Newtonian solar system, was being invaded by agents of social chaos from below and above. There was an inevitable tightening of the spirit that accompanied the constriction of opportunity and freedom for the good men and women who, to hear them tell it, had built this country from the start.

The violent poor and the irresponsible rich were only the most explicit and sensational symbols of the changing shape of America. Something fearful was going on much closer to home for most Americans. A specter was touching the human spirit at deeper levels than the newspaper could treat, levels at once less susceptible to analysis and more vital in their potential for human disfigurement. While the stories of railway strikes and anarchist agitation caught the headlines, the economic imperatives of industrialism were fastening their golden chains around the body politic in its traditional sanctuary, the American small town. Here is where it was normal to live in the late nineteenth century, far enough from the burgeoning cities to afford a measure of quiet and insulation from the growing social chaos, yet close enough to offer access to the good things of life newly presented by the factory system, things that appeared harmless when imported into such a benign and protected setting. Life in small-town America of the nineteenth century had been relatively stable and predictable. As centers of supply and social community for the surrounding farm families, the towns moved at a pace just slightly modified from the rhythms of agriculture. In most of them a relatively benign and easily recognizable elite defined standards of acceptable behavior and ruled by a certain implicit charter. Personal interaction with folks above and below on the social scale humanized class gradations. Social problems seemed resolvable by appeals to personal responsibility. The people who mattered most in influencing the quality of one's life were one's neighbors. If personal freedom was not untrammeled—hedged about as it was by codes of respectability and group expectations—still many of the factors making for earthly success or failure did seem to be lodged in one's own hands. For those who lived there, and even for many who fled to the inviting chaos of the cities, small town America was the real America, the epitome of social stability and symbol of the safety and comfort that only the familiar can bring.[9]

The familiarity and manageability of small-town life was what the implacable dynamic of industrial capitalism was destroying in the late nineteenth century, and its initial thrusts were delivered by the railroad. Despite the railroad's soot and noise, its land hunger and expense, every town wanted it. This technological marvel offered to the booster's imagination unlimited hopes for economic vitality and all the accouterments of civilized existence, which were naturally delivered to the local populace by the well-paid hands of the biggest dreamer. Town fathers bid, borrowed, and cajoled to attract a feeder line to their locale. Not until much later did the darkest potentials of this Trojan Horse become evident, but by then it was too late; the dependency had taken hold, and the railroad's transformation of small-town life proceeded apace. Townspeople discovered that, although their money had brought the railroad, it had not brought power over the railroad. Distant, faceless officials determined rates, routes, and services, often in total disregard for the integrity of the community. Moralists would soon note that railroads "override the laws of God, deprive thousands of their employees of their only day of rest and the pleasure of Christian worship."[10]

Small craftsmen and local manufacturers discovered that goods brought from the city sweatshops offered novelty at lower prices, making their own goods obsolete. Merchants, traveling salespeople, and jobbers were forced out of business by wholesale and retail chains operating out of the major cities, as the economies of specialization and centralization worked their will. Local farmers, jumping at the chance to secure their own prosperity by providing food for hungry city dwellers, soon enough found themselves dependent on faraway markets and processors, and on the whim of the railroad to get their products to marketplaces at a rate that did not drain away their profits. As these farmers expanded their land holdings to take advantage of the inviting new markets, they mortgaged their future to greedy financiers at high rates of interest. National credit systems and markets, crop specialization and mechanization, all made them less husbandmen than businessmen and wedded them—in a dependent position—to the maneuverings of wealthy bankers in distant cities, the monopolistic price-gouging of the railroads, and the wild fluctuations of market prices for their crops. Some succeeded and became wealthier than anyone thought a farmer could ever be, but with the same nagging dependency and the anxieties of operating in a world of powerful and impersonal entities. Many failed and took the railroad's offer of transportation to the city, where they were thrown into the even grimmer embrace of the forces that had worked their destruction once before.

These came to the city, but not only these. The city's seductions worked on restless farm or small-town youths, drawing them away from the familiar at a time when they could not but devalue its ineffable securities. The railroad and the city thus disturbed the expectations of many a family for intergenerational solidarity and disrupted the economies of a family business or farm. Craftspeople, shopkeepers, and farmers were left dependent on less loyal or reliable—and more expensive—rural wage earners or "hired hands." Their children, meanwhile, found in the city a badly eroded social entity. Population growth outpaced the provision of basic services, political institutions were shocked by new demands, nearby communities were being sucked into the urban orb willy-nilly, businesses were built and destroyed overnight, and frenetic activity reigned in a climate comparatively bereft of the restraints of social cohesion or civic spirit. Families and neighborhoods experienced the same disintegrating processes that were disrupting the small towns. Those who joined the growing ranks of industrial workers found themselves treated as interchangeable parts by distant managers who paid wages bearing little resemblance to the material requirements of human life.

Those, on the other hand, who made it to the top were themselves perplexed by the new demands of a national industrial system, although they could indulge their anxieties with a somewhat lesser sense of urgency than their desperate employees could. Often good at driving a hard bargain, they were less adept at administering an unwieldy financial, manufacturing, marketing, or transportation empire. As Robert Wiebe, an excellent commentator on this era, puts it,

> . . . far-flung networks did not respond to the personal, casual procedures of a small company, and the result was an unplanned diffusion of power. If those who thought of the new industrial giants as diabolically perfect organisms could have peeked inside, they would have found jerry-built organization, ad hoc assumptions of responsibility, obsolete office techniques, and above all an astonishing lack of communication among its parts. . . . What was true of business in general applied as well to banking. . . . The apparent leaders, like their industrial counterparts, presided over vast mechanisms that had developed beyond their control. With intuitive methods for gauging the business cycle and rule-of-thumb measures for evaluating credit risks, they relied on stabs of shrewdness, not long-range wisdom, in conducting their affairs. Bankers at all levels strained to comprehend an increasingly complex, impersonal operation.[11]

To some degree, then, the common small-town complaint about all-powerful financial conspirators calmly pulling the strings that made the citizenry jump according to some grand design was vastly overblown. Strong men there were, and greedy, with tentacles that did indeed touch the lives of ordinary citizens everywhere. But not even the richest could fully predict the consequences of their own schemes, nor comprehend the hidden logic of the times. Rich, middle-class, and poor—all were baffled by the fundamental transformations, the rapid revisions in the rules of the game, and the multiplicity of new phenomena that had no home in the familiar categories of the mind. If each did not see clearly the outlines of the new world being born, each did experience the labor pains, complicated by the vague anxiety that this new creature might be bent on destruction. And yet their own visions, their seemingly rational decisions, had contributed most to the acceleration of the process in which they now felt caught. Across the country, farmers and merchants, bankers and would-be employees measured the requirements of self-interest with a certain calm analysis and made the choices that sold them into an invisible slavery to faceless, strange, and distant powers. By their own acts of will, often with dreams of augmenting or recapturing control, men and women plunged into a world in which, increasingly, no one had any control at all. As Wiebe writes, a certain "perplexity" settled over the nation. "As the network of relations affecting men's lives each year became more entangled and more distended, Americans in a basic sense no longer knew who or where they were. The setting had altered beyond their power to understand it, and within an alien context they had lost themselves."[12]

Like all modern peoples, Americans were learning through painful experience the costs of progress. All of us since then have lived in the same ambivalent relationship to the economic and social forces of our time—welcoming them, celebrating them, unable to deny their enchantments, and yet dreading and resenting their disintegrating powers, wishing for the return of some imagined "good old days" when men and women could find comfort in familiar verities. We go on thinking that we can somehow regain control of the modernizing process, and we declare our intention to preserve the best of the old ways while swinging wide the doors to the new. We have not been quick to consciously acknowledge what Karl Marx saw a century ago: "Modern bourgeois society, . . . a society that has conjured up such gigantic means of production and of exchange, is like the sorcerer who is no longer able to control the powers of the subterranean which he has called up by his spells."[13] Having conjured up this sorcerer, Americans—and the evangelicals among them—were facing an unfamiliar world in the late nineteenth century and were feeling the vertigo in which the sure and the fixed spin and ultimately dissolve into the mist. Again, Marx was one of the earliest thinkers to understand this reality.

> Constant revolutionizing of production, uninterrupted disturbance of all social relations, everlasting uncertainty and agitation distinguish the bourgeois epoch from all earlier ones. All fixed, fast-frozen relations, with their train of ancient and venerable prejudices and opinions, are swept away, all new-formed ones become antiquated before they can ossify. All that is solid melts into air, all that is holy is profaned. . . .[14]

Marx, of course, hoped that by laying bare the true nature of life in modernizing society he could awaken its victims to the possibilities of revolution, where he placed hopes for a more humane world—hopes that the twentieth century would bitterly disappoint. By and large, Americans were uninterested in this message. But many could and did point to specific examples in their own experience of relationships being swept away, of things solid melting into air, of the holy being profaned. They could have used Job to complement Marx: "I am not at ease, nor am I quiet; I have no rest; but trouble comes."

III

Let us return to the book of Job to see whether it can help us further our understanding of what Americans were experiencing in the late nineteenth century. As chapter 29 opens, Job is dreaming of the good old days:

> Oh, that I were as in the months of old, as in the days when God watched over me; when his lamp shone upon my head, and by his light I walked

through darkness; as I was in my autumn days, when the friendship of God was upon my tent; when the Almighty was yet with me, when my children were about me; when my steps were washed with milk, and the rock poured out for me streams of oil! When I went out to the gate of the city, when I prepared my seat in the square, the young men saw me and withdrew, and the aged rose and stood; the princes refrained from talking, and laid their hand on their mouth; the voices of the nobles was hushed, and their tongue cleaved to the roof of their mouth. When the ear heard, it called me blessed, and when the eye saw, it approved; because I delivered the poor who cried, and the fatherless who had none to help him. The blessing of him who was about to perish came upon me, and I caused the widow's heart to sing for joy. I put on righteousness, and it clothed me; my justice was like a robe and a turban. I was eyes to the blind, and feet to the lame. I was a father to the poor, and I searched out the cause of him whom I did not know. I broke the fangs of the unrighteous, and made him drop his prey from his teeth.

(29:2-17)

In these lines Job describes the kind of life virtually every human being must crave, a life in which every element contrives to make him feel safe and secure. His tent lived up to its symbolism as a place of shelter and warmth, because he knew God's friendship was upon it. His family was intact, surrounding him with love and respect. He knew economic success and security, with milk enough to wash his steps and oil pouring forth at his command. He was an important figure in the social system, shown deference by both the young and the old. He certainly was a man of political importance, since princes refrained from talking in his presence. Everywhere he went, people knew who he was, and thus confirmed for him a sense of his own identity, which afforded him a certain emotional security. His neighbors knew him and praised him as a good man, a generous man, a just man, a courageous man. Job could truly be "at home" in this world.

So we are not surprised when Job wryly recalls how sure he had been that his blessings were permanent. This is the meaning of his very next line: "Then I thought, 'I shall die in my nest, and I shall multiply my days as the sand, my roots spread out to the waters, with the dew all night on my branches, my glory fresh with me, and my bow ever new in my hand'" (29:18-20). In some respects, Job had apparently come to take his good fortune for granted. With every social and cultural trapping supporting his heroism and offering him safety and meaning, he was very well "nested" indeed. His nest sheltered him and offered him the prospects of security right to the end of his life. He felt protected from the unpredictable and the irrational, and enjoyed a sense of control over his own life. He had no reason to expect disturbance.

But disturbance came. One day he "dwelt like a king among his troops" (29:25); the next, he had to mourn: "But now they make sport of me, men who are younger than I, whose fathers I would have disdained to set with the dogs of my flock. . . . I am a byword to them. They abhor me, they keep aloof from me; they do not hesitate to spit at the sight of me" (30:1, 9-10). Job had lost his nest and with it every security and basis for respect that he had enjoyed for so long. The familiar had passed away; everything solid had melted into air; the holy had become profane.

Most of us know, at least in a small way, what it is to be suddenly without a nest. If we have traveled beyond our national boundaries—say, as tourists in a strange and distant culture—we know what it feels like to be without mooring, thrown off-balance because customary assumptions are no longer operative and usual behaviors do not elicit predictable responses. At these times our sense of at-homeness in the world is badly shaken, and the illusion that we have control over our lives evaporates. We are ill-at-ease, and self-conscious, comforted only by knowing that we have come here voluntarily. We long for home and the familiar, where we are known and enjoy a certain importance recognized by all. Arriving at home, we may reflect with new insight on the arbitrary and artificial nature of our own rules for living and on the fragility of the social agreements that keep us feeling safe. We have come to terms, in some measure, with the precariousness of our grip on reality.

The adult generation of the 1880s and 1890s experienced the anxieties of this precariousness, but with a difference. They did not perceive that they had left home voluntarily, and they could find no truly safe haven within which to analyze their experience in retrospect and at a distance. As individuals they had certainly exercised a degree of choice in moving into this new world. Farmers were not forced to leave subsistence for commercial agriculture; small businessmen did not have to become marketing agents for distant factories; the younger generation did not have to run to the cities. But the fact that so many did, that a massive social transformation did take place, speaks of the extraordinary seductiveness of the new world. Clearly, many saw the alternatives as most uninviting and did not think they had a choice. But among those with the sharpest vision, even those who chose with great reluctance, there could not have been the foreknowledge of how quickly they would find themselves without a nest. We know that those who ventured into the cities for the first time were shocked and confused by the alien world they found there— though they were at the same time mysteriously attracted. How much more perplexed were those who stayed put in the small towns and found their lives just as radically altered as if they had settled in a foreign land![15]

Their perplexity—and the story of Job—remind us of how central to our humanity is this task of nest-building. Peter Berger, a leading contemporary sociologist of religion, begins his book *The Sacred Canopy* with the line: "Every human society is an enterprise of world-building."[16] Without significantly changing his meaning, he might have written: "Every human society is an enterprise of nest-building." We humans are noticeably frail creatures. The skin that covers and protects our vital organs is hardly equal to the task. We lack the armor of some animals, the speed of others, the scenting ability of still others; we have neither fur to keep us warm nor claws and fangs to ward off our attackers. But, in a sense not shared by the animals, we are fully and fearfully aware of our own vulnerability. As the late cultural anthropologist Ernest Becker has pointed out so forcefully, we are uniquely the animal that knows it will die, that lives with the at least intermittent awareness of its own vulnerability. Symbolically, we choose to protect ourselves, eke meaning out of what looks like a sheer animal existence, and provide ourselves a kind of immortality by creating and sustaining a culture.[17] A human culture, according to Berger, is a "shield against terror," an "area of meaning carved out of a vast area of meaninglessness, a small clearing of lucidity in a formless, dark, always ominous jungle. . . . Every human society is, in the last resort, men banded together in the face of death."[18] Every human society is, in other words, a nest for the trembling human creature.

Some may wish to take exception to this description of culture or society. We are not aware that we are trembling; in fact, we normally feel quite calm and competent. Nor are we aware that we have built anything resembling a nest. Our culture and our society seem to have been here before we were, and we meet them as givens by virtue of being born into them. But Berger's analysis counters these objections. No, we are not especially conscious of our own fears; this is because of the degree to which the cultural nesting apparatus really *does* perform its task. It provides a feeling of security and hides our vulnerability from us. We live out our daily lives within a familiar and safe network of social expectations, economic routines, political understandings, and material artifacts—feeling quite at home, quite comfortable, quite protected. This sense of comfort is enhanced by our failure to see ourselves as creating those protective nests. Rather, we take our social and cultural surroundings for granted; we treat our nest as if it were reality itself, not the contrivance of trembling human hands.

It was this unconscious familiarity—this comfortable taken-for-grantedness—that Job was wishing for as he dreamed of the good old days. And it was the loss of these same consolations that evangelicals and other Americans were mourning in the late nineteenth century. Economic processes were taking new shapes, social institutions were straining, roles and identities were newly threatened. Even the geographical and mate-

rial surroundings were being transformed under the impact of industrialization: homes were no longer protected in quite the same way; families
no longer cohered; the world indeed looked like a "wrecked vessel."
Americans were not feeling very safely nested.

But the times presented special problems for evangelicals. Like Job,
they had come to associate the safety of their tents, their nests, with the
friendship of God. They had not simply basked in the earthly delights of
that seemingly secure nest, but they had identified its political, social, and
economic features with the will of God. Berger calls this the process of
legitimation. Legitimations, Berger says, are answers to the "why" questions regarding social and cultural arrangements. If the social structure
provides an order for reality, the question may be asked: why *this* kind of
order? The answer, of course, is that God wishes it that way. If a rebellious soul wonders why he or she must observe the social customs, the
answer is that God commands it. If a group of people are asked why they
have status or wealth or power in the society, they can respond that God
gave it to them. In other words, religion tells us that God himself is the
creator and guarantor of our nest. This can be comforting indeed.[19]

I think we can say that evangelical theology functioned as just this sort
of religious legitimation for Americans of the bright and hopeful mid-
nineteenth century. As we have seen, it simply brought God down to give
his blessing to the institutional arrangements within which Americans
were already living. Countless evangelicals cited their nation's successes
as proof that God was on their side and used their faithfulness to this God
to give evidence that they deserved these blessings. In their use of millennial language evangelicals placed their history and the nation's history
into a cosmic frame of reference. As Berger explains, this "cosmization
. . . permits the individual to have an ultimate sense of rightness . . . in
the roles he is expected to play in society. . . . He *is* whatever society has
identified him as by virtue of a cosmic truth, as it were, and his social
being becomes rooted in the sacred reality of the universe."[20] When the
social nest becomes coterminous with the cosmic nest, we can expect to
hear the kinds of inflated and self-righteous claims that the mid-nineteenth-century evangelicals were wont to make.

Berger's analysis further helps us understand the traumatic impact, in
such a well-legitimated nest, of the widespread social and economic
changes of the late nineteenth century. Since a religious outlook and the
underlying social environment are so closely related by this process of
legitimation, changes in the social world can easily produce crisis in the
religious outlook. In Berger's terms, every religious world view depends
upon a social base for its continuing existence.[21] Berger calls this social
base a "plausibility structure." So long as the social and cultural arrange-

ments remain essentially unchanged, the religious ideas that are used to legitimate them retain their plausibility; the match between social and cosmic worlds seems secure, and the sense of nestedness can be preserved. But when the social environment alters drastically, so that the arrangements associated with the religious beliefs are now threatened, the beliefs no longer appear plausible. We can see from the way Berger says it how well this process describes the changing environment of late nineteenth-century America:

> The reality of the Christian world depends upon the presence of social structures within which this reality is taken for granted and within which successive generations of individuals are socialized in such a way that this world will be real *to them*. When this plausibility structure loses its intactness or continuity, the Christian world begins to totter and its reality ceases to impose itself as self-evident truth.[22]

The late nineteenth century in America is one of those historical situations in which "the Christian world" was beginning to totter. The neat, orderly, God-ordained social order of the mid-nineteenth century was giving way to the increasingly chaotic and unmanageable landscape of industrialism.

Job wrestled—indeed agonized—with his own religious legitimations as his familiar life dissolved before his eyes. He questioned the beliefs on which he had based his entire life and challenged the very God who stood behind those beliefs and to whom he had looked as the guarantor of his nest. Would the evangelicals do the same?

IV

The evangelicals of the United States were caught in a historic pincer movement, their way of life being transformed by the necessities of advancing industrialism. This should have been—and was—cause enough for some serious reevaluation of their evangelical belief structure. As the plausibility structure shook and twisted—for some, out of all recognition—the religious legitimations inevitably called for examination and, in some cases, revision. In succeeding chapters we shall take a closer look at this process of revision, with the historical context clearly in mind. But here we shall note that the American evangelicals were not only troubled by the implications of a changing social and economic environment for religious thought and experience. They were also under more direct assault, an assault bound to make them defensive and perhaps more open to knee-jerk retrenchment than to patient, trusting reexamination. This assault, associated with the high-water mark of the European Enlightenment, meant that evangelicals were not going to enjoy an environment of comparative intellectual calm and gradual change in which to ask their questions and to adjust their religious legitimations to new circumstances, as they had to some degree in bringing the Scottish philosophy to bear on the democratizing and enterprising conditions of the early nineteenth century. Even in those times, of course, the European Enlightenment had presented serious challenges to the traditional evangelical formulations; but by opting for the Scottish version and by a kind of revulsion against the excesses of the presumably enlightened French Revolution, the evangelicals kept the initiative in their hands and strictly contained the damage. But the theological self-examination and adjustment that evangelicals would undergo in the late nineteenth century would have to take place under fire from much more accurate, long-range intellectual guns than those of a century before. It would take place under more trying social and intellectual circumstances, and also in the face of the awareness that growing numbers of American religious and intellectual leaders were not interested in defending evangelical ground but in welcoming the enemy with open arms.

This enemy, the European Enlightenment, had risen to prominence in the Western mind in the late eighteenth century by virtue of the growing attractiveness of its major tenet: the workings of the natural and social worlds can be understood by humans through the use of their native rational faculties.[23] Tremendous confidence in human ability had flowed from Newton's understanding of the physical mechanics of the universe and by Locke's plumbing the wellsprings of human knowledge. It was a confidence shared particularly by the educated classes of eighteenth-century Europe; but, as we have seen, it was not lost on an American populace that pictured itself as a purer and more capable variety of the human species than even its European counterpart. As Henry May shows in his splendid treatment of the Enlightenment in America, the nation's Founding Fathers believed that, at the very least, they understood humanity well enough to design a polity that would minimize the consequences of whatever ignorance, obstinacy, or greed remained buried in the human breast, and, at most, supposed themselves to be creating the perfect society. When the French revolutionaries attempted the same feats, with somewhat more tragic results—made even less palatable by their explicitly anti-Christian sentiments—Americans recoiled even from some of their own idealistic propaganda and regrouped around a safer and more traditional evangelical revivalism. And yet their repudiation of the Enlightenment was a partial and contradictory one, as May demonstrates very well. Not to be left holding an outmoded and impractical Calvinist pessimism regarding human abilities, but put off by the skepticism, relativism, and irreligion of the later Enlightenment figures (especially Hume and continental thinkers like Voltaire, d'Holbach, Condorcet, and even Kant), the Americans adopted the philosophically moderate but still suitably optimistic Enlightenment thought of the Scottish Common Sense school.

With this choice Americans could posture as opponents of the godless Enlightenment while partaking of what they thought to be its sweeter fruits. So malleable was Common Sense thought that, although it readily supported the kind of "natural religion" espoused by the heretical Deists, American evangelicals could and did use it to make war on Deism and all other forms of rationalistic infidelity. At the same time, however, Common Sense philosophy allowed Americans to enjoy all the earthly delights and practical benefits of a high view of human nature and thus to participate fully in the underlying titanism of the Enlightenment. In effect, American evangelicals modified and moderated the Enlightenment for their own purposes. Their embrace of Common Sense philosophy and their adaption of its tenets to evangelical theology, and vice versa, gave them a philosophical mixture that would stop the erosion of biblical authority in its tracks while allowing the freedom to experience progress in every other field of human endeavor. They felt the relief of being up to date philosophically (or so they imagined) while holding on to the verities of their orthodoxy (or so they imagined). In the hands of an evangelical consensus, and on a continent isolated by geographical distance and intellectual provincialism from the dangerous European thought currents, this ploy worked well for more than half a century.

But in Europe, of course, things were very different. There the best minds ignored the consolations of the Scottish philosophy and explored, in due time, the most dangerous of the Enlightenment's waters. Leading the list, as perhaps it always must, was the question of God. If humans are fully capable of understanding the social and natural worlds by the instrumentality of reason alone, what is the need for revelation? Further, if rational critique be applied to the presumed means of revelation—the Scriptures or the historical figure of Jesus or the church—can these not be explained as purely human phenomena, perhaps even manifestations of a pre-Enlightenment ignorance? And further, do not the rational intellect's demands for evidence of what is to be believed remove the supernatural or transcendent realm from serious consideration as the subject of reliable knowledge? Do not the so-called proofs of the existence of God turn out to be feeble attempts to bolster what one simply desires to believe, despite the contrary witness of the senses? Can we not find the appeal of religion to be rooted more in the natural needs of the human animal than in the reliability of its truth claims?

In other words, European scholarship in the nineteenth century was far more courageous, although in some ways also far more self-assured and perverse, than was American scholarship. And this courage was characteristic of Christian thinkers as much as it was of the more secular-minded scholars. Karl Barth describes nineteenth-century Protestant theology on the continent as having been abjectly, almost obsessively, open to the Enlightenment-influenced intellectual climate of its day.[24] It did not shrink from facing the hardest questions of the secularizing consciousness—or from almost universal application of the scientific method. While he does not fault their sincerity or courage, Barth does believe that these theologians both took themselves too seriously and gave away too much. "Their particular venture became questionable . . . as they set out to prove the possibility of faith in its relatedness to, and its conditioning by, the world views which were normative for their contemporaries and even for themselves."[25] Those world views, strongly influenced by the Enlightenment and the heritage of Kant, leaned away from talk about God to talk about humanity. Without the confidence that talk about God would be credited among a positivistic generation, theologians tried to sell Christianity as a response to the deepest human feelings, and thus to locate the existence of God within the self-awareness of the individual Christian. In so doing, they paralleled—though with very different presuppositions on a conscious level at least—the American evangelical move: from a God who truly stands over against humans and their cultures and who calls them to account, to a vague and almost irrelevant God who offers his blessing to whatever cultural and historical tendencies seem most in fashion at the time.

By the middle of the nineteenth century, then, supernaturalism was clearly on the retreat even among Christian thinkers in Europe. Following the lead of Friedrich Schleiermacher, the "father of liberalism," theologians were seeing in the Bible primarily a record of the human experience of God and not God's Word to mankind. Since it was a human product, the Bible could—and should—be subjected to the careful scrutiny of the new, more "scientific" critical methods. Increasingly, by this same reasoning, the Christian faith became one religion among many, to be compared and contrasted to others, weighed as to its cultural determinants, and evaluated as to its ethical teachings. Jesus of Nazareth required reexamination as well. The supernatural trappings of his story had to be purged, his true teachings sifted out from the mythical context, and his moral example for Christians thus clarified. Embarrassed by traditional theological constructions, leading Christian thinkers turned to the history of doctrine and demonstrated the all-too-human cultural conditioning of the Christian faith, hoping to strip away the accretions of the

the centuries and to expose to the secular mind of the nineteenth century some attractive Christian kernel.

By the time this historical-critical method of biblical study arrived in the United States, some of its most stunning contributions had already become something like orthodoxy in Europe. It had come to understand that neither Paul nor Moses had written most of the works ascribed to them; it saw the Pentateuch as a compilation of several identifiable sources; it saw much of the New Testament as a result of a second-century squabble between Petrine and Pauline traditions; and it found that books making accurate prophetic predictions were written after the events described in them as future. The life of Jesus had been totally rewritten, several times, to portray a denatured Jewish prophet or a modern ethical philosopher with a lot of good, simple advice about loving one's neighbor—something, it was thought, most people could learn to do by observing Jesus' example. An uncritical naturalism seemed to have replaced an uncritical supernaturalism, and the result was a Bible and a Savior that many evangelicals could barely recognize.[26]

The shock was all the greater because, while this new and troubling scholarship was being introduced to a wider American public, another foreign visitor was capturing headlines for his own brand of infidelity. Charles Darwin had published *The Origin of Species* just before the Civil War, which meant that the greatest impact of his evolutionary hypothesis on American thought was somewhat muted until the latter 1860s, when it hit at least the scholarly community with the force of a tidal wave. Darwin's extensive and detailed study of biological organisms of a wide geographical scope over two decades had convinced him that the variations we see in living species are the result not of multiple, individual creations by God but rather of a natural process in which the environment "selects" the fittest for survival. Under the pressures of a struggle for existence in an ever-changing environment, certain species thrive, reproduce their adaptive characteristics in their offspring, and thus ensure for the time being the perpetuation of their life forms. Others, unequal by natural endowment to the demands of the struggle, perish, and fade from the earth. Given the required geographical isolation and vast eons of time, Darwin thought, a species could modify its nature by this unwieldy, wasteful, and indeterminate process of life and death, even to the point of becoming a separate species altogether. When Darwin published his *Descent of Man* in 1871, he made it clear that humans had also evolved by that same harsh regimen and had no more been a special creation by God than had the fruit fly or the famous finches of the Pacific islands.

Darwin's stunning synthesis, built on the labors of a dozen prominent thinkers and researchers of the preceding century but bound together by his own unique imaginative insight, wrought a revolution in the late nineteenth-century mind. It added the biological pieces of the puzzle to a growing historical consciousness: the awakening of leading thinkers to the developmental, fluctuating, historically conditioned nature of all things human as well as nonhuman. It unlocked nature's mysteries with a key that thinking persons felt they could hold in their own hands, a key not linked to the demands of faith in a supernatural being. At the same time that it perceived a certain design in life's processes, it eliminated the need for a beneficent divine superintendent. Indeed, had God's presence in the system been required, it would have been as a callous and whimsical being who used the sufferings of his very creation to work his unknown ends. Loren Eiseley captures the meaning of Darwin for the modern mind with unusual grace and melancholy:

> We today know the result of Darwin's endeavors—the knitting together of the vast web of life until it is seen like the legendary tree of Igdrasil, reaching endlessly up through the dead geological strata with living and related branches still glowing in the sun. Bird is no longer bird but can be made to leap magically backward into reptile; man is hidden in the lemur, lemur in tree shrew, tree shrew in reptile; reptile is finally precipitated into fish.
>
> But then there intrudes another problem: Mouse is trying to convert all organic substance into mouse. Black snake is trying to convert mouse into snake. Man maintains factories to convert cattle into human substance. It is an ingenious but hardly edifying spectacle in which nothing really wins, and through which whole orders of life have perished. If our tempo or seeing could be speeded, life would appear and disappear as a chaos of evanescent and writhing forms, possessing the impermanence of the fairy mushroom circles that spring up on our lawns at midnight. . . . "What a book," [Darwin] had written with unaccustomed savagery, "a devil's chaplain might write on the clumsy, wasteful, blundering and horribly cruel works of Nature."[27]

Darwin's aimless, bloodstained, and cosmically silent world was not where most Americans particularly wanted to live. The sense of chaos in their own lives, of being caught up in the grip of larger, impersonal forces, could only have been increased by the growing influence of Darwin's writings. But Darwin came as a special problem to evangelicals. For half a century, when they were not ignoring it, evangelicals were generous in their praise of science and confident in its results. The Scottish philosophy had posited a marvelous fit between the natural world, the mind of man, and the ways of God. By investigating the natural world, it was thought, the scientist would readily discover the evidences of God's existence and his creative ingenuity in fashioning this world. Science was thus a handy apologetic tool for the persuasion of sinners and the reassurance of the faithful. Some, characterizing science as the handmaiden of theology, went even further: "If there were no scientific proof of the existence of God, it was argued, revelation would be stripped of all authority, 'and man must forever live amidst the spectres of uncertainty and spiritual want.'" George Daniels adds that, in Common Sense thinking, science and religion were so closely associated that an attack on science was considered an attack on Christianity itself.[28]

Such a pleasant synthesis of science and religion, the likes of which we have not seen in evangelical circles since Darwin, had produced a popular body of literature in the eighteenth and nineteenth centuries known as natural theology—and an impressive record of scientific research as well. Theological naturalists like William Paley found a ready market for their writings in the United States. Paley's work made popular the argument from design, which attributed the vast complexities of biological organisms to the kindly hand of God in nature. Paley could assure his readers that they lived in a wonderfully designed and essentially caring world.

> In every nature . . . we find attention bestowed upon even the minutest parts. The hinges in the wings of an earwig and the joints of its antennae, are as highly wrought, as if the creator had had nothing else to finish. We see no signs of diminution of care by multiplicity of objects, or of distraction of thought by variety. We have no reason to fear, therefore, our being forgotten, or overlooked, or neglected.[29]

Both in England and America, this confidence led to bold investigations of all natural phenomena, as scientists sought to lay bare the evidences of God's design in nature. Most American scientists considered themselves disciples of Francis Bacon, interpreting his instructions as encouragement to collect and classify data and to avoid hypothesizing where empirical data were not available.[30] Thus they avoided dangerous ideas about the origin of phenomena while they assiduously collected extensive and minute discriptions of organisms. They ignored or explained away such anomalies as nature's profligate waste of life or the growing evidence of extinct species, and they preserved God's goodness at the end as they had assumed it from the beginning. Evangelically-oriented scientists showed the entire created order to be a fixed, balanced, divinely designed, and purposive mechanism. "Man stood at the center of all things and the entire universe had been created for his edification and instruction: hills had been placed for his pleasure, animals ran on four feet because it made them better beasts of burden, and flowers grew for his enjoyment."[31] Resting on its commonsense assumption that science, rightly done, could only generate and reinforce such a world view, evangelical Americans exhibited, in George Daniels's words, "an almost childlike faith in science."[32]

With science's essential innocence thus tightly woven into the very conceptual warp of the evangelical consensus in mid-century America, the sting of Darwin was all the greater. In one quick stroke he distorted the very notion of design (which he himself had gratefully received in devoted study of William Paley) and eliminated the need for the Designer. The most beautiful and intricate of an organism's characteristics could apparently be accounted for by nothing more dignified than the luck of the draw. Instead of a creation made for human use and enjoyment, it was made for no known intelligent purpose at all. Mankind itself was the "child of chance," selected out by an impersonal environment, perhaps doomed to extinction, and nowhere in the universe might there be a personal entity to mark and mourn its passing.[33]

Ernst Haeckel, a stridently naturalistic follower of Darwin, spelled out the further implications of Darwin's scheme in 1877: "The cell consists of matter called protoplasm, composed chiefly of carbon, with an admixture of hydrogen, nitrogen and sulphur. These component parts, properly united, produce the soul and body of the animated world, and suitably nursed become man. With this single argument the mystery of the universe is explained, the Deity annulled and a new era of infinite knowledge ushered in."[34] Haeckel's palpable glee could only have appeared incomprehensible, if not terrifying, to most American evangelicals. President Barnard of Columbia University certainly did not share it. Agreeing that organic evolution presaged the death of God, he declared: "If the final outcome of all the boasted discoveries of modern science is to disclose to men that they are more evanescent than the shadow of the swallow's wing upon the lake . . . give me then, I pray, no more science. I will live on in my simple ignorance, as my fathers did before me."[35]

But, of course, there was no such simple ignorance left for the life of the mind in scholarly circles after Darwin. While some mourned the passing of a stable, unchanging universe, others saw a certain order in the flux that reminded them of God's sovereignty. Christians like Asa Gray, one of the earliest partisans of Darwin in this country, hailed the evolutionary hypothesis as an even more ingenious evidence of God's design, although Darwin chided him for his unbridled theism. Secularists, untroubled by the flux, felt a certain freedom in the removal of a divine hand, although they differed as to the implications of that freedom for human behavior. Social scientists brought the struggle for existence into the heart of their own discipline's subject matter, the dynamic of human society. Some posited a determinism that allowed for little cultural tinkering lest the natural selective mechanisms be thrown out of gear; their opponents delivered a call for humans to master their fate by shaping social institutions from above.[36] In the first flush of enthusiasm and release, not many of a secular mind saw clearly how much more heavily a

vacant universe and an absent God might weigh on the human soul than
had the beneficent divine monarchy of the evangelical consensus. A half-
century later, though, after a world war had confirmed evolution's cruelty while destroying its pretentions to progress, Walter Lippmann sounded almost as plaintive as had Columbia's Barnard:

> Our forefathers . . . had no doubt that there was an order in the universe
> which justified their lives because they were a part of it. The acids of mod-
> ernity have destroyed that order for many of us. . . . The older fable may be
> incredible today, but when it was credible it bound together the whole of
> experience upon a stately and dignified theme. The modern man has ceased
> to believe in it but he has not ceased to be credulous, and the need to believe
> haunts him. It is no wonder that his impulse is to turn back from his
> freedom, and to find someone who says he knows the truth and can tell him
> what to do, to find the shrine of some new god . . . where he can kneel and
> be comforted, put on manacles to keep his hands from trembling, ensconce
> himself in some citadel where it is safe and warm.[37]

Most American evangelicals instinctively knew the meaning of Darwin—perhaps much better than did those prominent few who embraced
evolution as an evidence for design or a cause for comfort. Eiseley characterizes the outcry against Darwin as "the sick revulsion of the wounded
human ego."[38] The evangelical ego of the mid-nineteenth century seems
to have been dangerously overinflated, riding along in an era of ostensibly benevolent progress, fed on the rich fare of human capacity and
millennial hope. Now the tables were turned. Increasingly violent and
disorienting social change announced to them, perhaps only in some
hidden corner of the spirit, that matters were out of control. Biblical
scholars introduced the possibility that the symbol of their certainty and
the source of their civil mandate was perhaps simply the product of
human, not divine, creativity. Darwin not only raised the specter of chaos
and impersonality to a cosmic scale but exploded the easy confidence in
the harmony of human knowledge and the revealed ways of God. By the
last quarter of the nineteenth century American evangelicals were beginning to suspect that the kingdom of God was perhaps not coming in
America after all. With their religious legitimations crumbling, they felt a
deep and fearful confusion settling into their souls.

V

When I was seven years old, I became a Christian. The occasion was the
annual revival service at our small fundamentalist church in a large eastern city. Trembling, I answered the evangelist's invitation and made my

choice for God. Later, in bedside prayer with my parents attending, I confirmed that choice. The next day I felt cleaner—and much, much safer. It felt good to be on the right side of things eternal.

Of course, the deck was stacked in God's favor. Of the two choices presented me, the camp of the devil seemed, in the main, unappetizing. One had access to certain temporal joys, perhaps, but at the price of eternal damnation—even if one avoided the wages of sin and a possible criminal existence in this life, which was unlikely. God's camp had everything going for it—an all-powerful Father, happiness in this life at the cost of a little moral discipline, relief from a burden of guilt that, even for a seven-year-old, is not without its weight, and an eternal home in heaven. I seem to remember that it was particularly important that I not be left behind when Jesus returned to rescue the faithful, including my family and friends, from the Great Tribulation.

During my childhood and on that decisive night, I did not pause to consider the question of God's existence. I do not remember wondering whether Jesus was his only Son. I did not ask for a logical explanation of the virgin birth, or of how Jesus' death could save me from my sins. All these things seemed patently and obviously true. Apart from the names of my family members, Jesus' name was perhaps the first one I had learned in infancy. Songs, stories, Bible reading, and sermons made his existence and personal presence known to me daily. His interest in me, his pleasure in my good behavior, his help in trying situations—all were undeniable. I entertained no doubts. The truths of Scripture have never, since then, appeared more certain than they did to my seven-year-old eyes.

And my plausibility structure has never been stronger than it was then either. To say the deck was stacked in God's favor is to say that, sociologically, I lived in a "Christian world." All the important persons in my life, it seemed, were Christians. My parents, of course, and very seriously so since my father was the pastor of our church—but also my favorite relatives, my parents' adult friends, my Sunday school teacher and my babysitters, the children I was encouraged to play with, even my public school teacher, who led us in the Lord's Prayer each morning just before we saluted the flag. My contact with non-Christians was rare and brief. The reading material in our home was either Bible stories or tales of the relatively tame adventures of pious (though occasionally rascally) little Christians like myself. Our leisure activities we generally enjoyed in the company of others from our church, and we avoided worldly amusements with the exception of an occasional professional baseball game (in those days the ballparks were not awash in alcohol). Most importantly, all the language I heard was laced with religious terminology and simply assumed the reality of the Christian world picture.

In other words, my entire daily existence contrived to reinforce and illustrate the truth of the religious beliefs I was being taught at home and in church. If a fellow Christian recovered from a serious illness, we praised the Lord; if he or she died, we thanked God—since his will had been done. If friends experienced financial success, the Lord had graciously and faithfully taken care of their needs or rewarded them for diligence and good stewardship; if poverty struck, the Lord was teaching his people to trust him more or was putting them to the test for their own good. If church attendance boomed so that a new wing had to be built to hold the growing Sunday school program, the Lord was increasing the harvest in these last days; if attendance dropped, it was confirmation that perilous times are to be expected in the last days, and apostasy would be seen on every hand. As my contact with the wider world increased, the legitimations followed. Why are our boys fighting and dying in Korea? To stop an unrighteous power from bringing its neighbors under the yoke of communist dictatorship. God would bless our efforts—and it appeared to us that he did. Why must we build nuclear weapons with the capacity to destroy the world? Because if we don't, we will not be in a position to stop tyrants from ruling the earth. Of course, Hungary in 1956 confirmed that once and for all. Why vote for Richard Nixon in 1960? Because a Catholic presidency would bring us under the yoke of Rome, which received a very bad press in the book of Revelation.

But there's the rub: it didn't happen that way. The Kennedy presidency seemed—with respect to Rome and the triumph of Catholicism—little different from the Eisenhower presidency that had preceded it. Events did not seem to confirm the Bible-based predictions of evangelical leaders. Coming for me during my college years, this discovery only hastened the disintegration of my plausibility structure. The process had begun much earlier, of course, as it must for virtually any American evangelical teenager in the twentieth century. In high school the thick walls between Christian and non-Christian, saved and damned, weakened considerably. Peers who did not share my faith seemed, in some instances, just as friendly, as happy, as moral, as successful as I—many even more than I. New acquaintances from "liberal" or "unbelieving" churches seemed to believe pretty much what I did, and they often outdid me in Christian fervor for evangelization. Teachers took an interest in me, but seemingly without religious motivation. My experiments with behaviors proscribed by Christians produced guilt but no disaster, and some of them seemed more harmless in the doing than I had been led to believe. My plausibility structure was shaking, and this introduced my first hesitant doubts about the reliability of the Christian truth claims of which I had been convinced in childhood.

Further education, away from home, completed the task. I attended a Christian college, but one that introduced me to a bewildering variety of believers, some of whom seemed to be reading a Bible wholly different from the one familiar to me. Certain classmates believed that Jesus would not return before the Great Tribulation, but would leave us here to suffer. Episcopalians went to a church where, following the morning worship, members of the congregation smoked cigarettes and debated the merits of the sermon. I knew students who believed academic scholarship to be the Christian's highest calling and at least one who thought it a waste of time when souls were dying without Christ (he sold his goods in the middle of his freshman year and became a foreign missionary). We spent long Sunday afternoons in the dorm discussing previously certain truths: are the heathen lost? can anyone be saved? should infants be baptized? why does God allow suffering? It was dawning on me that I had some choices to make. That kind of freedom appeared less joyous than burdensome, and I was beginning to feel a little betrayed.

The turmoil continued in graduate school. There I met a yet more varied group of people: pleasant agnostics, liberal Lutherans, a generous and sensitive Roman Catholic, a Jewish roommate. As they became friends, they represented more challenges to the taken-for-granted truths of my childhood. They did not assume what I assumed, but their lives were little different from mine. I studied history and learned that the early church fathers had entertained long disputes about what I had been taught was unquestionable. I discovered that some of the impetus behind the Protestant Reformation was political, not strictly religious. I was introduced to whole civilizations that had lived and died in fervent dedication to religious traditions I thought to be mistaken; and evangelical Christianity appeared more and more a minor sidetrack in Christianity, much less history as a whole. Freud, Marx, Darwin, and Nietzsche all looked different in their historical contexts than in the gospel tracts I had read. Their understandings of the world seemed, in part, creditable, and their explanations of religious behavior, including my own, rang a frightening bell.

I am describing a process with which the reader is perhaps familiar. In one form or another, it comes to virtually every adolescent in a mobile, pluralistic world like ours; but it comes especially penetratingly to adolescents reared in the sheltered nest of a devout and separatist religious tradition. Inevitably, a youth's emergence from the confines and comforts of a religious family into the adult world of social variety and competing ideologies brings a sharp challenge to the taken-for-grantedness of the religious world view. The social world no longer supports the simple formulations of reality so convincing to a child. The rich variety of lenses through which people view their worlds relativizes old "truths," robbing the person of that confident naiveté. Things that made eminent sense now appear arbitrary; religion begins to look like a human creation. The neat order imposed on a potentially chaotic and meaningless world now seems insufficient to hold back the darkness. The holy is profaned. All that is solid melts into air.

We know how this feels. For brief moments we may revel in our freedom, scoff at our former innocence, cast barbs at those we blame for deluding us. But in our hearts we are afraid, and we cast about for some defense. We try to prop up old formulations with wishful thinking or intellectual shuffling. We wonder, quietly, how deep our delusion goes; we try to drown the questions in renewed activity; we seek trusted authorities to put the old ideas in new, more respectable language for us so that we can believe it again. We take note of the multitudes still "coming to Jesus" and admire the talents of outstanding soul-winners as proof that the old ways still attract people after all. We feel guilty, blame our disobedience for the doubts that plague us, and give ourselves anew to spiritual discipline. In all these ways we show that we are afraid.

Like Job, adolescents pass through a shaking of the plausibility structures, a dissolving of the religious legitimations. In simplest terms, they lose their nest. If we remember how this feels, perhaps we can understand more sympathetically the evangelical trauma of the late nineteenth century. Perhaps we can sense the confusion, the anxiety, the shock behind Moody's words: "I look on this world as a wrecked vessel." We might be able to predict, in some small measure, the kinds of responses which a deep and unacknowledged panic would elicit. Depending on our own experiences, we might affirm the necessity of such a shaking of the nest. From the standpoint of faith, we might remember that God does not shake the nest without desiring that thereby we should find him.

This brings us back to Job. To prove that Job did not love God "for nothing," Satan deprived Job of everything. *Did* Job love God for nothing? We are not precisely told. We do know that the terrible and total dismantling of his nest led him to question God, led him in effect to ask, Are you, God, my friend? We know that his experience of hopelessness brought him face to face with God, so that he could say, "I had heard of thee by the hearing of the ear, but now my eye sees thee" (42:5). We also know that in seeing God—perhaps for the first time—Job was brought to repentance: "Therefore I have uttered what I did not understand, things too wonderful for me, which I did not know. . . . Therefore I despise myself, and repent in dust and ashes" (42:3, 6). And we learn that Job's three friends, who did little more than repeat to him the well-worn theological propositions of the day, and who thus very nicely preserved their

nests at the same time that they presumed to defend God himself against
the questions of Job, were upbraided by God himself: "For you have not
spoken of me what is right, as my servant Job has" (42:8).

Where are the evangelicals of the late nineteenth century in this
drama? With their nest dissolved, did they question the God whose
faithfulness seemed suddenly withdrawn? Did they face the God of their
fathers and ask, Are you still our friend? Do we find them acknowledging
that the God whom they had so glibly identified with the American evangelical nest was really one they had not seen, but only heard with the ear?
In seeing him, did they meet anew the Son of man who, unlike the birds
of the air, had no nest, no place to lay his head (Matt. 8:20)? And did this
lead them to repentance? Or did they rush out, in the manner of Job's
friends, to feather afresh their threadbare and tottering nests, and thus to
ignore the disquieting comfort in the words of the apostle James: "Behold,
we call those happy who were steadfast. You have heard of the steadfast-
ness of Job, and you have seen the purpose of the Lord, how the Lord is
compassionate and merciful. . . . Therefore confess your sins to one another, and pray for one another, that you may be healed" (5:11, 16).

Chapter III

I Am Doing a Work in Your Days

I

The prophet Habakkuk knew how it felt to have his nest dissolving beneath him. He saw violence and destruction on every hand in the Israel of his day. He lived amidst "strife and contention," among a people who had no respect for the law. A few righteous people were left, he thought—perhaps he included himself as one of these. But they were so few in number, so surrounded by the wicked, that their efforts had little or no social consequence. Habakkuk was trying to hang on to his belief in a righteous God under these circumstances, but he was having a difficult time of it. Perhaps his religious legitimations seemed feeble beside the horrifying realities of his day. Did appearances indicate that maybe God does not answer the cry of the righteous? Is God perhaps not in control of history? Or, worse, has God joined the side of the wicked? We sense such questions in Habakkuk's spirit when we hear him plead with God: "O Lord, how long shall I cry for help, and thou wilt not hear? Or cry to thee 'Violence!' and thou wilt not save? Why dost thou make me see wrongs and look upon trouble?" (1:2-3).

Habakkuk was being buffeted by appearances, and his faith was being tried. Evangelical Christians living at the turn of the century surely could have heard in his words an echo of their own plight. For many humans, one religious legitimation is especially close at hand: God is still in control. When our lives are without trouble and our future seems bright, such words come easily to our lips. They sanctify the status quo and give a divine approval to the kindly world of appearances. When isolated troubles afflict us, we generally find it possible still to take refuge in these words. They come to us as a comfort, from a God who usually takes better care of us than this, and who must therefore have an important lesson in mind for us. But when trouble follows trouble, and our entire nest is shaken, the deeper questions begin. Is God still in control? If so, why does he "make me see wrongs and look upon trouble?" Is he who I thought he was?

We know that at least some evangelicals asked these questions, although, like ourselves, they may not always honestly have faced the depth of their own turmoil. For example, the editor of *The Sunday School Times*, a leading evangelical publication, wrote this in 1912: "Appearances are badly against those who are trusting everything to Christ. Most people get along without Christ and many of these seem to do very well without him."[1] Now, this is really Habakkuk's observation: The wicked seem to be calling the shots, and there is no sign that they're suffering for their wickedness. The very same complaint is found in the Psalms, for example, Psalm 73:

> For I was envious of the arrogant, when I saw the prosperity of the wicked. . . . They are not in trouble as other men are; they are not stricken like other men. . . . Therefore the people turn and praise them; and find no fault in them. And they say, "How can God know? Is there knowledge in the Most High?"
>
> (3, 5, 10-11)

The writer of these words is clearly struggling to understand how a God who *knows* can go on letting the wicked prosper and, by implication, the righteous suffer. He does not like what appearances are telling him about his religious legitimations. We know that evangelicals, like the editor quoted above, must have been asking the same questions, even when we see them move very quickly to an "answer" to the problem of appearances, one that is intended to put such questioning to rest. "What a blessing it is, therefore," continued the editor, "that we need pay no attention to appearances, and that we have a Christ to whom appearances count for nothing!"[2]

This was quite a switch for American evangelicals. In the mid-nineteenth century, it seems, appearances had counted for almost everything. In fact, we might want to characterize mid-century evangelicalism as having been utterly seduced by appearances. If we think about it in this way, a number of familiar but seemingly unrelated phenomena begin to form themselves into a meaningful pattern. Let us think, first, about revivalism. In any age, I would suggest, revivalism is closely associated with an inordinate attention to appearances. A revival is the most visible and obvious and seemingly irrefutable outcropping of a spiritual reality. In revivals men and women may actually *see* God at work, may quantify and gauge that work empirically. In hard times for Christians, revivals encourage the believer to think that all is not lost, and that perhaps even though his vessel is wrecked, he has a powerful ally on his side who can still flex his muscles by bringing people to visible manifestations of guilt and repentance. This, I think, was what made the Moody revivals so popular among Christians in the late nineteenth century.

Earlier though, in the period of evangelical ascendancy, revivals were powerful visible verifications of the accepted opinion that God was favoring his people and his people's nation. Visible revivals and visible signs of moral progress in the believer, like signs of economic, political, or moral progress in the nation, provided data by which the ineluctable march toward the millennium could be measured. In addition, as George Marsden shows, "the revivalists particularly centered their attacks on . . . visible sins and demanded strict abstinence from them as evidence of conversion. Prohibitions on all sorts of observable activities such as drinking, smoking, dancing, Sabbath-breaking, card playing, and theater attendance thus became indelibly associated with Protestantism in this tradition."[3] Here again we see the tyranny of the visible. The emphasis on the visibility of sin, the attention given to revivalism, the heroic status offered to the leading revivalist—all point to the Christians' earnest desire for appearances to confirm their own understanding of history and their position of rightness in the midst of that history. To revivalists, appearances count for very much indeed.

The triumph of appearances also explains the frequency of the term "evidences" in testimony from the nineteenth century. Evidences were the visible proofs of the presence of a nonempirical reality, ones that could be wielded by persons who wanted to show that they had the knowledge of that reality. Evidences gave plausibility to an unseen realm that might, without such verification, seem implausible. For example, the Calvinist notion that only God knows for certain whose names are among the "elect" was clearly a confusing and impractical teaching. As they had since Calvin's day, Christians were looking for signs of their inclusion among the blessed and thus their claim to immortality. In *Rockdale*, Wallace describes the frantic search for such signs that surrounded the death of a believer: "When the women knew the person who died it was important to examine with particular care the evidences of faith and to report to friends the cheerful news that he or she remained confident of God's mercy to the very end."[4] The Christian businessman and social activist Lewis Tappan described the mind-set of his brother Arthur this way: "With a firm belief in the evangelical faith, he relied upon the mercy of God through the atoning sacrifice of the Savior, discarding all thoughts of his good deeds as meriting reward in another life, although he firmly believed that as evidences of piety they were essential."[5] Thus even in their personal lives people looked to appearances for security and interpreted them as signs of God's favor and human rightness.

Evidences were also a common theme in the apologetic task, as they are in some circles today. The popular natural theologies of Paley and Butler were premised on the judgment that the natural world gave evidence of the existence of God. The Calvinist scholars at Princeton made a fine art of elaborating "Christian evidences," by which they meant those arguments for the inspiration of the Bible and the truth of its message whereby the Spirit brings skeptics to himself. Archibald Alexander, in his *Evidences of Christianity*, put emphasis on miracles and the fulfillment of prophecy, thus appealing to appearances to demonstrate the divine origin of Scripture. Alexander tried to strike a balance by admitting that "saving faith" comes most probably by "internal" as opposed to "external" evidence, such evidence consisting in the Bible's "moral fitness and beauty; in the adaptation of truth to the human mind; in its astonishing power of penetrating and searching the heart and affecting the conscience."[6] A later Princeton theologian, A. A. Hodge, "felt compelled . . . to shift the accent to external evidences of authenticity," in the words of one critic.[7] The world of appearances seemed tailor-made to support the truth-claims associated with the Christian gospel.

Common Sense philosophy, of course, fits into the same pattern of attention to appearances, providing a scholarly foundation for the extraordinary importance of the visible realm. Its naive Baconian empiricism promised people that what they saw before their eyes was truth, simple and unvarnished. It tended to discredit the paradoxical, the mysterious, the complicated or esoteric, and to bring the common man to the level of the theologian, if not virtually to the level of God himself, just by virtue of his possession of five external senses and an internal moral sense, or conscience. The overestimation of the empirical method and of the truthfulness of appearances encouraged a naive confidence that whatever science discovered could not be dissonant with the truth of Scripture because the scientist used the same criteria for truth that the Christian did. No wonder the theories of Charles Darwin came as such a surprise— a shock, in fact, from which evangelicals have not fully recovered to this day.

In an era as auspicious for evangelicals as the middle decades of the nineteenth century, it would be odd to find Christians escaping the tyranny of the empirical. If God is pouring out his Spirit and reviving one's soul and those of one's neighbors at the same time that factories are pouring out an unprecedented abundance of desirable goods, it is perhaps a temptation to assume a common source. If preachers promise that serious Christians will "inspire the confidence and command the respect of society," will be "honored in prosperity," and will enjoy the deference even of the irreligious, and if in fact all these seem for many Christians to be true, the world of appearances becomes indeed the arena and evidence of God's will.[8] One can then understand the confidence of Absalom Peters, who in 1837 asserted: "It is the revealed purpose of God to evangelize the world by the instrumentality of his church, and both prophecies and providential signs indicate that the time is at hand for the accomplishment of this glorious event."[9]

By the last decades of the nineteenth century, appearances had been radically altered, and the "signs" were not quite so reassuring. If "evangelizing the world" meant completing the conversion to Christ of every remaining unbeliever, as it seemed to mean to many postmillennialists, prospects were beginning to dim. As early as 1886, a prominent preacher noted that there were ever greater numbers in the world of the unconverted; this, not the increase of believers, was a "sign of the times" in his estimation.[10] About twenty years later, another popular evangelical leader admitted that "it is not the purpose [of God] now . . . to convert all the nations." And then, speaking to Christians whose nests had been shaken by the growth of unbelief, he added: "Therefore, let us not be discouraged, but adapt ourselves to the purpose of God. Let us not in the least think Christianity or the Holy Spirit to be a failure."[11] By this time, to avoid being associated with what appearances would indicate to be a failure, many evangelicals had redefined "evangelizing the world" to mean speaking the gospel to every person at least once, but without hope that every person would accept it. In fact, it now appeared that the enemies of the gospel were growing in numbers faster than its friends were, and Christians thus had to accommodate themselves to an exact reversal of the "signs" that had brought comfort to a previous generation.

Does this mean that, by the turn of the century, Christians were no longer being seduced by appearances? Had they learned to distrust signs and predictions drawn by their common sense from the visible realm? I suggest that it is quite the opposite. Despite the aforementioned opinion that "appearances count for nothing," evangelicals were very much tuned to the world of appearances. Now, however, instead of their self-inflated hopes animating and being animated by what they observed, their deepest fears and anxieties spoke through their selection of the signs of the times. Naturally, like Christians in any age, they appealed to Scripture as evidence that the signs really did point to God's plan for the world. But if we examine the signs they selected, we wonder whether it was not appearances and the threat of those appearances to their peace and happiness on earth that had seduced them.

Let us look at two evangelical spokesmen who were willing to go on record concerning the "signs of the times." At a conference in 1886, A. J. Frost submitted his evidences for the nearness of the coming of the Lord, including the following: society is experiencing serious convulsions; attendance at church is decreasing; churches seem to be supporting prostitution and the use of alcohol; Christians are not using their great wealth in godly ways; rationalism and theological decay invade the church; the Roman Catholic church dominates much of Christendom; Christians are given to worldliness, and there is insubordination in their homes.[12] Frost took these appearances very seriously. To him they demonstrated convincingly the error of postmillennial doctrine. Trusting in appearances, he was just as sure that the Great Tribulation was coming soon as his forebears, only one generation before, had been sure that a time of universal peace and righteousness was just around the corner.

Another important preacher, pastor of the First Baptist Church of New York City, was I. M. Haldeman. In 1911 he published his *Signs of the Times*, which also predicted the imminent return of Christ and the coming of great unhappiness upon the earth. Haldeman claimed that "there are signs for these days just as plainly foretold in Holy Writ, as were the signs of [Jesus'] days. They have been foretold by the Son of God himself and all his holy apostles. They are written in the Scriptures; and yet, the church, as a whole, fails to read or note them, is utterly blind to them, and all the out-reach of their tremendous meaning." These signs, being fulfilled in Haldeman's day, included:

> The widespread preparation for war, the down-grade in the Protestant Church, the up-grade in the Roman Church, the accumulation of wealth in the hands of the few, the increase of knowledge [in the context, Haldeman means science], the running to and fro—rapid transit and rapid flight—the multiplication of human inventions, the expanding cry that the voice of the people is the voice of God [in the context, Haldeman means socialism], the return of the Jew to his own land, the stealthy but steady strides of pestilence and the sudden grip of famine . . .—everywhere heart failure mixed with bold boasting and unconcealed defiance of God—what are these but the very signs pictured in the Word of God as antedating the advent of Christ.[13]

Haldeman, of course, professed to derive these signs from his study of the Bible. But the evangelicals of fifty years earlier had also studied the Bible and noticed very few of these signs. The ones they might have seen, such as the progress in science and technology, would have meant to them something very different than they meant to Haldeman. To the mid-nineteenth-century evangelicals, these signs would have presaged the gradual dawning of the millennial kingdom in America; to Haldeman they represented the decline of the times and the coming of a terrible tribulation. The evangelicals of the mid-nineteenth century might have pointed out that there had always been tribulation, unequal distribution of wealth, social convulsions, wars, and famines—in other words, that we had been living in the "last times" since the death of Christ—and that these were about to end with the reign of Christ on earth. The Bible Frost and Haldeman read told them that the worst was yet to come.

We have seen what had happened in America in the late nineteenth century to account for this new reading of the Bible and its signs. The world Haldeman was writing about was a very different one from those triumphant days before the Civil War. In 1912, when he published his book, Haldeman could observe the immense build-up of armaments among the major European powers and the corresponding heightening of hostilities. He lived in an age when wealth seemed increasingly concentrated in the hands of a few, which had been a common political theme in America during the elections of 1904 and 1908. He was aware, as were most Americans, of the millions of immigrants arriving on these shores, bringing baggage that threatened the American value system and social order: radical socialist ideas; Roman Catholic religious traditions; irreverence for the Sabbath; seemingly excessive alcohol consumption; adherence to the synagogue rather than to the church; and susceptibility to the infant labor movement and social unrest in general.

The middle classes, for whom Haldeman spoke, must have felt increasingly uncomfortable and helpless as they watched the organized money power and organized labor power grow in their importance on the political scene. During Haldeman's lifetime the city had become dominant in American society, and its servant, technology, had permanently altered the shape of life. He probably sensed—though perhaps only half-consciously—that the intellectual leadership in American society had passed from the hands of ministers like himself into those of philosophers and social scientists in the universities, and that the major church bodies were slowly passing into the control of theologians and ministers whose version of Christianity, unlike his own, had accommodated itself to the new learning. All this means, I think, that Haldeman's nest was shaking, as was the nest of most sincere evangelicals. As a human being, how could he not be afraid? How could these fears not have guided his search of Scripture for the signs of the times? Once again, are we not witnessing Christianity that had staked its peace of mind and its biblical understanding on the visible realm and thus chained God to the world of appearances just as firmly as had that ebullient, optimistic mid-century evangelicalism that Haldeman so roundly condemned?

II

I suspect that the evangelical sign-watchers we have been describing—and perhaps their defenders and imitators today—would want to challenge the foregoing analysis. After all, did not the editor of *The Sunday*

School Times insist that appearances "count for nothing"? Was not I. M. Haldeman standing against all the extravagant boasts of modern civilization, all the foolish believers in progress and in the beneficence of science and technology? Were not turn-of-the-century evangelicals the last defenders of the invisible supernatural realm, whose very existence the best minds were calling into question? Did not these evangelicals quarrel with the scientific determinists and uphold the increasingly belittled notion that God still takes an active role in history? Surely these are evidences of faith in the unseen, not seduction by the seen.

These points are not to be denied. Evangelicals did indeed stake out their territory within the domain of the invisible and the supernatural. They did indeed speak for a God whom the secularizing spirits of the age seemed to consider increasingly remote, if even existent. And yet, at another level, they succumbed completely to the commonsense dictates of the visible realm. If they continued to speak for an invisible deity, their conclusions about that deity's actions in the world were increasingly drawn in straightforward fashion from what was going on around them. Their version of the signs of the times bore an uncanny resemblance to a brief against modern industrializing and secularizing society that might have been composed by any formerly privileged middle class group that saw its comfortable world slipping away. While it was the invisible realm to which these evangelicals appealed for help, it was the simple world of appearances in late nineteenth-century America that brought on their fears, inspired their complaints, and shaped the answer they so eagerly desired. And many of Haldeman's signs of the times identified forces before which the individual is helpless: famine, earthquake, the conspiracies of the rich, the power of the Catholic church, the growth of technology, the warlike preparations of the European powers. All point to a world out of control.

If our analysis is correct, we would expect that evangelicals at the turn of the century might be tempted to recapture their control of history, might try to place themselves back in the driver's seat. I believe that this is, symbolically, exactly what they attempted to do. The means by which many evangelicals did this was remarkably simple: they reversed at least a century of theological thinking in American Protestantism and became fervent premillennialists. They did so in massive numbers, across denominational lines, and with remarkable speed—historically speaking. In the space of a generation they revolutionized the standard evangelical understanding of the meaning of history and the nature of the end times.

Since at least the days of Jonathan Edwards, as we have seen, American evangelicals by and large had been postmillennialists. Their doctrine, which nicely complemented the Enlightenment's optimism concerning human potentialities, had predicted a gradual conversion of the entire

world to Jesus Christ and the eventual dawning of a millennial reign of
the Spirit of Christ in the hearts of all peoples of the earth. Christ's actual
bodily return was not expected until that millennium had run its course.
This view of history was defended on the grounds that it energized Christians to live ethical lives and to evangelize the world in hopes of hastening
the promised millennium. By the mid-nineteenth century some evangelicals were so bold as to predict that the millennium might break out in as
little as three years, if the church would do its job.[14]

Premillennialism, on the other hand, had been quiescent in America
since the times of the Puritans. After the political chaos of the French
Revolution and the transforming power of the industrial revolution had
begun to take their toll, premillennialism underwent a small revival, particularly in Great Britain. It first came to America in popular form in the
teachings of William Miller, who believed that Christ would return to
earth before the millennium began, and who claimed to have broken
Scripture's prophetic code so that he could predict the exact day of this
Second Coming. After Miller's hopes were disappointed, his somewhat
chastened variety of premillennialism essentially taught the imminent
return of Christ and the folly of attempting to build a millennium here on
earth in the evil times that must precede Christ's coming.

Since the times did not seem so evil to most Americans during the
decades before the Civil War, only a few espoused premillennialism at
first. But, as historians Ernest Sandeen and George Marsden have shown,
it began to take hold in America during the Civil War and by the 1870s was
beginning to receive widespread approval for its claims that it, and not
postmillennialism, represented the only truly "evangelical" and "biblical" understanding of the last times. It prided itself on a literal interpretation of the fulfillment of prophecy when liberal theology was moving
toward increasingly symbolic or spiritual understandings of Scripture.
And it professed to be unsurprised by the growth of unbelief in the world,
since, by its lights, the Bible had predicted such apostasy thousands of
years before.

I suspect that the wildfire growth of premillennialism in the decades
after the Civil War really represented a bold move on the part of evangelicals to recapture their control of history. Sandeen puts it succinctly: premillennialists believed "that this whole panorama of coming glory and
judgment was explicitly foretold in the prophecies where one could, if
taught by the spirit, discover the truth and be ready for the coming of the
bridegroom."[15] This meant that for premillennialists there could be no
surprises. They had a line on the future, and that line allowed them to
place under their own intellectual or spiritual control every event that
might transpire in the last days. Was evil on the increase? Of course—

premillennial doctrine predicted it. Was Christian civilization threatened by "religious formalism, adulterous friendships with the world, waning of faith, tyranny, anarchy, general revolution?"[16] Naturally—any Bible reader would have come to expect it. Were families disintegrating? Yes, they were—and it would only get worse until Christ returned.

One can see how neatly the fears of losing control were thus transformed into claims of possessing control. To premillennialists looking for the return of the Lord, bad news was essentially good news. The worse things got, the nearer their reward approached. No evil could befall this world that they had not predicted and that they could not welcome. Haldeman offers an excellent example of this strange form of control:

> Nor, indeed, should the true Christian be overwhelmed with the downgrade in the church, as though God had failed and his Word had proved untrue. Instead, let him see that the very characteristic of the times, the very repudiation of the "faith once for all delivered to the saints," is the fulfillment, line for line, of the apostolic and Christly words, and the dynamic demonstration that it is, indeed, and in truth, not the word of man, but the very Word of God. Let him look upon the present state of the church as a sign of the times; as a witness of the closing hours of this age, the Coming of the Lord to take his true household of faith to himself.[17]

William Pettingill expressed similar sentiments in 1919: "It is a great thing to know that everything is going on according to God's schedule. . . . We are not surprised at the present collapse of civilization; the Word of God told us all about it." By such teaching, the premillennialist found himself in the enviable position of understanding, embracing, and even controlling virtually any disaster that might befall him, his family, his church, or his nation. The premillennialist was truly back in the driver's seat.[18]

But for most evangelicals who sought such control, premillennialism alone was insufficient. Sometime during the 1880s and 1890s, it seems, most premillennialist evangelicals also adopted *dispensationalism*. This doctrinal system was the brainchild of one of the founders of the Plymouth Brethren movement in England, John Nelson Darby, who brought it to North America on seven different occasions between 1862 and 1877. It is Darby's premillennialism, specifically, that we must examine if we are to understand the extent of the evangelical drive to regain control of history. We cannot offer a full doctrinal elaboration of dispensationalism in these pages, nor can we engage in a comprehensive debate over its merits as a system of biblical interpretation. Other studies have performed these tasks more than adequately.[19] But we can try to understand dispensationalism's unique features, and we can ask what these features tell us about the spiritual and psychological meaning of this doctrinal system that appealed so powerfully to evangelicals at the turn of the century, as indeed it still does to many.

The genesis of Darby's unique understanding of Scripture seems to have come in the midst of his deep disillusionment with the established Church of England. The forces of modernization, both socioeconomic and intellectual, had begun to have an impact in Great Britain at least a generation earlier than they did in the United States, bringing with them tensions similar to those we have described in late nineteenth-century America. Darby was caught in these troubled times and seems primarily to have articulated his anxiety in terms of the contrast between his own quest for spiritual purity and power and the formalism and corruption of the state church, which he served as a youthful clergyman. Later in life, Darby confessed that in his youth he had passed through "deep exercise of soul" without "a trace of peace" for some years. By his own testimony, he left the law profession and was ordained in the Church of England because "I owed myself entirely to [God]" and "I longed for complete devotedness to the work of God." After several years of ministry in a remote corner of Ireland, (during a physical convalescence) he experienced a release from his oppressive need to earn salvation. As he put it: "I was forced to the conclusion that it was no longer a question with God of this wretched 'I' which had wearied me during six or seven years, in presence of the requirements of the law."[20] In an insight similar to Martin Luther's, Darby rediscovered the reality of salvation by grace and experienced in it a deliverance and a cleansing. And as Luther had done, Darby followed up his personal crisis with an all-out attack on the established church, which, he came to believe, was badly in need of its own cleansing.

In America, at least through the end of the nineteenth century, the absence of a formal religious establishment led evangelicals like Moody to think primarily of society—and not the church itself—as a wrecked vessel. But in Britain a close formal identification existed between the church and the culture. In addition, Darby felt that the established church was implicated in his own lack of spiritual power and his works-orientation in the days before his deliverance. These facts led to a slightly different articulation of the declining times. Darby's own words were: "The Church is in ruins." His extensive and detailed indictment of the church did not, however, lead him to a call for reform. In his opinion, the church was beyond repair. Believers might better forsake the established church and separate themselves from this embodiment of evil, keeping their worship pure by assembling instead in small groups where, without ritual or hierarchy, they could symbolize the unity of the true church in Christ Jesus. As Darby expressed it, "it is positively stated (2 Tim. iii) that the church would fail and become as bad as heathenism; and the Christian is directed to turn away from evil and turn to the Scriptures, and Christ (Rev. ii and iii) is revealed as judging the state of the churches. . . ."[21]

This is a very different picture from the then fashionable one of the church of Jesus Christ marching forth triumphantly to spread the gospel and inaugurate the millennium. Far from being the agency of Christ's victory, the church has become in Darby's hands the clearest sign of apostasy, subject to God's judgment. How and when will this judgment occur? Very soon, thought Darby—in the time of tribulation predicted for the last days by Jesus and a number of Scripture writers. The believer needs to be prepared for these times and for the coming of Christ associated with them. Only this Second Coming will bring us the promised millennial reign of Christ, not any effort by the church today, and not the normal development of history.

Can one predict, then, when this Second Coming will occur? Many premillennialists of Darby's day were attempting to do just that by interpreting the apocalyptic events described in Scripture as occurring just before Christ's return. But Darby dissented on the basis of a principle he believed he had newly found in the Bible. This principle asserted the absolute distinction, biblically and historically, between Israel and the church. This principle, virtually all commentators agree, gives dispensationalism its uniqueness and separates it not only from those in Darby's day who wished to calculate the date of Christ's return but also from historical premillennialism with its understanding of the church as the spiritual successor of Israel as the people of God, comprised both of Jews and Gentiles.[22] For Darby, Israel was God's earthly people and the church his heavenly people. God had pledged himself to make Israel a great nation, through which all the world would be blessed. Even though the Jews were unfaithful in keeping the Law of Moses, God was going to keep his promise, foretold in the prophets, of giving them an earthly kingdom of peace and prosperity under his personal rule. According to Darby, Jesus came to offer that kingdom and himself as Israel's long-awaited king. When the Jews rejected Jesus, God determined to create a "heavenly" people, a church made of Gentiles who acknowledged Christ as their Savior and who lived not under law but under grace. This church would be the witness to God's salvation in the interim—of unknown duration—between Jesus' First and Second Comings. Although by this means God was postponing his establishment of the kingdom, he was not to be thwarted in fulfilling his promise to Israel. In the end, Jesus would return to establish an earthly kingdom for the Jews, to be centered in Jerusalem. This would be the long-awaited millennium.

The concept of these "end times" made clear the importance of Darby's separation of Israel from the church. Since Israel and the church seemed to be entirely different "dispensations," Darby believed that all the Old Testament prophecies, as well as Jesus' predictions, regarding the last times referred only to Israel, not to the church. The church is a wholly new thing, he said, not the beneficiary of the prophecies of Israel; the church is heavenly, not earthly. This means that predicted future events are irrelevant to the church. But how could this be so? Won't the church be at least mildly affected by the unfolding of God's judgment and God's promise to the Jews? It would not, according to Darby, because of a most ingenious "biblical" teaching: the secret, pretribulational rapture of the church. Before the unfolding of the specific events of the last times, Christ will return in the air for his saints. He will secretly remove them from history, and take them with him to heaven. Then the predicted events will occur on earth: the rise of the Antichrist, the persecution of believing Jews, the attempted destruction of Israel by the armies of the world, and the battle of Armageddon in northern Israel. Finally, at the time of this battle, after seven years of absence,[23] the church will return to earth with Christ at his Second Coming. The Antichrist will be thwarted, Satan bound, the nations judged, and the millennial kingdom established in Jerusalem. Jesus will reign for a thousand years, after which he will have to put down one last Satanic rebellion before the Resurrection of the Dead, the Last Judgment, and the creation of a new heaven and a new earth for his redeemed ones.[24]

We have only glimpsed the tip of the dispensational iceberg in this short review of Darby's doctrinal system. His own writings ran to dozens of volumes, and his followers have augmented his output with their own extensive treatises.[25] Dispensationalists have elaborated endlessly on the apocalyptic visions of Daniel and John; they have quarreled over the appropriate number of dispensations and have split hairs to avoid the charge that they present a God who saves people differently under law and grace.[26] They have created colorful and detailed scenarios of world events during the last days—at least one of which became the best-selling Christian book of the 1970s.[27] They have devised their own calculus to determine the meaning of Daniel's seventy weeks (see Dan. 9:24) and of John's "time, and times, and half a time" (see Rev. 12:14). They have read each Scripture passage with a view to putting it into its appropriate doctrinal category so that they could be sure of understanding its implications for history and prophecy aright. Their system is an intricately woven cloth with few loose threads.

I tend to think that it was just this quality of dispensationalism—its rationalistic neatness and systematic comprehensiveness—that recommended it to the evangelicals who, during the perilous times at the turn of the nineteenth century, were casting about for some means to bring history back under their control. Dispensationalism assumed the Bible to be a thinly disguised guidebook to human history: all one needed in order to decode its message and thus acquire God's master scheme, according to dispensationalists, was a commitment to a commonsense, literalistic reading of Scripture and the assumption that Israel and the church were two very distinct entities.[28] Using these tools, one could essentially take Scripture apart, verse by verse, and rearrange it into a tight, coherent system of truth—one, for example, that could be displayed graphically on a carefully drawn chart and hung in the front of the church auditorium for all the faithful to see.[29] According to one of its later champions, dispensationalism had "changed the Bible from being a mass of more or less conflicting writings into a classified and easily assimilated revelation of both the earthly and heavenly purposes of God, which purposes reach on into an eternity to come."[30] The system offered a sure identity for Christians in the present age (i.e., a faithful remnant in a disobedient age) and a comforting prognosis for the future (i.e., Christ is about to appear to rescue his people from their troubles). It offered its adherents the guarantee that they had mastered history's enigmas and forestalled its surprises because they understood "the divine plan of the ages."[31]

C. I. Scofield made it his business to establish dispensationalism in the minds of American evangelicals as the only credible understanding of Scripture. In 1902 he wrote that "the clear perception of this doctrine of the Ages makes a most important step in the progress of the student of the divine oracles. It has the same relation to the right understanding of the Scriptures that correct outline work has to map-making."[32] His masterstroke was the publication in 1909 of the Scofield Reference Bible, which Ernest Sandeen characterizes as "perhaps the most influential single publication in millenarian and Fundamentalist historiography."[33] Scofield's notes and cross-references turned this publication into an unrelenting brief for dispensationalism. The Scofield Bible's wide distribution and uncritical acceptance by American evangelicals in the twentieth century obscured the fact that its dispensational theology was neither the traditional Christian understanding of the Bible nor necessarily the biblical understanding of itself, but a human artifice created by John Nelson Darby and his followers. Many an evangelical youth in college or semi-

nary discovered, to his or her surprise, that Scofield's cut-and-dried biblical interpretations were not always the most natural ones, and that he or
she had been reading a Bible whose message and impact had been ar-
tificially constructed by the demands of a theological system that did not
bother to identify itself as such.

Scofield's notes treat the Bible, in Marsden's terms, as "a dictionary of
facts that had been progressively revealed in various historical circumstances and literary genres and still needed to be sorted out and arranged."[34] Scofield took it on himself to sort out and arrange these facts of
Scripture. His motto—and the title of one of his books—was "Rightly
Dividing the Word of Truth." He felt that one could conquer the meaning
of Scripture by dividing it: "The Word of Truth . . . has right divisions,
and it must be evident that . . . *any study* of that Word which ignores these
divisions must be in large measure profitless and confusing."[35] Scofield's
Bible is full of divisions and distinctions pressed into the text: seven
dispensations, two advents and two resurrections, five judgments, law
versus grace, Israel versus the church, the kingdom of heaven versus the
kingdom of God, and so forth. For example, his notes on Revelation 14:6
indicate that "four forms of the Gospel are to be distinguished: (1) the
Gospel of the kingdom . . . (2) the Gospel of the grace of God . . . (3) the
everlasting Gospel . . . and (4) that which Paul calls, 'my Gospel'. . . ."
Scofield describes each type of gospel fully and supplies Bible texts to
illustrate each one. In explicating the texts of Matthew 24:16 and Luke
21:21, for example, where both passages read "Then let those who are in
Judea flee to the mountains . . . ," Scofield's notes assure the reader that
"the passage in Luke refers in express terms to a destruction of Jerusalem
that was fulfilled by Titus in A.D. 70, and the passage in Matthew to a
future crisis in Jersualem after the manifestation of the 'abomination.'" As
Marsden says, dispensationalists like Scofield were predisposed "to di-
vide and classify everything."[36]

All the better to *control* it. In Scofield's hands, the Bible shed its mysteries and became a jigsaw puzzle that men like Darby had fortunately
figured out just in time to let Christians in on the secrets of the ages. To
many evangelicals, I suspect, Scofield's notes and dispensationalism generally came with the force of a revelation: so that's what the Bible is about!
So that's why the Sermon on the Mount sounds different from Paul's
gospel! The beauty of Darby's "postponed kingdom" and of his secret
rapture as techniques for fitting together Scripture's inconsistencies must
have thrilled the souls of many a sincere believer. What a privilege: to
possess in one's own hands the key to all of history, handed down by God
himself! For many, the Bible must have seemed like a whole new book
that was suddenly clear in its application to history for the first time—at

least, for the first time since the untidy demise of postmillennial optimism. As a way to identify with the God who was still clearly in control of history, and to be assured that that control would work to the benefit of the righteous like oneself, Scofield and his dispensational teachings were unparalleled.

That is why, I suppose, people flocked to conferences during this period, conferences whose teachings centered on the fulfillment of prophecy. Beginning in the late 1860s, a number of premillennialist pastors and teachers met to discuss "the personal imminent return of our Lord from heaven" among other things. This later became the Niagara Bible Conference, named for its location every summer from 1883 to 1897, and it spawned local imitators across the country. In addition, major "Bible and Prophetic Conferences," attracting widespread publicity, were held about every ten years from 1878 to 1919. The influence of Darbyite dispensationalism was palpable, if not dominating, at each of these conferences; and the honor roll of American dispensational leaders could be assembled from the lists of speakers appearing yearly at Niagara. Prophecy was a consuming interest at these conferences. "At the 1884 Conference," wrote one witness, it came to be the "fashion of every speaker to 'ring the changes' on the possibility of Christ coming any moment—before the morning dawned, before the meeting closed, and even before the speaker had completed his address."[37] A significant number of America's evangelicals seemed to thrive on the cultivation of "this blessed hope," the any-moment rapture of the church out of this wicked age. Evangelicals provided an eager audience for the systematizers and chart makers, who could show a mastery of the confusing events of the day and promise imminent rescue. For a time the study of "prophecy" was in vogue. And this brings us back, at last, to Habakkuk; for Habakkuk *was* a prophet.

III

I suspect that Habakkuk, like the dispensationalists, also wished for control of his history. He knew something was drastically wrong in the world; he knew what it meant to "see wrongs and look upon trouble"; he saw clearly that he belonged to a rapidly shrinking minority, "the righteous," and no doubt he was afraid. The righteous did not run things anymore; history did not seem to be going their way. Habakkuk's response was to "cry for help" (1:2). What kind of help did he want? Perhaps that God should interfere on his behalf and remove those who did violence, enlarge the camp of the righteous, establish justice in the place of strife and contention? Or perhaps—if, as it seemed, human history was really bound for disaster—God could rescue Habakkuk and the rest of the righteous, so that they would not have to look on trouble anymore. Whatever his will, God should make it known to Habakkuk so that the latter could once again trust God, so that he could feel that things were indeed under God's—and thus his own—control. What Habakkuk would have liked, I believe, was a reassuring glimpse of God's plan for the ages.

So God gave him a glimpse. Certainly not complete with charts and graphs and cross-references, outlining the history of the world; but still a glimpse, with enough historical detail to convince Habakkuk that God knew what he was talking about. And what God was talking about did not, at first, come as good news to the prophet Habakkuk. This is what God said:

> Look among the nations, and see; wonder and be astounded. For I am doing a work in your days that you would not believe if told. For lo, I am rousing the Chaldeans, that bitter and hasty nation, who march through the breadth of the earth, to seize habitations not their own.
>
> (1:5-6)

Habakkuk's wish was fulfilled: God granted him a look at the future. But what he saw was not what he had expected when he had cried to God for help. God was not about to make history gently right, according to Habakkuk's eyes. God would not rescue the righteous from seeing trouble. Quite the opposite: they were in for trouble the likes of which they had never seen. The Chaldeans were being roused by God himself, and when they arrived, their vengeance would not distinguish between the wicked and the righteous. Lest Habakkuk gloss over this point, God filled in the details:

> Dread and terrible are they; their justice and dignity proceed from themselves. Their horses are swifter than leopards, more fierce than the evening wolves; their horsemen press proudly on. Yea, their horsemen come from afar; they fly like an eagle swift to devour. They all come for violence; terror of them goes before them. They gather captives like sand. At kings they scoff, and of rulers they make sport. They laugh at every fortress, for they heap up earth and take it. Then they sweep by like the wind and go on, guilty men, whose own might is their god!
>
> (1:7-11)

Surely this is not what Habakkuk wished to hear from God, nor is it the kind of control he wished God to take of history. He had complained that the wicked surrounded the righteous; now the utterly reprehensible Chaldeans were about to swell the ranks of the wicked. He had bemoaned the existence of injustice in his land, and now he would be subject to those whose justice proceeded only from themselves. He had cried "violence!" and God's answer was the Chaldeans, who "come for violence." As a righteous man, Habakkuk had pled for the righteous, and God's answer was to place him in the hands of "guilty men, whose own might is their god." Surely Habakkuk was astounded, as God predicted he would be: he had longed for God to do a work in his days, and now that God was doing it, it was not the work Habakkuk had had in mind at all.

So Habakkuk wrestled with God. His agony is palpable in the question he puts to God, a question that mirrors his own disbelief and pleads as it asks: "Art thou not from everlasting, O Lord my God, my Holy One?" (1:12). In other words, are you not that faithful God to whom I lifted my cry for help? Here Habakkuk sounds like Job, wondering whether God is still his friend; and then a statement, but still a question: "We shall not die" (1:12). Ah, you must have a plan, Lord. This is not meant for the righteous, is it? You intend to rescue us, don't you? And yet these Chaldeans "all come for violence." And thus again the question, this time with its premises spelled out: "Thou who art of purer eyes than to behold evil and canst not look on wrong, why dost thou look on faithless men, and art silent when the wicked swallows up the man more righteous than he?" (1:13). Habakkuk thought he knew who God was. He had mastered all the standard definitions of God's character, and he throws these back in God's face. He had comforted himself that the God he knew so well could be counted on to provide a plan for the ages that fit Habakkuk's understanding of right and wrong in history. He had laid hold of this divine character as a tool for his own control of history. Hence, in the presence of this unexpected and potentially tragic word from God, Habakkuk tried to take refuge in the God *he* had fashioned. He called on this God to live up to his own definitions of holiness and purity. He was surprised that this God was free to transgress the definitions with which righteous humans had thought to trap and manage him. Habakkuk had hoped to control his history by using God. But he met a bigger and a freer God than he had expected.

It is not enough to say that Habakkuk was now puzzled; he was anguished. He had thought he knew the meaning of history, that he had a purchase on the God of history. Now he knew history was out of his control, perhaps beyond his understanding. Habakkuk pondered the meaning of history and of the human beings who are its victims and, seemingly, its conquerors: "For thou makest men like the fish of the sea, like crawling things that have no ruler" (1:14). Habakkuk's comforting distinction between the wicked and the righteous has disappeared in this formulation. Perhaps there is a certain insignificance, a certain smallness, that characterizes all of us. We are all caught up in matters too large for us to comprehend or to control, and we all fall into the hands of those who, like the Chaldean, fish in troubled waters: "He brings all of them up with a hook, he drags them out with his net, he gathers them in his seine; so he rejoices and exults" (1:15). The righteous and the wicked together are caught in the net of the mighty, suffer the victim's fate, and together become fodder for the strong man's insatiable pride: "Therefore he sacrifices to his net and burns incense to his seine; for by them he lives in luxury, and his food is rich" (1:16). Habakkuk sees that history is the struggle of the rich for greater riches, of the strong for greater power, and all of it in rebellion against God, all of it as a premise for self-worship. And yet it goes on, and God himself is somehow implicated in it, as Habakkuk now is forced to admit. The very God to whom he had looked for rescue has promised only greater suffering at the hands of the wicked. So Habakkuk asks God, "Is [the wicked] then to keep on emptying his net, and mercilessly slaying nations for ever?" (1:17).

How often the prophets are dismayed and surprised by God! They are caught in swirling times, in a history too big for them to control, and God visits them and seems to leave them worse off than when they began. Jeremiah is forced to endure the siege of Jerusalem and look on things too horrible for words. Hosea is called to love and marry an unfaithful woman, to bear in his own relationship to her the burden of God for his people. The prophets are forced to live in a history they cannot control, and their friend is a God whose purposes they cannot always understand. They are not exempted from history any more than was God's own Son; they are not delivered from suffering any more than was the New Testament church. Instead, they are called to faithfulness in declining times, faithfulness to a God whose purposes are larger than theirs, who is indeed doing a work in their days, but one they would not believe if told. They are called upon to witness to this unbelievable God.

Were these the prophets that the dispensationalists called to mind in their eagerness to think "prophetically"? If they asked Habakkuk's questions, were they ready to hear Habakkuk's answer? I believe that the true intentions of the dispensationalists are quite clear—and no different from all human intentions. They were interested in controlling history, not in hearing that it is controlled by a God whose purposes are larger than our understanding. They were interested in shaping the future to the demands of their fears and cries for solace, not in hearing the Word of the One who shapes it—albeit in surprising ways. The dispensationalists were interested in prophecy as a game they knew they would win, not in listening to the One whose winning is often like losing, and who promises that the first shall be last. In the hands of the dispensationalists, therefore, "prophecy" lost its biblical meaning. It was not steeped in the fear of the Lord and in waiting for the unexpected. It knew its God and its God's convenient plan for the ages. What did it have to wait for?

The clearest indication of dispensationalism's unfaithfulness to biblical prophecy, I would suggest, is its distinguishing doctrine of the secret rapture of the church. As Ernest Sandeen and others suggest, this was the teaching that seems to have accounted for dispensationalism's rapid and surprising growth to popularity in Britain and America during the late nineteenth century. In both countries a premillennialism of a more general sort got the earliest foothold. It taught that progress was illusory, and that the millennial kingdom could not be established except by Jesus' return. Although this return was imminent, the events associated with the Great Tribulation and the Antichrist would have to take place first. Many evangelicals were not satisfied with this. It seemed to the dispensationalists that "the hope of Christ's return had to be an imminent hope or it was no hope at all."[38] Predictable intervening events seemed to cut away at the imminence of Christ's return.

There is something just a bit odd about this argument. We have seen how a popular preacher like I. M. Haldeman could publish an entire book of sermons entitled *The Signs of the Times*, and, like many other prophetic and dispensationalist preachers, point to the evidences in current events that the coming of the Lord was drawing near. These events—earthquakes, famines, apostasy, and militarism—were presented as fulfilled prophecies. The world had been awaiting them, and now they were here. Before they were present (for example, before the telegraph and telephone had made it possible to run to and fro), could Christians have believed that the coming of the Lord was still in the distant future, that certain predictable events had to take place before that event could take place? This is the implication of Haldeman's argument and others like it. In this light, their insistence that no *further* predictable events could come between their own day and the return of the Lord seems somewhat feeble, if not self-serving. Their message, when boiled down, was not so much that the Bible teaches about no predictable intervening events to obstruct the Christian's hope; it was, rather, Christ's return is imminent because we want imminence.

But why did they want imminence? Sandeen gives us an idea: "If one believes that a period of tribulation must first take place before the coming of Christ, they said, then he cannot look forward to the second advent but must wait only for greater suffering."[39] This is, of course, precisely what Habakkuk the prophet was called on to do: wait for greater suffering. It is decidedly not what the prophecy aficionados of late nineteenth-century evangelicalism were interested in. Quite probably, on the contrary, they had no ears to hear the word of the Lord to Habakkuk: "I do have a plan, and a wondrous one; I will cause you to suffer at the hands of the wicked." The dispensationalists' direction was quite the opposite: we understand how God works in history, and it simply cannot involve suffering for those of us who are righteous.[40]

We of the latter twentieth century, ensconced more comfortably than any previous generation in the delights of the visible, material realm, should have little difficulty understanding the threat that suffering posed to the late nineteenth-century evangelical. How, for example, might we respond to the words reported by Matthew 24?

> As he sat on the Mount of Olives, the disciples came to him privately, saying, "Tell us, when will this be, and what will be the sign of your coming and of the close of the age?" And Jesus answered them, "Take heed that no one leads you astray. For many will come in my name, saying, 'I am the Christ,' and they will lead many astray. And you will hear of wars and rumors of wars . . . and there will be famines and earthquakes in various places: all this is but the beginning of the sufferings.
>
> "Then they will deliver you up to tribulation, and put you to death; and you will be hated by all nations for my name's sake. . . .
>
> "So when you see the desolating sacrilege spoken of by the prophet Daniel, standing in the holy place (let the reader understand), then let those who are in Judea flee to the mountains; let him who is on the housetop not go down to take what is in his house; and let him who is in the field not turn back to take his mantle. And alas for those who are with child and for those who give suck in those days! Pray that your flight may not be in winter or on a sabbath. For then there will be great tribulation, such as has not been from the beginning of the world until now, no, and never will be."
>
> (3-9, 15-21)

If we are honest, I suppose we must say that we do not want to experience such hardships and persecutions. The world so described cannot have appeared inviting to any Christian in any age. How convenient it would be to know that one will not have to undergo such privations! We cannot accuse Darby of consciously framing his doctrine of the secret rapture so as to provide an escape from that tribulation. But we must wonder whether the escape he provided was not at the very root of dispensationalism's appeal to a popular evangelical audience. How many anxious Christians, fretting over a world out of control and a foreboding future, took comfort from C. I. Scofield's notes on this very passage in Matthew 24, notes indicating that the Christian would no longer be on earth when Judeans would have to flee to the mountains and when babies and pregnant women would have to fear for their lives. To be sure, Scofield did not provide an escape from *all* suffering. He informed his readers that the first verses (24:4-14), while applying "in a specific way to the end of the age [i.e., the Great Tribulation]," also describe in a general sense the character of the times before the rapture of the church. But before treating the "seven seals" in Revelation 6 and 7, where war, famine, death, and persecution are unleashed on the earth, he made certain that his readers were aware—on the flimsiest of evidence—that the rapture of the church described by I Thessalonians 4:14-17 had by the time of those predicted events already been fulfilled, and that the church would thus be absent from the world during its time of greatest suffering.[41]

We can see the same escapist motives in I. M. Haldeman. Quoting John 14:3 ("And when I go and prepare a place for you, I will come again and take you to myself . . ."), he describes the passage in these terms:

> It is a simple and direct promise to come and take the church out of the world. . . . It is a promise to come himself . . . to the collective body, to the whole body of his disciples, and take them clean and clear . . . out of the earth.
>
> It is the express declaration that there is a term to the presence of the church on the earth; that the Lord is coming to remove the church from the earth to heaven.
>
> The outlook of the church, then, is not on this age, but on one to come.[42]

Now these words alone do not specifically exempt the church from all suffering. But they do, if not augmented by a further understanding of the church as a body called to suffer for and with its master, *imply* that the church will escape such suffering. Does Haldeman supply this further analysis? He does say that, in the times before the rapture, "righteous men . . . shall vex themselves hopelessly against the increasing on-rush of godlessness and sin."[43] But this can be read simply as a prediction that changing the course of the age, stemming the tide of unrighteousness, will be futile. It does not clearly indicate that God has called on his church to suffer at the hands of the wicked. Further on in the same sermon, however, Haldeman gives himself an excellent opening for just such an indication. He is railing against the "Christian socialists," those Christians of liberal theological persuasion whose avowal of the "Social Gospel" led them into some of the very same optimistic and reformist programs that mid-nineteenth century evangelicals had espoused. To them Haldeman proclaims that "neither Christ nor Christianity are in the world to reorganize the society of the natural man, elevate him, or appeal to his own resources." Haldeman goes on to ask: "What, then, was the mission of Christ and, consequently, of the church?" and answers, "He came into the world not to live, but to die."[44] We must expect that, following up on this assertion, Haldeman will show us how the church has to suffer and die too. But does he do so? He says that the church is here to testify to human hopelessness; to demonstrate that life comes through Christ alone; to point the world to the cross of Christ and to his resurrection; to show the world that its only hope is the "coming of the second and perfect man, the true king and saviour of the earth." He says that the work of the church is "to get men into Christ—get Christ into men." He comes close when he writes: "The church when true to its functions will always be rejected by the natural man, and the Spirit of God resisted."[45] But nowhere does he illustrate, nor even again raise the possibility, that the church is in the world not to live but to die, not to prosper but to suffer.

It is not part of the dispensational view of history that the church of Jesus Christ is to suffer. If Christians eagerly await the end, it is because it is precisely at the end that they will *not* suffer. As Haldeman puts it elsewhere, "The Lord shall descend and gather His church to Himself, that He may take her out of the way of those judgments with which He will sweep the earth clean. . . ."[46] What is the meaning of the cross? To Haldeman, a dying Lord seems to imply not a suffering but a delivered church. It seems to have been the same for Darby. "In effect," he wrote in a letter, "the cross of Christ and His return should characterize the church and each one of the members." And what is the practical meaning of this cross? Darby does not for a moment weigh the possibility that to stand under the cross means to belong to the fellowship of Christ's sufferings. Rather, he explicates his meaning in what appears almost to be a non sequitur: "Where was this unity, this 'body'? Where was the power of the Spirit recognized? Where was the Lord really waited for?"[47] Is this the meaning of the cross: unity, power, expectancy? Does not the cross have something to do with suffering? There is no word of this.

Nor is there a word in one of the first American premillennial publications, the *Prophetic Times*, first issued in 1863. In the creed governing its editors, we find "that Christ will soon reappear upon earth to avenge His elect and fulfill His covenant to them."[48] Neither here nor elsewhere in this creed can we find a recognition of the biblical understanding of such avenging. In Revelation 6:10ff., those who had been slain for the Word of God cry out, "O Sovereign Lord . . . how long before Thou wilt judge and avenge our blood on those who dwell upon the earth?" The answer these saints receive is that they are to rest until even more saints are killed as they had been! Were the writers of this creed thinking of themselves as suffering death for the Word of God, and thus among those whom God would avenge? There is no evidence that they were, nor that their creed even recognized that Darby would have placed this portion of Revelation in the Great Tribulation, with the church already absent from the world, and with only those few who had recently acknowledged Christ, after the rapture, as having to suffer for his Word. We do know that, later in their creed, the editors promised that those who are awake and waiting for the Lord's return "shall escape the dreadful tribulations which are to mark the last years of this dispensation. . . ."[49] Here again is that theme: if God has judgments in store for mankind, he will surely not unleash them until his people are safely whisked away.

Such is the conclusion, I would suggest, not of revelation but of common sense. I believe that we are beginning to see the serious pitfalls into which a commitment to common sense, rampant in evangelicalism even after the demise of its optimistic plans for a Christian culture, can lead the Christian community. A trust in one's own senses dies hard. Even though the conclusions of the Common Sense philosophy of the 1850s concerning such matters as science and social progress were badly discredited in the later nineteenth century among evangelicals, common sense could now rise again (as we have shown) to acknowledge more pessimistic signs and proclaim the end of history. But it could also leap to the conclusion that God would surely not leave the "righteous" to suffer with the wicked. Such suffering just does not make sense, especially if you count yourself one of the righteous. Marsden has shown how dispensationalist theology grew out of the very same "Baconian" presuppositions that had animated the earlier postmillennialist outlook. Dispensationalists "were absolutely convinced that all they were doing was taking the hard facts of Scripture, carefully arranging and classifying them, and thus discovering the clear patterns which Scripture revealed." The dispensationalist teachers presented their teachings as a "simple and straightforward interpretation of fact according to plain laws available to common sense and the common man."[50] Since American evangelicals had, in their embrace of the Scottish philosophy, effectively locked out the somewhat more self-critical findings of what Henry May calls the "skeptical Enlightenment," there was no tradition within contemporary Christian thought that might question the glib use of such "common sense," no precedent for asking whether common sense might open the door to the naturally self-interested projections of a fallen human nature. What is to keep common sense from finding in Scripture exactly what the reader wants to find? In the absence of such epistemological checks, common sense ruled the councils of biblical interpretation. The result—unfortunately, I think—was the triumph of a Christian mentality whose presupposition, never explicit, was the equivalent of asserting that God's ways are indeed the ways of humans.

Such was the outlook of the "prophecy" movement. Was it also the outlook of the prophets themselves, men like Jeremiah, Hosea, and Habakkuk? The prophets most often put the lie to common sense. It was the people they were calling to repentance who put trust in their common sense. The prophet was often burdened with a message that did not make sense, that was not comforting to those who considered themselves righteous. The prophet knew that, far from being commonsensical, God's ways are "neither transparent nor immune to misunderstanding. There is an unfolding and a shrouding, a concealing within a disclosing, consoling as well as confusing."[51] As Isaiah reports, "the Lord will rise up . . .to do his deed—strange is his deed! and to work his work—alien is his work!" (28:21). Is it alien only to the wicked but crystal clear to the righteous? Habakkuk could not have said that. Furthermore, it could not have been said of him, as it was of Darby, that "the will of God seldom blurred before his vision."[52] The prophets knew, as Abraham Heschel points out, that there is no general theory that can explain to us how this God, so other and so free, works in the world. "Exceedingly intricate are His ways. Any attempt to formulate a theory, to stamp a dogma, to define God's itinerary through history, is a sham, fraught with pretensions."[53] Habakkuk was stripped of any such pretensions when God responded to his cry for help by promising a work that Habakkuk would not believe if told. And Habakkuk had then to go to the people with that word, a word insanely contradicting the common sense both of Habakkuk and of his listeners—a word that offered suffering, greater violence, injustice, and not rescue. The prophet, as Heschel writes, "was often compelled to proclaim the very opposite of what his heart expected."[54] I submit that we cannot say this of the dispensationalists.

IV

When we last looked in on Habakkuk, he was feeling lost. His hopes for controlling history had been shattered by God's surprising word. Habakkuk could only ask the plaintive question: "Is he then to keep on emptying his net, and mercilessly slaying nations for ever?" (1:17). We hear in Habakkuk's voice a note we recognize from the Psalms. "Out of the depths I cry to thee, O Lord! Lord, hear my voice!" (130:1). "I cry to thee; save me, that I may observe thy testimonies. I rise before dawn and cry for help . . ." (119:146-47). "How long must thy servant endure? When wilt thou judge those who persecute me?" (119:84). In the Psalms we hear these cries for help over and over again, and we wonder whether they are not somehow the most fitting and continual cry of one who looks to God alone for salvation.

It seems a pity that the dispensationalists so segregated the Old Testament from the New that they inevitably diminished the importance of these Psalms to the church. Had they heard these cries for help as their own cries, they might have come to know the God that Habakkuk knew. They might have heard a surprising word from that God, one their common sense could not believe, a word of suffering but by the same token a word of grace. They might have recognized themselves, as Habakkuk knew himself, as poor and needy rather than as the controllers of a history that exempted them from judgment. In other words, had they heard the Psalms, they might also have heard the gospel in them.

I do not suggest that they were utter strangers to the gospel. The dispensationalist leaders, as one of their kindlier foes has said, "were men who walked with God."[55] Their devotion to Scripture was exemplary. Their rejection of the increasingly works-oriented and humanistic liberal theology—a more legitimate offspring of mid-nineteenth century evangelicalism than was dispensationalism—was timely and insightful. I warm to Haldeman's sermon entitled "The Jericho Theology," in which he castigates theological modernism as "the devil's lie repeated with increased accent, 'ye shall be as gods,'"[56] and where he ridicules the presumption that identifies the telegraph and telephone with the Spirit of Christ. Surely Haldeman knew and preached the gospel—that it is by grace that the sinful person is saved, not by the modern works of progress or the optimistic ideologies of the day. Haldeman seemed to know in 1912 what World War I had to convince so many others of, including the brightest lights of contemporary theology—that the human race is doomed to sinful futility without its Savior. The dispensationalists were firmly in the Reformation tradition; most of the leaders had been, and remained, Calvinists. They knew that the just shall live by faith, that salvation is by grace alone. They knew and preached this gospel.

But had they fully heard it? Have any of us? Can humans so radically at enmity with God come to where they need not hear it afresh each day, each hour? The gospel is a slippery thing. Adherence to it as a doctrinal matter is not difficult. But we often affirm what we have only begun to glimpse in the depths of our spirits. We affirm that the first shall be last even while we are racing to be first. We proclaim our commitment to the Prince of Peace at the same time that our souls are doing secret violence to the enemy standing before us. And no doubt we testify with our mouths to the wonderful gift of God's salvation—a gift totally undeserved by sinners without merit—at the very time that we are feeling meritorious for articulating the self-same testimony. (Is not the writer of a book like this in jeopardy with each passing word?) Surely the gospel is a slippery thing.

We must ask of the dispensationalists, as we must ever ask of ourselves, how did they hear the gospel? Perhaps it would be fitting to begin, as we have been doing, with Habakkuk. How did Habakkuk hear the gospel? To the dispensationalists themselves this may seem to be a misguided and inappropriate question. Habakkuk was an Old Testament figure; how could he have known the gospel at all? And yet we know that Paul, in writing Romans, inserts Habakkuk's words into the midst of his treatment of exactly that topic—the gospel of Christ. Perhaps Paul knew something about Habakkuk. Perhaps he knew that Habakkuk, in his upsetting encounter with God, had heard the gospel.

We left Habakkuk feeling lost. But it was exactly at that point, when his "lostness" far exceeded the lostness he felt while calling on God to control history and rescue him, that Habakkuk reached a turning point. Let us see what his next words are:

> I will take my stand to watch, and station myself on the tower, and look forth to see what he will say to me, and what I will answer concerning my complaint.
>
> (2:1)

Habakkuk has become a watchman. This in itself is an advance on his former state of mind and soul. He has learned some things since his insistent—shall we say, arrogant?—demand that God control history for his benefit and according to his own sense of justice. He has learned that God controls history but that the ways in which he does so are mysterious and surprising. He has learned that he will suffer God's judgment along with all his people, whether righteous or wicked. He has pondered his own insignificance and powerlessness before the larger forces of history. In all these ways Habakkuk has been humbled; it is a newly humbled person who stands in his tower and watches.

But there is a paradox here: Habakkuk knows that he is lost but also that he has already been found. The God who has dissolved his pretensions and left him helpless before the flow of history is the same God who has spoken to Habakkuk and assured him that, however unbelievable, he is doing a work in Habakkuk's day. What a strange place for Habakkuk to be standing: directly between his own dissolution and his own salvation, a dissolution that is not lessened by the nature of the salvation (Habakkuk will be saved "so as by fire"), but a salvation that cannot be compromised by Habakkuk's dissolution (it is *God* who is doing the work in Habakkuk's day). So Habakkuk is at the same time both lost and found. As such, he is prepared to hear God's promise and comfort. Precisely as one who is both lost and found, Habakkuk will not turn the promise into a guarantee of safety or the comfort into a denial of suffering. He is ready, in other words, to hear of God's salvation without his own dissolution. This is most important. Habakkuk will not make the critical mistake of thinking that salvation negates dissolution.

And so God speaks to Habakkuk:

"Write the vision; make it plain upon tablets, so he may run who reads it. For still the vision awaits its time; it hastens to the end—it will not lie. If it seem slow, wait for it; it will surely come, it will not delay."

(2:2-3)

What is the vision? We are not precisely told, but we can surmise. If the remainder of Habakkuk's book reflects that vision, three elements emerge: human futility; God's inevitable judgment; and withall, God's marvelous salvation. This is the vision Habakkuk is to write in bold letters, so that it cannot fail to come to the attention of even the busiest and most distracted of his countrymen. He is supposed to believe, against all the evidence, that this vision will indeed come. If we review the three elements of the vision presented by Habakkuk, we should be prepared to understand more fully the burden of his prophetic message as well as its relevance to the self-consciously prophetic dispensationalists.

The first element is the revelation of human futility. Beginning in Habakkuk 2:6, the prophet spins out a list of woes against sinful humanity. The primary application of these woes may be to the Chaldeans, though they are not specifically named. They do seem a possible subject in verse 8, for example: "Because you have plundered many nations, all the remnant of the peoples shall plunder you. . . ." But I think we would not be misled to apply certain of the woes more generally—to Habakkuk's own people, and to all people down to the present day: "Woe to him who gets evil gain for his house" (2:9); "woe to him who builds a town with blood, and founds a city on iniquity" (2:12); "woe to him who says to a wooden thing, Awake; to a dumb stone, Arise!" (2:19). Greed, violence, and idolatry are not sins of the Chaldeans only; indeed, as other Hebrew prophets reveal, God's people themselves became disobedient in just these ways. The passage makes clear that all this wickedness is futile—that it will bring only destruction on the people, that the "nations weary themselves for nought" (2:13). Here is a stinging indictment of the pretensions of human civilization and human progress, and a revelation of the bitter darkness in human hearts that forms the basis for the violence and injustice permeating world history.

Habakkuk's second element is God's judgment. The third chapter is Habakkuk's prayer, as the first verse informs the reader, a prayer that begins with a plea for mercy:

O Lord, I have heard the report of thee, and thy work, O Lord, do I fear. In the midst of the years renew it; in the midst of the years make it known; in wrath remember mercy.

(3:2)

Habakkuk then envisions the Lord's coming in glory and power, a vision creating both praise and fear:

> He stood and measured the earth; he looked and shook the nations; then the eternal mountains were scattered, the everlasting hills sank low. . . . Thou didst bestride the earth in fury, thou didst trample the nations in anger.

(3:6, 12)

Habbakuk's vision of God's judgment seems to shock and exhaust him. Once again, as in the beginning of the second chapter, he becomes a watchman in his tower:

> I hear, and my body trembles, my lips quiver at the sound; rottenness enters into my bones, my steps totter beneath me. I will quietly wait for the day of trouble to come upon people who invade us.

(3:16)

Habakkuk concludes his book by returning to the reality of God's salvation. Doubtless he is chastened by his vision and his encounter with a God who does not promise him control of his history or escape from suffering. He has been humbled, to the point where he can ignore the message of the visible realm altogether. He knows a new kind of trust, one that is not tied to self-serving interpretations of the world of appearances. We have in his finale one of the most poignant and moving hymns in the entire Bible:

> Though the fig tree do not blossom, nor fruit be on the vines, the produce of the olive fail and the field yield no food, the flock be cut off from the fold and there be no herd in the stalls, yet I will rejoice in the Lord, I will joy in the God of my salvation. God, the Lord, is my strength; he makes my feet like hinds' feet, he makes me tread upon my high places.

(3:17-19)

No longer is Habakkuk's strength in his own sense of justice, his own identity as one of the "righteous," his own plan for history. Now God alone is his strength. He knows the salvation of the Lord, but he knows it by means of a dissolution and a judgment that are necessarily related to that salvation. He is not the same Habakkuk we met in the first chapter.

This, I suggest, is the vision God revealed to his prophet, the watchman, in his tower: the human project is futile and doomed; God's judgment is sure and terrible; God's salvation can be trusted. And Habakkuk was to write it for his people—plainly. Is it possible that he felt foolish writing such a vision? Think for a moment of the words he was to put in bold letters and trumpet loudly. He was to say that those who took pride in their power, riches, and security would be revealed as failures, and that their glory would be their shame. Of course, there was no evidence for this. The Chaldeans, for example, were frighteningly successful; their empire, in Habakkuk's own words, had made them fat (1:16), had caused them to rejoice and exult (1:15). Who would predict their demise? The very same air of foolishness could be heard in Habakkuk's proclamation of the judgment of the Lord. Who had ever seen mountains writhing under God's hand, or the sun and moon stand still (3:10-11)? How believable was the imminence of God's judgment when the wicked seemed to be prospering as they always had. And what about the third of Habakkuk's messages, the Lord's salvation? Such salvation was nowhere to be seen. In fact, Habakkuk's very declaration of it admitted its invisible quality, its preposterousness: "Though . . . the fields yield no food . . . , yet I will rejoice in the Lord" (3:17-18). The entire vision ran counter to common sense, counter to appearances. One could say of it, as God had said to Habakkuk, "I am doing a work in your days that you would not believe if told" (1:5). Truly this vision, which Habakkuk was to speak boldly, was an unbelievable one.

And yet I do not think Habakkuk was embarrassed by it. For it was precisely in its unbelievability that it became, for Habakkuk, the gospel. To someone who now knew his own futility (for God had foiled his control of history) and who saw afresh his eligibility for God's judgment (a judgment accomplished, in part, in the Chaldeans' depredations), the vision of God's salvation was good news indeed. Habakkuk had not come to understand his own futility and the coming judgment through self-examination or rational decision. He had been confronted by the living God, and in that confrontation he knew himself in an entirely new way. What he came to know was bad news, but the kind of bad news that opened his ears—perhaps for the first time—to the true nature and true goodness of the good news. Habakkuk was not embarrassed by the preposterousness of this good news, because he could no longer doubt his utter lostness without it.

The apostle Paul, who also knew the gospel, was not embarrassed either. His affirmation in Romans 1:16 is: "For I am not ashamed of the gospel: it is the power of God for salvation to every one who has faith. . . ." Paul's story has its parallels to Habakkuk's. Like the latter, he had thought to control history with the help of a God of his own description. His particular version of injustice was the aggravating heresy of that little band of men and women who worshipped the would-be Messiah, Jesus of Nazareth. Paul was sure he could stamp out this sect and get Jewish history back on track. As a devout Jew, Paul called on God to justify him in this task. But God had different plans, plans for a work that Paul would not have believed if told. God carried out his judgment by toppling his loyal servant off his donkey and striking him blind. A few days in that state seems to have confirmed in Paul's brain the message God had given him on the road to Damascus: who do you think you are, to take such things into your hands? Paul was not ashamed of the gospel of Christ because he had come to know the utter futility of his best intentions, of his well-meant "righteousness," and he had waited for the salvation of the Lord.

It is thus no accident that Paul quotes Habakkuk in the introduction to his epistle to the Romans, a letter in which he lays out the gospel of Jesus Christ in brilliant strokes. He quotes the portion that follows immediately on God's instructions to Habakkuk concerning the vision.

> Behold, he whose soul is not upright in him shall fail, but the righteous shall live by his faith. Moreover, wine is treacherous; the arrogant man shall not abide. His greed is as wide as Sheol; like death he has never enough. He gathers for himself all nations, and collects as his own all peoples.
>
> (2:4-5)

Paul's version of Habakkuk's message is found in Romans 1:16-17:

> For I am not ashamed of the gospel: it is the power of God for salvation to every one who has faith, to the Jew first and also to the Greek. For in it the righteousness of God is revealed through faith for faith; as it is written, "He who through faith is righteous shall live."

Habakkuk's vision was a vision of the gospel. Here we see Paul using the heart of Habakkuk's vision—the righteous shall live by faith—as the heart of his own message. It is no surprise, then, to find that Paul's letter to the Romans, and thus his presentation of the gospel, includes the same three ingredients that appear in Habakkuk's vision, and they all appear in short order following his quotation from Habakkuk. Paul's indictment of human sinfulness is a familiar one: "None is righteous, no, not one; no one understands, no one seeks for God. All have turned aside, together they have gone wrong" (3:10-12). His proclamation of God's judgment is just as plain: "For the wrath of God is revealed from heaven against all ungodliness and wickedness of men. . . . Therefore God gave them up in the lusts of their hearts to impurity. . . . We know that the judgment of God rightly falls upon those who do such things. Do you suppose, O man, that when you judge those who do such things [remember Habakkuk?] and yet do them yourself, you will escape the judgment of God?" (1:18, 24; 2:2-3). And Paul's affirmation of the salvation of God comes as the same joyous good news and with the same paradoxical promise of suffering that it did in Habakkuk's case:

Therefore, since we are justified by faith, we have peace with God through our Lord Jesus Christ. Through him we have obtained access to this grace in which we stand, and we rejoice in our hope of sharing the glory of God. More than that, we rejoice in our sufferings, knowing that suffering produces endurance. . . .

(5:1-3)

We learn that the gospel as Habakkuk and Paul understood it reveals the righteousness of God and not of ourselves—a serious problem for the self-justifying and pretentious human creature. We also learn that a recognition of this righteousness means the shocking discovery of our own limitless unrighteousness, an unrighteousness that taints even our cries to God for help in controlling history or for our own kind of rescue. In both writers' stories we see that the gospel comes first as bad news and then as good news, but as a good news that does not mean we can forget the bad news without forgetting the gospel altogether. It comes first as the dissolution of our obdurate pride and then as the promise of help from beyond us—but never the kind of help that will let us take back our pride. We know that if we are unwilling to hear the bad news, today and each day, we will not have ears to hear the good news. And we also see in the gospel the promise of suffering, suffering we are called to embrace willingly as witnesses to the God who, in Christ, himself suffered for the sins of the whole world. To hear the gospel is to embrace the judgment God pronounced over the world in Christ—to embrace it not as condemnation, for there is now no condemnation, but as mercy and as witness to the One who is greater than ourselves.

For the gospel truly is Christ. If Habakkuk could not name the name, he could still witness to the fact that God was doing it, in some sense without his participation and far beyond his own ability to cooperate in so great a salvation. Paul could name the name and thus point us to the One without whom we might never have understood the gospel according to Habakkuk. The name Jesus points us to One whose vision and offer of salvation is no less preposterous than Habakkuk's was. Neither vision holds up well in the realm of appearances. That Jesus is God's Son is in no way self-evident. That he demonstrated the end of human possibilities is a message many would find unpersuasive. That God came in judgment to that Son we can easily deny. And that those who embrace that judgment, witnessing by their suffering both to their deserving it and to its mercy, are eternally saved by that God—that is preposterous to all but the eyes of faith.

To be prophetic, as Habakkuk was prophetic, is to speak that absurd name boldly and without shame in large letters so that all can hear it. But to the degree that it is the gospel, it will not find a ready audience. The report that God is doing a work in our days is one we cannot believe if told—particularly if that work is aimed at the dissolution of the righteous. It is only by the faithfulness of God awakening our faith that the righteous shall live. And when that faith is awakened, it must be awakened to our own utter futility before it will be awakened to the meaning of salvation. This is the gospel as Habakkuk knew it and as Paul knew it. And now we must ask whether the dispensationalists knew it.

V

The dispensationalists came to popularity within American evangelicalism in a period of rapid secularization, particularly among the educated classes. We have shown how religious legitimations were implicitly shaken by the gradual dissolution of a plausibility structure, and were at the same time under full-scale attack by thinkers armed with what they took to be the undeniable truths of science. The evangelical consensus shattered under these blows, as did the shared assumptions about the reality and importance of a supernatural realm.

The prophetic movement, which was dominated by dispensationalists, represented a clear and vocal challenge to the increasingly respectable assumption that God had little or nothing to do with human history. Like Habakkuk, the dispensationalists wrote their vision in bold strokes. In an age when the intellectual leaders could find little to recommend any way of knowing but the empirical, the dispensationalists attracted ridicule. They insisted that appearances did not tell the whole story, that there was a powerful reality hidden from human view (at least from the view of nondispensationalists), and that that reality both eclipsed the current world-historical events in importance and interpreted their meanings. They witnessed to a living, personal, and imminently returning God when many of the best minds had reduced God to a lifeless symbol, a quiescent force, or a moral principle.

The dispensationalists also lived, as had their evangelical forebears, in an age of enterprise. The machine was the wonder of the age, and those willing to invent, own, use, or become machines were rapidly transforming the American environment. Human and social possibilities seemed unlimited. "We can do it" was the American mentality, whether applied to technology, financial achievement, political reform, or military encounter. Certainly the late nineteenth century had its share—and maybe more—of anxious, confused, or victimized people who did not necessarily view it as a good time. But the people who were "making it" could shove aside these fears for the moment. And often, I believe, the ones who felt at some level the deepest anxieties were the very ones who had the surest sense that action would solve things, that the old American tradition of self-reliance and hard work would pay off in the end, would perhaps get them to where they would not feel anxious any longer.

In this age of enterprise and action, dispensationalism witnessed to God's call to wait and watch. For many evangelicals, we can be sure, this waiting did not preclude joining everyone else in the quest for economic or social success; to some of these, we suspect, this waiting was little more than lip service. But from the lips of most dispensationalists, and the lives of many, did come witness to the One on whom all history depends and for whom all Christians wait. Dispensationalists kept alive the truth that our history is a ceaseless round of futile events that takes us nowhere without the intervention of the God and Father of Jesus Christ. Dispensationalists fixed their minds on God's return into our history, and they insulted an age of enterprise and high human hopes by instructing it to wait patiently for the end.

And yet it is difficult to discern among the dispensationalists the spirit of the prophet Habakkuk. Habakkuk's was a humbled spirit among them. The prophet had met God, who, far from reinforcing his desires, crushed his bid to control history and contradicted his commonsense notions of justice. Instead this God brought judgment down on Habakkuk, handing the victory—at least for the time being—to the very embodiment of evil, the Chaldeans. Habakkuk was left reeling, puzzled, anguished, and empty. However, the dispensationalists of late nineteenth- and early twentieth-century America felt none of these things—at least not admittedly. They were proudly confident, sure of themselves, professedly happy, and filled. In other words, they do not seem to have been humbled. To be sure, they had been given the opportunity to be humbled, if they had had eyes to see. Their dominance of American life, as evangelicals, had been shattered; their self-assurance had at least been issued a strong challenge. Their earlier rhetoric about Christianizing the culture had been revealed as emptiness. But by the time they became dispensationalists, at least, they were back on their feet, so to speak, and sounding very much in charge of the situation. One does not find them admitting that they are confused or wondering why God allows the wicked to swallow up the righteous. One does not hear them pondering the meaning of God's mysterious action. One does not hear them embracing the judgment and chastisement of God, as did Habakkuk. Instead, one hears the same self-assured tones that one heard from the mid-century evangelicals, and behind these tones the message: We are right; you are wrong. We will be rescued; you will be judged.

The dispensationalists had not been humbled. They had identified themselves as the true remnant, that small portion of genuine saints Christ would take with him when he returned. Particularly for Darby himself—and others like him—this status as the last remaining faithful in a wholly apostate world seemed very important. Darby and his followers viewed themselves as the righteous who were surrounded by a sea of unrighteousness—just as Habakkuk had. But these self-identified righteous were never disturbed by dispensationalist theology, never shaken by the possibility that the true saints were as much in need of judgment as were the false. Instead, the true church was to be rescued in the end, and taken to be with its Lord in heaven. This was certainly the answer that Habakkuk wanted from God as well. But it is not the one he got.

Darby developed quite an elaborate doctrinal structure to support his exalted view of the true church. According to Clarence Bass, the dispensationalists understood themselves to be, as the true church, "in the forefront of Christ's interest" and "the *ultimate* of God's plan for man." The church was not an "earthly" but a "heavenly" entity, composed of "heavenly people" whose true place is with Christ in glory.[57] In Darby's own words,

> It is this conviction that the Church is properly heavenly, in its calling and relationship with Christ, forming no part of the course of events of the earth, which makes the rapture so simple and clear: and on the other hand, it shows how the denial of its rapture brings down the Church to an earthly position, and destroys its whole spiritual character and position.[58]

Here Darby comes very close to admitting that, as one might suspect, the doctrine of the secret rapture comes not so much from a considered examination of Scripture as from the conviction that the church is a special group of people who somehow *deserve* exemption from suffering and judgment. Because we are much like they are, we can imagine the emotional lift and self-affirmation that many dispensationalists received from such teachings. It is no small comfort to be told that "the Christian must never lose sight of the fact that he belongs to heaven" when one's status on this earth is threatened by events too large to control.[59]

Nor is it an inconsiderable boost to the ego to be taught that this special status will persist even after the rapture. Dispensationalists understood the church to be returning to earth with Christ, to share in his victory at Armageddon, and to reign with him in the millennial kingdom. Again, there is something a bit strange about this. It was by distinguishing between Israel and the church and reserving all prophecies about the literal earthly kingdom for Israel that dispensationalism made a case for the rapture of the church out of the earth. But, according to dispensationalism, when Christ returns to rule for a thousand years, he will bring the church with him to help him run the show once again. How satisfying it must have been to evangelicals who were losing their cultural dominance to be assured that, as a more contemporary dispensationalist has said, "God's purpose in this age [is] to form an aristocracy for the kingdom."[60] That there is a "pay-off" of this sort for dispensationalists can be sensed in these comments by J. C. Massee, a prominent premillennialist, in 1919:

> I am not looking for an immediate residence in heaven. I expect to be there only a little time and then I am coming back with Him to live in a redeemed earth and rule here with Him in the earth. I would regret to believe that I would have to spend my thousand years in heaven. The reward of the saints is to have the privilege of coming back with Jesus to reign here over the nations with Him.[61]

Dispensationalism never seemed to have challenged its adherents' sense of their own rightness, nor to have led them to expect anything other than "the high and peculiar honors in reservation for the wise and faithful."[62]

Unlike Habakkuk, then, the dispensationalists seemed to feel that they had nothing to fear in the work of the Lord (3:2). Our God will come, they seemed to be saying, and he will establish *us*. Their vision did not bring them low, as Habakkuk's did him. Rather, it spoke of their glory. Their version of "I am doing a work in your days" was not unbelievable to them but rather quite affirming of them and their rightness. Their witness to the Unseen Reality, while timely in a period of growing unbelief, was not done as by those who understood *themselves* and *their* works to be judged by that Reality, and who knew that they deserved such judgment. To recall an earlier theme of ours, they saw themselves not as the poor but as the rich—rich in their status as the faithful remnant, rich in their sure grasp of the future, and rich in their certainty of escaping the suffering to come.

We might even see them, within the context of Habakkuk's prophecy, as "the arrogant" or the "proud one" whose soul is not upright rather than as the watchman. Darby's life gives ample evidence of arrogance. Although he could say, "Hitherto in infirmity and weakness the brethren have been a testimony, and are more and more publicly so. . . ,"[63] he was also certain that his own doctrinal formulations were the only biblical ones, and he did not hesitate to force them on his fellow Plymouth Brethren under threat of excommunication and eternal punishment. He found it easy to describe the opinions of those who disagreed with him on relatively minor points as "an abominable evil" and to ascribe their existence to the work of Satan.[64] We hear the same arrogance in Haldeman's oft-repeated phrase "thus saith the Lord," with which he proclaimed, essentially, the inerrancy of his own opinions.[65] We also hear it in William Bell Riley's assertion that, as Christians, we have Christ's crown "in our hands."[66]

In other words, there is a certain stridency of tone in the dispensationalist writings that one does not associate with humility or brokenness but with pride. Habakkuk was prepared for his reception of and his prophetic witness to the gospel by a posture of humility. I have been suggesting that the dispensationalists were not. On the face of it, this would indicate that they could not clearly—at the deepest levels—hear that gospel. Still rich in their righteousness, far from being broken, they stood as the Pharisee stood in the temple to pray, not as the publican. Instead of pointing to the God of righteousness, as Paul did in beginning his presentation of the gospel, they pointed to their own merit. This essentially prideful starting point should have implications for their understanding and reception of the three elements of the gospel we originally saw outlined by Habakkuk's vision. Let us examine them in this light.

We noted, first of all, Habakkuk's outspoken indictment of sinful humanity, taking the form of "woes" directed against human economic, social, and political structures, and against the idolatry that suffuses human society. Here Habakkuk reminds us very much of other Jewish prophets of his day who anguished along with God over the disobedience, the injustice, and the violence that seem so rampant in human history. As Abraham Heschel points out, the prophet is horrified at the daily occurrences of evil:

> God has thrust a burden upon his soul, and he is bowed and stunned at man's fierce greed. Frightful is the agony of man; no human voice can convey its full terror. Prophecy is the voice that God has lent to the silent agony, a voice to the plundered poor, to the profaned riches of the world.[67]

The prophet rails fiercely against human pretensions to power or security, and he enumerates their cost in sheer human agony and oppression. The prophet thus takes history very seriously. He does not write it off as inconsequential, or as merely preliminary to the main event. He lives in history with his people, suffers the same depredations as the poor, and shares complicity in the guilts they enumerate.

The dispensationalists were also discomfited by human social evil. They were painfully aware of the social unrest and economic warfare that were tearing apart the fabric of life in late nineteenth-century America. Their indictments, however, were always oversimplified and pointed unfailingly away from themselves. The culprits were easily identifiable: the irresponsible rich and the unreliable, potentially explosive poor. Arno

Gaebelein bemoaned the luxurious lives of the extravagant wealthy classes, who threw parties for their dogs while the poor starved. "Such an affair creates the most bitter feelings among the poorer classes and feeds the smouldering flames of rebellion and anarchy. Some day there will be an outburst of lawlessness which will deal a fearful blow to the rich. . . ." Dispensationalists did not approve of such lawless outbursts, but neither did they seem sympathetic to the budding labor union movement, whose purpose was to shield the poor against certain of the depredations of the rich. Such efforts, many thought, only presaged the day of the Antichrist.[68]

Dispensationalists also noted certain corruptions wrought by an urbanizing society and attacked them as signs of the end times. The more moderate of them were sometimes willing to join civic campaigns for moral reform, risking the ire of compatriots who thought any effort to cleanse society by social or political action could only delay the Second Coming. Thus they could speak of the "rogues" in city hall who "steal our money," and "the rum-seller or the procurer" who "debauch our youth." To be thwarting these was, in a small way, to be "undoing the works of Satan, . . . giving him all the trouble we can till Jesus comes. . . ."[69] But here again their attention seemed drawn to sins in which they had no personal part. Their compassion for the victims of these evils seems to have been sincere, as shown in their enthusiasm for city rescue missions; yet it was the compassion of those who do not find themselves implicated in any way in the misery of their fellow human beings.

What was missing in their indictment, in other words, is any sense of the social evils in which the middle class was implicated—say, the kinds of small and large businessmen who flocked to Moody's revival services, or the skilled craftsmen and professional people who filled the pews each Sunday. These middle classes seem to have represented the bulk of Protestantism in late nineteenth-century America, and the evidence suggests that they filled the ranks of the dispensationalist movement.[70] The poor cannot repair to pastoral summer retreats to sit for a week under the spell of prophetic teachers. Such relatively prosperous denominations as the Presbyterians seemed overrepresented among dispensationalist leaders.[71] Could this be the reason for the absence of a sensitive awareness of the everyday injustices brought on by the normal and accepted human struggle for competitive advantage and economic gain, which is motivated by nothing more than what Habakkuk saw: "To set his nest on high, to be safe from the reach of harm!" (2:9). Instead of giving themselves to a serious analysis of their time and place, as Habakkuk and most of the prophets seem to have done, the dispensationalists settled for moralistic attacks on adultery and alcoholism, which, tragic though they may be, did not represent the root of the problem of human futility and social evil in industrializing America. As Marsden points out, the "dispensationalists were not much interested in social or political questions, except as they bore on spiritual history."[72] When they did talk about social and economic realities, it was to express fear of whatever threatened the middle classes of society: "trusts and syndicates" that "control the business and commerce of the world" or "the organized revolt of the mass against the domination of the class."[73] D. L. Moody, who played his part in popularizing at least a moderate form of dispensationalism, urged the businessmen in his audience to take care of their "servants" and employees—giving evidence by his very terminology that he saw little to be regretted in the free-enterprise system as it found expression in his day. His social and economic analysis rarely went beyond such comments as these:

> I thank God I live where the Bible is read. Anarchy, nihilism, socialism, would sweep this whole country, your property and your life would not be safe, if it was not for this old book.[74]

Such comments illustrate the accuracy of Richard Hofstadter's assertion that the middle class of late nineteenth-century America, experiencing a status revolution that we have called the disturbing of their nest, lashed out against the organized forces of big business and big labor, between whose great jaws they felt themselves mashed. This meant that they did not give serious thought, either as Americans or as evangelicals, to the sinful bases of all human enterprise—nor to their own complicity in that enterprise. In their account of human sinfulness, at least as that sinfulness was embodied in social institutions and the historical process, the dispensationalists stopped short of the whole truth. This is a natural result, of course, of their unwillingness to embrace human history in all its relativity and yet all its seriousness, as did the prophets of old. It also follows logically from their lack of a radical humility, which might have opened them to a critique of their own complicity in social and economic evil. Such humility, along with a serious interest in their own times, might have made them truly powerful and prophetic witnesses to an age that applauded its own human achievements without embarrassment. Instead, these critiques were left to secular voices like those of Marx and Engels or, in the United States, Debs, Veblen, and Sinclair, or theologically liberal voices like those of Gladden and Rauschenbusch. In the process, dispensationalists missed an opportunity to witness to the fullest meaning of human depravity and the gracious rescue offered in Christ.

The theologian Karl Barth has written that "the Gospel is God's condemnation of man, of all men and every man." We have argued that the dispensationalists failed to take to its limit their own solidarity with other men and women, as human beings standing together under this condemnation. An incomplete social and historical analysis was the result. But there is another result, which is related to the second point in Habakkuk's articulation of the gospel—the judgment of God. Barth goes on: "The one who is justified by faith, who receives the sentence of this Judge, trusting that it is valid and right, who subjects himself to it in obedience, will live, will partake of redemption."[75] It seems that Habakkuk did this—he freely, though at first haltingly, accepted God's mysterious work, which was also his own judgment. When we get to the third chapter of Habakkuk, where he paints this judgment in vivid colors, we must be led to surmise that Habakkuk understood that he was under this judgment himself. We must assume that when Habakkuk says of God, "Thou didst crush the head of the wicked" (3:13), he knew that he was deservingly one of those wicked.

When dispensationalists spoke of judgment, it was generally of other people being judged. They admitted that the church would go through a heavenly judgment, but their explanation of this makes it sound as if it simply will be a verbal accounting for the deeds done on earth.[76] The real judgment will fall on earth, when the church is safe in heaven, and again at the end of the millennium, a judgment from which the church is exempt. Such immunity stands in stark contrast to the way of the prophets who announced God's judgment on the people and endured that same judgment with their people. When the people were taken captive and led into exile, the prophets went along—to suffer with them. The prophets were ready to subject themselves to that judgment in obedience, not to plead their case for special exemptions.

Dispensationalism was truly prophetic in pointing to the long awaited arrival of the Savior. But, if William Stringfellow is right, Christians are those who "eagerly expect and patiently await the Second Coming of Jesus Christ, with a glad and trustworthy knowledge that what is vindicated in judgment is the Lordship of Christ, *not* the Christians since they are also judged by the Word of God."[77] Stringfellow makes a key distinction here between the judgment that vindicates Christ and one that vindicates us. To recognize the lordship of Christ means to recognize that the judgment that fell on him is the judgment we deserve. One who sees this must be willing to go through whatever temporal judgments God sends his people, knowing that they pale into insignificance alongside the judgment that fell on Christ. Christ did not clutch after equality with God, Paul tells us, but took the form of a servant, "humbled himself and became obedient unto death, even death on a cross" (Phil. 2:6-8). When we see it truly, this cross instructs us concerning our well-deserved judgment. To "take up" this cross and follow Jesus is to accept our afflictions as "evidence of the righteous judgment of God" and to take our rightful place as those of whom "the experience of suffering is required . . . throughout the world" (Mt. 16:24; II Thess. 1:5; I Peter 5:9). This is the meaning of the cross, one that is not articulated clearly in the writings of the dispensationalists.

Because Christ himself became a man, showing his solidarity with a fallen race, we hear from him the same cries of compassion that we hear from the prophets, cries that indicate he does not welcome the judgment he knows is coming. He weeps over Jerusalem and the sad fate that awaits her (Lk. 19:41-44). In this he simply continues the tradition of the prophets—Ezekiel, for example: "Have I any pleasure in the death of the wicked, says the Lord God, and not rather that he should turn from his way and live?" (18:23). It is for this reason that Habakkuk can cry to the Lord, "In wrath remember mercy" (3:2). One does not hear dispensationalist preachers crying to the Lord to remember mercy on that day of judgment. One can find, instead, statements that indicate an insensitivity to the sadness of this world and of the coming judgment, statements such as this one made by R. A. Torrey to a Prophetic Conference in 1918:

> But as I hear the low rumblings of the thunder of the coming storm, as I go over to the East Side in New York, as I go across the river in Chicago, as I walk the streets of Milwaukee, as I go down the Los Angeles streets to see the soap box orators of the I. W. W., my heart is not heavy, not a bit. . . . The Lord is coming.[78]

Torrey is comforting fearful evangelicals, promising that social chaos will not engulf them. But he is also showing a marked lack of the pathos of the prophets, an insensitivity both to the evils of his time and to what the end will mean for these people he is passing in the streets as well as for himself. His hardness of spirit in the face of judgment was more than matched by one of his dispensationalist contemporaries describing the judgment:

> Multitudes of men and women will, for the first time in their lives, call upon the name of the Lord and cry unto Him for Mercy. But their cry will not be heard. . . . Often had these left-behind ones been warned, but in vain. Servants of God had faithfully set before them their imperative need of fleeing from the wrath to come . . . only to be laughed at for their pains. And now the tables will be turned. God will laugh at them, laugh at their calamity and mock at their fear.[79]

This sort of attitude, I suggest, is diametrically opposed to the spirit of the prophets, and to the burden of Habakkuk's cry to the Lord, "In wrath remember mercy."

Habakkuk's final words are a vision of salvation. He has been humbled by God's revelation of man's lostness and the judgment to come. The watchman has learned quietness. After his feverish accounting of the pretensions and futility of human civilization, he wrote: "But the Lord is in his holy temple; let all the earth keep silence before him" (2:20). Now, the judgment revealed, we find quietness instead of mirth and a confession of utter lostness: "I hear, and my body trembles, my lips quiver at the sound; rottenness enters into my bones, my steps totter within me. I will quietly wait for the day of trouble to come upon people who invade us" (3:16). This is not the triumph of one who sees that he has been vindicated. Its imagery is death, feebleness, fear. He cannot mean that he is quietly exultant that the Chaldeans are about to be vanquished. Rather, it speaks of Habakkuk's solidarity with the Chaldeans, and of the chastening that the Lord has done to his spirit. He has learned to let go of history—and to wait.

The writer of the epistle to the Hebrews knew what it meant to wait. He also knew Habakkuk, and he chose to quote the same line Paul did right in the middle of a treatise on judgment and suffering. In the tenth chapter he warns that "if we sin deliberately after receiving the knowledge of the truth, there no longer remains a sacrifice for sins, but a fearful prospect of judgment . . ." (10:26-27). Small comfort this must have brought to his readers, who, if they were honest, knew that they were included in such a category of sinners. To all of us the author writes: "'The Lord will judge his people.' It is a fearful thing to fall into the hands of the living God" (10:30-31). So this writer knows something about the judgment. He also knows about salvation, but it is a salvation that encompasses suffering. "For you have need of endurance," he says, "so that you may do the will of God and receive what is promised" (10:36). And then he quotes Habakkuk:

> For yet a little while, and the coming one shall come and shall not tarry; but my righteous one shall live by faith, and if he shrinks back, my soul has no pleasure in him.
>
> (10:37-38)

Now we can see that Habakkuk, indeed, knew the gospel. The vision that God told Habakkuk to write plainly and wait for is that of the "coming one," who alone of all men and women on earth was able to live by faith. Habakkuk was pointing to the Messiah, the same one the writer of Hebrews and the apostle Paul looked back to. But that Messiah is a suffering servant before—and at the same time as—he is the conqueror on the white horse. And we are called to suffer with him, to join the fellowship of his sufferings, "becoming like him in his death . . ." (Phil. 3:10).

When Jesus talked about his sufferings and his death, Peter rebuked him (Mk. 8:32) and the disciples "did not understand the saying" (Mk. 9:32). In my opinion, the dispensationalists did not understand the saying either. Thus they did not understand salvation in the paradoxical sense shared by the biblical writers. Their gospel pulled them out of the world and its sufferings. Habakkuk's gospel placed him in the world to grieve over the human plight, to experience the judgment, to share the sufferings, and in this spirit—and only in this spirit—to wait for God's arrival.

And in the midst of all this mystery, expectancy, and suffering, Habakkuk lifts a hymn of praise. Sandra Sizer has written that hymns of praise were diminishing in importance in the singing of the Moody-Sankey era, the late nineteenth century. Instead, sentimental prayer hymns and exhortations to conversion were being sung.[80] Without making too much of this, I wonder if it is not at least a small clue to the mood of the late nineteenth century. Perhaps the experience of nest rattling had taken some of the joyous praise out of the mouths of evangelicals. But for Habakkuk, who understood the gospel, praise was not for a God who was making life easy or rescuing his people from the ravages of history. Rather, he was singing praise in famine, and his words implied that if the famine continued, so would the praise. Jeremiah found the very same occasion for praise. At the nadir of Israel's fortunes, suffering with his people in a ruined city, he cried, "Great is thy faithfulness" (Lam. 3:23). Habakkuk did the same, in words that penetrate strangely—in the context of his whole prophecy—to the core of the gospel. They are words that must cause the dispensationalists—and us too—to reconsider our understanding of the mysterious work God is doing in our days, which we would not believe if told:

> Though the fig tree do not blossom, nor fruit be on the vines, the produce of the olive fail and the fields yield no food, the flock be cut off from the fold and there be no herd in the stalls, yet I will rejoice in the Lord, I will joy in the God of my salvation.[81]

Chapter IV

Bear Fruit That Befits Repentance

I

Jesus' first act in his public ministry signified repentance: he was baptized in the river Jordan. We may be a bit puzzled by this act because our theology asserts that Jesus was sinless. What did he repent of? John the Baptist voiced a similar puzzlement: "I need to be baptized by you, and do you come to me?" (Mt. 3:14). But Jesus insisted, saying that he thought it proper for himself and John to "fulfil all righteousness" (3:15). We cannot escape the imagery: John's baptism was a baptism of repentance. Those who came to him "were baptized in the river Jordan, confessing their sins," and it was this same baptism that Jesus underwent, a baptism publicly and fully identifying him with the human condition in an act of repentance. Matthew does not want us to ignore it, as if it were perhaps the only utterly truthful repentance ever made. He records that immediately thereafter the Spirit of God descended like a dove, alighting on Jesus, and a voice from heaven said, "This is my beloved Son, with whom I am well pleased" (3:16-17). Jesus had clearly "fulfilled all righteousness," and "righteousness," as the term characterizing the right relationship of the created to the Creator, seems to have been captured in the act of repentance.

Matthew next records that Jesus was led by the Spirit to go to the wilderness, where he would be tempted by the devil (4:1). Does this story have anything to do with Jesus' repentance? I suggest that it has a very close connection. It was the very nature and sincerity of Jesus' repentance, and thus the quality of his righteousness, that was being tested in the wilderness. In each of the tempter's sallies he confronted Jesus with the possibility of using his power—the power of the Spirit—toward illegitimate ends. You need physical nourishment, said the tempter, so command these stones to become bread. You'd like to guarantee your safety, your immortality, wouldn't you? So cast yourself off the temple, and the angels will protect you. Would you like to rule all the kingdoms of the earth? I will guarantee you that power if you worship me. In each case, Matthew records, Jesus turned away temptation with the Word of God.

But why? Are not sustenance and physical safety legitimate needs? And does not Christ deserve to reign over all the kingdoms of the earth, deserve to make things right for human beings everywhere? Jesus' answers to the tempter implied that these are in some sense unimportant. "Man shall not live by bread alone," he said and thus refused, as he would throughout his ministry, to call on the power at his disposal to guarantee that his own human needs would be provided for. His example and his words taught that he believed God would provide these things in his own measure and in his own ways. They were not to be wrested from a divine hand by spiritual techniques, but they were to be waited for, undemandingly, in humility and trust. The prayer "give us this day our daily bread" was one that called the disciples ever to be waiting for each new day's provision. They were not to be anxious for life—or food and drink and clothing. "Look at the birds of the air," he said, "they neither sow nor reap nor gather into barns, and yet your heavenly Father feeds them." Or look at the lilies, which God arrays in glory. "But if God so clothes the grass of the field, which today is alive and tomorrow is thrown into the oven, will he not much more clothe you, O men of little faith?" So don't worry about these things, Jesus said. Instead, "seek first his kingdom and his righteousness, and all these things shall be yours as well" (Mt. 6:25-33). We have already been told that in the baptism of repentance he fulfilled all righteousness. Jesus' words must indicate that repentance is at the very heart of the "carefree" life.

We must use the word "carefree" with great caution. For Jesus himself did not live a life that any of us would, if it were ours, identify as carefree. "Foxes have holes, and birds of the air have nests," he admitted, "but the Son of man has nowhere to lay his head" (Mt. 8:20). Perhaps we should have caught the paradox: today God clothes the grass, but tomorrow it is thrown into the oven. And the birds who are fed by the Father are also the birds that fall to the ground—by the will of the same Father. So "do not fear those who kill the body" (10:28-31). We need only look at the dying Jesus, nailed to a cross, to catch the full mystery of his trust in God. For food and drink they gave him vinegar; in the absence of protecting angels, they speared his side; and in a parody of his promise of God's eternal kingdom, they hailed him "King of the Jews" and crowned him with thorns. In this time of extremity and human need, just as in his wilderness temptation, he refused to save himself. Instead, as Paul writes, he "humbled himself and became obedient unto death, even death on a cross" (Phil. 2:8). The man who in humility signified his repentance at the onset of his ministry is the man who in humility listened silently to the curses of his adversaries at the end of his ministry: "He saved others; he cannot save himself. . . . He trusts in God; let God deliver him now . . ." (Mt. 27:41-43).

I suspect that Jesus is one of the very few who have ever really understood that it is not our business to wrest from God those earthly benefits that we associate with happiness. "And my God will supply every need of yours according to his riches in glory in Christ Jesus," writes the apostle Paul (Phil. 4:19). Yet it is Paul who must admit: "To the present hour we hunger and thirst, we are ill-clad and buffeted and homeless . . . we have become, and are now, as the refuse of the world, the offscouring of all things" (I Cor. 4:11, 13). Paul knew the paradox of being, in God's sight, "of more value than many sparrows" (Mt. 10:31). It meant that, if he was in God's embrace, it was the embrace of a "consuming fire" (Heb. 12:29). He knew what it meant to be a "living sacrifice" (Rom. 12:1). Annie Dillard expresses well the very same paradox:

> There is not a guarantee in the world. Oh your *needs* are guaranteed, your needs are absolutely guaranteed by the most stringent of warranties, in the plainest, truest words: knock; seek; ask. But you must read the fine print. "Not as the world giveth, give I unto you." That's the catch. If you can catch it it will catch you up, aloft. . . . Did you think, before you were caught, that you needed, say, life? Do you think you will keep your life, or anything else you love? But no. Your needs are all met. But not as the world giveth. You see the needs of your own spirit met whenever you have asked, and you have learned that the outrageous guarantee holds. You see the creatures die, and you know you will die. And one day it occurs to you that you must not need life. Obviously. And then you're gone. You have finally understood that you're dealing with a maniac.[1]

Often enough, in Jesus' time, the men and women who watched and heard him must have thought they were dealing with a maniac. His enemies did for sure; they accused him of serving Beelzebub, the prince of demons (Mt. 12:24). But his disciples must have had their moments as well. When this Jesus, who had promised them that every hair of their heads was numbered, began to speak of his suffering and death, they knew they had caught him in a contradiction. Peter was moved to rebuke him (Mt. 16:21-22). Did he think this was the talk of a madman? And who did Peter think he was dealing with when Jesus told him to sheath his sword, and went with his enemies as a lamb to the slaughter? We read that "all the disciples forsook him and fled" (Mt. 26:56). Did Peter ponder the irony of his flight, coming so soon after he had been promised the keys to the kingdom of heaven (Mt. 16:19)?

And the people—how did they see him? Not as a maniac, at least not at first. He was much too valuable for them as a healer and a miracle worker for them to grasp the contradictions. It is clear, of course, that Jesus did not want them to see him merely as healer. Shortly after his temptation in the wilderness, he began to preach, "Repent, for the kingdom of heaven is at hand" (Mt. 4:17). His message, it appears, was very similar to John's; but it seemed to get short shrift among the crowds that followed him. They preferred to see his signs and wonders—perhaps for their entertainment value, or as a portent of political revolution, or for the more immediate purpose of healing their bodies and relieving their worries. Jesus often obliged. Matthew says he "went about all Galilee, teaching in their synagogues and preaching the gospel of the kingdom and healing every disease and every infirmity among the people" (4:23). This caused Jesus' fame to spread, and the crowds grew larger. We do not read that they came for repentance, but that "they brought him all the sick . . . and he healed them" (4:24).

Why did he heal them, if his message was repentance? When two blind men shouted, "Have mercy on us, Son of David!" as he was passing by, Jesus "in pity touched their eyes" (Mt. 20:30-34). His healing was an act of love, and yet it was an act he chose to do freely, when and for whom he willed. But more than that, his healing was a portent of the coming kingdom, when every infirmity would be healed and every eye would be dried. When he healed, he pointed to an eternal healing. But he also pointed clearly to a greater healing, the healing of repentance. This is clearest in the story Matthew tells of the paralytic who was brought on his bed to Jesus. Jesus said to him: "Take heart, my son; your sins are forgiven" (9:2). Was Jesus finished with this man who still lay paralyzed on his bed? He might well have been, for that moment. Jesus had accepted—indeed, he created and embodied in a way the paralytic could not then know—the man's repentance; and he offered him forgiveness. What more, this side of the eschaton, did the man need? Perhaps both Jesus and the man knew at that moment that healing his paralysis would be anticlimactic, or superfluous, or in some sense untimely. If so, then Jesus knew he had, in a brief word, granted all that the paralytic truly needed in his knocking, seeking, and asking. It may not have been until he heard those words that the paralytic himself knew what he was asking. Carried by his believing friends, he came thinking that he might walk again. But now he knew that he had a greater healing and a greater hope—that just possibly he did not need legs, or even life.

But among the spectators were some scribes who grumbled that Jesus' act of forgiving sins was blasphemous. Was this their real objection to Jesus' words? Matthew tells us that Jesus knew there was evil in their hearts (9:4). And surely the evil went much further than the scribes were aware of. For it was not Jesus' "blasphemy" that angered them so much as their own pangs of recognition that they—who themselves had made a fetish and a work of human merit out of the very act of repentance—they too stood in need of forgiveness. Such a recognition is always accompanied by anger and denial. The offer of forgiveness implies that we are offenders who need forgiveness. The scribes and their allies among the Pharisees and Sadducees did not recognize the true nature of their own offenses. They prided themselves as keepers of the law, defenders of the faith, and of course as repenters par excellence. Could Jesus' words to the paralytic have meant that they too required forgiveness? And from this itinerant prophet? This would have been beneath their carefully guarded dignity. So they stumbled over this "stone of offense" (Isa. 8:14). Knowing their thoughts, Jesus said: " 'For which is easier, to say, "Your sins are forgiven," or to say, "Rise and walk"? But that you may know that the Son of man has authority on earth to forgive sins'—he then said to the paralytic—'Rise, take up your bed and go home.' And he rose and went home" (Mt. 9:4-7). The healing was easy. Others were healing in Jesus' day, as they are in ours. It was the forgiveness that no other could offer.

I believe that this story is about the offensiveness and the sufficiency of forgiveness. Jesus knew that in the simple act of forgiveness he had given the paralytic all he needed in the present moment. I suspect that the paralytic knew that in repentance he was somehow healed of *all* his infirmities, even though he still lay on his bed. And maybe the scribes knew it, remembering Israel's history; but they could not accept it, since it would have meant giving up the public reputation and the private illusions they had nourished. And perhaps the crowd knew it too. They had come to witness—and perhaps experience—healings; what they had witnessed instead was the forgiveness of sins. They had readily admitted the frailty of their bodies. Now Jesus' words forced them to look within at the frailty and corruption in their souls. This was more than they had bargained for, and Matthew tells us that they were afraid (9:8).

Is not this message of repentance and of forgiveness one we are all afraid of? When we hear the call to repentance, if we hear it correctly, we experience an arrow piercing very near to the core of who we are as humans. The call to repentance is not a call to be sorry for a few glaring imperfections in an otherwise perfect creation. If it were just that, repentance would be easy, since none of us *wants* to be imperfect. Nor is it a call to repent once and be made whole in some straightforward way that will make further repentance unnecessary. Who would not opt for that kind of repentance? It offers us the very godlikeness for which we all hunger. These versions do not capture the biblical notion of repentance, which has to do rather with a recognition that in our very essence we are not now—nor shall ever inherently be—anything but the sinners with whom

Jesus chose to eat (Mt. 9:10). Biblical repentance attacks that secret for-
tress inside where we have established a place to nest in this world, where
we have created an illusion of safety. It topples the house of cards that
protects our self-esteem. It rips from our eyes the blinders that hide our
own frail mortality from our own view. It asks us to admit that we are, in
the psalmist's words, worms and not men (22:6).

No wonder the crowds were afraid. Of course, they were drawn to
him: he could solve the problems that lay on the surface of their lives; he
could turn stones into bread, send angels to rescue them, even offer them
a kingdom in this world. So they flocked to him and hailed him as their
King, shouting, "Hosanna to the Son of David!" (21:9). But before the
week was out, they would also turn on him, asking that the criminal
Barabbas be released and the Son of David be crucified. If he was no
longer to turn stones into bread, or stress into happiness, or defeat into
victory as they defined it—and if his kingdom was clearly not of this
world—they could do without him, since his call to repentance had never
made them anything but afraid. Barabbas might not heal them, but at
least he did not confront them with the bankruptcy at the center of their
lives. So in the end they joined the scribes and Pharisees and chief priests
and elders and the hated Romans themselves—a grand human coalition,
and a symbol of the solidarity of the race—to put him to death. The healer
had become the wounded, and the people, unwilling to admit their own
mortal wounds, had no more need for him.

We do not like to think our wounds are mortal; when reminded of this
fact, we become afraid. Or worse. When Peter and the disciples were
questioned by the high priest in Jerusalem, they announced that this
Jesus, so recently crucified, had been exalted by God as Leader and Savior, "to give repentance to Israel and forgiveness of sins." It is recorded
that the chief priest and the council "were enraged and wanted to kill
them" (Acts 5:30-32). Truly, this threat of forgiveness is an insult and a
provocation. Those who were enraged in this case were the religious
authorities, and for good reason. Religion is what we make of the Word of
God when we decide, as we tend to do daily, that we are no longer
interested in hearing the truth about ourselves and our need for rescue.
The religion Jesus confronted in the Pharisees had become a mechanism
not for the dissolution but for the exaltation of humans. The Pharisee
prided himself on knowing God and observing his commandments.
When he prayed he thanked God that he was not a sinner—not, at least,
deep down as the tax collector was (Lk. 18:11). The Pharisee, like most of
us, considered his religion a boost to his self-esteem. No doubt the scribes
and chief priests played similar games: they were not about to let the
preaching of repentance and forgiveness destroy what it had taken them

a lifetime of purity and cant and admirable self-control—indeed, even of self-consciously humble repentance—to create. So they joined their anger to the fear of the crowds.

The experience of the leading religionists of the day should suggest to us possibilities for examining our own history as evangelical Christians. Has our religion been that of the crowds, who wished for healing but shrank in fear from the Savior who preached repentance? Has it perhaps been the religion of the establishment, whose pretensions of an earthly righteousness were pricked by the man who pointed to the worm at the core? Or has it been the experience of the paralytic, in whom faith was created in the presence of repentance—in the presence of the Man who, alone of all humans, fulfilled the call to repentance—and who knew that something greater had happened to him in the moment of forgiveness than would ever have happened had he merely been made to walk? The crowds wanted healing. The leaders wanted heroism. But the paralytic learned that, as David wrote, "blessed is he whose transgression is forgiven, whose sin is covered" (Ps. 32:1).

We have been studying the American evangelicals at the turn of the century. They too followed Jesus. Now we must ask: what did they want from him?

II

What many evangelicals of the late nineteenth century seemed to want, most church historians would agree, was perfection. Andrew Murray, a South African whose books were very popular among evangelicals, put it this way in a prayer concluding his book *Be Perfect:* "O my Father! I would walk before Thee this day, and be perfect. Thou has commanded it; Thou givest the enabling grace. I would be perfect with the Lord my God. I would serve Thee with a perfect heart. I would be perfect as the Father is perfect." Murray made it clear that he was not content with a perfection that is hidden from the believer who attains it. His biblical study revealed to him that "the man who walks before God with a perfect heart can know it—it may be a matter of consciousness." Since that is the case, he said, "let us seek to have this blessed consciousness."[2] During the last third of the nineteenth century millions of Americans joined Murray in the search for this consciousness of perfection.

The largest and most sustained outburst of perfectionism in nineteenth-century America was associated with the Methodists. In the middle of the century, Methodists had rediscovered a doctrine that had been promulgated a century earlier by their founder, John Wesley, a doctrine that had been somewhat submerged during the early days of Method-ism's wildfire growth in America: the teaching that Christians could be "entirely sanctified." Wesley seems to have spent a good part of his adult life thinking about in what sense and by what means the Christian could be perfect. His doctrinal development reflected his own religious driven-ness and the ups and downs of his experience of sanctification over thirty years or more. By 1766, when he published *A Plain Account of Christian Perfection*, he had come to something like a settled conclusion on the matter. When a person is converted, he said, he experiences justification, which means that his sins are forgiven; then he begins on a process of sanctification, or deliverance by God's Spirit from the power of sin. If the believer "keepeth himself," he will not commit further sin. But, of course, believers do not keep themselves, since there is still within them a sinful nature. Deliverance from this sinful nature or "being," with its "inbred sin," can come only through *entire sanctification*, which occurs both in-stantaneously (by way of a "specific spiritual experience," which aug-ments the moment of conversion) and as a process. Even though entire sanctification comes instantaneously, there is still growth in grace by which the perfection relative to one stage in life is made even more com-plete in the next. One cannot take this perfection for granted, since entire sanctification may be lost if the believer ceases to rely on God's grace moment by moment. What entire sanctification gives the believer is a heart of perfect love, which works itself out in actions that are loving. This does not mean that the perfected believer will not make errors of judg-ment or mistakes in action. The believer is not all-knowing in the applica-tion of love. But the believer's intentions, or motives, will be entirely loving. "All that is necessarily implied," wrote Wesley, "is humble, gen-tle, patient love: love regulating all the tempers and governing all the words and actions."[3]

The possibility of achieving this perfect love had remarkable appeal to evangelicals in mid-nineteenth-century America. We have already wit-nessed the triumphal optimism that served as a religious counterpart to the ebullient democratic spirit sweeping the land. Americans were caught up in an enthusiasm for their own possibilities. They saw no limits for the American nation in world history, nor for the achievements of the com-mon woman or man within that nation. To their confidence in personal economic improvement they added a confidence in personal moral achievement, and to this end Wesley's perfectionism seemed a most use-ful doctrine. And once again we find Charles Finney in the middle of things. Around 1836, Finney discovered Wesley's notion of entire sancti-fication, and by the early 1840s he was championing a similar view among his followers, most of whom were from the decidedly nonperfectionistic

Calvinist traditions. By introducing the possibility of Christians being so transformed by the Spirit of God that they would no longer consciously choose to commit sin, Finney offered his Calvinist followers relief from the dour and unwinnable life of struggle against sin to which so many had resigned themselves. He also greatly augmented his evangelist's repertoire. As one historian writes, "The appeal to the spiritual advantage of a second crisis in the Christian's life was an extension of the basic revival call in every respect. The invitation was a universal one. Every convert was a candidate. The sense of immediacy was also there; the time to enter into the 'higher life' was now."[4]

While Finney was thus presiding over the transformation of the Reformed tradition into something more palatable to the triumphant American spirit, Phoebe Palmer was reenergizing the holiness movement within American Methodism. Palmer was a central figure in nineteenth-century Methodism, particularly by virtue of her sponsorship of the "Tuesday Meetings" in New York City for nearly forty years. In these Bible study and devotional gatherings she urged her followers to open themselves to the "second blessing," whereby one could experience in faith the blessedness of entire sanctification. She chronicled her own experience of that blessing in *The Way of Holiness . . . Being a Narrative of Religious Experience Resulting from a Determination to be a Biblical Christian*, published in 1848. Here she described how she had been led "directly into the 'way of holiness,' where with unutterable delight, [she] found the comprehensive desires of [her] soul blended and satisfied in the fulfillment of the command, 'Be ye holy.'" She urged her readers to seek the same experience—not as an "attainment beyond . . . reach" but as a "state of grace in which every one of the Lord's redeemed should live." Palmer denied that her own powers had anything to do with arriving at this state. The very presentation of herself to God had come by the power of God; the only requirement of the believer is that she believe: "Faith is taking God at his word, relying unwaveringly upon his truth." Once this faith is expressed, God does his work—a fact the believer can be sure of even if she does not "feel" perfect. In time the feeling will come, wrote Palmer, if we only believe.[5]

Palmer reported that, in the midst of this experience, the Spirit had said, "You will be called to profess this blessing before thousands." This caused her a certain anxiety, but after being assured of the Spirit's presence and support, she agreed to this witness, even if it meant being "a martyr to the cause."[6] To her surprise, perhaps, she became the progenitor of what grew into a sizable "holiness movement" within the Methodist church—a movement, in fact, that eventually left that church battered by partisan warfare. Palmer's teachings spread rapidly among the Methodist churches in America. After the Civil War, holiness revivals occurred across the country, particularly in summer "camp meetings" organized "for the promotion of holiness." A huge output of holiness literature kept the enthusiasm more or less alive in the churches between camp meetings. Holiness associations sprang up, comprised mainly of Methodists, but joined by holiness advocates from a dozen denominations. In 1885 the First General Holiness Assembly was held in Chicago, and it adopted a doctrinal statement affirming "entire sanctification" as that work involving, among other things, "the entire extinction of the carnal mind, the total eradication of the birth principle of sin." By 1887 this association was affiliated with sixty-seven camp meetings across sixteen states. By 1888 it reported over two hundred "stated meetings for the promotion of holiness" and listed the names of about as many holiness evangelists. Four publishing houses were producing holiness materials exclusively, and twenty-seven holiness journals were circulating.[7]

Needless to say, this kind of activity introduced enthusiasms into Methodism that could not be contained by the traditional church structure and hierarchy. In 1894 the bishops drafted an address that brought to a head several decades of a very complex intradenominational struggle. The bishops affirmed the doctrine of entire sanctification as a "well-known teaching of Methodism" and encouraged that it "still be proclaimed and the experience still be testified." They went on, however, in a different spirit:

> But there has sprung up among us a party with holiness as a watchword; they have holiness associations, holiness meetings, holiness preachers, holiness evangelists, and holiness property. . . . We deplore their teaching and methods in so far as they claim a monopoly of the experience, practice, and advocacy of holiness, and separate themselves from the body of ministers and disciples.[8]

It took only six years from the time of this statement for enough Methodists to leave their churches that ten new denominations were formed, each with "entire sanctification" at their doctrinal center, and most emphasizing the instantaneous "second definite work of grace, subsequent to regeneration" as the biblical means to that blessed state. Many of these groups joined with others to form one of the leading holiness denominations, the Church of the Nazarene, in 1907-1908.[9]

As we have seen in the case of Finney, however, the holiness movement was not confined to American Methodism. George Marsden writes that "by 1870, holiness teachings of one sort or another seemed to be everywhere in American revivalist Protestantism." Americans sang hymns by Fanny J. Crosby, P. P. Bliss, and Frances R. Havergal, whose sentiments urged the experience of total surrender and a relationship of mystical love with Jesus. Dozens of books were published on the subject of the Holy Spirit: his indwelling in the believer, his gifts to the believer, his enduing with power from on high. Leading premillennialists urged believers to wait for the Lord in perfect holiness so that he would find them with their garments clean. Even D. L. Moody, the era's most popular evangelist, experienced a filling with the Spirit subsequent to his salvation, and made his summer conference at Northfield, Massachusetts, a center for the promotion of the sanctified life.[10] One of the speakers to appear at Northfield was Andrew Murray, author of *Be Perfect*. Murray's closest association, however, was not with Northfield but with Keswick, in England, where the specific brand of holiness teaching that we shall examine more closely was first fully adopted and popularized.

The Keswick movement found its roots in the widespread attention given to two books by American evangelicals who described their discovery of a whole new level of Christian existence: W. E. Boardman's *A Higher Life* and Hannah Whitall Smith's *The Christian's Secret of a Happy Life*. Smith's book had grown out of a deep dissatisfaction with her Christian experience, which she described as a ceaseless round of sinning and repenting. The Christians she consulted assured her that this was all she could expect; yet she somehow knew that Christ must offer victory. In 1867 a Methodist acquaintance told her about the possibility of a "second blessing," and both Smith and her husband, Robert Pearsall, experienced this blessing.

> We had simply discovered the "secret of victory," and knew that we were no longer the "slaves of sin" and therefore forced to yield to is mastery, but that we might, if we would, be made more than conquerors through our Lord Jesus Christ. But this did not mean that temptations ceased to come; and when we neglected to avail ourselves of the "secret" we had discovered, and, instead of handing the battle over to the Lord, took it into our own hands as of old, failure inevitably followed.[11]

The Smiths soon made a full-time writing and speaking career of their secret of victory through faith. Visits to England brought them a large following and encouraged others who had entered this "higher life" to begin meeting in conventions dedicated to "victory over all known sin." By 1875 these conventions were attracting thousands from many parts of Great Britain and the Continent. Rev. T. D. Harford-Battersby, whose reading about Smith's experience had made him "utterly dissatisfied" with himself, wrote after attending the convention in Oxford in 1874: "I got a revelation of Christ to my soul, so extraordinary, glorious, and precious, that from that day it illuminated my life. I found *He* was *all* I wanted. . . ."[12] Along with several friends, Harford-Battersby called the first convention in 1875 at Keswick, a small town in England's Lake District, and after that, Keswick, with its yearly gatherings, became the center of the newer holiness teaching in England.

The Keswick teaching distinguished itself from the Wesleyan perfectionism that characterized the American holiness revivals at the time. The meetings at Keswick were subdued and orderly and proper. Under the leadership of a respected Church of England clergyman, H. W. Webb-Peploe, Keswick was also somewhat more sober about its claims for the "higher life." At first suspected by many English Christians of teaching the total eradication of the sinful nature, it defended itself by promulgating the more Calvinist opinion that the sinful nature is not removed, but its tendencies are counteracted by the indwelling life of Christ in the believer. Thus, while the sinful nature still exists in the believer, it need have no power over the life of the believer. What is necessary to maintain this Spirit-filled life is a moment-by-moment surrender of the self to Jesus, and a moment-by-moment appropriation by faith of the cleansing and strengthening power of Christ. So long as the self is surrendered and Christ appropriated by faith, the Christian can be free of any known sin. Many of those who came to Keswick seemed to experience this surrender and Spirit-filling, and to have the nagging burdens of their sin lifted from their souls for the first time in their lives.

In 1891, F. B. Meyer, one of the most popular Keswick speakers and writers, brought the Keswick brand of holiness back to the United States when he was invited to speak at Moody's summer conference at Northfield. This visit was only the first in a long series of exchanges, continued throughout the 1890s, between "higher life" teachers in the United States and England. In its Keswick form this somewhat de-Wesleyanized version of holiness found an increasingly wide audience among Calvinist-oriented American premillenialists, including leading dispensationalist teachers like C. I. Scofield. Books by F. B. Meyer and Andrew Murray achieved wide circulation in America around the turn of the century, as did Keswick-influenced works by R. A. Torrey, A. T. Pierson, A. J. Gordon, A. B. Simpson, Harry A. Ironside, and W. H. Griffith Thomas. Together, Keswick's higher life teaching and John Nelson Darby's dispensationalist premillenialism—both English imports—became the backbone of the fundamentalist movement in American evangelicalism after the turn of the century.

Organizationally, however, no American counterpart of the Keswick movement existed until after 1910, when Charles G. Trumbull attended a summer youth conference in New Wilmington, Pennsylvania, and experienced a profound conversion to what soon came to be called the "Victorious Life." Trumbull had inherited the editor's desk at *The Sunday School Times*, a leading weekly journal featuring devotional and educational aids for the Christian worker. He at once turned the magazine into a mouthpiece for Keswick-type teachings. With a few close friends who had also experienced the "victory," he organized the Victorious Life Testimony, which sponsored summer conferences in several east coast locations between 1913 and 1924, and which finally established a permanent conference at Keswick Grove, New Jersey. Trumbull's enthusiastic salesmanship was also responsible for spawning a series of Keswick-style conferences in a number of locations in the United States and Canada. He himself spoke at many of these conferences and continued for many years to be the spark at the center of a movement that exerted a remarkable influence on American evangelicalism in the twentieth century.

In fact, it can be said that Victorious Life teaching became *the* way of understanding true Christianity in a secularizing society for many Christian workers, particularly those who had influence in the training of Christian youth. Many of the leading twentieth-century evangelical educational institutions became centers for the teaching of the victorious Christian life—well into the 1960s at least. Among these are Columbia Bible College, founded by one of Trumbull's closest associates, Robert C. McQuilken, Prairie Bible Institute, Moody Bible Institute, Wheaton College, and Dallas Theological Seminary. A recent analyst of the movement estimates that "the Keswick teaching has made a far greater impact on American evangelical theology than many realize. . . . Many evangelical pastors who have been products of these schools have gone on to preach the victorious life from their pulpits, even though they may never have attended a Keswick conference."[13] As with Scofield's popularization of dispensationalism in his Reference Bible, many evangelical Christians who imbibed the teachings of the Victorious Life had no idea that the version of Christianity being presented to them was a relatively recent, historically conditioned understanding of the Christian life. Essentially, it spoke to the spiritual agonies of a troubled Christian generation in its passage to modernity, and it offered that generation (and those who followed) an opportunity to transcend its agonies through the Spirit's power to indwell the Christian with a life of perfect victory. We will do well to understand just how it articulated this offer before we go on to inquire about its meaning in the nest-shaking passage of the nineteenth century into the twentieth.

III

"It is the privilege of every Christian to live every day of his life without breaking the laws of God in known sin either in thought, word or deed." In a nutshell, this was the message of Charles G. Trumbull and his cohorts in the Victorious Life movement. Of course, Trumbull knew that most Christians did not actually experience such a sin-free existence; but in his mind this was a tragedy. As he surveyed the spiritual landscape of his day, he saw it strewn with the defeated lives of Christians who were essentially "ignorant" of Christ's provision for victory over sin. Many Christians were "monstrosities" who had not grown spiritually in the ten or twenty years of their Christian experience.[14] Not that most Christians were not earnest in their hunger for righteousness. The problem was that their earnestness only led them into more and more bitter defeat. Unaware of the power of God available to them, they were striving with all their might to fulfill the greatest commandments—to love God and neighbor. Although they sought divine help in their struggles, they were essentially relying on their own willpower to live a perfect life in God's sight. But when one relies on self, self remains in the center of one's life and leads the Christian only into bondage to sin. "Nearly all Christians" make this mistake, agreed Trumbull's friend Robert C. McQuilken; in so doing they simply repeat what, in his opinion, was the apostle Paul's mistake, recorded in Romans 7: they find themselves doing what they wish not to do and not doing what they wish to do. Such is the experience of all those who attempt to obey God's command, "be ye perfect," in their own strength.[15]

But God has provided a better way. He has not only promised to free us from the penalty of sin after death, but he has promised to free us from the power of sin in this life. In fact, God offers us "freedom from the whole power of every known sin at once." Just as he freely released us at once from the penalty of sin at conversion, he offers us victory over sin in this life as a free gift, to be taken in one moment. "The receiving of a gift is not a gradual attainment, it is instantaneous. So victory over sin is not a gradual thing. We can have as complete victory over all our sins now, at once, as we can have in twenty years of prayer and Bible Study and surrender."[16] It is ours for the taking.

But what does it mean to be free from the power of all known sin? It means that "the very desire for sin is taken from you; you do not want to do anything that you know to be sin." Although the sinful nature is still part of you, it has been put to death by the indwelling of the Spirit of God. This means that, when you are tempted to commit sin, you do not struggle against the temptation but simply trust in God's Spirit to keep you from sin. Trumbull recounted one man's discovery of this truth: "There was no struggle, no effort, no desire. I was dead on that side of my nature. Oh, it was wonderful; it was a miracle." Trumbull also told of a missionary whose terrible temper had often led her to slam the door in the faces of her "stupid Indian servants." After she "entered into the whole blessed experience of the Christian life," she found that three months went by without her even wanting to slam the door. Trumbull observed that any good person could, by self-discipline, learn not to slam doors; but "to go for three months without once feeling anger surge up within us, or temper"—that is a miracle only Christ can perform in us. So Trumbull says that he is talking not about the "counterfeit victory" of acceptable outward actions but about the real victory that lets the Christian freely express what is inside, because what is inside is Christ.[17]

How then can one enjoy this victory? There are really only two steps. The first of these is to "surrender": if we have been trying to be perfect in our own efforts, then this step of surrender may feel as if we are doing nothing at all. It is a reliance on self that keeps us in sin's bondage. Surrender means simply letting go of self. Although we must decide to do so, it really takes no trying at all:

> We ought not try to surrender. Surrender means ceasing to try, rather than trying. Surrender is not so much an act of the will, as a letting go of the will. It is not accomplished by determination and set teeth. It is rather a complete yielding, loosening, relaxing; a falling in conscious and gladly acknowledged helplessness at the feet of Jesus Christ, and asking him to finish the even then incomplete work of surrender by putting us completely to death, crucifying us with himself, and then replacing our wrecked, helpless, worthless, dead self with himself. . . .[18]

When we surrender, we are essentially giving our lives over to the lordship of Jesus Christ and telling him that his will, and not ours, is to be supreme in all we do. Of course, we will not always know what his will is for us, but the surrendered person is one who is willing to be shown what that will is, and then to do it. "In surrender we abandon ourselves to God to use us in any way that he will to work out his purposes."[19]

This is surrender in its most general sense—a turning over of our wills to God. But surrender also has a more specific meaning in Victorious Life teaching. "Of course surrender includes every sin, known and unknown, in our lives. Are we ready to say to the Lord Jesus Christ that we surrender to him now every sin of our lives?"[20] Trumbull details for us what such surrender might mean. We may have to surrender our envy or jealousy; God cannot remove our feelings of envy unless we surrender them to him. We must also be willing to surrender our laziness and our overactivity. We must surrender our life plans—including whatever service we had planned, in our own will, to render to God. " 'But,' you say, 'it is Christian service!' Never mind; the Lord *may* know better than you what service he wants you in!" Perhaps we have a lack of love, which we must surrender; or even love itself. A Christian minister and his wife learned this. When the minister finally yielded his life fully to God, he told his wife that she would thereafter have to take second place in his life, for God had first place. His wife "fought it, rebelled against it, and for a while things were unhappy, for he was wholly yielded to the Lord and was praying for his wife." Finally, his wife also yielded and told him: "Husband, hereafter you will have to take second place in my life; God has first place."[21]

Is there a way to tell if you are totally surrendered? If there is something in your life that makes you uneasy, or about which you find yourself arguing in your conscience, it probably points to a lack of surrender. Or perhaps you find yourself asking others if a thing is wrong, because you cannot get satisfaction in your mind. Again, a lack of surrender may be indicated. But one should not be overscrupulous in self-examination, but allow such problems to come naturally to one's attention. There is generally nothing subtle or mysterious about surrender. "Unsurrender is conscious, deliberate, wilful rebellion against the known will of God." A person can be needlessly unsure of whether or not he or she has truly surrendered. Trumbull advises: "If he cannot name anything definitely which he now knows he is doing or intends to do in deliberate rejection of God's will, but if he is ready for God's whole will in his life provided God will guide and empower him, then he *is* surrendered."[22]

Occasionally, Christians wish to surrender, but cannot do so. There is something standing between them and Jesus that they cannot let go. They try to will to let it go, summoning all their strength to the battle. But the answer is so simple: "Surrender your fighting, and trust God to deliver you." Trumbull describes C. I. Scofield as saying that "if you have sin in your life that you cannot let go, bring it to Jesus and let him kill it. So the best way to surrender is to trust your surrender to the Lord Jesus; he can take care of it." You may not want to give up a sin you cherish, but it is enough to tell Jesus that you are willing to be made willing. Say, "Lord, you take it from me, because I never can let it go." As Trumbull says, "He will do it."

Surrender is the first step, and it is our part of the victory. But it alone cannot bring the victory, because victory is something we cannot do by ourselves. In fact, "many a surrendered Christian is a defeated Christian." Surrender must be augmented by faith. This faith is a simple belief that Christ will do for us what he has promised to do. In faith we simply hold out our hands, confident that God will fill them with his gift of victory. This faith has nothing to do with feelings. Too many Christians wait for a feeling of faith, when all they really need to do is recognize the promise of Jesus for what it is. In fact, the best way to have faith is to forget about faith altogether, open the Bible, and "face the great facts that are there, and recognize that those facts are true."

Trumbull illustrates how it can happen in real life.

> A woman said to me yesterday, "Mr. Trumbull, I have done everything that you people say needs to be done; I have surrendered, but nothing has happened; I am not having any such experience as the others are telling about."
>
> I suggested that all she needed to do now was to recognize that the Lord Jesus Christ was accomplishing in her all that he is accomplishing in these others whose experiences she coveted, and to accept that by faith, and *trust the matter of experience to him.* Said I, "Will you believe right now that Christ is meeting all your needs and doing this very thing for you?"
>
> "I will," she answered.
>
> "Do you believe this now?" I asked.
>
> "I do," was her quiet reply.
>
> That is all; that woman will have the "experience;" she now has the victory. What we call "experiences" will follow from time to time—they are comparatively unimportant. But the life of the "victory that is Christ" we cannot have in its fulness until we do just as she did, without any evidence or feeling.[23]

Faith, in other words, is an act of the will, just as is surrender. It is not our will that gives us the victory over sin, but it *is* our will that yields itself up in total surrender and then believes that Jesus can give us this victory. Victory depends simply on believing the facts of the Bible. "God tells us first what the facts are, then he says, 'Count on them, bank on them, recognize them. . . . These are the facts; will you believe my Word?' God says." If we believe his Word, we will have the miracle of victory in our lives.[24]

The apostle Paul's way of talking about that miracle is found in Romans 6:4: "that as Christ was raised from the dead through the glory of the Father, we too might walk in newness of life." If we surrender, it means our self is crucified with Christ; if we believe, it means we trust God to raise us from the dead in newness of life. He is not simply going to renovate our lives but give us a life that is "brand new, fresh from the hands of God, created for us." This new life will be characterized by the "fruit of the Spirit" found in Galatians 5:22-23. We will be given a miraculous love for our enemies—"not indifference, but a positive outgoing of love, so that you would do anything for him." We will experience long-suffering—"how long? right through life, taking 'all that is coming to you' with a smile." We will enjoy self-control—"not control of self by self, but control of self by the Holy Spirit."[25]

Victory means that the Holy Spirit is actually living in us. The Bible tells us that all Christians have been "baptized" with the Spirit at conversion. But all have not been "filled with the Spirit," because they have not been willing to surrender and trust. As Andrew Murray often stressed, there is no room for Jesus to be in our life when we are in charge of our own lives. "If I am something, then God is not everything; but when I become nothing, God can become all. . . . That is the higher life."[26] With God at work in us, we have an infinite source of power working within us to keep us surrendered and holy. We can experience a real sense of rest, since God is doing it all. One English Keswick convert expressed it this way: "But look at it! God is able! It's all, all, all—five alls. He is *always* able, to make *all* grace abound, there is no lack, no cessation of the abundant supply—in *all* things—heart needs, trials, Christian service. It is not merely that the Lord will help me. It's that *He* will do all, and will live in me His own Holy life, the only holiness possible to us."[27]

But, of course, there is something that we as Christians ourselves do to bring us into defeat. We can take our eyes off Jesus and begin once again to depend on our own efforts. Our victory is not such that we can count it finished, once and for all, so that we can never again knowingly sin. Rather, "it is a moment-by-moment victory depending upon a moment-by-moment faith—or depending upon our remembering moment by moment his faithfulness." One of the "perils" of the victorious life is that, after experiencing victory through the sufficiency of Christ, we come "somehow, to doubt that sufficiency." In that moment we lose the victory—and fail. Perhaps at that time Satan takes advantage of our weakness to convince us that we never had the victory in the first place. At these times we must remember that Satan is a liar and that the victory we had in Christ we can have once again, instantly, simply by faith in Christ's sufficiency.[28] We can maintain our victory—or restore our lost victory—simply by continuing to look to Jesus each moment, each day. If we are "occupied each day with the Lord Jesus Christ we shall never become degenerate."[29] While we are trusting, we will not commit a known sin. It is when we stop trusting that we get into trouble.

But this does not mean we must exert ourselves in a daily struggle of willpower to try to maintain this trust. Trumbull tells us that this would be an "unendurable yoke of bondage." Once again, this trust is more a matter of not trying than of trying. Depending moment by moment on Christ's faithfulness is "perfectly possible, for the simple reason that Christ is our life." That is, *he* will maintain our trust for him.

The great glory of this life is that it is Christ looking at us that is the secret of our looking at Christ. It is because he looks at us that we can continue to look at him, without strain or effort on our part. . . . So in every problem of the victorious life, turn your mind away from what you are doing to what Christ is doing for you. It is not your faith but his faithfulness; not your eye on him as much as his eye on you. Yet, we have the responsibility, too, of "looking unto Jesus," but quietly, trustfully, restfully. . . . We are to "entrust to him our trust," and he will sustain it.[30]

There are other "perils" in the victorious life—or, perhaps we should say, other manifestations of this same peril. One is falling into overconfidence, thinking that if we have continued in victory for a very long time, we are stronger in ourselves and have some reason to believe we cannot fail. But in ourselves we are just as weak as when we first found victory. "Even the veteran warrior in the victorious life is always capable of unbelief and of disastrous defeat in sin." It is not our strength or our unblemished record but our moment-by-moment "looking away unto Jesus" that ensures the victory. Another peril is to be driven by Satan into a false sense of duty—perhaps a frenzy to witness of our new life in Jesus to literally everyone we meet, or an obsession to confess our sins to everyone we know, to cultivate asceticism rather than maintaining "a golden mean between the extremes of asceticism and luxury." If it is Satan who is thus leading us, rather than God, we will know it by the sense of worry or harrassment we feel, which contrasts sharply with the peace and quiet that come from the Holy Spirit.

Still another peril is living for "thrilling, unexpected, supernatural evidences of God's power" instead of remembering that he sends us what he wants for us. We may also fail by "unconsciously assuming an infallible knowledge of God's will" or by slipping into pride or a "holier than thou" attitude (in which case we have instantly lost the victory), or by being unteachable, or by taking our liberty in Christ as license to be undependable in relationships or careless in appointments. Or we may become complacent in defeat. The victorious Christian can also commit "gross sins"; "there is something about the life of spiritual power and victory that, when broken into in the slightest way by unbelief, seems to expose one most terribly to sins of gross immorality and degradation. Those who have gone highest with the Lord can go lowest." If this happens, we must stop what we are doing instantly, confess our sin, claim forgiveness and cleansing, and trust him for the complete restoration of victory.[31]

Although these perils are always present, we can be certain of victory if we keep looking at Christ. And of great aid in this looking at Christ are the practices of the devotional life. Trumbull advises that, at any cost, one must "let God . . . so organize your life that there will be in it daily, habitual, stated times and ample time for feeding on God's Word for your own personal nourishment and prayer."[32] Robert F. Horton, who wrote for Trumbull's journal, asserted that "the Bible of anyone who has lived the life of which we are concerned is yellow with the years, thin at the edge with the constant turning of the pages. . . . Without this use of the Bible, the devotional life becomes unhealthy, ascetic, morbid, extravagant."[33] Another Victorious Life speaker, Howard Dinwiddie, called attention to the fact that only in union with Jesus do we attain victory, and that "the minute you break that union the victory is gone." That union can only be maintained by constant and unceasing prayer.[34] Andrew Murray put it a bit differently: "I have only so much faith as I have of the Spirit. Is not this then what I most need—to live entirely under the influence of the Spirit?" To help us have this Holy Spirit within us, Murray urged Christians to say each day, "I believe in the Holy Ghost."[35] Of course, Christians could become quite legalistic if they thought that somehow the victory lay in the faithful observance of this daily regimen. Trumbull understood this and encouraged his audiences not to worry if, by some accident, they failed to observe the "Morning Watch." They could still have victory that day, he said, because victory depends on faith, not on these disciplines. But this should not lead them to neglect Bible reading and prayer as a matter of course. Christ "cannot maintain victory day in and day out, week in and week out, when we habitually neglect what he has told us we must do. Victory is by faith, but faith must be fed."[36]

Not only must we take in nourishment, but we must give it as well. Trumbull and his associates all tended to emphasize that the victorious life is not a life of introspection but of service. Robert Horton expressed it most pointedly: "Surrender: faith: service: these three he asks from every human soul."[37] The service most often mentioned by Victorious Life spokespeople was soulwinning: "The victorious life cannot but express itself in soulwinning. . . . The victorious life is an experience of a present and powerful salvation, and an inevitable impulse urges those who possess it to share it."[38] An emphasis on foreign missions as a particularly suitable vocational choice for youth who wished to enjoy the victorious life was present from the very beginning of Trumbull's movement in America. Victorious Life literature is peppered with stories of young people who overcame the resistance within themselves or in other people and "volunteered their lives to the Lord for service on the mission field."[39] But soulwinning was not only for foreign missionaries. Everyone who enjoys the victorious life, Trumbull believed, would find himself or herself just naturally speaking to others about the new power that Christ represents in life. In fact, we may not be able to maintain that life unless we share it. "We must continue to witness to our Lord Jesus Christ if we would have the blessing continued in fulness in our own hearts—or rather, the Blesser reigning in his fulness."[40]

That, of course, is what the victorious life was all about: the Blesser, Jesus Christ, reigning in human hearts in fullness, giving "newness of life." This fullness is available to every Christian, Trumbull and others believed, but few make the decision to take advantage of it. If we do not, we live defeated lives. If we do, we rest completely in him, and he lives the victorious life in and through us. With Christ's life in us, "we have God's own resurrection power at our disposal to work in us this moment and every moment. . . ." His power is infinitely greater than the power of sin, and while we rely on his power, full victory is ours. All we have to do to experience this victory is surrender ourselves to him and believe that he is working in us. It's that simple. In fact, it can be stated even more simply in the story of the little girl who was praying. She said: " 'Jesus, I hear you are knocking at the door of my heart. Come in, Jesus.' Then she rose from her knees and said, 'He's in.' That is all there is to the victorious life."[41]

IV

We asked what the evangelicals of the late nineteenth and early twentieth century wanted from Jesus. Now we have at least one important part of the answer. They wanted victory. And it appears that they wanted it now, in visible ways, in ways known by the conscious mind and felt by the feelings. They were not comforted by the promise of victory in the next life. They found the standard conversion formula—that Christ saves us from the penalty of sin but leaves us trying hard to live moral lives—unsatisfying and exhausting. They wanted more than deliverance from the wrath to come. If salvation is really good news, they said, it must offer us victory in this life. This victory has got to be effective in daily routines. The Keswick people identified this sort of concern when they called their first conferences "Union Meetings for the Promotion of Practical Holiness."[42]

So they wanted victory—now. But over what? The testimonies of the Christians who attended the Victorious Life conferences speak eloquently to this point. Invariably they would speak of their lives as defeated, or of being "discouraged over failures." Occasionally they would express their guilt at being "unwilling to testify for Christ" or "unwilling to go as a missionary." Most often, however, in giving content to their sense of defeat, they would speak in the language of feelings. They were plagued by "an ugly temper" or by "giving way to irritation"; they held "grudges against others" or were unloving "toward people who are very trying"; some spoke of "fearfulness," others of "nerves" or a "nervous breakdown." The word most frequently used was "worry." By their own descriptions, these folks were anxious, troubled people, plagued by worry. They wanted Jesus to give them victory over incessant worry.[43]

But evangelicals were not the only worried Americans, and Jesus was not the only means to victory. In one of the classic works of modern religious psychology, William James's *The Varieties of Religious Experience*, we find evidence that many Americans were suffering from a certain nervous anxiety at this time, and were finding relief in a wide variety of religious and semireligious therapies propagated by popular writers and teachers. Two of the groups in existence when James published his work in 1902 were the "Gospel of Relaxation" and the "Don't Worry Movement." According to James, these were examples of what was then becoming a major "religious" phenomenon that owed its rapid spread to its "practical fruits and the extremely practical turn of character of the American people."[44] What the American people wanted practical answers for, it seems, was a deep uneasiness of spirit, and the therapies James surveyed were speaking to the same concerns the Victorious Life movement was speaking to when it promised its adherents they could "live moment by moment without worry."[45]

What were Americans so worried, anxious, frustrated, and even angry about at the turn of the century? To answer this, we will have to try to understand the inner, psychic meaning and relentless pressure of life in a rapidly industrializing society. We noted in chapter two that Karl Marx described industrial capitalism in his day as a climate in which "all that is solid melts into air." Marx was highlighting a major feature of the late nineteenth century—and of every period since then in American life—namely, the rapid and seemingly uncontrollable pace of change in the material realm, in social and economic conditions, and ultimately in the inner, emotional, and spiritual realm itself.

We who live in the latter decades of the twentieth century were born into and have lived our lives within the unsettling flux of continuous change. Most of us have known nothing but a situation in which "all that is solid melts into air"; many of us have become so accustomed to it that we scarcely recognize anything odd or stressful about our way of life. And yet the author of *Future Shock* can parlay his description of the strains of such a society and of our incomplete adaptation to it into best-seller notoriety. Imagine the psychic costs of this "future shock" to those who in the space of their own lives traversed the distance from farm or small-town existence, with its sense of permanence and rootedness, and its clearly understood guidelines for human conduct, with its slow, orderly pace of life, to the frenzied and chaotic reality of modern urban industrial-

ism. The world has never seen so dramatic a revolution in human life as
has swept the industrial West in the last two hundred years; and in many
ways the people of the late nineteenth century lived through that revolution at the point of its greatest, most exhilarating, and most unnerving
acceleration.

We can perhaps get a feel for life during this period of rapid acceleration through the image of a whirlpool—whirling faster and faster, suck-
ing all the comfortable givens down into its vortex, distorting shapes, and
making the familiar unfamiliar. Marshall Berman says that the maelstrom
had been fed from many sources, and his description illuminates its social
extent and complexity:

> . . . great discoveries in the physical sciences, changing our images of the
> universe and our place in it; the industrialization of production, which
> transforms scientific knowledge into technology, creates new human en-
> vironments and destroys old ones, speeds up the whole tempo of life,
> generates new forms of corporate power and class struggle; immense de-
> mographic upheavals, severing millions of people from their ancestral hab-
> its, hurtling them half-way across the world into new lives; rapid and often
> cataclysmic urban growth; systems of mass communication, dynamic in
> their development, enveloping and binding together the most diverse peo-
> ple and societies; increasingly powerful national states, bureaucratically
> structured and operated, constantly striving to expand their powers; mass
> social movements of people, and peoples, challenging their political and
> economic rulers, striving to gain some control over their lives; finally, bear-
> ing and driving all these people and institutions along, an ever-expanding,
> drastically fluctuating capitalist world market.[46]

This modern social and economic dynamic, according to Berman, imparts
a "desperate pace and frantic rhythm . . . to every facet of modern life."[47]
A society caught up in this maelstrom generally offers no solid place to
stand from which one might objectively examine the forces at work, or
from which one might choose appropriate actions to preserve what is of
real or sentimental value. Instead, one finds oneself contributing to the
disintegration of the very realities one holds dear, albeit comforted by the
rationalizations such disintegrating forces inevitably bring with them.

Those who lived through the birth of this new age were not oblivious to
the "frantic rhythm" of their lives. An English observer in 1869, for example, suggested that his hearers compare "the rate at which you are now
living . . . the rate of thought, feeling, and energy—in these as compared
with those quiet and comfortable times" earlier in the nineteenth century.
Another attested to "that constant sense of being driven—not precisely
like 'dumb' cattle, but cattle who must read, write, and talk more in
twenty-four hours than twenty-four hours will permit. . . ."[48] In an arti-

cle entitled "Life at High Pressure," an English writer spoke of living "a life of *haste*—above all a life of excitement, such as haste inevitably involves—a life filled so full . . . that we have no time to reflect where we have been and whither we intend to go . . . still less what is the value, and the purpose, and *the price* of what we have seen, and done, and visited."[49] One hears in this opinion that strange ambivalence we feel toward this life of "whirl," as Walter Lippmann called it.[50] We bemoan its frenzy, resent its disintegrating effects, and regret that it is blind to all values but those of quantity, novelty, and technical rationality—and yet, we rather enjoy the "excitement" of it and find we cannot do without it. These words of a successful American businessman were quoted in a regular publication of the Moody Bible Institute in 1914:

> It is play up, play up, play up and play the game. The experience of "getting there" is pleasurable, but the cost of it all makes one sad. I am yielding my life to ends rather than means. How often would I burst the bonds of my circumstances and find my way to some quiet corner of the earth where "it is not all of life to live." But when I would do this I cannot, for the city and its business life have a peculiar and constraining fascination for me. It is a whirlpool charmed with currents so subtle and intermingled that one is borne on to the vortex, gaining a world but losing his soul![51]

The sense that Americans were losing their souls, or at the very least their emotional stability, was a common theme in late nineteenth-century America. Beneath the surface exhilaration and the spirit of "play up, play up, play up," intelligent social critics sensed a very real layer of debilitating anxiety. E. L. Youmans, founder of the *Popular Science Monthly*, observed as early as 1867 that "we live in an age of intense mental activity and ever-increasing cerebral strain." He pointed to the "fierce competitions of business, fashion, study, and political ambition" that were attacking "the integrity of the mental fabric," resulting in "much secret suffering" and often in "permanent mental derangement." He observed that "the price we pay for our high-pressure civilization is a fearful increase of cerebral exhaustion and disorder. . . . We are startled when some conspicuous mind strained beyond endurance . . . crashes into insanity and suicide, yet these are but symptoms of the prevailing tendencies of modern life."[52]

The leading observer of the anxieties of late nineteenth-century America was George M. Beard. Beard's work commended itself to no less a thinker than Sigmund Freud as a reliable accounting of the neuroses of the aspiring American middle class. His book *American Nervousness: Its Causes and Consequences* (1881) offers a comprehensive catalog of the emotional ailments Beard saw on the rise in his day; the list was long and variegated: hysteria, hay fever, sick-headaches, inebriety, some forms of insanity, neuralgia, nervous dyspepsia, increased tooth decay, "fear of lightning, or fear of responsibility, of open places or of closed places, fear of society, fear of being alone, fear of fears, fear of contamination, fear of everything," heart palpitations, hopelessness, chills, incontinence, pains in the back, irritability, and additional symptoms running to several pages. Beard summed all of these up in the term "neurasthenia": Americans were suffering from nervous exhaustion.[53]

In Beard's opinion, this nervousness was a direct and inevitable result of "modern civilization," particularly of some of its features, such as steam power, electricity, the periodical press, the telegraph, religious excitements, the complexities of modern education, and the sciences. American nervousness was a city phenomenon, "more frequent at the desk, the pulpit, and in the counting room than in the shop or on the farm." He attributed some of it to the "unrhythmic, unmelodious and therefore annoying" noises produced by "the appliances and accompaniments of civilization." He saw clocks as a major cause: "We are under constant strain, mostly unconscious, often times in sleeping as in waking hours, to get somewhere or do something at some definite moment." Beard was clearly dismayed by the pace of life dictated by industrial civilization. He felt that the "gospel of work must make way for the gospel of rest." He knew that modern civilization had its distinct advantages, the leading one being a longer life expectancy. And he presumed that, in time, the human organism might adapt to the requirements of modern life and conquer the worst manifestations of this nervousness. But he warned "those who prefer, or fancy they prefer, the sensations of movement and activity to the sensations of repose" that "from the standpoint only of the economy of nerve-force all our civilization is a mistake."[54]

In Beard's judgment, American "nervousness" was essentially a problem of the "professional and business men" who were profiting most from the advances of modern life. If we take a closer look at the middle class to which these men belonged, we may understand better why they were given to nervousness, or, as many Victorious Life adherents called it, "worry." The new industrial society beckoned enticingly to all whose drive was to "get ahead" in life—those who were not born to large fortunes but were determined to escape the clutches of poverty or the demands of wage labor, and who by acquiring education or cultivating a skill envisioned a life of status, respectability, and material comfort. The opportunities were there. In the space of a generation—from 1870 to 1900—the number of professionals, managers, clerical workers, and other service workers needed by the new society increased dramatically, in some cases a hundredfold. The middle-class person was one—most often male during this time—who saw the opportunities and took thought for himself: he grasped his own individual capacities as his only true endowment and resolved to use that endowment to enter on a lifetime of continual self-expansion, self-expression, and self-enrichment. To accomplish those ends, the middle-class person had to become a calculating, willful, and often ruthless individual. As Emerson observed, "property is an intellectual production. The game requires coolness, right reasoning, promptness and patience in the players. . . ."[55] In his determination to rise in society, the middle-class person often found it necessary to shove tradition or convention aside. He functioned with a certain abandon, competing shamelessly against his rivals, undermining any opposition to his self-serving innovations. In many ways, the middle class person was all alone, an individual in this frantic world, and he knew it would take every ounce of intelligence, foresight, and energy for him to maintain an advantaged position atop the carriage of progress while others were getting crushed beneath its wheels.

Thus aspiring members of the middle class lived with intensity, but also with a certain insecurity. Most basically, they could be ruined by the unpredictable fluctuations of the highly volatile economy. One of Moody's successors, the revivalist J. Wilbur Chapman, recalled how "by one of those reverses of fortune, so often experienced in American business life, my father's property was swept away; and I can to this day recall how the location of our home was changed from one part of the city to another, and the house in which we dwelt, instead of being commodious, was extremely small."[56] The reality of such losses, not only in economic privation but in social stigma as well, was never far from the experience of the late nineteenth-century middle class. Businessmen in particular knew that their successes were built like houses of cards, and that if larger economic forces did not topple them, personal mistakes in judgment or momentary pauses in the relentless competitive struggle could very well bring them down. These realities made hard work, constant calculation, and a tense alertness obsessive qualities in the late nineteenth-century middle-class America; and of course, they took their psychic toll.

But there was more to this insecurity than the possibility of economic failure. There was the threat of humiliation as well. Middle-class Americans, particularly those in the professions, were making *themselves* the assets they presented to the public for approval. They offered no commodity except their skills: their access to social position and respectability depended on personal qualities and accomplishments. Success established them as worthwhile persons, while failure threw them into depression, for it implied an inherent, internal defect. In an age when poverty was presumed to flow from immorality or an inherited degeneracy, the aspiring middle-class person lived to garner not just wealth but self-esteem. Upward mobility offered affirmation of one's superiority, and in order to enter the fray and climb to the top, one would have to cultivate a certain self-confidence. According to Burton Bledstein, "the middle class American artfully tested the limits of the individual ego. . . . He attached to himself all the status and honor that an accomplishment would bear; and he needed to be publicly recognized as someone with a special gift and with a decisive influence over others." Bereft of the inherited standards of status or worth that predominated in a simpler age, the middle-class person was caught up in a mad race for self-esteem or self-glory based on his mastery and development of unique personal qualities. Therein were untold possibilities for ecstasy but also for despair, for

> as the American inflated his self-esteem, he also took the chance of magnifying his limitations, defects, and inability. A dread of failure, a fear of lost position, a wavering of confidence: all accompanied the middle class passion for status. In the new social morality, anxiety pushed the American as much as position pulled him.[57]

It seems clear that real emotional suffering must have been an inevitable accompaniment of the middle-class quest for economic advantage in late nineteenth-century America. And it would be foolish to suggest that evangelicals were not as fully susceptible to this suffering as anyone else was. In fact, if Max Weber is correct, evangelicals may have been *more* susceptible to it than was anyone else. In his 1904 classic *The Protestant Ethic and the Spirit of Capitalism*, Weber suggests that Calvinism fashioned its Christian adherents to be precisely the kind of people who would be most given to ruthless economic striving and thus also to the strains accompanying that striving. Weber himself was not particularly interested in exploring the suffering wrought by the Protestant ethic; what he wanted to explain was the nature of the relationship between religion and economic activity. He had observed that capitalism was most highly developed in geographical areas where the Calvinist and quasi-Calvinist versions of Protestant Christianity had taken firmest hold, more so than in Lutheran or Roman Catholic areas. Weber inquired whether anything inherent to Calvinism could explain this seeming historical coincidence.

He found his answer in the emphasis Calvin and his successors had placed on the doctrine of predestination. According to this central Calvinist teaching, all mankind has sinned and deserves to reap the harvest of that sin—everlasting punishment in hell. But God has in mercy chosen certain of the wicked to be saved—these "elect" he rescues by the blood of Christ, and these will live with him forever in heaven. The rest God consigns to everlasting death, withholding his mercy from them so that they may not be saved. God makes his choices in mystery and utter freedom, not depending in any way on the supposed good works or other merits of men and women to inform his decisions, and not consulting human standards of justice. Those who receive his mercy can do nothing to lose it, and those who receive his condemnation have no appeal.

The immediate, practical question this doctrine poses for each church member is obvious: Am I one of the elect? According to Weber, the question itself did not unduly trouble John Calvin. He counseled believers to rest in the fact that God had done the choosing and to depend "only on that implicit trust in Christ which is the result of faith." But the question seemed to trouble his followers, who were perhaps dissatisfied with such a subjective and uncertain confirmation. As typical humans, they preferred to use the empirical realm as a path to a certainty of their election. A life of observable good works, useless though it might be in effecting salvation, would certainly testify to the reality of true faith and thus the election of the believer, they thought. Weber explains:

> It was through the consciousness that his conduct, at least in its fundamental character and constant ideal, rested on a power within himself working for the glory of God; that it is not only willed of God but rather done by God that he attained the highest good toward which this religion strove, the certainty of salvation.[58]

In practical consequence, then, though never in theory, Calvinism became a doctrine of salvation by works—and a particularly demanding one. Since lapses in one's conduct might imply the absence of true faith and thus of election, the Calvinist strove to make his life a systematic and thorough example of moral conduct. In every respect, by seriousness of purpose and scrupulous rational attention to details, the Calvinist attempted to turn his life into a reflection of God's glory. The Calvinist, in other words, became a kind of ascetic, not least in his fear of emotional expression. The emotions, bursting uncalled from deep inside the person, always threatened to disrupt the life of orderly, rational conduct performed to the glory of God and for the assurance of the saints. Subjection of the emotions to the sane, conscious choices of the dedicated Christian intellect seemed to be a necessary discipline for the Calvinist ascetic.[59]

But, as Weber makes clear, this asceticism was essentially different from Catholic monasticism in being a "worldly asceticism." According to Calvinism, each believer has a divine "calling" in this world—an actual occupational role in which one should labor for the glory of God. In this secular calling the believer's life is to express the same rational, methodical approach with which one shows evidence of election in more "spiritual" matters. Weber quotes Richard Baxter, the English Puritan divine, to the effect that "outside of a well-marked calling the accomplishments of a man are only casual and irregular, and he spends more time in idleness than at work. . . ." In a calling, however, the worker "will carry out his work in order while another remains in constant confusion and his business knows neither time nor place. . . ." In this same spirit, Baxter counseled against taking excessive leisure or enjoying one's wealth by consuming material goods.[60] He acclaimed hard work as "the action that God is most served and honoured by," and urged Christians to "be every day more careful that you lose none of your time."[61] In financial matters the Calvinist believer had a duty to be shrewd:

> If God shows you a way in which you may lawfully get more than in another way (without wrong to your soul or to any other), if you refuse this, and choose the less gainful way, you cross one of the ends of your calling, and you refuse to be God's steward, and to accept His gifts and use them for Him when He requireth it: you may labor to be rich for God, though not for the flesh and sin.[62]

By such teachings, according to Weber, Baxter and other Calvinist moralists showed their high respect for the "sober, middle-class, self-made man" and prepared for Christian believers a set of ethical rationalizations that would fit their conduct comfortably to the demands first of a commercial and later of an industrializing society, at least in its initial stages. Out of Calvin's humble thankfulness for the gift of faith evolved a theological and ethical system that afforded the consolations of a divinely acclaimed superiority to its adherents. One can hear in Calvinist writings of the seventeenth century the self-congratulating tone of a people who knew themselves to be the elect of God and who offered as evidence their own worldly, often economic, successes. As Weber explains, "this thankfulness for one's own perfection by the grace of God penetrated the attitude toward life of the Puritan middle class, and played its part in developing that formalistic, hard, correct character which was peculiar to the men of that heroic age of capitalism."[63]

By the late nineteenth century, the heroic age of commercial capitalism that American and English Puritans had done so much to further had evolved into the heroic age of industrial capitalism—and indeed beyond, into the first stirrings of the age of bureaucratic capitalism in which we now live. One need not look far, however, in the social and moral teachings of late nineteenth-century American Christianity to find this Protestant ethic alive and well and expressed in terms that reflected little change from seventeenth-century Puritan sentiment. Evangelicals believed, as did most American Protestants by this time, that hard work in a secular calling gave glory to God; that accumulating money was something of a Christian duty and financial success an indication of God's favor; that conspicuous consumption was ungodly and poverty shameful. These attitudes served the middle class well in its concern for upward mobility and material security, and they made for evangelicals' relatively uncritical acceptance of what we have called the maelstrom of modern capitalist social and economic development.

But more than this. Weber's analysis, while not beyond criticism, is most profound, I think, in its understanding of the nature of modern capitalism as a rationalizing reality—and of Calvinism's shaping of the human personality to match that reality. Western civilization, Weber believed, is unique in world history in its attempt to bring rational organization, rational procedure, rational definition into every field of human endeavor, whether it be jurisprudence, music, architecture, the pursuit of knowledge, or the wielding of political power. Likewise in the economic arena: capitalism does not encourage greater greed than has any other economic system, but it channels human greed toward "the pursuit of profit, and forever *renewed* profit, by means of continuous, rational, capitalist enterprise." To pursue profit rationally means to remove sentimental concerns from view and to make decisions based on careful, systematic calculations of the means by which one may, at the end of each business period, show that one's money assets exceed one's investment of capital. "Everything is done in terms of balances," writes Weber: "At the beginning of the enterprise an initial balance, before every individual decision a calculation to ascertain its probable profitableness, and at the end a final balance to ascertain how much profit has been made."[64] Rationality has also been applied, of course, to the use and organization of labor, to the functioning of a legal system and the administration of government, eventually to the educational process in preparing citizens for economic activity. This is the logic of Western civilization, Weber postulates: the gradual, ineluctable triumph of rational, calculable, systematizable methods in every area of modern life.

To this drift, in Weber's mind, Calvinist Christianity made a crucial contribution. It fashioned a Christian citizen who, in his concern to give glory to God in every detail of life and in so doing to confirm his own election, approached his secular calling with precisely the rational calculation that capitalism required. Disorder, spontaneity, and emotional expression threatened one's methodical attempt to give glory to God. Calvinists, rather, were known for their self-control, sobriety, careful regulation of feelings, moral rigidity, and a general sense of personal restraint. The Calvinist of Weber's description watched over his life carefully, always on guard against "the spontaneous expression of undisciplined impulses" or "raw instinct" or impulsiveness.[65] He imposed strict order on the inner life, the better to enforce it in the business life. Given this tendency to restrain and order his own emotional life, the Calvinist was well matched to the requirements of middle-class life in an increasingly rationalized and calculating industrial society.

The most concrete and identifiable expression of the Protestant ethic in late nineteenth-century America was the interest so many Protestants showed in the matter of "character." Building character seems to have been the essential task of any adults engaged in the raising of children—at least in the raising of male children. The book publishers of the period turned out a virtual library dedicated to furthering this project of character building; it was taught in schools and preached from pulpits; it even informed the educational goals of the rapidly expanding and secularizing universities, as we find if we look at the expressed concerns of the major university presidents, men like Eliot of Harvard, Porter of Yale, White of Cornell, or Barnard of Columbia. The historian Burton J. Bledstein has contributed an excellent group portrait of these men in his book *The Culture of Professionalism*. He describes them as the "ideological spokesmen for a growing middle class in the post–Civil War decades." These decades in America witnessed the appearance of "an increasingly aggressive, pushy, and impersonal society." And the presidents, according to Bledstein, "joined in the pushing."[66] As caretakers of the lives of young men, these presidents took seriously the requirements for success in their time. Their goal was to prepare their young charges to rise to positions of power and influence as, they noted with pride, they themselves had done. They agreed that the obvious means to this end was the cultivation of character.

And what was this "character"? As Bledstein describes it, it was "the deepest self of the man that bound together the whole of the individual." Although these presidents were "congenital Christians in a non-theological school," one can still hear in this definition the echoes of the older Calvinism. Character has become the secularized version of that visible morality and success wherein the Calvinist may once have attained the miraculous assurance of true faith and thus, humbly, of his or her own election by God. And in binding together the whole individual, this character, like true faith, brings all of life into consistency with one's status as God's elect. Indeed, the university presidents called for this sort of rational and systematic totalization. In business or professional life, the man of character "calculated his course beyond specific cases, particular events, and *ad hoc* decisions." Work was to him "a statement to the world of his internal resources, confidence, and discipline; his active control over the intrinsic relationships of a life. . . ." He engaged in methodical

examinations of his own life and the lives of others. To the man of character, "the smallest feature about a person's behavior now related to a
higher meaning, to an ulterior purpose, to a potential basis for approval
or condemnation of his innermost character. Mid-Victorians dismissed
no utterance or act as a trifle, unrevealing about a person's character; and
too often they eliminated those human tolerances that saved a life from
misery." To have character meant to be resilient, to be able to suffer
hardships or, to use one of their favorite words, to be "manly." Self-
control or discipline was highly prized, as was moral earnestness. Bledstein describes their lifestyle (in words reminiscent of Weber's) as one of
"personal asceticism." The university presidents considered themselves
to be excellent examples of these features of character.[67]

However, the presidents of these secularizing universities did not
have a corner on character in late nineteenth-century America. When
William Borden attended the Hill School, he was placed under the tu-
telage of an educator who wished to inculcate "truth-speaking and truth-
loving" as "the very bedrock of character"; who spoke of "the high majesty of accepted duty"; and who agreed with Tennyson that "self-rever-
ence, self-knowledge, self-control" could issue in "sovereign power." He
urged in his students a "manly . . . choice of Christ as a pattern and
Master and Lord."[68] Meanwhile, at Amherst College, President Stearns
was fostering "character" by educating for "moral principles, right purposes, appropriate emotions and practical wisdom," while his successor,
President Seelye, in 1893, declared that "education is the creation and
training of character."[69]

A more thoroughly evangelical example of this obsession with character is found in the writings of Robert Speer, who blossomed into a leader
of the modern foreign missionary movement under the influence of D. L.
Moody. Over the years he wrote a number of books intended for Christian youth; one of them, *The Marks of a Man; Or, the Essentials of Christian
Character* (published in 1907), gives the reader a feel for the life agenda
receptive evangelicals were encouraged to establish for themselves: "We
ought repeatedly to confront ourselves with the inquiry, Am I a better or
stronger man than I was?" As Christians, we share a duty always to be
advancing, for "that is what the Christian life is, a life of steady progress
and growth." We need to "keep our faces set toward perfection," each
year asking ourselves:

> Am I really better than I was? Have I more self-control, more patience and
> sympathy? Do I think more often and more lovingly of God? Am I more
> kind and unselfish and helpful and tender? Do I do my work with more ease
> and power? Am I quicker to obey God and do the duty He assigns . . . ?[70]

Like secular teachers of character, Speer appealed to the young man's lust for the heroic, noting that all great men are "seeking men, the men who are not content." He urged his readers to cultivate this same lack of contentment, to be claimed "irresistibly" by the ideal of perfection.

In many respects, Speer's description of character matched that of the university presidents and of Max Weber's Protestant ethic. He urged Christians to be "manlike" in struggling to achieve their ideals, he recommended "simple duty" in avoiding wrongs and exterminating habits, and he proposed that the Christian submit all his conduct to "be examined and mercilessly judged by right standards." Christian manhood, he declared, has a free mind, which means one that "masters the senses" and "protects itself against animal appetites" and "contemns pleasure and pain in comparison with its own energy."[71] To this end, Speer called for "a stern self-government under the will of God," because the maintenance of one's character required nothing less.[72]

What are we to make of this discussion of character by the theologically and nontheologically inclined alike? If we remember that Americans in the late nineteenth century were experiencing life as a kind of maelstrom, then perhaps we can see their concern for character as an essentially conservative move to fight the chaos of the objective world with an increasingly rigid ordering of the subjective inner world. Much of the concern for character was focused on child-rearing, which is always a frightful matter, the more so in a period of rapid change when behavior standards, value systems, and moral principles are all in flux in response to evolving social and economic conditions. New careers were opening up; information was becoming more accessible; standards of living were rapidly rising; and consumer goods and leisure experiences were proliferating. All these developments threatened the continuity between generations, and that threat went to the heart of many parents who, like parents in all ages, desired the very best for their children but not at the cost of turning them into strangers. By building character into the next generation—and defining that character in terms of the old verities and moral absolutes—parents could perhaps hope to channel the forces of change and tame the potentially disintegrating effects of the maelstrom. "Character" had a good, solid feel to it: it spoke of permanence and strength in a society where "all that is solid melts into air."

Although the requirements of safety and cohesiveness dictated some sort of moral anchor in stormy weather, however, the requirements of success demanded that the anchor not slow down either parent or child in the race to cross the finish line first. The very whirlpool that threatened destruction also promised untold opportunities for rapid advancement, for wealth, power, and independence. Safety at the cost of obsolescence in a competitive environment is nobody's desire, particularly not of parents for their children. But here the notion of character showed its finest feature: its traits, as Weber's analysis would predict, were in most respects the very ones indispensable to upward mobility and earthly success in the turmoil of an advancing industrialism. Character was simply the late nineteenth-century version of the "worldly asceticism" that drove so many Calvinist entrepreneurs to the top of the early capitalist commercial heap. It was just that now evangelicals and nonevangelicals alike were using it to pave their own way to the top of the heap represented by an industrializing and bureaucratizing America.

I would suggest, however, that this version of the Protestant ethic took an especially painful toll on its enthusiasts. When George Beard tried to explain this peculiar American anxiety in 1881, he was identifying the Protestant ethic, though not in name: "A factor in producing American nervousness is, beyond dispute, the liberty allowed, and the stimulus given, to Americans to rise out of the position in which they were born, whatever that may be, and to aspire to the highest possibilities of fortune and glory." This feature of modern—as opposed to aristocratic civilization—caused all classes of society to live in "a constant friction and unrest" since it fostered "a painful striving to see who shall be highest." Further, Beard observed, such striving generally required that the emotions be repressed: "The more we feel the more we must restrain our feelings." Such "constant inhibition, restraining normal feelings, keeping back, covering . . . is an exhausting process, and to this process all civilization is constantly subjected."[73]

The Protestant ethic was closely tied to both of these nerve-wracking features of modern civilization. It encouraged its adherents to jump into the maelstrom—with both feet and to God's glory—and to view any success achieved as signs of God's favor. The catch, of course, was that any failure meant abandonment by God or temporary disfavor at the very least, and this must have produced enormous pressure on the individual psyche. The Protestant ethic also encouraged the middle-class climber to keep his emotions on a tight leash, to cultivate "indomitable will," to retain self-control at all times. While this may have increased the odds of worldly success in a more and more fully rationalized capitalist economy, it also had a catch: inhibition and repression, guilt, the stifling of feelings, and ultimately painful neurotic expressions. All this simply multiplied the discontents of middle-class life in industrial America, making for nervous exhaustion in many. It was this exhaustion that the Victorious Life movement promised to relieve—instantly, fully, and without the long, wearying journey implied by the older Calvinist quest for that thing called character.

V

"Living is an unspeakably hard thing," confessed a participant at the Victorious Life Conference held in the summer of 1922.[74] She poignantly summed up the experience of many an evangelical Christian since at least the time of Hannah Whitall Smith, who in 1870 began her best-selling book with a similar observation made by an acquaintance of hers: "You Christians seem to have a religion that makes you miserable."[75] Smith did not reply, though she could not have failed to notice, that one did not have to be an earnest Christian to be miserable. As E. L. Youmans and George Beard both observed at about the same time, the rising American middle class as a whole was in emotional turmoil as it tried to come to terms with this new age. A historian has characterized the businessmen of these years as "men harassed in mind and spirit, full of care, groaning under the burdens, . . . haunted and frightened."[76] Meanwhile, middle-class women were showing "the nervous strain of sham emotions."[77] At Harvard University in the 1880s, youthful instructors were driving themselves to nervous breakdowns by worry and overwork. As Bledstein puts it, middle-class people were finding that "the psychological tensions were nearly unbearable."[78]

We have already observed that, according to Max Weber, Christians from Calvinist traditions (which included most evangelical Americans) may have been particularly given to attitudes and behaviors that suited them to this middle-class rat race. But did they not receive, along with the Protestant ethic, certain consolations as Christians that might have helped them transcend the deepest tensions and frustrations of a competitive, industrializing society? Perhaps this is why Hannah Whitall Smith did not bother to qualify her friend's comment. Everybody may be unhappy, but Christians should be different. "The religion of Christ ought to be . . . something to make them happy," she said. But it was not working that way, and Smith knew it from personal experience. Instead, Christians were "struggling under a weary consciousness of defeat and discouragement."[79] Smith wanted her book to rescue Christians from that burden by helping them recapture the awareness that they could stop struggling and rest in Jesus to do everything for them.

As we have seen, this book helped inspire the Keswick movement in England after Smith visited there in the 1870s, and thus it is in the direct lineage of the Victorious Life movement founded by C. G. Trumbull some forty years later. But it is possible to read Smith's book less as a serious theological work than as a window on the troubled spirit of evangelicals during the last decades of the nineteenth century. While offering her prescriptions for the attainment of a happy life, Smith cataloged the commonest manifestations of unhappiness: feelings of defeat and failure; chafing and fretting; perplexion, worry, and anxiety; the sense of being strained and burdened; and tiredness, weariness, and exhaustion.[80] All of these are Smith's own words to describe the "miserable" state of the evangelical spirit in her times. To read her book is to know that Christians were not emotionally better off than were the nervous Americans Beard was describing. Indeed, they were worse off in some ways.

We have already described evangelicals in the latter decades of the nineteenth century as going through a kind of nest shaking—for some, a nest dissolving. It is not difficult to surmise that evangelicals would feel a sense of defeat when they identified themselves with a God who was letting Catholics and Jews take over their country, liberals take over their churches, Darwinists and secularists take over their schools, and a variety of progressive reformers take over their political institutions—at least that is the way it seemed to some. Their God appeared to be no longer in charge of the American corner of the universe, where it had appeared the millennium was about to dawn just a few decades before. Generational differences evoked primordial terrors as increasingly university-educated young people spoke a different language and expected different things from life than did their parents. Meanwhile, the country was changing: blacks were gradually moving to the urban north, and immigrants were rapidly streaming into the cities, each group representing ethnic or religious threats. The language and tactics of European social radicalism were making their appearance in the city streets. Big technology and big money were modernizing the economic structures at the same time that they distorted familiar political practices. Between the organized forces of labor and the overpowering influence of newly rich industrialists stood the middle class: it was struggling to organize itself professionally and politically but still had insufficient muscle power to rest easy in its dominance of society. In all these ways the middle class felt vulnerable to the flow of history, which did not seem as under control as it had in the period prior to the Civil War.

At the very same time, however, the flow of history allowed the middle class to envision its own apotheosis. Rapid change meant that rapid ascent was possible in the accumulation of power or status or wealth. Who would be equal to the ascent? Naturally, those of the middle class who had honed their characters to a fine edge, who had made of themselves well-tuned and perfectly controlled machines, who acted with confidence, a genteel sort of ruthlessness, and stubborn perseverance in the competitive game. Since they often sold a service rather than a product, they actually found it necessary to "sell themselves," and for this reason success required them to cultivate a "positive outlook" and a "persuasive style." Competitive failure, in this climate, could easily be construed as personal inferiority. To avoid such painful experiences, middle-class people, particularly clerical and professional types, often had to respond defensively or cultivate an inflated estimation of themselves.[81] All this meant that the pressure on the middle-class person's ego was very great, emotional honesty very difficult, and consequently nervous breakdowns or other expressions of anxiety not at all rare.

A sizable proportion of evangelical Christians belonged precisely to this middle class and bore precisely these pressures. But more than this: on the whole, middle-class Christians had been taught the tradition of Calvinism. Even though some of Calvin's less "democratic" teachings had been watered down in the nineteenth century, there is no evidence that what Weber identified as the Protestant ethic was losing its appeal. In fact, given the legalistic and perfectionist tone of mid-nineteenth-century evangelicalism, one must assume that this ethic—often under the rubric of "character"—was taken more seriously than ever before. Evangelical middle-class children were subjected to a constant stream of admonitions to duty, hard work, perseverance, diligence, utter honesty, thrift, and other virtues traditionally associated with worldly success. And God was taken seriously. The revivalism growing out of the 1830s and 1840s encouraged parents to seek dramatic, life-changing conversions in their teen-aged children—almost as rites of passage. When such conversions took place, they seemed to ease parents' minds concerning their children's achievement of true character (or often true manhood) and ultimately of worldly success.

This meant that worldly success and a recognized Christian character could often be signs, as Weber points out, of the genuineness of that youthful conversion and thus of true election by God. Now, the middle-class Christian had to answer to the demands of not only his or her own ego but also to those of God. A sense of shame and guilt before God were added to the normal emotional costs of failure in perfecting character or in competing economically; and, as in any human life—particularly during periods of rapid historic change—failure of character was quite to be expected. Indeed, the evolution of the capitalist economic system was beginning to assault the very character traits by which it had thrived, and conscientious people were caught by the shift. The old productive virtues that were associated with the Protestant ethic were still important; but the late nineteenth century was seeing the rise of the need for consumptive virtues, such as obedience to impulse, material display, and the freer spending of money—all quite anathema to the Protestant ethic. The economy increasingly demanded that people buy the goods it was so fruitfully producing, and the message "live it up while you can" began to compete with the image of a sober, virtuous life represented by a former generation of Calvinist faithful. This dissonance (which we shall examine more closely in a later chapter) added its strain to the lives of conscientious Christian people. In addition, increasingly frenetic competition made for a blurring of the lines between honest and dishonest business dealings. One Christian writer described the Christian "business man down in the sharp competition of the world where duty calls him," confronted with "the sly temptations to overreach" while staying "keenly alert not to be overreached; and through all to preserve an uncensorious spirit, unhurt by the selfishness of the crowd. . . ." Or that young man who must stay "wide-awake, a pusher in business," who must try "steadily, determinedly to hold back any crowding of the other side of his life: the inner side, the outer-helpful side, the Bible-reading- and secret-prayer- and quiet-personal-work-side of his life. . . ."[82] These contradictions evangelicals must have felt, with the consequence that God's will, as defined by childhood norms and maxims, and the socially acceptable or socially necessary were beginning to sound like two different things.

Evangelicals lived with yet another dissonance. The perfectionism of the 1850s generation had been developed within a context of postmillennialism. One very good reason to succeed economically, as well as to perfect one's character, was that the millennial reign of Christ was just around the corner. This-worldly success and perfect living had an eschatological meaning and were quite in harmony with God's plans for the entire world. By the 1880s, however, Christians were gradually becoming convinced that they could not hope for a perfect society to grow out of their efforts. The rapid shift toward premillennialism reflected this despairing attitude toward the world and inspired the hope of growing numbers of evangelicals that God would rescue them from a terminal predicament. Meanwhile, they were beginning to see that their major task was to preach the gospel to every creature on earth and bring as many of the lost into the fold as possible, so that they too could join the saints in heaven. But middle-class Christians were at the very same time building their nests here on earth, caught up in the spirit of the time, joining the race for worldly success and material security. Many were building businesses or being educated for the professions—and not evangelizing. Their eschatology implied something much different from the way they spent their time and conceived of their lives. Serious Christians were being torn in two directions, and it undoubtedly added to an unconscious reservoir of guilt.

If our analysis is correct, evangelicals of the late nineteenth and early twentieth centuries were particularly caught in the crossfire of severe, often opposing emotional demands. I think we can put the evangelical dilemma of the day this way: history and theology conspired to convince the middle-class Christian that he or she had to be perfect in order to be happy and godly; and history and human nature conspired to make even the illusion of perfection essentially and increasingly impossible to attain. If we understand this, we will not find it surprising that evangelicals were feeling miserable about themselves. An agenda like this could only promise failure and defeat. But it would also certainly make the offer of a quick and easy "victory" through Christ sound unbelievably inviting.

We catch a glimpse of this sense of defeat in the testimonies of the early leaders of the Keswick movement in England, who were representatives of English evangelicalism in the 1870s, which one writer has described as "slowly suffocating in an atmosphere of introspection and gloom. . . . Fervent Christians groaned and gloried in unceasing inner conflict. Many were afraid to be happy: happiness would be sapped by a lurking sense of guilt."[83] Mostly university-educated Anglican clergymen or scholars, the early Keswick leaders have left an excellent sampling of their states of mind just before their "victory" under the ministry of speakers such as Hannah Whitall Smith and her husband Robert Pearsall Smith. A survey of their writing shows that these British evangelicals, almost to a man, were conscious of an overwhelming sense of their own failure. T. D. Harford-Battersby, for example, wrote in 1860: "Oh what a compound we are of good wishes and miserable performances! When, when shall it be otherwise?"[84] A friend of Harford-Battersby said that the latter was "deeply sad at the thought of stumbling and failure and sin."[85] H. W. Webb-Peploe spoke of a "constant watching, waiting, and struggling to do right. . . . I was strained and overstrained until I felt I was breaking down."[86]

H. G. C. Moule remembered feeling "guilty of discreditable failures in patience and charity, and humbleness, and I know not what. I knew that I was not satisfied." Theodore Monod, a French clergyman, recalled his "innumerable and conscious failures." Hudson Taylor wrote in 1896 of how, each hour of each day, he was oppressed by the consciousness of sin. He tried to keep his eyes on Jesus, "but pressure of duties, sometimes very trying, and constant interruptions apt to be so wearing, caused me to forget Him. Then one's nerves get so fretted . . . that temptations to irritability, hard thoughts and sometimes unkind words are all the more difficult to control. Each day brought its register of sin and failure. . . ." Andrew Murray, the Dutch Reformed clergyman from South Africa, spoke of "a dissatisfaction and restlessness inexpressible." He admitted that his "life was one of deep dissatisfaction." A historian of the Keswick movement writes that these men experienced victory only after "a crisis created by the realization of personal failure to come up to God's standard of expected holiness."[87]

In America a similar sense of failure prevailed. Hannah Whitall Smith characterized the Christian life this way:

> And your hearts have sunk within you as, day after day, and year after year, your early visions of triumph have seemed to grow more and more dim, and you have been forced to settle down to the conviction that the best you can expect from your religion is a life of alternate failure and victory, one hour sinning, and the next repenting, and then beginning again, only to fail again, and again to repent.[88]

These lines are particularly revealing because they contrast the high expectations, so effectively fueled by perfectionism, with the disappointing reality; and they point to the weary round of exertion that could only heighten the feelings of utter failure. The same notes were struck in 1916 at the Victorious Life conference, where one Christian admitted, "I have been a Christian all my life, but I have lived a defeated life," and where C. I. Scofield characterized the lives of many Christians as "so much of a failure."[89]

The natural result of this constant awareness of failure was a certain nervous anxiety that often came out in the spontaneous expression of unwanted emotions—exactly the result the builders of character feared most. Over and over again in the testimonies of English Keswick devotees in the 1880s and of those attending the 1916 Victorious Life Conference in the United States, one encounters the outbreak of temper as the most common or obvious example of personal sin and failure. During the Smiths' ministry in England, "besetting sins to be overcome were a tattling tongue, angry looks, viciousness on the croquet lawn, impatience with servants ('Does the sudden pull of the bell ever give notice in the kitchen that a good temper has been lost by the head of the household?'). Women discovered inner strength under days of 'feeling poorly,' men ceased to worry about the next bank failure. . . ."[90] Andrew Murray spoke with predictable frequency, in virtually every book, of how God could give victory over outbreaks of temper. He reminded his readers that "when your temper and hasty judgment and sharp words came out, you sinned against the highest law—the law of God's love." He promised that ". . . God can keep you from outbreaks of temper," and he asked his readers to pray, "Father, let the Holy Ghost have full dominion over me, in my home, in my temper, in every word of my tongue. . . ."[91] In 1916,

C. G. Trumbull was still sprinkling his sermons with illustrations of Christians losing their tempers before finding victory in Christ.

Worry, anxiety, defeat, failure, and particularly an uncontrolled temper—all of it illustrated the truth of that plaintive confession: "life is an unspeakably hard thing." The paeans to character and manliness and self-control that cluttered the growing self-help literature of the late nineteenth century were mocked by the reality of a people growing more and more weary of constant struggle and constant defeat. The focus of the middle-class consciousness, evangelical or otherwise, was more and more the inner self, that unruly source of anger, irritability, and worry. "A cross Christian, or an anxious Christian, a discouraged, gloomy Christian, a doubting Christian, a complaining Christian, an exacting Christian, a selfish Christian, a cruel, hard-hearted Christian, a self-indulgent Christian, a Christian with a sharp tongue or bitter spirit, all these may be very earnest in their work . . . but they are *not* Christ-like Christians. . . ." The message is obvious: what we must be is the perfect Christian. And there was only one course of action to become that: "In laying off your burdens . . . the first one you must get rid of is yourself."[92]

This was essentially the conclusion of the Victorious Life movement and its kindred spirits: get rid of yourself. Clearly, the self had become a burden in these times. Beard saw it as the nervous self. Freud saw it as the neurotic self. Historians have labeled the period as one of "intense self-consciousness"[93] and have seen the "distrust of the self" as intrinsic to the new and rising middle class.[94] Hannah Whitall Smith anticipated them when she observed Christians whose "inward affairs" had become "evermore utterly unmanageable."[95] The Keswick people hammered away on the root of all sin and defeat as the result of the "self-life."[96] And the purveyors of the victorious life identified the problem when they offered to effect an "emancipation from the tyranny of the self."[97] The Victorious Life speakers frequently warned against introspection—the clearest evidence that it had probably reached epidemic proportions among evangelicals. Robert McQuilken said, "Any view that centers attention upon the self is dangerous."[98] Middle-class Americans—and evangelicals prominently among them—were groaning under the burden of the self, and the Victorious Life theology's answer was to somehow relieve oneself of that burden. It offered an escape from introspection, from subjectivity, from constant self-consciousness and self-judgment, as well as from the self's morbid fears, doubts, anxieties, and uncontrolled angers. And for some people, at some times, it appeared to make good on its offer. As one participant in a Victorious Life conference exclaimed, "I am taking a great deal away from this conference, but I am leaving one thing; that is the self."[99]

VI

For as long as history has been recorded, men and women have looked to religious persons and systems to find healing. In primitive societies, the witch doctor or shaman was indeed both witch and doctor. She or he could both demonstrate intimate knowledge of the invisible powers of the universe and make the sick whole. In our day, science has taken these twin functions into its hands, offering plausible answers to the mysteries and prescription drugs for the ailments of body and spirit. It seems that human illness, whether physical or emotional, is more than the simple presence of pain and misery. It has religious meaning, perhaps because it is a reminder of finitude, of how fragile is the thin casing we call the body, of the vulnerability of life itself. Explicitly or not, we make healers into gurus and theologians, for they represent the only power we ultimately worship—the power over life and death. Today this applies as much to the purveyors of an illicit cure for cancer as to the certified medical doctor or psychotherapist. We will pay them the honor of our last dime in return for health and happiness, along with the answers to life's questions.

William James, writing in 1902, knew enough about all this to include in his pathfinding work *The Varieties of Religious Experience* a lengthy discussion of the healers of his day, whom he labeled the "mind-cure movement." We have already mentioned two specimens: the "Gospel of Relaxation" and the "Don't Worry Movement." Others in late nineteenth-century America included Divine Healing, New Thought, and the largest of them, Christian Science. Donald Meyer, whose book *The Positive Thinkers* covers some of the same ground that James did, names still others: Divine Science, Unity, Religious Science, and individual gurus like Charles and Myrtle Fillmore and Ralph Waldo Trine.[100] All of them flourished contemporaneously with the Keswick and Victorious Life movements. They spoke to the same middle-class audience, and about the same concerns: nervousness, irritability, worry. James does not mention the Victorious Life movement in his study; it had not yet begun as an organized American phenomenon. Most of his examples existed outside of and often at some enmity with the Protestant establishment, and they seldom took pains to demonstrate biblical orthodoxy, as did the Victorious Life movement. But when James describes the "mind-curers" as sharing a "contempt for doubt, fear, worry, and all nervously precautionary states of mind," we hear echoes of Victorious Life teaching. And beyond that, when these healers embrace as their cures "the conquering efficacy of . . . trust," we begin to wonder whether we have not heard a synonym for "victory through surrender and faith." We must ask: Was the Victorious Life movement the gospel of Jesus Christ, or was it perhaps more a typically middle-class technique for the healing of sick spirits? Perhaps a closer look will give us the answer.

At its most abstract levels, the standard mind-cure religion (as described by William James) posited the dual nature of all humans. In each of us exists a realm of the flesh, it said, where fear and egotism and doubt reign supreme; and in each of us also dwells a realm of the spirit, where one is in communion with God and "partakers of the life of God." A person may live in one or the other of these realms, but only life in the realm of the spirit offers wholeness, harmony, and power. Most mind-curers taught that, by virtue of the spiritual realm, humans "are already one with the Divine without any miracle of grace, or abrupt creation of a new inner man."[101] In this respect, James believed, they represented not Christianity but pantheism.

The Victorious Life movement was, in theory, somewhat different: it taught that Christ was only in the believer, not in the unbeliever, and then only by a specific and gracious gift, not naturally. Thus the Victorious Life teaching technically avoided James's charge of pantheism. But in that it spoke its message almost entirely to Christians, it said much the same as the mind-curers did: Christ is already within you, if you will just recognize him and let him act. And when you do let him act, it will be Christ acting in your place, as virtually indistinguishable from yourself. In this respect Victorious Life teaching was very much like the mind-cure movement as a whole. When it spoke of the term "self," it meant precisely what the mind-curers meant by the lower nature. When it spoke of the "Christ-life" within, it meant precisely what the mind-curers meant by the spiritual nature, although they might have called it the "Divine Energy" or the "Infinite Life."[102]

The mind-curers took this union of the person and the divine very seriously. Naturally, if God is actually one with the person, and the person lives in that reality, he or she can never become sick. As one recipient of the mind-cure said, ". . . how can a conscious part of Deity be sick?"[103] We hear the same sentiment in the Victorious Life illustration of the little girl who, when Satan knocked on the door, sent Jesus to answer it.[104] How can Jesus give in to temptation? *The Sunday School Times* quoted a college freshman as saying, "God now does everything for me, and I praise him for it; that awful thing, Self, is dead. . . ." Another correspondent, identifying him/herself as "A Texas Victor," testified that "I myself was in the way" until self was removed so that he/she could "let him do my living for me, in my place."[105] A participant in the 1916 Victorious Life Conference claimed that, looking within, she now found "none of self and all of Christ"; and a 1922 participant went even farther in extinguishing "self": "[Jesus] got into my body Friday night and stood me up for the foreign field."[106] Trumbull constantly emphasized that the Christian is *literally* within Christ, "so far within him that all our dealings with life thereafter are in reality his dealings with life."[107] All this is quite consistent with the spiritual psychology of the mind-cure movement.

How did the mind-cure movement promise to bring about this state of union with God? By getting its followers to "relax." Here it was responding to that severe and moralistic, that struggle-oriented atmosphere we have come to identify with late nineteenth-century Christianity, what we saw illustrated in the lives of the early Keswick leaders. William James describes the cure in these words, which Victorious Life teachers might also have used:

> Official moralists advise us never to relax our strenuousness. "Be vigilant, day and night," they adjure us; "hold your passive tendencies in check; shrink from no effort; keep your will like a bow always bent." But the persons I speak of find that all this conscious effort leads to nothing but failure and vexation. . . . The tense and voluntary attitude becomes in them an impossible fever and torment. Their machinery refuses to run at all when the bearings are made so hot and the belts so tight.[108]

As an alternative path to happiness, James writes, the mind-cure teachers urged "surrender" or "relaxation." "Give up the feeling of responsibility," they said; "let go your hold, resign the care of your destiny to higher powers . . ." and you will find relief.[109] The Victorious Life teachers preached precisely the same thing: that the victorious life "is radically different from the earnest life of struggle and service that is commonly urged upon Christians. It is a life that allows Christ to win the victories, to bear the fruit, to bring the joy and peace, in a supernatural and complete way." It urged that Christians appropriate the victory by doing "nothing . . . nothing at all." The common summation of the entire Victorious Life theology was "let go and let God."[110] The word "surrender" appears over and over and over in virtually every Victorious Life publication, along with the occasional admonition to relax. Such relaxation not only gave initial entry to the "Christ-life" but it characterized that life through and through. Keswick teachers spoke often of the life of victory as a life of "rest."[111] Trumbull put it this way:

> There is activity on our part, physical and mental; yet, it may be truly said that, when we are living in complete and sustained surrender to Christ in our life, there is no effort in what we do. None, that is, in the ordinary sense of that word. We simply surrender to Christ's effort. For Christ himself furnishes all the strength, whether physical, mental, or spiritual; and we no more put forth effort than the driving rod of a locomotive puts forth effort to turn the wheels. The steam furnishes the effort, not the rod. Christ in us is

the sole and entire dynamic, or motive-power, of our life. All that we seem to do, he, and he alone, personally present, actually and literally accomplishes.[112]

Here, as elsewhere, Trumbull uses a mechanical image to convey the effortlessness of this life of surrender. A decade earlier, one of James's key mind-curers had used a similar image: "To recognize our own divinity, and our intimate relation to the Universal, is to attach the belts of our machinery to the powerhouse of the Universe."[113]

The task of the mind-curers, just like that of C. G. Trumbull and company, was to bring ailing supplicants to the point where they would and could relax—or surrender. Naturally, this was the central practical problem for the healer. As James recognized, for many people who did relax and trust in this Infinite Other to possess them, the benefits to health and happiness were quick and remarkable. The new discipline of psychology was just beginning to come to grips with these results. In James's time there was a good deal of discussion of the so-called "power of suggestion" as effective in healing. Psychology was discovering "the powerful influence of the mind in disease," and it was demonstrating that "the faithful adherence to a truer philosophy of life will keep many a man well."[114] James found that mind-curers almost universally used this power of suggestion to do their healing. If they could get their audiences to believe that their ideas were true, and worked as they said, they could perform miracles in people's lives.

Inevitably, then, the work of the mind-curers involved a great deal of simple salesmanship. They knew that "an idea, to be suggestive, must come to the individual with the force of a revelation," and that "the force of personal faith, enthusiasm, and example, and above all the force of novelty, are always the prime suggestive agency in this kind of success."[115] And the Victorious Life people knew the same thing, although perhaps intuitively. From the first, the Victorious Life teaching had a "gnostic" flavor about it, specializing as it did in revealing a great secret (*The Christian's Secret of a Happy Life*), a secret hidden for many years from the vast majority of Christians, only now revealed to the fortunate few. After Victorious Life conferences, participants would write saying: "This year at Princeton I discovered the great secret that the Victorious Life is a moment by moment experience. . . ."[116] Decades after joining the Victorious Life movement, Robert C. McQuilken was still impressing audiences with his possession of a "new secret" that would revolutionize their lives.[117] Andrew Murray wrote books on "The Secret of Believing Prayer," and "The Believer's Secret of Obedience." A common theme among Keswick and Victorious Life teachers was the twofold division of all Christians into the defeated, those who did not know the secret, and the victorious, those who did. The defeated were described in terms every Christian could recognize in himself: weariness, restlessness, unanswered prayer, outbursts of anger. The victorious were presented as larger than life, possessing the power, self-control, and happiness that every Christian would naturally envy. One person spoke for many when, on hearing of the secret, he cried: "Oh, that I had known this years ago." Trumbull introduced to his conferees Christians who were living examples that this Victorious Life teaching really worked—for example, a "consecrated Christian . . . who five years ago entered into the Spirit-filled life, and has, I believe, been living continuously in victory since that day. . . ." Christians were urged not to live another day in ignorance of this precious secret, but to join the victorious few who lived moment by moment without known sin.[118]

As good salesmen, the Victorious Life teachers made extravagant promises in connection with their product. "Do you want your prayers answered?" asked one. "Do you want your relatives saved? Do you want your church revived? Do you want your town quickened . . . ? You may have every prayer answered . . . [if you] give yourself to God."[119] Another promised that the result of surrender would be that one's "spiritual health will immediately revive."[120] Trumbull was, by far, the premier salesman of the movement. He could describe the victorious life in almost irresistible terms:

> It is the Devil's own lie that we cannot live on a spiritual mountaintop all the time. Every one of those thrilling, joyous experiences that have accompanied your best moments ought to be habitual with you. . . . The steadily sustained consciousness of Christ's actual presence, and of glorious fellowship with him; a prayer-life that makes your times of secret prayer the richest parts of *every* day, . . . an unforced, spontaneous joy in talking with others about *your* Christ . . . ; a perennial interest in the Bible . . . ; and victory, habitual, progressive, increasing, over the sins that used to mock you with their constant defeat of your life; *this* is the only normal life for any and every follower of the Lord Jesus Christ. Is it your life?[121]

Trumbull's sermons have very much the feel of sales pitches for a miraculous new product. They are composed of what amounts to one true-life story after another, each illustrating the frustration and unhappiness and ineffectuality of the life of the defeated Christian, each bringing that Christian to a sudden revelation of the secret of victory (often with Trumbull himself as the messenger of that revelation), and each then showing the startling and joyous results of a life of new-found victory. One can almost feel the audience, longing for this life that some seem to have achieved, straining to believe that they too can possess it, crying out in their spirits the words one woman used in writing to Trumbull: "*I must have this full life of Christ that you speak of.*"[122]

Trumbull and others, again as practiced salespeople, guaranteed Christians that this new life of victory was automatic—just like lights coming on when you turn the switch. But you have to follow the steps. Almost every Victorious Life book or sermon outlines a series of steps that made the path to victory plain and simple. Here is one of Andrew Murray's versions:

> The steps in this path are these: First, the deliberate decision that self shall be given up to the death; then, the surrender to Christ crucified to make us partakers of his crucifixion; then, "knowing that our old man is crucified," the faith that says, "I am crucified with Christ;" and then, the power to live as a crucified one, to glory in the cross of Christ.[123]

Trumbull's formula was somewhat simpler: first let go; then let God. He emphasized that both steps were necessary before the guarantee could take effect. Many people have "let go," he would say, but not "let God."[124] If a person does both, he or she cannot fail to have the victory.

Thus they implemented the power of suggestion by the promises of startling life changes, the use of tantalizing success stories, the presentation of a few simple steps, and the guarantee that the process would indeed work as advertised. It was also vastly strengthened by the way Victorious Life teachers dealt with the matter of feelings or experience. Naturally, some who followed the steps very carefully felt no difference; to this Victorious Life teachers replied that feelings did not count. This, I believe, was the source of a great deal of confusion in the Victorious Life message, and it is also where one begins to smell the rat of charlatanism. The victorious life was offered to Christians, especially by Trumbull, precisely as a whole new way to *feel*. What else can we make of the promises that worry, anxiety, and anger would be replaced by constant joy and peace? What is "happiness" if not a feeling? And yet when confronted by a woman who said, "I have surrendered, but nothing has happened," Trumbull quoted C. I. Scofield: "'There are so many people waiting for some feeling to confirm the action of God. . . .' Dear friends, do not wait another moment for feeling to confirm the Word of God. If you are resting on your feelings you are resting on quicksand. . . . Victory has nothing to do with feelings; God's Word is true whether we feel it or not."[125] Not to be totally contradictory, Trumbull promised that feelings would eventually follow faith; but even so, "God will give feeling in such measure and at such a time as his love sees best for the individual case." Instead of "facing toward our feelings," Trumbull thought, Christians should be "facing toward God's facts."[126]

This is another refrain one encounters again and again in Victorious Life literature: the victory comes not by feeling but by believing. And of course Trumbull was right, as William James could show. People who *believe* firmly enough that they are happy tend to *feel* that they are happy. People who believe that they already have the victory will tend to go around feeling they have the victory. Those who are certain of the possibility of healing can often be healed. Any number of mind-cure successes attest to the power of one's beliefs. But why believe? Why believe Trumbull and not Mary Baker Eddy? Here the Victorious Life took advantage of the fact that its adherents were uniformly evangelical Christians. Evangelicals already believed. What Victorious Life teachers had to do was somehow to focus that belief on the healing powers of the Spirit of Christ, and to activate it at deeper levels within the person. At times this took on the aspects of a mind game. To have faith, Trumbull advised, "open your Bible and face the great facts that are there, and recognize that those facts are true. . . ." Trumbull could play on people's guilt: if you don't have the victory, it is because of your unbelief. Unbelief is the greatest sin, since it means not admitting "that Jesus Christ is equal to meeting the pressure" of life. Sometimes the manipulation involved in bringing a person to belief was quite palpable and startling, as in one dialogue between Trumbull and a Victorious Life conferee in a public meeting:

> Questioner: I have sought to, and as far as I know, I have fully consecrated my heart and life to God, but still I find great anxiety and care pressing upon me as regards the affairs of this life.
>
> Answer: Have you definitely accepted Christ as your victory in this matter?
>
> Questioner: Yes, as far as I know.
>
> Answer: You must not say "as far as you know;" you must say "yes" or "no"—either you have or you have not fully accepted Christ as your victory. Rather, I will not even say, "Have you?" but "Do you now?"
>
> Questioner: By the grace of God I do now; I have not done so heretofore.
>
> Answer: That settles it. Jesus is meeting all your needs now.[127]

All of this sounds very much like the mind-curers and faith-healers of William James's day and ours. James tells of the answer these mind-curers gave to those seeking to be made well: "You *are* well, sound, and clear already, if you did but know it. . . . God is well, and so are you." Another mind-curer urged: "Live as if it were true . . . and every day will practically prove you right."[128] Victorious Life sounds hauntingly similar.

Trumbull urged his audience "to recognize at this moment Christ is accomplishing in our lives all that is needed for the life of victory and power; and that we need do, and can do, nothing about it except to receive it, now, as a present fact, without feeling, without evidence, without proof of any sort." But do you feel that you have not got the faith? Trumbull answers, Of course you have the faith! It's the same faith that got you saved in the first place! But what if you "can get no assurance of victory"? Trumbull: "Then take it without assurance."[129] What if you have been "pleading for it" but "can't quite grasp it," as one of his correspondents admitted? The answer is, "Stop praying for the blessing of the Victorious Life, and commence praising him that he is now giving it to you. Don't look for any evidence of it. . . . Don't look for changed feelings of any sort. In blind, cold faith thank your Lord Jesus Christ that he *is* meeting all your needs now."[130]

Much of Trumbull's advice amounts to this kind of magically oriented mental gymnastics, calculated to create something out of nothing. It boils down to "it will work if you just believe it will work," and "if it is not working, it is because you are not believing enough," and "if you are believing but it is still not working, then it is because you can't see that it is working already." This sort of convoluted mental technology is no different from that offered by any number of would-be healers in our own day.

But in many cases it seemed to work. James himself had little doubt on this score. You have to take the mind-cure movement seriously, he said, because it makes some people feel happier. One mind-cure testimonial had it that "all feelings of irritability disappeared." "I had been nervous and irritable," another witness said, but "I grew serene and gentle" and developed a "confidence and inner calm." The same person reported "the elimination of selfishness" in its "subtler and generally unrecognized" forms, and the end of such feelings as "sorrow, grief, regret, envy," along with a cure for a chronic "sick headache" and associated "dyspepsia."[131] Similarly, those who attended Victorious Life conferences testified to instantaneous healing. "I came to Princeton with a great burden of worry. . ." said one, "and I am going home without it." Another reported: "I had a nervous breakdown and the devil got hold of me; but since coming here I have surrendered my whole life, and I have the peace that passes understanding. I have never had such peace before. I have not worried since,—and I have been a great victim of worry."[132] At the end of each conference, Trumbull gave participants a chance to say in public what God had done for them. The immediate emotional impact of these conferences was obvious in the repeated testimonies to the healing of body and spirit.

But there is another note we hear in the records of the Victorious Life movement, a note of continuing frustration and defeat. For many Victorious Life adherents cures often seemed transitory. Participants testified to having lost the victory in the weeks or months following the heady, intoxicating days of the Victorious Life conference. In the very testimonials to their certainty that they would not lose the victory, one hears the real secret of Victorious Life: for many people, it was not that life of constant, intimate, sinless communion with God that they had craved. This came as a deep disappointment to many of them, and as a source of continuing guilt to others. Many seemed confused. They had been taught, for example, that the victorious life was a life of rest, not of struggle, because once Jesus was given full sway in a person's life, *he* would maintain the victory without their effort. As Trumbull said, "It is Christ's responsiblity to bring me into, and keep me in, victory, after I have surrendered to him absolutely."[133] But it did not always work that way, as this letter to *The Sunday School Times* illustrates:

> You say God must do it all, and will, if we remain yielded. At the beginning of this year I was living the Victorious Life, and it certainly was wonderful; God gave me the victory in all things. But somehow I lost it. As far as I knew, my life remained yielded, and I was serving him as he led me; but, seemingly without any disobedience on my part, I found myself growing cold, and soon lost my joy and power. Now why was it? If God is to do the saving and keep us victorious after we do our part, why was my failure possible?[134]

These kinds of testimonies, repeated often, forced Trumbull to spend a great deal of time explaining to his followers why Christ had not delivered on the inflated promises of the Victorious Life movement. He preached sermons entitled "The Victory Tested" and "The Perils of Victory," which implicitly acknowledged that the victorious life was very much like that on-again, off-again experience many Christians had had trying to live the Christian life by their own moral efforts.[135] Generally, he argued that such failure could be blamed on Satan's wiles, although the Christian could make himself or herself especially susceptible to these wiles by wrong ways of thinking about victory.[136] He often suggested that there was some inadequacy in the person's degree of surrender (has every last corner of your life been given to Jesus?) or of faith (are you thanking him already, before you feel anything, for what he has done?). To the logical ear, he never really answered the question of why, if Jesus is to maintain one's surrender and faith, defeat can ever again occur in the Christian's life.

Trumbull and other Victorious Life figures did have some practical advice for those who worried about maintaining the victory. One variety smacked of auto-suggestion: "Just say in blind trust . . . ," wrote Trumbull, " 'I *know* that Jesus *is* meeting *all* my needs *now*, because his grace is sufficient for me.' "[137] Hannah Whitall Smith suggested that one should repeat over and over, "Jesus saves me now."[138] These and other such examples imitated a standard mind-cure ploy. Charles Fillmore, for example, offered his students these lines for daily repetition: "I am the Christ of God. . . . My perfection is now established in the Divine Mind. . . . My doubts and fears are dissolved and dissipated. . . . I no longer condemn, criticize, censure. . . . I am fearless, powerful and wise in God's love."[139] William James gives similar examples.[140]

Trumbull's concern for the maintenance of victory led him, as we have seen, to emphasize the "Morning Watch." This daily time of prayer and Bible reading kept one's mind fixed on Jesus, and thus helped "feed our faith" and maintain the fellowship with Jesus that alone could guarantee victory.[141] Again and again, Trumbull emphasized that victory was a "moment-by-moment" thing—that it all depended on a constant looking to Jesus. "Morning Watch" was thus an excellent discipline, for it reinforced daily the sense of God's presence and the contents of belief that, when they filled the mind, could by definition keep the Christian from known sin. The logic of the "Morning Watch" seems to be twofold: first, devotional disciplines drive deeply into the mind the truths that are necessary to control one's emotional and objective behavior; and second, when one's mind is consciously full of Jesus, it will not be full of anything else, which means that one will not in fact be consciously feeling angry or resentful or unloving. All this simply meant that the power of suggestion could work to greatest effect if one consciously focused on Jesus.

These techniques were common practice in any mind-cure teaching—or any cult, for that matter. James quotes a mind-cure advocate to the effect that "disease can no longer attack one whose feet are planted on this rock, who feels hourly, momently, the influx of the Deific Breath." Another testified that "we must be in absolutely constant relation or mental touch . . . with that essence of life which permeates all and which we call God."[142] Victorious Life teachers agreed that this constant relation was the key to maintaining Christ's life in the believer, and they urged "continuous and unbroken prayer" as the path to "a steady and unswerving victory."[143] So, although they often insisted that only the Holy Spirit can maintain "God's way of holiness" within the Christian, they placed the blame for failure on the Christian, not on the Holy Spirit, and urged personal disciplines as means to help the Holy Spirit do what he alone could do.[144]

Thus, like the mind-curers generally, they recalled some of the medieval exertions of Christian mysticism—hardly a struggle-free life. William James comments that much of the mind-cure movement emphasized exercises in passive relaxation, concentration, and meditation. To him it sounded like a secularized version of "the practice of the presence of God." He quotes the Roman Catholic mystic Alvarez de Paz, who wrote: "Would you escape from every ill? Never lose this recollection of God. . . ."[145] Victorious Life teaching said much the same and thus placed itself squarely within the mind-cure movement sweeping American society at the turn of the century.

VII

In the hands of Charles G. Trumbull, Robert McQuilken, and their successors such as Donald Grey Barnhouse, Harold J. Ockenga, and Alan Redpath, the Victorious Life theology established itself very prominently at the center of American evangelicalism in the twentieth century. One can still hear students from Wheaton College and Moody Bible Institute in the 1980s describe the Christian experience in a vocabulary first popularized at the Keswick conventions one hundred years earlier. Hannah W. Smith's *The Christian's Secret of a Happy Life*, newly republished, can be found in Christian bookstores, as can any number of devotional studies by Andrew Murray. Christians recommend these books to one another having no idea that they represent the specific sociological and religious milieu of modernity rather than the timeless gospel message descended from the time of Jesus Christ. The Victorious Life theology has become the gospel for many evangelicals in late twentieth-century America.

This is, of course, as its leading proponents intended it. The mercy of God, forgiving the repentant evildoer, is the good news for the "sinner," they said. But where is the good news for the "saint"?[146] Are Christians saved from damnation after death but left during life to wallow in sorrow and defeat? Must the Christian wait for his or her reward? Do Christians have to continue to feel angry, irritable, and guilty? Must they struggle to love their neighbors? Must they bear the same psychic scars of living in the maelstrom as do the non-Christians around them? Or is there a good news effective right now that offers a taste of heaven in this life, that makes the Christian "more than conqueror" where it really matters—in the home, at work, in the routines of daily life? Of course—there is the good news that the saint can "possess his possessions," can "have the victory" right now, through the grace of Jesus Christ. This is the good news that animated much of the evangelical community in early twentieth-century America.

Like all humans, evangelicals longed for this kind of victory. Materially, for the most part, their lives were improving; economic opportunity, at least for the winning competitors, seemed endless; social and cultural change brought increased personal freedom; technology promised the good life. But in many ways they were not happy. Instead, they were worried, nervous, and afraid. They were laboring under psychic burdens and dissonances that their forefathers probably did not know and thus had not prepared them for. If the Victorious Life teaching could give them victory over their ailments of spirit, it could supply them with the only things they seemed not able to get for themselves. That sounded like good news for sure.

But we must also stop to notice that, if this was indeed the good news of the gospel, they were not the only ones who had access to it. A wide variety of mind-cure competitors offered the very same good news. And there is no evidence that the latter offered a formula for spiritual healing that was in any way inferior to the version represented by the Victorious Life. Each could produce testimonials to success that echoed—and in some cases were verbally indistinguishable from—those offered at the "Say-So" meetings closing out each Victorious Life conference. William James, by no means a gullible observer, attested to the success record of the mind-cure healers of his day: "The blind have been made to see, the halt to walk; lifelong invalids have had their health restored. The moral fruits have been no less remarkable . . . ; regeneration of character has gone on on an extensive scale; and cheerfulness has been restored to countless homes."[147] The Victorious Life teaching may have added a few lines about healed Christians being empowered for Christian service, but otherwise its agenda and its results seem to have matched James's description quite precisely.

The lines about Christian service were indeed quite important, and they give some indication of an uneasy conscience within the Victorious Life movement. Evangelicals were carrying with increasing weariness the burden of the self, and in so doing they perhaps portended a common problem of affluent Westerners in the twentieth century—a problem that made Freud a household word in the 1920s and narcissism a national disease in the 1970s. An apparently ever-intensifying obsession with the self has given a therapeutic cast to much of our civilization's products, and made psychological help and self-help the dominating concern of even evangelicals in the late twentieth century. The Victorious Life teaching was in on the ground floor of this therapeutic drift. When critics accused it of morbid introspection and an essentially self-centered orientation toward life, it defended itself by pointing to the soul-winning and foreign missionary activity its ministry had spawned.[148] It thereby attempted to put a bit of distance between itself and the mind-cure competitors of its day.

Perhaps its stiffest competition was the Christian Science movement, a rapidly growing sect in the first decades of the twentieth century. The literature of evangelicalism is so full of angry attacks on Christian Science that one wonders whether the attention given it does not reflect how closely and how successfully it paralleled the teachings and results of the Victorious Life movement. The attacks remind one of throwing rocks over the back fence at one's nearest neighbors. There is some evidence that the Victorious Life teaching attracted people who had previously sought healing, often unsuccessfully, through Christian Science.[149] Victorious Life speakers took pains to distinguish between their message and that of Mary Baker Eddy's followers.[150] Leading preachers like I. M. Haldeman dismissed Christian Science as "one of the most subtle and disastrous deceptions that ever entered the world" and then went on to describe it in terms reminiscent of Victorious Life teaching.[151] A contributor to *The Fundamentals* characterized Christian Science this way:

> One of the keenest observers of America has made the remark that "the reason so many new isms are constantly springing up is because the old Gospel is so hard to live." People are looking for a comfortable life here, and an easy way to heaven. . . . The fight with sin which the Gospel demands is a fierce and bitter fight; and many men and women are anxiously searching for a way of escape, desiring to be "carried to the skies on flowery beds of ease."[152]

This writer, obviously relishing the older, nineteenth-century moral strenuousness of Calvinism, did indeed have an insight into Christian Science when he concluded by saying that it promised its adherents that "all disagreeable and unpleasant things vanish."[153] But in so doing he came perilously close to a characterization just as applicable to the Victorious Life movement as to the "vagary" of Christian Science.[154]

Which brings us back to William James. Making disagreeable and unpleasant things vanish, he ventured, is the primary task of any religion. For most people happiness is human life's chief concern. "How to gain, how to keep, how to recover happiness, is in fact for most men at all times the secret motive of all they do, and of all they are willing to endure." Religion answers the demand for happiness, which is essentially a demand for psychic healing. "The more complex ways of experiencing religion," James wrote, "are new manners of producing happiness, wonderful inner paths to a supernatural kind of happiness, when the first gift of natural existence is unhappy, as it so often proves itself to be."[155] Perhaps this tells us why Hannah W. Smith's book *The Christian's Secret of a Happy Life* is still in print after a hundred years.

But it also tells us that Smith's book is a *religious* tract, and that the Victorious Life is a *religious* movement. As such, I suggest, these are in some very important respects in tension with—and even contradictory of—the revelation of God in Jesus Christ as understood in the biblical text. For Jesus Christ became flesh not to found an alternative religious system and not to offer the kind of psychic healing or happiness that religions offer, but to dissolve human religions and to disturb human happiness. Jesus is not a great religious healer (though history is full of those) but a revelation of God's eternal enmity with religions and therapies of all kinds. Any version of the good news that does not reflect this disturbing revelation of God is—whatever else it may be, however effective in bringing "happiness" it may be, and however clothed in biblical language it may be—not the gospel of Jesus Christ.

A religion is a human product. It meets human needs, at least humanly perceived needs, in humanly acceptable and often quite lofty, profound, charitable, and pious ways. Naturally, it claims a divine origin, as it must in order to give itself the greatest possible credibility and to satisfy the human need for a healing and a happiness that are "ultimate." And perhaps it can often trace its ancestry to the revelation of God in Jesus Christ. But invariably, since its goal is extrinsic and practical, it has seized that revelation and turned it to human purposes in a perfect recapitulation of the history of the people of God in the Old and New Testaments. When it does so, it joins all the countless religions of mankind's creation in their revolt against the God of Jesus Christ. Like them, it can be historically and sociologically examined; like them, it promises freedom but delivers only greater slavery; and like them, it is positively offended by the truly freeing revelation of the grace of God in Jesus Christ.

In what respect can we say all this of the Victorious Life movement? Certainly these were not insincere or stupid women and men. Their piety, especially that of the Keswick leaders in England, seemed to commend them to all who heard them. Their sense of the unhappiness of their Christian brothers and sisters was heartfelt and perceptive, and they expressed this concern in lives of caring ministry. Many of them brought a learned intelligence to the study of Scripture, and all believed they were being true to the historic teachings of the Christian church, and especially to the Reformation doctrine of justification by faith alone.

But perhaps in some measure this was not entirely true. I find it revealing to hear a great many of them make a distinction between the good news for the sinner and the good news for the saint. To them the doctrine of justification by faith alone implied salvation only from the "penalty" of sin. It was good news only at the instant of the conversion experience of which so many could testify. After that, it seems it was no longer satisfying. They desired salvation from the "power" of sin, which they apparently found in their unique version of the biblical doctrine of sanctification, which, as Trumbull observed, was just another word for the victorious life.[156] We must ask, why is sanctification and its concomitant doctrine of the Holy Spirit so attractive to late nineteenth- and twentieth-century Christians, so much so that it becomes the dominating message in some circles? And why does justification seem so incomplete a blessing, so inadequate to the task of making Christians "happy"?

I would suggest that it is because they inherited an exceedingly shallow, intellectualistic, and trivialized understanding of repentance. To them, repentance seemed something of a formality. They knew it was required: required that they feel the weight of their sin (or usually, sins); required that they feel sorry for those sins; required that they "turn around" (to use the oft-preached meaning of the term "repent"). In all these requirements repentance meant a certain brokenness of spirit, an awareness of falling short, a deep and radical humiliation. But the social institutions that touched their lives—family, church, business, community—demanded that they be competent, responsible, decisive, equal to any challenge, farsighted, resourceful, industrious and energetic, purposeful, self-controlled, and confident! These would not seem to permit a life of brokenness. They imply the cultivation of an artificial and basically deceitful self-inflation. This self-inflation was the real requirement of life at the turn of the century; total adequacy was the real goal of life. A religious conversion, accomplished under the influence of the yearly revival enthusiasm, was an important means to that end. Repentance was simply the doorway to personal strength and adequacy, not the freedom from those demands by the admission of an enduring finitude and frailty. Repentance gained admission to heaven ("free from the penalty") and thus comforted the Christian that he or she had removed the formal barriers to eternal life as God's elect. Now all energies could be concentrated on proving a certain prowess in this matter of the calling, which was the real demonstration of God's favor—at least the one that counted most for happiness in this life. Thus the tendency for the impulse, let's repent and get on with it!

Repentance could not make a person happy, then, because repentance implied exactly the opposite of what middle-class Christians were wanting to hear about themselves in the midst of their middle-class existence. That was perfection. Perfection would guarantee worldly success, the respect of Christian family and friends, the favor of God. But, having turned down the freedom of true repentance, and having embraced the goal of perfection, their lives became a matter of intense daily struggle, guilt in the event of failure, and often utter exhaustion. It was the genius of the Victorious Life movement, as well as much of mind-cure religion, that it recognized this sense of exhaustion and saw that the struggle was yielding little real progress in attaining its goal: a perfect Christian character. The Victorious Life doctrines and the mind-cure teachings offered to relieve the burden. Relax, they said; effort and willpower will get you nowhere. Besides, noted Trumbull and others, the Christian life is not meant to be a matter of works, but of grace. Give up, surrender to God's grace, and you will be whole.

There, of course, was the problem: you will be whole. Essentially, the Victorious Life movement carried forward the very same goal of the moral perfectionists of the mid- and late nineteenth century, changing only the means of reaching that goal. If one examines the promised results of this surrender to and trust in God, one finds a picture of the ideal Christian character: serenity in every situation, perfect and unshakable trust in God, effective service for God's kingdom, immunity to all temptation, and the complete rational control of all negative emotions so as to make one perfectly loving toward other people. Occasionally, a Victorious Life teacher actually spelled it out. Lewis Sperry Chafer, for example, a leader both in Victorious Life and dispensationalist theologies, affirmed in *He That Is Spiritual* that the Spirit produces character, not by "self-training and self-repression," but "at once . . . by a right adjustment to the indwelling Spirit."[157] A speaker at the 1922 Victorious Life Conference said that "God wants us to have a holiness of character, that our life and our doings may be righteous."[158] The Victorious Life movement was recapturing the importance of grace, only to turn it into a technique for achieving what it had not been successful in achieving by other means: a perfect moral character and the happiness to go with it.

I believe that this constitutes a religious seizure of the revelation of God for the satisfaction of human needs. And the reason for this seizure? I am convinced that the answer is a simple one, which startles us even though the biblical writers would lead us to expect it. The Victorious Life movement, for all its condemnation of unbelief, stood within the pale of unbelief. The movement that taught the crucial importance of trust in God became, by dictating the necessary results of that trust, a form of rebellion against and freedom from God. The movement that proclaimed the central significance of grace in the Christian life was a denial of the particular grace revealed in Jesus Christ, the grace that offers us unmerited favor rather than the grace that magically turns us into people who no longer need unmerited favor but now indeed merit God's favor. The movement that encouraged a posture of humble surrender was in fact a manifestation of autonomy—of the demand for a kind of visible perfection that God did not even embody in Jesus Christ. The Victorious Life movement, with its pat answers and confident guarantees, represented the continuance in American evangelicalism of human unbelief hidden beneath the pleasing garb of Christian theology. It gave new life to the lost triumphalism of a former day by shifting it to the subjective realm and cloaking it in the language of Christian devotion.

When the revelation of God comes to us it reveals to us in dramatic and utterly disillusioning ways our own pretensions. It shows us how our lives are compromised at the very core, how our very best moves are as filthy rags before God. We see that we are building structures for our own glory, our own happiness, our own longevity—but on sinking sand. The futility of our deepest yearning and striving is laid bare to us. We see that every goal we have established for our lives is in fact a spiritual goal whose meaning is an attempt to be our own gods, to replace God as our security, ultimately to rebel against God in the name of our own lordship. That is, when the revelation of God comes to us, we hear from the God of mercy a word of judgment and of dissolution, the terrible No to our deepest selves.

To believe is to hear this No. To believe is not to hear it temporarily, as if we could acknowledge it briefly and then move beyond it; nor is it to hear it instrumentally, as a means to an end, as if we could hear it only in order not to have to hear it again. To believe is to hear it and keep on hearing it, because it is true—because it is God's revelation of who we are and, in some sense, will always be until death is finally vanquished.

For the evangelicals of the mid-nineteenth century and beyond, this word was exceedingly difficult to hear. We have already seen how the middle-class competitive struggle in an exploding industrial society put a premium on self-confidence and encouraged the pursuit of self-glory. The adulation of the "hero," from Emerson's *Representative Men* to Philip Howard's *The Life Story of Henry Clay Trumbull: Missionary, Army Chaplain, Editor, and Author* and Charles G. Trumbull's *Anthony Comstock, Fighter,* created the illusion of human greatness. The ideal of character implied moral progress and a sufficiency to every human situation. The Protestant ethic encouraged such spiritually deceptive traits as strength of will and self-control. The message from every corner of the rising industrial society was "you can succeed, if you have the drive, the perseverence, the skills to compete." The culture as a whole was turning its back on the truth of the human condition, creating illusions of adequacy and glory that would function to keep the engines of capitalism running at full speed.

The evangelical mind of the late nineteenth century, rising out of the serious confusion of Jesus Christ and American culture that we have described, had new weapons with which to withstand this onslaught. An Arminianizing and Enlightenment-soaked theology had cast a rosy glow on human nature, giving more credit to human rationality and will than the older Calvinism had afforded. Decades of revivalism had trivialized human sin and guilt, making conversion simply a recognition of past defects or errors and a statement of nobler intentions for the future rather than an admission of the utter bankruptcy of one's own human enterprise. For youths raised in evangelical homes, the expectation of conversion sometime before adulthood was a given. This conversion experience became for many a mere ritual, a rite of passage, not a realization of one's true and abiding neediness. One frequently reads of a nineteenth-century Christian youth on the point of conversion who says something like, "I became burdened because I was not burdened. I cried because I could not cry. I was dreadfully depressed because I thought I was not depressed enough." Or, in another case, "I feel even now that I do not feel that interest in the subject which its importance demands. I feel that I *do not feel* sufficiently my condition and my danger and my need of a Savior."[159] These are young evangelicals who know that they must be converted but are prevented in a climate of moralism and human self-inflation from seeing the truth about themselves. So they go through the motions, or they whip up some sort of momentary frenzy; their hearts concealed from their heads. And they grow up into a climate of perfectionism, of great expectations, of the inflated human hopes for individual and social progress that postmillennialism represented, finding plenty of encouragement to delude themselves about their own moral advancement and need for still greater struggle but little encouragement to the truth about themselves and their efforts.

Christians thus moved into the late nineteenth century with a substantial baggage of deceptive self-assessments and expectations, and with an underlying quest for their own apotheosis. In this climate God's revelation of the truth about humans and their pretensions was shouted down and shut out, most effectively, I would say, in the evangelical church, where Christians were so sure they possessed the truth that they had no ears to hear the truth when it came to them. In the preceding chapter I suggested that they could have heard this truth had they examined their own history sensitively and in the light of biblical revelation. Instead, they built the structure of dispensationalist premillennialism, which, in a way reminiscent of Victorious Life teaching, offered them the same goals they had sought as postmillennialists, but by different means. The actual truth about their condition and their pretensions did not seem to penetrate their spirits. They had no ears to hear. Victorious Life theology, by offering them the ideal of character and the happiness they imagined would be associated with it, was a continuation of this deafness to God's dissolving judgment. As a theology, therefore, it was a manifestation of unbelief.

But God's judgment never comes—nor can it be heard—in isolation from his embracing mercy. When the truth of God's revelation penetrates the human spirit, it speaks both messages at once: you are a sinner in deep and enduring ways; but God is merciful and will surely rescue you. Evangelicals also found this message hard to believe. Perhaps their minds were so conditioned by the perfectionism and moralism of evangelicalism and middle-class life that they could not break through to accept a grace truly free and truly freeing. In unbelief they could not hear the truth about themselves because they could not hear the truth about God's mercy; and vice versa: they could not experience true forgiveness because they were not inclined to enter a place of true repentance.

So they hung on to their illusions of perfection and healing and peace of mind. But in reality they were anxious, ailing, and often out of control of their own beings. Unwilling or unable to hear the judgment of God in his mercy, they were left to experience it in its condemnation—a kind of hell on this earth. Their quest for character, with its presumed godlike qualities, left them neurotic and nervous; their struggle to avoid the guilt of failure left them exhausted. Instead of self-control, they showed anger; instead of love, irritation. They distorted the biblical understanding of sin, deep unbelief in the human breast, into regrettable acts of moral imperfection; and then were overwhelmed by that trivialized, nevertheless guilt-producing and nagging sinfulness. They felt sick, but they refused to identify it as a terminal sickness; instead, they treated it as a temporary "adjustment" problem to be overcome. To overcome it, they created a human technique that many others in their day were also creating, a religious therapy they called the "Victorious Life."

The Victorious Life teaching did make a bit of progress on the old moralistic evangelicalism. It discovered some very important truths: for example, that Christians were getting nowhere in their quest for character and happiness through rigorous moral effort; that this quest was a manifestation of a works-righteousness; and that rest and rescue lay in the grace of the God through Jesus Christ. But it stopped short of the Reformation doctrine of justification by faith alone (except in the most trivial sense), preferring a "medicinal" definition of grace—grace manipulated for visible results—that was essentially Roman Catholic and best articulated at the Council of Trent, which was called in the sixteenth century to counter the teachings of Luther and the Reformation.[160] And it could attest that turning aside from the quest for perfection would, in Andrew Murray's words, endanger the Christian's salvation.[161] The Victorious

Life movement did not seem to understand that grace would cease to be grace if it was turned into an instrument for achieving the same moral perfection, self-control, and happiness that the old works-righteousness sought. It did not know that its desires for these things were in themselves desires to escape the radical judgment and infinite mercy of God. It did not see that, in emphasizing the necessity of belief in God, it was urging a belief in what God would *do* for the Christian instead of who God *was* in his self-revelation. Most of all, it did not understand that unless it heard the revelation of God in all its truth—not as a patent medicine for personal healing (as one speaker said, "you've got to take the full Christ if you're going to have the full benefit"),[162] but as the truth that questions all humanly defined benefits and humanly inspired programs of healing—it would not indeed result in a life of moral perfection, emotional control, and unselfish love but in the same dreadful round of guilt and anxiety and weariness—only now under new auspices, the auspices of the Victorious Life.

This is precisely what happened. To replace the old moral effort, the Victorious Life way proposed two steps: surrender and faith, or "let go and let God." The guarantee of victory did not hold unless the Christian fulfilled these two requirements, and fulfilled them perfectly. As Victorious Life teachers were fond of saying, God demands not 99 percent but 100 percent surrender if he is to be Lord.[163] They told stories of Christians who held back one last aspect of themselves and thus never experienced the victory.[164] To try to mitigate the obvious emotional burden this implied, they devised a well-used formula: if you are not willing to surrender all to God, then tell God you are willing to be made willing.[165] Still, one of the recurring questions asked by frustrated seekers of the Victorious Life was, "Have I really surrendered all, or have I not?" Trumbull tried to put this to rest by assuring listeners that surrender is "limited to the sphere of your consciousness," and that "the fact that anyone is asking the question, 'Am I really surrendered?' is evidence that he has surrendered." The question seemed to persist, however, and it appears that for some it became the grounds for nervous introspection, self-doubt, and a perfectionist treadmill all the more wearying because it was in the area of the subjective and immeasurable.

The same problem—and the same anxiety—were created by the second step: faith. How does one know when he or she has sufficient faith to secure the victory? Of course, one must have this faith "moment by moment," which means that at any moment one could fall out of victory. Here is one Christian's experience:

Question: I surrendered Monday might; I trusted the Lord with my whole heart. I had my Bible reading and prayer this morning, and then right after that something happened and made me cross. It seemed strange, after Bible reading and prayer, for that defeat to come so quickly. What was the trouble?

Answer: There is only one answer to that; somehow you were not trusting Christ, as you failed. Christ had not failed; the only thing that can get us out of victory, when we have surrendered to Christ, is to cease to trust him wholly. Possibly you were trusting in your Bible reading and prayer instead of in Christ. . . .[166]

Trumbull, the answerer, was drawing some fairly fine psychological and spiritual distinctions and in the process only worsening the inner treadmill that this Christian found himself on. The fact that Jesus himself is supposed to maintain the victory did not seem to solve the problem. So the life of victory is a life always on the edge of abject and sudden failure, always with an eye to one's own state of surrender or state of faith. Both surrender and faith become a work, a matter of self-conscious effort, even—as though they had learned nothing at all from the moral effort of their forefathers—a matter of will. One Victorious Life speaker put it this way: "To me this whole walk is expressed in the one word, yield. I do not mean as an effort on my part,—Jesus does it all, he is all; it is just the exercise of my will keeping myself in his presence."[167]

What we have here is the spirit of nineteenth-century legalism removed from an objective to a subjective, inner sphere, with no gain in real rest for the weary soul. The struggle to control unwanted emotions (even to repress and lie about them) goes on at full speed, reinforced by the teaching that Jesus will not let you even *feel* angry if you are surrendered and trusting. The temptation to emulate others brings its own kind of bondage, which was not relieved by the tendency of Victorious Life teachers to dangle before their listeners the images of other Christians, superior to every circumstance, living lives of total victory. One can imagine the deep sense of pain and failure of those who heard Victorious Life teachers speak of their own lives as a continual spiritual high, or even in their admission of occasional failures giving the impression of a fullness of life unknown to most listeners. One such listener expressed it this way: "I believe the Holy Spirit is calling me into the Victorious Life, because he has given me such a longing for it. Those who are living it draw me as by some mighty power; yet it seems I cannot quite attain unto it. . . . Jesus does not always seem as real to me as others."[168] This woman was plagued by her own inability to live the life she imagined others to be living. Was she perhaps the victim of an unintended but nonetheless cruel hoax? Was she seduced by a fantasy of a trouble-free life whose foundation was in her desire to believe an illusion, fed by the salesman-like techniques of charismatic figures like Trumbull? For this woman and for many others, the Victorious Life made the burden of the self more, not less, burdensome.

Ultimately, this is the only course a religion can take. Religion, in its opposition to revelation, is never freeing, except in the most immediate and transitory sense. It offers the illusion of sight but the deepening of blindness, the illusion of healing at the cost of greater sickness. Religion, it seems, can be a very dark prison. When Christianity becomes a religion, as seems historically inevitable, it forsakes the revelation of God in Jesus Christ and congratulates itself instead on meeting human needs in human ways—that is, without passing through the resounding No of God's judgment and the eternal Yes of his mercy and forgiveness.

Jesus came preaching repentance—not as a step that places one legally within the family of God, not as a step to be accomplished once and for all in a revival service, but as a way of life. Martin Luther knew this: "When our Lord and Master Jesus Christ said 'Repent,' . . . he willed the entire life of believers to be one of repentance."[169] Surely this involves surrender, but not the proud surrender of "100 percent" of one's life to God, a life one expects to be perfect thereafter; rather, it involves the very surrender of one's calculated and pretentious surrender, the very surrender of one's plans for a life of happiness and moral rectitude. Paul called this surrender "a living sacrifice" (Rom. 12:1). Surely this life of repentance involves faith, but not the pragmatic faith that God will keep his Word and make one's life over as a visible demonstration of love and victory; rather, it is the faith that though one has not surrendered, and though one does not have faith, God will grant mercy, forgiveness, and pardon. And it is the faith that one's very faith, in its ambiguity and imperfection, will receive forgiveness, "a faith in which we can only cry and pray that God will help our unbelief."[170] This alone is the faith that gives glory to God and not to ourselves.

Surely this repentance also involves happiness, but not the happiness of one who finally has true character, who is never angry, never uncontrolled, always light of spirit and untroubled. Rather, this repentance offers the happiness of those who mourn, those who hunger, those who grieve for their own unbelief and the unbelief of others, those who, in the words of Paul, "groan." For when we face our own pretensions, our longing to be beyond the very need for repentance, and know that this must endure until our mortality puts on immortality—we groan. We groan for what we are, for our disobedience in the presence of God's faithfulness, for our solidarity with those who grieve him daily, for the offense we take at his forgiveness. We groan for the unfinishedness of this world, for the mess that we and our sins have made of it, for the prisons we have created in our religious fervor, for the human cost because men and women—and we above all—do not really believe.

And yet this very groaning is because we do believe—at least enough to repent for our own unbelief. For, like Paul, we await the full revealing of the sons of God, knowing that those who are not his sons he will call his sons (Rom. 8:19; Hos. 1:10). We groan "and long to put on our heavenly dwelling, so that by putting it on we may not be found naked" (II Cor. 5:2-3) And because we groan for that heavenly dwelling, we refuse to accept as substitutes any human techniques for the fabrication of this dwelling here below, as if by spiritual discipline we could ever cover our nakedness. And we groan "so that what is mortal may be swallowed up by life," and thus we refuse to identify as life and victory what are really death and defeat.

We are thus people of despair: despair for ourselves and our lack of repentance, for this world left to itself, and for the truth (since we must and will seize it for our purposes). Despair for these penultimate things, yes—but not for God! For we have confidence in the God who, in Jesus, "led a host of captives," and whose very repentance *in our place* offers a freedom (in hope) from our own captivity. Such confidence in God, and in the judgment that he delivered in our behalf by raising Jesus from the dead, releases us joyfully from the prison of our own religiosity, offers us permission not even to judge ourselves but to rest in a far kinder judgment. This is truly good news, news that encourages and comforts us in our despair, so that with Paul "we are always of good courage . . . for we walk by faith, not by sight" (Eph. 4:8; I Cor. 4:3; II Cor. 5:6-7). In Barth's words, we are a people of comforted groaning, of confident despair.[171]

In confident despair we wait. Not for Jesus to come and heal us by removing all troublesome feelings and making us happy. (Certainly he will heal us, but we know not when or how.) Not for instant happiness, since we know we are to fellowship in his sufferings. Not for a visible victory, since his victory in some way involves our own brokenness and defeat. Not indeed for anything that we would predict of Christian living, not for any visible affirmation of our belief, not for answers to our human needs as we would define them. We wait, in confident despair, for the God of mercy, who comes freely as a friend to one who is an enemy. In this confession and in repentance we wait. We wait not for healing but for mercy—for the mercy that ultimately heals.

Chapter V

They Have Healed My People Lightly

I

Many of the evangelicals living amid declining times at the turn of the century were not willing to give up on America. They understood what it meant to mourn, perhaps, but their mourning was for a recently lost evangelical dominance in America, not for a timeless, terminal condition. They did not consider it impossible for their countrymen to turn back to God and thus bring back the days, now viewed through a certain nostalgic haze, when Americans shared a moral and intellectual consensus, and good folks like themselves "ran the show."

Theological and psychological consistency might dictate that the dispensationalists and Victorious Life proponents would not be among these hopeful folk. Both had chosen to cope with the loss of evangelical social control by means other than the outright reestablishment of formal control over American life. It is quite obvious, however, that representatives of these groups were willing to make one last pitch for a Christian America. The long-established tradition that the United States is a nation especially loved and favored by God had taken deep root in evangelicals of all stripes; and it seemed inconceivable that God would abandon his people now—even if, as the dispensationalists among them believed, Jesus was about to return for his church. Wouldn't it be wonderful, they thought, if Jesus found faith on earth, particularly in the United States of America. And even though the Victorious Lifers were placing emphasis on privatized and spiritualized means of dealing with a wicked world, they could imagine that a nation whose citizens were just plain "defeated Christians" might be better than one comprised of rank unbelievers.

So a fairly large body of evangelicals could be aroused in support of a person or program that offered promise of the re-Christianization of the nation. And there was one such program—older, by far, than either dispensationalism or the Victorious Life theology. That program was revivalism, whose long history in America we have noted above, as well as its contribution, earlier in the nineteenth century, to the consolidation of an evangelical consensus and the expectation that the millennial age was just around the corner. The revival tradition proved remarkably adaptable to changing theological fashions during the late nineteenth and early twentieth centuries; in fact, it hardly missed a beat in moving from an association with postmillennial optimism to a cozy alignment with premillennial pessimism during these decades. This switch meant that it would harp a bit less on the social and political implications of conversion and confine itself a bit more to the state of the soul and personal moral issues than did the revivalism associated with Charles Finney. It also took on a somewhat more desperate tone, since there were now two different ways of going to hell at any moment: the unconverted person might die without Christ, or Christ might return—even before the meeting's end. This seemed to give a slight advantage to premillennial evangelism, as certain premillennialists claimed, and the growing numbers of revivalists and recorded conversions tended to support that conclusion. But beneath this premillennial revivalism lurked the suspicion that if God decided to throw the really big fuel on his revival fires, America might soon return to its former status as the unique national manifestation of God's elect.

Thus bad times for God's people were good times for a new breed of revivalist preachers, and by the late nineteenth century revivalism had become somewhat institutionalized in the evangelical church. A leading revivalist of the early nineteenth century, Asahel Nettleton, had rejected the notion that a church "could have a revival anytime" it wanted; he said that true revivals awaited "the sovereign interposition of God."[1] A half-century later, however, thanks to Finney, evangelical churches did not tend to take the freedom of God quite so seriously. The typical evangelical church engaged a professional evangelist for a regular visit each year—to revive the somnolent, heat up the lukewarm, prod the backsliders a bit, and add new converts to the membership rolls. This institutionalization seemed to be an acknowledgment that times were always troubled for God's people in the modern world, judgment was always nigh, and hence the Spirit of God had better be on duty on a more regular basis.

And revivalists abounded. During the late nineteenth century a goodly number of these modern-day circuit riders migrated with their stock sermons and stock altar calls from town to town. Many of them, certainly, knew the legendary reputation of Charles Finney, had perhaps even read his handbook on revivalism.[2] His efficient revival techniques were already being surpassed by those who counted themselves his disciples. The modern news media and religious press had begun to influence the climate of opinion in ways that we are well familiar with today. Headlines were made and newspapers sold because of the superstar, who was by definition one of a kind, generally the "greatest ever" of his kind. The rise and fall of the latest superstar was perhaps not quite as fickle and arbitrary a process in the nineteenth century as it would become in the twentieth, meaning that the "greatest ever" could actually stay in the limelight for as much as a decade as long as he continued to repeat his greatest successes. No doubt scores of small-town revivalists aspired to the superstar status in hopes of being used by God to effect the salvation of souls and the revival of a nation on a scale reminiscent of Finney, Lyman Beecher, or Jonathan Edwards. But only one could be Finney's successor.

The man who actually accomplished this feat for late nineteenth-century America was Dwight L. Moody. Moody was in many ways a typical man of his age. In his prime he was portly and solid of frame, indistinguishable from the ordinary businessman in dress and demeanor. He exuded nervous energy and deep earnestness—not for making money but for saving souls. In rough-hewn, mildly colloquial phrases and with a consummate storytelling skill, he pressed on his listeners the matchless love of Jesus Christ. His quiet self-confidence, charismatic warmth, and direct, often sentimental delivery brought home with surprising power the lack of spiritual reality—of an intimate and personal relationship with Jesus Christ—in the lives of his listeners, and filled his after-service "inquiry rooms" with church members seeking "assurance" and sinners seeking salvation. Along with Ira D. Sankey, his crowd-pleasing soloist and master of musical entertainment, Moody developed the techniques of revivalism, from prerevival planning through the actual conduct of the public services and the counseling of seeking souls, that would set the standard of successful evangelism in urban America for a quarter century.[3]

As a young man in his twenties, Moody had made himself a visible figure on the Chicago religious scene with startling success in street evangelism and Sunday school work. His leadership in the YMCA movement had also given him access to church leaders around the country and in England, where during an 1867 visit he made the acquaintance of leading evangelicals. Sometime around his thirtieth birthday, Moody seems to have entered a period of emotional and spiritual turmoil, which was punctuated by the temporary loss of his base of operations in the Chicago fire of 1871. A deep inner experience with God's Spirit brought him out of this period of restlessness with a renewed sense of direction and dedication to "preach Christ and work for souls." Almost immediately, in 1873, he launched a series of evangelistic meetings throughout England and Scotland that, after a slow start, began to attract large crowds and considerable press notices. His arrival for London meetings in early 1875 took on something of the character of a triumphal entry, and by the time he returned to New York later that summer, he was a national sensation in his own country.[4]

The next three or four years consolidated Moody's reputation as a successful revivalist in the leading cities of America, beginning in Brooklyn, Philadelphia, New York, Chicago, and Boston. Until well into the 1880s, he was able to capture headlines; and right up to his death in 1899, he continued to make revival services the backbone of his ministry. By then, however, he had also been instrumental in YMCA and student missions movements, had launched a successful summer Bible conference near his home in Northfield, Massachusetts, and had organized several educational institutions. He was also loosely associated with the popularization of dispensational premillennialism and the Keswick holiness movement in the United States. He was a major spokesman for the defense of the verbal inerrancy of the Bible against the liberal onslaughts of higher criticism. As Martin Marty writes, "At a critical stage of American religious history, [Moody] could plausibly have been called Mr. Revivalist and perhaps even Mr. Protestant."[5]

In terms of recapturing American culture for evangelicals, however, D. L. Moody's ministry was of strictly limited effect. In the lives of countless individuals, his preaching had certainly culminated in a new sense of spirituality and dedication to godly living. Among evangelicals, he had contributed to the popularization of new theological emphases that promised to uphold the faithful in their combat with an increasingly hostile and secularizing world. But he had not slowed down the inexorable dynamic of modernity and secularism in any perceptible way; nor had he offered particularly creative perspectives on that world or ways by which Christians could engage it meaningfully and still remain Christians. Toward the end of his life, Moody grew a bit more defensive and seemingly puzzled by the directions of American life and troubled by the waning welcome given his brand of revivalism by a Protestant clergy that seemed to be growing theologically more liberal by the day. His convivial spirit and broad-minded acceptance of those with differing points of view never really left him, but one could often hear in his later voice the wistfulness of one who wished that he had been able to leave behind a better world.[6]

By 1900, in other words, the tide in America had still not turned back to God, for all of Moody's exertions, and the evangelical hegemony so secure in the antebellum period seemed now in very serious jeopardy. The social problems that had become worrisome to the middle class—immigration, urbanization, labor organization, religious and behavioral pluralism—were not going away. The rift in evangelical ranks represented by the liberal "new theology" and the "social gospel" was beginning to look serious—and perhaps permanent. Still, the deep pessimism that would take hold by the 1920s was not yet the reigning spirit among evangelicals. The revivalist tradition naturally led most of them to expect little real improvement until Americans in large numbers turned back to Christ, though some had hopes that social conditions would improve if only existing Christians would join the moral and political battle against civic vices like prostitution, gambling, sabbath-breaking, the saloon, and political corruption. To most evangelicals, it seemed, the battle for a Christian America was not yet lost. Although the prospect looked dim, a residual optimism lay just below the surface in many an evangelical breast, ready to be activated by a positive turn of events.[7]

The first decade of the twentieth century offered what appeared to many evangelicals to be just that positive turn of events. It was a new century, to be sure, and with a new century often comes a sense of new prospects and new hopes. But more than that, this new century saw the birth of what would become revealingly known as the Progressive movement. For about a decade and a half, middle-class Americans and their political and cultural leaders supported a crusade to rid the American system of corrupt and unjust practices and to cleanse the wellsprings of democracy that had been fouled by a generation of breakneck social and economic changes. Large concentrations of economic power, both in industrial and banking circles, were brought under somewhat more effective government control; health and environmental hazards were addressed; entrenched political power was challenged, and there were new attempts to consult the will of the people rather than to knuckle under to the clout of the bosses. Working men and women, as well as their children, began to enjoy a modicum of government protection, and the poor received the attention of a first generation of idealistic social workers. The Progressive movement, by advertising the abuses of the system and by proposing remedies at various levels of government, encouraged both a sense of emergency (as if this generation were the last, best hope for the survival of the democratic system) and also a high sense of expectancy (as if fundamental reform and rejuvenation were genuine possibilities). Even among the intellectuals who spoke for progressive ideals one could hear echoes of nineteenth-century Protestant moral optimism and a revivalist energy that, though somewhat secularized, helped evangelicals feel at home with much of the progressive ethos.[8]

And yet, for most traditional evangelicals, the possibilities of progressive reform never really shook a deep-rooted assumption that institutional changes without the conversion of souls could not amount to much. A century of revivalism had only strengthened the belief of many of America's first settlers that good societies are made by good people and bad societies by bad people. Even an optimist like the young John Roach Straton, later to become one of fundamentalism's most prominent preachers, who believed that "the church of Jesus Christ needs to assume the position of leadership in social and political reforms," was quick to assume a traditional stance:

> The main point of emphasis, therefore, must continue to be regeneration, not reform; soteriology, not sociology. We may reconstruct society on the most ideally perfect lines, but we are still confronted with the sad fact that the human heart is "deceitful above all things, and desperately wicked," and that it must be changed before even ideally perfect social machinery will work. . . ."[9]

"Soul-winning power" is what Straton believed would eventually make a difference in healing America's "moral desolations." With soul-winning power, Christians could "wage a new warfare of aggression within the devil's own territory." "Our modern Christianity will prevail again," he said, "when it abandons the long-range methods and gets down once more in pulpit and pew to individual sacrifice and personal work for the salvation of the lost." This would require a "heroism within the ranks of the ministry," marked by sermons displaying "more of the fire of the prophet and less of the perfume of the priest," sermons with "less finish, but more force; less polish, but more power; less rhetoric, but more results." "There is therefore, as never before in the history of our world, the call to an enlightened, aggressive and blood-earnest evangelism."[10]

Even as Straton spoke, communities across the Midwest were being shaken by just such sermons. Church members and the unchurched alike were responding with enthusiasm to the soul-winning power of a man who was emerging as Moody's successor, the evangelistic superstar of the hour. His heroism was obvious to anyone who saw him, and though some questioned his enlightenment, none could say that his evangelism was not "aggressive and blood-earnest." One close observer called him "the most effective pulpit speaker that ever appeared in this country." In 1911 in Lima, Ohio, over 5,000 converts were counted, including "many of our strong and prominent men, the toilers in the shops, the public officials of the city, the representatives of the press, the doctors and lawyers." Nearly 300 high-school youths responded to the plea for conversion in a single evening. "In power of illustration, energy of diction, earnestness of spirit, and wealth of appropriate stories," this witness wrote, the evangelist "has not had a peer in the United States since Abraham Lincoln." It was his judgment that "Reverend W. A. Sunday is the greatest evangelist in the world."[11]

II

Billy Sunday began his adult life as a volunteer fireman and undertaker's assistant in Marshalltown, Iowa. There is little in the early record of his life to suggest that he would one day be hailed as the world's greatest evangelist. The Civil War had left him fatherless in 1862, when he was but a month old, and he passed his childhood in the custody first of his mother and stepfather, then of his grandparents, and finally of a home for war orphans. What really brought him to Marshalltown was the chance to use his running ability in a fire fighters' tournament. Sunday's big athletic break came when "Pop" Anson, manager of the Chicago Whitestockings, noticed his athletic ability and offered him a job playing baseball. Sunday left immediately for the big city, joining in the demographic shift that was remaking America in the late nineteenth century. He played baseball for eight years and finally resigned in 1891, at the height of his career, to go to work for the Chicago YMCA.

In the meantime Billy Sunday had become a fervent Christian. On a Sunday afternoon in 1886, he and a few teammates left a Chicago saloon and ran into an evangelistic group from the Pacific Garden Mission. Sunday accepted the invitation to come to the mission and, after several visits and under the influence of a motherly mission worker, he made a public confession of Christ as his Savior. He continued to play baseball another five years, but he gave up drinking with the boys, and he refused to play ball on Sunday. He also began lecturing in YMCAs in various league cities, took preparatory school courses, and joined a Presbyterian church in Chicago where his sweetheart, Helen Thompson, was a member. Billy married "Nell" in 1888, and it was she who apparently convinced him to quit baseball and "go into Christian work."[12]

After two years doing street evangelism, leading prayer meetings, and helping rescue alcoholics with the YMCA, Sunday took a job as administrative assistant to J. Wilbur Chapman, whom D. L. Moody described in 1895 as "the greatest evangelist in the country."[13] Sunday organized the advance preparations for Chapman's revivals in various cities, and then stayed on to see that things ran smoothly during the services. But quite suddenly, in 1895, Chapman left the revival circuit to accept a pastorate. Sunday considered returning to baseball; but when the ministers of Garner, Iowa, invited him to conduct revival services in their town, he agreed—and thus set his course on preaching for the next forty years.

There is every evidence that Billy Sunday was scared to death by his sudden elevation to the pulpit. Borrowing sermons from Chapman and mustering as much dignity as he could, however, he plunged in at Garner and was rewarded with almost one hundred conversions by the week's end. He immediately moved on to Sigourney, Iowa, where he attracted the largest audiences anyone could remember. The local newspaper editor noted that "he talks good sound sense, and has a way about him that people admire," and that "his sermons are similar to those of Mr. Moody." Billy moved on to Paunee City, Nebraska. After that, an invitation was never lacking. In the succeeding five years Sunday conducted more than sixty revival campaigns in small towns across the Midwest. He supported himself and his family by collecting a freewill offering at the end of each series of meetings, and he remembered later how meager his income had been: "I worked in one whiskey-soaked, gambling-cursed, jay-rube town out in the short-grass country on the kerosene circuit for two weeks and had one hundred and twenty-seven people accept Christ as their Saviour. They gave me thirty-three dollars."[14]

Sunday excelled from the very beginning, however, in the size of his audiences. Meeting halls large enough to hold his audiences were often hard to find. By 1898, Sunday was using tents, and by 1901 he was asking that special wooden tabernacles be built that could hold 1,000 or more. By 1905 some of these tabernacles were built to hold 4,000, and Sunday's campaigns could be expected to fill them. Even so, he was still primarily a small-town phenomenon until 1906. More than half the towns where he preached between 1896 and 1906 had populations of under 2,500, and only a couple lay outside the midwestern Corn Belt. He was a legitimate success, but still on a rather limited scale.

It was surely this success, however, that led him to begin revealing the "real" Billy Sunday. Gradually the dignity and reserve he had learned from Chapman melted away: he began to shed coat and collar and roll up his sleeves during his sermons; his language became more proudly colloquial, his speaking style more rhetorically flashy, his illustrative stories more lurid and sensational. He learned that the crowds loved to hear their enemies denounced, whether it be the local "booze gang," the cultured "society ladies," or the higher criticism. He marched, slid, lunged, and leaped on the platform, imitating every character in his Bible stories and declaiming sinners with his "power of ridicule and denunciation," working up the sweat of a champion gymnast in the course of each sermon. Early press reviews compared him to a whirlwind, headlining his "great vaudeville stunts in the tabernacle pulpit."[15]

By the time he had reached the height of his career, after 1910, he was speaking regularly to crowds of up to 20,000, and his sermons were fully choreographed stage shows that attracted the applause and laughter of his audiences, as if they were attending the theater. In one of his Boston meetings, early in 1917, Sunday was preaching on Solomon. He had just challenged the men in his audience to "take home a new daddy tonight" when, as a newspaper account described it, some frenzied impulse seemed to flash into the preacher's overwrought brain . . . suddenly, unaccountably, without an instant's warning came the outburst. With eyes shut tight, knees flexed, his body rising and falling to the rhythm of his words, with perspiration raining from his touselled, tossing head, with clenched fists beating the air, he hurled forth an astonishing torrent of adjectives: "Bull-necked, infamous, black-hearted, white-livered, hog-jowled, god-forsaken, hell-bound gang!" Dropping like lightning to the carpet he dealt the trapdoor a punishment of clattering blows . . . whirling about on hands and knees with the quickness of a cat and the rage of a tiger, he glanced at the first person who confronted him— one of the newspapermen. His expression was appalling. His contorted face was deep red, his eyes were bulging circles of white with blazing centers of fire, and his lips were drawn back from twin rows of white, tight-shut teeth. His breath came in gasps, and he squealed the impotent anger that no words could voice. Then, leaping to his feet, he dashed across the platform and spit over its edge a mouthful of white. As suddenly as it swept over him, his indignation spent itself. . . . Billy was himself again, laughing at his display of emotion and resuming his exposition of the case of King Solomon.[16]

This, of course, was what much of the crowd had come to see. During those long years on the "kerosene circuit" Sunday had clearly discovered that he possessed, in sheer native talent, the ability to hold an audience spellbound. Once he realized this, it was only a matter of time before he had married hard work in sermon preparation and a deep earnestness for the salvation of lost souls to his charismatic charm and genius as an entertainer: the combination made him the first national evangelical hero of the twentieth century.

In the early years he did all of it virtually by himself. His wife acted as business manager and led women's meetings, but Sunday himself handled most of the advance preparations, even to the construction of his own tents. In 1900 he followed what had become a standard revival formula by that time and hired a gospel singer to lead the musical service. In 1904 he augmented his staff with an assistant for advance preparations and a man to care for the tabernacles. In succeeding years he hired assistants to help in sermon preparation, in directing Bible studies, in public relations and other matters—until his staff was at twenty-three members by 1918. The key staff contribution was made by Homer A. Rodeheaver, who replaced Sunday's first soloist in 1910 and became famous for his ability to "warm up" a crowd with a combination of choral and instrumental music, spirited congregational singing, magic tricks, and good-humored stories. "Rody," as the crowds called him, displayed the "grace and politeness which gave tone and polish to the meetings, while Sunday's acrobatics and hoarse shouting provided the emotional fervor."[17]

As Sunday's staff grew, so did the efficiency of his operations. Unlike the revivalist R. A. Torrey and others, Sunday was never ashamed of the businesslike preparations that seemed to be required for a successful revival. "I am not only a preacher, but [a] businessman," he said. And he told the local ministers before each campaign, "You can't conduct business as you did twenty-five years ago, neither can you religion. This is a day of specialists." Sunday's specialists quickly displaced local leadership, dictating (and sometimes stage-managing) the kind of citywide invitation Sunday would accept, supervising the design and construction of the tabernacle, arranging for financial support, recruiting volunteer workers (choir members, ushers, doorkeepers, clerks, prayer-meeting leaders, personal workers, drivers, child-care staff, and others—a total of 50,000 persons for the New York City revival). Sunday's advance men saw to the formation and training of up to twenty local committees (e.g., shop work, publicity, printing, entertainment). They organized a network of "cottage prayer-meetings," led by volunteers twice a week— 79,784 of them during the Boston campaign. They arranged businessmen's lunches and fund-raising dinners; they generated public interest by getting constant coverage in the local press; they arranged for Sunday's triumphal entry into the city: bands, speeches by dignitaries, and parades. By the opening hymn of the first meeting, the city was generally gripped by such a feverish excitement that the success of the revival was virtually assured.[18]

Success, of course, meant big numbers. At the turn of the century, Americans were increasingly falling under the spell of big numbers. As a government statistician observed in 1914, "the science of statistics is the chief instrumentality through which the progress of civilization is measured. . . ."[19] For evangelical Christians the progress of religion could be expressed through statistics. Billy Sunday's statistics soon outshone those of any other revivalist, living or dead, and the press delivered a steady stream of them to a hungry public. When Sunday closed his campaign in Jefferson, Iowa, in January 1904, for example, the local paper published the statistical summary of his meetings in the center of its front page, including total conversions, attendance in the final meetings, various offerings, and "Jefferson's total investment." The headline read: "516 Turn To Christ," and under "Jefferson's Dividends on Investment" one read: "The conversion of more than half of the population outside the churches."[20] Thirteen years later, the New York newspapers published daily box scores of attendance and conversion figures during Sunday's meetings in that city, which revealed that by the end of the campaign 1,443,000 had attended and 98,204 had walked forward in answer to Sunday's invitations. Financial statistics were also public fare, particularly the expenses of each campaign, the contributions given to cover them, and Sunday's salary, often collected by local leaders using what some called high-pressure tactics on the last night of the revival. Cities vied to break each others' records in various categories, and Sunday was not above using the crowds' interest in big numbers and their competitiveness to urge them to ever-greater exertions.[21]

After 1912 the numbers got bigger as Sunday took his revivals from the small and medium-sized towns to the metropolises of the East. During the next six years he held major campaigns, lasting eight to ten weeks each, in Pittsburgh, Philadelphia, Baltimore, Atlanta, Boston, Los Angeles, Dallas, Detroit, Washington, D.C., and New York City. He had been slow to take up the challenge of the big cities because he had noticed that when he preached in Spokane and Toledo before 1912, his proportion of converts to population fell to 4 or 5 percent, while in the smaller towns of his pre–1908 campaigns he had been able to convert 20 percent of a town's population on the average. The percentage seemed important to him. But a series in Columbus, Ohio, where 10 percent of the population registered conversions, convinced him to head for the big cities he had so often used in his sermons as modern versions of the wicked biblical city of Babylon.[22]

He was never able to duplicate his earlier small-town proportions of converts to population in the bigger cities; but he was able to produce the spectacle of hundreds, sometimes thousands, of persons "hitting the sawdust trail"—that is, walking to the front to shake his hand and "stand up for Jesus"—at a single meeting. His methods were often calculated and always effective. Sunday usually delayed the first call for converts, or "trail-hitters," until well into the campaign, building the anticipation of audience and general public and inevitably producing a record number of trail-hitters when he finally issued the long-awaited call. In Boston, for example, Sunday waited until the tenth night, a men-only meeting attended by 11,000 members of the local churches' men's Bible classes. He concluded his sermon with a stirring story of a Scottish military hero, jumped up on a chair, and shouted,

> I seize the Cross of the Son of God and I wave it over this audience and hurl the heart of the Saviour out into the ranks of the manhood of Boston and as I do I cry aloud, "On, on Christ, and we will follow." How many of you will walk out and give me your hand and say, "I will live for Christ from now on the best I know how?" Come on. Come on. Come on.[23]

The crowd streamed forward, was directed by ushers into two lines, filed past Sunday for the ritual handshake, and was herded into a quickly cleared front section of seats. Rodeheaver's choir sang "Stand up, Stand up for Jesus" over and over, then switched to "We're Marching to Zion." The lines did not peter out for twenty minutes. Sunday assured the crowd that "God is proud of you. . . . Millions of people the country over are watching Boston," and he dismissed the meeting with a brief prayer for the trail-hitters. The converts filled out their decision cards, the crowds poured out of the exits, and the press rushed off to report a new record of 1,441 trail-hitters.[24]

This talent for enticing large numbers of people to file forward and shake his hand was what observers usually meant when they said, "Billy Sunday gets results." Local ministers, especially, were astounded by his ability to evoke religious enthusiasm in their parishioners—and indeed it was the parishioners who often responded to his invitations to "reconsecrate" their lives or to "get out fully for God."[25] In the early days of his career, small-town ministers testified almost breathlessly to the benefit Sunday brought to their churches and communities. A Presbyterian pastor in Colorado, writing about five months after a Sunday campaign in his town in 1905, claimed that his church gained 225 new members in one month. "I have a membership of over 800 now, none of whom are so regular in church attendance, so liberal in gifts, so interested in prayer-meeting and the church in general as the new converts. I have been surprised beyond measure and profoundly grateful. They were many of these enemies of the church but they have completely and unresistibly surrendered and are active for Christ."[26] Particularly in the smaller towns and cities, Sunday's meetings were big enough events to make a visible impact: to enlarge churches, change the lives of individuals in ways noticeable to their neighbors, even affect the general social and political climate for a short time. Statements like the one below point to very real effects, although they remain difficult to evaluate:

> Six hundred converts in the city of 1,800 inhabitants is the record. . . . The town was fairly revolutionized. Converts came from all walks of life. Many drunkards were reclaimed and while a very few of them have taken to their cups again, most of them are standing firm and the liquor traffic was given a hard blow. The four saloons here are slowly *starving to death.* . . .[27]

Or again:

> Previous to his coming to Carthage, it was a common thing to see advertised almost every week, card parties, telling who received the prizes, etc., among which were often church people. So far as I have observed since, no such news items appear and dancing was practically put out of business. . . . I think there has been a few small private dances possibly, but pains is rather taken to keep it quiet than to advertise it as heretofore.[28]

These kinds of results, attested by observers and noised abroad by the press, served to win over to Sunday's cause many who were originally skeptical. The logic of the numbers simply seemed irrefutable, as contemporaries testified again and again. "He uses language that seems to me entirely out of place," wrote a Presbyterian minister from Keokuk, Iowa, ". . . but at the close of that address which was the most offensive, there were nearly 150 men pressed forward to make confession of faith."[29] "His methods are peculiar," wrote another. "I was not in love with him before he came and could by no means have unreservedly endorsed him. My opinion entirely changed as the meetings progressed." This minister then followed with a report of numbers of conversions and new church members.[30] Another minister described his ambivalence in terms that appear caricatured: "Why, my dear sir, the man has trampled all over me and my theology. He has kicked my teachings up and down that platform like a football. He has outraged every ideal I have had regarding my sacred profession. But what does that count against the results he has accomplished? My congregation will be increased by hundreds."[31] Whether caricature or not, it is a fact that at the peak of his career—between 1912 and 1917—Billy Sunday had attracted the support of virtually all evangelical groups and their leaders—and many of the theologically liberal as well.[32] The president of Brown University was quoted as saying, "God bless any man who, by any method, can reach the hearts of men."[33]

Billy Sunday felt exactly the same way about it. "I'd stand on my head in a mud puddle," he said, "if I thought it would help me win souls to Christ." When critics complained about his liberal use of slang expressions in preaching, he responded, "It wins converts."[34] Many agreed with him and thus not only endured his offenses to their dignity but became his enthusiastic supporters. But the numbers were not the only thing Sunday had going for him. From all accounts, to be in his presence was just plain intoxicating. You may find his language "vulgar, hard and harsh" on the written page, said one, but in person, his "broad smiles" and his "tenderness, pity and compassion" take away the sting.[35] In an auditorium filled with 20,000 people, Sunday seemed able to establish a personal rapport with each individual. Even the caustic H. L. Mencken fell for him: "Many persons in that crowd, I dare say, came away with a certain respect for the whirling doctor's earnestness, and a keen sense of his personal charm—as I did myself." The bitter critic John Reed, who considered Sunday a positively evil force in America, nonetheless summarized the almost universal opinion of America's favorite revivalist: "Everyone who talks to him loves him."[36]

III

Those who loved Billy Sunday best were the millions of evangelical Americans who made him their champion and who counted on him to change the course of history. On this one man's shoulders, in the eyes of many, suddenly fell the formidable task of bringing America back to God and ending a period of disorientation and confusion for God's people. This man would stop the drift toward moral anarchy; he would convince America that it was flirting with God's judgment, and he would point to the way of salvation.

At its simplest level this meant converting sinners into Christians. If enough sinners became Christians—so went the formula—America would come back to God. Billy Sunday subscribed to this formula and seemed to agree that changing sinners into Christians was technically his first responsibility as a great revivalist. As we have seen, he took a certain pride in being able to produce this conversion experience in a predictable portion of each local population. The numbers of converts seemed to be a measure of how quickly and completely America was returning to God. And like all revivalists, he felt that returning to God was a fairly simple matter: his job was to present the gospel so plainly that only a fool would find it resistible.

Like many other revivalists of his day, though perhaps more outspokenly than most, Billy Sunday felt that too much theological training could get in the way of carrying out this mandate. His preaching was a culmination of two hundred years of a successively more distant relationship between revivalism and theology. In Jonathan Edwards, spiritual revival had been considered to be an outgrowth of good theology made alive by the Holy Spirit. But since it was only God's Spirit that animated revival, good theology alone could not guarantee spiritual awakening. A century later, Lyman Beecher and Charles Finney seemed to be asking the pragmatic question: what kind of theology does it take to guarantee revival? Their theological innovations were their answers to this practical need. Still, they honored the importance of theology and considered their own speculations to be part of a long theological tradition dating back to the Reformation. By contrast, D. L. Moody and Billy Sunday were virtually unlettered and on the whole uninterested in theology. They completed the logic of Beecher's and Finney's surrender to pragmatism, in effect wondering why, if souls were being saved, any theology at all was needed.

Many of Billy Sunday's supporters explicitly accepted this logic. As we have seen, even the minister whose theology Sunday "trampled all over" could not withhold support when such trampling promised multitudes of new church members. When the Princeton theologian Dr. Charles Erdman introduced Sunday at the New York revival in 1917, he must have known that Sunday ignored many of the values Princeton held dear; and yet Erdman ranked him second only to Jesus himself as a promulgator of the gospel.[37] When Sunday had applied for ordination in Erdman's own Presbyterian denomination in 1903, he had declined to answer many of the theological questions during his examination, claiming that they were "too deep for me." One of the examiners recommended—and the rest agreed—that the interview be cut short and Sunday ordained, since "God has used him to win more souls to Christ than all of us combined."[38] Sunday liked to observe that a knowledge of theology had nothing to do with the fate of a person's soul. "I don't care if you're ten miles off in theology if you're right in your heart. Nobody was ever kept out of heaven because he didn't know theology."[39] He admitted that this generalization included himself: "I don't know any more about theology than a jackrabbit knows about ping-pong, but I'm on my way to glory."[40]

Getting others to join him on his way to glory was Sunday's task, and he did this by preaching the gospel. He thought that the gospel could be summarized in just a few words: "Good news I bring you people. You need not go to hell if you will accept the Christ that I preach to you." He was not above rephrasing it a little more menacingly for impact: "And the gospel of God is, 'Repent or you will go to hell.' "[41] Like most evangelicals and all revivalists of note, Sunday believed in a literal heaven and a literal hell where the souls of the saved and the damned would receive their just rewards in the next life. Sunday believed that virtually everyone accepted these realities—those who did not he called "degenerate."[42] He seemed to enjoy preaching about hell and used the word often in his sermons.[43] And he did not think it improper to use the prospect of eternal torment as an encouragement to repentance. "You are going to live forever in heaven, or you are going to live forever in hell," he would say. "There's no other place—just the two. It is for you to decide . . . and you must decide now."[44]

No decision at all, of course, was actually a decision for hell. Ever since Adam and Eve disobeyed God, our inclination has been to sin, which Sunday thought was obvious to anyone; and he chose to illustrate it by using some very obvious examples: the arrest of "three women taken from some drunken debauch . . . dirty and bleary-eyed" and speaking profanity. "There is sin," he said; its existence is beyond debate. Since we are all sinners, we are all lost. "A sinner has no standing with God."[45] To have no standing means to be destined for hell, the proper reward for people who cannot stop committing sin.

Sunday admitted that this did not sound like good news. He insisted, though, that unless one took this lostness seriously, he or she would not be ready to hear the really good news when it came. When the good news comes, it is that God has, in his love, provided a means of salvation, but only for those who know they are lost.

Now God doesn't tell you that you are lost, and on the road to hell, and then leave you, but he tells you that you are on the road to hell, and he says, "I have sent a guide, my Son, to lead you out, and to lead you back to peace and salvation." That's good news. . . . That's gospel; that's good news that tells a man that he needn't go to hell unless he wants to.[46]

God wants every sinner to be saved, and he has established a "plan of redemption" whereby anyone who is willing to "comply with his requirements" is entitled to enter heaven.[47] These requirements are simply that sinners repent and accept Jesus Christ as their personal Savior. It is as simple as that: "With Jesus you are saved, without Him you are lost."[48] It is Jesus and Jesus alone who, by dying on the cross, finished the work of redemption and made it possible for those who believe in him to be saved.

Sunday admitted that the precise way in which Christ "atoned" for our sins was perhaps the primary source of doctrinal disagreement within the church. His own interpretation was fairly simple. Someone had to die for the sins of the people in order to satisfy God's sense of justice and to free sinners from their deserved condemnation in hell. In Old Testament times the Jews shed the blood of animals to make atonement for sins of disobedience to the law of Moses. Then Jesus came and shed his blood on the cross, allowing God to remove the condemnation from all of our heads. "God says, 'If you will accept Jesus Christ as your Saviour, I will put it to your credit as though you kept the law.' And it's Jesus Christ or hell for every man or woman on God Almighty's dirt." It is Jesus' shed blood, and it alone, that saves. "When someone tells you that your religion is a bloody religion and the Bible is a bloody book, tell them yes, Christianity is a bloody religion, the gospel is a bloody gospel, the Bible is a bloody book, the plan of redemption is bloody. . . . Jesus has paid for your sins with his blood. The doctrine of universal salvation is a lie. I wish everyone would be saved but they won't. You will never be saved if you reject the blood."[49]

Sunday saw his role as an evangelist as announcing this good news of salvation through the blood of Christ, and to get people to accept it. He did not seem to think that it generally took much more than common sense to lead one to acceptance. Although in one breath he would describe his message as "not from human reason," in the next he would aver that "most men have sense" enough to believe in God and the doctrine of eternal reward and punishment, and he would characterize the gospel as eminently "reasonable." Conversion appeared in his sermons as less a moment of crisis for the whole person than a simple assent to God's logical plan. In one sermon he appealed to simple prudence: I do not expect to die soon, he told his audience, but because I may, "I carry thousands of dollars of life insurance." By the same token, the skeptic may not know for sure that there is a hell, but he ought to try to be ready for it, just in case there is. And by doing so, Sunday claimed, I will be ahead in this life too: "I will live longer, be happier, and have lost nothing by believing and obeying the Bible, even if there is no hell. But suppose there is a hell? Then I'm saved and you are the fool. I have beat you again." Coming to Christ seemed to be a simple choice of the common sense, a choice that any man or woman with natural intelligence could make.[50]

Once a person made this decision to "believe on the Lord Jesus Christ," he or she was crossing the line, as Sunday put it, from "the devil's side" to God's side. The decision could be very quick, without struggle—a simple assent of heart and mind—and instantly salvation was accomplished. Sunday illustrated this moment of conversion by the example of the disciple Matthew, the tax collector, who heard Jesus and immediately rose to follow him: "You can be converted just as quickly as Matthew was. How long did that conversion take? . . . And you tell me you can't make an instant decision to please God? The decision of Matthew proves that you can. While he was sitting at his desk he was not a disciple. The instant he arose he was. That move changed his attitude toward God. Then he ceased to do evil and commenced to do good."[51]

This, then, is the good news—that sinners can be saved in an instant and know that they are "on their way to glory." In that he was an evangelist, Billy Sunday preached this good news and used every persuasive technique in his repertoire to win adherents. Yet, a survey of his sermons reveals that he did not very often make this gospel the overriding focus of his preaching. A reference to this "plan of redemption" was often to be found somewhere in the sermon, but not as the center of attention. Reading his sermons, one gets the curious but distinct impression that this gospel was really not his message at all—at least not where he became most exercised, where he put his emphasis, where he spoke most concretely, or where he received the most enjoyment. He seems to have had another agenda.

That agenda, I believe, was to interpret for his audiences the nature of the world in which they lived and to provide a formula by which they might once again exert an influence over that world. In other words, the evangelical Christians who flocked to his meetings were coming to hear a modern-day prophet, one who could give them God's explanation for their confusion and sense of loss and offer them God's prescription for a remedy. These Christians were perfectly happy to have their prophet package his message in the traditional revivalist rituals. They were not averse to hearing the standard gospel formulas preached, since to hear their own ideas repeated in public could be quite comforting. And their sense of being part of a powerful popular movement, of course, must have been dramatically enhanced by the hundreds of trail-hitters who choked the aisles at the meeting's end. But what Christians most came to hear, I suspect, was not this repetition of a formula they knew so well; at least, that formula is not what drew the deafening ovations. What they came for was an interpretation of the signs of the times—one that sounded true to them—and a means by which they could again dominate those times.

Billy Sunday's genius was that he knew how to do this, and how to do it in an electrifying and entertaining fashion. He defended his rambling preaching style by admitting, "If I don't stick to my text I stick to my crowd."[52] And he was a master at understanding and managing his crowds. He held thousands spellbound, speaking instinctively to deep spiritual needs of which they and he were only dimly aware on a conscious level. He took his audiences with him from hilarious laughter to "righteous" anger to tearful sentimentality. He played the role of friend, of father, of practical joker, of judge, of comforter, of inspirer, and finally of something close to God himself as he welcomed the trail-hitters into the kingdom with his famous handshake. And all this because he knew that what they wanted was really not the simple gospel but a way to control their lives and their history. Sunday played that prophetic role more successfully than has any other evangelical spokesperson of his time.

What were the signs of the times, according to this prophet? Sunday confirmed in his listeners what, no doubt, they already knew. The times were very bad, and the evidence was all around in the disastrous state of personal morality. Sunday was never more impassioned, never more obviously exercised and earnest, than when delivering this message: America is a moral cesspool. Something has happened to this nation, he said, this country founded by Christians and blessed and protected by God.[53] This people of moral strength and principle has recently grown flabby; somehow whole communities have fallen under the influence of "damnable, hell-born, whisky-soaked, hog-jowled, rum-soaked moral assassins."[54] Instead of "civic righteousness," we have "graft in high places," and the political system is in the hands of "a gang of devils," who rule in the name of fraud, injustice, office-seeking, and wastefulness. An "avalanche of vice" threatens the nation, a "tidal wave of intemperance and dissipation . . . threatens the young manhood of our land and imperils our destiny as a nation."[55] On every hand one sees it: "misery and sorrow and corruption," "poverty and wretchedness, and disease, and death, and damnation. . . ."[56] America is in deep trouble.

One could scarcely attend one Billy Sunday revival without hearing some memorable version of this message. Indeed, Sunday's eloquent portrayals of the boundless sins of America were his most entertaining, crowd-pleasing moments. Audiences were awed by his "biting, blister-ing, blasting condemnation of sin."[57] One journalist called a Billy Sunday sermon a "drama of sin."[58] Another said, "Mr. Sunday's preaching makes men loathe sin."[59] The official souvenir program printed for Sun-day's Spokane meetings called Sunday a "rigid adherer to Gospel truth," but then quickly moved on to the primary source of his appeal:

> Theology he does not discuss, but the sins of the sinful, the backslidings of the backslider, the formalities of the formal, the hypocrisies of the hypocrit [sic], the skepticism of the skeptic, the liar, the adulterer, extortioner, boozer, indolent worthless rich, the divorcee, prostitute, saloonist, and dudish—people in the church and out, all share in his acrobatic, dramatic, linguistic sermons . . . every effort is directed to the unmasking of sin in all its forms in church, lodge, club, society, business and professional life, in both high and low.[60]

When contemporaries characterized Sunday's sermons, they most often referred to his famous denunciations of sin. And Sunday himself would have accepted this description. He believed, he said, in calling sins "by their right names."[61] "I will try to disgust you with your sin until you turn away from it," he said. "That's my business."[62]

In lurid detail, and to the delight and horror of his audiences, Sunday spelled out the sins into which those "moral assassins" had led a once-righteous America. If one was to put together what emerges in seemingly random fashion from his many sermons, one would not get a pretty picture. The American home was an unsightly mess; if Jesus had come to it, he would have found beer in the refrigerator, playing cards on the table, "nasty music on the piano," and cigarettes (location unspecified). The husband was all too often a "cigarette-smoking, cursing, damnable libertine" who played poker, spent his money on his own pleasures while his wife and children suffered, abused his wife, growled at and beat his children, taught his sons to smoke, drink, and chew. The wife tended to spend money on "fool hats and card parties" and cosmetics, driving the husband away with her "badly cooked meals" while her children ran the streets, "learning to be hoodlums," looking like "a rummage sale in a second-hand store; with uncombed hair, ripped pants, buttons off, stock-ings hanging down." Instead of praying with their children, parents were taking them to "dancing schools and haunts of sin," serving them liquor, letting them "gad about the streets with every Tom, Dick and Harry, or keep company with some little jack rabbit whose character would make a black mark on some piece of tar paper." It was no wonder to Sunday that criminals in prison "blame their mothers for their being where they are."[63]

Indeed, lives of crime seemed to be the fate of many young American men. They associated with "godless, good-for-nothing gang[s] that blaspheme and sneer at religion," who were "character assassins." They learned to swear, to become "staggering, muttering, bleary-eyed, foul-mouthed down-and-outer[s]," to laugh at the "smutty story." Eventually they would become "wrecks" drifting in "the seas of lust and passion." Their sisters kept bad company and hung out in ballrooms, the "moral graveyards" that "are wrecking the virtue of our girls" and leading almost invariably to lives of prostitution.[64] Because their mothers allowed them to, they tended to "float around town and joyride and hit the cabarets till two o'clock in the morning with a counterfeit sport with weak jaws and weaker morals, puffy eyelids, green vest, pair of spats on. . . ." A mother who did not prevent her daughter from being "pawed over by every yap in the community" was "opening the front door and inviting sin and disgrace to cover her threshold."[65] According to Sunday, "the average girl today no longer looks forward to motherhood as the crowning glory of womanhood. She is turning her home into a gambling shop and a social beer-and-champagne drinking joint, and her society is made up of poker players, champagne, wine and beer drinkers, grass widowers and jilted jades and slander-mongers. . . . She is becoming a matinee-gadder and fudge eater."[66]

Billy Sunday reserved some of his most blistering scorn for these "society women":

> I believe the most God-forsaken, good do-for-nothing, useless woman on earth is an American society woman whose life is frappes and there is nothing, my friends, to her but a frame upon which to hang fashionable clothes, and a digestive apparatus to digest highly seasoned foods. . . . Hags of uncleanness today, they walk our streets, they ride in their limousines, sail in their private yachts, they look from behind French plate glass and hide behind rich tapestries . . . they quaff their wine from gold and silver tankards and they eat from Haviland or hand-painted china, and society today, my friend, is fast hastening to the judgment that overtook Pompeii, Herculaneum and Sodom and Gomorrah, when God Almighty made old Mount Vesuvius vomit and puke in a hemorrhage of lava.[67]

But the sins of high society were simply the counterpart of the sins of low society, "the impurity that lurks in the alley and in the cellar and in the fan tan, the opium joints and the coke joints . . . the stale beer joints. . . ."[68] One major manifestation of this impurity was the "disreputable house," or house of prostitution, which, to hear Sunday describe it, was fast becoming one of the most prominent features of city life in America. He informed his New York audience in 1917 that "every year 60,000 girls are robbed of their virtue, 5,000 a month, 168 every day."[69] In one town alone, Sunday boasted, his preaching had closed down four of these "disorderly houses," with the girls fleeing home to their mothers. Sometimes Sunday described these prostitutes as wicked, diseased women; at other times he painted them as victims of unprincipled, money-hungry men who drugged them and dragged them into lives of slavery. He encouraged his audiences to "rid the world of those despicable beasts who live off the earnings of the unfortunate girl who is merchandising herself for gain."[70] Sunday's description of this traffic in human bodies was so graphic that, as one observer noted, "men fainted here and there as he explained, in blunt language that the man in the street could understand, the diseases and ravages caused by the sin of impurity—diseases that fasten themselves upon innocent wives and children of men who have broken God's laws of chastity."[71]

The same observer went on to say, however, that "the climax of the enthusiasm . . . was reached when Sunday for fifteen minutes poured out his defiance and arraignment of the liquor traffic." As serious as was the scourge of prostitution, it had to take second place to Sunday's favorite whipping boy, the saloon. Sunday devoted at least one sermon to the liquor traffic in each of his campaigns; it was invariably his most popular sermon and was interrupted by applause over and over again. To hear him describe it, the saloon was a ubiquitous establishment in America. "We have in this country 250,000 saloons," he said, "and allowing fifty feet frontage for each saloon it makes a street from New York to Chicago and 5,000,000 men, women and children go daily into the saloon for drink. And marching twenty miles a day it would take thirty days to pass this building, and marching five abreast they would reach 590 miles. There they go; look at them!" Every year a half million young men entered the saloon, he said, and at year's end "165,000 have lost their appetites and have become muttering, bleary-eyed drunkards, wallowing in their own excrement. . . . In an hour twelve men die drunkards, 300 a day, and 110,000 a year."[72] In a later sermon, the figure had grown to 600,000 men each year, "staggering and reeling and screaming into drunkards' graves and drunkards' hell."[73]

Sunday did not hesitate to link the saloon to virtually everything American evangelicals feared and hated. Most of the crime, most of the paupers, idiots, suicides, most of the wife- and child-beating, most of the murders of friends, children, and mothers were traceable to the saloon. Dramatic, sentimental stories of drunken sons rejecting the pleas of their mothers, eventually murdering family members or friends, captivated Sunday's audiences. Whiskey was responsible for 865,000 orphan children in the United States, for the destruction of countless homes, for children going naked. Because of whiskey, the city streets were choked with talented young and old men who had lost respectable jobs, deserted their families, and were living out their miserable days in the gutter. In the saloon, men hatched political plots against the government and planned crime. "The saloon is the sum of all villainies. It is worse than war or pestilence. It is the crime of crimes. It is the parent of crimes and the mother of sins. It is the appalling source of misery and crime in the land. And to license such an incarnate fiend of hell is the dirtiest, low-down, damnable business on top of this old earth."[74]

So the bad news about America, according to the prophet Sunday, was very bad indeed. Riddled with red light districts, saturated with saloons, stained by selfish and immoral parents, its youth ruined by luxury and exploited by traffickers in vice and degradation, criminals filling its prisons, its political processes corrupted by "good-for-nothing, modern, beer-soaked, tin-horned, grafting, two-by-four, pliable, plastic, whiskey-soaked politicians"—surely the likes had not been seen since the days of Sodom.[75] Surely, Americans were tempting God to "purify" their nation, "whether . . . with a fire or with a flood or with a famine or with a pestilence or with a war. . . . You can't defy God all your days and lift your puny, infinitesimal, mediocre, pigmy selves up in defiance of the omnipotent and omnipresent God. No! No!"[76] Could anything possibly avert the just condemnation of a wicked and wanton people?

There was indeed, in Billy Sunday's mind, a course of action that could avert God's judgment, and here lay the good news in his prophetic message. On the whole—and contrary to the impression Sunday gave when railing on America's sins—the people of this country were good folks with generally high moral standards and sound instincts. "Pigmy selves" though they were in their moments of moral weakness and self-indulgence, another possibility lay open to them, an invitation, in the words of a sermon title, to "be strong, and show yourself a man." For as Sunday quoted it,

> From California's golden shores
> To Dixie's sunny land,
> In East and West and North and South,
> In valley, plain and glen,
> The call of God is ringing loud
> For valiant, noble men.[77]

True, America was in trouble. But there was nothing wrong with it that a strong dose of "real manhood" (occasionally Sunday added "real womanhood") could not fix. And "real manhood" was within the reach of every listener in his audience—by extension, every male citizen of the United States.

Some of Billy Sunday's most popular and widely quoted sermons were those he delivered to men only, which he did several times during each major campaign. These sermons, of course, were laden with references to manhood, its necessity and its character. But a survey of the sermons he preached to mixed audiences shows that even then his concern for manhood was one of his most consistent themes, perhaps second in importance only to his nearly obsessive preoccupation with the evils of the saloon. In the attention he gave to manhood, Sunday considered himself simply to be taking his cue from Scripture. "Nobody can read the Bible thoroughly and thoughtfully and earnestly," he asserted, "and not be impressed with the fact that it makes a great deal out of manhood and holds it up as something that should be sought after with diligence and perseverance." The Old Testament in particular, Sunday believed, "exalts and emphasizes and shows what real, true manhood is." In its pages one reads of the "colossal manhood of Abram" and the "rugged manhood of Caleb" and the "princely manhood" of Moses. Job, David, Joseph, and Daniel are all men whose "lives are worthy to emulate. . . . God wants us to see what real manhood and real womanhood is and to become enamored of it." "God loves to watch a real man go and grow. The Bible dwells on the manly things about a man." Since it was the Bible's concern, Sunday felt justified in making it his concern. Indeed, he felt that his sinful nation might actually be rescued if it began to honor the simple biblical encouragement to real manhood.

What is this real manhood the Bible presumably speaks of? It is first of all characterized by nobility and tenacity of purpose. When David, nearing death, instructed Solomon to "be thou strong and shew thyself a man," he "wanted Solomon anchored to a noble purpose, he didn't want him to drift aimlessly like a log in a whirlpool. He wanted him to have his eye on something worth while." David himself was the outstanding model of high purpose, as he showed in rising from shepherd boy to king of Israel. "Aim high," Sunday urged. "Without a definite, ever-mastering purpose in life, failure is the certain result. . . . You will get out of life just what you look for." Sunday assured his listeners that God despises failure, that he wants everyone "to win out in this old world."[78] To win out, one cannot be a "zigzagger" but must have a "definite aim" and not turn aside from pursuing it. "And the man who devotes himself and time and skill and energy to one thing is the man that will stand before a king."[79]

Sunday did not make clear exactly what a high or noble purpose might be. At times, it seemed, he was describing simple ambition to be the best in one's field, whether it be "religion, business, politics." This ambition had to be realistic, however, since "it's eagerness to achieve success in realms you can't reach that creates the hells that curse the world." So aiming high might mean being the very best farmer one can be. "The plowman who plows the field to win fame and fortune for his wife and children is better than the financial shylock in Wall Street. . . ." On the other hand, so many of his nonbiblical examples of high purpose were millionaires, political leaders, and generals, that one wonders whether Sunday believed David could have shown high purpose if he had chosen to remain a shepherd. Nobility of purpose did seem to imply a certain upward social mobility and a desire to escape anonymity. "Obscurity didn't keep Tom Edison a train butcher" or "Ben Franklin walking the streets of Philadelphia gnawing a loaf of dry bread." Occasionally, Sunday simply expressed this as a refusal to be a "little man" when one could be a "big man." Here again, David was an example: He "threw the shepherd's crook down in the pasture and picked up the crown . . . and put it on his bean and climbed up on the throne and sat down," and "God said to him, 'Dave, you're a man after my own heart.'" The lesson of this story, according to Sunday, was as follows:

> The humility that wants to remain little, simply because it's easier to loaf under the shade . . . is something vastly different, young people, from that magnificent manhood who will pull off his coat, sell it, and with the money buy a sword and then leap out into the arena of the world's conflicts and drive that sword to the very hilt in the putrifying abscesses that bore their way toward our spiritual and moral vitals to leave your young men and young women pieces of human driftwood out upon the high seas of lust and of passion and of wreckage.[80]

Often, it seemed, nobility of purpose involved this willingness to despise evil and fight for the right, specifically by casting a ballot for Prohibition. Men could show their manhood, Sunday preached, by fighting the curse of liquor. "In the name of your manhood," he said, "I beseech you, make a fight for the women who wait until the saloons spew out their husbands and their sons, and send them home maudlin, brutish, devilish, stinking, blear-eyed, bloated-faced drunkards."[81] And of course, nobility of purpose implied keeping oneself to the highest moral standards in every area of life, which obviously ruled out cursing, dirty stories, smoking, drinking, lying, masturbating, sexual profligacy, and all the other indecencies that were plaguing America in his day.

Nobility of purpose was of no avail, however, unless the other manly traits accompanied it. Foremost among these was determination. "Once you have made your plan, cling to it," Sunday preached. "Be a man even in situations of great danger."[82] "Nail your flag to a mast with nails that clinch."[83] "The rich jewels of manhood and womanhood are for the man or the woman who is determined to kill all the lions, swim all the streams, tunnel all the mountains . . . uproot all the trees that impede your progress and keep you from this goal. . . ."[84] Such determination would not flag even if one had to endure great hardship; in fact, the real man shunned a life of ease: "Don't spend much time in looking for an easy chair, with a soft cushion on it, if you would write your name high in the hall of fame where the names of real men are found."[85] Real men showed courage. Sunday professed to hate cowards but to admire men who showed "grit." "Grit," he explained, is "the Samson in you that doesn't get cold feet when the lions roar . . . . Grit! That's the Abraham Lincoln in you that will save nations." Grit also meant standing firm on moral principle, saying no "so loud that all hell can hear you, when you are tempted to do wrong."[86] Joseph had this kind of grit when, faced with the blandishments of Potiphar's wife, "he looked her square in the eye and passed her up." Daniel showed grit when "he refused to hit the booze and he stood four square for God. . . ."[87] Sunday claimed that the men of the Bible were examples to us in that they faced "the same temptations as the men of today, but they didn't let their temptations get the best of them."[88] "Let your life be directed by principle," he said, "and not by impulse . . . decide that you will not yield to sin when temptation beats against you." In all these ways, Sunday urged, be men of "honor."

Such manhood, Sunday had no doubt, would require a certain toughness: "What one needs and what the world needs is men and women who are solid mahogany all the way through." Physical size was not required, he thought, since "there are men who are small in stature, but they are noble in manhood, men like Paul, men like Julius Caesar . . . men like Napoleon, only five feet, four inches high and yet every time his old heart beat and his temples throbbed, the old moss-covered thrones in Europe trembled."[89] Sunday often repeated his contention that "you can't measure manhood with a tape line around the biceps."[90] On the other hand, God wants us to be what David desired for Solomon—not "an old woman and a sort of a sissified proposition," but "a man with knotted muscles and with a great, big heart and plenty of gray matter in his brain." Throughout this sermon on manhood, Sunday called out to his audience, "Be strong! Be strong!" The world, he said, is looking for real men, strong men, men it can admire. A strong man is immediately recognized, and he transforms his environment. "When David comes before you, you take your hat off, the weather changes . . . the birds come back . . . grass turns green . . . all nature claps her hands." Sunday urged especially his younger listeners to look for these strong men, and to "walk by their side." "Eat and drink manhood and womanhood in this old world," he recommended. And when you do this, when you "get your eye on somebody that is bigger than you, when you see what it is to be a real man or woman, you need something I want to tell you about . . . and that is Jesus Christ."[91]

The climax of Sunday's prophetic prescription was that manhood had something to do with Jesus Christ. Exactly how this was so he never very satisfactorily explained. He did contend that in Jesus Christ we find "the definition of manhood" and that one cannot know the meaning of manhood except through God's "revelation of manhood" in Jesus Christ.[92] But he never went any further than this. He never identified in Scripture's portrayal of Jesus the traits of real manhood that he identified so readily in the likes of Napoleon and Lincoln, and that he thundered so eloquently from the pulpit. He undertook no examination, systematic or otherwise, of the personality traits or "character" of Jesus. On this he was strangely silent, and one suspects that, his claim notwithstanding, he did not derive his definition of manhood from Jesus Christ but from the common understandings of middle-class Americans in his time.

Jesus Christ did, however, seem to have something to do with the possibility of one's attaining real manhood. Without Jesus, an important ingredient in manhood is missing: "Here a lot of you are trying to build character," he said, "but you are leaving God out; you will lose as sure as you breathe. You can't build and win without Jesus Christ. I don't give a picayune who you are. You can't win. So, stick in your education; crowd in your physical development, but if you leave Jesus Christ out of your proposition, you are gone."[93] A certain ambiguity remains in this formulation: is Jesus an "ingredient" in character in the sense that one "trait" of a real man is Christian faith? Or is Jesus the motive power for real manhood? I can find no statements by Sunday to clarify this issue, although he may have had both meanings in view.[94] The words Sunday used in inviting sinners to respond at the end of one of his meetings seem to indicate that, in some almost magical way, Jesus makes a person manly.

> So, now, Jesus, we pray that Thou wilt help this vast throng, thousands of them to come and say, "Here's my hand, I will do my best to serve Jesus. I will crown Him, I will give Him the place in my life, I will be strong, I will be a man, I will be a woman, not simply in physique, not because I top the scales at a hundred or a hundred and fifty, but because Jesus is in my heart. . . ."[95]

In some not very clearly defined way, Sunday seems to have believed that conversion to Jesus Christ could be of instrumental value in the attainment of manhood.

He was very clear, on the other hand, that the actual decision to follow

Christ, to proclaim it publicly by stepping out in a revival meeting, and to live the life of a Christian required an especially courageous form of manliness. "Many think a Christian has to be a sort of dishrag proposition, a wishy-washy, sissified sort of a galoot that lets everybody make a doormat out of him. Let me tell you the manliest man is the man who will acknowledge Jesus Christ."[96] In Sunday's opinion, "the manliest man and the womanliest woman that breathes is one who has grit or courage to take his or her stand for Jesus Christ."[97] Sunday taunted his audiences, suggesting that it was their cowardice that kept them from responding to his pleas:

> Oh, do you want to know why you are not a Christian? You aren't man enough to be a Christian! You haven't manhood enough to get up and walk down the aisle and take me by the hand and say, "I give my heart to Christ." You haven't manhood enough to take my hand and go home this afternoon and say "I hit the trail this afternoon and I'm going to live for Christ. . . ." It takes manhood to be a Christian, my friend, in this old world.[98]

Sunday frequently phrased his invitation to salvation as a choice for manliness. "How many of you men will say, 'Bill, I believe the Christian life is the right and manly life, and by the grace of God, from now on I'll do my best for the Lord and for his truth'?"[99] "Do you believe it's manly?" he would ask. "Have you got the guts to do it? Come on! Come on! Come on!"[100]

All this would indicate that perhaps Sunday's deepest purpose in preaching was not to speak of God, of his victory and his salvation, but to speak of humanity and its possibilities for strength and heroism and goodness. More than anything else, Sunday was a denouncer of the bad and an exhorter to the good. As one in a long line of evangelists, Sunday had to proclaim the salvation Jesus purchased on the cross, and he had to bring his listeners to the point of conversion. Conversion, however, was portrayed primarily as a means to an end—an end that obviously concerned and excited both Sunday and his crowds—an end of moral attainment and manliness. The good news, in Sunday's hands, became the proclamation that men and women could be good and strong; and that if enough people were good and strong, politics would be purified, insanity and poverty would disappear, families would be made whole, young people would grow up to be solid citizens, and, in general, America would be saved. One wonders whether Sunday ever really stopped to ask what *God* was doing in the world. Rather, it looks as though he grasped the mechanism of conversion as a tool by which those moral evils he and his audiences most deplored could quickly be eradicated, and by these means America could be brought under control. What excited Sunday was not that people would hear of the love and merciful forgiveness of God, but that they could use God to make themselves and their country good. Morality was Sunday's concern, and religion was his means to encourage it.

This emphasis explains why Sunday could attract the loyalty and admiration of all sorts of public-spirited people, many of whom did not share his revivalist theology but all of whom appreciated the moral benefits of his preaching. His admirers found that they could describe his influence without mentioning the name of Jesus Christ, speaking rather of the impetus Sunday gave to "good living" or "righteousness of life." One of his earliest biographers praised him for getting all sorts of people "talking about religion" and for his ability to "make religion interesting to the common people."[101] Of course, who would not be interested in talking about what promises to make one strong and good, and to distinguish one from one's neighbors by these characteristics? After Sunday spoke to students at the University of Pennsylvania, an administrator noted: "He has a special message which deeply stirs many who are in need of moral stimulation and the powerful incentive of religion."[102] In an early review of his ministry, one journalist remarked that Sunday preached for over two and a half hours on the evils of cardplaying and dancing with hardly a reference to religious doctrine at all, basing his argument "from beginning to end upon the effect of such things upon the public morals. . . ."[103] Supporters spoke enthusiastically of Sunday's contribution to the "moral uplift of the community."[104]

All the talk during this era of progressive reform was about civic righteousness, and in his concern for civic righteousness Sunday took a back seat to nobody. Sunday himself summarized his message in this way:

> Bluntly put, my friends, I think this: the trouble with America is the lack of moral principle. Now moral statutes may be needed but statutes cannot put morals where morals do not exist. You cannot raise the standard of morals by raising the scale of wages; you've got to go higher than the pay envelope to find out the cause of vice and of virtue—and it's in the heart of men and women.
>
> I tell you men of New York tonight, the thoughtful businessmen all over this land are awakening to the perils that threaten our cities and our civilization in the widespread disregard for the old-time principles of integrity, honesty and manhood and businessmen everywhere are recognizing as never before that if civic righteousness prevails, if graft in high places is overthrown, if the great avalanche of vice that threatens our nation is stopped, if the tidal wave of intemperance and dissipation that threatens the young manhood of our land and imperils our destiny as a nation—if these evil forces are going to be defeated it will be done by and through the religion of Jesus Christ. That's the only religion. (Applause)[105]

Often, in describing or defending the meaning of Jesus Christ and his gospel, Sunday would speak in purely moralistic terms. "I want to tell you if you take Christianity out of this world you will sound the death knell of morality," he said.[106] This is because "no man ever had such influence to teach men and women virtue and goodness as Christ."[107] "Trust in God and behave yourself," he asserted, is just "another way of saying 'Thou shalt love the Lord thy God with all thy mind and with all thy strength and thy neighbor as thyself.'"[108] Again: "All God wants is for a man to be decent."[109]

In expressing his primary motivations as an evangelist, Sunday's own words confirm our analysis that morality was uppermost to him. Shortly before he died, in 1935, he wrote these words: "I do not conceal the fact that I am in this world for the purpose of making it easier for people to do right and harder for them to do wrong." A few lines later, he defined his role more typically as an evangelist would: "I am and always have been plain Billy Sunday trying to do God's will in preaching Jesus and Him crucified and arisen from the dead for our sins."[110] Somehow the latter words come across, if not as an afterthought, then perhaps as a doctrinally oriented statement of purpose whose real meaning is found in the earlier words: "making it easier for people to do right and harder for them to do wrong." It was not the first time he had put his real mission in similar words. Every day of the year, he said, "I try to post myself on the evils that are going on in the world and to warn people about the pitfalls."[111] "God knows I would do anything in my power to help you be a better man. I want to make it easier for you to be square, and harder for you to go to hell." Elsewhere he phrased it even more directly: "I have no motive in preaching except the interest I have in the moral welfare of the people."[112]

Billy Sunday's gospel was a moral gospel. The good news in this gospel was the news that people could be good, and that if enough people were good, America would be saved. Its destiny would once again be in the moral hands of the people of God.

IV

Jesus of Nazareth was born and lived among a Jewish people who knew what it was like to be out of control of their lives. For centuries their fate had been determined by people who were not Jews: Egyptians, Syrians, Babylonians, Assyrians, Greeks, still more Egyptians and Syrians, and finally the Romans. Their history was a long line of military sieges and defeats, captivities and exiles, massacres and crucifixions. Now and then glimmers of hope appeared, brief respites from foreign domination, but they were soon crushed by a new conqueror's triumphant march through the streets of Jerusalem. Even the revolt of the Maccabees in the second century before Christ, which gained them a semblance of national independence for a time, simply introduced a century of political intrigue, entangling alliances, and bloody slaughters that were no less violent for their being at least partially homegrown. The six centuries before the birth of Jesus were never without the sound of Jews wailing for the lost fortunes of the people of God.

Simeon of Jerusalem may have been one of these wailing Jews. His story is told in Luke 2.

> Now there was a man in Jerusalem, whose name was Simeon, and this man was righteous and devout, looking for the consolation of Israel, and the Holy Spirit was upon him. And it had been revealed to him by the Holy Spirit that he should not see death before he had seen the Lord's Christ. And inspired by the Spirit he came into the temple; and when the parents brought in the child Jesus, to do for him according to the custom of the law, he took him up in his arms and blessed God and said, "Lord, now lettest thou thy servant depart in peace, according to thy word; for mine eyes have seen thy salvation which thou hast prepared in the presence of all peoples, a light for revelation to the Gentiles, and for glory to thy people Israel." And his father and his mother marveled at what was said about him; and Simeon blessed them and said to Mary his mother, "Behold, this child is set for the fall and rising of many in Israel, and for a sign that is spoken against (and a sword will pierce through your own soul also), that thoughts out of many hearts may be revealed."
>
> (2:25-35)

At first glance, the text does not tell us a great deal about Simeon. If we read between the lines, however, we meet a man who knew the sad history of his people and was no stranger to the sound of mourning. The clue is given in just a few words: Simeon, we are told, was "looking for the consolation of Israel." Were it not for this line, we might misinterpret the preceding description of Simeon as "righteous and devout"; to our moralistic ears "righteous and devout" sounds something like "morally upright and pious." It is of course quite possible that Simeon was, to all appearances, morally upright and pious. But the biblical message is that there is no one good, no one that seeks after God. We must assume, then, that Simeon's righteousness inhered not in his moral exertions but in his understanding that in God's righteousness alone is there salvation. Simeon's righteousness must have lain in his conscious awareness that he had no righteousness of his own, that by his own piety he could lay no claim on God. In other words, it is quite possible that Simeon was humble.

This impression is enforced when we understand that Simeon was waiting for the consolation of Israel. It is not the human practice to wait—particularly for consolation. To wait for consolation is to live with a certain emptiness or incompleteness, a longing and a sadness. It is the human custom, when things are bad, to strive to make them better by whatever means are available. This striving may take the form of active participation in crusades for social betterment—politics, evangelism, military campaigns, and the like. Or it may be embodied in more personal remedies—programs for building one's moral integrity, schemes for self-renovation, or perhaps escapes such as alcohol, tourism, or suicide. Humans seem to live with a subliminal awareness that death marches upon them inexorably. The little deaths involved in personal and national failures remind us of our own mortality, and they typically send us into a frenzy of activity designed to forget and to forestall. What we seem entirely incapable of doing, for more than a few hours or days, is mourning—and waiting.

Simeon waited, and since it was a consolation he awaited, I believe we can say he mourned. Perhaps as a youth he had read the history of Israel as a heroic history, a history of manliness and courage. And perhaps as a youth he had thought to emulate these heroes, to outshine all the rest in moral achievement, perhaps by his righteousness to attract the attention of the Holy One of Israel and gain the divine blessing needed to liberate his people from half a millennium of human bondage. But by the time we meet him, Simeon has become an old man and has learned a truth about his own life and that of his people, a truth bound only to bring him the deepest sadness. He has discovered his own powerlessness and the powerlessness of his people. It is a powerlessness to be manly and moral and thus to please God; and it is a powerlessness in the affairs of peoples and nations, an utter inability to control the course of history. Simeon has learned the brokenness of this world and of his own life. He knows he will not be fixing these things. He knows that God does not await our exertions, or else we would all be lost; but that it is God's alone to fix and meanwhile to console. Simeon has learned to mourn, genuinely, and to await a genuine consolation—God's consolation.

In the same Gospel accounts of Jesus' life, we meet a group of people very unlike the waiter and mourner Simeon, a group known as the Pharisees. The Pharisees also knew the history of Israel. In fact, their fortunes had been intertwined with the political history and fortunes of Israel for a century and a half before Jesus' day. They had arisen, we can surmise, as a latter-day expression of the Hassidean sect, which dated back to at least the third century before Christ and whose purpose was to purify Jewish rites and counter the influence of paganism in Israel. During the second century before Christ the Pharisees emerged as a separate sect noted for its extreme dedication to fulfilling the minutest observances of the law of

Moses, especially as it was passed down through the centuries by oral tradition. People of middle economic status, such as merchants and traders, along with certain members among the priestly class, made up their ranks; but interpreters agree that the Pharisees were the most popular party and thought of themselves as the truest representatives of the great mass of Jewish people. With a few brief exceptions, they were out of favor with the political establishment, and for their stubborn opposition to pagan customs and the growth of Greek culture among the Jews they suffered persecution and bloody reprisal.[113] If any Jews, then, should have recognized that their history was a tale of woe, that it was not within human control, and that it was badly in need of salvation from outside— no matter what their personal moral exertions—it should have been the Pharisees.

Their response to this history, however, was not what we have inferred Simeon's response to have been. Their response was a kind of moral and religious heroism, as if by that means they could tame the forces that ravaged their history and could recapture control of their society for good people like themselves. To this end, they entered into a crusade for scrupulous religious observance and irreproachable moral integrity. *They* would keep the strictest requirements of the moral and ceremonial code, even if no one else did. And yet, as their history shows, it mattered very much whether or not anyone else did. On the one hand, the Pharisees took a certain pride in their religious superiority (scholars think their sect's name meant "the separated ones") and they spoke condescendingly of the multitudes as "the people of the land," who had little or no concern for strict moral and religious observance. On the other hand, they made a bid for power and popularity on the very basis of their moral superiority. They evangelized vigorously, urging upon others the merits of their strict regimen, presenting themselves as the worthiest representatives of the Jewish tradition, and in fact achieving a certain popular acceptance during much of their history. The Pharisees thus represent the anomaly of a group that touted its own moral superiority and yet enjoyed the favor of the very masses to whom they considered themselves superior.[114]

The Pharisees do not remind me of the waiting Simeon but rather of the evangelicals we have been examining—not to mention the evangelicals of today. When confronted with a history out of control, the Pharisees rushed into action, thinking to remedy matters by a fresh application of moral rigor and religious zeal. Although the Pharisees included in their teachings an expectancy for the coming Messiah as the premillennialists did, they understood their own moral exertions both to be essential to the coming of the future kingdom and to constitute a claim on the Messiah when he arrived—a claim that would raise them above the unfaithful masses in the new society. Their attitude, then, was clearly not one of waiting—as if dependent on God's action—but one of acting—as if God were dependent on theirs. And for all their talk of the coming Messiah, their real agenda was earthly power, which was demonstrated in their unrelenting quest for popular support and their undying hostility toward the one man who seemed to threaten that support. That man was Jesus of Nazareth, the very one they claimed to be waiting for but whose appearance put the lie to this claim once and for all.

The prophet Isaiah presents the Messiah as the "man of sorrows, and acquainted with grief" and thus as one from whom men hid their faces. The Pharisees, although they claimed to await this Messiah, were among those men. It is unlikely that Simeon, who recognized the Messiah in the baby Jesus, would not also have recognized him in the full-grown "man of sorrows" he became. We cannot be certain, of course, since it was clearly not flesh and blood that convinced him the child in his arms would be the Savior of the world. But Simeon did know how to mourn; the Pharisees did not. Perhaps Jesus had them in mind when he said, "Woe to you that laugh now, for you shall mourn and weep," or when he spoke of those who already had their reward (Lk. 6:25; Mt. 6:2). Thus the Pharisees were offended at this man of sorrows, Jesus of Nazareth. They hardly knew what to do with him, except perhaps to measure him against themselves—as if the Messiah must surely demonstrate some version, perhaps just the slightest bit more exalted, of their own morality. This Messiah did not do so. He was not one of the "separated ones," as they were; instead, he ate and drank with tax collectors and sinners. He did not demonstrate their piety; instead, he healed and allowed his disciples to gather food on the Sabbath. He was not ritually pure, as they were; instead, he permitted his disciples to eat without washing their hands. His very freedom and lack of anxiety in these areas stood as a witness against their own heroic moral exertions and the power they hoped to gain by them, and we must suspect that they felt belittled by him, even as they felt contemptuous of him, and morally superior.

Perhaps Jesus posed the greatest threat to the Pharisees in their bid for earthly power. He seems to have known that power was on their minds. He spoke directly to the Pharisees' aspirations in his diatribe in Matthew 23, where he describes them as sitting on the seat of Moses, as laying heavy burdens on men's shoulders, as loving the places of honor at the feasts and in the synagogues, and as wishing to be called "rabbi." Matthew's account of the Sermon on the Mount may suggest that Jesus meant to contrast the "righteousness" of the Pharisees with poverty of spirit, mourning, and meekness—all implying powerlessness. One can hear in the Pharisees' accusation that Jesus was casting out devils by the Devil himself a claim to the illegitimacy of his power and the legitimacy of theirs. When Jesus' disciples hailed their Messiah as "the King who comes in the name of the Lord," the Pharisees were offended, not the least, one can gather, because Jesus' kingship called their own claims to power into question. Their disturbance could not have been eased by their awareness that the multitudes, on whose loyalty their own power rested, seemed for the moment also disposed to hail this carpenter's son as their rightful king. And how deeply threatening to their very attempt to control their history must have been Jesus' words to them, "Therefore I tell you, the kingdom of God will be taken away from you and given to a nation producing the fruits of it" (Mt. 9:32-34; Lk. 19:37-39; Mt. 21:9-11, 43; Jn. 12:19).

But this Messiah, it turned out, was not riding a royal mount but a simple donkey. And "his face was set toward Jerusalem," not to reign but to die like a criminal in a posture of utter powerlessness, hanging on a cross. It was, after all, his task to speak God's word about earthly power, its pretensions and its ultimate futility. As far as this power went, he seemed to have none at all. Thus the Pharisees in due time found him to be no threat to them. They discovered that they did indeed have earthly power: in fact, they had the power that underlies every power among humans, the power of life and death, and they used that power to crucify the Messiah, as others had used theirs to crucify Pharisees who awaited the Messiah. In a moment of nervousness, they set guards at Jesus' tomb so that he would not in death prove more powerful than they. But we can imagine that, after a flurry of excitement over his rumored resurrection, they settled into their usual self-assurance, confident that their moral superiority would soon enough attract God's attention and put them back in charge of history. Some of them, perhaps, continued to worry about this little Christian sect, until the murder of Stephen and the crusading zeal of Saul of Tarsus seemed to turn the tide in their direction. Even Saul's transformation into Paul, the apostle, failed to ignite the anger they had felt toward Jesus. No doubt they took a certain pride in having prevailed over this Jesus. Contrary to his accusation, they, not he, had accurately interpreted the signs of the times (Lk. 9:53; Mt. 27:62-66; Acts 23:9; Mt. 16:1-4).

But in the year A.D. 70 it all came tumbling down. The legions of the Roman Empire burst into the land of the Jews, bringing with them murder and destruction. Jerusalem was laid waste and with it any sense that history was destined to prove the power of the people of God. All along, it turned out, the power of the Pharisees had been a deception. The forces working in the ancient world were larger than any single man or group of men. These forces took no notice of claims to superior morality or to the power that comes from a presumed friendliness with God. The Pharisaic sect lived on, but its relatively less rigid legalism may speak for a new awareness that history was not—and would never be—within its control. Perhaps in those most sorrowful and tragic of times a few Pharisees understood Jesus' saying concerning them: "Let them alone; they are blind guides. And if a blind man leads a blind man, both will fall into a pit" (Mt. 15:14).

V

In large measure, Billy Sunday's audiences, whether in the small towns of his early years or in the giant cities of his prime, were composed of middle-class Christian people who considered themselves the backbone of America. Their understanding of the world and of themselves was rooted in a simpler time and place, where moral issues seemed clear-cut and one's life seemed largely to be under one's own control. That time and place was the rural and small-town setting of mid-nineteenth-century America. The small towns of America and their surrounding rural regions were "island communities," as Wiebe puts it, marked by relative economic self-sufficiency and political autonomy, geographical isolation, and social homogeneity. Within these island communities life's contours were explainable in terms of the familiar and the personal. The institutions that circumscribed community life, such as family, church, school, press, courthouse, shop, and workshop, affirmed similar values and had faces attached—faces one recognized as one's neighbors, faces susceptible to one's gratitude, one's grudges, one's appeals to reason or to conscience. Within these island communities most people agreed on working definitions of right and wrong, good and evil; and if offenders against these "village values" could not find it in themselves to mend their ways, social pressure added its irresistible weight. Bad things happened in these island communities, of course, but generally they could be explained by nature's cruelty or the familiar machinations of bad people. And the bad people were one's neighbors, whose badness one had come to understand and account for, and in some small degree to control.[115]

By the time Billy Sunday began his career as a revivalist, these island communities had lost their insularity. The relentless pressure of modern industrial and capitalist organization had woven virtually every isolated pocket into a web. Now, as we have seen, distant institutions of indeterminate size, character, and power became arbiters of community life, holding the economic destinies of once independent towns in their impersonal and often arbitrary grip. In this new world one no longer knew his or her enemies by name—or if by name, then by name alone and not by face. How does one argue with a railroad or an oil company? How does one scold an absentee landlord or appeal to the conscience of Wall Street? Exactly whom might the local merchant blame for the loss of his customers to the Sears catalog? Upon whom should the farm parent avenge himself for the loss of his son or daughter to the seductions of the city, for the fact that his own offspring have become strangers to him? Standard approaches to the redress of grievances seemed strangely irrelevant, strangely impotent, even if one could determine the nature of the grievance.

And yet Americans knew no other approaches, so they tried using what they had. Starting in the 1870s and continuing in cyclical waves until the years just after World War I, they labored stubbornly to attach names and faces to their enemies, to comprehend the unsettling course of their lives in terms of the machinations of bad men, as if the relentless impersonality of modern life were but a flimsy disguise for the familiar world of the neighborhood or the village. They found their scapegoats in political bosses, in conniving financiers, in wealthy capitalists, in blacks or Jews or Italians, in this "ring" or that "trust," in Christian heretics, radical socialists, even the German Kaiser. In locating the perpetrators of their discomfort, they hoped to shame them or jail them or convert them or legislate them into good behavior. If they could make these bad folks good, they thought, perhaps the confusions of their lives would come to an end.[116]

Billy Sunday comforted these people, especially the evangelicals among them, by telling them what they wanted to hear. There is no mystery to our present evil state, he assured them. It's all very simple. The bad people of America are assaulting the good Christian people of America. Lots of the good people, regrettably, are asleep in the church pews, lulled by the droning of ineffectual and fearful ministers. The good people need to wake up and mount a counteroffensive. They need to call the bad persons by their rightful names and give them no quarter. Since the good vastly outnumber the bad, and since God is on the side of the good and is just waiting for the good to wake up, the forces of evil are doomed and the future is reasonably bright. Who will join the battle?

The crisis America found itself in at the turn of the century, however, was not simply the result of individuals making clear-cut choices between obvious goods and evils. Rather, America was caught in a historical dynamic much larger than the sum of the individual choices, a dynamic that good people could do little to direct and almost nothing to stop. The myth of individual autonomy, and of society as nothing more than the sum of its autonomous individuals, contributed to a deep blindness on the part of evangelicals at the turn of the century. It was a blindness for which they had been preparing throughout a century of optimistic, Enlightenment-provoked, commonsense-oriented thinking, and a blindness that robbed them of the opportunity to understand the very forces that were battering their own lives and mocking their attempts at happiness and self-control. These forces, as we have shown, were associated with the breakneck advance of modern technology, wedded to the rapidly changing shape of monopoly capitalism. Although these forces utilized the decisions of countless millions, those decisions could hardly be called free and were rarely clear-cut as to their moral significance. Rather, they were dictated by a logic generally uncomprehended and unexamined by their human subjects. Billy Sunday, by a badly oversimplified and essentially misguided diagnosis of society's traumas, and, I believe, of human nature generally—not to mention the gospel—contributed to this inability to comprehend, turning the faces of evangelicals toward a false hope and leaving them vulnerable to a historic battering from behind. If we look more closely at economic developments in late nineteenth-century America, we can begin to understand the nature and scope of that battering and perhaps understand both Billy Sunday and his audiences somewhat better.

The typical American citizen living about a century before Billy Sunday's heyday existed "from hand to mouth" in the best sense of those words. Those items and objects that he or she found most necessary or useful in daily life, for the most part, were the result of personal creative activity or the activity of one's neighbors. The farm family produced not only crops for the local market but also most of its own food needs, and in addition made such items as furniture, soap, lye, candles, leather, cloth, and clothing. A government official in 1810 estimated that "about two-thirds of the clothing, including hosiery, and of the house and table linen, worn and used by the inhabitants of the United States, who do not reside in cities, is the product of family manufactures."[117] Even as late as 1880, less than half of men's clothing came from factories, ready to wear.[118]

By 1900 all this had changed in a most startling fashion. Now factories produced, railroads delivered, and department stores or other retail outlets sold almost everything that at one time had been hand-produced in the home or local shop. For the very necessities of life—food, clothing, household goods, tools and hardware, and dry goods—the average American was becoming nearly dependent on strangers in faraway places. An observer in 1907 noted that the "home has ceased to be the

glowing center of production from which radiate all desirable goods and
has become a pool towards which products made in other places flow—a
place of consumption, not of production."[119]

This revolution in economic processes was wrought by the historic
confluence of mechanical and administrative techniques that mark our
era as a modern industrial age. Its key innovations were the telegraph, the
railroad, and the use of coal as an accessible source of energy—all of
which came to fruition in the United States in the 1840s. With energy,
communication, and transportation assured, and with the rapid development of new machinery in a wide variety of productive fields, the factory
system quickly outpaced small family shops and businesses as a producer
of cheap goods. The railroad made possible the regular, rapid, and high-
volume distribution of these goods to an ever-widening portion of the
public, while the telegraph provided the communication that would
make possible the efficient operation of vast business empires. In all these
fields geometric patterns of growth had made the America of 1900 into an
unprecedented consumer's paradise where the necessities of life were
displayed in wild profusion and where goods heretofore considered luxuries, or perhaps nonexistent, were now available at a price that the
average woman and man could afford.[120]

But would they buy them? Could the demand of Americans for manufactured products possibly keep pace with the constantly proliferating
productive capacities of the ever-new machines and processes? This worried many business minds at the turn of the century, fueling demands
that the government join the other industrialized nations in the race for
overseas empires so that new markets might be opened up for surplus
American goods. Some observers hailed the growing evangelical missionary movement as a means of preparing backward people for the
material blessings of modern civilization, to be provided by the flow of
goods from American factories.[121] One leading business historian makes
it clear that key innovations in the shape of business enterprise—particularly the integration of mass production and mass distribution by
giant corporations—were encouraged by the fear that existing markets
were inadequate to relieve them of the volume of goods their firms
produced.[122]

An excellent example of this is the cigarette industry. At the time that
James Bonsack invented a machine to manufacture cigarettes in 1881, a
highly skilled worker could make only three thousand a day by hand.
Bonsack's machine could turn out 70,000 in a ten-hour day; fifteen such
machines could have supplied the entire American cigarette market at the
time. Technical improvements soon increased the output of a single cigarette machine to 120,000 a day. James B. Duke, a small manufacturer of

smoking tobacco in Durham, North Carolina, was the first to see the potential of Bonsack's machines and quickly became the dominant force in the cigarette industry. Since he could easily saturate the existing market with his cigarettes, his only hope for growth lay in increasing the size of that market. To do this, he quickly built a giant sales organization and, most importantly, launched an expensive nationwide advertising campaign to convince users of other tobacco products, as well as users of no tobacco products at all, to buy his cigarettes. Using these means, he was soon selling $4.5 million worth of cigarettes a year, and by 1890 he had gained control of much of the market by creating the American Tobacco Company. In 1915 the firm ranked fourth in amount of national magazine advertising, and by 1917 it was the eighteenth largest industrial enterprise in America.[123]

The grain-processing industry provides a similar example. Henry P. Crowell built a modern, highly mechanized mill in 1882 that could produce far more processed oats than could be sold to existing customers. As Alfred B. Chandler, Jr., describes it, "A new market had to be found if the great volume of output from the new machines was to be sold."[124] Crowell responded by inventing a breakfast cereal, until then (like cigarettes) relatively unsatisfying to the American taste. He called it Quaker Oats, packaged it attractively, and advertised it nationally, using many of the gimmicks for which breakfast cereals are still known today: box-top offers, prizes, testimonials, and endorsements by scientists. In a variety of ads he associated Quaker Oats with "love, pride, cosmetic satisfactions, sex, marriage, good health, cleanliness, safety, labor saving, and status seeking."[125] He attempted to familiarize every American with his corporate symbol, placing it "on billboards, streetcars, newspapers, calendars, magazines, blotters, cookbooks, Sunday church bulletins, metal signs on rural fences, company sponsored cooking schools, free samples given away house-to-house, booths at county fairs and expositions."[126] In due time Crowell added other products such as wheat cereals and baby foods, always with advertising campaigns, and built Quaker Oats Company into a leading American firm.[127]

Both cigarettes and oat cereals exemplify machine-engendered overproduction that spurred the quest for new markets. The machine age had wrought a truly new phenomenon in history, an era in which the economic challenge would no longer be the production of goods in quantity enough to supply a known demand but the expansion of demand in order to accommodate the riotous profusion of goods. If manufacturers could not sell the output of their factories, their newly discovered productive potential would do them no good. Customers had to be found—or perhaps made—and advertising was the answer.[128]

The significant breakthroughs in modern corporate organization and in the machine production of consumer goods seemed to cluster in or around the decade of the 1880s. It is no accident, then, that the modern advertising industry was born at approximately the same time. Before the Civil War, advertising in newspapers had been generally restricted to notices of goods for sale that were printed in very tiny type (called *agate*) and single-column widths. The assumption was that the customer already knew what he or she wanted and simply needed to be provided with information on where to get it. Shortly after the Civil War, the new marketing sensation called "department stores" began to break with advertising tradition. Macy's was the first to use larger type and multiple-column widths; and John Wanamaker placed the first full-page retail ad in a daily newspaper in 1879. At about the same time, advertisers began experimenting with pictorial representations of their products. The use of nationally recognizable brand names became widespread soon thereafter, followed quickly by the creation of advertising agencies to advise firms and manage their advertising campaigns. One of the most successful of these advertising agencies was N. J. Ayer and Son of Philadelphia, which produced a sophisticated advertising campaign for the National Biscuit Company in 1899 by saturating the country with distinctive displays in newspapers, magazines, streetcars, posters, and other media. Overnight the American public discovered a sudden craving for Uneeda Biscuits.[129]

The two or three decades after 1890 might well be called, as they were by a 1915 observer, "the Age of Advertising."[130] Advertising agencies proliferated. Technical advances in the creation of increasingly appealing ads came rapidly during these years. The 1890s saw newspapers and mass-circulation magazines being founded almost weekly. Among the latter the big success stories were the *Ladies' Home Journal* and the *Saturday Evening Post*. When Cyrus H. K. Curtis bought the *Post* in 1897, it had a circulation of just over 2,000 and yearly advertising revenues of just under $7,000; by 1917, its circulation was almost two million, and its advertising revenue just over $16 million. Curtis made his fortune by dropping the price of his magazines below that of most of his competitors and making up for the loss of revenue by printing far more advertising.[131] At its peak the *Post* devoted 60 percent of its 125 pages to advertising.[132] Even the older, idea-oriented magazines joined the advertising age. In 1900, *Harper's Weekly* printed a volume of advertising greater than the combined volume of its first twenty-two years of publishing.[133]

The change in advertising content during this period is also remarkable, as a random look at *Collier's Magazine* in 1899 and again in 1909 dramatizes. In 1899 most advertising was dull and unimaginative, featuring a fairly narrow range of patent medicines, cures for drunkenness, baldness, or shamefully small bust lines, plus a few consumer items like bicycles, clothing, and Armour Beef. By 1909 advertisements were much larger and flashier, with fancy artwork and pictorial displays. Patent medicines had almost disappeared, replaced now by appeals to buy a wide range of consumer products from automobiles to washing machines ("2 Cents a Week Does Washing!"), refrigerators, Old Town Canoes, Edison Phonographs, and Florsheim Shoes. In 1894, according to one study, 30 percent of the ads in *Collier's* and *Literary Digest* used pictures, and by 1919 close to 90 percent used pictures to attract the attention of customers.[134] After 1900, advertisers turned from religious journals, which had held a large portion of the nineteenth-century readership, to secular weeklies and monthlies. Several religious publications turned secular in the quest for advertising revenue.[135] In 1899 major department stores in New York and Chicago together spent close to $2 million in advertising; John Wanamaker alone spent $300,000. By 1920 such companies as Proctor and Gamble, Goodyear Tire, and Quaker Oats were each spending over a million dollars per year in advertising.[136]

What did all this amount to for the people living in America at the turn of the century? Most of us pay little attention to the incremental changes in our daily lives and in the environment that surrounds us. Only when we meet an old friend who tells us who we used to be, or perhaps see an old photograph, do we have the flash of recognition that it is a different world we now inhabit than the world of our youth. With the recognition of that distance can come new insight into the forces that have been operating on us without our knowledge all the while. It is quite possible that a person living through the period of greatest advancement in advertising—from 1890 through 1920, for example—might never have brought into conscious focus the revolutionary changes in his or her environment. But a more distant observer can see that the impact of such changes must have been overwhelming. People of that time were living within an environment that was increasingly saturated by the print media. Printed words and illustrations were becoming a significant portion of what the senses perceived. These words and illustrations comprised messages that were intended to enter the reader's brain even when the recipient was not explicitly aware of it. "Advertising was part of a new visual environment," one historian has said, "where innumerable images jostled for the attention of a mass audience."[137] A significant portion of those messages, perhaps even a majority, had a very specific task to perform: to incite the reader to desire and to purchase. If the corporate willingness to spend millions on advertising and the wildfire growth of the firms spending the most on advertising is any measure, the messages performed their task very well indeed.

During the years after 1890, advertisers, advertising agencies, and scholars interested in advertising as a subject of study conducted a running dialogue about how best to go about creating wider markets for consumer goods. It was becoming obvious that advertising was in the process of a major change. No longer was its purpose simply to provide objective information about the location and price of particular items consumers were looking for; rather, its purpose was now to persuade those who had perceived no previous need for a product that they did indeed need and want the product.[138] "No initial interest can be assumed on the part of the reader of advertisements," wrote one expert. "The psychology of advertising must assume that the customer is inert and is to be aroused to reaction."[139] One of the earliest uses of psychology as a discipline in American intellectual life was in the service of informing advertisers how to arouse the consumer to reaction—the reaction to buy.

In 1913, Harry L. Hollingworth of Columbia University wrote one of the first studies of the psychology of advertising. Certain kinds of goods, he said, such as toilet articles, jewelry, fancy dress, toys, disinfectants, food products, ornamental (as opposed to utilitarian) clothing, and a host of others—all could best be sold by a "short-circuit appeal" that did not rely on rational argument or objective information but rather on appeals to instinct or feeling. His advice was to use words and images that stimulated deep inner instincts and moved the potential consumer to action: "The moment a thing can be demonstrated to be *chic*, stylish, nobby, modern, popular, clean, artistic, imported, scientifically made, guaranteed, elegant, socially advantageous, progressive, gentlemanly, bohemian, refined, sporty, up-to-date, used by some favorite, etc., etc., it will at once find a market. . . ." Hollingworth noted that appeals should vary according to the readers' age, sex, and class. Women, for example, are more sensitive to sensory impressions, to pictures and color, to "irrelevant material" and patriotic pride than are men.[140] A decade earlier, another advertising psychologist asked, "How many advertisers describe a piano so vividly that the reader can hear it? How many food products are so described that the reader can taste the food? How many advertisements describe a perfume so that the reader can smell it? How many describe an undergarment so that the reader can feel the pleasant contact with his body? Many advertisers seem never to have thought of this, and make no attempt at such description."[141] With the help of this expert and scores like him, however, advertisers were learning to think of such things in their quest for the aroused consumer.

The advertising literature of the early twentieth century provides telling examples of this attempt to appeal to the consumers' instincts and impulses and to awaken their desire. One strong motif was "luxury," with words and pictures evoking an enviable elegance, followed by the pitch: "This is a luxury you can afford."[142] As one advertising agency proclaimed, "The luxuries of yesterday [we accept] as necessities today. Automobiles, tiled bathrooms, radio, oil heating, electric refrigeration, the telephone. . . ."[143] Closely associated were images of pleasure and the life of ease. The White Star Line wooed customers with these words: "Life is so pleasant sailing the ocean the way of White Star . . . life becomes a smartly gay affair."[144] A recent historian of the consumer culture has found that a significant theme in the national advertising of this period was "the fun of living."[145] A related code word was "leisure," with one agency claiming that the name of "an ironing machine can be made synonymous with leisure." "Fashion" also had a strong pull; certainly women would want to be among those who "cultivate the decorative side of life" and thus set the fashions for tomorrow.[146] Advertisers were not above appealing to pride or envy. A General Electric "All-Steel Refrigerator" was pictured in a modern kitchen, surrounded by the hostess and her awestruck party guests, under the headline, "Happy to own it . . . proud to show it." The ad copy read as follows: "Really, you can't blame her. Who wouldn't drag her friends out into the kitchen to show off her new General Electric? There it stands, gleaming white, strong as a safe, incredibly quiet . . . the envy of all who see it."[147]

All this has become commonplace to us in the late twentieth century. We have been immersed in advertising stimuli all our lives, particularly those of us whose life spans correspond to the age of television. To the people living at the turn of the century, however, it was all quite new. The effect of this new advertising environment should not be underestimated. What it added up to was the generation and justification of a whole new and ever-growing set of consumer desires. The purpose of advertising since the revolution of productivity has been to convince the public that it wants—indeed craves—what it did not want or know about before. The men and women who pioneered in the advertising business knew this very well. A writer in 1897 commented that "now we read [advertisements] to find out what we really want." Around the same time, an advertising agent urged his clients to "almost invariably seek to create desire . . . before divulging the price." In 1904 a writer noted that ads were no longer for those who knew they wanted a product, but "it's for the one who don't [sic] in order to make him."[148] A leading advertising psychologist in 1911 suggested that "the man with the proper imagination is able to conceive of any commodity in such a way that it becomes an object of emotion to him and to those to whom he imparts his picture, and hence creates desire rather than a mere feeling of ought."[149] One of the leading advertising agencies published essays in leading national magazines after 1919 that paid tribute to the advertising industry that, in its words, "creates new interests and satisfies old wants," and succeeds by "implanting desire and cultivating it into ready consumer acceptance," thus reducing "sales resistance."[150] A recent historian of advertising summed it up in these words: "Marketing mass-produced consumer goods demanded a revised model of buyer behavior. Manufacturers had to catch the consumer's attention, arouse desires, and transform desires into purchases."[151]

On the face of it, these words are unexceptionable to our late twentieth-century ears. But in the context of the period we have been studying, they constituted a dagger thrust into the vitals of the evangelical community, forcing a radical reevaluation of much of what nineteenth-century evangelicals held dear. The hand holding this dagger could not be readily identified and was not susceptible to clear-cut moral analysis or to blame or punishment. No one sinister person or group of persons determined that these thrusts be made. The historic movement of industrial capitalism dictated these thrusts, and they were carried out on victims who to all appearances welcomed them. The evangelical community felt these thrusts only subliminally; without tools to identify them, they all too readily fixed their hostility on other villains, villains more easily specified and personalized. And yet their language shows that they felt the pain and could betray without knowing it what the source of that pain was. This deeper, mostly unconscious wisdom is never more startling— and more vulnerable to confusion—than in America's leading revivalist, Billy Sunday.

VI

When Billy Sunday preached, "Be strong and show yourself a man," he joined a long line of Christian moralists stretching back at least a generation. Late nineteenth-century bookshelves were laden with little volumes of practical advice by these moralists, the "character builders," on how one might "be a man." The authors, one historian has noted, were "unabashedly moralists," their goal being the transformation of raw youths into moral men and women. Many of the character traits Billy Sunday associated with manliness, or morality, were standard fare in the literature of the nineteenth-century character builders: nobility of purpose, determination, courage, strength, the ability to endure hardship. These were "manly virtues," virtues of toughness, of "grit." One sought in one's male offspring, very early, the signs that he was a "little man" who possessed these austere virtues.[152]

A leading author in the character-building movement of the period was Samuel Smiles, whose 1876 book *Character*, a long commentary on "the principles of a manly character," was first published in London but received a wide American audience as well. "When the elements of character are brought into action by determinate will," Smiles writes, "and, influenced by high purpose, man enters upon and courageously perseveres in the path of duty, at whatever cost of worldly interest, he may be said to approach the summit of his being. He then exhibits character in its most intrepid forms, and embodies the highest ideals of manliness." Smiles's writing is essentially a stiff, less colloquial version of Billy Sunday. He speaks of character as involving reverence for "pure thoughts and noble aims." In a chapter entitled "Courage," Smiles describes the "determined man" going out "like David to meet Goliath." Like Sunday, Smiles often uses Napoleon and other great military heroes as models of manliness. Like Sunday, he urges constant vigilance: "Every action, every thought, every feeling, contributes to the education of the temper, the habits, and understanding; and exercises an inevitable influence upon all the acts of our future life. Thus, character is undergoing constant change, for better or for worse. . . ."[153]

Another American evangelical who wrote on the subject of character was Henry Clay Trumbull, long-time editor of *The Sunday School Times* and father of Charles G. Trumbull, of Victorious Life reknown. In 1889 the elder Trumbull published several small books of practical advice. Two were entitled *Duty-Knowing and Duty-Doing* and *Character-Shaping and Character-Showing*. "Character is the measure of the man," he wrote. "He who is spoken of as a man of upright character, as a man of courageous character . . . is by that very mention designated as a man of exceptional character. . . ." Like Sunday and Smiles, Trumbull was an enthusiast of manliness. "A real man is a real hero," he asserted. "The primary idea of heroism is an exceptional manliness, a manliness which partakes of the divine element." Again we hear familiar words and phrases, calls to "nobility," to "high moral purpose," to "courage." The manly life is an austere life, and references to the life of the soldier are sprinkled throughout. Again, Napoleon makes his frequent entrance as a figure worthy of manly Christian emulation.[154]

Since the publication of Max Weber's *The Protestant Ethic and the Spirit of Capitalism*, it has been no secret that such character traits necessarily bear implications for economic behavior. Associated with this model of manliness are those practices that encourage the careful accumulation and investment of capital, the rational calculation of prospects for profit, and the tireless application to the task of creating and maintaining a successful business enterprise. One of the most important specific economic virtues associated with this sort of manliness is thrift. For the purveyors of the "Protestant ethic," as for the capitalist system in its formative stages, the undisciplined expenditure of money was a cardinal sin. The typical young man and woman of the late nineteenth century could not escape childhood without many a lesson on the merits of thrift: money was to be saved, not spent. And a "manly" character helped, of course, if it meant the abilty to keep oneself under control and say a firm no to the many varied pleasures of this world that one's money could buy.

None of the three champions of manliness mentioned above—Sunday, Smiles, or Trumbull—used the term "thrift" in describing the traits of a manly character; they did not conceive of themselves as writing about economic matters at all. Along with most of the character builders of the late nineteenth century, they did, however, agree on a list of good and bad qualities that add up to a most discriminating and miserly use of money and a lifestyle of considerable austerity. The good qualities are such as these: self-denial, self-restraint, self-control, self-discipline, self-watchfulness. The bad qualities, as one might expect, include: selfishness, self-indulgence, love of ease or of pleasure.[155] This value system was not conducive to the development of energetic consumers.

The point at which these partisans of manliness and character offered the most serious resistance to the advertising ethos of the late nineteenth and early twentieth centuries was in their deep suspicion of human impulse and human desire. "Desire is . . . never a safe guide of conduct," wrote Trumbull. "Desire is an impulse of the nature. . . . We, being what we are, are sure to have desires which we, being what we are, have no right to seek the gratifying of." Likewise, we must not be led by "our impulses, or moods, or freaks of feeling." "There is no more unsafe guide for us than our impressions of the hour." Everyone ought to know what is right and do it, "unflinchingly, regardless of his temporary feelings—of his fluctuating impressions and his emotional impellings." One ought not give way to "feeling," but rather always to follow "principle."[156] According to the elder Trumbull's admiring biographer, his life embodied these virtues: "He was ready to master his impulses, to hold himself in check. . . . He set barriers to his desires. . . . He kept himself under control."[157] Samuel Smiles echoed these sentiments almost exactly: "To be morally free—to be more than an animal—man must be able to resist instinctive impulse, and this can only be done by the exercise of self-control." Smiles quoted Herbert Spencer in the same vein: "In the supremacy of self-control consists one of the perfections of the ideal man. Not to be impulsive—not to be spurred hither and thither by each desire that in turn comes uppermost. . . ."[158]

The full flowering of the advertising ethos in America, of course, immersed the average American in visual messages shouting exactly the opposite message: to be impulsive, to be spurred hither and thither by each desire, there is real manhood and womanhood and the only hope for true happiness. The society within which Billy Sunday preached was one torn by a historic dissonance, the dissonance of two contradictory value systems, two "moralities" locked in mortal combat. The morality of the "Protestant ethic," ideally suited to a society struggling with the economic challenges of production, was finding its monopoly threatened by a morality necessary to a society whose economic health required that its citizens learn to consume—and keep on consuming.[159] The former morality was deeply imbedded in the American psyche, the result of intense childhood conditioning and reinforcement perpetuated by centuries of religious justification. The latter value system increasingly dominated the powerful national print media; indeed, its purveyors owned or financed those media. Rarely did Americans of that time recognize the dissonance as an explicit clash of two moralities. Even more rarely did they understand the changing dynamic of capitalism and the economic source— even the economic necessity—of the dissonance. All too often they framed the crisis of their day in individualistic terms and sought for individualistic solutions, thus obfuscating the true nature of the crisis and missing their own ineluctable participation in it. They did not see the problem with the clarity that hindsight affords us almost a century later; but they did sense that somehow they were caught in a period of crisis. They knew something was wrong.

A striking example of their uneasiness appears in an article published in a national magazine as early as 1887. The author, George Frederic Parsons, was worked up about what he called "the growth of materialism" in American culture. At first the essay appears to be the standard declamation against the "cult of riches," a note struck often during the nineteenth century. "The whole aim and intent of the social system of today," Parsons asserts, "is to facilitate the acquisition of material wealth." We have made a virtue of selfishness, and we worship at "the shrine of Mammon." Very soon, however, he begins to describe a society dominated by what we have come to recognize as the consumerism ethos, and his analysis touches on themes we have learned to associate with the language and effect of advertising, which in his day was still in its infancy. Modern life, he says, has seen a profusion of goods; along with this profusion, "invention has been stimulated to multiply the wants of men by increasing their desires." We are surrounded by "the incessant stimulation of man's lust of possessions, of his wants, of his selfishness. . . ." We appear to believe that "the more wants a man feels, the better off he is." Yet, since we cannot satisfy all these desires, we experience a "baffled cupidity" that results in "discontent" and "dissatisfaction," for which there seems to be no cure.[160]

With keen insight, I believe, Parsons puts his finger on those human vulnerabilities advertising most persuasively exploits. If "the fetich of man is money," he wrote, "the fetich of woman is fashion." To be in fashion, we "cultivate frivolity" and surrender to "imitation," to "perennial sham and imposture." We indulge "a senseless desire to appear better off than we are," thus existing in a "haze of false pretenses, for no better object than the gratification of a vanity. . . ." Our aim in life is "pleasure" and "sensuous and sensual gratification, ministrations to the lusts of the eyes, and to the demands of the body for soft lying and savory eating and agreeable drinking. . . ." Our motto, more than in any other historical era, is *carpe diem;* we honor luxury, amusement, comfort. "One of the most common of current phrases," he observes, "is that of 'having a good time,'" which most often leads to "some contemptible concession to a self-indulged, pithless inclination." The results to us and to society are grim. We shirk duty, avoid and devalue hard work, refuse self-sacrifice, and do violence to "all the qualities which go to make honorable manhood." "Force of character" is no longer deemed necessary to social success, and we succumb to "moral dry rot."[161]

Parsons was prophetic. At the dawn of the age of consumerism, he described the frantic quest for self-gratification that has become the reigning morality of our time and, in the eyes of some, a threat to the very economic system that brought it into existence.[162] Before its fullest manifestation, Parsons sensed the nature of that threat: "It would not . . . require more than one or two generations of undisciplined self-seekers to establish a breed of egoists more self-centered, more void of sympathy, than any form of advanced civilization has yet known. . . ." The twentieth century has known this void, from the death camps of Nazi Germany to the abortion clinics of contemporary America—to name only two from a tragically long list. Parsons may not have seen how inevitable, and how vital to the health of the mature capitalist system, was this ethic of self-gratification, although he came close enough to warrant our admiration. He bemoaned those theorists in his day "who hold that the best guarantee for steady progress consists in the infinitude of human wants and desires." Little did he know how incisively he had captured the reigning doctrine of an entire advertising industry whose effects could only be dimly perceived in his day. Perhaps he did not realize how the symptoms he bemoaned pointed to the deepest necessities of the evolving economic system in which he participated. But he did know something was wrong.[163]

Billy Sunday also knew something was wrong, and in his opinion, the problem was the lack of moral principle. To a certain degree, of course, he was right. When has immorality not been a problem in human history?

But he was intellectually and emotionally unable to view the demise of traditional morality in anything other than the most individualistic and judgmental light. The problem was simple, he seemed to think: people are freely choosing to do bad things when they should freely choose to do good things. He could not see that his own version of morality was tied to a particular place and time, and that larger forces were at work altering that place and time forever. He could not see this because he considered humans to be in charge of their history, which, whether he knew it or not, he had learned from the Enlightenment. He also could not see it because he believed that he possessed a timeless morality—with the freedom to obey its dictates. He did not understand himself to be a culturally and historically conditioned human being.

And yet his ministry is most revealing and helpful to our understanding of his time. His preaching points to the dissonance in which he and evangelicals generally lived, and it reveals to us, quite unsystematically, the clash of moralities that dominated his day. While I do not believe Sunday was prophetic in the way he and his followers thought he was, he was prophetic in another sense—a sense hidden entirely from himself. He spoke intuitively to the deepest confusions of his age and to the realities most troubling to his evangelical audiences. In this way he did stick to his crowds, and his crowds loved him for it. He spoke in the language of a moralist and an evangelist, as one might expect. When he summarized his indictment of society, his excessive moralism and his lack of critical tools led him into oversimplification and superficiality, as when he bemoaned the "widespread disregard for the old time principles of integrity, honesty and manhood."[164] This is not cultural analysis at its best, nor does it indicate an understanding of how thoroughly conditioned by larger historical forces was this lack of moral principle. But when one searches through Sunday's sermons with an awareness of the dissonance being wrought by the new consumerist ethic, one finds a startling bill of particulars that amounts to an indictment of the consumer society and the ethic of self-gratification that advertising was selling to an increasingly uneasy but increasingly vulnerable American public.

Like Parsons, Sunday seemed to think that an inordinate love of money was somewhere near the heart of the crisis of his day. "Money is as truly a god for some people," he preached, "as if they prayed to ten dollar gold pieces." Sunday here creates a very apt image of human slavery to a "principality" or "power," an image, if we extended it a bit, that might mitigate his own sense of human moral autonomy. He continues:

Oh, we are making money in America by bucketfuls, but we are going to hell in car-lots on excursion rates! Oh, the magic of money! Oh, the rush for

money! Oh, the counting of money! Oh, the jealousy of money! Oh, the
lying for money! Oh, the stealing for money! Oh, the contentions after
money! Oh, the oppressions for money! Oh, the murder for money! The
adultery for money! The gambling for money! Selfishness for money! Oh,
the loneliness of the man that has lost all but his money! Oh, the loneliness
of the man who has nothing but money! The fellow that has no money is
poor; the fellow that has nothing but money is poorer still.[165]

Sunday captured here the abject drivenness, even the dizzy drunkenness, that characterizes the lust for money—a drunkenness potentially
much more widespread and just as enslaving as that caused by alcohol.
But in another sermon, as if recommending moral reformation instead of
the more appropriate recognition of and liberation from a powerful and
enslaving reality, he suggested that what the world needed was "not
more money but more love. Not more money but more devotion, more
kindness, more smiles, more honor, more virtue, more truth. . . . We
need more manhood in America and less money."[166]

Sunday's diatribes against the love of money were not nearly as frequent as his stinging thrusts against the things money could buy—the
consumer items so tirelessly being sold by the advertisers of his day. We
do not know whether he had ever heard of Bonsack and his amazing
cigarette machine, or knew that the generation immediately before his
had been virtual strangers to cigarettes; but Sunday did know that "last
year we spent one billion two hundred million dollars for tobacco" and
that smoking "leads to drink . . . grinds a man's will into powder, racks
his nerves, ruins his heart, deadens his sensibilities" and turns him
"yellow-fingered" and "anaemic." Perhaps he was not aware that
E. Anheuser Brewing Company and Joseph Schlitz Beverage Company
were among the major industrial success stories and the leading advertisers of his day; but he did know that "last year we spent in this country
two billion five hundred and ninety million dollars for drink" and that
"we wasted grain enough in the breweries and distilleries, my friends, to
have fed this country as much grain as we used for bread."

Sunday went on to give the figures for yearly expenditures on jewelry,
automobiles, candy, soda water, chewing gum, and pet dogs—most of
these, unknown to him, key participants in the advertising industry.
Toward these items, in contrast to tobacco and alcohol, Sunday betrayed
a certain ambivalence; he was unwilling to condemn them out of hand. "I
love to see nice jewelry if you can afford it," he said, and "I wish everybody could afford an auto. I think it is one of the grandest inventions for
the comfort, the happiness of the American people. It makes a man forget. He spins out into the country in the motor and forgets his cares. I
wish we could all afford it." Here he betrayed his presuppositions about

human freedom and his ignorance of the forces working to take away any real association of these items with free moral choice. At the same time, he betrayed how deeply into his own psyche these forces had penetrated: advertising had apparently convinced him that automobiles really do provide happiness and, startlingly, that thereby one can forget his cares. He could not have recognized how his use of the automobile paralleled the beer-drinker's use of alcohol as an escape mechanism. I suspect, in other words, that unwittingly he simply parroted the automobile advertisements of his day, which could hardly have wished for a better endorsement from a leading public figure. Yet, the general context of these figures on American spending patterns was negative. We spend more money on chewing gum than on Christian missions, he said. If we've got so much money in America, why is not more of it at the disposal of God's kingdom?

Sunday's obvious ambivalence toward certain of these consumer items disappeared, however, when he came to his indictment of "society women" in the same sermon. That is where he seems to have found his paradigm of consumerism, and he condemned the consumer items these women were most interested in, item by item: dancing pumps, silk hose, diamonds, limousines and yachts, tapestries and rugs, fashionable clothes, highly seasoned foods, candlesticks and tankards, polo, bridge, fine clothes (again), matinee and opera, dresses six inches above the shoetops, cosmetics, candy (particularly fudge), ragtime music, manicured nails, and penciled eyebrows.[167] In other sermons Sunday reeled off similar lists, adding "painted cheeks," "dope and cold cream," "foolish amusements" and "trashy novels," the "silks and the satins and the diamonds."[168] He seems to have been especially troubled by the women's clothing industry and its appeal to "fashion." In one sermon he mentioned the "faddist mother" who always "buys the latest in dresses and hats. She wears a velvet hat in August because that is going to be the style in October."[169] Sunday often spoke as if these vices were unique to the upper crust of society, the "society women." But when one realizes that advertisers were consciously boasting that goods once confined to the homes of the rich were now available to all, and were claiming to democratize the previously aristocratic tastes for luxury, one can see the differences between the classes disappearing. Sunday could just as well have been talking about the vast middle class.[170]

It is significant, I think, that in Sunday's references to consumer items he spoke almost without exception of women. He referred at times to the hard-working husband as the victim of these women and suggested that when the wife goes out and spends family money on clothing, the husband has a right to be upset and to prohibit such behavior in the future.[171]

Sunday seems to reflect here a male uneasiness at a time when great social pressures were being marshalled to redefine the woman's role as that of household consumer. A standard teaching in the burgeoning advertising industry at the turn of the century was that men were the earners and women the spenders of money. "The proper study of mankind is MAN," went one formula, ". . . but the proper study of markets is WOMAN." Journals cited statistics showing that 85 percent of all consumer spending was done by women. Even male items were sold to women: "What does a man know about complexion, the skin? Nothing. . . . You, the woman of the family, understand what the care of the skin means. . . . Protect that foolish husband of yours . . . put a bottle of Facefriend in the bathroom closet." Or, the inevitable appeal to fashion: "Jim always buys the same old ties, doesn't he? . . . Dig Jim out of the dark-blue-and-white-dot habit. Make him stylish whether he wants to be or not."[172] Both of these ads ran in 1917, the year of Sunday's New York campaign and of the sermons we have been examining. He may not have seen these ads, and his critiques of "society women" may be heavy-handed and full of male bias, but he was not unenlightened in sensing that the consumerist appeals and temptations were strongest to women, due not to any innate vulnerability on their part but to their being the targets of many millions of dollars worth of advertising assaults. In one of Sunday's most poignant portraits of woman as consumer he spoke of the "delicatessen woman":

> She lives in the apartment. Her work is minimized. She never has to build a fire, she spends her time visiting her neighbors, always dressed up, always dressed up. Keeps her husband's nose to the grind stone three hundred sixty-five days a year, to keep that little dog. Now she gazes into the shop window, has to have a maid to take care of her children and when the whistle blows she rushes to the telephone, calls up her grocer and gets her stuff already cooked.[173]

Sunday recognized that the Industrial Revolution had narrowed the sphere of a woman's duties in the middle-class home.[174] In one brief phrase—"she gazes into the shop window"—he symbolized the efforts of a whole generation of advertising experts to shape a substitute identity for housewife, the identity of shopper.

Sunday came closest to an outright denunciation of the rising culture of consumerism and the ethic of self-gratification in a sermon he delivered on the text "Behold, he hath hid himself among the stuff." Ignoring the context of this passage in I Samuel 10:22, Sunday describes the man and woman of his time as hiding among the stuff of modern civilization, as virtually buried by it—an apt image.

They are hiding behind and beneath stocks and bonds, dry goods, infidelity, whiskey, beer, love of ease, my friends, Sunday and Sabbath desecration. Genuineness, purity, Christian nobility and integrity are lost in the search for fortune, and in their ambition to gratify their desires to drink at the bubbly spring of pleasure.[175]

Sunday's image of the consumerist society as a "bubbly spring of pleasure" is a powerful one. What is most remarkable about this paragraph, though, is the variety of modern symbols he has collected in one sentence: symbols of the new finance capitalism; "old" vices like infidelity, now an increasingly respectable response to the ethic of self-gratification at all costs; "new" vices like whiskey and beer, now standardized, tradenamed, and widely distributed consumer items; Sabbath desecration, which can at least partially be traced to new attitudes toward leisure, the rise of an increasingly variegated and consumable leisure technology (Sunday himself associated Sabbath-breaking with "amusement parks"), and professional spectator sports (in this department, Sunday had been in on the ground floor);[176] dry goods, one of the first of the factory-produced consumables and a staple of those modern temples to consumerism, the giant department store;[177] and the love of ease, a standard theme in the new advertising ethos. The sermon returns repeatedly to condemn exactly those motivations that were fueling the rising consumer mentality: gratification of desire, love of pleasure, luxury, and ease, vanity, selfish ambition, passion, and overindulgence.[178] Sunday did not frame his indictment in terms of the creeping miasma of consumerism, nor did he treat these symptoms as part of a systematic unity. As a moralist, he spoke of things that were simply wrong. But he spoke more eloquently than he knew—if one reads between the lines.

Because he was unsystematic and often contradictory in the wild meanderings of his sermon material, and perhaps because he was himself the child of an age of cultural confusion and dissonance, Sunday demonstrated a certain ambivalence about the consumer culture, as we have seen in his description of the pleasures of the automobile. The ambivalence comes up again in his discussion of debt. Presumably the immorality of debt was a theme in his boyhood training along with the importance of thrift. Financial debt was associated with the irresponsible life, and when Sunday sought justifications in his sermons for his indictment of consumerism, a natural expedient was this debt taboo. "I believe that the angels weep the day that a young fellow starts out and spends more than he earns," he preached. He pressed young men to make it their first rule not to go into debt, since "the best plan the devil ever hit upon is to get people in debt." Once he had constructed his argument on the evils of debt, however, he was virtually forced to approve the purchase of consumer goods so long as there was no debt involved. Thus he admitted: "It is gratifying to be well dressed—oh my!—but when your clothes are bought on credit, they cost you too much. . . . So wear the best clothes you can and pay for them, that is all."[179] His advice to women was similar: "Oh, I don't blame you for wanting nice things, but when you can't afford it, don't be a darn fool and keep your husband in debt all the time, just to show off."[180] Here the limits of his moralism in reaching a deeper understanding of the lure of the consumer culture became plain.

And yet Sunday rose to a truer—though not always less moralistic—understanding of modern culture on other occasions. He did seem to understand, dimly perhaps, that the problem of the average American was not really the problem of indebtedness but the problem of a slavery, a drivenness, a blindness. We live in a "pleasure-mad community," he said.[181] We are "slaves to fashion," and "chained to Mammon," and caught in "the whirl of society" and "the giddy circles of fashion," we never really experience the "choicest sweets of human existence." Sunday described well the trappedness that many in his audiences must have felt had they been able to admit it:

> Vast accumulations always bring with them vast responsibilities and they rob life seemingly of its sweetest pleasures and they harden and dwarf the better side of our nature and they turn the milk of human kindness into a sort of a buttermilk or a whey, and feed upon the baser longings of the human heart and mind. [Are these "baser longings" the deep human instincts to which the advertising psychologist urged his clients to make their appeal?] It drives its victims to a premature grave, worn out and jaded and tired. . . .

And yet, Sunday admitted, these things have a certain "allure."[182] Sunday pled with his crowds to resist that allure: "Don't allow the devil to beat you in these days and turn you aside by the glitter and dazzle of the world."[183] "O Jesus," he prayed, "Lord, God, help us not to be absorbed and blinded and dazzled by the temporary things of the world."[184] How hard, when our eyes are blinded, to see "that stuff is transient, stuff is as weak as a rope of sand and as unenduring as a cloud of smoke or vapor."[185]

And yet people desire stuff, cling to stuff, and consume stuff. In Sunday's own ambivalence ("it is gratifying to be well-dressed") he must have known the addictive power of the consumer society. When he spoke directly about an addiction, however, it was a different addiction, the addiction to alcohol. In fact, the entire society spoke of that addiction over the course of several generations, and the discussion culminated in the

United States just after World War I with a national law prohibiting the manufacture and sale of alcoholic beverages. Billy Sunday's "booze sermon" was by far his most popular sermon, the subject of genuine excitement when he preached it. How odd it seems, that while the rapidly developing field of consumer advertising was fastening its seductive grip on American society, with revolutionary albeit rarely noticed effects on the American psyche, the citizenry chose to work itself into a fever over an addiction whose social impact may have been more visible but which was certainly less ubiquitous and relevant than consumerism to the average men, women, and children of America.

I suspect, however, that it is not very odd at all. Americans, particularly evangelicals, were deeply troubled by the emerging landscape of modern society, and it is not strange that they should reach for a scapegoat, a symbol of their discontent; nor is it strange that they should try to rid society of the evil thing. But how could they symbolize what so few of them could recognize as evil? How difficult to comprehend the increasingly demonic nature of that profusion of goods that humanity has always craved that was now within its grasp, and that could so readily appear to be the bounty of God's goodness. How utterly impossible to grasp and then consciously to symbolize the logic of an economic system gone awry when that economic system had been at the center of the nation's pride, distinction, and prosperity for a century or more, and when that system seemed in quantitative terms such an obvious success, the envy of the world. How to embody in symbol an only dimly dawning awareness that something was wrong with life in an increasingly affluent, industrial society—that, in fact, that wrong might be endemic to the society? It is hard to choose a symbol consciously when one is confused about exactly what one is trying to symbolize.

But humans choose their symbols anyway, without systematic analysis, and their symbols often speak a truth that they themselves do not know. Symbols that achieve wide popular appeal are ones that reach deep into the human psyche and touch places with which most of us are not very familiar, least of all in ourselves. A symbol is always meaningful on a superficial level but never on that level alone. American evangelicals and others certainly had a right to be disturbed by the enslaving and degrading power of alcohol addiction, had a right to bemoan the violence and crime and family tragedy always associated with that addiction. But humans, it seems, rarely get exercised over a slavery that touches only others and not themselves, their fears, their vulnerabilities. Certainly they do not shake with "sobs and rage" and leap to their feet screaming and waving their arms as Billy Sunday's audiences did when he preached on the evils of booze, unless the evil in some way comes very close to

home.[186] Only as one evil symbolizes another evil, real or imagined, one
that is perhaps threatening to us, do we gather our forces to assault that
evil. When Billy Sunday and his followers and millions of Americans
assaulted "demon rum" at the turn of the century, I believe that they were
unwittingly lashing out against a slavemaster much more potent and all-
pervasive than alcohol alone, and they were lashing out not as the deliv-
erers, as they fancied themselves in the Prohibition crusade, but as the
slaves.

Demon rum, after all, had a power that was legendary. What better
symbol to capture the growing mastery over all of us of the twentieth-
century demon of consumer gratification? How better to symbolize a
historic dynamic not within the power of mortals to control. How might
one depict with greater poignancy the creation of infinite desire and
infinite restlessness, the yawning, unquenchable thirst for more, on
which the consumer culture thrives? Does not alcohol speak eloquently of
seeking but never really finding gratification? And does not the ceaseless
search for self-gratification, as surely as alcohol, destroy families, take
children from the parents and parents from their children, as the love of
pleasure finds that it cannot coexist untrammeled with the sanctity of
commitment and the loving self-sacrifice that stable relationships demand in any age?[187]

Demon rum also captured the insidiousness of the addiction that consumerism brings, the luster of the package, the seeming harmlessness of
the temptation, but the enslavement that ensues. Sunday captured this
dynamic in speaking of sin, but he could as easily have been speaking of
consumerism: "If sin weren't so deceitful it wouldn't be so attractive. The
effects get stronger and stronger while you get weaker and weaker all the
time, and there is less chance of breaking away."[188] And just as surely as
did alcohol, the demon of consumer gratification expressed itself as a
mania that broke out virtually uninvited. Listen to the testimony of a
woman visiting a department store, the economic institution that to one
historian most aptly symbolized the modern "consumption principle
based on self-indulgence."

> I felt myself overcome little by little by a disorder that can only be compared
> to that of drunkenness, with the dizziness and excitation that are peculiar to
> it. I saw things as if through a cloud, everything stimulated my desire and
> assumed, for me, an extraordinary attraction. I felt myself swept along
> towards them and I grabbed hold of things without any outside and superi-
> or consideration intervening to hold me back. Moreover I took things at
> random, useless and worthless articles as well as useful and expensive
> articles. It was like a monomania of possession.[189]

Other women testified similarly: "my head was spinning"; "I felt completely dizzy"; "I am just as if I were drunk." This testimony was taken from middle-class women who were apprehended for shoplifting in department stores, an odd foreshadowing of Billy Sunday's contention that alcohol was the cause of virtually all crime. Here the addiction was to consumer gratification, leading one historian to suggest that "the pathological frenzy to which some women were driven had become simply the seamier side of the new consumer society, where the old virtues of thrift and self-control were giving way to a culture of gratification."[190] In the plight of these women, drunk on goods, we can see writ large the addictive forces that, more quietly, plague all engaged members of the modern consumer society. In choosing as their symbol the addicting demon of alcoholism, Sunday and his followers revealed a logic they themselves were not even aware of.

Billy Sunday's obsession was with those who indulged in an appetite for alcohol. But he did use very similar imagery, that of eating and drinking, in connection with the consumption of material goods. In the midst of a diatribe on "purples and . . . furs" and "homes of grandeur and of splendor," he inserted these lines: "Over-indulgence, fostering pride, my friends, feeding their passions, glutting their appetites on champagne, cocktails and wines, highly seasoned food, O God, that's what made the wrecks."[191] Elsewhere he urged men to "fight against physical appetite . . . against the demands of an inflamed appetite" that cries out for "the gratification of some desire."[192] And in yet another sermon, where he spoke sensationally of the craving for and display of material goods, he offered a most striking analogy between the physical act of eating and drinking and material consumption: "So you people are being choked to death trying to gulp down the forbidden things of the world. It may take some of the good hard clapboard raps of the gospel to dislodge it, but I have come as your friend to help you and I hope I might, lest it choke out every spark of manhood and womanhood in the world."[193]

In alcohol, Billy Sunday and his fellow Americans found a suitable symbol for the demon that, more than any other, has moved into the very heart of the American system and enslaved the American people, evangelicals included, in the twentieth century. This demon has indeed threatened to choke us to death on surfeit; and yet no sooner have we swallowed the latest object, experience, adventure, or person than the hunger pangs begin anew and the mania to consume carries us to our next banquet table. But Sunday could never bring before his audiences the explicit connection between the alcoholism they so berated and the consumerist addiction to which larger social forces were tempting them. He could not admit that he, and his audiences, were surely drunk. It would have required a more critical eye toward the American economic system, a more thoroughgoing acceptance of his own—and his audiences'—solidarity in sin with fellow Americans, and a more abject confession of powerlessness than Sunday was capable of embracing. It would have complicated his program for moral heroism and his hopes to recapture American society for evangelical Christianity.

So instead, he leveled his guns consistently at the evils of alcohol and related sins, as well as the people who shamed themselves by indulging in such sins, and thus confirmed evangelicals in the impression that a quick fix was available that required little action on God's part and the kind of moral heroism on their own part to which they were already accustomed. Sunday chose the expedient of many of the prophets of Jeremiah's day. Thinking he was asking a great deal of his listeners when he asked them to be moral and manly and to fight demon rum, he actually asked very little. He made it unnecessary for them to admit the extent of their guilt and their slavery, and thus he "healed the wound of [God's] people lightly, saying, 'Peace, peace,' when there is no peace." Perhaps the prophet Micah could have said of him, "If a man should go about and utter wind and lies, saying, 'I will preach to you of wine and strong drink,' he would be the preacher for this people!" (Jer. 6:14; Mic. 2:11).

In convincing evangelicals that they could, by moral exertion and manly courage, control their destinies and the destiny of their nation, Sunday helped make them feel full rather than empty and helped them avoid the mourning of those who know their own powerlessness and the futility of their own moral efforts. But he deprived them also of the joy of those who know that God is the Victor in history—Victor even over those demonic principalities and powers that enslave humankind in every age. Sunday presented himself as one who could rightly interpret the signs of the times. But for all his earnest love for souls and his eloquent denunciation of sins, he may well have been a blind guide who, together with his followers, fell into a pit.

VII

American evangelicals, from the beginning of their history, have lived within a national ethos whose unquestioned and proudly advertised assumptions receive no support whatever in the biblical text. These assumptions go something like this: we are in control of our own lives, of the nature of our society, and of our history. This ethos has become implicit and unquestioned in the evangelical mind. The colonies and territories that became the United States were peopled by restless spirits chafing under unwanted authorities. The ocean that separated them from duly constituted governments offered the illusion of freedom and power; and the rhetoric of the War for Independence, reflecting the self-inflated human aspirations of the European Enlightenment, strengthened that illusion. The surprising success of the American experiment with representative government—"of the people, by the people, and for the people"—and the growing prosperity of the nation in the nineteenth century, wedded the American people to this Enlightenment mythology even as they were congratulating themselves on being a Christian nation.

If human history itself were revealing, it seems quite possible that evangelicals would have put the lie to this mythology of human control by the early years of the twentieth century. Their world was immeasurably more complex and less comforting than it had been just fifty years before. One can understand the lingering—in some cases, even the building—confidence of the new professional classes and the new social scientists whose embrace of the scientific ethos offered hope of moving from "drift" to "mastery" in the relationship of humans to their history.[194] But this scientific ethos was increasingly unfriendly to any view of the world that retained a place for the supernatural; thus science simply added its sting to the sense of alienation and powerlessness that rapid moral, social, and religious changes were pressing upon the evangelicals of America. One would think that these evangelicals might have reflected on their history and might have slowly apprehended the full extent of their surrender to human arrogance in the form of the American national mythology, bringing them to repentance, mourning, and an attitude of waiting.

History does not seem to be revealing in itself, however, for we do not find much evidence of this dawning awareness among evangelicals. We do find hints of a move in that direction in the premillennialist and Victorious Life movements, both of which reflected a certain partial letting go of temporal history and a disillusionment with American history in particular. But what they gave with their right hands, they took back with their left, transforming their quest for power into a knowledge of predictable events and an exemption from suffering (in the case of the premillennialists) or into perfect victory centered in a subjective inner kingdom (in the case of the Victorious Lifers). Their maneuvers were defensive and grudging, I believe, not a full-hearted embrace of the paradoxical powerlessness revealed in Jesus' journey toward Jerusalem and Golgotha. The half-heartedness of their relinquishing worldly power becomes evident in their enthusiastic support for an evangelist like Billy Sunday, who overtly symbolized a new lease on life for evangelical hegemony in America and thus tantalized them with the possible reestablishment of the power they had lost. They happily overlooked all doctrinal inconsistencies in their rush to identify themselves with this powerful champion who told them that they were the true Americans, destined by virtue of their morality and manliness to rule over their country and their history once again.

This slavery to the mythology of our own freedom, and thus our own power, is rooted very deep within evangelicalism, and it shows no signs of being shaken—even in the waning years of the twentieth century. That national mythology is reinforced by the media, which tell us what we want to hear; by the educational system, which tells our children what we want them to hear; and by the political authorities who, in addition to believing it, find it helpful in maintaining their popularity and the popularity of the policies they believe enhance American strength, autonomy, and prosperity in an increasingly hostile world. But the national mythology also meshes with a deeper human mythology by which the Bible defines our radical illness and fallenness: the mythology that tells us we are in charge of the world and our lives, that we have a certain efficacy in human affairs, that we are God's agents to set things right. This mythology goes back to the dawn of human life, and the American national mythology is just the latest version of it, albeit a particularly tenacious and ultimately, I believe, dangerous version of it.

The biblical perspective on this mythology is helpful in our attempt to understand the meaning of Billy Sunday's ministry. In John 8 we listen in on a rather lengthy dialogue between Jesus and the Jews. In the latter half of the chapter Jesus confronts certain of these Jews who had ostensibly believed in him. His word to them is a revelation of their own slavery. I find it quite likely that among these "believing" Jews are Pharisees, who see Jesus as a vehicle to their own self-justification and earthly power. When Jesus implies that they do not yet know the truth, and that they are not yet free, these Jews protest, at first rather modestly but then with increasing anger and hostility. "We are descendants of Abraham, and have never been in bondage to any one." Jesus then informs them that they are indeed slaves—slaves to sin—and that this slavery goes so deep that they will seek to kill him. Again they claim their noble religious lineage and thus their freedom. Jesus sees the hardness of their hearts and in the simplest terms reveals the nature of their bondage: "Why do you not understand what I say? It is because you cannot bear to hear my word. You are of your father the devil, and your will is to do your father's desires. He was a murderer from the beginning, and has nothing to do with the truth, because there is no truth in him. When he lies, he speaks according to his own nature, for he is a liar and the father of lies. But, because I tell the truth, you do not believe me" (Jn. 8:13, 31-39, 43-45).

What is the truth, the truth that drives these "believing" Jews to stone Jesus before this dialogue is over, and to crucify him as a false Messiah? It is the truth that we are not free, but slaves. And one of our deepest slaveries is our slavery to our own efficacy, our own will to power, our own freedom to decide the course of history. The evangelicals of Billy Sunday's time, like all humans, were not apt to admit this slavery. History, they thought, revealed not the utter impotence of puny human beings but the temporary, soon to be remedied, overthrow of a good group of godly people. They believed that through moral exertion they would once again—and deservedly—be at the helm of an earthly kingdom, and all would be well. Could they have borne to hear the truth from Jesus himself, or would they too have stoned him for questioning their freedom and their fitness for power? Would he not have had to say to them, as he must say to us, "Why do you not understand what I say? It is because you cannot bear to hear my word."

The truth that sets us free involves, in part, the truth of our own feebleness, our own slavery. This truth throws us, like Simeon, on the mercy of God. And history seems unable to reveal this truth to us. It is Jesus who is the light of the world, and to see his light is to walk no longer in blindness to our own slavery—or, as the text says, in "darkness." Darkness is our natural condition, according to the Bible, and we love it rather than light; that is, we love our own slavery, which we insist on calling freedom. Proverbs 4:19 puts it well: "The way of the wicked is like deep darkness; they do not know over what they stumble." Billy Sunday's prophetic message, I believe, gives evidence of that darkness. In his trumpeting of the possibilities for morality and manliness, and his hope that by these means God's people could return to power, he remained ignorant of the menace embodied in consumer capitalism that has tripped up the evangelical church from his time to ours. He thought he saw clearly the signs of the times, but as Jesus told the Pharisees, "If you were blind, you would have no guilt; but now that you say, 'We see,' your guilt remains" (Prov. 4:19; Jn. 9:41).

Billy Sunday and his crowds believed that they were up against the devil, to be sure, but they thought they had taken the devil's measure in assessing the gross immorality of the time and in prescribing a manly morality to replace it. They would have been shocked to hear Jesus' news that they were of their father the devil. But they would also have been shocked to know that they had not really taken the devil's measure—that even as they berated the grossest immoralities they knew, the Prince of Darkness was forging new chains with which to deepen their enslavement—the chains of consumer yearning and the endless search for self-gratification. Perhaps they read only superficially Paul's admonition to the Ephesians: "Finally, be strong in the Lord [not in your own morality] and in the strength of his might [not your own manliness and "grit"]. Put on the whole armor of God [not of "character"], that you may be able to stand against the wiles of the devil. For we are not contending against flesh and blood [such as society women, or saloon keepers, or even the greedy concerns of the advertising industry], but against the principalities, against the powers, against the world rulers [therefore, do not too readily yourself aspire to be a ruler] of this present *darkness* [which afflicts you too], against the spiritual hosts of wickedness in the heavenly places [thus, do not think that, with your earthly power and morality, you can defeat these particular powers!]. Therefore take the whole armor of God, that you may be able to withstand in the evil day [and when has it not been an evil day—even, perhaps most specifically, in professedly 'Christian' societies?], and having done all, to stand [not to rule, but to stand . . . waiting?]." And then Paul recommends truth. Does he mean the truth of our weakness, our own slavery, even our own darkness—but God's strength and freedom and light? And he recommends righteousness—surely not our own but what is ours only in Christ, and then not as if we could possess it and boast of it. And he recommends the gospel of peace. Did Billy Sunday's violent diatribes presage *this* gospel? And he recommends faith and salvation and the word of God—all gifts by which we are made not moral and manly but grateful recipients of undeserved mercy. Paul adds a word of warning: keep alert. How can we be alert if we persist in calling our darkness light, if we insist that "we see" (Eph. 6:10-18; Jn. 9:41)?

The Pharisees thought they were alert—indeed, the most alert of all the Jews—but in their unwillingness to hear Jesus' truth about their own slavery they stumbled. Simeon knew he was bereft, and thus he waited—alert. In this baby Jesus he could see what the Pharisees would not see in the adult Jesus: the consolation for his mourning, the victory of God in history (all appearances to the contrary), salvation prepared in the presence of *all* peoples, and a light for the Gentiles and for Israel. Surely he was joyful. Not that he ceased his mourning: Herod was still king, Jewish babies were still being killed, patriots still hung on crosses, and on the outskirts of Jerusalem the poor still begged and the lepers nursed their broken bodies. But somehow all of history had changed, and the triumph of God had been revealed, even though nothing had changed to the naked eye. Perhaps Simeon smiled, but through tears that continued to flow. He knew the joy of his Consolation, but he also knew that this light would be, for some, not a revelation and a glory but "a sign that is spoken against . . . that thoughts out of many hearts may be revealed." Simeon knew his own heart, and thus his mourning was rooted very close to home. Perhaps he knew the words of Isaiah that were repeated by John's gospel: "He has blinded their eyes and hardened their heart, lest they should see with their eyes and perceive with their heart." And would Simeon have been surprised by Jesus' own words, "For judgment I came into this world, that those who do not see may see, and that those who see may become blind" (Jn. 12:40; 9:39)?

It is the age-old temptation of the people of God to think that, because we have received the Word in Jesus Christ, we see while all humanity is blind. It should frighten us and give us pause to recognize that the Pharisees were to a large degree the most faithful people of God in their day— and self-consciously so. Evangelical preaching has made much of the villainy of the Pharisees in order to put distance between them and ourselves. This has served to blunt the shock of recognition that should occur when we read their story. We are the Pharisees of our time, if anyone is. We say we see, and therein is our greatest offense against the Light of the world. Like the Pharisees, we are secure in our ancestral traditions, our religious observances, our moral heroism, our self-identity as the righteous and the godly. But like the Pharisees, we are ever in danger of stumbling into a pit along with those whom we have convinced to follow us. We are too often in the posture of Billy Sunday, leaping about in denunciation of public sins and in praise of our own achievements, while unwittingly we succumb to the latest shape in which history has dressed up human slavery to the principalities and the powers. We boast and play for power when we should be mourning and waiting.

The evangelicals of Sunday's day, like the Pharisees, were truly in darkness, truly blind to the signs of the times, as Jesus said. But Jesus was not blind to them, and his ability to see was also an occasion for him to mourn. Listen to this story in Luke 19:

> And when he drew near and saw the city he wept over it, saying, "Would that even today you knew the things that make for peace! But now they are hid from your eyes. For the days shall come upon you, when your enemies will cast up a bank about you and surround you, and hem you in on every side, and dash you to the ground, you and your children within you, and they will not leave one stone upon another in you; because you did not know the time of your visitation."
>
> (41-44)

Some of the very Pharisees who heard him say these words may have survived to see the destruction of the Holy City, over which Jesus wept, by the Romans in A.D. 70. But Jesus was speaking of more than this single event. I suspect that he was describing the fabric of human history as a whole. If so, perhaps he was also speaking of the fate that came, or is still to come, to the American evangelical community in the twentieth century.

We are blind and walk in darkness; and yet we are called to be alert. Paul takes up this theme again in his first letter to the Thessalonians:

> But as to the times and the seasons, brethren, you have no need to have anything written to you. For you yourselves know well that the day of the Lord will come like a thief in the night. When people say, "There is peace and security [by virtue of my power? my manliness? my friendliness with Almighty God?]," then sudden destruction will come upon them as travail comes upon a woman with child, and there will be no escape. *But you are not in darkness*, brethren, for that day to surprise you like a thief. *For you are all sons of light and sons of the day;* we are not of the night or of darkness. So then let us not sleep, as others do, but let us keep awake and be sober. For those who sleep sleep at night, and those who get drunk are drunk at night. But since we belong to the day, let us be sober, and put on the breastplate of faith and love, and for a helmet the hope of salvation.
>
> (5:1-8)

What an irony that, in their very quest for morality, manliness, and a godly control of history, the evangelicals of Billy Sunday's time demonstrated their own darkness, and indeed their drunkenness even while they chose as their champion a man who symbolized the national crusade against drunkenness. How fitting and how tragic a symbol for the inner contradictions of the evangelical Christian church in the time of its historic travail. Such are the paradoxes one may expect if one hears the word spoken by the Light of the world: "Now that you say, 'We see,' your guilt remains."

It remains to us, as evangelicals, to confess that guilt, that slavery, and indeed that drunkenness. There is freedom in hearing this truth, attested by the God of truth in Jesus Christ, for the God who speaks to us of our slavery also offers us a victory far greater than our paltry human victories could ever be, and a freedom that no national mythology, so deeply enslaving, can begin to comprehend. At least this is the cry and the hope of the psalmist:

> Some sat in darkness and in gloom,
>   prisoners in affliction and in irons,
> for they had rebelled against the words of God,
>   and spurned the counsel of the Most High.
> Their hearts were bowed down with hard labor;
>   they fell down, with none to help.
> Then they cried to the Lord in their trouble,
>   and he delivered them from their distress;

he brought them out of darkness and gloom,
    and broke their bonds asunder.
Let them thank the Lord for his steadfast love,
    for his wonderful works to the sons of men!
For he shatters the doors of bronze,
    and cuts in two the bars of iron.

                          (Ps. 107:10-16)

Chapter VI

Put No Confidence in the Flesh

I

Throughout his ministry Jesus was confronted by individuals who wished to make clear their own religious superiority. Often, as in his dialogue with the Samaritan woman, they appealed to a singular religious ancestry or an authoritative name: "Are you greater than our father Jacob. . . ?" In John 8, even those "believing" Jews boasted of their ancestry and turned it against Jesus: "Abraham is our father. . . . Are you greater than our father Abraham, who died?" The rich young ruler, on the other hand, appealed to his own moral uprightness as a sign of his religious merit: "All these [commandments] I have observed from my youth." From the beginning, the tenor of this conversation indicates that the young man believed he had a claim on Jesus' approval by virtue of his goodness. But here, as in most of these encounters, Jesus showed that he was unimpressed by claims to religious superiority or moral heroism, that he was uninterested in helping his listeners justify themselves by these means. All of these, as he told the Samaritan woman, were somehow at odds with worship made in spirit and in truth (Jn 8:39, 53; Lk. 18:20-21).

The apostle Paul, of all the New Testament writers, seemed to understand best the meaning of the spiritual worship to which Jesus referred. Like Jesus, Paul confronted during his ministry people whose primary intention was to proclaim their own rightness. In strong and blunt language, Paul warned the churches against the "dogs" and "evildoers" who would appear righteous, for example, by "mutilating the flesh" (in other words, by reviving circumcision as a mark of religious identity and superiority). These were very devout folk, no doubt; but like Jesus, Paul reserved some his most scathing remarks for them. He contrasted their false piety with the "true circumcision" that characterized those who "worship God in spirit, and glory in Jesus Christ." True spiritual worship, he reminded the Philippians, puts "no confidence in the flesh" (Phil. 3:23).

It is remarkable how thoroughly we twentieth-century Christians have forgotten the rather shocking meaning, in Paul's lexicon, of this term "the flesh." Our tendency has been to identify the flesh with the physical body in a fairly simplistic way, to assume that Paul was talking primarily about sexual sins. Paul's use of the term, however, was much more profound and far-reaching. In his letters Paul speaks of the flesh as that deep-rooted, natural orientation in the human being that is unrelentingly hostile toward God. The flesh is driven by a spirit of fear to seek its own enhancement and glorification instead of the glorification of God. In this frantic self-enhancement, it is enslaved and serves the law of sin. Blindly reaching out for eternal life, it is actually and inevitably bound for corruption, for death. "The flesh" is a reference to the enslavement of humanity by its own passions, that is, humanity at its most fallen and futile and tragic (Rom. 8:7, 15; 7:25; Gal. 6:8; Rom. 8:13).

Now it is clear that among these passions, rooted in the very core of human existence, is the passion for religion and the self-enhancement that religion offers. Paul hints at this in Romans 7:18, where he confesses that, although nothing good dwells in his flesh, he finds that he is indeed capable of *willing* what is right; it is the *doing* of the right that he ultimately finds impossible. In fact, several important passages in Paul's letters indicate that it is precisely this sincere willing of the good and right—and the religious machinations and presumptions issuing from it—that most manifest the enslavement to the flesh. Paul's letter to the Galatian church, for example, is full of consternation that they have been "bewitched," so that, "having begun with the Spirit," they were "now ending up with the flesh." What was their offense? It seems to have been a revival of the rituals of the Jewish law as a test and a badge of their faithfulness to the gospel of Jesus Christ. The motivations of these religious enthusiasts, and what characterized their "fleshiness," seems to have had to do with making a "good showing." In the attempt to demonstrate their own goodness, however, they were preaching a "different gospel"—indeed, a perversion of the gospel of Jesus Christ (Gal. 3:3; 6:12; 1:6-7).

In his letter to the Colossians, Paul reproached the church for a different variety of enslavement to the flesh. Here those who desired to appear morally upright were encouraging a severe ethical legalism, along with pious-sounding religious accouterments such as the worship of angels and attending to visions. Paul startled the Colossians by referring to them as the issue of a "puffed up" and "sensuous" mind. Since the Colossians had experienced the "putting off [of] the body of flesh in the circumcision of Christ," they were encouraged to avoid the kind of moral strictures ("Do not handle, Do not taste, Do not touch") that indicate, surprisingly, not piety but enslavement to the world. He left no doubt that he associated the religious mentality and moral legalism with the flesh when he wrote, "These have indeed an appearance of wisdom in promoting rigor of devotion and self-abasement and severity to the body, but they are of no value in checking the indulgence of the flesh." On the contrary, he might have said, the very attempt at self-abasement in these ways is of the essence of self-enhancement, and thus, far from checking the indulgence of the flesh, it subtly serves to promote it (Col. 2:18, 11, 21, 23)!

It appears, then, that Paul associated the flesh with the pride of religious achievement and of moral heroism, as if somehow in those human attitudes and behaviors that to all appearances are most "spiritual" one can discern that deep-rooted rebellion against God that is actually most unspiritual. In his instruction to the Colossians, Paul explicitly warns that the legalistic moralism to which they were drawn was a sign that, although Christ had liberated them from the "elemental spirits of the universe," these Christians gave evidence that they "still belonged to the world" (Col. 2:20). Here Paul shows a profound understanding of the deepest human motivations. He refused to be taken in by the appearance of goodness and piety. The burden of the religious person is to demonstrate that in religiosity he or she stands apart from and is obviously superior to all others, particularly to those who do not appear devout or moral. Paul's use of "flesh" reveals his understanding of the essential sameness of all human beings, both the religious and the ostensibly nonreligious. A concern for religiosity as such indicated to him simply the continuation of the human project of self-glorification and self-apotheosis—but in another guise, one that is somewhat more difficult to penetrate. The religious person, or the moral hero, is devoted to his or her own symbolic divinity, not to the divinity of Jesus Christ.

Paul's letter to the Philippians sums up this entire train of thought: to those tempted to subtle forms of self-glorification Paul commended a truer humility, which counts others better than oneself, a humility embodied most completely in Jesus Christ. He did not—as does the religious person—"count equality with God a thing to be grasped, but emptied himself, taking the form of a servant, being born in the likeness of men." Paul could not have been unaware of just how immoral and irreligious Jesus must have appeared to the proudly religious observers of his day—even in this sense of not grasping after equality with God. Christian believers who would "have this mind . . . , which is yours in Christ Jesus," would hardly be those boasting of their religiosity or moral accomplishments. They might rather be those who humbly understood that the gospel of Jesus Christ placed them in the strictest solidarity with all men and women, the religious and nonreligious alike (although also set apart by their willingness to testify to the grace of God), in that now and ever they were the shipwrecked, in need of rescue. Their witness was not to their rightness, their goodness, their piety, but to the grace of an all-forgiving God (Phil. 2:3-7).

Lest his Christian brothers and sisters miss this point, Paul took time to spell out the implications for his own life as an apostle of Jesus Christ. He had himself been a Pharisee, and he knew intimately and no doubt embarrassingly the seductiveness of religious and moral attainment. It was a measure of the divinely wrought revolution in his own being that he could count himself among those who "worship God in Spirit, and glory in Christ Jesus, and put no confidence in the flesh." Paul had obviously put his entire confidence in the flesh even when, as a devout Pharisee, he had thought that he was putting confidence in God alone. He had been proud and supremely confident in his religious attainment, and he owned that he could be confident still, had it not been for a meeting with Jesus Christ. As he wrote to the Philippians, "If any other man thinks he has reason for confidence in the flesh, I have more: circumcised on the eighth day, of the people of Israel, of the tribe of Benjamin, a Hebrew born of Hebrews." These, of course, had been granted him by birth. To them he added religious attainments: ". . . as to the law a Pharisee, as to zeal a persecutor of the church, as to righteousness under the law blameless."

Surely here Paul intended his readers to see this subtlest of points—that it was not as infidel or libertine that he had "breathed threats and murder against the disciples of the Lord," but as the model of piety and purity, as the epitome of the religious man. His very violence was a function of his goodness. And yet this goodness, this quest for religious status, had blinded him to his own essential worldliness, his hostility to God. Blinded him, that is, until this Jesus whom he persecuted, this most un-self-glorifying Messiah, had met him in a blinding light and given him eyes with which to see. For the sake of this Jesus, Paul wrote to the Philippians, "Whatever gain I had, I counted as loss"—as if the very pursuit and certainly the pride of his religiosity had gotten him further from, not nearer to, his goal. "Indeed," he wrote, "I count everything as loss because of the surpassing worth of knowing Christ Jesus my Lord. For his sake I have suffered the loss of all things"—including, of course, his stature as a religious and moral hero—"and count them as refuse, in order that I may gain Christ and be found in him, *not having a righteousness of my own,* based on law"—and religious or moral attainments of all sorts—"but that which is through faith in Christ," that often immeasurable, often invisible "righteousness from God that depends on faith." The faith of Paul, that religious giant, was no longer a "confidence in the flesh" but instead a confidence in Jesus, and in Jesus alone (Phil. 3:3, 4-6; Acts 9:1; Phil 3:7-9).

What Paul had learned, and what he never failed to remind the young churches of, is that the religious person who takes pride in avoiding "worldliness" is the very essence of enslavement to the flesh. As he wrote to the church at Rome, this person "cannot please God." As one who had worked unceasingly to please God, and who believed that he had done so quite nicely, Paul understood the gospel of Jesus Christ as a judgment of God upon the religious person. He understood that religious and moral heroes measure themselves "by one another" and thus show that they are "without understanding." "Let him who boasts, boast of the Lord," he wrote. "For it is not the man who commends himself that is accepted, but the man whom the Lord commends" (Rom. 8:8; II Cor. 10:12, 17-18).

II

When Billy Sunday spoke of the manliness of the real man, he was speaking of himself. From the day he stripped off his collar and rolled up his sleeves, whether self-consciously or not, Billy Sunday presented himself to his audiences as the epitome of the muscular, masculine Christianity that alone was pleasing to God. The poses he struck for the widely distributed photographs—raised arm, clenched fist, set jaw—confirmed this impression. The world needs "big men," he would say, and no one listening to him doubted that he, Billy Sunday, was one of those big men.[1]

Sunday was quite plain about his opinions on the manliness of Christianity: "Many think a Christian has to be a sort of dish-rag proposition, a wishywashy, sissified sort of a galoot that lets everybody make a doormat out of him." Not so, he said. "You never become a man until you become a Christian" were words in the middle of his standard sermon to young men, "The Moral Leper." A good portion of that sermon was devoted to Sunday's description of his own life, in terms that left no doubt that he was no "dish-rag proposition." He told of being "born and bred" on a farm, of holding his own with men in the harvest fields at age eleven, of milking ten cows every morning. "I know what hard knocks are," he said, and "I have struggled ever since I was six years old. . . ." He allowed as how he was still pretty tough. "Before I was converted I could go five rounds so fast you couldn't see me for the dust, and I'm still pretty handy with my dukes and I can still deliver the goods with all express charges prepaid. Before I was converted I could run one hundred yards in ten seconds and circle the bases in fourteen seconds, and could have run just as fast after I was converted. So you don't have to be a dish-rag proposition at all."[2]

A real man also has character, of course: "It's your character that gets you anything." Sunday would use himself as an example of character, telling a story of how a banker had invited him to walk around in his bank vaults unattended, knowing he could trust Sunday. "Why did they trust me?" he asked. "Because they knew I was preaching the gospel of Jesus Christ, and living up to it." Sunday would often boast from the pulpit that no one would ever find a discrepancy between his preaching and his life. "I will defy and challenge any man or woman on earth, and I'll look any man in the eye and challenge him, in the twenty-seven years I have been a professing Christian, to show anything against me. If I don't live what I preach, gentlemen, I'll leave the pulpit and never walk back here again. I live as I preach and I defy the dirty dogs who have insulted me and my wife and spread black-hearted lies and vilifications."[3] Sunday was sensitive about his honor as a man of character, tending at times to portray himself as an innocent martyr. "I've been vilified and blackmailed and denounced and libeled up and down all over the country," he would say. His innocence would someday be vindicated, though, since "when I die and go to heaven . . . Jesus will come up to me and take me by the hand and say: 'Bill, you see this mansion? It's yours. Enter in and dwell there.' And I'll know that it was for that, and I'll say 'I'm satisfied, Lord, I'm satisfied.'"[4]

Sunday often reiterated that it took a real man to say "no" to the temptations offered by the world. Again, he thought of himself as such a man: "I used to drink," he admitted. But "I haven't tasted a drop of liquor or beer for thirty years. I used to play cards like the rest of you, and lie and cheat as much as any of you. I haven't had a pack of cards in my hands from the day I was converted until today. I used to go to the theatre. . . ."[5] In another sermon Sunday advertised his own integrity: "You say you hate sin," he told his audience. "But you never saw anyone who hates sin worse than I do, or loves a sinner more than I. I'm fighting for the sinners. I'm fighting to save your soul. . . . I'm your friend, and you'll find that I'll not compromise one bit with sin."[6]

The pattern of pointing to his own virtues and achievements runs throughout Sunday's sermons. He spoke often of his contribution to the fight for Prohibition: "I put Michigan dry; I put the state of Iowa dry and West Virginia dry. . . ."[7] He professed: "There is no one that will reach down lower, or reach higher or wider to help you out of the pit of drunkenness than I."[8] But he also spoke in more general terms: "I have reached down into the slime, and have been privileged to help tens of thousands out of the mire of sin. . . ."[9] Or: "Will you do your duty? God knows I will do my part. I will preach until I fall dead at His feet. I will fight for Jesus Christ."[10] Or again: "There is not a preacher on earth that can preach a better gospel than 'Bill.' I'm willing to die for the Church. I'm giving my life for the Church."[11] And in a particularly pugnacious spirit, he once challenged his audience: "If I am not God's mouthpiece, come up and show me."[12]

In speaking of himself as a hero of Christian manhood, Sunday was clearly not offending very many people in his audiences; more often than not, these self-serving outbursts were met by spontaneous rounds of applause.[13] Those who witnessed his performances spoke of him in tones of awe and admiration. One called him "a sort of John the Baptist who shook the town and region round about."[14] Another testified to his "wonderful personality" and "the beauty of [his] private life. . . ."[15] He impressed one admirer as being "pure man,"[16] and another as being "a manly prophet of Christ."[17] An observer of his Spokane campaign spoke emphatically to this point:

> He stands up like a man in the pulpit and out of it. He speaks like a man. He works like a man. The genuine courage of a man is his. . . . His manliness is nowhere more evident than in his purpose to be himself under the blessing of God. He is manly with God, and with every one who comes to hear him. No matter how much you disagree with him, he treats you after a manly fashion. He is not an imitation, but a manly man giving to all a square deal.[18]

"I want to be a giant for God," was the way Sunday himself put it.[19] His admirers led him to believe that he had attained that goal. A Spokane minister put it this way: " 'Billy' Sunday is a success, with 'no shadows' to darken the landscape. He brings men to Jesus Christ by the thousand. He is a giant."[20]

Billy Sunday's very openness about his own heroic accomplishments is perhaps remarkable. Not many men or women of his day could bask so constantly for a quarter century in the adulation of their fellow citizens. Not many were the subject of continuing media attention, and only one could be the world's leading evangelist. As the embodiment of the Christian hero, Billy Sunday was unique. But as yearning to *be* a hero, to transcend the mortal condition in some symbolic way, Sunday was one of a great company of people both inside and outside the camp of evangelical Christianity. One could say of late nineteenth-century Americans what has been said of their counterparts, the English Victorians, that they "carried admiration to the highest pitch. They marshalled it, they defined it, they turned it from a virtue into a religion, and called it Hero Worship."[21]

We have already met the character builders and heard their homilies to manliness. Naturally, they were among the leading American spokespersons for the cult of the heroic. Character, after all, "is of the nature of immortality"; those who possess the courage of "silent effort" are "truly heroic." Patience and self-control will yield a "heroic character."[22] One's efforts should be concentrated toward the achievement of the "heroic life" or "heroic greatness," since often "one hero has transformed a people."[23] The training of young people for the heroic life should include readings in the lives of great men. "The career of a great man remains an enduring monument of human energy. . . . It is natural to admire and revere really great men. . . ." Since "the very sight of a great and good man is often an inspiration to the young . . . ," parents should hang portraits of noble men in their children's rooms. The lists, appearing in the character-building books, of such noble men are surprising similar: George Washington, Napoleon, Wellington, Bismarck, Luther, Savonarola, Galileo, Thomas More, Wesley, Jesus.[24]

Henry Clay Trumbull clothed the same urge toward heroism in evangelical Christian teaching. He found in the Bible a record of heroic lives, lives showing that "an exceptional independence of character" is "the measure of heroism." He quoted Emerson, Carlyle, and other hero worshipers of the Romantic movement as if he saw no contradiction between their worship of great men and the biblical message. In human heroism there is a "divine element," he wrote, and heroic activity gives evidence of a "hero-soul within." Although Trumbull saw in Jesus Christ "the ideal standard of human conduct," he did not think that Jesus' primacy should keep us from revering truly heroic mortals, since "human nature needs the inspiration and the encouragement of purely human ideals, reflecting and, so far, reproducing the one perfect Ideal, as an incentive and a pattern to worthy being and doing." He urged each in his own sphere to attain to the heroism of which he was capable.

> Any man of exceptional character anywhere is a man among men, is a man above men, is a man of force in his sphere; and every man's sphere is, in a sense, the sphere of the universe. Mr. Moody has said that "the world has yet to see the power of one man wholly consecrated to Christ"; of one character fully devoted to its highest possibilities. But the world has had many a gleam in this direction.

All that God asks of us, he wrote, is that each of us be "faithful and heroic" in his or her own sphere of activity.[25]

Henry Trumbull was preeminently a man of the nineteenth century. No evangelical after him urged individual heroism with quite the same grim sobriety, nor were appeals to an inner divinity as common among evangelical character builders after the triumph of the liberal theology and the popularity of the pantheistic mind-cure movement gave a bad name to this kind of immanentism. But the call to Christian heroism did survive, most notably in the writings of a man we have met briefly, Robert E. Speer. Speer was a key figure in the Student Volunter Movement and a leading spokesman for evangelical foreign missions until his death in 1947. Not coincidentally, he was an admirer and eventually a close friend of Henry Clay Trumbull, who testified to having been the primary beneficiary of this friendship with a man half his age. Speer, for his part, often quoted Trumbull approvingly and recommended Trumbull's books as important reading for young men.[26] And Speer complemented Trumbull's contribution to the character-building literature by publishing enough works in that area to comprise a small shelf of his own.

Speer's continuity in the tradition of Trumbull can be seen in the titles of several of his books: *Things That Make a Man* (1901), *The Marks of a Man* (1902), *The Stuff of Manhood: Some Needed Notes in American Character* (1917). Speer's interest in foreign missions gave his books an emphasis on Christian service that was not quite as prominent in Trumbull's works; but his core theme, like Trumbull's, was essentially the call to a kind of Christian heroism. Central to Speer's heroism were duty and loyalty to Christ, though in the 1917 volume he added "the qualities of discipline and austerity generally regarded as characteristic of the soldier," and spoke of "the need of those qualities in American life today." He echoed nineteenth-century themes by urging Americans to cultivate "those qualities of self-control, of quick and unquestioning obedience to duty, of joyful contempt of hardship, and of zest in difficult and arduous undertakings. . . ." "The appeal of Christ," he explained, "was always addressed to the sacrificial and the heroic."[27]

Speer's 1905 volume *Young Men Who Overcame* painted brief, inspiring portraits of fifteen exemplary young men, all prematurely deceased, "who loved the highest and who made duty the first thing in their lives." Speer wrote the book, he said, "as a challenge and a contradiction to those who think Christianity a weak and unmanly thing. . . ." The stories were full of earnest, though modest, heroisms. One young hero carried in his Bible the White Cross pledge card, which read in part, "My strength is as the strength of ten, because my heart is pure." Another was "tall in stature and muscled like a Greek god," with such "manly features" and "manly qualities" that his friends nicknamed him "Manny." In virtually every one of the fifteen young men, "manly" traits were to be found: earnestness, courage, "invincible determination," a "hatred of everything mean," a "massive majesty," "firmness and constancy," and many others, all in the same key. The full measure of heroism available to a young man was made explicit in one remarkable paragraph.

> There is a commmon notion among many young men that no young man
> can live a flawless life; that every life has its lapses and its stains; that some
> conceal them and some recover from them, but that there are only spotted
> men and Pharisees. And there is another common notion that, when a

young man does live a stainless life, he must be a man incapable of its common pleasures and joys. There are hundreds of young men whose lives correct these errors.

To the model of such a flawless life—and the heroism implicit in it—Speer called countless evangelical youth. To accept a lesser ideal than perfection, he thought, was to give evidence of "some moral defect." "Christian character," he repeated, "is hunger for the highest."[28]

Robert Speer was Henry Clay Trumbull's protégé and friend. But Charles G. Trumbull was the latter's son, and he felt the full brunt of his father's quest for, and exhortation to, the status of the heroic. Charles Trumbull was also the long-time friend of Robert Speer (in fact, he became a premillennialist at the urging of Speer's mother) and thus continued to soak up the same heroic impetus after the death of his father. The results are evident in the pages of *The Sunday School Times*, which he edited, particularly in those years just before his experience of the victorious life in Christ. By his own admission, his life during those years was marked by deep discontent in his Christian experience. "I certainly found that there were habitual failures of many sorts in my life which I was trying to overcome, and which I was failing to overcome." Specifically, "I was not seeing other lives revolutionized by Jesus Christ as the result of my testimony." He confessed that he had been "heartsick" over this failure.[29]

At the very same time, Trumbull was filling the pages of his periodical with calls to heroism that would have made his father proud. Clearly, these articles were addressed primarily to his own frustrated longings for the life of the heroic. One editorial, "Long-Distance Heroism," informed his readers that "it calls for more real heroism to be true to Christ and his standards in our ordinary, everyday life, than to stand the test of physical martyrdom for Christ in a foreign mission field."[30] One after another of his feature articles, however, trumpeted a much less modest version of heroism in the form of biographies of heroic persons, including Ira D. Sankey, Moody's revival songster; Anthony Comstock, an early antipornography crusader ("a story of moral and physical heroism"); Alice Jackson, an example of "Heroic Girlhood"; and, naturally, Henry Clay Trumbull, known for "Taking Men Alive."[31] In an editorial whose very language sounded like the elder Trumbull's, the younger Trumbull reminded his readers that the price of Holy Spirit power is "stern, rigid duty-doing at every point."[32]

Charles Trumbull's experience of victory in Christ must have been a tremendous emotional breakthrough, allowing him a certain relaxation of the "stern, rigid duty-doing" by which his father had sought—and doubtless urged his son to seek—earthly heroism. The younger Trumbull's understanding of the means to such heroism seems to have changed most abruptly. He no longer prescribed moral struggle as the path to Christian victory, and he never again identified doing one's duty as a prerequisite to receiving the Holy Spirit. In fact, the opposite prescription pertained: relax from your struggle and let Christ flow into you and be your life. If one can imagine living with old Henry Clay Trumbull, and having to bear the burden of his moral earnestness and heroic striving, one can breathe a sigh of relief for his son Charles, who could finally rest from his labors. And yet, in a strange way, Henry Trumbull prevailed: Charles may have relaxed, but what he got for his relaxation was still that sense of victory whose attainment had dominated his father's restless life. Charles may have given up his father's *means* to heroism, but not the heroism itself.

We have already seen evidence of this in Charles Trumbull's description of the victorious life as a life without known sin. What is striking for our understanding of heroism is the way his formulation of the victorious life is virtually identical with the comments by his friend Speer concerning the possibility of a flawless life. Trumbull quotes the Shorter Catechism: "No mere man, since the fall, is able, in this life, perfectly to keep the commandments of God; but doth daily break them in thought, word, and deed." Trumbull's response: "But a man who has Christ dwelling within him and living his life for him, winning his victories for him . . . is not a 'mere man.' It is really an insult to the Lord to call such a man a 'mere man.'" There follows Trumbull's standard definition of the victorious life, a life truly heroic: "Yet it is the privilege of every Christian to live every day of his life without breaking the laws of God in known sin either in thought, word, or deed. . . ."[33] The younger Trumbull had finally accomplished the task his father had set out for him: he had ceased to be a "mere man."

The heroic theme persists in the "victorious" Trumbull in still other ways. Like his father and Speer, he continued to publish inspiring examples of heroes worth emulating, though the Wellingtons and Napoleons receded and were replaced by the simple heroes of faith who had tried his recipe for victory and won. Quite a few issues of *The Sunday School Times* in 1919 and 1920 carried, in serialized form, Trumbull's fawning biography of Dr. C. I. Scofield, who so neatly represented in one person the dispensationalist and Victorious Life teachings that were becoming more and more characteristic of conservative evangelicalism. Trumbull was just a bit awed by the graciousness of this "mighty man of God" and "veteran saint" who had deigned to autograph Trumbull's personal copy of the Scofield Reference Bible.[34] In another issue Trumbull published a bibliography, compiled by an official of the Boy Scouts of America and recommended for boys, that listed about sixty titles in three groupings: "Heroes of Success," "Heroes of Service," and "Heroes of Faith."[35]

The cult of the hero thus persisted within the pages of *The Sunday School Times* and the ranks of the Victorious Life movement, a testimony to the tenacity of its appeal among those whose roots reached back into the evangelicalism of the post–Civil War generation. Its longevity made for at least one poignant—and confusing—episode. The decade of Charles Trumbull's most vocal and insistent dedication to the Victorious Life movement was also the decade of Billy Sunday's greatest influence among American evangelicals. Trumbull heard Billy Sunday preach, and we have evidence of what he thought of Sunday's message:

> Even in evangelistic services, even in revivals where the blood of Christ is rightly being pointed to as the only way of salvation, you have heard that mistaken emphasis, the call to "Be a man" if you would get saved. In a great evangelistic revival where souls were being saved, I have heard the evangelist cry out, as he called upon men to hit the trail and come up and acknowledge Jesus Christ as Saviour, "Be a man! Don't be a milk-sop! Don't be a mollycoddle! Be a man!"
>
> But there is no such call in the Bible to the unsaved; God never tells one to "assert his manhood" by accepting Christ. The offense of the cross is just the opposite. It is a degrading thing, a humiliating thing, to recognize why the cross saves us. I do not mean that the cross degrades us, but that the cross *exposes our degradation;* it humiliates us into the dust. There is no Scripture appeal to the unsaved to "be a man and accept Christ"; but there is a clear declaration from God that, because you are less than a man, less than a woman . . . you must let God save you through the death of Christ. . . . You can't do anything for yourself. No; salvation is not asserting our manhood; salvation is recognizing our utter lack of manhood and womanhood, our hopelessness, our worthlessness; recognizing that, if we are to be saved, it has got to be done for us by God.[36]

I find this passage not only a remarkable, and stunningly true, critique of the message of Billy Sunday, but also an evidence that Charles Trumbull did indeed understand, in a very important respect, the meaning of the grace of God in Jesus Christ.

When Billy Sunday came to Philadelphia, home of *The Sunday School Times,* Trumbull turned his magazine over to a regular and extensive reporting of the campaign. If one reads carefully, one can feel Trumbull wrestling with his own theology in the course of that reportage. The best example is in one of his own articles, "The Billy Sunday Whom the Public Doesn't Know," in which he portrays Sunday at home, prone, exhausted from his labor. "The flaming prophet of God seemed a weak, worn, frail, common man," who knows that "he is still a man, and not an archangel." At one point, in describing Sunday's frailty, Trumbull almost puts words into his mouth: "Mr. Sunday was talking about his own unfitness—

though he did not use that word—for his work." Sunday had mentioned his lack of education but had ended on a more characteristic note: "God seems to have called me for a special work." Trumbull chose to interpret this not as Sunday's familiar pointing to himself but as a word of humility from the great evangelist. He depicted Sunday lying in bed, "weak, grateful, tender-hearted, loving, simple: a little child in spirit and in humility, at the foot of the throne of God."[37]

In portraying the hero as a weak man, Trumbull seemed to be working hard to ignore, or even to refute, Sunday's advertisement of himself as the epitome of manliness. Trumbull's Victorious Life theology taught that God's Spirit uses only those who are content to surrender, to be weak, to be nothing. Trumbull portrayed such a Billy Sunday in his article, and in countering the popular image of the evangelist, he seemed to be trying to make sure God, not the pugnacious, muscular Sunday, got the credit for the harvest of souls that attended this man's work.

But Billy Sunday disliked the old Moody revival song, "Oh to Be Nothing," preferring a call to arms like "Onward Christian Soldiers."[38] And Trumbull, his father's son, was not immune to that call. One can sense in his description of the preacher's public image a genuine admiration for this "mighty man of God," "God's spokesman and the ambassador of Jesus Christ." He admitted that, as he watched Sunday's performance from a privileged vantage point right next to the platform, he had "marveled . . . at the irrepressible activity of those steel-like muscles, the superb poise or the lightning-like flashes of the Indian scout figure, the swing or the thrust of those arms, the swift plunge of the whole body. . . . I had realized that here was a supernatural physical strength, given and used by God as the earthly vehicle of the supernatural spiritual strength that was overflowing the man and pouring out into hundreds of thousands of lives." Here Trumbull paints Sunday in the universal, mythic image of the hero, through whom the very force of life—and not the awareness of one's mortality, of death—flows into his followers. In this and other passages Trumbull breathes the same barely suppressed awe that later characterized his encounter with Scofield. And toward the end of his article the cult of the hero emerges full-blown, only barely disguised by all the talk of Sunday's weakness:

> Before I went, I told him I wanted him to know how much some of us loved him,—how much *I* loved him. That there were times when he was on the platform at the tabernacle and when it seemed as though, sitting not far from him in one of the press seats, I should just have to spring up there and throw my arms around him, I loved him so! And again the loving, child-like spirit shone out of his eyes as he thanked me, and hinted at what this meant to him.[39]

In the presence of this man who, by Trumbull's own account, was preaching a kind of manly heroism unknown to the Bible, and thus falsifying the gospel of Jesus Christ, the critic melted into the star-struck little boy. Thus did the cult of the hero confront the theology of surrender and nothingness and, in the person of Billy Sunday, prove its triumphant appeal to the evangelical mind.

III

The quest for the heroic has been a constant among human beings. Humans have never been satisfied with being "mere" humans. In ways almost as various as the cultures they have created, humans have sought paths to superhuman status, a status they imagine to be ultimately fully gratifying, fully emblematic of their truest selves. The magnetic emotional pull of the words "you shall be as gods" is as irresistible to men and women of every age as it was when the first man and woman heard them spoken by the tempter. Ernest Becker, whose contributions to our understanding of the human condition uniquely parallel the biblical revelation, characterized this quest for the heroic as "man's tragic destiny: he must desperately justify himself as an object of primary value in the universe; he must stand out, be a hero, make the biggest possible contribution to world life, show that he *counts* more than anything or anyone else." We humans carry in our breasts "the ache of cosmic specialness." It is an ache that, we imagine, will find no rest until we ourselves become "larger than life."[40]

For the human being, however, "larger than life" means "larger than death." The "ache of cosmic specialness" does not arise from entirely mysterious origins, but from our knowledge, and our rejection, of what we really are. We are creatures who die, like all other animals; unlike the other animals, however, we know we die. We alone are granted the power of conscious awareness that our lives will be no more. We alone may consciously come to grips with the mightiness of the natural forces arrayed against us, and with our own puniness among all the powers, real or imagined, of heaven and earth. We know—when we permit ourselves to know—that at any moment we may be crushed, snuffed out forever. What a paradoxical power is this power of awareness! It threatens only to reveal to us how abjectly powerless we are, how contingent our life is and how certain—unpredictable but unstoppable—our exit is. How unbearable is this burden of our own impotence, and how driven our attempts to forget it!

It is Ernest Becker's contention that we do indeed forget it. From earliest childhood we purchase equanimity by learning how to turn our faces from the reality that at any instant we may die. We forget so well that we find ourselves protesting, when reminded of these things, that we are aware of our mortality, that we do not really fear it, that it has no hold on us. The protest, of course, is part of an urbane denial we have learned in response to an instinct for psychic survival, a denial that our entire social and cultural apparatus—including, very prominently, the religions of the world—has conspired to strengthen and affirm.

And yet, if we look very closely at our cultural apparatus and at human behavior in all times and places, we will discover that this fear of death, a fear far deeper than any of us may want to admit, is "the worm at the core" that eats at our vitals beneath the "bland exterior" of human life. Becker believes that there is good and mounting evidence for this in the scientific study of the human psyche. Far more persuasively, however, he finds evidence for it in the study of social institutions and in the history of our time. Becker offers this often startling evidence and his own profoundly stimulating and revealing conclusions in the two books he wrote just before his own untimely death, *The Denial of Death* and *Escape from Evil*. His analysis is scholarly and wide-ranging and explains with penetration and pathos the sad history of human life on the planet. It is not easy to gainsay his central thesis, that "the idea of death, the fear of it, haunts the human animal like nothing else; it is a mainspring of human activity—activity designed largely to avoid the fatality of death, to overcome it by denying in some way that it is the final destiny for man."[41]

The quest for the heroic, according to Becker, is one of the clearest manifestations of our "forgetting" and "transcending" the reality of this final destiny. "Heroism," he says, "is first and foremost a reflex of the terror of death." This is easy enough to see in the common story of the soldier who, in the face of his own death, rises up in superhuman strength to kill a dozen of the enemy. If he lives, we decorate him for the fruits of his terror; if he dies, we celebrate his valiant stand against his (and our) fate, and we feel that in some measure our enemy, death, has been cheated by his short-lived protest. But the ordinary man and woman are not afforded this test of their immortality. Their heroism must come in quieter and subtler ways, by their accomplishing some version of a heroic role presented to them by the society in which they live. Society itself, Becker believes, is a

> symbolic action system, a structure of statuses and roles, customs and rules for behavior, designed to serve as a vehicle for earthly heroism. Each script is somewhat unique, each culture has a different hero system. What the anthropologists call "cultural relativity" is thus really the relativity of hero-systems the world over. But each cultural system is a dramatization of

earthly heroics; each system cuts out roles for performance of various de-
grees of heroism: from the "high" heroism of a Churchill, a Mao, or a
Buddha, to the "low" heroism of the coal miner, the peasant, the simple
priest; the plain, everyday earthly heroism wrought by gnarled working
hands guiding a family through hunger and disease.

The meaning of "high" heroism and "low" heroism is the same, according
to Becker. Both prime minister and peasant have one purpose in becoming heroes: to prove their own power or merit, and thus symbolically to
outrun their own inevitable death.[42]

Late nineteenth-century America offered a wide variety of culturally
approved means to heroism. A few of them stand out as particularly
characteristic of the age. For women, the roles of mother and homemaker
predominated. Since urbanization and industrialization had already begun to provide in the marketplace most of those goods and services
formerly provided by women working in the home, these "hero-systems"
were in flux. The roles of moral guardian first, and later of consumer,
were increasingly rising to the fore to define the virtuous mother and
homemaker, with all the confusion that such historic transitions imply.[43]
For men, economic success was an ever more prominent path to heroism.
The so-called captains of industry, with their rags-to-riches mythology,
attracted widespread admiration, as well as the fear that most heroes
generate. The rapid acceleration of the techniques of the machine, industrial organization, and financial manipulation brought an ostensibly divine power within the grasp of an ambitious man. The open display of
wealth by the new capitalist elites inspired many a young man to emulate
such demigods as Andrew Carnegie and John D. Rockefeller.

Some chose a different heroism: social and political power in service to
society. Robert M. Crunden's study of the Progressive activists such as
Jane Addams and Richard Ely portrays the path to heroism of "a generation of intelligent youth" who could never quite escape their parents'
piety and moral earnestness, but who resisted the pressures to become
ministers or missionaries, finding that "settlement work, higher education, law, and journalism all offered possibilities for preaching without
pulpits." This heroism often involved abandoning a doctrinally orthodox
evangelical Christianity. Crunden's sensitive treatment of these figures
reveals their drivenness to a godlike moral status and the "religious and
moral significance" with which they invested their choice of a career.[44]
This heroism of social critique and activism has become a familiar one in
the twentieth century, evoking admiration for a wide variety of figures
from Dorothy Day to Bertrand Russell.

For many evangelicals, the heroism of choice was the foreign missionary movement. They could stay home, of course, and become parish

ministers, and many did. The really exciting challenges, however, seemed to be offered in exotic foreign lands, many of them only recently come to light or penetrated by western economic institutions. Little boys of the late nineteenth century thrilled to the exploits of Adoniram Judson, William Carey, and David Livingstone, whom biographers presented in blatantly heroic terms. The rigors of missionary life attracted those who saw in the growing comforts of a consumer society the temptation to moral laxity. Robert Speer and others traded on this penchant for heroism when they established and promoted the Student Volunteer Movement.

Still, not everybody could be a foreign missionary. What of the more timid souls, the farmers and merchants of America, the office and factory workers, the eager young men on the corporate ladder? They too were offered a distinctly Christian heroism, less sensational perhaps but still demanding: to be heroic was to possess and display "character." Character was a particularly stern and unyielding variety of heroism that was suited to a community under attack—and thus all the more heroic. One who had character was fully in control of himself. By exercising a strict physical and moral regimen, constant watchfulness, and struggle, he could restrict the very flow of inward emotion and say no to temptations to evil that may have slipped through the defenses. He could be utterly "master" of himself, as some said; and of course, by the same token, he could be master of the situations of life. The person of character displayed a certain iron grip on life itself. Nothing could surprise him, no force could overwhelm him, no exigency could find him without resources. His strength was "as the strength of ten. . . ." The imagery here is truly godlike, a status to which the character builders sometimes urged their readers in quite explicit terms, without embarrassment. One sees, in the quest for character, a quest for utter invulnerability. Character was the most popular evangelical means to transcending the finite, impotent, frail human condition; it symbolized immortality for a generation of American evangelicals.[45]

I see it as no coincidence that the cult of Christian character received its most extreme formulation at the very moment in history when the evangelical cultural hegemony was most obviously on the wane. The Christian triumphalism of the period immediately before the Civil War, which we examined at the outset of this study, represented a culturewide claim to immortality that was almost giddy in its expressions of self-confidence, all the more so because in the myopia of the moment it seemed without serious opponent. By the 1870s and 1880s this giddiness had given way to the gloom of dispensational premillennialism, whose adherents had to find other ways to claim special, godlike status as opponents of a dominant culture that seemed increasingly less homogeneous, less Christian,

and certainly less under the control of evangelicals. Whatever their evolving views of the millenium, those who were somewhat less disposed than
the dispensationalists to give up on the dominant culture, and who perhaps held out hopes for reestablishing Christian hegemony, seem to have
been attracted by the possibilities of character building—although the
emphasis on Christian character was not absent in any portion of the
evangelical community.[46] Since the outer world was increasingly disorderly, shaken by the social, economic, and intellectual changes we have
been exploring, the temptation was to impose an inner order that would
then enable one to order the outer world in one's immediate environment. By imposing this inner order, one could still feel in control of the
situation of one's life, despite the surrounding chaos.

The late nineteenth century did not, however, see a reestablishment of
evangelical hegemony in America. We have already seen how history and
society appeared to be falling under the influence of powers over which
individuals or groups would have no control whatsoever. Not only had
evangelicals lost their sense of dominance over American culture; they
seemed hardly able to control their own lives. Technology dictated
changes in their lives that they almost always applauded, but underneath
they surely sensed the implacability of the machine that modern culture
had become. Bureaucratic capitalism was extending its reach, bringing
the masses within the circle of its quest for utter technical rationality and
administrative control, demonstrating that beneath its modern facades
lay a new, constantly all-embracing "iron cage."[47] Evangelicals, like most
other Americans, were learning that modern civilization's promise of
freedom is utterly seductive, but utterly deceptive. No wonder a recent
social historian can speak of a widespread "spiritual and cultural confusion" and "a spreading sense of moral impotence" at the turn of the
century, in which the old "ideal of the independent self"—an abiding
premise of the character builders—"seemed barely tenable."[48] In a society
in which individual behavior seemed more and more circumscribed by
the dictates of technology and bureaucratic rationality, genuine heroism,
with its implications of personal power and autonomy, seemed an impossible attainment except by a most tenuous self-deception.

Evangelical heroism could perhaps have lived indefinitely within an
increasingly controlled corporate society had it been satisfied to narrow
its applicability to ever more private moral concerns where the pretense of
autonomy would be maintained—as, indeed, certain twentieth-century
fundamentalists have done. But the rise of the consumer society made
this kind of adaptation, if not impossible, then exceedingly difficult: it
introduced a new kind of heroism to do pitched battle with the heroism of
character. This heroism of consumption, still nascent in the late nine-

teenth century, had behind it the logic of several centuries of technological and financial development that were coming to sudden and surprising
fruition. Also on its side was the growing power of the media, just beginning its revolutionary twentieth-century proliferation—and all at the behest of those who had the money, who had the goods to sell, and with
those goods a way of life that challenged virtually every precept of the
character builders. The hero of consumption lived life for fun, not duty.
He also coveted power; but he gained it by material purchases, not moral
triumphs. This hero wrung the meaning out of life by living for today, not
by deferring gratification until tomorrow. This hero transcended the human condition by collecting and using technological contrivances. This
hero gained the victory by letting go, by seeking pleasure, by yielding to
temptation. This hero's testimonials and pictures filled the print media:
he or she seemed to be having so much fun, seemed to embody life itself.
How unrewarding the heroism of character must have looked by contrast, and how increasingly difficult it must have been to strive for it and
to convince one's children that they too should strive for it.

All this translates, I believe, into a late nineteenth-century evangelical
hero system that was on the rocks by the early twentieth century. Millions
of people gave it lip service, equated it with good and moral behavior,
urged it on the young, and felt vaguely guilty when they violated its
precepts. But they did violate its precepts, I suspect, as they succumbed
to the lure of life in an affluent, consumer-oriented, technologically advanced society. And they must have felt diminished in that they could not
live by the precepts that had promised them, since childhood, a certain
heroic accomplishment, with all the emotional well-being issuing from an
imagined invulnerability to sin and death. Their own allegiance to an
outmoded hero system was not delivering the relief from anxiety humans
crave, and its dissonance with the drift of values in the larger society was
causing even greater anxiety. How could they not have felt the helplessness that always threatens to remind the fearful human animal of its
deepest helplessness, its most radical and terrifying vulnerability, its impotence in the face of death?

This very helplessness is what we do hear in so many evangelical
voices at the turn of the century. In an atmosphere pierced by noisy calls
for more godlike heroism and books about young men who overcame,
one hears confessions of human and Christian failure that speak eloquently of a wrecked hero-system. The confessions of helplessness were
quite explicit, though never analyzed in social terms; typically, Christians
complained of a deficiency of power. Heroes, by definition, were presumed to have power, and Christian heroes were presumed to have
God's power. For example, A. B. Simpson, the founder of the Christian

and Missionary Alliance, portrayed the disciple Peter as an irresolute man whom God had transformed, by the baptism of the Holy Ghost, into a "fearless hero" who could endure sufferings with "heroic fortitude." Simpson identified "the wondrous power of [Peter's] public testimony" as a power that "no man can gainsay," a power "the church needs today." And yet, according to Simpson, the church of his day did not have this power. Instead of a whole and powerful body, it was "mutilated and severed," "diseased and lacerated," and "broken to pieces." "Oh, for a band of heroes," he cried.[49]

He was not alone. One of Moody's coworkers and a leading evangelical revivalist and educator, R. A. Torrey, noted: "From many earnest hearts there is rising a cry for more power in our personal conflict with the world, the flesh, and the devil, and more power in our work with others." Torrey lamented "the poverty and powerlessness of the average Christian," and characterized 99 percent of Christians as "mere weaklings."[50] J. Wilbur Chapman, who gave Billy Sunday his start, warned that "there is many a man in the pew who is shorn of power," and he recounted approvingly the story of a man who prayed "My Father, I will give up every known sin, only I plead with Thee for power."[51] Andrew Murray spoke of "the sad state of the Church of Christ on earth," full of "honest, earnest Christians" with "so little power."[52] *The Sunday School Times* editorialized that "many a Christian of good average standing really longs for spiritual power."[53] The popular devotional writer S. D. Gordon asked, "Why is there such a lack of power in our lives?" Gordon likened the powerless Christians of his day to the dead Lazarus, "bound hand and foot and face."[54] And F. B. Meyer, the Keswick teacher widely read in America, summarized this widespread malaise:

> Do you not sometimes moan over your want of power? You stand face-to-face with devil-tormented people, but you cannot cast the devil out. You feel that you ought to confess Christ in the workshop, the commercial room, the railway carriage, and the home, but your lips refuse to utter the message of the heart. Yes, and worse than all, you are constantly being overcome by besetting sins, which carry you whither you would not. There is a lamentable lack of power among us. . . .[55]

Such admissions and bemoanings are prominent in the leading evangelical figures of the period.

But so are the books written to remedy this palpable deficiency of power. The outpouring of writings on the subject of power—what it is, where it comes from, how to get it, how to keep it, what to do with it—is quite remarkable. Foremost among them were the books associated with the Keswick movement: Evan Hopkins's *The Christian's Pathway to Power*,

J. Stuart Holden's *The Price of Power*, A. W. Webb-Peploe's *The Life of Privilege: Possession, Peace and Power*, and many others, including Andrew Murray's spate of devotional books, many of which spoke to the need for power. In *Be Perfect*, for example, he broached the subject of power once every four pages on the average, although the book was ostensibly about the possibility of Christian perfection. One of F. B. Meyer's many books dealing with the subject of power was entitled *Elijah and the Secret of His Power*, and W. H. Griffith Thomas wrote *Grace and Power*. But non-Keswick writers also contributed liberally. R. A. Torrey wrote *How to Obtain Fullness of Power* and *The Power of Prayer*; A. B. Simpson wrote *The Holy Spirit; Or, Power from on High*; S. D. Gordon wrote *Quiet Talks on Power*; and J. Wilbur Chapman wrote *Power: "Received Ye the Holy Ghost?"*. These are just the most prominent of a very long list, which could be expanded almost indefinitely by adding Christian periodicals that featured articles or editorialized on the subject of power.

As some of the above titles indicate, a heavy emphasis in these works was the person and work of the Holy Spirit.[56] Individual writers would touch on other themes in varying proportions: study of the Bible ("unless you keep in constant association with the . . . Bible, you will not have power");[57] the efficacy of Jesus' blood; the indispensability of prayer ("if you tell me . . . what your prayer habits are . . . I can tell you what your power is . . . ");[58] and so forth. But center stage generally belonged to the Holy Spirit, who "imparts to the individual believer the power that belongs to God."[59] And these writers agreed that many believers did not show evidence of being filled by the Holy Spirit and thus were powerless because they had blocked his working by not surrendering every area of their lives and wills to God. They frequently used mechanical analogies to illustrate the proper flow—and all-too-frequent blockage—of the Holy Spirit. A. B. Simpson uses one of the commonest of these analogies in this passage:

> He has the power and you have Him. In the science of electricity it has been found that the best form in which this motive power can be used to run our street cars is not through storage batteries, but through overhead wires. The power is not stored up in the car, but in the dynamo and the wires, and the car just draws it from above by constant contact, and the moment it lets go its touch the power is gone. . . . And so the power of the Holy Ghost is power from above. It is not our power, but His, and received from Him moment by moment. In order to receive this power and retain it there are certain conditions which are necessary. One of them is that we shall obey Him and follow His directions. . . .[60]

Another leading evangelical preacher, A. C. Dixon, used essentially the same illustration, emphasizing that "the measure of His power depends upon the wire of faith and consecration through which He may work the machinery of our lives and bring things to pass."[61] Trumbull added that a very small sin can "shut off the great currents of power" in our lives.[62] In a variation on this theme, one writer depicted the Spirit as a continuous floodtide that is nonetheless dependent on our opening the floodgates; or a reservoir whose flow of refreshing water is often blocked by a sin we let clog the channel.[63] Most of the popular writers saw their tasks as explaining the means of receiving the Holy Spirit and encouraging Christians to fulfill the conditions for—or remove the obstacles to—this powerful indwelling. The obstacle one most often sees is the lack of full surrender. As Torrey put it, "Absolute surrender to God is the secret of blessedness and power."[64]

What strikes the reader of these books is how often they appeal, almost blatantly, to the felt deficiency of power and the lust for infinite power on the part of a finite creature caught in a confusing historical era. There is the whiff of the very clever salesman about these writers. They depict the average Christian, and thus the reader, as a pitiably helpless thing. They offer, by contrast and in worshipful tones, the lives of the great men of God, the heroes in God's hall of fame. Then they close in for the kill: you can be just such a hero. The claims for their product are tantalizing—and extreme:

> The Christian can "have power in actual conscious possession."[65]

> Have you realized that the present power which God offers you for every moment of your life is the very power which God had to use to break the power of death in the body of his Son? . . . *And all that power is offered you*, to be at work in you this moment. . . .[66]

> It is divine, not human strength, and it is strength which is wholly divine and in no sense or measure human.[67]

> The mightiest power under the heavens is . . . one that is in constant communion with God.[68]

> Satan cannot understand the omnipotence of a life that is homed in God.[69]

> But if we link ourselves to the Eternal Power of God, nothing will be impossible to us.[70]

> . . . the placing of divine omnipotence at the disposal of a Spirit-filled child of God.[71]

Who of us, powerless creatures that we are, would not wish to have divine omnipotence at our disposal?

One is tempted to see in all this a frantic adaptation of the old character heroism by the addition of "Holy Spirit power," as if only a very heavy dose of divine power would make attainment of the old heroism possible. There do seem to be some differences, however, between the heroism of character and the newer power-heroism. The hero envisioned by the evangelical literature of power is something less of an earnest moral struggler than the hero of character. This hero, to whom God grants his power, must be watchful lest his own will take the place of God's will, since only a lack of complete surrender can stand in the way of the experience of divine omnipotence. Thus this heroism is of a somewhat more relaxed sort, a getting out of the way so that God can take over. And yet it is still very definitely a heroism. A. B. Simpson said it most graphically:

> God is preparing his heroes still, so that when the opportunity comes He can fit them into their places. . . . Let the Holy Ghost prepare you, dear friend, by all the disciplines of life, that when the last finishing touch has been given to the marble, it will be easy for God to put it on the pedestal and fit it into the niche.[72]

When the evangelical power literature made specific reference to its heroes, D. L. Moody was inevitably among the most prominent. With a few exceptions, the rest were also famous evangelists or missionaries. Most often mentioned were Charles G. Finney, R. A. Torrey, George Whitefield, Jonathan Edwards, Hudson Taylor, William Carey, Adoniram Judson. All were generally grouped under the term "soul-winners." These were people who had "passed from an experience of weakness to power with God and man, by definitely receiving the Holy Spirit for service."[73] Chapman added the stories of anonymous heroes, such as the man who, after surrendering every area of his life, led over sixty men to Christ in only a few months, or the wretched woman of the streets who was responsible for converting more than one hundred women like herself.[74] Torrey claimed that soul-winning was the normal activity of the Spirit-filled person: "If I am baptised with the Holy Spirit, then will souls be saved *through my* instrumentality [his emphasis]. . . ." And he added a grim warning: "I am responsible before God for all the souls that might have been saved, but were not saved, through me, because I was not baptised with the Holy Spirit."[75]

In fact, it is difficult to avoid the impression that, for these leading evangelicals, "power" and "soul-winning" were strictly synonymous. Many whose books constitute the literature of power also wrote books on the subject of soul-winning. These books ignored the contradiction inherent in combining detailed evangelism techniques with a teaching that the Holy Spirit works naturally and divinely through the Christian if the Christian will just let him. Torrey, for example, introduced his subject by noting that only those baptized with the Holy Ghost would have success in soul-winning; but then he went on to elaborate methods for dealing with the varying classes of sinners. In some concluding tips he urged the soul-winner to "be dead in earnest," not to lose his temper when dealing with a soul, not to have a heated argument, and so on—without mentioning that if one is filled with the Spirit such tips would be unnecessary.[76] Chapman, Pierson, and others also contributed volumes on soul-winning techniques, though Torrey led the pack with at least four books on this subject.[77]

The Keswick movement was just a bit slower to join the emphasis on soul-winning; it clung for a while to language that identified power with living a life unspotted by known sin. But in time even these writers took pains to say that victory is not simply an emotional experience or an experience of sinlessness but a preparation for service. And service, more often than not, meant soul-winning. In fact, one conference speaker called Keswick a "meeting for making missionaries."[78] Trumbull's movement picked up the same emphasis soon after its inception, and, like many other authors of evangelical books on power, Charles Trumbull wrote his own book on soul-winning, *Taking Men Alive.*

The acknowledged champion at "taking men alive" during the first two decades of the twentieth century, as we have seen, was Billy Sunday. Sunday, in all his photogenic glory—and by his own admission—was the hero of manliness to early twentieth-century evangelicals. And manliness, of course, implied power. But he was also the hero of the power of soul-winning, and he spoke often in his sermons of that power. "The Church today needs power," he would preach. "There is no substitute for the Holy Spirit and you cannot have power without the Holy Spirit." Why do Christians not have this power? Because "you have disobeyed some clear command of God." With Sunday's penchant for moralizing, he devoted most of the sermon to pointing out the sins that the church had not yet learned to shun. "You'll have power when there's nothing questionable in your life," was his summation. Then, characteristically putting the logical cart before the horse: "You'll have power when you testify in a more positive manner." Although he was not entirely clear on this point, he did seem to think that power's purpose was soul-winning: "Let's quit fiddling with religion and do something to bring the world to Christ."[79] In another sermon, he made the point more forcefully: "The only thing that pleases Jesus is winning souls."[80]

So Billy Sunday preached the gospel of power and the urgency of soul-winning. But he did more than preach it: he demonstrated it as no other evangelist had done up to that time. The numbers showed it. Even the much-loved Moody stood in his shadow as a soul-winner, it seemed. When the hundreds, even thousands, of his listeners would pour down the aisles to shake his hand and declare for Christ, the heroic extent of his power was available for all to see. Given the formula developed by the

leading evangelical spokesmen—power equals soul-winning equals heroism—Billy Sunday was a hero without peer. No wonder Charles Trumbull was awed in his presence. In Trumbull's own words, "He loves all the
world; why shouldn't we love him?"[81]

IV

From the beginning of time men and women have not only sought a
heroism of their own, but have offered a special reverence to those beings
who seem to possess superior power. The practice seems rooted in childhood. Few of us are so distant from our own childhoods that we cannot
remember that awe. It is some combination of ultimate trust and ultimate
fear that is evoked by the face or voice of a seemingly all-powerful parent.
As adults we continue to demonstrate a fascination with those who represent power, and we are often willing to give them an almost worshipful
allegiance. For ancient men and women these power figures were the
gods or the larger-than-life mythic heroes whose feats demonstrated a
superhuman triumph over danger and death. We are no different as
moderns. We seem willing to attribute a godlike status to kings and
presidents, warriors and conquerors; we have been willing to follow them
in life and, too often, to death. This susceptibility of ours to the all-
powerful hero has done more than its share in turning our planet into a
mass grave.

When the socially constructed and approved everyday heroisms available to the average man and woman seem confused or futile, as they do in
times of cultural transition such as we have been examining, the stage is
set for the entrance of The Hero. The Hero is clearly not as helpless as we
are, and since he is *our* hero, he diminishes our own sense of helplessness. The Hero does not fear the forces ranged against us; and he tells us
that while he remains our hero we need not fear them either. The Hero
has the "courage" to stick out his neck, as it were, and taunt the hostile
powers of the universe, to invite their anger and their attack. He draws
attention to his powers, which are the powers of life and death. We who
pledge him our allegiance are protected by his powers. The forces that
would diminish us, would rob us of our "cosmic specialness," cannot
stand up to The Hero; he is immune to death, and his immunity is also
ours.[82]

Billy Sunday offered himself to the evangelical Christians of the early
twentieth century as exactly this sort of hero. In proclaiming his own
manliness, he showed himself to be what his listeners wished but doubted themselves to be. As a "man's man," he seemed invincible; never did

he show confusion, consternation, or fear. He was never anything but utterly sure of his own rightness and the rightness of his cause. His very physical bearing and presence bespoke power and confidence and ultimate triumph. He explicitly presented himself as a man the times could not control—as one who, on the contrary, could well control the times. Within the circle of his magnetic power all must have seemed well. What a comfort to know, at least for those brief moments in the Billy Sunday Tabernacle, that the world was not so overwhelming as it seemed. This man Sunday stood undaunted by all the confusing crosscurrents of life, and his audience participated in his invulnerability by their adulation of him.

The Hero must appear supremely confident, but he must also demonstrate that he knows the plight of his followers and understands the power of the foes who would diminish and defeat them. In proof of his control of the unseen forces of life and death, he names them and thus gives objective reality to the people's enemies—and his. And Billy Sunday did this very well. He assured his followers that their malaise was no accident, that a host of enemies lay encamped about them plotting their destruction. He strutted around the platform, grimacing and bringing these forces to life right before their eyes. These embodiments of the power of death included society women, prostitutes, liberal and effeminate ministers, unbelieving church members and scoffers, and folks who were cowardly, immoral, and unmanly—among others. Heading up this unholy alliance, of course, was that "dirty, stinking bunch of moral assassins," the "whiskey gang."[83]

Sunday never underestimated the strength and wiliness of these forces arrayed against the good Christian people of America. To do so would have been to lose his credibility, since his followers knew from their own experience of anxiety and powerlessness that they were being thwarted by a very substantial enemy force. It would also have been to diminish his own importance as The Hero who alone could be victorious over these forces. So Sunday had to confirm the worst fears of his listeners. His descriptions of the reign of sin in the modern world were dramatic and frightening: grown men and women sighed and fainted as he charted the gains of the enemy. But his listeners must have found a strange comfort in his portrayals of the power of darkness, a confirmation that their anxieties were not groundless and an assurance that The Hero's familiarity with enemy terrain demonstrated his superior knowledge and power.

However, the crowds did not come simply to see a confident man, nor just to hear an explanation of their malaise, important as these were. More than anything, I believe, they came to witness a killing. This is the tragic meaning of The Hero in human history: The Hero is a killer. The

Hero's task is to affirm his invulnerability and thus ours in the face of death. He must do this, it seems, by confronting those embodiments of death that he himself has identified as his own and his followers' worst enemies, and by defeating them in battle and emerging unscathed himself. As Elias Canetti writes, The Hero chooses to place himself at risk: his movement is always "towards the greatest danger," and his aim is always "the ever-growing sense of invulnerability which can be won in this way." This sense is gained only as "the enemy succumbs, but the hero comes through the fighting unhurt and filled with the consciousness of this prodigious fact, plunges into the next fight." With each victory, each mortal wound he delivers, his confidence grows, and with it the "armor" of invulnerability. The Hero is one who "piles up moments of survival" and comes to fear nothing. This is the way it must be, writes Canetti, for "the people want their hero invulnerable." It is only when he proves himself invulnerable that their fears of impotence and death subside, and he does this by killing and not being killed himself.[84]

All along, as Becker points out, it is a lie: heroism is but an illusion of victory. No human is truly victorious over death; no Hero literally prolongs existence past the brief span of human life. In fact, it is this very quest for victory over death that has turned the earth red with human blood since the beginning of history. Just to live in equanimity, humans objectify the repressed threat of death in hated symbols, or scapegoats, and lash out in fury against them. In Becker's words: "History is . . . a testimonial to the frightening costs of heroism. The hero is the one who can go out and get added powers by killing an enemy. . . . In a word, he becomes a savior through blood."[85] The Hero need not be a "bad man" to indulge the human taste for enemy blood in its quest for an imagined immortality. He can be dedicated to the highest good, a champion of morality, an altruist and an idealist. After all, his goal is to triumph over the evil embodied in death—his own death, the "worm at the core." He intends only to secure immortality, and his followers intend the same by their association and fascination with him. But the cost is always human blood just the same.

Billy Sunday did not spill literal human blood; but he was a masterful killer—figuratively. Every time he entered the pulpit, he placed himself at risk by challenging the forces of darkness, and he emerged unscathed. In his sermons, he dramatized his own victory over those forces lying in wait for good Christian people, and he did it without shrinking from the language of violence. His boasts about his own manliness often amounted to proclamations of his ability to do violence. "I now have as fine a physique as you ever saw," he said. "I'm pretty handy with my dukes."[86] According to a press report, he claimed to have whipped a man who had insulted a woman.[87] And one sermon featured a long story of his visit to a man who had beaten his wife for going to church. After a violent verbal exchange and mutual threats, the man backed down. If he had not, Sunday said, "I'd have backslid long enough to have licked him."[88] About another wife-beater Sunday said, "I'd knock seven kinds of pork out of that old hog." He thought any man who lures a woman into prostitution should be "shot at sunrise." Some sinners, he announced, ought to be "hurled out of society . . . kicked out of lodges . . . kicked out of churches." Others were so "rotten and vile" that they ought to "take a bath in carbolic acid and formaldehyde."[89] Certain popular writers deserved the death sentence, he thought; and double-barreled shotguns should be used on people who curse in public.[90]

Moreover, Sunday understood himself as a man of violence. He spoke of turning "his guns" loose on unorthodox ministers. When he heard that revivalism had been criticized, he claimed that revival meetings were responsible for most Christian conversions, and said, "I want to hurl this in the teeth, cram it down the throats of those who sneer at revival services—preachers included." He boasted: "I assault the devil's stronghold and I expect no quarter and I give him none." He ridiculed preachers who cried "peace"; "there is no peace," he said. "Some people won't come hear me because they are afraid to hear the truth. They want deodorized, disinfected sermons. They are afraid to be stuck over the edge of the pit and get a smell of the brimstone. You can't get rid of sin as long as you treat it as a cream puff instead of a rattlesnake." Sunday thought that much of the preaching of his day was "too nice; too pretty; too dainty; it does not kill." And he made it clear that preaching ought to kill. If words could kill, the violence of Billy Sunday's language could have killed his enemies many times over in a single sermon.[91]

"The threat of death is the coin of power," writes Elias Canetti.[92] Perhaps Sunday knew that ridicule itself threatens its object with death, and that those who applaud such ridicule—as his audiences did—are accessories to murder. Sunday brought his audiences into complicity with him in ritual murder and gave them permission to vent their hostile and hateful feelings in the guise of righteous indignation. He was famous for his strings of invectives, and his name-calling and denunciations were high points of audience enthusiasm. Although David was one of his favorite biblical heroes, his pulpit demeanor was much more that of Goliath: "Come to me, and I will give your flesh to the birds of the air and to the beasts of the field" (I Sam. 17:44). He hurled direct threats at his enemies, especially the whiskey gang, which he promised to drive out of American society—single-handedly, he implied. His "Booze Sermon," in which he unleashed his most unrelenting violence, was the favorite of his audiences. With confidence he promised God's judgment on his enemies. He was proud to preach about hell,[93] and he expressed happiness and praise to God that certain kinds of people would spend eternity there.[94] And he loved to use the language of death. In one memorable passage he personified various sins as the false prophets of Baal, and shouted for their execution:

> . . . they have got to be put to the sword. They must be slain. You've got to, my friends, slay uncleanness; you've got to slay lasciviousness; you've got to slay adultery; you've got to slay enmity; you've got to slay strife; you've got to slay jealousy; you've got to slay wrath; you've got to slay factiousness; you've got to slay divisions; you've got to slay heresies; you've got to slay these infamous lies that men are preaching from orthodox pulpits, that lead people away from God Almighty; you've got to slay envy; you've got to slay drunkenness; . . . you've got to slay lying; you've got to slay stealing; you've got to slay revilings; before the fire from God comes, the prophets of Baal have got to die, sir![95]

"I have no interest in a God who does not smite," he would say.[96]

Of course, his audience had no interest in that sort of God either, since the God they needed for their own sense of power was a God who would carry out the sentence of death that they had pronounced over their enemies. Sunday's followers took pleasure in his violence. The following outburst, for example, ended with a round of applause from the audience:

> You have a chance to double your fist and put it under some fellow's nose or in his face for Jesus Christ, and if a man stands up and talks against your wife and insults her, I wouldn't give that [sic] for you if you didn't have red blood enough in your veins, my friend, to send him to the mat. All right! Nobody can insult Jesus Christ in my presence without a scrap, now don't forget that.[97]

One approving observer used an apt image of violence to describe Sunday's delivery: "With the speed of a rapid-fire gun he pours volleys of denunciation with strings of adjectives, hurling them with unerring aim at the heart of religious and irreligious."[98] A like-minded fan was similarly impressed: "He spoke with the rapidity and energy of a gatling gun in action, lashing every form of sin and vice with scorching sarcasm and blistering epigram, asking no quarter and giving none."[99] Another prayed, at the start of a Billy Sunday meeting, "We thank Thee, O Lord, for the bravery of this man. We thank Thee for his open mouth that no man can shut. O Lord, drive on; may the slain of the Lord be many in this place."[100] Here the connection between God's violence and Sunday's violence is direct: The Hero holds in his own hands the very powers of life and death that belong only to divinity itself.

All this openly expressed symbolism of violence gave a certain "feel" to the typical Billy Sunday meeting. Sunday's crowds were not quiet and reserved but raucous and noisy, and the gatherings had the carnival spirit of spectacle. The audiences came expecting excitement—and blood. Their enthusiasm was still further aroused by the group-singing and platform entertainment under the skilled hand of Homer Rodeheaver. A sense of anticipation rose, as the time for The Hero's performance drew near. Then, quick as a flash, he was there, leaping about the stage, impersonating the infamous, ridiculing absent enemies, joking, threatening, parading his manliness, and announcing his victory over the forces of sin and death. All this may seem quite harmless—perhaps a bit atypical for a revival service but well within the realm of approved behavior. It comes as a shock, however, to realize that one has heard descriptions of lynch mobs that sound strangely like the human dynamic at a Billy Sunday meeting: the carnival atmosphere, the building excitement, the seizure and execution (symbolically) of the hated enemy, the sense of power and triumph, and the joy of a victory over evil. Elias Canetti offers an abstract description of the lynch mob, which he calls the "baiting crowd":

> This crowd is out for killing and it knows whom it wants to kill. It heads for this goal with unique determination and cannot be cheated of it. . . . This concentration on killing is of a special kind and of an unsurpassed intensity. Everyone wants to participate; everyone strikes a blow and, in order to do this, pushes as near as he can to the victim. If he cannot hit him himself, he wants to see others hit him. . . .
>
> One important reason for the rapid growth of the baiting crowd is that there is no risk involved. There is no risk because the crowd has immense superiority on their side. The victim can do nothing to them; he is either bound or in flight, and cannot hit back; in his defenselessness he is victim only. Also he has been made over to them for destruction; he is destined for it and thus no one need fear the sanction attached to killing. His permitted murder stands for all the murders people have to deny themselves for fear of the penalties for their perpetration. A murder shared with many others, which is not only safe and permitted, but indeed recommended, is irresistible to the great majority of men. There is, too, another factor which must be remembered. The threat of death hangs over all men and, however disguised it may be, and even if it is sometimes forgotten, it affects them all the time and creates in them a need to deflect death onto others. The formation of baiting crowds answers this need.[101]

No literal human blood was shed in Billy Sunday's meetings. In certain respects, the proceedings were carried on with a pretense of civility and restraint. Those who attended—mostly middle-class church members, good family people of high moral principle—would certainly have been appalled at the suggestion that they had participated, symbolically, in a lynch mob. But the parallels are quite suggestive: an anticipation and enjoyment of the most violent of Sunday's rhetoric; a general crowd participation through laughter, applause, shock, anger; the relatively "unheroic" nature of the violent activity, since all are participating and The Hero, after all, is doing the actual killing; the defenselessness of the victim. One cannot avoid the impression that the symbolic killing afforded a certain joyful release for Sunday's listeners. And why shouldn't it if it actually represents a triumph over the forces of death that the victim, as scapegoat, embodies? Becker states it bluntly: "Men spill blood because it makes their hearts glad and fills out their organisms with a sense of vital power. . . . Man aggresses not only out of frustration and fear but out of joy, plenitude, love of life. *Men kill lavishly out of the sublime joy of heroic triumph over evil*" (Becker's emphasis).[102]

Billy Sunday did not consider his meetings sanctified lynch mobs either, but he did see them as a muster for battle. One can place him quite comfortably within an entire social and intellectual movement at the turn of the century that the historian T. J. Jackson Lears calls "antimodern militarism." During Sunday's time there were calls from many quarters for a revival of the martial spirit, for a return to the "manlier" ways of the Middle Ages, for attention to the warrior as a heroic image worth emulating. Stories of adventure and violence and "historical romances full of heroic exploits" flooded the marketplace. Between 1894 and 1896 alone, twenty-eight books were published in the United States on the subject of Napoleon. Social critics offered sports and military drill as the proper way to train young people to physical hardness. Lears finds a widespread "fascination with physical power" and a growing anxiety that modern life was making people "soft."

The most popular American expression of this revived militarism was Teddy Roosevelt, who celebrated the rigors of outdoor life and the virtues of military action, and thus made himself the center of the cult of the "strenuous life." He was not alone in urging the possibilities of "moral regeneration through military adventure."[103] Robert Speer saw in World War I an opportunity to be reminded that the "American character" needs more "discipline and austerity."[104] And Billy Sunday, who prayed that Americans would enter the war so as to "help wipe Germany off the map," vowed that if war came, you could "count Billy Sunday in up to his neck . . . I'll raise enough of an army myself to help beat the dust off the Devil's hordes." He boasted, "Jesus will be our Commander in chief and he has Hindenburg beaten to a frazzle."[105]

Roosevelt, whom Sunday admired, called Sunday the "most wide-awake, militant preacher of Christianity I know."[106] He did not, however, have in mind Sunday's belligerent patriotism, which filled his sermons after the United States entered the war. Roosevelt referred to Sunday's own military campaign, the battle to which Sunday was always committed: the battle against those moral assassins who were threatening America and the devil who was standing behind them. Echoing Roosevelt, Sunday proclaimed: "Moral warfare makes a man hard. Superficial peace makes a man mushy. . . . The prophets all carried the Big Stick." His sermon "The Fighting Saint" urged Christians to "go on the warpath for purity, sobriety, and righteousness" and "take up the cudgels for reforms in civil and social life."[107] He told Christians that "when a war is over heroes have scars to show and they are proud of them," and asked, "what scars have you to show?"[108] Unlike Moody, who disliked songs of such self-confident tones, Sunday loved to have his audiences sing martial tunes like "Onward Christian Soldiers," "The Battle Hymn of the Republic," and "The Fight Is On"; in his hymnals one could find a section labeled "Warfare." "The church must be martial and we need martial music," he would say.[109] Such music would inspire the Christian to go out and do battle for the Lord:

> Go straight on and break the lion's neck and turn it into a beehive, out of which you will some day take the best and sweetest honey ever tasted, for the flavor of a dead lion in the honey beats that of clover and buckwheat all to pieces. Be a man, therefore, by going straight on to breathe an air that has in it the smoke of battle.[110]

Since booze was the one battle Sunday fought hardest, his most popular song was "De Brewer's Big Horses Can't Run Over Me." By one description, it was not a "hymn of worship" but a "battle cry. When thousands of men lift their voices in this militant refrain, with whistles blowing and bells ringing in the chorus, the effect is fairly thrilling." When a beer wagon interfered with a parade following Sunday's campaign in Scranton, Pennsylvania, and the driver "hurled offensive epithets at Sunday and his converts," the men in the crowd "bodily overturned the brewer's wagon, and sent the beer kegs rolling in the street, all to the tune of the Sunday war song. . . ."

Much of the hoopla surrounding Sunday's campaigns also evoked the martial spirit. Just before the opening of each campaign, Sunday would arrive to a tumultuous welcome at the local train station, would accompany a parade through the city streets, and would then be "triumphantly escorted by mounted police" to his lodging. When he came to Philadelphia, according to an observer, the ovation that met him "exceeded anything ever accorded president, prince or returning hero." The closing parade could be equally impressive. One admirer put it revealingly:

> The idea of the Roman imperial triumph survives in the Billy Sunday parade. It is a testimony to the multitudes of the loyalty of Christians to the Gospel. Beyond all question, a tremendous impression is made upon a city

> by the thousands of marching men whom the evangelist first leads and then reviews. A street parade is a visualization of the forces of the Church in a community. Many a man on the street, who might be unmoved by many arguments, however powerful, cannot escape the impression of the might of the massed multitudes of men who march through the streets, thousands strong. . . . Religion loses whatever traits of femininity it may have possessed, before the Sunday campaign is over. . . . Every Christian the world around must be grateful to this evangelist and his associates for giving the sort of demonstration, which cannot be misunderstood by the world at large, of the virility and the immensity of the hosts of heaven on earth.[111]

These words, including the veiled threat implied in them, sum up the meaning of Billy Sunday as The Hero to a generation of evangelicals—the man of power, the leader of a mighty band, the manly general of the Lord's army, and thus the one who leads the people of God in the ritual killing of the chosen enemy. Who would not join the forces of this mighty man, so impressive in his display of power over the very forces that dog our steps in an increasingly troubled world?

Thousands did just that during each of Sunday's major campaigns. After the first week or two of his meetings, he would invariably end the services by inviting his listeners to come forward in response to his message. This was standard operating procedure for American revivalists. Unlike Moody, however, who had concentrated on ending his sermons in a mood of solemnity conducive to sinners' wrestling with their own rebellion and struggling with their need for repentance, Sunday would often reach a fever pitch of raucous excitement just before he issued the altar call. Moody had also continued Finney's practice of meeting penitent sinners and inquirers in after-meetings, where individuals might be counseled and encouraged personally to repent and be saved. Sunday, as we have seen, dispensed with the use of these "inquiry rooms"; his practice was to invite his crowds to step down to the front, shake his hand, and hear a few words of advice and a short prayer after the larger audience had been dismissed.[112] This was in line with his opinion that salvation was a simple matter, and "a man can be converted without any fuss."[113]

It was not at all clear, however, that conversion was what his invitations aimed at; nor was it clear exactly what conversion meant. The vast majority of those "hitting the trail" were often Christians, even church members, which hints that the invitations performed a different sort of service than that of encouraging lost souls to repent and be saved. His first call for trail-hitters in Boston (recounted in the previous chapter) was replete with military imagery: calls to "die for Christ" in fighting booze, a rousing story of a military hero, an image of the cross as a weapon, hymns addressed to the "soldiers of the cross," and so on. And after all the trail-hitting had ended, Sunday assured his audience that God was proud of them.[114] Perhaps this reveals the true meaning of his invitation rituals. They were not calls to broken sinners to repent and be converted as much as they were opportunities for the righteous to publicly proclaim their allegiance and receive God's commendation. In other words, they were public proclamations of one's own rightness, of one's loyalty to the right and the good. This interpretation explains the wording of others of Sunday's calls:

> How many of you men and women will jump to your feet and come down and say, "Bill, here's my hand for God, for home, for my native land, to live and conquer for Christ"?[115]
>
> How many of you will pledge and promise and say, "God, I will stand by you and I'll stand by your cross, and I'll stand by the religion of Jesus Christ. I'll stand by my flag, I'll stand by my country—here I am, Lord"?[116]
>
> How many men and women here tonight will come down and give me your hand and say: "Here's my hand, to live for God and Christ the best I know how"? Will you? Come on. I would like to have the honor to take you by the hand. . . .[117]
>
> I want the inspiration of taking the hand of every fellow who says, "I'm with you for Jesus Christ and for truth."[118]

As folks came forward, one reporter observed, "tears of penitence were few, and there were smiles on the faces of most of those with whom the evangelist shook hands. . . ." Sunday said "thank you" to each one. Meanwhile, spectators would stand on their seats to get a better view of the people streaming down the aisles in the cause of the good, and friends would cheer as one of their company went to shake Sunday's hand.[119]

All of this completes the picture of Sunday as the archetypal evangelical Hero. Fresh from the battle, slain enemies lying all around, The Hero calls for a confirmation of his invulnerability and for the righteousness of his cause to be proclaimed. Hundreds stream forward in answer because his invulnerability, his righteousness, his power over the enemy can be theirs as well. Their response is not a confession of lostness, of brokenness, or of mortality at all, but quite the opposite: it is a proclamation of their rightness and their immortality. Although they function as "the slain of the Lord," they do not stream forward to a death but to a denial of the power of death over them. And those who do not come forward watch from audience or platform, with only slightly subdued enthusiasm, for their side is swelling its ranks, the enemy is in retreat, and their own invulnerability is even further secured. They project onto the invisible powers their own invincible rightness and thus their claim to immortality, aided by Sunday's own words: "God is proud of you." They are thus engaged in a kind of cosmic ritual for the determination of fitness to live forever, and their Hero has won the balloting, as anyone watching the masses push forward to shake his hand can plainly see.

The magic moment for the trail-hitter, however, was the actual shaking of The Hero's hand, which physically passed The Hero's invulnerability on to the humble follower. The hand that had seared the air in threatened violence, symbolically still dripping the enemy's blood, became the hand of blessing. In the actual touching of flesh on flesh, the invisible powers available to The Hero flowed into the follower: one could imagine oneself, for just a moment, a hero like The Hero. Sunday's admiring biographer put it clearly:

> As I have studied Mr. Sunday in the act of taking the hands of converts—
> one memorable night more than five hundred at the rate of fifty-seven a
> minute—the symbolism of his hand has appealed to my imagination. Sur-
> prisingly small and straight and surprisingly strong it is, . . . no scars upon
> it. . . . The lines are strong and deep and clear . . . no flabbiness about
> it. . . . No outstretched hand of military commander ever pointed such a
> host to so great a battle. . . . The soldier sent on a desperate mission asked
> Wellington for "one grasp of your conquering hand. . . ." Conceive of the
> vast variety of hands that have been reached up to grasp this one, and what
> those hands have since done for the world's betterment! Two hundred
> thousand dedicated right hands, still a-tingle with the touch of this inviting
> hand of the preacher of the gospel! The picture of Sunday's right hand
> belongs in the archives of contemporary religious history.[120]

In touching that heroic hand the multitudes could imagine that they had gained a godlike power and invulnerability for themselves. Yet all they had touched was human flesh.

V

Paul the apostle knew that the path of religious heroism was also the path of violence and bloodshed. In his "zeal," as he said, he had been Saul the "persecutor of the church." The Acts of the Apostles records that he "laid waste the church, and entering house after house, he dragged off men and women and committed them to prison." It was as a devout man, a man of unimpeachable piety, a man of God, that Paul, "still breathing threats and murder against the disciples of the Lord," took the road to Damascus to widen his sphere of violence. Jesus asked him, "Saul, Saul, why do you persecute me?" And when Saul responded, "Who are you, Lord?" he was not feigning ignorance or surprise. He had always been confident that his heroism and his violence were in the service of the Holy One of Israel. Now he saw with a certain shock that his confidence had not been in the God of Israel but in the flesh. His confidence had been the confidence of the religious hero whose exertions mask a panicked denial that one is "booked to die," and amounted to an attempt to serve as one's own savior. How like Billy Sunday was this zealous and violent man, and how like each of us to whom the gospel of Jesus Christ is so much more of an affront than we can possibly admit (Phil. 3:6; Acts 8:3; 9:1-4).

We can imagine that that gospel never affronted Saul so deeply as in his encounter with Stephen, where he had been a member of the "godly" lynch mob. Stephen, brought before the council by the religious leaders in Jerusalem, spoke, with "the face of an angel," of the God of glory who had made himself known in Jesus Christ, whom these same elders had "betrayed and murdered." Murder was still in the hearts of these pious men: "They were enraged, and they ground their teeth against him." Stephen's response was not that of the belligerent Billy Sunday before his accusors. He "gazed into heaven and saw the glory of God, and Jesus standing at the right hand of God. . . . And as they were stoning Stephen, he prayed, 'Lord Jesus, receive my spirit.' . . . And when he had said this, he fell asleep." As a youthful participant, Saul observed all this and, as the text makes clear, "was consenting to his death" (Acts 7:52-68; 8:1).

We do not know exactly how Saul experienced this encounter, although there are plenty of clues in his subsequent career, first as the persecutor of the church and then as a slave of Jesus Christ the crucified One. Saul probably joined the lynch mob as a young Pharisee and protégé of the religious leaders and heroes of Jerusalem. No doubt he was in deadly earnest about the law of God and anxious that this band of Christians not "change the customs which Moses delivered," as his elders accused Stephen—and Jesus—of doing. Certainly, like many of his elders, he felt enraged at this Stephen, who seemed to be threatening the standard religious hero-system of the Jews, and when his elders ground their teeth, Saul must have ground his too. Like them, he would have defended it as a righteous grinding, a zeal for the God of Israel and for the right; and he felt justified in his own eyes and God's as he participated, vicariously perhaps, in the murder of Stephen. Clearly, Saul must have thought that Stephen deserved to die; otherwise he would not have been "consenting to his death." The concomitant of this judgment of death on the enemy is always: surely *I* do not deserve to die; surely I am a hero. And perhaps in this pronouncement he felt a certain exhilaration flowing into him, as the blood flowed out of Stephen—an exhilaration that he would attempt to reexperience time and again, by making a career of persecution and murder (Acts 6:14; 22:3-5; 26:4-5).

Stephen had heard the gospel, and it was given to him to believe it. He did not boast of his manliness or breathe out threats and murder. He did not call on the Righteous One to wreak his vengeance and destroy his enemies. Instead, he turned to face his death—perhaps understanding that it was a death deserved, the rightful judgment of the Holy One of Israel upon his life. And in his acceptance of that judgment he cried a prayer that, in our heroic denials of that judgment, we can never cry: "Lord, do not hold this sin against them." He did not praise God that his enemies would burn in hell; but he echoed the incomprehensible—and most unheroic—words of Jesus on the cross: "Father, forgive them, for they know not what they do."

Billy Sunday did not seem capable of offering that sort of prayer. He is the symbol of a whole evangelical community, in his day and ours, that finds it hard to love its enemies. It embodies in those enemies all the forces of evil, the forces that threaten—figuratively or literally—its own death. And in doing violence to those enemies it can experience the "joy" of victory over death, the emotional payoff from imagining, in repressed and hidden ways, that it has transcended God's words, "You shall surely die." In its choice of daily hero systems, and in its choice of The Hero, evangelicals simply continue the human project of self-justification: "I do not deserve to die; I deserve to live forever." Thus Billy Sunday could say: "Oh my! Remember please that stuff is transient, stuff is as weak as a rope of sand and as unenduring as a cloud of smoke or vapor. Oh no! No! No! *Christian manhood, that's eternal.* That stands when the mountain peaks will be incinerated into ashes" (emphasis mine).[121]

Here is as frank a denial of death and a grasping after a deserved immortality as one can find. In Billy Sunday the evangelical community had found its hero of Christian manhood, the man who would not die. And the issue of this denial is violence, as we have seen, and not forgiveness. It is not surprising that Billy Sunday had to admit, with a lovable candor, that "resist not evil" was "the hardest verse in the Bible for me to live up to." "If a fellow would swat me on one cheek," he confided, "I think I'd clear for action like a battleship." Of course, to be a true Christian hero, Billy Sunday knew he had to take the Bible seriously and be "moral" in terms that he felt it dictated. Since Jesus said it is right to love your enemies, and not resist evil, Sunday owned that he was "trying my level best to live up to it."[122]

And yet, how could he, since his attempt would flow from the very moralistic striving for heroism that, in fallen humanity, always implies the opposite: threats and murder. The Hero will always have trouble "resisting not evil," because The Hero's very task, for himself and his followers, is to resist evil and thus attain victory over death. The Hero does not stand in the solidarity of sin and death with all humanity, but in a place of presumed righteousness and immunity to death, a place he must secure by further expressions of violence. It makes The Hero a very unforgiving man or woman.

In Stephen the martyr we have God's gracious contradiction of Saul the hero. The Hero rejects the judgment of death in many and subtle ways, most of them deeply concealed beneath conscious and unconscious deceptions. The martyr accepts death—not as yet another means to heroism but as the end of heroism, as a judgment pronounced by God himself on the martyr's life as well as on every human life. As the stones fly faster or the flames burn higher, perhaps the martyr hears the words of God to Adam and Eve as words directed to himself, as words that he or she can embrace as from a loving God who must burn away the chaff: in the day you eat of it you shall surely die. Perhaps the martyr's eyes are opened by God to the bankruptcy of all human posturings and boastings, even those in the guise of piety and religious zeal, and to the foolish and destructive lies embodied in heroisms of every sort. And perhaps in that opening of the eyes to his or her own deserved oneness in death with all mankind, even with those who would accuse and murder, the martyr is graciously enabled to forgive the enemy. Only then does violence cease to beget violence.

I do not question Billy Sunday's sincerity in his proclamation of love for Jesus Christ and for lost souls, nor the sincerity of the evangelical community that made him their Hero at the turn of the century. Nor do I question the sincerity of Saul or the religious zeal of the Pharisees. Their motives, if I am correct in identifying them, were hidden from themselves, as generally are our own. Sin and self-deception are no strangers to each other, and no one escapes their bondage in a straightforward, heroic way. But there are moments of revelation, and in this revelation there is a certain freedom, though one continues "in the flesh" to "serve the law of sin." Saul, as the apostle Paul, enjoyed such moments of revelation, causing him to ask, "Who will deliver me from this body of death?" and to answer, "Thanks be to God through Jesus Christ our Lord" (Rom. 7:24-25).

But he knew that this deliverance would be not by some inherent immortality of his own, as the Greeks taught, and not by virtue of his heroic manhood, as the Romans taught, but by the fruition of his mortality in death—actual physical death—and then by God's gracious act of resurrection. Only *then* would "this perishable nature . . . put on the imperishable, and this *mortal* nature . . . put on immortality." He knew this because he knew Jesus. In Jesus God took human form and did precisely what we will not and cannot do, and for that reason what he had to do in our place: "He humbled himself and became obedient unto death, even death on a cross." What powerful words these must have been for Paul to write—Paul who for so long had shunned his own mortality by feats of religious heroism. How stunning it must have been to Paul to learn that he would be rescued, as "chief of sinners," by a God who, in Christ, simply (but for us, impossibly) became obedient unto death (I Cor. 15:53).

Herein is the affront of the gospel, an affront we have long hidden from ourselves by our complacent familiarity with a nicely packaged, domesticated Jesus, and by our superficial, self-serving understanding of what it means to follow him. The good news is that we have been rescued by a man willing to die. We are not willing to die—to literally, physically die, or to die in any other way—and thus when we truly see Jesus, he is an offense, an affront, a reminder of the judgment that hangs over all of us. It is no surprise that "he was despised and rejected by men"—Christian men and women included—nor that we recoiled in horror from him "as one from whom men hide their faces." Even Peter could not accept *this* Messiah, the one who dies, and in Jesus' words to him we hear his words to us as well: "Get behind me, Satan! You are a hindrance to me; for you are not on the side of God, but of men" (Is. 53:3; Mt. 16:23).

There is really only one side for humanity, and it is not the side of God. In our attempts to fashion a certain heroism, we split humanity in two and work out our violent death-denials on all those across the line from us, those we identify as the enemy. In so doing we deny our human solidarity under God's judgment of death, and we make of God our truest enemy. That is why we killed him. But he will not be enemy to us. We are not on his side, but he comes onto our side, in the flesh, and shows us who we might be and ultimately—willingly or not—must be: obedient unto death. In his death, by his stripes, we are healed. And God raised this Jesus from the dead and exalted him and bestowed on him the name that is above every name, to which every knee shall bow, in heaven and on earth and under the earth, and before which every tongue will confess that Jesus Christ is Lord, to the glory of God the Father. We who share a solidarity in death, and in our futile attempts to escape that death, shall also share a solidarity in resurrection to life everlasting. Then will our futile heroism and our striving for spurious status and healing and power be at an end, and only then will we sing what we so deeply yearn to sing: "Death is swallowed up in victory. O death, where is thy victory? O death, where is thy sting?" (Phil. 2:9-11; I Cor. 15:54-55).

Epilogue

There is only one serious human agenda, and it is shared by Christians and non-Christians alike. We want to be like God. We want to know victory, to embody perfection, to wield power, to be right. In other words, we want to be the keepers of good and evil—in our personal worlds as well as in the social world around us. Knowing that our lives are under a sentence of death, we want these things in the here and now— some symbolic taste of immortality to help us forget who we really are.

The evangelicals of the mid-nineteenth century were confident that victory, perfection, power, and rightness in the visible as well as invisible realm were within their grasp. A new continent, the first stirrings of the machine age, a small and relatively homogeneous population, the successes of a fledgling republic: these and other accidents of history blessed antebellum America with a preternatural calm. Evangelicals prepared to tear down their barns and build greater ones. Their giddy millennialism was the self-congratulation of the spiritually rich.

But the calm was deceptive, cruelly so. Stormy weather crashed down upon these evangelicals and crumbled their barns before their eyes. Their precipitate decline was a kind of death, a reminder of the finitude from which they had hidden their eyes, a portent of the judgment of God. It offered them a window on their folly. It dashed their euphoric predictions of a society bathed in glory, and it revealed instead their oneness with all humanity in the futility to which the creation has been subjected. It wrested control, or the illusion of control, from their hands, and it gave their history over to an economic and social mechanism that trampled all they had held holy and mocked their protests of human freedom. It was very heavy weather indeed, a potential "moment of truth" for American evangelicals.

But it was a moment not to be grasped. On the whole, evangelicals did not have ears to hear. Doubtless they were uneasy, even anguished, deep within. But they turned from their anguish very quickly. They rarely acknowledged their true state, rarely cried out in repentance or begged God's mercy in ways that might be historically observable. They did not acknowledge their poverty of spirit, nor hold up the fragility of their belief to public view. If a cry of anguish ever rose in their throats, they silenced it, protesting instead with utter confidence their own rightness, their status as the faithful remnant, their continued qualification for temporal power, and their possession of a God whose primary task soon became to attest and attend to these things. Even as their old triumphalism soured in their mouths, they devised a new triumphalism that would obviate any necessity to face their own abject poverty, and to admit their lies.

By elaborating and insisting on this new triumphalism, the evangelicals at the turn of the century clung to their spiritual riches, effectively shifting their assets behind the scenes. The move from postmillennialism to dispensational premillennialism redefined their richness as that of a godly minority rather than a godly majority. Using a complicated theological alchemy, they transformed bad news into the good news of their own special status, and they traded the open domination of American society for a more hidden and yet just as confident control of cosmic history. In embracing the Victorious Life theology, they aspired to the same moral perfection that their mid-nineteenth-century forebears had craved, except that it was with a new technique of relaxation rather than the old rigor of moral struggle. To this status of outward moral perfection they added a victorious control of the increasingly chaotic inner world of emotions, and thus they joined the nascent therapeutic society in its promise of psychic health and happiness. All this was not without its payoff for the invidious ego, which found comfort in joining a select group of those who, unlike most "average" Christians, had experienced the filling of God's Spirit and were no longer in danger of being mistaken for "mere men." And in the revivalism of Billy Sunday evangelicals not only permitted themselves a sweet taste of the old triumphalism of the mid-nineteenth century, with its promise of actual social dominance as thousands joined the victorious Christian army by taking to the sawdust trail, but they participated in the dramatic personal heroism of their champion. The evangelist's godlike powers and media attractions afforded them a certain reflected glory, and his manly courage and moral fortitude offered them a substitute, albeit symbolic, means for the attainment of the perfection of character and personal heroism that was increasingly eluding them in a modernizing and bureaucratizing society. In all these ways, the triumphalism of the mid-nineteenth century demonstrated its stubborn lock on American evangelicals, and the delights of spiritual richness revealed their addicting power.

As the rich, however, they did not give up the prospect of owning it all once again. While shifting their assets to account for foul weather, they harbored the hope of recovering their former empire after the storm had passed. Many evangelicals thought conditions looked favorable again in the 1920s. Billy Sunday's huge popularity, as well as the success of the Prohibition movement, allowed them to imagine that a major portion of the American populace was turning back to God, and that the dissolution of the evangelical consensus might perhaps be reversed. The wave of patriotism surrounding World War I emboldened them to think that perhaps God had not abandoned his favorite people, and that perhaps Americans were not beyond recognizing evangelicalism's association with that God. The formation of several important interdenominational bodies to launch new offensives against the growing secularism and unbelief in American society, and especially in its churches, produced the illusion of an advancing rather than a retreating evangelicalism. Conservative evangelicals even had a new name—"fundamentalists"—and a new spate of energetic, aggressive leaders—William Bell Riley, John Roach Straton, Frank Norris, and others. All of these men promised that the newer, symbolic triumphalism might only have to provide comfort for its adherents in the brief interim before God revived the fortunes of his people. Then the rich would once again be rich in the ways that really matter—they would *literally* "run the show" in America, as they had in the days of their fathers.

The initial euphoria generated by the formation of the fundamentalist coalition did not survive the decade of the 1920s. At Dayton, Tennessee, in 1925, fundamentalist forces won the battle against the teaching of evolution in the public schools, but they lost the war for the loyalties of the American people at large. Meanwhile, the experiment with Prohibition appeared to be going badly, and the roar of the "Roaring Twenties" was not the sound of the chariots of God. Billy Sunday's appeal drained away swiftly, while his nemesis, the society woman, saw her fortunes rise. By the end of the decade it seemed clear that evangelicals posed no serious threat to the advance of secularization and the loosening of moral standards in American culture. Their brief counterattack quickly ended on the national scale. Evangelicals skirmished for a time with the forces of liberalism in the major denominations, seminaries, and mission boards; but in general they met defeat on this front as well. After 1930, evangelicalism continued to show vitality within its pockets of organizational endeavor and resistance, but it seemed more and more resigned to minority status within a pluralistic and rapidly secularizing American culture. Their society had come so far from those optimistic days when the United States could be counted a "Christian nation," that H. L. Mencken could define Christendom as "that part of the world in which, if any man stands up in public and solemnly swears that he is a Christian, all his auditors will laugh."[1]

Thereafter, the true designs of the spiritually rich American evangelicals went into hiding. As I suggested at the outset of this study, we evangelicals of the post–World War II generation inherited at least several decades of cultural pessimism—the decades, in fact, during which our parents' generation came of age. The evangelical adults in our lives, particularly those more comfortable with the designation "fundamentalist," actually seemed to be operating under a nontriumphalist model for understanding Christian prospects in this world. The symbolic triumphalism hidden behind its theological formulations was perhaps felt at an intuitive level but was nowhere made plain to us. It looked to us as though our parents' generation was resigned to the rank apostasy of America and had dedicated itself to evangelism and spiritual discipline while awaiting the rapture of the saints at the sound of God's trumpet. To all appearances, they had given up on America.

In the decade of the 1970s, however, evangelicals were taken by surprise—the surprise of their own resuscitation. Religion as a whole acquired a new respectability. Cults proliferated, but so did evangelical home Bible studies, youth programs, evangelistic techniques, and outreach campaigns. "Church growth" became a Christian academic specialty. The evangelical book, film, and music industries flourished. Charismatic preachers blossomed into television personalities overnight. A "born-again Christian" moved into the White House, and a "Year of the Evangelical" was proclaimed by the secular press. Politically oriented evangelicals (especially those on the right) formulated a coherent legislative program directed at America's worst problems, and were optimistic enough to style themselves a "moral majority."

It is still too early for any reliable explanation of this surprising resurgence. Our study of the shaping of early twentieth-century evangelicalism might, however, allow us to hazard a guess. The 1960s and 1970s were a kind of turning point in America's self-understanding. Our country had emerged from World War II as an economic, political, and military giant, leader of the free world, in control—or so it seemed—of world affairs in general. For a while it looked like an "American century" had begun. In retrospect, we see that almost immediately our illusion of control began to crack. In the 1950s the Soviet Union emerged as a powerful contender for world domination. In the 1960s we confronted our impotence in Southeast Asia, and the "Third World" seemed on the brink of getting away from us. In the 1970s the oil-producing countries of the Middle East exposed yet another vulnerability. Meanwhile, racial, political, and generational conflict wrought turmoil in the streets, and parents had to watch police beating their children. Recession and runaway inflation was wrecking our economy. A very popular president abused his power and was forced out of office. Our sense of ourselves as the beloved protectors of liberty and the envy of all the world evoked doubt from some, ridicule from others. We were thrown on the defensive at home and abroad.

All this, I suspect, contributed to an already generalized anxiety rooted in the loss of control over our private lives in a highly bureaucratized, technological society. Large, faceless institutions—making those of the late nineteenth century look positively benign—conducted most of the nation's business. The persons (if they were persons) who determined one's fate were almost impossible to locate, much less to influence. Computers seemed to be in charge of the most important questions. Experts fashioned regulations by which Americans had to live and used a barrage of paperwork to intimidate challengers. Big business, having fostered public addiction to the newest consumer goods, held customers hostage to rising prices and falling quality. Professional help seemed required for every problem, small or large: accountants and tax experts, doctors and lawyers, child psychologists and marriage counselors. The media shaped the entire society to the demands of consumerism, and even those who recognized their vulnerability could not quite find the "off" button. Families disintegrated willy-nilly, re-formed, and disintegrated again, as if a monster had been unchained in American society whose purpose was to destroy the possibility for commitment and who was enjoying every minute of it.

American society at large, it seems, was experiencing a dissolution and disillusionment not unlike what evangelicals had weathered at the turn of the century. It had, perhaps, taken a little longer for the secular sectors of society to feel the pain, although the twentieth century seemed like one long object lesson. The turmoil of the 1960s and 1970s finally brought it home: in a very real sense, humans are not in control of their lives in a modern, technological society. Evangelicals had experienced this trauma, at least unconsciously, long before; what is more, they had devised ways of coping with the trauma, of regaining control, at least symbolically. The ideological package comprising twentieth-century evangelicalism was thus ready-made, and free for the taking, for a people in the throes of impotence and self-doubt.

Years in a seductively affluent and secularizing society had taken their toll, however, so that the original contents of the evangelical package looked just a bit different than they had half a century earlier. Not so different, though, that they could not be recognized. The eschatological component, in particular, seemed almost unchanged. The author of the best-selling book of the decade, *The Late Great Planet Earth*, added the glitter of technology, a dash of contemporary politics, and a Disneyland imagination to an essentially standard dispensational premillennialism. The Scofield Reference Bible was reissued (somewhat revised), and dramatic Second Coming scenarios made it into the movies. Meanwhile, the television preachers and the Moral Majority took up Billy Sunday's cudgel against every sort of evil, adding nuclear disarmament, homosexuality, and the Equal Rights Amendment to fill out the great revivalist's slate of godless wrongs. Heroism was alive and well in evangelicalism, featuring religious media celebrities and with it the moral chest-thumping and aggressive name-calling of an earlier era. Sunday's knee-jerk patriotism continued its hold on American evangelicals, countering the bad news from overseas and offering no serious critiques of American culture beyond simplistic moralizing about secular humanism. All this sold well in a nation that wanted to hear good things about itself. The Victorious Life theology was most altered by its twentieth-century passage. While the Christian liberal arts colleges and Bible schools kept it alive in something close to its original version, imaginative television preachers forged new alloys of Holy Spirit power, positive thinking, self-esteem psychology, and magical devotional practices. From these emerged a gospel of health, wealth, and happiness that promised instant success over any and all of life's problems. All this symbolic triumphalism owed its inspiration to late nineteenth- and twentieth-century evangelicalism, but it found itself most up-to-date and attractive to desperate folks of all sorts in the late twentieth century.

It is anyone's guess whether American evangelicals and their close fundamentalist relatives will be forced much longer to settle for a triumphalism that is merely symbolic. The alleged presidential ambitions of one of its slicker media personalities indicate that, at least in some minds, the time may be right for a return to the *real* power enjoyed by mid-nineteenth-century evangelicals. If the evangelical resurgence continues in this direction, one would not be surprised to see evangelical theology and practice begin to resemble its triumphalist nineteenth-century predecessor. The appeal of dispensationalism might well wane, with postmillennial optimism taking its place. The revivalism of Billy Graham's successor might find itself more ardently associated with programs of collective political and social reform, as Graham himself has very tentatively been in recent years, and at a level to which even Billy Sunday would not have aspired in his concern for the individual soul. One might also expect the Victorious Life theology to be swallowed up by the secularized techniques of the counseling profession, conducted by evangelicals in evangelical language, but promising the same fix for the broken human soul that was Charles G. Trumbull's stock in trade.

My own instinct is that the times will not sustain an optimistic millennialism, and that the "go for it" confidence of the Reagan years will end with the Reagan years. I do not look for conservative Christianity's current resurgence to be consummated in real political power, and, if it is, it would certainly be shown up for weakness in the face of technology's ever-tightening grip and America's probable decline as a world power broker. We may have to be satisfied with a symbolic triumphalism of the sort that evangelicalism forged in the crucible of modernity at the end of the previous century, one whose religious language provides only a thin veneer over an increasingly secularized and consumer-oriented product. Of course, this will not be evidence of the freedom of the Spirit in our midst. It would merely signal our continuing enthrallment to emotionally pleasing illusions and our failure to hear in our many dissolutions the judgment of a merciful, beckoning, suffering God. It would demonstrate that we evangelicals had learned nothing from the last century of human history. It might also signify that God has chosen to be silent in our generation. That would truly be cause for mourning—and for a protest and a plea that God renew his Word in our world.

Such a renewal, if it were to come, would surely reveal itself in a spirit of brokenness, confession, and repentance. And it would certainly find itself discovering Jesus Christ, as if for the first time. "Beyond Jesus, behind him," Jacques Ellul has written, "there is nothing—nothing but lies."[2] A church that awakens to the Stranger, Jesus Christ—the Jesus Christ of the biblical witness, not the denatured, ideologically and morally useful Jesus Christ of evangelicalism—would not shrink from recognizing and unmasking those lies as they appear in cultural and theological garb. The lies it would unmask, however, would first of all be its own. This would make it a confessing church, a church that takes the gospel of God's grace so seriously that its words of praise for so great a salvation are never more than a breath removed from a humble recognition, and confession, of its own lostness. It would recognize in the Word of God a living and active Word, sharper than a two-edged sword, piercing to the division of its *own* soul and spirit, its *own* joints and marrow, and discerning the thoughts and intentions of its *own* heart (Heb. 4:12). A confessing church would not find itself adding to the world's divisions, and thus to its violence, by proclaiming its superiority to sinful humanity, whether found in American homosexuals or Libyan terrorists or Soviet communists. It would see itself in the prodigal son, in the adulterous woman, in the pious Pharisee, in the mockers at the cross, in the stoners of Stephen. Like Paul after years of Christian experience, it would proclaim itself to be "foremost of sinners" and thus one with the human race for which Christ died (I Tim 1:15). A confessing church would recognize itself as that which Jesus builds of the stuff of people like Peter, who can in one moment proclaim, "You are the Christ," and in the next, "I do not know this man of whom you speak." With Peter, the church of Jesus Christ would confess that it is all too often on the side of men and not God, and with Peter it would weep bitterly (Mk. 8:29, 33; 14:71-72). This church would thus find its uniqueness as a people of God in recognizing, in sorrow and in hope, its solidarity with those who are not the people of God.

I do not often find that I am myself this lamenting, confessing Christian. And I do not predict that my church, the evangelical Christians of America, will become this lamenting, confessing church. Whether in auspicious or declining times, as we have seen, we display a tenacious commitment to self-deceit. It is true that we are those who like to think we heed Jeremiah's words, "Blessed is the man who trusts in the Lord." Our history, however, gives evidence rather of Jeremiah's wisdom in adding these words: "The heart is deceitful above all things, and desperately corrupt; who can understand it?" (Jer. 17:7, 9). In our very protests of trust in the Lord, we find occasion for our deepest self-deceits.

But God's ways are not our ways. Scripture announces that he will not be defeated by our unfaithfulness. Even in our unfaithfulness we serve his purpose, witnessing paradoxically to the boundlessness of the mercy offered by the God who saves by grace. He is the One who, through the prophet Hosea, says to his people, "You are not my people." But He is also the One who, in Jesus Christ, makes of these unfaithful people "sons of the living God." And Hosea assures us that one day we shall find the words to say, in truth, "Thou art my God" (Hos. 1:10; 2:23).

Notes

Chapter I

1. Martin Marty, *The Modern Schism: Three Paths to the Secular* (New York: Harper and Row, 1969), p. 116.
2. George M. Marsden, *Fundamentalism and American Culture: The Shaping of Twentieth-Century Evangelicalism, 1870-1925* (New York: Oxford University Press, 1980), p. 11.
3. H. Richard Niebuhr, *The Kingdom of God in America* (New York: Harper and Row, 1937), p. 157.
4. See, for example, Robert T. Handy, *A Christian America: Protestant Hopes and Historical Realities* (New York: Oxford University Press, 1971); Sidney E. Mead, *The Lively Experiment: The Shaping of Christianity in America* (New York: Harper and Row, 1963); Sidney E. Mead, *The Nation with the Soul of a Church* (New York: Harper and Row, 1975).
5. Herbert Gutman, *Work, Culture and Society in Industrializing America* (New York: Vintage Books, 1966, 1976), p. 164; Anthony F. C. Wallace, *Rockdale: The Growth of an American Village in the Early Industrial Revolution* (New York: W. W. Norton, 1972, 1978), p. 408.
6. Gutman, *Work*, p. 233.
7. Wallace, *Rockdale*, pp. 411-12.
8. Richard D. Brown, "Modernization: A Victorian Climax," in Daniel Walker Howe, ed., *Victorian America* (Philadelphia: University of Pennsylvania Press, 1976), p. 35.
9. Harold Underwood Faulkner, *American Economic History*, 8th edition (New York: Harper and Brothers, 1960 [1924]), p. 216.
10. Ibid., p. 213.
11. Paul W. Gates, *The Farmer's Age: Agriculture 1815-1860*, vol. III of *The Economic History of the United States* (New York: Holt, Rinehart and Winston, 1960), pp. 418-19.
12. Ibid., p. 420.
13. Robert Heilbroner and Aaron Singer, *The Economic Transformation of America* (New York: Harcourt Brace Jovanovich, 1977), pp. 52-53.
14. This summary of the economic shape of the immediate pre–Civil War period was drawn from Faulkner, *American Economic History*, pp. 216-99; Gates, *The Farmer's Age*, pp. 418-20; Heilbroner and Singer, *Economic Transformation*, pp. 27-53; Charles H. Hession and Hyman Sardy, *Ascent to Affluence: A History of American Economic Development* (Boston: Allyn and Bacon, Inc., 1969), pp. 227-306; and George Rogers Taylor, *The Transportation Revolution, 1815-1860*, vol. IV of *The Economic History of the United States* (New York: Holt, Rinehart and Winston, 1951), pp. 384-95.
15. Timothy L. Smith, in *Revivalism and Social Reform in Mid-Nineteenth Century America* (Nashville: Abingdon Press, 1957) gives very helpful evidence on this score. See especially chapters I through IV.
16. Smith, *Revivalism*, pp. 17, 18.
17. Quoted in Smith, *Revivalism*, p. 18.
18. Mead, *Lively Experiment*, p. 126.

19. Quoted in Joel Carpenter, "American Fundamentalism: Coming to Terms with a Troublesome Heritage," *Mission Journal* (November 1981):20.

20. Quoted in George M. Marsden, *The Evangelical Mind and the New School Presbyterian Experience: A Case Study of Thought and Theology in Nineteenth Century America* (New Haven: Yale University Press, 1970), p. 16.

21. Sydney E. Ahlstrom, *A Religious History of the American People* (New Haven: Yale University Press, 1972), pp. 422-23; and Smith, *Revivalism*, chapters X through XIV.

22. Quoted in Marsden, *Evangelical Mind*, p. 188.

23. Quoted in Theodore Dwight Bozeman, *Protestants in an Age of Science: The Baconian Ideal and Antebellum American Religious Thought* (Chapel Hill, N.C.: University of North Carolina Press, 1977), p. 34.

24. Quoted in Ernest R. Sandeen, *The Roots of Fundamentalism: British and American Millenarianism 1800-1930* (Chicago: University of Chicago Press, 1970), p. 44.

25. Quoted in Marsden, *Evangelical Mind*, p. 200.

26. Wallace, *Rockdale*, pp. 473-74.

27. The work of theological renovation continues today in the Calvinist community. See Robert H. Schuller, *Self-Esteem: The New Reformation* (Waco, Tex.: Word Books, 1982).

28. Karl Barth, *Church Dogmatics*, vol. II, "The Doctrine of God," Part 2 (Edinburgh: T. and T. Clark, 1957), p. 133.

29. Nathan Hatch makes a similar point: "In short, Calvinism was being dropped not in response to theological arguments but because it violated the spirit of Revolutionary liberty." Mark Noll, Nathan Hatch, and George Marsden, *The Search for Christian America* (Westchester, Ill.: Crossway Books, 1983).

30. William G. McLoughlin, *Revivals, Awakenings and Reform: An Essay on Religion and Social Change in America, 1607-1977* (Chicago: University of Chicago Press, 1978), pp. 100-101.

31. Jack B. Rogers and Donald K. McKim, *Authority and Interpretation of the Bible: An Historical Approach* (New York: Harper and Row, 1979), pp. 236-40. A very helpful recent treatment of the Scottish philosophy, especially in relation to evangelical Christianity, is Mark A. Noll, "The Common Sense Tradition and American Evangelical Thought," *American Quarterly* 37 (Summer 1985):216-38.

32. Henry F. May, *The Enlightenment in America* (New York: Oxford University Press, 1976), pp. 345-46.

33. Quoted in Marsden, *Evangelical Mind*, p. 146.

34. Quoted in ibid., p. 47.

35. Quoted in McLoughlin, *Revivals*, p. 119.

36. Quoted in Marsden, *Evangelical Mind*, p. 51.

37. McLoughlin, *Revivals*, pp. 119-20.

38. Marsden, *Evangelical Mind*, p. 51.

39. May, *Enlightenment*, p. 345.

40. Richard F. Lovelace, *Dynamics of Spiritual Life: An Evangelical Theology of Renewal* (Downers Grove, Ill.: InterVarsity Press, 1979), pp. 83-84.

41. Lovelace, *Dynamics*, p. 86.

42. Mead, *Lively Experiment*, p. 123.

43. Quoted in Marsden, *Evangelical Mind*, p. 152.

44. Quoted in ibid., p. 104.

45. Smith, *Revivalism*, p. 161.

46. Quoted in Marsden, *Evangelical Mind*, p. 111.

47. Ahlstrom, *Religious History*, p. 410.

48. Marty, *Modern Schism*, p. 112.

49. Marsden, *Evangelical Mind*, p. 49.

50. Quoted in McLoughlin, *Revivals*, p. 124.

51. Ibid., p. 115.

52. Quoted in ibid., p. 125.

53. Ahlstrom, *Religious History*, p. 460.
54. McLoughlin, *Revivals*, p. 28.
55. Quoted in ibid., p. 129.
56. Mead, *Lively Experiment*, pp. 125-26.
57. Marsden, *Evangelical Mind*, p. 109.
58. Lovelace, *Dynamics*, p. 194.
59. Donald W. Dayton, *Discovering an Evangelical Heritage* (New York: Harper and Row, 1976), pp. 41-42.
60. Quoted in W. Andrew Hoffecker, *Piety and the Princeton Theologians: Archibald Alexander, Charles Hodge, Benjamin Warfield* (Grand Rapids: Baker Book House, 1981), p. 131.
61. Quoted in Smith, *Revivalism*, p. 225.
62. Quoted in Dayton, *Discovering*, p. 21.
63. Quoted in Smith, *Revivalism*, pp. 235-36.
64. Dayton, *Discovering*, p. 81.
65. Quoted in Handy, *Christian America*, pp. 38, 57.
66. Marsden, *Evangelical Mind*, p. 47.
67. Ahlstrom, *Religious History*, p. 671.
68. Smith, *Revivalism*, pp. 226-36.
69. Quoted in ibid., p. 137.

Chapter II

1. Quoted in James F. Findlay, Jr., *Dwight L. Moody: American Evangelist, 1837-1899* (Chicago: University of Chicago Press, 1969), p. 257.
2. John F. Kasson, *Civilizing the Machine: Technology and Republican Values in America, 1776-1900* (New York: Penguin Books, 1976 [1977]), pp. 36-37, 56.
3. This discussion of the early response to industrialization is drawn from Kasson, *Civilizing*, chapters 1 and 2.
4. Wallace, *Rockdale*, p. 350.
5. Mead, *Lively Experiment*, p. 97.
6. Wallace, *Rockdale*, p. 17.
7. Ibid., pp. 179, 439.
8. Marsden, *Evangelical Mind*, p. 241.
9. Robert H. Wiebe, *The Search for Order: 1877-1920* (New York: Hill and Wang, 1967), pp. 2-3.
10. Quoted in Findlay, *Moody*, p. 299.
11. Wiebe, *Search*, pp. 19-21. Wiebe is very helpful for an understanding of the pressures, fears, and confusions wrought by industrialization and modernization in late nineteenth-century America.
12. Ibid., pp. 42-43.
13. Karl Marx and Friedrich Engels, *The Communist Manifesto* (New York: Washington Square Press, 1964), pp. 66-67.
14. Ibid., p. 63.
15. Marsden suggests the helpful analogy of the immigrant experience to explain the tensions felt by old-stock Americans at the turn of the century. *Fundamentalism*, pp. 204-5.
16. Peter L. Berger, *The Sacred Canopy: Elements of a Sociological Theory of Religion* (Garden City, N.Y.: Anchor Books, 1967 [1969]), p. 3.
17. Becker, *Escape From Evil* (New York: The Free Press, 1975), pp. 1-5.
18. Berger, *Sacred Canopy*, pp. 22-23, 51.
19. Ibid., pp. 29-34.
20. Ibid., p. 37.
21. Ibid., p. 45.
22. Ibid., p. 46.

23. May, *Enlightenment*, p. xiv.

24. Karl Barth, *The Humanity of God* (Atlanta: John Knox Press, 1960), pp. 19-21.

25. Ibid., p. 21.

26. For brief descriptions of the "higher criticism," see Stephen Neill, *The Interpretation of the New Testament, 1861-1961* (London: Oxford University Press, 1964); and Robert M. Grant, *A Short History of the Interpretation of the Bible* (New York: Macmillan, 1948).

27. Loren Eiseley, *The Unexpected Universe* (New York: Harcourt Brace Jovanovich, 1964 [1969]), pp. 133-35. I have used Eiseley generally in summarizing the spirit of Darwinism.

28. George H. Daniels, *American Science in the Age of Jackson* (New York: Columbia University Press, 1968), pp. 54-55.

29. Loren Eiseley, *Darwin's Century: Evolution and the Men Who Discovered It* (Garden City, N.Y.: Anchor Books, 1958 [1961]), p. 176.

30. Daniels, *American Science*, pp. 65-66.

31. Eiseley, *Darwin's Century*, p. 177.

32. Daniels, *American Science*, p. 192.

33. Eiseley, *Darwin's Century*, p. 334.

34. Ibid., p. 346.

35. Quoted in ibid., p. 194.

36. Richard Hofstadter, *Social Darwinism and American Thought* (Boston: The Beacon Press, 1944 [1955]), describes these varying meanings of "social Darwinism."

37. Walter Lippmann, *A Preface to Morals* (New York: The Macmillan Company, 1935), pp. 8-9.

38. Eiseley, *Darwin's Century*, p. 195.

Chapter III

1. *The Sunday School Times*, January 6, 1912, p. 1.

2. Ibid.

3. Marsden, *The Evangelical Mind*, p. 239.

4. Wallace, *Rockdale*, p. 432.

5. Quoted in Dayton, *Heritage*, p. 64.

6. Quoted in Rogers and McKim, *Authority and Interpretation*, p. 271.

7. Ibid., p. 300.

8. Quoted in Wallace, *Rockdale*, pp. 366-67.

9. Quoted in Marsden, *The Evangelical Mind*, p. 104.

10. A. J. Frost, quoted in George W. Dollar, *A History of Fundamentalism in America* (Greenville, S.C.: Bob Jones University Press, 1973), p. 64.

11. W. J. Erdman, quoted in Timothy P. Weber, *Living in the Shadow of the Second Coming: American Premillennialism 1875-1925* (New York: Oxford University Press, 1979), p. 71.

12. Dollar, *History*, pp. 64-65.

13. I. M. Haldeman, *Signs of the Times*, 3rd edition (New York: Charles C. Cook, 1912), pp. 30-31.

14. Weber, *Living*, p. 14.

15. Ernest R. Sandeen, *The Roots of Fundamentalism: British and American Millenarianism, 1800-1930* (Chicago: University of Chicago Press, 1970), p. 39.

16. J. S. Kennedy, quoted in Dollar, *History*, p. 53.

17. Haldeman, *Signs*, pp. 61-62.

18. Weber, *Living*, p. 88.

19. Clarence B. Bass, *Backgrounds to Dispensationalism: Its Historic Genesis and Ecclesiastical Implications* (Grand Rapids: Baker Book House, 1960, 1977); Daniel P. Fuller, *Gospel and Law: Contrast or Continuum? The Hermeneutics of Dispensationalism and Covenant Theology* (Grand Rapids: Eerdmans, 1980); C. Norman Kraus, *Dispensationalism in America: Its Rise and Development* (Richmond: John Knox Press, 1958); Sandeen, *Roots*.

20. Quoted in Fuller, *Gospel*, pp. 13-14.

21. Quoted in Bass, *Backgrounds,* p. 100.

22. I have relied here on George E. Ladd, "Historic Premillennialism," in Robert G. Clouse, ed., *The Meaning of the Millennium: Four Views* (Downers Grove, Ill.: InterVarsity Press, 1977), p. 24.

23. The seven-year duration is based on calculations derived from Daniel 9:24. For elaboration, see the Scofield Reference Bible note on that verse.

24. In my general description of dispensationalism, I have leaned most heavily on Weber, *Living.*

25. See for example, Lewis Sperry Chafer, *Dispensationalism* (Dallas: Dallas Seminary Press, 1936); *The Kingdom in History and Prophecy* (New York: Fleming H. Revell, 1915); *Systematic Theology,* vol. IV (Dallas: Dallas Seminary Press, 1947); Arno C. Gaebelein, *The Return of the Lord* (New York: Publication Office "Our Hope," 1925); Charles C. Ryrie, *Dispensationalism Today* (Chicago: Moody Press, 1965); C. I. Scofield, *Rightly Dividing the Word of Truth: Being Ten Outline Studies of the More Important Divisions of Scripture* (New York: Bible Truth Press, n.d.); John Walvoord, *The Rapture Question* (Findlay, Ohio: Dunham, 1957).

26. Examples of some of these split hairs can be found in Fuller, *Gospel,* pp. 34-46.

27. Hal Lindsey, *The Late Great Planet Earth* (Grand Rapids: Zondervan, 1970).

28. Marsden quotes a leading evangelical spokesman, A. T. Pierson, to this effect: "I like Biblical theology that does not start with the superficial Aristotelian method of reason, that does not begin with an hypothesis, and then warp the facts and the philosophy to fit the crook of the dogma, but a Baconian system, which first gathers the teaching of the Word of God, and then seeks to deduce some general law upon which the facts can be arranged." Marsden, *Fundamentalism,* p. 55.

29. A nice example of such a chart can be found in Marsden, *Fundamentalism,* pp. 58-59.

30. Lewis Sperry Chafer, quoted in Fuller, *Gospel,* p. 25.

31. J. N. Darby, quoted in Bass, *Backgrounds,* p. 47. The sure knowledge of such a plan appealed to others than the dispensationalists. Charles Taze Russell, founder of the Jehovah's Witnesses, wrote a book entitled *The Divine Plan of the Ages* in 1886.

32. Quoted in Kraus, *Dispensationalism,* p. 112.

33. Sandeen, *Roots,* p. 222.

34. Marsden, *Fundamentalism,* p. 58.

35. Scofield, *Rightly Dividing,* p. 5.

36. Marsden, *Fundamentalism,* p. 59.

37. Sandeen, *Roots,* pp. 133, 140.

38. Ibid., pp. 21-22, 220.

39. Ibid., p. 220.

40. Sandeen suggests that this intentionality, which he associates with "the psychology of deliverance," was the true reason for the growing popularity of premillennialism. See *The Roots of Fundamentalism,* p. 229.

41. *Scofield Reference Bible* (New York: Oxford University Press, 1909), pp. 1033, 1334. The "flimsy" evidence he uses is Revelation 4:1.

42. Haldeman, *Signs,* p. 295.

43. Ibid., pp. 297-98.

44. Ibid., p. 299.

45. Ibid., pp. 301-6.

46. Ibid., p. 32.

47. Quoted in Sandeen, *Roots,* p. 33.

48. Quoted in ibid., p. 95.

49. Quoted in ibid., p. 96.

50. Marsden, *Fundamentalism,* pp. 56, 61.

51. Abraham J. Heschel, *The Prophets,* vol. I (New York: Harper and Row, 1962, 1969), p. 175.

52. Sandeen, *Roots,* p. 31.

53. Heschel, *Prophets*, I:176.

54. Abraham J. Heschel, *The Prophets*, vol. II (New York: Harper and Row, 1962, 1975), p. xvii.

55. George E. Ladd, *Crucial Questions about the Kingdom of God* (Grand Rapids: Eerdmans, 1952), p. 49.

56. Haldeman, *Signs*, pp. 106-7.

57. Bass, *Backgrounds*, pp. 116-17.

58. Quoted in ibid., p. 39.

59. C. H. Macintosh, quoted in Weber, *Living*, p. 20.

60. H. A. Hoyt, quoted in Clouse, *Four Views*, p. 90.

61. J. C. Massee, *The Second Coming* (Philadelphia: Philadelphia School of the Bible, 1919), p. 10, quoted in Dollar, *History*, pp. 148-49.

62. *Prophetic Times* (1863), pp. 13-14, quoted in Sandeen, *Roots*, p. 96.

63. Quoted in Sandeen, *Roots*, p. 70.

64. See Bass, *Backgrounds*, pp. 81-91.

65. Haldeman, *Signs*, pp. 164, 252.

66. Quoted in Weber, *Living*, p. 72.

67. Heschel, *Prophets*, I:5.

68. Weber, *Living*, p. 95.

69. Ibid., pp. 98-99.

70. Some of the most influential spokesmen for the new premillennial teachings were pastors of prosperous middle-class churches in primarily urban areas: James H. Brookes, A. J. Gordon, A. T. Pierson, C. I. Scofield. See also Marsden, *Fundamentalism*, p. 202: "Fundamentalism appealed to some well-to-do, and some poor, but also and especially to the 'respectable' Protestant and Northern European working class, whose aspirations and ideals were essentially middle-class Victorian."

71. Sandeen, *Roots*, p. 167.

72. Marsden, *Fundamentalism*, p. 67.

73. Haldeman, *Signs*, pp. 20-21, 277.

74. Dwight Lyman Moody, *Moody's Last Sermons as Delivered by the Great Evangelist* (Chicago: Rhodes and McClure, 1899), p. 623.

75. Karl Barth, *Church Dogmatics*, vol. IV, "The Doctrine of Reconciliation" (Edinburgh: T. and T. Clark, 1956), 1:392-93.

76. Haldeman, *Signs*, p. 94.

77. William Stringfellow, *Conscience and Obedience: The Politics of Romans 13 and Revelation 13 in Light of the Second Coming* (Waco, Tex.: Word Books, 1977, 1978), p. 85.

78. Quoted in Sandeen, *Roots*, p. 235.

79. Arthur W. Pink, quoted in Weber, *Living*, p. 54.

80. Sandra S. Sizer, *Gospel Hymns and Social Religion: The Rhetoric of Nineteenth Century Revivalism* (Philadelphia: Temple University Press, 1978), p. 45.

81. I have found Leon Morris's *Apocalyptic* (Grand Rapids: Eerdmans, 1972) helpful in thinking about the dispensationalists in relation to the gospel. His analysis suggests to me that dispensationalism is characterized by many of the distinguishing features of "apocalyptic." As he says, " 'Gospel' is not an apocalyptic term" (p. 101).

Chapter IV

1. Annie Dillard, *Pilgrim at Tinker Creek* (New York: Bantam Books, 1975), p. 277.

2. Andrew Murray, *Be Perfect: A Devotional Study of Christ's Command* (Minneapolis: Bethany Fellowship, 1965), pp. 30, 163.

3. John Peters, *Christian Perfection and American Methodism* (New York: Abingdon Press, 1956), p. 54. I have relied on Peters for this general account of Wesleyan perfectionism.

4. Melvin E. Dieter, *The Holiness Revival of the Nineteenth Century* (Methuen, N.J.: The Scarecrow Press, 1980), pp. 19-20.

5. Pheobe Palmer, *The Way of Holiness, with Notes by the Way: Being a Narrative of Religious Experience Resulting from a Determination to Be a Bible Christian* (New York: G. Lane and C. B. Tippett, 1848), pp. 28, 33, 37-38.

6. Ibid., pp. 48, 51.

7. Peters, *Christian Perfection*, pp. 134-39.

8. Quoted in ibid., p. 148.

9. Ibid., p. 149.

10. Marsden, *Fundamentalism*, pp. 75-78. Most evangelical church hymnals today still provide examples of these themes. Havergal's "Take My Life, and Let It Be" reads in part, "Take my love, my God, I pour / At Thy feet its treasure store; / Take myself and I will be / Ever, only, all for Thee." Or a Crosby hymn, "I Am Thine, O Lord," reads in part, "O the pure delight of a single hour/ That before Thy throne I spend, / When I kneel in prayer and with Thee, my God, / I commune as friend with friend."

11. Quoted in Steven Barabas, *So Great Salvation: The History and Message of the Keswick Convention* (Westwood, N.J.: Fleming H. Revell, n.d.), p. 18.

12. Ibid., p. 21.

13. Mel Loucks, "The Victorious Life" (unpublished thesis, Fuller Theological Seminary), pp. 12-13.

14. *Victory in Christ: A Report of Princeton Conference, 1916* (Philadelphia: Board of Managers of Princeton Conference, 1916), pp. 70-73, 87.

15. Robert C. McQuilken, *Victorious Life Studies* (Philadelphia: Christian Life Literature Fund, 1918), pp. 22-23.

16. C. G. Trumbull in *Victory in Christ*, pp. 82, 110.

17. Ibid., pp. 81-82.

18. Charles G. Trumbull, *The Sunday School Times*, September 16, 1911, p. 442.

19. C. G. Trumbull, *The Sunday School Times*, June 3, 1916, p. 351.

20. C. G. Trumbull in *The Victorious Christ: Messages from Conferences Held by the Victorious Life Testimony in 1922* (Philadelphia: Sunday School Times, 1923), p. 101.

21. Ibid., pp. 102-5.

22. *The Sunday School Times*, June 23, 1916, p. 351.

23. C. G. Trumbull in *Victory in Christ*, pp. 94, 100, 101, 104-5, 107.

24. *Victorious Christ*, p. 122.

25. C. G. Trumbull in *Victory in Christ*, pp. 77, 113.

26. Andrew Murray, *Absolute Surrender: Addresses Delivered in England and Scotland*, 3rd ed. (London: Marshall Brothers, n.d.), p. 176. The preface is dated 1895, indicating that these were given as part of Keswick Convention.

27. Quoted in J. C. Pollack, *The Keswick Story: The Authorized History of the Keswick Convention* (Chicago: Moody Press, 1964), pp. 14-15.

28. *Victorious Christ*, p. 126.

29. W. H. Griffith Thomas in *Victory in Christ*, p. 142.

30. C. G. Trumbull in *Victorious Christ*, pp. 117-18.

31. C. G. Trumbull in *Victory in Christ*, pp. 127-37.

32. Ibid., p. 146.

33. Robert F. Horton, "Bible Study in the Victorious Life," *The Sunday School Times*, October 21, 1911, p. 162.

34. *Victory in Christ*, p. 162.

35. Andrew Murray, *Holy in Christ* (Minneapolis: Bethany Fellowship, n.d.), pp. 193, 203.

36. C. G. Trumbull in *Victorious Christ*, p. 141.

37. Robert F. Horton, "The Daring of Victorious Life," *The Sunday School Times*, September 30, 1911, p. 467.

38. Robert F. Horton, "The Victorious Life and Evangelism," *The Sunday School Times*, December 30, 1911, p. 687.

39. *Victorious Christ*, p. 12.

40. C. G. Trumbull in ibid., p. 142.

41. C. G. Trumbull in *Victory in Christ*, pp. 77-78.

42. Barabas, *So Great Salvation*, p. 25.

43. *Victory in Christ*, pp. 7-8, 260-62.

44. William James, *The Varieties of Human Experience: A Study in Human Nature* (New York: New American Library, 1958), p. 88

45. *Victory in Christ*, p. 66.

46. Marshall Berman, *All That Is Solid Melts into Air: The Experience of Modernity* (New York: Simon and Schuster, 1982), p. 16.

47. Ibid., p. 91.

48. Quoted in Walter E. Houghton, *The Victorian Frame of Mind: 1830-1870* (New Haven: Yale University Press, 1957), p. 8.

49. Quoted in ibid., p. 7.

50. Walter Lippmann, *A Preface to Morals* (New York: Macmillan, 1920, 1935), pp. 3-4.

51. *The Christian Workers Magazine*, May 1914, p. 582.

52. Quoted in Burton J. Bledstein, *The Culture of Professionalism: The Middle Class and the Development of Higher Education in America* (New York: W. W. Norton, 1976), p. 115.

53. George M. Beard, *American Nervousness: Its Causes and Consequences* (New York: G. P. Putnam's Sons, 1881), pp. vii, 6-7.

54. Ibid., pp. vi, 97, 26, 106, 103, 313, 104.

55. Ibid., pp. 4-34, 37-38.

56. Quoted in Ford C. Ottman, *J. Wilbur Chapman: A Biography* (Garden City, N.Y.: Doubleday, Page, and Co., 1920), p. 17.

57. Bledstein, *Culture of Professionalism*, pp. 30, 23.

58. Max Weber, *The Protestant Ethic and the Spirit of Capitalism* (New York: Charles Scribner's Sons, 1958), pp. 114-15; see pp. 98-128.

59. Ibid., pp. 115, 118-19.

60. Ibid., pp. 157, 160-61.

61. Quoted in ibid., pp. 260-61.

62. Quoted in ibid., p. 162.

63. Ibid., p. 166; see also p. 163.

64. Ibid., p. 18.

65. Ibid., p. 167.

66. Bledstein, *Culture of Professionalism*, pp. 129, 133.

67. Ibid., pp. 135-36, 146-47, 149, 154-55.

68. Mrs. Howard Taylor, *William Borden of Yale* (Chicago: Moody Press, 1980), pp. 22-24.

69. Thomas LeDuc, *Piety and Intellect at Amherst College: 1865-1912* (New York: Columbia University Press, 1946), pp. 25-26, 45-46.

70. Robert Elliot Speer, *The Marks of a Man; Or, The Essentials of Christian Character* (New York: The Methodist Book Concern, 1907), pp. 157-58.

71. William Ellery Channing, quoted in ibid., p. 61.

72. Ibid., pp. 157-64.

73. Beard, *American Nervousness*, pp. 120-23.

74. *Victorious Christ*, p. 246.

75. Hannah Whitall Smith, *The Christian's Secret of a Happy Life* (Old Tappan, N.J.: Fleming H. Revell, 1942, 1970), p. 13.

76. Quoted in Donald Meyer, *The Positive Thinkers: A Study of the American Search for Health, Wealth, and Personal Power from Mary Baker Eddy to Norman Vincent Peale* (New York: Doubleday and Company, 1965), p. 131.

77. Quoted in ibid., p. 47.

78. Bledstein, *Culture of Professionalism*, pp. 103, 48.
79. Smith, *Christian's Secret*, pp. 13-14.
80. Ibid., pp. 14, 25, 28, 30, 31, 40.
81. Bledstein, *Culture of Professionalism*, p. 37.
82. S. D. Gordon, *Quiet Talks on Power* (Chicago: Fleming H. Revell, 1903), p. 35.
83. J. C. Pollock, *Keswick Story*, p. 12.
84. Quoted in ibid., p. 24.
85. Murray, *Absolute Surrender*, p. 167.
86. Quoted in Pollock, *Keswick Story*, p. 41.
87. Quotations in this paragraph from Barabas, *So Great Salvation*, pp. 65-66, 171, 178, 187.
88. Smith, *Christian's Secret*, p. 14.
89. *Victory in Christ*, pp. 259, 56.
90. Pollack, *Keswick Story*, p. 15-16.
91. Murray, *Absolute Surrender*, p. 156, 67.
92. Smith, *Christian's Secret*, pp. 28, 141.
93. Meyer, *Positive Thinkers*, p. 48.
94. Bledstein, *Culture of Professionalism*, p. 114.
95. Smith, *Christian's Secret*, pp. 28, 30.
96. Barabas, *So Great Salvation*, p. 172.
97. Pollock, *Keswick Story*, p. 74.
98. McQuilken, *Victorious Life Studies*, p. 88.
99. *Victory in Christ*, p. 262.
100. Meyer, *Positive Thinkers*, p. 146.
101. James, *Varieties*, pp. 88-92.
102. Ibid., pp. 92-93.
103. Ibid., p. 93.
104. *Victory in Christ*, p. 110.
105. *The Sunday School Times*, November 11, 1916, p. 668.
106. *Victory in Christ*, p. 258; *Victorious Christ*, p. 243.
107. Quoted in Loucks, *The Victorious Life*, p. 33.
108. James, *Varieties*, pp. 98-99.
109. Ibid.
110. *Victory in Christ*, pp. 5, 102, 270.
111. Barabas, *So Great Salvation*, p. 95.
112. *The Sunday School Times*, January 27, 1916, p. 50.
113. James, *Varieties*, p. 92.
114. H. H. Goddard, "Effects of Mind on Body as Evidenced by Faith Cures," *American Journal of Psychology* 10 (1899), quoted in James, *Varieties*, pp. 89-90.
115. James, *Varieties*, p. 101.
116. *The Sunday School Times*, November 11, 1916, p. 668.
117. Quoted in Loucks, *The Victorious Life*, p. 61.
118. *Victory in Christ*, pp. 5, 16.
119. Howard B. Dinwiddie, in *Victorious Christ*, p. 160.
120. Evan Hopkins, quoted in Barabas, *So Great Salvation*, p. 121.
121. *The Sunday School Times*, November 5, 1910, p. 552.
122. *The Sunday School Times*, January 27, 1912, p. 50.
123. Murray, *Holy in Christ*, p. 182.
124. *Victory in Christ*, p. 255.
125. Ibid., p. 101.
126. *The Sunday School Times*, March 20, 1920, p. 1.
127. Quotations in this paragraph from *Victory in Christ*, pp. 102-5, 240.
128. Quoted in James, *Varieties*, pp. 97, 105.

129. *Victory in Christ*, pp. 100-101, 120, 25.

130. *The Sunday School Times*, November 25, 1916, p. 698. The same logic was used by Moody and others in assuring a doubting convert of his or her salvation. When Moody first met J. Wilbur Chapman, he asked Chapman, "Are you a Christian?" Chapman replied, "Sometimes I think I am and again I am fearful." Moody made Chapman read John 5:24 twice and then, since Chapman was still doubting, Moody "seemed . . . to lose his patience, and he spoke sharply: 'Whom are you doubting?'" Chapman said that suddenly "it all came to me." At Moody's request, Chapman read John 5:24 again and, when Moody asked whether he believed it, answered "Yes, indeed I do." "Are you a Christian?" Moody asked. "'Yes, Mr. Moody. I am.' From that day forward, I have never questioned my acceptance with God." Ottman, *Chapman*, pp. 29-30.

131. James, *Varieties*, p. 111.

132. *Victory in Christ*, pp. 257, 262.

133. Ibid., p. 237.

134. *The Sunday School Times*, November 11, 1916, p. 664.

135. *Victory in Christ*, p. 114; *Victorious Christ*, p. 125.

136. *Victory in Christ*, p. 118; *The Sunday School Times*, November 11, 1916, p. 664.

137. *The Sunday School Times*, November 11, 1916, p. 664.

138. Smith, *Christian's Secret*, p. 38.

139. Quoted in Meyer, *Positive Thinkers*, p. 91.

140. James, *Varieties*, p. 95.

141. *Victory in Christ*, p. 118.

142. Quoted in James, *Varieties*, pp. 93-94.

143. Robert Horton in *The Sunday School Times*, November 11, 1911, p. 568.

144. See, for example, Murray, *Holy in Christ*, p. 182.

145. James, *Varieties*, p. 103.

146. W. H. Griffith Thomas, "The Victorious Life," *Bibliotheca Sacra* (October 1919):464.

147. James, *Varieties*, p. 88.

148. *Victory in Christ*, p. 9.

149. See, for example, ibid., pp. 21, 259.

150. *Victorious Christ*, p. 121.

151. Haldeman, *Signs*, pp. 16-17.

152. Maurice E. Wilson, "Eddyism, Commonly Called Christian Science," *The Fundamentals*, vol. 4 (Grand Rapids: Baker Book House, 1972), p. 149.

153. Ibid.

154. *Victory in Christ*, p. 21.

155. James, *Varieties*, p. 76.

156. C. G. Trumbull, *What Is the Gospel?* (Philadelphia: The Sunday School Times, 1918), p. 71.

157. L. S. Chafer, *He That Is Spiritual* (Chicago: The Bible Institute Colportage Association, 1929), p. 49.

158. *Victorious Christ*, p. 176.

159. Helen C. A. Dixon, *A. C. Dixon: A Romance of Preaching* (New York: G. P. Putnam's Sons, 1931), p. 30; Philip Howard, *The Life Story of Henry Clay Trumbull: Missionary, Army Chaplain, Editor, and Author* (Philadelphia: The Sunday School Times, 1905), p. 85.

160. Otto Weber, *Foundations of Dogmatics*, vol. II (Grand Rapids: Eerdmans, 1983 [1962]), p. 292.

161. Murray, *Be Perfect*, p. 25.

162. *Victory in Christ*, p. 255.

163. J. Wilbur Chapman, *Power: Received Ye the Holy Ghost?* (New York: Fleming H. Revell, 1894, 1912), pp. 84-85.

164. A. B. Simpson, *The Holy Spirit; Or, Power from on High*, vol. I (Harrisburg, Pa.: Christian Publications, Inc., n.d.), p. 44.

165. A. Chester Mann, *F. B. Meyer: Preacher, Teacher, Man of God* (New York: Fleming H. Revell, 1929), p. 146.

166. *Victory in Christ*, pp. 235, 238.

167. Edith Fox Norton in *Victory in Christ*, p. 202.

168. *The Sunday School Times*, January 4, 1913, p. 1.

169. Quoted in Otto Weber, *Foundations*, II:345.

170. Barth, *Church Dogmatics*, II, 2: 767-68.

171. Karl Barth, *Come Holy Spirit* (Grand Rapids: Eerdmans, 1978 [1933]), p. 267.

Chapter V

1. Quoted in Findlay, *Moody*, p. 140.

2. Charles G. Finney, *Lectures on Revivals of Religion* (New York: Fleming H. Revell, 1868).

3. Findlay, *Moody*, pp. 198-231.

4. Ibid., chapters 3 and 4.

5. Martin E. Marty, "Foreword," in Findlay, *Moody*, p. 1.

6. See, for example, Marsden, *Fundamentalism*, pp. 33-38.

7. Ibid., chapter XV.

8. Robert M. Crunden, *Ministers of Reform: The Progressives' Achievement in American Civilization, 1889-1920* (New York: Basic Books, 1982), pp. 3-15.

9. Straton, *The Salvation of Society and Other Addresses* (Baltimore: Fleet-McGinley, n.d.), pp. 20-24.

10. Ibid., pp. 20-22.

11. Letter by John Davison, 2 May 1911, Box 5, Reel 9, Collection 61, Papers of William and Helen Sunday, Library of Grace Theological Seminary, Winona Lake, Indiana (Microfilm in Archives of Billy Graham Center, Wheaton, Ill.). Hereinafter cited as Sunday Papers. All citations are to the microfilm collection.

12. William G. McLoughlin, *Billy Sunday Was His Real Name* (Chicago: University of Chicago Press, 1955), p. 8.

13. Ibid., p. 9.

14. Ibid., pp. 13-14.

15. Ibid., pp. 26-27.

16. Quoted in ibid., p. 159.

17. Ibid., p. 83.

18. Ibid., pp. 43, 50-54, 67-73.

19. S. N. D. North, quoted in Daniel J. Boorstin, *The Americans: The Democratic Experience* (New York: Vintage Books, 1974), p. 165.

20. Jefferson, Iowa, *Bee*, January 7, 1904, pictured in McLoughlin, *Billy Sunday*, opposite p. 66.

21. McLoughlin, *Billy Sunday*, pp. xxvi-viii, 105-7.

22. Ibid., pp. 46-47.

23. Ibid., pp. 98-99.

24. Ibid., pp. 99-100.

25. Ibid., pp. 18-19, 101.

26. Letter by J. F. Thomas, 27 August 1905, Box 1, Reel 1, Sunday Papers.

27. Letter by A. M. Welles, 15 November 1905, Box 1, Reel 1, Sunday Papers.

28. Letter by Orville F. Berry, 16 November 1905, Box 1, Reel 1, Sunday Papers.

29. Letter by Ezra Butler Newcomb, 15 November 1905, Box 1, Reel 1, Sunday Papers.

30. Letter by J. F. Thomas, 27 August 1905, Box 1, Reel 1, Sunday Papers.

31. Quoted in William L. McLoughlin, *Modern Revivalism* (New York: Ronald Press, 1959), pp. 419-20.

32. Marsden, *Fundamentalism*, p. 131; McLoughlin, *Modern Revivalism*, p. 424.

33. Quoted in *Modern Revivalsim*, p. 428.

34. Quoted in McLoughlin, *Billy Sunday*, pp. 154, 164.

35. Souvenir Program of Billy Sunday Spokane Campaign, Box 5, Reel 9, Sunday Papers.

36. Quoted in McLoughlin, *Billy Sunday*, pp. 154, 252.

37. *The New York Times*, April 15, 1917, p. 8.

38. McLoughlin, *Billy Sunday*, pp. 44-45.

39. *The New York Times*, April 27, 1917, p. 20.

40. Quoted in McLoughlin, *Billy Sunday*, p. 123.

41. William T. Ellis, *Billy Sunday: The Man and His Message* (Philadelphia: John C. Winston Company, 1914), p. 390.

42. Quoted in McLoughlin, *Billy Sunday*, pp. 203, 223.

43. Ellis, *Sunday*, p. 187.

44. Quoted in McLoughlin, *Billy Sunday*, p. 123.

45. Ellis, *Sunday*, pp. 426, 430-31.

46. Ibid., p. 388.

47. Ibid., p. 379.

48. Sunday, "Look to Yourselves," Sermon Transcript, New York, 17 June 1917 (morning), p. 20, Box 8, Reel 12, Sunday Papers.

49. Ellis, *Sunday*, pp. 389, 428-29.

50. Ibid., pp. 384, 399; and McLoughlin, *Billy Sunday*, p. 128.

51. Ellis, *Sunday*, pp. 152, 154.

52. *The New York Times*, April 11, 1917, p. 22.

53. Sunday, "Why Call Ye Me Lord?" Sermon Transcript, New York, 15 April 1917 (evening), pp. 33-35, Box 6, Reel 9, Sunday Papers.

54. Ellis, *Sunday*, p. 360.

55. Sunday, "Why Call Ye Me Lord?" Sermon Transcript, New York, 15 April 1917 (evening), pp. 33-35, Box 6, Reel 9, Sunday Papers.

56. Ellis, *Sunday*, pp. 89-90.

57. Ibid., opposite p. 141.

58. *The Sunday School Times*, February 13, 1915, p. 99.

59. Letter by William S. Phillips, 15 November 1905, Box 1, Reel 1, Sunday Papers.

60. Souvenir Program of Billy Sunday Spokane Campaign, Box 5, Reel 9, Sunday Papers.

61. Ellis, *Sunday*, p. 75.

62. McLoughlin, *Billy Sunday*, p. 131.

63. Ellis, *Sunday*, pp. 169, 228, 175, 184, 298, 240, 282, 246, 243-44, 216.

64. Ibid., pp. 211-12, 243, 282; McLoughlin, *Billy Sunday*, p. 132.

65. Sunday, "Why Call Ye Me Lord?" Sermon Transcript, New York, 15 April 1917 (evening), pp. 30-31, Box 6, Reel 9, Sunday Papers.

66. Ellis, *Sunday*, p. 228.

67. Sunday, "Why Call Ye Me Lord?" Sermon Transcript, New York, 15 April 1917 (evening), pp. 25-26, Box 6, Reel 9, Sunday Papers.

68. Sunday, "Why Call Ye Me Lord?" Sermon Transcript, New York, 15 April 1917 (evening), p. 26, Box 6, Reel 9, Sunday Papers.

69. McLoughlin, *Billy Sunday*, p. 143.

70. Ellis, *Sunday*, pp. 215, 222.

71. *The Sunday School Times*, February 13, 1915, p. 99.

72. Ellis, *Sunday*, p. 105.

73. Sunday, "Why Call Ye Me Lord?" Sermon Transcript, New York, 15 April 1917 (evening), p. 9, Box 6, Reel 9, Sunday Papers.

74. Ellis, pp. 93-94, 106, 97-98, 109, 171, 102, 89; Sunday, "Why Call Ye Me Lord?" Sermon Transcript, New York, 15 April 1917 (evening), p. 10, Box 6, Reel 9, Sunday Papers.

75. Sunday, "Show Thyself a Man," Sermon Transcript, New York, 17 June 1917 (afternoon), p. 3, Box 8, Reel 12, Sunday Papers.

76. Sunday, "Why Call Ye Me Lord?" Sermon Transcript, New York, 15 April 1917 (evening), pp. 26-27, Box 6, Reel 9, Sunday Papers.

77. Sunday, "Show Thyself a Man," Sermon Transcript, New York, 17 June 1917 (afternoon), p. 3, Box 8, Reel 12, Sunday Papers.

78. Sunday, "Show Thyself A Man," Sermon Transcript, New York, 17 June 1917 (afternoon), pp. 1-6, Box 8, Reel 12, Sunday Papers.

79. Sunday, Sermon Transcript, New York, 25 April 1917 (afternoon), p. 8, Box 6, Reel 10, Sunday Papers.

80. Sunday, Sermon Transcript, New York, 25 April 1917 (afternoon), pp. 8, 22-23, 37, 11, Box 6, Reels 9 and 10, Sunday Papers.

81. Ellis, *Sunday*, pp. 114-115.

82. Ibid., p. 352.

83. Sunday, Sermon Transcript, New York, 13 April 1917 (evening), p. 22, Box 6, Reel 9, Sunday Papers.

84. Sunday, "Show Thyself a Man," Sermon Transcript, New York, 17 June 1917 (afternoon), p. 9, Box 8, Reel 12, Sunday Papers.

85. Ellis, *Sunday*, p. 141.

86. Sunday, Sermon Transcript, New York, 13 April 1917 (evening), pp. 30-32, Box 6, Reel 9, Sunday Papers.

87. Sunday, "Show Thyself a Man," Sermon Transcript, New York, 17 June 1917 (afternoon), p. 3, Box 8, Reel 12, Sunday Papers.

88. Ellis, *Sunday*, p. 312.

89. Sunday "Show Thyself a Man," Sermon Transcript, New York, 17 June 1917 (afternoon), pp. 10-11, 18, Box 8, Reel 12; and Sermon Transcript, 22 April 1917 (evening), pp. 11-12, Box 6, Reel 12, Sunday Papers.

90. Ellis, *Sunday*, p. 75.

91. Sunday, "Show Thyself A Man," Sermon Transcript, New York, 17 June 1917 (afternoon), pp. 9, 4, 15, 28, Box 8, Reel 12, Sunday Papers.

92. Sunday, Sermon Transcript, New York, 27 May 1917 (afternoon), pp. 2-3, Box 8, Reel 11, Sunday Papers.

93. Sunday, Sermon Transcript, New York, 13 April 1917 (evening), p. 29, Box 6, Reel 9, Sunday Papers.

94. At times, it seems, Sunday restricted the potentiality for real manhood to Christians alone: "No man can be a man without being a Christian. . . . If you want to be a man, be a Christian." Sunday, Sermon Transcript, New York, 27 May 1917 (afternoon), p. 5, Box 8, Reel 11, Sunday Papers. In other contexts, he professed to admire real men who stood by their ideals even if they were not Christians. Sunday, Sermon Transcript, New York, 27 April 1917 (evening), p. 11, Box 6, Reel 10, Sunday Papers.

95. Sunday, "Show Thyself a Man," Sermon Transcript, New York, 17 June 1917 (afternoon), pp. 31-32, Box 8, Reel 12, Sunday Papers.

96. Ellis, *Sunday*, p. 204.

97. Sunday, "Paul's Conversion," Sermon Transcript, New York, 18 May 1917 (afternoon), p. 19, Box 7, Reel 11, Sunday Papers.

98. Sunday, Sermon Transcript, New York, 27 May 1917 (afternoon), p. 5, Box 8, Reel 11, Sunday Papers.

99. Sunday, "Chickens Come Home to Roost," Sermon Transcript, 29 April 1917 (afternoon), p. 40, Box 6, Reel 10, Sunday Papers.

100. Sunday, "The Devil's Boomerang; Or, Hot Cakes off the Griddle," Sermon Transcript, New York, 6 May 1917 (afternoon), p. 53, Box 6, Reel 10, Sunday Papers.

101. Ellis, *Sunday*, pp. 354-55, 18-19.

102. McLoughlin, *Modern Revivalism*, p. 428.

103. Unidentified newspaper clipping from 1901, pp. 5-6, Box 12, Reel 19, folder 9, Sunday Papers.

104. McLoughlin, *Billy Sunday*, p. 29.

105. Sunday, "Why Call Ye Me Lord?" Sermon Transcript, New York, 15 April 1917 (evening), pp. 33-34, Box 6, Reel 9, Sunday Papers.

106. Sunday, "Tarry Ye . . . ," Sermon Transcript, New York, 8 April 1917 (evening), p. 21, Box 6, Reel 9, Sunday Papers.

107. Ellis, *Sunday*, p. 257.

108. Sunday, "Ye Must Be Born Again," Sermon Transcript, New York, 28 April 1917, p. 7, Box 6, Reel 10, Sunday Papers.

109. McLoughlin, *Modern Revivalism*, p. 409.

110. McLoughlin, *Billy Sunday*, p. 293.

111. Sunday, "Amusements," Sermon Transcript, New York, 25 May 1917 (evening), p. 49, Box 7, Reel 11, Sunday Papers.

112. Ellis, *Sunday*, p. 227.

113. D. S. Russell, *The Jews from Alexander to Herod* (Oxford: Oxford University Press, 1967), pp. 1-111; and Menahem Mansoor, *The Dead Sea Scrolls* (Grand Rapids: Eerdmans, 1964), pp. 110-17.

114. Mansoor, *Dead Sea Scrolls*, pp. 110-17; and Merrill C. Tenney, ed., *The Zondervan Pictoral Encyclopedia of the Bible*, vol. 4, *Pharisees* (Grand Rapids: Zondervan, 1975), pp. 745-52.

115. Wiebe, *Search*, pp. 2, 12, 133.

116. Ibid., chapter 3.

117. Quoted in Alfred D. Chandler, Jr,. *The Visible Hand: The Managerial Revolution in American Business* (Cambridge: Harvard University Press, 1977), p. 51.

118. Boorstin, *The Americans*, p. 99.

119. Quoted in Stuart and Elizabeth Ewen, *Channels of Desire: Mass Images and the Shaping of American Consciousness* (New York: McGraw-Hill, 1982), p. 58.

120. Chandler, *The Visible Hand*, Parts I-III.

121. Kenneth W. Mackenzie, *The Robe and the Sword: The Methodist Church and the Rise of American Imperialism* (Washington, D.C.: Public Affairs Press, 1961), pp. 14-15.

122. Chandler, *The Visible Hand*, p. 287.

123. Ibid., pp. 290-92; and Daniel Pope, *The Making of Modern Advertising* (New York: Basic Books, 1983), p. 43.

124. Chandler, *The Visible Hand*, p. 294.

125. Arthur F. Marquette, *Brands, Trademarks, and Goodwill* (New York: McGraw-Hill, 1967), p. 51, quoted in Michael Schudson, *Advertising: The Uneasy Persuasion: Its Dubious Impact on American Society* (New York: Basic Books, 1984), p. 166.

126. Schudson, *Advertising*, p. 166.

127. Chandler, *The Visible Hand*, p. 294.

128. E. S. Turner, *The Shocking History of Advertising* (London: Michael Joseph, 1952), p. 142.

129. Boorstin, *The Americans*, pp. 138, 142-43, 147; and Stephen Fox, *The Mirror Makers: A History of America and Its Creators* (New York: William Morrow and Company, 1984), p. 39.

130. Quoted in Pope, *Making of Modern Advertising*, p. 3.

131. Frank Presbrey, *The History and Development of Advertising* (New York: Greenwood Press, 1968 [1929]), pp. 480-83.

132. Boorstin, *The Americans*, p. 151.

133. Presbrey, *History and Development*, p. 443.

134. Pope, *Making of Modern Advertising*, p. 235.

135. Presbrey, *History and Development*, p. 436.

136. Pope, *Making of Modern Advertising*, pp. 136, 6.

137. T. J. Jackson Lears, "From Salvation to Self Realization: Advertising and the Therapeutic Roots of the Consumer Culture, 1880-1930," in Richard W. Fox and T. J. Jackson Lears, eds., *The Culture of Consumption: Critical Essays in American History, 1880-1930* (New York: Pantheon Books, 1983), p. 18.

138. Pope, *Making of Modern Advertising*, p. 8.

139. D. T. Howard, *The Psychology of Advertising* (New York: Dodd Mead and Company, 1931 [1921]), p. 11.

140. Harry L. Hollingworth, *Advertising and Selling: Principles of Appeal and Response* (New York: D. Appleton and Company, 1913), pp. 241-42, 293.

141. Quoted in Presbrey, *History and Development*, p. 443.

142. Quoted in ibid., p. 426.

143. *In Behalf of Advertising: A Series of Essays Published in National Periodicals from 1919 to 1928* (Philadelphia: N. W. Ayer and Son, 1929), p. 187.

144. Quoted in Howard, *Psychology of Advertising*, p. 68.

145. T. J. Jackson Lears, "Some Versions of Fantasy: Toward a Cultural History of American Advertising, 1880-1930," in *Prospects*, vol. 8 (New York: Cambridge University Press, 1984), quoted in Schudson, *Advertising*, p. 252n.30.

146. *In Behalf of Advertising*, pp. 153, 201.

147. Quoted in Howard, *Psychology of Advertising*, p. 37.

148. Quoted in Pope, *Making of Modern Advertising*, pp. 5, 73, 234.

149. Walter Dill Scott, *Influencing Men in Business* (1911), in Stuart Ewen, *Captains of Consciousness: Advertising and the Social Roots of the Consumer Culture* (New York: McGraw-Hill, 1976), p. 31.

150. *In Behalf of Advertising*, pp. 57, 24-25.

151. Pope, *Making of Modern Advertising*, p. 249.

152. Donald M. Scott and Bernard Wishy, eds., *American Families: A Documentary History* (San Francisco: Harper and Row, 1982), p. 290.

153. Samuel Smiles, *Character* (London: John Murray, 1876), p. 290.

154. Henry Clay Trumbull, *Character Shaping and Character Showing* (Philadelphia: John D. Wattles, 1889), pp. 17, 20, 23-24, 123, 173, 182, 57, 103, 126, 115, 61.

155. Henry Clay Trumbull, *Duty Knowing and Duty Doing* (Philadelphia: John D. Wattles, 1889), pp. 131, 205; Smiles, *Character*, pp. 11, 158, 162-63, 167, 170; A. T. Schofield, *The Springs of Character* (New York: Funk and Wagnalls, n.d.), pp. 149, 151.

156. Trumbull, *Duty Knowing*, pp. 25, 27, 29, 24; Trumbull, *Aspirations and Influences* (Philadelphia: John D. Wattles, 1889), pp. 62-65.

157. Howard, *Trumbull*, p. 72.

158. Smiles, *Character*, pp. 158, 160.

159. Daniel Bell has explored this clash of productive and consumerist values in *The Cultural Contradictions of Capitalism* (New York: Basic Books, 1976), pp. 55-84.

160. George Frederic Parsons, "The Growth of Materialism," *Atlantic*, August 1887, pp. 160-63.

161. Ibid., pp. 164-71.

162. Bell, *Cultural Contradictions*, p. 84.

163. Parsons, "Growth of Materialism," p. 170.

164. Sunday, "Why Call Ye Me Lord?" Sermon Transcript, New York, 15 April 1917 (evening), p. 23, Box 6, Reel 9, Sunday Papers.

165. Sunday, Sermon Transcript, New York, 3 June 1917 (afternoon), p. 10, Box 8, Reel 11, Sunday Papers.

166. Sunday, "Hidden among the Stuff," Sermon Transcript, New York, 27 May 1917 (evening), pp. 9-11, Box 8, Reel 11, Sunday Papers.

167. Sunday, "Why Call Ye Me Lord?" Sermon Transcript, New York, 15 April 1917 (evening), pp. 9, 11-14, 25-30, Box 6, Reel 9, Sunday Papers.

168. Ellis, *Sunday*, pp. 282, 297; and Sunday, "Hidden among the Stuff," Sermon Transcript, New York, 27 May 1917 (evening), p. 13, Box 8, Reel 11, Sunday Papers.

169. Sunday, "Fishing on the Wrong Side," Sermon Transcript, New York, 26 April 1917 (afternoon), p. 19, Box 6, Reel 10, Sunday Papers.

170. Bell, *Cultural Contradictions*, pp. 65-66.

171. Sunday, "Why Call Ye Me Lord?" Sermon Transcript, New York, 15 April 1917 (evening), p. 17, Box 6, Reel 9, Sunday Papers.

172. Pope, *Making of Modern Advertising*, pp. 247-48; and Schudson, *Advertising*, pp. 173-74.

173. Sunday, "Fishing on the Wrong Side," Sermon Transcript, New York, 26 April 1917 (afternoon), pp. 18-19, Box 6, Reel 10, Sunday Papers.

174. A good summary of this narrowing process is Sheila M. Rothman, *Woman's Proper Place* (New York: Basic Books, 1978), pp. 13-21.

175. Sunday, "Hidden among the Stuff," Sermon Transcript, New York, 27 May 1917 (evening), p. 9, Box 8, Reel 11, Sunday Papers.

176. Sunday, Sermon Transcript, New York, 3 June 1917 (afternoon), p. 18, Box 8, Reel 11, Sunday Papers.

177. The best treatment of the department store as a middle-class "cathedral" is Michael B. Miller, *The Bon Marché: Bourgeois Culture and the Department Store, 1869-1920* (Princeton: Princeton University Press, 1981).

178. Sunday, "Hidden among the Stuff," Sermon Transcript, New York, 27 May 1917 (evening), pp. 11, 13, 17-18, 22, 24, Box 8, Reel 11, Sunday Papers.

179. Sunday, Sermon Transcript, New York, 4 May 1917 (evening), pp. 25-27, Box 7, Reel 10, Sunday Papers.

180. Sunday, "Is It Well with Thee?" Sermon Transcript, New York, 1 June 1917 (evening), pp. 19-20, Box 8, Reel 11, Sunday Papers.

181. Sunday, "O Lord Revive Thy Work," Sermon Transcript, New York, 10 April 1917 (evening), p. 5, Box 6, Reel 9, Sunday Papers.

182. Sunday, "Hidden among the Stuff," Sermon Transcript, New York, 27 May 1917 (evening), pp. 17-18, Box 8, Reel 11, Sunday Papers.

183. Sunday, "The People Took a Mind to Work," Sermon Transcript, New York, 12 April 1917 (evening), p. 36, Box 6, Reel 9, Sunday Papers.

184. Sunday, "Mighty Men Who Cannot Save," Sermon Transcript, New York, 6 May 1917 (morning), p. 27, Box 7, Reel 10, Sunday Papers.

185. Sunday, "Hidden among the Stuff," Sermon Transcript, New York, 27 May 1917 (evening), p. 20, Box 8, Reel 11, Sunday Papers.

186. McLoughlin, *Billy Sunday*, p. 183.

187. For the relationship of consumerism and divorce, see Elaine Tyler May, "The Pressure to Provide: Class, Consumerism, and Divorce in Urban America, 1880-1920," in Mel Albin and Dominick Cavallo, eds., *Family Life in America: 1620-2000* (St. James, N.Y.: Revisionary Press, 1981).

188. Quoted in Ellis, *Sunday*, p. 204.

189. Miller, *Bon Marché*, pp. 4, 202.

190. Ibid., pp. 205-6.

191. Sunday, "Hidden among the Stuff," Sermon Transcript, New York, 27 May 1917 (evening), pp. 24-25, Box 8, Reel 11, Sunday Papers.

192. Sunday, "Dr. Jekyll and Mr. Hyde," Sermon Transcript, New York, 31 May 1917 (evening), pp. 19-20, Box 8, Reel 11, Sunday Papers.

193. Sunday, "Why Call Ye Me Lord?" Sermon Transcript, New York, 15 April 1917 (evening), p. 29, Box 6, Reel 9, Sunday Papers.

194. For example, Walter Lippmann, *Drift and Master: An Attempt to Diagnose the Current Unrest* (New York: M. Kennerley, 1914).

Chapter VI

1. Ellis, *Sunday*, p. 350.
2. Ibid., pp. 204-5.
3. Ibid., pp. 203-5.
4. *The New York Times*, April 26, 1917, p. 7.
5. Sunday, Sermon Transcript, April 12, 1917 (afternoon), p. 14, Box 6, Reel 9, Sunday Papers.
6. Ellis, *Sunday*, p. 206.
7. Sunday, Sermon Transcript, 18 April 1917, p. 2, Box 6, Reel 9, Sunday Papers.
8. Quoted in McLoughlin, *Billy Sunday*, p. 183.
9. Ellis, *Sunday*, p. 52.
10. Souvenir Program of Billy Sunday Spokane Campaign, Box 5, Reel 9, Sunday Papers.
11. Ellis, *Sunday*, p. 201.
12. McLoughlin, *Billy Sunday*, p. 123
13. E.g., Sunday, Sermon Transcript, 12 April 1917 (afternoon), p. 14, Box 6, Reel 9, Sunday Papers.
14. Letter from William S. Phillips, Pontiac, Iowa, 11 November 1905, Box 1, Reel 1, Sunday Papers.
15. Letter from Robert Bentley, Youngstown, Ohio, no date, Box 1, Reel 1, Sunday Papers.
16. Letter from C. F. Brown, Centerville, Iowa, 16 November 1905, Box 1, Reel 1, Sunday Papers.
17. Robert McQuilken, "Where the Tabernacle is Open for Men Only," *The Sunday School Times*, February 13, 1915, p. 105.
18. C. Howard Davis, in Souvenir Program of Billy Sunday Spokane Campaign, Box 5, Reel 9, Sunday Papers.
19. Ellis, *Sunday*, p. 277.
20. Everett M. Hill, in Souvenir Program of Billy Sunday Spokane Campaign, Box 5, Reel 9, Sunday Papers.
21. Edmund Gosse, quoted in Houghton, *Victorian*, p. 305.
22. Smiles, *Character*, pp. 21, 123, 163.
23. Newell D. Hillis, *A Man's Value to Society: Studies in Self-Culture and Character* (Chicago: Fleming H. Revell, 1896), pp. 57-60.
24. Smiles, *Character*, pp. 20-21, 73-74, 12, 18, 44, 73, 104, 123, 143; and Orison Swett Marden, *Every Man a King; Or, Might in Mind Mastery* (New York: Thomas Y. Crowell, 1906), p. 52.
25. Trumbull, *Character-Shaping*, pp. 25, 23, 28, 64-65, 123, 131-32.
26. W. Reginald Wheeler, *A Man Sent from God: A Biography of Robert E. Speer* (Westwood, N.J.: Fleming H. Revell, 1956), p. 135.
27. Ibid., pp. 126, 145, 287.
28. Robert E. Speer, *Young Men Who Overcame* (Chicago: Fleming H. Revell, 1905), pp. 5-6, 15, 21, 95, 89, 94, 99, 195-96; and *Marks*, p. 158.
29. *The Coming Kingdom of Christ* (Chicago: The Bible Institute Colportage Association, 1914), pp. 65-67.
30. *The Sunday School Times*, June 5, 1909, p. 285.
31. E.g., "Glimpses of Mr. Moody's Last Years," August 22, 1908, p. 407; "Taking Men Alive," November 30, 1907, p. 615; "Anthony Comstock, Fighter," March 20, 1909, p. 147; "Heroic Girlhood," October 30, 1909, p. 549.
32. "When We Long for Power," *The Sunday School Times*, August 22, 1908, p. 405.
33. *Victory in Christ*, p. 17.

34. "Dr. Scofield as His Friends Knew Him," *The Sunday School Times*, October 30, 1920, p. 595, and November 6, 1920, p. 612.

35. *The Sunday School Times*, January 2, 1915, p. 4.

36. C. G. Trumbull, *Victory in Christ: Messages in the Victorious Life* (Fort Washington, Pa.: Christian Literature Crusades, 1959), pp. 54-55.

37. C. G. Trumbull, "The Billy Sunday Whom the Public Doesn't Know," *The Sunday School Times*, February 20, 1916, pp. 112-13.

38. McLoughlin, *Billy Sunday*, p. 84.

39. Trumbull, "Billy Sunday Whom the Public," pp. 112-13.

40. Ernest Becker, *The Denial of Death* (New York: The Free Press, 1973), p. 4.

41. Ibid., pp. 21, 14; and *Escape from Evil* (New York: The Free Press, 1975).

42. Becker, *Denial*, pp. 11, 5.

43. Ann Douglas, *The Feminization of American Culture* (New York: Avon Books, 1977), pp. 50-93.

44. Crunden, *Ministers*, pp. 15, 277.

45. "Holiness" was another such means to symbolic immortality, especially for evangelicals in the Wesleyan tradition.

46. The picture is somewhat complicated by the fact that the emerging liberal theology was also, for a time, wedded to character building. This was a natural expression of liberalism's emphasis on the ethical life and the imitation of Christ. Evangelicals stressed the importance of a conversion experience and of a spiritual enablement by Christ, more so than liberals did, but the attention given by both camps to character building is an example of the many continuities between evangelicals and liberals in this period.

47. Weber, *Protestant Ethic*, p. 181.

48. T. J. Jackson Lears, *No Place of Grace: Antimodernism and the Transformation of American Culture, 1880-1920* (New York: Pantheon, 1981), pp. 4-5, 32.

49. A. B. Simpson, *The Holy Spirit; Or, Power from on High* (Harrisburg, Pa.: Christian Publications, Inc., 1896), pp. 108-9, 112, 121.

50. R. A. Torrey, *How To Obtain Fullness of Power* (Springdale, Pa.: Whitaker House, 1982), pp. 7, 66; and *Why God Used D. L. Moody* (Chicago: The Bible Institute Colportage Association, 1923), p. 20.

51. Chapman, *Power*, pp. 18, 39.

52. Murray, *Absolute Surrender*, p. 92.

53. "When We Long for Power," *The Sunday School Times*, August 22, 1908, p. 405.

54. Gordon, *Quiet Talks*, pp. 29, 19.

55. F. B. Meyer, *Steps into the Blessed Life* (Philadelphia: Henry Altemus, 1896), p. 121.

56. I have not dealt with the burgeoning Pentecostal movement, although its adherents testified to the same quest for power, consummated by receiving the gift of the Holy Spirit. See, for example, Robert Mapes Anderson, *Vision of the Disinherited: The Making of American Pentecostalism* (New York: Oxford University Press, 1979).

57. Torrey, *Why God Used Moody*, p. 19.

58. *Victory in Christ*, p. 158.

59. Torrey, *How to Obtain*, p. 37.

60. Simpson, *The Holy Spirit*, p. 106.

61. A. C. Dixon, *Christian Character* (London: Marshall Brothers, n.d.), p. 4.

62. "Power Destroyers," *The Sunday School Times*, February 10, 1912, p. 81.

63. Gordon, *Quiet Talks*, pp. 263, 28-29.

64. Torrey, *How to Obtain*, p. 81.

65. Gordon, *Quiet Talks*, p. 157.

66. *Victory in Christ*, p. 76.

67. A. B. Simpson, *A Larger Christian Life* (Harrisburg, Pa.: Christian Publications, n.d.), pp. 113-14.

68. *Christian Workers Magazine*, February 19, 1914, p. 372.

69. Trumbull, *Victory in Christ*, p. 86.

70. Meyer, *Steps*, p. 122.

71. *Victory in Christ*, p. 31.

72. Simpson, *The Holy Spirit*, p. 111.

73. Dixon, *Christian Character*, p. 6.

74. Chapman, *Power*, pp. 39, 110-11.

75. Torrey, *The Baptism with the Holy Spirit*, p. 32.

76. R. A. Torrey, *How to Bring Men to Christ* (Chicago: Fleming H. Revell, 1893), pp. 98-99.

77. J. W. Chapman, *The Problem of the Work* (1911); *Present Day Evangelism* (1903); A. T. Pierson, *Evangelistic Work in Principle and Practice* (1887); R. A. Torrey, *How to Work for Christ: A Compendium of Effective Methods* (1901); *How to Promote and Conduct a Successful Revival* (1901).

78. Barabas, *So Great Salvation*, pp. 149-50.

79. Ellis, *Sunday*, pp. 310, 307, 309, 306.

80. McLoughlin, *Modern Revivalism*, pp. 438-39.

81. Trumbull, "Billy Sunday Whom the Public," p. 112.

82. Becker, *Escape from Evil*, pp. 149-50.

83. *The New York Times*, April 19, 1917, p. 24.

84. Elias Canetti, *Crowds and Power* (New York: Continuum, 1981), pp. 227-29.

85. Becker, *Escape*, p. 150.

86. McLoughlin, *Billy Sunday*, p. 179.

87. Newspaper from Keokuk, Iowa, 1904 (date imprecise), p. 1 Box 12, Folder 11, Reel 19, Sunday Papers.

88. Sunday, "Why Call Ye Me Lord?" Sermon Transcript, 15 April 1917 (evening), p. 19, Box 6, Reel 9, Sunday Papers.

89. Quoted in Ellis, *Sunday*, pp. 117, 353, 215.

90. McLoughlin, *Billy Sunday*, p. 142.

91. Quoted in Ellis, *Sunday*, pp. 196-98, 186.

92. Canetti, *Crowds*, p. 470.

93. *New York Times*, April 11, 1917, p. 22.

94. A Moody Bible Institute publication editorialized that Sunday preached hell "with gusto instead of anguish and yearning" and regretted Sunday's return to the "grotesque idea . . . that the redeemed in heaven would rejoice at the sight of sinners punished in hell" ("Sunday Good—Should Be Better," *The Christian Workers Magazine*, August 1915, p. 786).

95. Sunday, Sermon Transcript, 19 April 1917 (evening), p. 28, Box 6, Reel 10, Sunday Papers.

96. McLoughlin, *Billy Sunday*, p. 142.

97. Sunday, Sermon Transcript, 10 April 1917 (afternoon), p. 16, Box 6, Reel 9, Sunday Papers.

98. Souvenir Program of Billy Sunday Spokane Campaign, Box 5, Reel 9, Sunday Papers.

99. Letter from John Davison, Lima, Ohio, Board of Education, 2 May 1911, Box 5, Reel 9, Sunday Papers.

100. *The New York Times*, April 19, 1917, p. 24.

101. Canetti, *Crowds*, p. 49.

102. Becker, *Escape*, pp. 122, 141 (his italics).

103. Lears, *No Place of Grace*, pp. 102, 109.

104. Quoted in Wheeler, *Man Sent from God*, p. 145.

105. Quoted in McLoughlin, *Billy Sunday*, p. 257.

106. Ibid., p. 224.

107. Quoted in ibid., p. 141.

108. Quoted in Ellis, *Sunday*, opposite p. 60.

109. Quoted in McLoughlin, *Billy Sunday*, p. 84.

110. Ellis, *Sunday*, p. 141.

111. Ibid., pp. 60, 83-85, 301-2.

112. Findlay, *Moody*, pp. 221, 263-64.

113. McLoughlin, *Billy Sunday*, pp. 128, 201.

114. Ibid., pp. 97-99.

115. *The New York Times*, April 20, 1917, p. 22.

116. Sunday, Sermon Transcript, 15 April 1917 (afternoon), p. 33, Box 6, Reel 9, Sunday Papers.

117. Sunday, Sermon Transcript, 22 April 1917 (evening), p. 33, Box 6, Reel 10, Sunday Papers.

118. Quoted in McLoughlin, *Billy Sunday*, p. 183.

119. *The New York Times*, April 20, 1917, p. 22.

120. Ellis, *Sunday*, p. 162.

121. Sunday, Sermon Transcript, 27 May 1917 (evening), p. 20, Box 8, Reel 11, Sunday Papers.

122. Sunday, "Why Call Ye Me Lord?" Sermon Transcript, 15 April 1917 (evening), p. 15, Box 6, Reel 9, Sunday Papers.

Epilogue

1. See Marsden, *Fundamentalism*, pp. 184-95, 3.

2. Jacques Ellul, *The Meaning of the City* (Grand Rapids: Eerdmans, 1970), p. 130.

Bibliography

Ahlstrom, Sydney E. *A Religious History of the American People*. New Haven: Yale University Press, 1972.

Anderson, Robert Mapes. *Vision of the Disinherited: The Making of American Pentecostalism*. New York: Oxford University Press, 1979.

Barabas, Steven. *So Great Salvation: The History and Message of the Keswick Convention*. Westwood, N.J.: Fleming H. Revell, n.d.

Barth, Karl. *Church Dogmatics*. Vol. II: "The Doctrine of God." Part 2. Edinburgh: T. and T. Clark, 1957.

_____. *Church Dogmatics*, Vol. IV: "The Doctrine of Reconciliation." Part 1. Edinburgh: T. and T. Clark, 1956.

_____. *Come Holy Spirit*. Grand Rapids: Eerdmans, 1978 [1933].

_____. *The Humanity of God*. Atlanta: John Knox Press, 1960.

Bass, Clarence B. *Backgrounds to Dispensationalism: Its Historic Genesis and Ecclesiastical Implications*. Grand Rapids: Baker Book House, 1960, 1977.

Beard, George M. *American Nervousness: Its Cause and Consequences*. New York: G. P. Putnam's Sons, 1881.

Becker, Ernest. *The Denial of Death*. New York: The Free Press, 1973.

_____. *Escape From Evil*. New York: The Free Press, 1975.

Bell, Daniel. *The Cultural Contradictions of Capitalism*. New York: Basic Books, 1976.

Berger, Peter L. *The Sacred Canopy: Elements of a Sociological Theory of Religion*. Garden City, N.Y.: Anchor Books, 1967.

Berman, Marshall. *All That Is Solid Melts into Air: The Experience of Modernity*. New York: Simon and Schuster, 1982.

Bledstein, Burton J. *The Culture of Professionalism: The Middle Class and the Development of Higher Education in America*. New York: W. W. Norton, 1976.

Boorstin, Daniel J. *The Americans: The Democratic Experience*. New York: Vintage Books, 1974.

Bozeman, Theodore Dwight. *Protestants in an Age of Science: The Baconian Ideal and Antebellum American Religious Thought*. Chapel Hill, N.C.: University of North Carolina Press, 1977.

Brown, Richard D. "Modernization: A Victorian Complex." In Daniel Walker Howe, ed., *Victorian America*. Philadelphia: University of Pennsylvania Press, 1976.

"A Business Man's Soliloquy." *The Christian Workers Magazine* 14 (May 1914): 582.

Canetti, Elias. *Crowds and Power*. New York: Continuum, 1981.

Carpenter, Joel. "American Fundamentalism: Coming to Terms with a Troublesome Heritage." *Mission Journal*, November 1981.

Chafer, Lewis Sperry. *Dispensationalism*. Dallas: Dallas Seminary Press, 1936.

_____. *He That Is Spiritual*. Chicago: The Bible Institute Colportage Association, 1929.

_____. *The Kingdom in History and Prophecy*. New York: Fleming H. Revell, 1915.

_____. *Systematic Theology*, Vol. IV. Dallas: Dallas Seminary Press, 1947.

Chandler, Alfred D., Jr. *The Visible Hand: The Managerial Revolution in American Business*. Cambridge: Harvard University Press, 1977.

Chapman, J. Wilbur. *Power: Received Ye the Holy Ghost?* New York: Fleming H. Revell, 1894, 1912.

Clouse, Robert G., ed. *The Meaning of the Millennium: Four Views.* Downers Grove, Ill.: InterVarsity Press, 1977.

Crunden, Robert M. *Ministers of Reform: The Progressives' Achievement in American Civilization, 1889-1920.* New York: Basic Books, 1982.

Daniels, George H. *American Science in the Age of Jackson.* New York: Columbia University Press, 1968.

Dayton, Donald W. *Discovering an Evangelical Heritage.* New York: Harper and Row, 1976.

Dieter, Melvin E. *The Holiness Revival of the Nineteenth Century.* Methuen, N.J.: The Scarecrow Press, 1980.

Dillard, Annie. *Pilgrim at Tinker Creek.* New York: Bantam Books, 1975.

Dixon, A. C. *Christian Character.* London: Marshall Brothers, n.d.

Dixon, Helen C. A. *A. C. Dixon: A Romance of Preaching.* New York: G. P. Putnam's Sons, 1931.

Dollar, George W. *A History of Fundamentalism in America.* Greenville, S.C.: Bob Jones University Press, 1973.

Douglas, Ann. *The Feminization of American Culture.* New York: Avon Books, 1977.

Eiseley, Loren. *Darwin's Century: Evolution and the Men Who Discovered It.* Garden City, N.Y.: Anchor Books, 1958 [1961].

————. *The Unexpected Universe.* New York: Harcourt Brace Jovanovich, 1964 [1969].

Ellis, William T. *Billy Sunday: The Man and His Message.* Philadelphia: The John C. Winston Company, 1914.

Ellul, Jacques. *The Meaning of the City.* Grand Rapids: Eerdmans, 1970.

Engels, Friedrich, and Karl Marx. *The Communist Manifesto.* New York: Washington Square Press, 1964.

Ewen, Stuart. *Captains of Consciousness: Advertising and the Social Roots of the Consumer Culture.* New York: McGraw-Hill, 1982.

Ewen, Stuart and Elizabeth. *Channels of Desire: Mass Images and the Shaping of American Consciousness.* New York: McGraw-Hill, 1976.

Faulkner, Harold Underwood. *American Economic History.* 8th ed. New York: Harper and Brothers, 1960 [1924].

Findlay, James F., Jr. *Dwight L. Moody: American Evangelist, 1837-1899.* Chicago: University of Chicago Press, 1969.

Finney, Charles G. *Lectures on Revivals of Religion.* New York: Fleming H. Revell, 1868.

Fox, Stephen. *The Mirror Makers: A History of America and Its Creators.* New York: William Morrow and Company, 1984.

Fox, Richard W., and T. J. Jackson Lears, eds. *The Culture of Consumption: Critical Essays in American History, 1880-1980.* New York: Pantheon Books, 1983.

Fuller, Daniel P. *Gospel and Law: Contrast or Continuum? The Hermeneutics of Dispensationalism and Covenant Theology.* Grand Rapids: Eerdmans, 1980.

Gaebelein, Arno C. *The Return of the Lord.* New York: Publication Office "Our Hope," 1925.

Gates, Paul W. *The Farmer's Age: Agriculture 1815-1860.* Vol. III of *The Economic History of the United States.* New York: Holt, Rinehart and Winston, 1960.

Gordon, S. D. *Quiet Talks on Power.* Chicago: Fleming H. Revell, 1903.

Gutman, Herbert. *Work, Culture and Society in Industrializing America.* New York: Vintage Books, 1966, 1976.

Haldeman, I. M. *Signs of the Times.* New York: Charles C. Cook, 1912.

Handy, Robert T. *A Christian America: Protestant Hopes and Historical Realities.* New York: Oxford University Press, 1971.

Hatch, Nathan, George Marsden, and Mark Noll. *The Search for Christian America.* Westchester, Ill.: Crossway Books, 1983.

Heilbroner, Robert, and Aaron Singer. *The Economic Transformation of America.* New York: Harcourt Brace Jovanovich, 1977.

Heschel, Abraham J. *The Prophets.* Vol. I. New York: Harper and Row, 1962, 1975.

Hession, Charles H., and Hyman Sardy. *Ascent to Affluence: A History of American Economic Development.* Boston: Allyn and Bacon, Inc., 1965.

Hillis, Newell D. *A Man's Value to Society: Studies in Self-Culture and Character.* Chicago: Fleming H. Revell, 1896.

Hoffecker, W. Andrew. *Piety and the Princeton Theologians: Archibald Alexander, Charles Hodge, Benjamin Warfield.* Grand Rapids: Baker Book House, 1981.

Hofstadter, Richard. *Social Darwinism and American Thought.* Boston: The Beacon Press, 1944 [1955].

Hollingworth, Harry L. *Advertising and Selling: Principles of Appeal and Response.* New York: D. Appleton and Company, 1913.

Houghton, Walter E. *The Victorian Frame of Mind, 1830-1870.* New Haven: Yale University Press, 1957.

Howard, D. T. *The Psychology of Advertising.* New York: Dodd Mead and Company, 1931 [1921].

Howard, Philip. *The Life Story of Henry Clay Trumbull: Missionary , Army Chaplain, Editor and Author.* Philadelphia: The Sunday School Times, 1905.

In Behalf of Advertising: A Series of Essays Published in National Periodicals from 1919 to 1928. Philadelphia: N. W. Ayer and Son, 1929.

James, William. *The Varieties of Religious Experience: A Study in Human Nature.* New York: New American Library, 1958.

Kasson, John F. *Civilizing the Machine: Technology and Republican Values in America, 1776-1900.* New York: Penguin Books, 1976.

Kraus, C. Norman. *Dispensationalism in America: Its Rise and Development.* Richmond: John Knox Press, 1958.

Ladd, George E. *Crucial Questions about the Kingdom of God.* Grand Rapids: Eerdmans, 1952.

Lears, T. J. Jackson. *No Place of Grace: Antimodernism and the Transformation of American Culture 1880-1920.* New York: Pantheon, 1981.

LeDuc, Thomas. *Piety and Intellect at Amherst College, 1865-1912.* New York: Columbia University Press, 1946.

Lindsey, Hal. *The Late Great Planet Earth.* Grand Rapids: Zondervan, 1970.

Lippmann, Walter. *Drift and Mastery: An Attempt to Diagnose the Current Unrest.* New York: M. Kennerley, 1914.

―――――. *A Preface to Morals.* New York: The Macmillan Company, 1935.

Loucks, Mel. *The Victorious Life.* Diss., Fuller Theological Seminary.

Lovelace, Richard F. *Dynamics of Spiritual Life: An Evangelical Theology of Renewal.* Downers Grove, Ill.: InterVarsity Press, 1979.

Mackenzie, Kenneth W. *The Robe and the Sword: The Methodist Church and the Rise of American Imperialism.* Washington, D.C.: Public Affairs Press, 1961.

McKim, Donald K., and Jack B. Rogers. *Authority and Interpretation of the Bible: An Historical Approach.* New York: Harper and Row, 1979.

McLoughlin, William G. *Billy Sunday Was His Real Name.* Chicago: University of Chicago Press, 1955.

―――――. *Revivals, Awakenings and Reform: An Essay on Religion and Social Change in America, 1607-1977.* Chicago: University of Chicago Press, 1978.

McQuilken, Robert C. *Victorious Life Studies.* Philadelphia: Christian Life Literature Fund, 1918.

Mann, A. Chester. *F. B. Meyer: Preacher, Teacher, Man of God.* New York: Fleming H. Revell, 1929.

Mansoor, Menahem. *The Dead Sea Scrolls: A College Textbook and a Study Guide.* Grand Rapids: Eerdmans, 1964.

Marden, Orison Swett. *Every Man a King; Or, Might in Mind Mastery.* New York: Thomas Y. Crowell, 1906.

Marquette, Arthur F. *Brands, Trademarks, and Goodwill.* New York: McGraw-Hill, 1967.

Marsden, George M. *The Evangelical Mind and the New School Presbyterian Experience: A Case Study of Thought and Theology in Nineteenth Century America.* New Haven: Yale University Press, 1970.

————. *Fundamentalism and American Culture: The Shaping of Twentieth-Century Evangelicalism: 1870-1925.* New York: Oxford University Press, 1980.

Marty, Martin. *The Modern Schism: Three Paths to the Secular.* New York: Harper and Row, 1969.

Massee, J. C. *The Second Coming.* Philadelphia: Philadelphia School of the Bible, 1919.

May, Elaine Tyler. "The Pressure to Provide: Class, Consumerism, and Divorce in Urban America, 1880-1920," in Mel Albin and Dominick Cavallo, eds., *Family Life in America: 1620-2000.* St. James, N.Y.: Revisionary Press, 1981.

May, Henry F. *The Enlightenment in America.* New York: Oxford University Press, 1976.

Mead, Sidney E. *The Lively Experiment: The Shaping of Christianity in America.* New York: Harper and Row, 1963.

————. *The Nation with the Soul of a Church.* New York: Harper and Row, 1975.

Meyer, Donald. *The Positive Thinkers: A Study of the American Search for Health, Wealth, and Personal Power from Mary Baker Eddy to Norman Vincent Peale.* Garden City, N.Y.: Doubleday and Company, 1965.

Meyer, F. B. *Steps Into the Blessed Life.* Philadelphia: Henry Altemus, 1896.

Miller, Michael B. *The Bon Marché: Bourgeois Culture and the Department Store, 1869-1920.* Princeton, N.J.: Princeton University Press, 1981.

Moody, Dwight Lyman. *Moody's Last Sermons as Delivered by the Great Evangelist.* Chicago: Rhodes and McClure, 1899.

Morris, Leon. *Apocalyptic.* Grand Rapids: Eerdmans, 1972.

Murray, Andrew. *Absolute Surrender: Addresses Delivered in England and Scotland.* 3rd ed. London: Marshall Brothers, n.d.

————. *Be Perfect: A Devotional Study of Christ's Command.* Minneapolis: Bethany Fellowship, 1965.

————. *Holy in Christ.* Minneapolis: Bethany Fellowship, n.d.

Niebuhr, H. Richard. *The Kingdom of God in America.* New York: Harper and Row, 1937.

Noll, Mark. "Common Sense Traditions and American Evangelical Thought." *American Quarterly* 37 (Summer 1985): 216-38.

Ottman, Ford C. J. *Wilbur Chapman: A Biography.* Garden City, N.Y.: Doubleday, Page, and Co., 1920.

Palmer, Phoebe. *The Way of Holiness, with Notes by the Way: Being a Narrative of Religious Experience Resulting from a Determination to Be a Bible Christian.* New York: G. Lane and C. B. Tippett, 1848.

Parsons, George Frederic. "Growth of Materialism." *Atlantic,* August 1887, pp. 160-63.

"Pharisees." In *The Zondervan Pictorial Encyclopedia of the Bible,* vol. IV. Ed. Tenney, Merrill C. Grand Rapids: Zondervan, 1975.

Peters, John. *Christian Perfection and American Methodism.* New York: Abingdon Press, 1956.

Pollack, J. C. *The Keswick Story: The Authorized History of the Keswick Convention.* Chicago: Moody Press, 1964.

Pope, Daniel. *The Making of Modern Advertising.* New York: Basic Books, 1983.

Presbrey, Frank. *The History and Development of Advertising.* New York: Greenwood Press, 1968 [1929].

Rothman, Sheila M. *Woman's Proper Place.* New York: Basic Books, 1978.

Russell, D. S. *The Jews from Alexander to Herod.* Oxford: Oxford University Press, 1967.

Ryrie, Charles C. *Dispensationalism Today.* Chicago: Moody Press, 1965.

Sandeen, Ernest R. *The Roots of Fundamentalism: British and American Millenarianism, 1800-1930.* Chicago: University of Chicago Press, 1970.

Schofield, A. T. *The Springs of Character.* New York: Funk and Wagnalls, n.d.

Schudson, Michael. *Advertising: The Uneasy Persuasion—Its Dubious Impact on American Society.* New York: Basic Books, 1984.

Schuller, Robert H. *Self Esteem: The New Reformation.* Waco, Tex.: Word Books, 1982.
Scofield, C. I. *Rightly Dividing the Word of Truth: Being Ten Studies of the More Important Divisions of Scripture.* New York: Bible Truth Press, n.d.
Scott, Donald M., and Bernard Wishy, eds. *American Families: A Documentary History.* New York: Harper and Row, 1982.
Simpson, A. B. *The Holy Spirit; Or, Power from on High.* Harrisburg, Pa.: Christian Publications, 1896.
————. *A Larger Christian Life.* Harrisburg, Pa.: Christian Publications, 1979.
Sizer, Sandra S. *Gospel Hymns and Social Religion: The Rhetoric of Nineteenth Century Revivalism.* Philadelphia: Temple University Press, 1978.
Smiles, Samuel. *Character.* London: John Murray, 1876.
Smith, Hannah Whitall. *The Christian's Secret of a Happy Life.* Old Tappan, N.J.: Fleming H. Revell, 1942, 1970.
Smith, Timothy. *Revivalism and Social Reform in Mid-Nineteenth Century America.* Nashville: Abingdon Press, 1957.
Speer, Robert Elliot. *The Marks of a Man; Or, The Essentials of Christian Character.* New York: The Methodist Book Concern, 1907.
————. *Young Men Who Overcame.* Chicago: Fleming H. Revell, 1905.
Straton, John Roach. *The Salvation of Society and Other Addresses.* Baltimore: Fleet-McGinley, n.d.
Stringfellow, William. *Conscience and Obedience: The Politics of Romans 13 and Revelation 13 in Light of the Second Coming.* Waco, Tex.: Word Books, 1977, 1978.
"Sunday Good—Should Be Better." *The Christian Workers Magazine,* August 1915, p. 768.
Taylor, George Rogers. *The Transportation Revolution, 1815-1860.* Vol. IV of *The Economic History of the United States.* New York: Holt, Rinehart, and Winston, 1951.
Taylor, Mrs. Howard. *William Borden of Yale.* Chicago: Moody Press, 1980.
The Victorious Christ: Messages from Conferences Held by Victorious Life Testimony in 1922. Philadelphia: Sunday School Times, 1923.
The Coming Kingdom of Christ. Chicago: The Bible Institute Colportage Association, 1914.
Thomas, W. H. Griffith. "The Victorious Life." *Bibliotheca Sacra.* July 1919, pp. 267-88; October 1919, pp. 455-67.
Torrey, R. A. *The Baptism with the Holy Spirit.* New York: Fleming H. Revell, 1895.
————. *How to Bring Men to Christ.* Chicago: Fleming H. Revell, 1893.
————. *How to Obtain Fullness of Power.* Springdale, Pa.: Whitaker House, 1982.
————. *Why God Used D. L. Moody.* Chicago: The Bible Institute Colportage Association, 1923.
Trumbull, C. G. *Victory in Christ: Messages in the Victorious Life.* Fort Washington, Pa.: Christian Literature Crusades, 1959.
————. *What Is the Gospel?* Philadelphia: The Sunday School Times, 1918.
Trumbull, Henry Clay. *Aspirations and Influences.* Philadelphia: John D. Wattles, 1889.
————. *Character Shaping and Character Showing.* Philadelphia: John D. Wattles, 1889.
————. *Duty Knowing and Duty Doing.* Philadelphia: John D. Wattles, 1889.
Turner, E. S. *The Shocking History of Advertising.* London: Michael Joseph, Ltd., 1952.
Victory in Christ: A Report of Princeton Conference, 1916. Philadelphia: Board of Managers of Princeton Conference, 1916.
Wallace, Anthony F. C. *Rockdale: The Growth of an American Village in the Early Industrial Revolution.* New York: W. W. Norton, 1972, 1978.
Walvoord, John. *The Rapture Question.* Findlay, Ohio: Dunham, 1957.
Weber, Max. *The Protestant Ethic and the Spirit of Capitalism.* New York: Charles Scribner's Sons, 1958.
Weber, Otto. *Foundations of Dogmatics.* Vol. II. Grand Rapids: Eerdmans, 1983 [1962].
Weber, Timothy P. *Living in the Shadow of the Second Coming: American Premillennialism, 1875-1925.* New York: Oxford University Press, 1979.

Wheeler, W. Reginald. *A Man Sent From God: A Biography of Robert E. Speer.* Westwood, N.J.: Fleming H. Revell, 1956.

Wiebe, Robert H. *The Search for Order: 1877-1920.* New York: Hill and Wang, 1967.

Wilson, Maurice E. "Eddyism, Commonly Called Christian Science." In *The Fundamentals,* vol. 4. Grand Rapids: Baker Book House, 1972.

Index

Advertising: early development of, 206–7; techniques of, 208–10. *See also* Consumerism

Ahlstrom, Sidney, 21

America: as a Christian nation, 2, 34, 167–68, 170–71, 225; church growth in, 11–13; heroism in, 247–48; martial spirit in, 262; middle-class pressures in, 126–29, 138–41; nineteenth-century history of, 8–13, 32–41, 43, 138–39; progressivism in, 171, 194, 247; since World War II, 274–77; small town life in, 33, 38–40

Alexander, Archibald, 63

Bacon, Francis, 52, 63, 83
Barnes, Albert, 21
Barth, Karl, 49, 98–99, 166
Bass, Clarence, 94
Baxter, Richard, 131
Beard, George M., 126–27, 136–38
Becker, Ernest, 44, 245–47, 258, 262
Beecher, Edward, 24
Beecher, Lyman, 12, 169, 180
Berger, Peter, 34–36
Berman, Marshall, 125
Bledstein, Burton, 129, 133
Bonsack, James 204–5
Borden, William, 134
Boardman, W. E., 113
Brooks, Phillips, 26

Calvin, John, 14, 130
Calvinism, 14–18, 20–22, 47, 63, 111, 114, 129–33, 137–40, 156, 161
Canetti, Elias, 258–61
Capitalism, 8–13, 32–41, 129–32, 139–40, 160, 203, 210, 212, 249, 275. *See also* Industrialism
Carey, Henry C., 35
Chafer, Lewis Sperry, 159
Chandler, Arthur B., Jr., 205

Chapman, J. Wilbur, 128, 173, 174, 251, 252, 254–55
Character, 133–36, 162, 211–12, 238–41, 248–49. *See also* Sunday, Billy: and manhood
Christian Science, 156
Civil War, 226, 66, 68, 112, 133, 138, 206, 248
Common Sense Realism ("Scottish" philosophy), 15–16, 18, 20–22, 47–48, 51–52, 63, 83
Consumerism, 213–24, 249–50. *See also* Advertising
Crowell, Henry P., 205
Crozier, John P., 36

Daniels, George, 52
Darby, John Nelson, 69–74, 80, 82, 94–95, 114
Darwin, Charles, 50–54, 57, 63
Dayton, Donald, 3, 25
Deism, 48
Dillard, Annie, 105
Dinwiddie, Howard, 122
Dispensationalism: development of, 69–75; and the gospel, 85; and humility, 92–96; and judgment, 99; and Keswick, 114; and prophecy, 78–84; since World War II, 275–76; and social reform, 96–98; and suffering, 79–83, 100–102
Dixon, A. C., 252–53
Duke, James B., 204–5

Eddy, Mary Baker, 150, 156
Edwards, Jonathan, 12, 18, 22, 24, 67, 169, 180, 254
Eiseley, Loren, 51, 54
Ellul, Jacques, 26, 277
Emerson, Ralph Waldo, 128, 160
Enlightenment, 2, 17, 18, 46–49, 67, 83, 161, 203, 215, 225
Erdman, Charles, 180–81

305

Evangelicalism: and American mythology, 225–26; and appearances, 60–67; and confession, 277–78; in darkness, 229–30; and heroism, 247–51, 276; and loss of hegemony, 271–73; and moral perfection, 23–24; and nest-building, 54–59; in the 1920s, 273; and power, 3–5, 12, 24–25; resurgence in the 1970s, 1–5, 274–77; and self-righteousness, 25; and self-sufficiency, 15, 31; and social reform, 3–5, 12, 24–25; and soul-winning, 254–56
Evolution, 50–54

Falwell, Jerry, 4
Finney, Charles, 12, 21–25, 32–33, 110–11, 168, 180, 254, 264
Flesh, biblical view of, 232–36
Forgiveness, 19, 25, 27, 107
Freud, Sigmund, 57, 126, 155
Free enterprise system. *See* Capitalism
Frost, A. J., 64–66

Gaebelein, Arno, 96–97
Gordon, A. J., 114
Gordon, S. D., 251–52
Gray, Asa, 53

Habakkuk: and appearances, 60–61; and gospel, 84–92, 96–102; and humility, 92–93, 95–96; view of history, 75–79; as poor, 19
Haeckel, Ernst, 53
Haldeman, I. M., 65–67, 69, 79, 81–82, 85, 95–96, 156
Harford-Battersby, T. D., 113–14, 141
Heroism: and Billy Sunday, 238, 243–45, 256–66; and character, 238–41; and consumerism, 249–50; and evangelicals, 238–45; and the human condition, 245–47; and middle class, 160; and Pharisees, 198; and power, 251–59; and St. Paul, 234–36; and violence, 256–70
Heschel, Abraham, 84, 96
Historical-critical method, 50
Hodge, A. A., 63
Hofstadter, Richard, 98
Holden, J. Stuart, 252
Hollingworth, Harry L., 208
Holiness Movement, 111–13
Hopkins, Evan, 251
Horton, Robert F., 122
Howard, Philip, 14
Human depravity, 14, 17

Industrialism, 9–11, 33–41, 46, 124–25, 127–28, 203–5, 218, 247. *See also* Capitalism
Israel, history of, 195–201, 229

James, William, 124, 144–46, 150–51, 155–57
Jesus, 26–27, 29, 48–50, 103–9, 159–61, 165, 181–83, 192–95, 197, 199–201, 226–30, 232–36, 245, 266–67, 269–70, 277–78
Job, 30–32, 41–43, 45–56, 58–59

Kant, Immanuel, 48, 49
Keswick movement: in America, 114–15; in England, 113–15, 123, 137, 141–44, 146–47, 157

Ladd, George T., 24–25
The Late Great Planet Earth, 275
Lears, Jackson, 262
Liberalism (Protestant), 49, 98
Lippmann, Walter, 54, 126
Luther, Martin, 18, 70, 165

McQuilken, Robert C., 115, 116, 143, 147, 154
Marsden, George, 21, 36, 62, 68, 74, 83, 86, 112
Marty, Martin, 21, 170
Marx, Karl, 41, 98, 124
Marxism, 35
Massee, J. C., 95
May, Henry, 47–48, 83
Mead, Sidney, 35
Mencken, H. L., 175, 273
Methodism, 109–13
Meyer, Donald, 144
Meyer, F. B., 114, 251–52
Millennium, 13, 24–25, 28, 68, 71, 94, 99
Miller, William, 68
Mind-cure religion. *See* Victorious Life movement
Modernization, 32, 70
Monod, Theodore, 141
Moody, Dwight L., 32, 58, 61, 70, 97, 98, 102, 113, 114, 128, 132, 169–74, 180, 244, 251, 254, 264
Moody Bible Institute, 115, 126, 154
Moral Majority, 4, 276
Moule, H. G. C., 141
Murray, Andrew, 109, 113, 114, 120, 122, 141–42, 147, 149, 162, 251–52

Nest-building, 42–46, 66, 102
Nettleton, Asahel, 168

New Haven Theology, 16–18, 21
Niagara Bible Conference, 75

Oberlin College, 23–24

Paley, William, 52–53, 62
Palmer, Phoebe, 111
Parsons, George Frederic, 213–14
Paul, Saint (Saul of Tarsus), 19, 50, 86, 89–92, 96, 101, 119, 166, 232–36, 266–67, 269–70
Perfectionism, 109–15, 140, 161–62
Peters, Absalom, 20, 63–64
Pettingill, William, 69
Pharisees, 96, 107–8, 197–201, 226, 228–29, 267, 277
Pierson, A. T., 114, 255
Plausibility structure, 45–46, 55–59, 92
Plymouth Brethren, 69
Postmillennialism, 24, 64, 67–68, 83, 140
Premillennialism, 24–25, 32, 66–69, 79, 113, 114, 140, 168, 225, 248, 276
Prophecy, 75
Prophetic movement, 92
Prophetic Times, 83
Prophets, 78, 91–92, 96
Protestant ethic, 129–36, 139, 160, 211–23

Reed, John, 179
Reid, Thomas, 15
Repentance, 103–9
Revivalism, 11–12, 21–25, 47, 61–62, 112, 161, 168–72. *See also* Beecher, Lyman; Edwards, Jonathan; Finney, Charles; Moody, Dwight L.; Sunday, Billy
Riley, William Bell, 96
Rodeheaver, Homer A., 175, 261
Roosevelt, Theodore, 262–63

Sandeen, Ernest, 68, 73, 79
Sankey, Ira D., 169, 241
Schaeffer, Francis, 4
Schleiermacher, Friedrich, 49
Scofield, C. I., 73–75, 80–81, 114, 115, 118, 142, 149, 242
Scofield Reference Bible, 73–74, 276
"Scottish" philosophy. *See* Common Sense Realism
Second Great Awakening, 2
Simeon, 196–99, 227–29
Simpson, A. B., 250–51, 252, 254
Sizer, Sandra, 102
Smiles, Samuel, 211–12
Smith, Adam, 34

Smith, Hannah Whitall, 113, 137–38, 141–43, 153, 154, 157
Smith, Robert Pearsall, 113, 141
Smith, Timothy L., 3, 20, 25
Sociology of religion, 43–46
Speer, Robert E., 134–35, 239–42, 248, 262
Spencer, Herbert, 212
Spiritual poverty, 6, 26–29, 119
Spiritual richness, 6–8, 13–21, 25–29, 30–32, 36, 271–72
Straton, John Roach, 172
Stephen, 267–69, 277
Stringfellow, William, 99
Suffering, 79–83, 90–91, 99–100
Sunday, Billy: on alcohol, 187–88, 190, 221–24, 263; background and early career of, 173–75; and character, 210–13; and Charles Trumbull, 243–45; and consumerism, 214–24; decline of, 273; as hero, 238, 255–66; and manhood, 188–93, 210, 236–38; as modern prophet, 183–84, 215; as moralist, 193–95, 210; and nineteenth-century tensions, 201–2; public opinion of, 178–79; revivalist successes of, 176–78; revivalist techniques of, 175–79; and slavery to sin, 227–31; as social critic of America, 184–88; theology of, 180–83; and violence, 257–66, 268
Supernaturalism, 49–50

Taylor, Hudson, 141, 254
Taylor, Nathaniel W., 16–17, 21, 24, 33
Theology, nineteenth-century (European), 14–19, 21–25, 49–50
Thomas, W. H. Griffith, 252
Torrey, R. A., 100, 114, 176, 251–52
Trumbull, Charles G., 61, 115, 116–23, 137, 143, 146–54, 158–60, 163–64, 241–45, 253, 255–56
Trumbull, Henry Clay, 211–12, 239–42

Victorious Life movement: and American History, 225; conferences, 142, 143, 145, 159; and faith, 118–19, 162–63; and middle-class pressures, 136–40; and mind-cure religion, 144–54; perils in, 120–22; as religion, 157–60, 164–65; and repentence, 154–59; since World War II, 276; and spiritual defeat, 141–43; and surrender, 117–18; theology of, 116–23; and the therapeutic society, 272; Trumbull's conversion to, 115. *See also* Keswick Movement

Wallace, Anthony F. C., 9, 13, 36, 62
Wanamaker, John, 206, 207
Warfield, B. B., 23–24
Webb-Peploe, H. W., 114, 141, 252
Weber, Max, 15, 129–39, 211

Wesley, John, 109–10, 114
Wheaton College, 115, 154
Wiebe, Robert, 40, 201

Youmans, E. L., 126, 137

Scripture Index

Genesis
11:4 — 27

I Samuel
10:22 — 218
17:44 — 259

I Kings
9:19 — 19

Job
1:10-11 — 31
3:3 — 31
3:24 — 31
3:26 — 32
29:2-17 — 42
29:18-20 — 42
29:25 — 43
30:1 — 43
30:9-10 — 43
42:3 — 58
42:5 — 58
42:6 — 58
42:8 — 59

Psalms
2:14 — 29
2:16 — 29
32:1 — 109
34:6 — 19
40:17 — 19
73:3 — 61
73:5 — 61
73:10-11 — 61
107:10-16 — 231
109:21-26 — 6
119:84 — 84
119:146-47 — 84
120:1 — 84

Proverbs
4:19 — 227
10:15 — 26

Isaiah
8:14 — 107
25:2-3 — 28
25:4 — 29
28:21 — 84
53:3 — 270

Jeremiah
16:14 — 224
17:7 — 278
17:9 — 278

Lamentations
3:23 — 102
3:45 — 19

Ezekiel
18:23 — 100

Daniel
9:24 — 72

Hosea
1:10 — 166, 278
2:23 — 278

Amos
1:4-7 — 27
1:10 — 27
5:8-9 — 28
5:11 — 27
6:1 — 26
6:11 — 28

Jonah
2:2 — 19

Micah
2:11 — 224

Habakkuk
1:2 — 75
1:2-3 — 60

1:5 — 89
1:5-6 — 76
1:7-11 — 76
1:12 — 77
1:13 — 77
1:14 — 77
1:15 — 78, 89
1:16 — 78, 89
1:17 — 78, 84
2:1 — 86
2:1-2 — 19
2:2-3 — 87
2:4-5 — 90
2:6 — 87
2:8 — 87
2:9 — 87, 97
2:12 — 87
2:13 — 87
2:19 — 87
2:20 — 101
3:2 — 87, 100
3:6 — 88
3:10-11 — 89
3:12 — 88
3:13 — 99
3:16 — 88, 101
3:17-18 — 89, 102
3:17-19 — 88

Matthew
3:14 — 103
3:15 — 103
3:16-17 — 103
4:1 — 103
4:17 — 106
4:23 — 106
4:24 — 106
6:2 — 195
6:25-33 — 104
8:20 — 59, 104
9:2 — 106
9:4 — 106
9:4-7 — 107

Scripture Index

9:8	107	8:53	232	**Philippians**	
9:10	108	9:39	229	2:3-7	235
9:32-34	200	9:41	227, 228	2:6-8	99
10:28-31	104	12:19	200	2:8	104
10:31	105	12:40	229	2:9-11	253
12:24	105	14:3	81	3:3	235
15:14	201			3:4-6	235
16:1-4	200	**Acts**		3:6	267
16:19	105	22:10	19	3:7-9	235
16:21-22	105	23:9	200	3:10	101
16:23				3:23	232
16:24		**Romans**		4:19	105
20:3	195	1:16	89		
20:30-34	106	1:16-17	90	**Colossians**	
21:9-11	200	1:18	90	2:11	234
21:43	200	1:24	90	2:18	234
22:6	108	2:2-3	90	2:20	234
24:3-9	80	2:10-12	90	2:21	234
24:15-21	80	5:1-3	91	2:23	234
24:16	74	7:18	233		
26:56	105	7:24-25	269	**I Thessalonians**	
27:41-43	105	7:25	233	4:14-17	81
27:62-66	200	8:7	233	5:1-8	230
		8:8	236		
Mark		8:13	233	**II Thessalonians**	
8:29	278	8:15	233	1:5	100
8:32	109	8:19	166		
8:33	278	11:33	28	**I Timothy**	
9:32	102	12:1	105, 165	1:15	277
10:23-31	7				
10:26-27	29	**I Corinthians**		**Hebrews**	
14:71-72	278	4:3	166	4:12	277
		4:11	105	10:26-27	101
Luke		4:13	105	10:30-31	101
1:51-53	29	15:53	270	10:37-38	101
2:25-35	196	15:54-55	270	12:29	105
4:18	29				
6:25	199	**II Corinthians**		**James**	
9:53	200	5:2-3	166	5:11	59
12:16b-21	7	5:6-7	166	5:16	59
12:21	26	8:9	29		
18:11	108	10:12	236	**I Peter**	
18:20-21	232	10:17-18	236	5:9	100
19:37-39	200				
19:41-44	100, 229	**Galatians**		**Revelation**	
21:21	74	1:6-7	233	3:16-20	28
		3:3	233	6-7	81
John		6:8	233	12:14	72
8:13	226	6:12	233		
8:31-39	226				
8:39	232	**Ephesians**			
8:43-45	226	4:8	166		
		6:10-18	228		

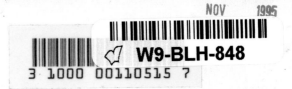
AND THEN I WROTE

AND THEN I WROTE

The Songwriter Speaks

Edited by Tom Russell and Sylvia Tyson

Arsenal Pulp Press / Vancouver

Introductions copyright © 1995 by Tom Russell and Sylvia
Tyson

Arsenal Pulp Press
103-1014 Homer Street
Vancouver, B.C.
Canada V6B 2W9

Book design by DesignGeist
Printed and bound in Canada

Canadian Cataloguing in Publication Data:
Main entry under title:
And then I wrote

Includes index.
ISBN 1-55152-023-0

1.Popular music–Writing and publishing–Quotations,
maxims, etc. 2. Lyric writing (Popular music)–Quotations,
maxims, etc. 3. Composers–Quotations. 4. Lyricists–
Quotations, 5. Popular music–Writing and publishing–
Anecdotes. 6. Lyric writing (Popular music)–Anecdotes. I.
Russell, Tom. II. Tyson, Sylvia.
ML3477.5.A52 1995   782.42164'13   C95-910827-0

TABLE OF CONTENTS

INTRODUCTION vi

1 CAN YA DANCE TO IT Song Anecdotes 1

2 IN THE BEGINNING Beginnings and Early Influences 26

3 TAPDANCE ON A TIGHTROPE Song Philosophies 44

4 FELLOW TRAVELLERS Idols and Influences 61

5 "I PICK UP MY PEN AND GOD MOVES IT" Inspiration and Motivation 83

6 ORDER OUT OF CHAOS The Craft of Songwriting 98

7 ALL YOU CAN WRITE IS WHAT YOU SEE The Art of Lyric Writing 127

8 GETTING PERSONAL Songs of Love, Sex and Loathing 139

9 WE ALL WANT TO CHANGE THE WORLD Songs of Politics and Conscience 148

10 MARRIAGES OF CONVENIENCE Collaborations 159

11 BLOOD FROM A STONE Writer's Block 172

12 USE A #2 LEAD PENCIL Sound Advice 178

13 MADE TO ORDER Writing for Hire 187

14 LET'S MAKE A DEAL Song Plugging 197

15 EVEN A DOG CAN SHAKE HANDS Bad Business Deals 203

16 SEND IN THE CLOWNS Performing Songs 215

17 CHICKEN SOUP AND THE MEANING OF LIFE One-Liners 228

INDEX 234

INTRODUCTION

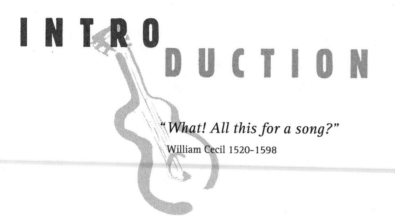

"What! All this for a song?"
William Cecil 1520-1598

This book is a collection of quotations and anecdotes on popular songs, spoken by the songwriters. The quotations deal with the creative process of writing songs as well as personal views on the business of songwriting. The material was gathered from personal interviews, radio and television archives, books, magazines and newspaper articles. Dates of the quotations have been included where possible, as many of the quotations are best understood within a historical context.

Some writers are more quotable than others, and many writers prefer not to analyze their art. "If you intellectualize and examine the creative process too carefully," said playwright Edward Albee, "it can evaporate or vanish. It's not only terrible to talk about, it's also dangerous." He cites the fable of the centipede who, when asked how he co-ordinates his dozens of legs, stops to think about it and forgets how to walk.

"It's dangerous form to talk about it," says Rickie Lee Jones. "It's private . . . when you talk about these things, you disengage them. You violate them. It's hard to go back and say, 'Let's be private again.' There are spirits."

Our goal is to shed light without violating the spirits. The songwriting process involves creative alchemy mixed with a knowledge of the craft. We've arranged the quotations so that they build into a shared compendium of the experience. They have been organized according to themes and ideas, and a story emerges that may, in a small way, enlighten our understanding of both the art and the craft of the song. They also add up to an effective oral history of popular song from Irving Berlin to R.E.M., from Stephen Foster and his "Ethiopian songs" to the revolution of rap.

Twenty years ago Phil Spector declared that music was going to die because people were not writing songs any more, they were writing "ideas." In the last ten years there seems to have been an obsession with songwriter analysis: clinics, seminars, magazines, "writers in the round" concerts—yet in the last generation we haven't quite managed to improve on Irving Berlin, Smokey Robinson, Bob Dylan or the Beatles. Over-analysis of the craft has not opened any magic trap doors.

There are no grand conclusions here. It comes down to the thoughts of survivors of the song wars telling us about life in the trenches. We may gain insight, the odd bit of advice, and a shared awe of the magic; beyond that, one learns as much or more by listening to the songs themselves—"The songs of the maniacs," as Plato would say.

Tom Russell

During the last three years I've been active in the Songwriter's Association of Canada. Although they are very active as a lobby group for publishing and copyright, their primary focus is putting emerging songwriters together with established writers in an ongoing series of weekend workshops. As a resource writer in this program, I've come to meet, work with and admire many of my younger contemporaries, and to enjoy the exchange of ideas and information.

Writing is such a solitary endeavour, and so it should be, but sometimes it's comforting to know that there are others going through the same trials as you are. I believe that this book goes a long way toward illustrating that fact.

As to the many writers who aren't quoted here, it's not that they don't have equally important insights, but rather that we haven't reached them yet. We look forward to adding them to the second edition.

Sylvia Tyson

CHAPTER 1

CAN YA DANCE TO IT?

SONG ANECDOTES

Some of the songs mentioned here have been hits, or "big" songs. Others are included because of an interesting anecdote. Some of the writers talk about the spark or initial inspiration for a particular song.

A song anecdote? I was sitting in a carnival tent in Puerto Rico in 1981, three weeks into a wretched job as a country singer in an "urban-cowboy" tent show. I felt I'd reached the end of the line. Rains had flooded the midway for a solid week, an armed guard had shot up my '46 Martin guitar, and I hadn't written a song in over a year. I was beyond writer's block; I was in Writer's Hell. One bleak night in the dressing room I picked up a magazine with a small item about rock'n'roller Bill Haley. He died broke and alone in a little town in Rio Grande Valley in Texas. No one knew who he was. He used to go around to all-night cafés showing waitresses his old press clippings.

I felt an instant kinship with Bill's last days of desolation. I jotted down the title "Haley's Comet" on a scrap of paper. I felt a touch better. At least I'd written something; at least I'd felt something. I was on the road back. I finished the song in a New York hotel room with Dave Alvin a few years later.

—T.R.

My very first song, "You Were On My Mind," was written in the bathtub of a room in the Earle Hotel in Greenwich Village in 1962. It was the only place the cockroaches wouldn't go, so I spent a lot of time there.

An exciting time, the '60s. Everyone was writing songs—Tom Paxton, Eric Anderson, Phil Ochs, Buffy Sainte-Marie. Bob Dylan was writing about a song a day. He'd run up to you on the street and say, "I just wrote a new song. At least, I think I wrote it. I might have heard it somewheres."

I don't remember what my second song was.

—S.T.

AMAZING GRACE

Written by a former slave ship captain, John Newton, who had been transformed into a country curate and a stalwart opponent of the slave trade. For contemporary listeners a key word in "Amazing Grace" is "wretch." It is not a word we commonly use. It is quaint, it is disturbing, and it tells us that here are no greeting card sentiments.

—Peter Steinfels, *New York Times,* 1990

MELANCHOLY BABY

Ernie Burnett wrote the tune in 1911 and it became a big hit. Burnett went to war in France and fell amongst a heap of bodies. His name tags got swapped with a corpse's, so the stretcher-bearers thought he was somebody else. He wasn't able to identify himself because he lost his memory. After the war a band of entertainers visited the hospital and one of the girls sang "Melancholy Baby." Burnett suddenly shot up in bed and claimed "That's my tune!" The lead singer explained that the composer had been killed during the war. Working from the knowledge that he'd written the tune, Burnett gradually found out about his past life and was reincarnated, as it were.

—Ian Whitcomb, *After the Ball*

SONNY BOY

Al Jolson, filming in Hollywood, rang the songwriters (Buddy DeSilva, Lew Brown & Ray Henderson) one evening and demanded a song by the following morning, a song "about a kid— a boy supposed to be my son—a ballad to make people cry." They sat down to write the corniest song they could dream up—a real practical joke. The following morning they sang it into the telephone to Jolson. He loved it. "It'll be the biggest ballad I've ever sung," he said. They could hardly believe it, and could hardly stop laughing. The song sold a million copies of sheet music, and a million records.

—Attributed to Eddie Cantor, *You Must Remember This*

IT'S ALL IN THE GAME

The tune was composed in 1912 by Charles Gates Dawes, a Chicago banker who eventually wound up as vice president of the United States under Calvin Coolidge. Lyricist Carl Sigman added words thirty-nine years later.

—Bob Gilbert & Gary Theroux, *The Top Ten*

MAD DOGS AND ENGLISHMEN

My lyric writing during "The Thirties" started very satisfactorily with "Mad Dogs & Englishmen." The idea of it and the rhythm of it got into my head when I was driving, in February 1930, from Hanoi in Tonkin to Saigon. It was completed

4

without even the aid of pencil or paper. I sang it triumphantly and unaccompanied to my travelling companion on the verandah of a small jungle guest house. Not only [my companion] but the gecko lizards and the tree frogs gave every vocal indication of enthusiasm.

—Noel Coward, *The Lyrics of Noel Coward*

BEGIN THE BEGUINE

I was living in Paris at the time and somebody suggested that I go to see the Black Martiniquois, many of whom lived in Paris, do their native dance called the Beguine, in a remote nightclub on the left bank of the Seine. The moment I saw it I thought of "Begin The Beguine" as a good title for a song and put it away in a notebook, adding a memorandum as to its rhythm and tempo.

About ten years later while going around the world, we stopped at an island in the lesser Sunda Islands to the west of New Guinea, at a place called Kalabahi. A native dance was staged for us, the melody of the first four bars of which was to become my song.

—Cole Porter, *Cole Porter: A Biography*

IN THE STILL OF THE NIGHT

Imagine making L.B. Mayer cry. What could possibly top that?

—Cole Porter, *Cole Porter: A Biography*

WHITE CHRISTMAS

In 1942, Irving Berlin clomped out "White Christmas" on the piano—he was never a good player—and whined the wistful lyrics in his high, anxious voice for Bing Crosby.

Puffing on his pipe, the crooner regarded the tiny composer with amusement in his blue eyes. "I don't think you have to worry about this one, Irving," he said.

—Melanie Chandler, *As Thousands Cheer*

PARIS-MEDITERRANÉE

Travelling to Nice by train with her half-sister Simone Berteaut, Piaf was smitten by a handsome well-dressed man who shared their compartment. She leaned close to him, he took her hand, she put her head on his shoulder. When the man stepped into the corridor for a smoke, Piaf told her sister she was mad for him and would never leave him. At Marseille, the man got off the train to stretch his legs. The girls watched in astonishment from a window as two cops clapped handcuffs on him. The man turned and gave her a last smile before being led away. Piaf later told the story to Raymond Asso, who turned it into "Paris-Mediterranée." (Piaf said the moral was: Never trust a stranger on a train.)

—Gene Lees, *Singers & the Song*

THE SUNNYLAND TRAIN

The Sunnyland train was a fast train, run right out of Memphis to St. Louis on the Frisco. I started singing about it because, man, it killed peoples. They would be coming to town along those gravel roads, farmers in their wagons getting supplies for their families, and people would get caught just comin' across the tracks. The Sunnyland train killed my aunt's husband down there, comin' fast through that brush.

—Sunnyland Slim, *Deep Blues*

HOOCHIE COOCHIE MAN

Through many generations there has been people that felt like other people could tell them some of the past or the future—even back in Biblical days. Just from thinking about all those different things, I got the idea for this song. It was "Hoochie Coochie Man." Muddy [Waters] was working in this big joint at Fourteenth and Ashland [in Chicago], and I went over there to take him the song. We went in the washroom and sang it over and over 'til he got it. Then he said, "Man, when I go out there this time I'm going to give it." He went out and jumped on it, and it sounded so good the people kept on applauding and asking for more.

—Willie Dixon, *Deep Blues*

SPECIAL DELIVERY BLUES

I wrote a song called "Special Delivery Blues." My husband, Matt, had gone to the army and he told me he was going to send me a special [delivery parcel]. He never did send me a special—so I wrote a "Special Tune" and Louis [Armstrong] helped me to make the song a hit. I had King Oliver and Sidney Bechet, too. That's one of my greatest songs.

—Sippie Wallace, *Meeting The Blues*

TRAVELIN' BLUES

I wasn't accustomed to this "early to bed and early to rise" [recovering from a physical collapse brought about by overwork and overindulgence], and for months, when they were all in bed at nine sharp, I stayed up to two or three in the morning writing songs. One night I had the blues, and what I mean to tell you was I was sure enough blue, when all of a sudden a train passed. Then I decided I'd catch the very first train for Dallas and take my chance on the cemetery regardless of what my Dallas doctor told me. That was the night I wrote "Travelin' Blues" [recorded by Jimmie Rodgers].

—Shelley Lee Alley

JOHNNY B. GOODE

I guess my mother has as much right to be declared the source of "Johnny B. Goode" as

6

any other contender in that she was the one who repeatedly commented that I would be a millionaire some day.

The gateway to freedom, I was led to understand, was somewhere "close to New Orleans" where most Africans were sorted through and sold. I had driven through New Orleans on tour and I'd been told my great grandfather had lived "way back up in the woods among the evergreens," in a log cabin. I revived the era with a song about a "coloured boy named Johnny B. Goode." My first thought was to make his life follow as my own had come along, but I thought it would seem biased to white fans to say "coloured boy" and changed it to "country boy."

—Chuck Berry, *The Autobiography*

MAYBELLENE

I have never in my life met nor even known of any woman called "Maybellene." The name actually was first brought to my knowledge from a story book when I was in the third grade, of animals who bore names. Along with Tom the cat, and Donald the duck, there was Maybellene the cow. Not offending anybody, I thought, I named my girl character after a cow. In fact, the girl was to be two-timing, so it would have been worse if I had used a popular name.

—Chuck Berry, *The Autobiography*

TOO MUCH MONKEY BUSINESS

"Too Much Monkey Business" was meant to describe most of the kind of hassles a person encounters in everyday life. When I got into writing on this theory, I realized I needed over a hundred verses to portray the major areas that bug people the most. I was even making up words then, like "botheration" to emphasize the nuisances that bothered people. I tried to use (or make up) words that wouldn't be hard to decipher by anyone from the fifth grade on. I hadn't received any kickback about using "motovating" in "Maybellene," so why not compete with Noah Webster again?

—Chuck Berry, *The Autobiography*

PROMISED LAND

"No Particular Place to Go," "Nadine," "Tulane," "You Never Can Tell," and "Promised Land" were all written while I was in Springfield [Federal Medical Centre as an inmate aide]. I remember having extreme difficulty while writing "Promised Land" in trying to secure a road atlas of the United States to verify the routing of the "Po'Boy" from Norfolk, Virginia to Los Angeles. The penal institutions then were not so generous as to offer a map of any kind, for fear of providing a route for escape.

—Chuck Berry, *The Autobiography*

ALL SHOOK UP

A fellow that used to work in the Shalomar office, fellow by the name of Ralph Stanton, came in with this Coca-Cola bottle. He was told I could write a song about anything, so he made me a bet. Stanton shook the coke bottle 'til it fizzed over and dared me to write something about that. I didn't realize what the hell I was doin' until they shot that song over to Elvis and it really worked.

—Otis Blackwell, 1987

FEVER

A lot of people didn't know I wrote "Fever" 'cause I wrote it under the name John Davenport—which was my stepfather. From signing up early, down the line I had one of those "forever" [publishing] contracts, you know. I got a chance to do some writing, so I was told to use another name. Little Willie John had the first cut, then Peggy Lee jumped on it and it went all the way.

—Otis Blackwell, 1987

HANDYMAN

"Handyman" was an idea that Jimmy Jones brought to me. We fooled around with it and stuck in a few words here and there. We took him in and made the demo, [which] they wanted to release. Back then the demo had to do with splicing tapes. We had to splice that tape about twenty times before we got it to sound like something. I wanted a flute player, but he didn't show up, so I did the whistling on the record. I wanted a drummer, but the drummer didn't show up, so we found a drummer downstairs. He had an old drum that had a hole in it. That's the way MGM took it. That was the hit.

—Otis Blackwell, 1987

PRISCILLA

I read a lot of comic books 'cause at the time I wanted to be a cartoonist, 'til my eyes went really bad on me. Comic book titles would give me an idea. I used to read them a lot, not for the story but for the ideas about love. Then you add a little country bit to it. They gave me a little direction. So we made that little hit with "Priscilla," the comic book character. She was a bad little broad, too!

—Otis Blackwell, 1987

HOUND DOG

We saw Big Mama [Thornton] and she knocked me cold. She looked like the biggest, baddest, saltiest chick you would ever see. And she was mean, a "lady bear," as they used to call 'em. She must have been 350 pounds, and she had all these scars all over her face. I had to write a song for her that basically said, "Go fuck yourself." But how do you do that without actually saying it? And how to do it telling a story? I couldn't just have a song full of expletives—"You ain't nothin' but a motherfucker."

—Jerry Leiber (Leiber & Stoller), 1990

KANSAS CITY

"Hound Dog" took like twelve minutes. That's not a complicated piece of work. But the rhyme structure was difficult. Also the metric structure of the music was not easy. "Kansas City" was maybe eight minutes, if that. Writing the early blues was spontaneous. You can hear the energy in the work.

—Jerry Leiber (Leiber & Stoller), 1990

GOOD GOLLY MISS MOLLY

I was working at the Greyhound bus station in Macon, Georgia, oh my Lord, back in 1955. I was only twenty-four, washing dishes. I couldn't talk back to my boss, man. He would bring all these pots back for me to wash, and one day I said, "I've got to do something to stop this man bringing back all these pots for me to wash," and I said, "a wop bop alu bop a wop bam boom, take 'em out!" and that's what I meant at the time. And so I wrote "Good Golly Miss Molly" and "Long Tall Sally" in that kitchen.

—Little Richard, 1970

LONG TALL SALLY

Sally used to come back with all of this whiskey, and she'd get drunk, and she was tall and ugly, man, that was an ugly woman. She was so ugly people used to turn their heads, she didn't have but two teeth and they were on each side of her tongue, and she was cockeyed. so we used to say, "Long Tall Sally, she's built for speed."

—Little Richard, 1970

TUTTI FRUTTI

"Tutti Frutti" really started the races being together. Because when I was a boy, the white people would sit upstairs and the blacks was downstairs. But the white kids would jump over the balcony and come down where I was and dance with the blacks. We started that merging all across the country. From the git-go, my music was accepted by the whites.

—Little Richard, 1990

PAPA'S GOT A BRAND NEW BAG

On playback [in the studio], when I saw the speakers jumping, vibrating in a certain way, I knew that was it: deliverance. What I started on "Out of Sight" I took all the way on "Papa's Got a Brand New Bag." Later they said it was the beginning of funk.

—James Brown, 1994

HOLD ON, I'M COMING

With "Hold On, I'm Coming," the Sam and Dave hit, I had the horn riffs first. So one day I was at the piano, and David Porter and I were working on something, and David goes to the john. Suddenly I struck a groove, and it looks like it's taking David forever. I yelled, "David, c'mon man! I got something," and he said, "Hold on, I'm coming!" Then he ran out of the john with his pants down to his knees and ran to the piano yelling, "That's it, That's it!"

—Isaac Hayes, 1994

FOLSOM PRISON BLUES

I went inside the movies at the base theatre in 1953 [when he was in the armed forces], and there was a movie called *Inside the Walls of Folsom Prison*. It was a big movie during that time. I couldn't get it off my mind. I went back to my barracks, and I started writing lyrics. I don't remember what my first lines were. I'd just seen this movie and felt what it was like to be in prison through the prisoners and this story. I thought, "I'm going to write this song as if I'm a criminal. What could be the worst thing a criminal could do? Shoot a man just to watch him die." That's where those lines came from.

—Johnny Cash, *Set Your Guitars and Banjos on Fire*

BLUE SUEDE SHOES

I remember the guys in the Air Force saying, "Don't step on my blue suede shoes." I thought it was a good line and told Carl [Perkins] he should put it into a song. But he wrote it. It's all his song.

—Johnny Cash, 1973

I felt out of place when "Blue Suede Shoes" was Number One. I stood on the Steel Pier in 1956 in Atlantic City, followed Frank Sinatra there. And the Goodyear blimp flew over with my name in big lights: APPEARING TONIGHT AT THE STEEL PIER, CARL PERKINS. And I stood there and shook and actually cried. That should have been something that would elevate a guy to say, "Well, I've made it." But it put fear in me.

—Carl Perkins, 1990

AT THE HOP

In 1957, Danny and the Juniors played me a song called "Doin' The Bop." I thought the Bop was outdated. I suggested "At The Hop." They changed it. It went to number one. That's my big contribution to music history.

—Dick Clark, 1994

'TIL I KISSED YOU

I wrote "'Til I Kissed You" about a girl I met in Australia. Her name was Lillian, and she was very, very inspirational. I was married, but. . . . I wrote the song about her on the way back home.

—Don Everly, 1986

CATHY'S CLOWN

Part of the inspiration for "Cathy's Clown" was the "Grand Canyon Suite" domp-de-domp-de-da-da-da, boom chaka boom. And back then I had a girlfriend called Catherine.

—Don Everly, 1986

DIANA

I wrote it to impress a girl. She wasn't impressed, until it was a million seller.

—Paul Anka, 1994

THAT'LL BE THE DAY

Buddy [Holly] and Jerry Allison had seen a movie called *The Searchers* with John Wayne. If you've seen that movie you'll know that John Wayne is always saying, "That'll be the day." Buddy and J.A. got the idea for the title from that.

—Sonny Curtis, 1986

(OH) PRETTY WOMAN

My wife was going to town and I asked her, "Do you need any money?" Bill Dees was there and he said, "A pretty woman never needs any money." And then he said, "Hey, how about that for a song title?" I said, "No, that won't make it, but 'Pretty Woman' will." So by the time my wife got back from the grocery store, we'd written "(Oh) Pretty Woman" and played it for her.

—Roy Orbison, *The Top Ten*

THE WANDERER

That was about a kid in my neighbourhood who had tattoos all over his body. He had "Flo" tattooed on his left arm and "Mary" on his right, and every time he'd go out with a different chick he'd add her name to his collection. If things got bad, he'd have a name covered up with a panther or a rose or something. He got "Rosie" tattooed on his chest. It's crazy but we all kind of looked up to him, and my friend Ernie Maresca wrote a song about the guy.

—Dion, *The Top Ten*

ABRAHAM, MARTIN AND JOHN

It's three minutes of hope. It says you can kill the dreamer, but not the dream.

—Dion, 1994

SHOP AROUND

Some songs have taken me five years to write. "Shop Around" took me five minutes. I originally wrote it for someone else. It was an assignment.

—Smokey Robinson, 1976

THE LOCOMOTION

[Little] Eva took babysitting jobs, one of which was with Gerry Goffin and Carole King. Eva often sang to herself, imitating her favourite performers, such as Dee Dee Sharp. One night Gerry and Carole overheard "Mashed Potato Time" wafting out from inside the house. They were impressed with Eva's voice. "You should be cutting demos," they said. Carole sat down at the piano, and as she played, Eva began inventing dance steps. They reminded Gerry of the movement of a train. He sketched out some lyrics, and within a few minutes "The Locomotion" was on paper.

—Bob Gilbert & Gary Theroux, *The Top Ten*

BLOWIN' IN THE WIND

I wrote it in a café across the street from the Gaslight. Although I thought it was special, I didn't know to what degree. I wrote it for the moment, ya know.

I remember running into Peter, of Peter, Paul & Mary, on the street after they recorded it. "Man," he said, "you're going to make five thousand dollars." And I said, "What?" Five thousand dollars, it seemed like a million at the time. He said, "It's amazing, man. You really hit it big." Of course I'd been playing the song for a while anyway and people had always responded

to it in a positive way, to say the least. Money was never a motivation to write anything. I never wrote anything with "this is gonna be a hit or this isn't"-type attitude. I'm not that smart, anyway.

—Bob Dylan

EVE OF DESTRUCTION

I was in bed. My parents were asleep. I woke my mom up at three in the morning and said, "You'll never believe what just came through to me," and I showed her the lyrics to "Eve of Destruction." She said, "Be quiet, you'll wake your father up."

—P.F. Sloan, 1991

FOUR STRONG WINDS

This is a song that started it all for me, in 1963. We used to hang out in the village at The Kettle of Fish, a neat little bar. Used to scrape up our beer money and hang out there. There was this kid from Hibbing, Minnesota named Bob Dylan used to come in and ask, "Got a cigarette? Can I borrow your pick? Borrow your guitar? Borrow five dollars?" Once he said, "I just wrote this song, you gotta hear it." I said, "Okay, Bob, go head on." He sang me "Blowin' in the Wind." I thought, boy, that is a great song, but, shit, I can do that. So I went over to my manager Albert

Grossman's house and I wrote this song that afternoon. It paid the mortgage on the farm.

—Ian Tyson, 1987

GREENBACK DOLLAR

"Greenback Dollar" was written by a dude named Ken Ramsey and was originally a Marty Robbins gunfighter type ballad. He sang it to me one time and it stuck in my ear. Barry McGuire and myself and a few other guys were all pooling our money doing laundry at the laundromat and sitting around drinking wine. Barry reminded me of that song, but we couldn't remember it, so I took it and re-wrote it on the spot.

I played it in the Troubadour a few days later and John Stewart, who had just joined the Kingston Trio, heard it and asked if they could do it. I said, "Hey, man, you guys can do a whole album." I checked with Ken Ramsey, and he approved the re-write so it was copyrighted as a dual writing effort, but we actually didn't write it together.

—Hoyt Axton, 1976

SUZANNE

Suzanne had a room on a waterfront street in the port of Montreal. Everything happened just as it was put down. She was the wife of a man I knew. Her hospitality was immaculate. Some months later I sang it to Judy Collins over the telephone. The publishing rights were lost in New York City but it is probably appropriate that I don't own this song. Just the other day I heard some people singing it on a ship in the Caspian Sea.

—Leonard Cohen, 1975

MY FATHER

The night I went home from the hospital [1950, recovering from polio], I slept in my parents' bed. Trying to keep my breath even and my eyes still under my eyelids, I pretended that I was asleep when they came into the room to look at me. Through my eyelashes I watched my father's face. He sat with his head turned toward me [Charles Collins was blind since childhood], a curiously tranquil look on his face. I felt a sense of peace from him there in the dimly lit room. Years later when I wrote my song about him, "My Father," the look on his face that night came into my mind. In that look were all the hopes and promises he had for me, and for himself. He never heard this song. He died three weeks after I wrote it.

—Judy Collins, *Follow Your Heart*

THE WRECK OF THE EDMUND FITZGERALD

In personal terms, I think "The Wreck of the Edmund Fitzgerald" is the best I've ever written for both music and content. I first read of that shipwreck in Newsweek in October, 1975, then started the song. It took me three days, working eighteen hours a day. Different producers have wanted to make a movie based on the song, but a Women's Committee in Madison, Wisconsin, made up of the widows of the men who drowned asked me not to give my permission. I didn't need any further money, mileage or publicity for it, and those women have feelings too, so I promised them I'd stay out of it.

—Gordon Lightfoot, 1981

MacARTHUR PARK

We did it pretty much as an experiment. I was asked to do that by [producer] Bones Howe. He asked, "Can you do something that suggests movements in the classical sense that a symphony or sonata has movements?"

—Jimmy Webb, 1994

STILL WITHIN THE SOUND OF MY VOICE

My father was a Baptist minister. We used to drive along at night down in the panhandle of Texas and down in Oklahoma, and my dad would always be listening to those radio preachers. This disembodied voice coming out of nowhere. . . . There was this one guy from Del Rio, Texas who used to say, "For those of you within the sound of my voice. . . ." That phrase stuck in my head.

—Jimmy Webb, 1994

THE BAND PLAYED WALTZING MATILDA

I think the first song where I began to get my craft together was "The Band Played Waltzing Matilda." I wrote that song in 1972 and it was the first time I had approached a really serious subject. I used to write a lot of humorous songs, because as a migrant to Australia [from Scotland] I could see a lot of humorous things. The reaction to that convinced me I should write a few more serious songs.

—Eric Bogle, 1985

BUD THE SPUD

When my song "Bud the Spud" was a hit, they gave me a big parade in Charlottetown, P.E.I., with me perched on the back of a truck full of potatoes. The Minister of Agriculture gave me a gold-plated spud, and thanked me for my contribution to the Island's potato industry. I guess I didn't feel like reminding them that the time before when I'd been in the city I'd had to sleep in the jail because there wasn't anywhere else for fellers with no money.

—Stompin' Tom Connors, 1983

HELP!

When "Help!" came out in 1965, I was actually crying out for help. It was my "fat Elvis" period. You see the movie. He/I is very fat, very insecure and he has completely lost himself, and I am singing about when I was so much younger, looking back at how easy it was. Now I may be very positive–yes, yes–but…but I also go through deep depressions where I would like to jump out the window. It becomes easier to deal with as I get older; I don't know whether you learn control, or when you grow up, you calm down a little. Anyway, I was fat and depressed, and I was crying out for help.

—John Lennon

IN MY LIFE

It was the first song I wrote that was consciously about my life. Before, we were just writing songs à la Everly Brothers, Buddy Holly–pop songs with no more thought to them than that. The words were almost irrelevant. "In My Life" started as a bus journey from my house at 250 Menlowe Avenue to town, mentioning all the places I could recall. I wrote it all down and it

was boring. So I forgot about it, and laid back and these lyrics started coming to me about friends and lovers of the past.

—John Lennon

NORWEGIAN WOOD

I was trying to write about an affair without letting me wife know I was writing about an affair, so it was gobbledygook. I was sort of writing from my experiences, girls' flats, things like that.

—John Lennon, 1971

MICHELLE

Paul [McCartney] and I were staying somewhere, and he walked in and hummed the first few bars, with the words, you know [first verse of "Michelle"], and he says, "Where do I go from here?" I had been listening to Nina Simone—I think it was "I Put a Spell On You." There was a line in it that went, "I love you, I love you, I love you." That's what made me think of the middle eight for "Michelle": "I love you, I love you, I lo-o-ove you."

—John Lennon

YESTERDAY

I had a piano by my bedside, and I must have dreamed it, because I tumbled out of bed and put my hands on the piano keys and I had a tune in my head. It was just all there, a complete thing. I couldn't believe it. It came too easy. In fact, I didn't believe I'd written it. I thought maybe I'd heard it before, it was some other tune, and I went around for weeks playing the chords of the song for people, asking them, "Is this *like* something? I think I've written it."

—Paul McCartney, 1985

I did the tune easily and then the words took about two weeks, because it was all "scrambled eggs, I love your legs" for awhile, and then I thought no, it's too beautiful a tune, can't have scrambled eggs. I never seriously intended to.

—Paul McCartney, 1978

HEY JUDE

I happened to be driving out to see Cynthia Lennon. I think it was just after John and she had broken up, and I was quite mates with Julian [their son]. He's a nice kid, Julian. And I was going out in me car just vaguely singing this song, and it was like, "Hey Jules." I dont know why. It was just this thing, you know, "Don't make it bad/Take a sad song . ." and then I thought a better name was Jude. A bit more country and western for me.

—Paul McCartney, 1974

LET IT BE

I had a dream one night about my mother. She died when I was fourteen, so I hadn't really heard from her in quite a while. It gave me some strength. "In my darkest hour, Mother Mary comes to me." I get dreams with John in them, and my Dad. It's very nice because you meet them again. It's wondrous. It's like magic. Of course, you're not meeting them. You're meeting yourself, or whatever.

—Paul McCartney, 1986

MY SWEET LORD/HE'S SO FINE

I obviously wasn't consciously aware of the similarity [between "My Sweet Lord" and "He's So Fine"]. It would have been dead easy for me to have changed a note here or there. I had just heard "Oh Happy Day" [by the Edwin Hawkins Singers], and if there was any song "My Sweet Lord" was inspired by, it was that one. I didn't feel guilty about the [court] decision, but the whole thing made me sort of paranoid. I didn't even want to touch the guitar or piano—maybe I'd be touching somebody else's note.

—George Harrison, 1979

SOCIETY'S CHILD

I was fourteen when I had my first hit song called "Society's Child." I woke up one morning to discover that audiences twice my age were hanging on my every word. Critics would ask me to explain an abstract lyric from my album, and all I could do was smile mysteriously. Three years after "Society's Child" I left the music industry feeling like a fraud. It wasn't until I'd written "Jesse" and then "Stars" that I felt qualified to call myself a songwriter.

—Janis Ian, 1990

AT SEVENTEEN

I think "At Seventeen" is a good song. It does what a good song should do, which is strike a nerve, communicate to any age group, cross class and cultural boundaries. . . . It may make some difference to some kid in junior high.

—Janis Ian, *The Top Ten*

When I wrote "At Seventeen" I'd been a professional songwriter for over ten years. I knew I had something special after the first two lines, and I also knew it would take some time. It took four months, and I've never regretted them. In fact, I sometimes wonder if I should have taken longer.

—Janis Ian, 1990

SHE'S A LADY

"She's a Lady" is probably my most chauvinist song. There's no way to defend it. When I sing it,

I "tongue-in-cheek" it, because I don't believe it, but I do feel terribly guilty about that song. I wrote it on assignment for Tom Jones, and it fits him.

—Paul Anka, 1979

YOU'RE HAVING MY BABY

The initial rap on that song was understandable, especially in the light of the abortion issue. For a while, I just wanted to explain. I seriously considered releasing a follow-up single, "I'm Killing My Baby," but you can't please everybody, and you can't put out a pamphlet of explanation with every record. It's something you have to feel, and gradually, people who got past the title came to understand what I really meant.

—Paul Anka, 1976

COPACABANA

"Copacabana" was the biggest hit I ever had, and it was also the biggest surprise, because we didn't write it to be that kind of hit. I mean, I don't know if I could get through another year of singing "Copacabana" all the way through.

—Barry Manilow, 1988

JOY TO THE WORLD

I saw that in Singapore and Malaysia the song was number one. That made me feel great, because I could imagine all those little kids with holes in their shirts and no shoes rockin' around singin' "Jeremiah was a bullfrog." That cracked me up.

—Hoyt Axton

KILLING ME SOFTLY WITH HIS SONG

I remember Johnny Mercer said before he died, "How the hell can you write a song with the word killing in it?" There was also a whole diatribe against me and the song in some magazine . . . about how dare I do this to the language, and stuff like that. People can be so rigid sometimes.

—Norman Gimbel, 1978

IN THE SHAPE OF A HEART

I wrote it about my wife committing suicide in the '70s, but it could be about any relationship that didn't quite make it. And even though it's also partially about the futility that arises out of not having words that can adequately describe these things, I do happen to like the lyrics.

—Jackson Browne, 1993

RAPE ME

Basically I was trying to write a song that supported women and dealt with the issue of rape. Over the last few years, people have had such a hard time understanding what our message is,

what we're trying to convey, that I just decided to be as bold as possible. How hard should I stamp this point? How big should I make the letters?

—Kurt Cobain, 1993

RUBY

The song happened so fast to me. I wrote it between my home and my office which are about eight miles apart. I wanted my wife Doris to hear it, so I sat her down and played it for her. After listening to it she said, "That's awful! That's the most morbid song I've ever heard!"

—Mel Tillis, 1977

L.A. FREEWAY

I was playing with a little string band, and we were coming back late at night from San Diego to Long Beach in the back of this old '56 Cadillac, I remember, and I was dozing and I kind of woke up and turned to Suzanna and said, "If I can just get off this L.A. Freeway without getting killed or caught," and it just struck me what I'd said and I wrote it down right then, and put it in my pocket. I carried it around for two years before I wrote the song.

—Guy Clark, 1989

18

DESPERADOS

That's about a guy who lived at my grandmother's hotel in west Texas, an old bachelor who had drilled oil wells all over the world all his life. During World War II, my dad was overseas and he sort of was my father figure. He taught me how to whittle and took me around with him. He drilled the first wells in Colombia and Venezuela and he'd been in Iran and Iraq in the '20s and wound up in west Texas.

—Guy Clark, 1989

TEXAS 1947

When I was young I lived in a small town in west Texas, and my playmate's father worked for the railroad. One day we got the word his streamlined train was coming through. Up until then all we'd seen was pictures of them in *Life* magazine, so the whole town turned up. It was like a moon shot or something. Everybody just stood there at the depot and watched it go by. It just roared right through—didn't stop. Everybody said, "Yep, sure was."

—Guy Clark, 1989

MR. BOJANGLES

It didn't start with Bill Robinson being Bojangles. It started with the term Bojangles from minstrel shows where they had a guy who danced who was called a Bojangles, and then from that, Bill Robinson took the name, Bill 'Bojangles' Robinson, and from then, the guy I met in a New Orleans jail as called a Bonjangles because someone related it to Bill Robinson., so they called him, "Hey Bonjangles." Because of that, I wrote a song about him. The last time I was in New Orleans I was walking down the street and there was an old street dancer and he came up and he said he was Bojangles. So the cycle goes.

—Jerry Jeff Walker, 1984

COUNTRY ROADS

The second verse of the tune was a bit risqué—making reference to naked ladies and such—so Bill and Taffy [Danoff] figured their song would never get played on the radio. They played it for John [Denver], and as he recalled, "I flipped." The three of them stayed up until six a.m. changing words and moving lines around.

—Bob Gilbert & Gary Thefort, *The Top Ten*

SONG OF THE SOUTH

"Song of the South" is a little cerebral yet still funky and palatable to the public. Alabama left out the verse about malnutrition—a wise move.

—Bob McDill, 1990

19

GOD SHUFFLED HIS FEET

I started out with the idea of a boy with blue hair, and a bunch of people sitting around having a picnic with God in the very early days of human history, and wondered how the hell that was ever going to come together in one lyric.

—Brad Roberts (Crash Test Dummies), 1994

HEY MISTER

That's what "Hey Mister" is all about. . . . You always gonna have the poor but ain't no need to have no hungry people. . . . We *pay* people *not* to grow food. Ain't no reason for us to have hungry people.

—Ray Charles, 1973

WITH PEN IN HAND

A very good friend of mine was in the process of getting divorced. He had three kids, and I'd known the family for a long time. I started thinking how bad it was going to be for him and his wife and especially the children, because it's the kids that suffer the most in a divorce. The more I thought about it, the more the fragments of thought began to rhyme in my head. I was living in Dothan, Alabama at the time and commuting to Nashville. About halfway to Nashville I had the song written. Melody, lyrics, and I could even hear the arrangement. I pulled over

on the freeway, got the guitar out of the trunk and began playing the song. It was about eleven o'clock at night, rain pouring down, hardly anyone on the freeway, and I was sitting there writing "With Pen In Hand."

—Bobby Goldsboro, 1977

NEW WAY TO FLY

I was driving down the road, and I looked over and saw these birds lined up on a telephone wire. Everybody's seen that, but for some reason I connected that to people in a bar and came up with a few lines. . . . "Birds on the High Line, they're lined up at night time at the bar. They all once were lovebirds, now bluebirds are all that they are."

I brought those few lines to Garth [Brooks]. We wrote a verse and a chorus, and then he drove home to Oklahoma for Christmas. He said he would be singing the song in the car, stop [singing], and once he looked over and saw the birds again, he'd start over. He sang it all the way back to Oklahoma.

—Kim Williams, 1994

THE GAMBLER

One August afternoon I had a long conversation with Bob McDill about writer's block. I had been blocked for about six months, pretty much since my father had died. I was so caught up in my own feelings, I guess, that nothing was translating onto paper. That day, Bob showed me the open D tuning on guitar. He told me that this tuning had helped him simplify songwriting by making everything so precise and so compact that it wouldn't let him do anything fancy and screw up. I made the long walk home, sat down at the typewriter, tuned my guitar to the D tuning, and in two hours, I wrote three songs. One of them was "The Gambler."

—Don Schlitz, 1980

SHORT PEOPLE

I didn't like all that attention. It was a pain in the ass to me. I went to a doctor, and there was this receptionist who was 4'11" and she said, "Oh yeah, you wrote 'Short People.'" She didn't like it. I said, "Jeez, I'm sorry I ever wrote it!" She had me right there at the table. Anyway, I'm not sorry I wrote it.

—Randy Newman, 1979

TO ALL THE GIRLS I'VE LOVED BEFORE

Not long ago one of those supermarket newspapers had a full-page story about the face of Jesus suddenly appearing on the outside wall of a grocery store in South America after a dra-

matic rain storm. Hundreds of people came to pray to the image of Jesus, and some of the sick went away cured. A few days later, following another thunderstorm, a new figure appeared on the wall beside Jesus. It was Julio Iglesias. What had happened, the rain had washed off the coat of whitewash that had covered a poster for "To All The Girls I've Loved Before." The supermarket headline said, "That's not Jesus—it's just old Willie."

—Willie Nelson, *Willie: An Autobiography*

SILVER BLUE

I wrote that in the studio sitting at the piano while I was doing my first album. I came home and played it for my girlfriend at the time [Linda Ronstadt], and it seemed to have a very upsetting effect on her, so I thought, "This is great. This is a song that makes people cry—makes them feel vague."

—J.D. Souther, 1980

OL' 55

When the Eagles did "Ol' 55," it was all right. It was kind of clean, like it was shrink-wrapped. I would've put a little more hair on it myself.

—Tom Waits, 1980

EVERY BREATH YOU TAKE

"Every Breath You Take" I consider to be really quite an evil song about surveillance and controlling another person. The fact that it was couched in seductive and romantic disguise made it all the more sinister for me. Having lived through that feeling in quite a real way and seen the other side, I think the highest tribute you can pay another person is to say, "I don't own you—you're free."

—Sting, 1984

PERFECT WORLD

Frantz: I wrote the lyrics to "Perfect World" a long time ago. David found them filed and changed them around a little bit to make them fit the song. He said I wrote them in 1974. He couldn't think of anything to work with a melody, so he used those.

Byrne: It was meant to be metaphysical, people's activities or lives as songs. I can imagine somebody asking themselves, "Am I always going through the same routines?" I played it for Chris, and boy was he surprised.

—Chris Frantz & David Byrne (Talking Heads), 1985

MONEY FOR NOTHING

"Money For Nothing" was inspired by an appliance store employee I heard talking about the MTV rock stars on a row of display televisions. I borrowed a bit of paper and actually wrote that song while I was in the store. I wanted to use the language the guy really used. It was more real. I did use "that little faggot," but there were a couple of good "motherfuckers" which mean nothing to you in a hardware store in New York City, but which might mean something to people who live in Tallahassee. There's no way I could expect people to receive that in the spirit it's intended. They'd probably think I was just being vulgar. Still, if we have time, I might record a version with the real language, just to have it for myself.

—Mark Knopfler, 1985

EVERYBODY HURTS

Michael [Stipe] came up with the lyrics in the time it took us to go through the song three or four times. None of us really thought it would see the light of day. It was kind of a joke song at first, but Michael, in my opinion, is the best lyricist alive, and that song's a great example of how he polished a turd.

—Bill Berry (R.E.M.), 1994

SHE BOP

It was about more than just masturbation. It's like how you're told everything is no good, and that God is up there watching everything you're doing and come on! God's got nothing better to do than watch what we're doing with our genitals? You know, with all the things that are happening in the world today, war and hunger and earthquakes and tornados? And it's not a bad thing to love yourself a little bit, is it?

—Cyndi Lauper, 1987

DANCING IN THE DARK
It was just like my heart spoke straight through my mouth, without even having to pass through my brain. The chorus just poured out of me.

—Bruce Springsteen, 1987

RAIN ON THE SCARECROW
I think on that record I really started taking a lot more responsibility. People out here [in Indiana] were losing farms at a rate of one every five minutes, and it was something that touched my own family. It wasn't enough any more just to write pop songs about being a kid in Indiana or whatever. I found that not only did I have something to say, but after all I'd been through, as crazy as it sounds, I felt later I was just beginning to really learn how to write songs.

—John Cougar Mellencamp, 1987

LUKA
When "Luka" went to Number Three, I hired a detective to track him [her father] down. I knew he lived in California. He turned out to be a bohemian guy who played jazz piano. He knew who I was. When I first called him on the phone, he went, "Luka, that's you?" He was happy I'd become a musician. He was adopted too, and he only recently became aware that his natural mother played drums in a touring jazz band in the '30s and '40s. He sent me all these pictures of her and I immediately saw myself. She has this long face, a way of standing and tilting her head, which helped explain a few things for me. The whole thing really affected my attitude in making the next record. I felt, if the musical impulse is strong enough to go through at least three generations, why not release a bit and have some confidence?

—Suzanne Vega, 1990

GIVE ME HIS LAST CHANCE
The biggest reward for me is to touch somebody's life with a song. We were flying to a gig and my drummer and I sat down next to a lady who started asking us questions. She found out who I was and that I did the song, "Give Me His Last Chance," and she went berserk.

It was almost embarrassing, because she literally started screaming. I thought it was just another starstruck sort of deal, but it wasn't. She said she had been in a bad relationship she stayed in, not because of love but because she felt secure. Then this other guy who'd fallen for her brought her a tape of "Give Me His Last Chance." She ended up going out with him, and they fell in love, and now that song is their song.

—Lionel Cartwright, 1990

MY SISTER

When I was in high school, I wrote stories. I wrote a couple of really good ones that won a couple of awards. But now, "My Sister" has influenced people in a way I've never seen before. While I was at a radio station in Arizona, this deejay played it on the air, and she started crying. It was amazing. And this other girl came up to me recently and said that her sister had died two months ago, and she really wanted me to sign this piece of paper that she was going to put by her grave.

—Juliana Hatfield

SUMMER OF '69

I'd have to say that "Summer of '69" is one of my favourites as far as songs I've written with Bryan Adams over the years. I think the song captures how I felt that summer as a seventeen-year-old. It was an exciting time with *Abbey Road* and Hendrix on the radio, and moon-landings on TV, and I had just begun experimenting with songwriting and recording.

—Jim Vallance, 1986

I WANT A NEW DRUG

Some people thought, "Jesus, it's a pro-drug song," or "No, it's definitely an anti-drug song." I mean, I had people, born-again people, coming up to me thinking that I was born-again somehow, that it was a very spiritual sort of Christian song.

—Huey Lewis, 1988

WE DIDN'T START THE FIRE

That song's about my life. Most of my mail I get about that song comes from teachers who have said this is the greatest teaching tool to come down the pike since *Sesame Street*, which means a lot to me, since I once wanted to be a history teacher. But I wish people could understand that I did not write that song to be a hit—I wrote that one for me. And nobody liked it at first.

—Billy Joel, 1990

IF I HAD A ROCKET LAUNCHER

When I saw the conditions people lived under in the refugee camps, it was infuriating. There was so little food that they had to eat grass. Witnessing what was going on there brought out such angry feelings in me. There were children dying of starvation every day, yet these people still had a sense of dignity about them.

"If I Had A Rocket Launcher" sums up how I felt when I was there. I didn't like the feeling of actually wanting to kill. It disturbed me deeply. But when those Guatemalan helicopters, which crossed the border illegally to shoot down innocent people in the camps, were buzzing around, I felt so helpless and full of anger. If you were there, I'm sure you'd feel the same way.

–Bruce Cockburn, 1989

CHAPTER 2

IN THE BEGINNING

BEGINNINGS AND EARLY INFLUENCES

The first song I can remember hearing was "You Are My Sunshine." My great grandmother would hold me on her lap and sing it to me in the old rocker in front of the Quebec heater. My father loved Bach organ and choral music, classical ballet music, and Gilbert & Sullivan. His hobby was going to country churches on weekends and repairing the old pump organs. I would sometimes go with him, building houses with stacks of hymn books between the pews as he worked. He always finished with "Roll Out the Barrel." During the depression he had a job as a piano demonstrator in a music store, and moonlighted playing piano for Aimee Semple McPherson's first mission in Toronto.

My mother had been a classically-trained pianist from the age of five. Her first love was the pop music of the '20s and '30s. But my strongest musical memory of her is the way she played the Chopin waltzes. When I hear them now, I am flooded with memories of that time.

–S.T.

As a child I played with miniature cowboys and Indians. I made up songs and stories about imaginary gunfights, hangings and Indian wars. All the romance, all the tragedy. I probably stole the melodies from nursery rhymes and the plots from comic books. Life was divided between "real time" and "dream time." I haven't grown up. I became a songwriter. Time is still measured between time writing songs and "other time."

I was raised on Broadway musicals and '50s "hillbilly" music. Story songs. I remember owning a Hank Williams 78 record. One night in the early '60s I heard Buck Owens and Bob Dylan played back-to-back on the radio. They sounded like wild hillbilly mystics. The announcer said they wrote their own songs. That was the first I was aware that living people actually wrote songs. Then, in 1964, I saw Dylan sing "Desolation Row" at the Hollywood Bowl. I was hooked. That was the job to have. It took me twenty years to work it out . . . to reach the point where I could call myself a songwriter.

—T.R.

There was no time when I was not fascinated by words 'going together': Lewis Carroll, Edward Lear, Beatrix Potter, all fed my childish passion, in addition to all the usual nursery rhymes that the flesh is heir to, beginning with . . . 'pat-a-cake, pat-a-cake, baker's man.'

—Noel Coward, *The Lyrics of Noel Coward*

What really hooked me was the movies. I used to go to the movies and see this magic land of people and places, and I always wanted to be part of it.

—Sammy Cahn, 1976

Our family was sort of divided up into two sides: Mama taught us kids to sing the old songs and told us long stories about each ballad, and in her way she told us over and over to always try and see the world from the other fellow's side. Meanwhile, Papa bought us all kinds of exercising rods and stretchers, and kept piles of kids boxing and wrestling out in the front yard, and taught us never and never to allow any earthly human to scare us, bully us, or run over us.

—Woody Guthrie, *Bound for Glory*, 1943

When I first wrote to RCA, I got a letter back saying they were interested, but they couldn't use me right then. Then they suggested that if I was ever in Montreal. . . .

Well, as soon as I heard that I headed for Montreal. The fare cost thirteen dollars and that was all the money I had, and so a stranger on the train offered me a part of his sandwich because I couldn't afford my own.

The man at RCA—Mr. Hugh Josephs—asked me if I had two songs I'd like to record. I said "Yes, sir!" and went right back to the hotel to write them.

—Hank Snow, 1979

When I first came to Toronto, I was in the souplines, the breadlines and the bedlines, staying at the Salvation Army, the Scott Mission, places with bugs where they'd steal your boots. The first guy out was the best dressed. I was all the time searching for something, but I didn't know what it was. I certainly didn't want a job—it was rare I'd keep a job for a week. Home to me was always something to run away from.

—Stompin' Tom Connors, 1973

My father, singing in his Irish tenor voice, performed songs of Rodgers & Hart, Irving Berlin, Cole Porter. His program was a mixture of humour and philosophy which he called his "medicine show." . . . Sometimes he did three shows a day, often in three different towns. I would stare from the wings of the auditoriums, in my mother's arms or by her side, and sing

along with the music. Then Daddy would call me out on the stage saying, "Here's my little girl, Judy." I would rush into his arms. I loved the stage lights, the faces of the people in the audience, and the thought that I was making them happy, just by being there. My father said I was a born ham.

—Judy Collins, *Trust Your Heart*

Our father was born in the nineteenth century. A lot of our friends' parents were bobby-soxers but we never had that '40s Frank Sinatra, Italian jazzy music. I guess we had everything else: classical, Stephen Foster, old show tunes, Bing Crosby, French folk songs from our mother, Gaby. And then Janey, our older sister, would bring home country and western records, Grand Ole Opry, and of course Elvis Presley. But you know, all those styles are very straight. You don't throw in fancy chords just because it's fun to do. Our music works kind of the same way.

—Kate McGarrigle, 1978

My father was a country and western freak and he road herd on the car radio whenever we went any place. We didn't get to listen to Elvis Presley. We had to listen to Ernest Tubb, Lefty Frizzell. In those days a lot of the music was pretty bad. What keeps in my mind is that the songs that attracted me were the ones that had beautiful chords, which comes right out of the religious thing, so I remember Neil Sedaka's music for instance, and the early Burt Bacharach tunes, and as far back as the Shirelles, "Baby it's You" . . . Gene Pitney, Ben E. King, some beautiful tunes where strings began to be introduced into pop music. Now, all of a sudden, I was interested.

—Jimmy Webb, 1976

My favourite singer was Tex Ritter. Still is, really. I grew up with the singing cowboys. There was a little theatre called the Tompkins Theater when I was a little kid in Brooklyn. They showed cowboys, cartoons, and gave away dishes on Thursday nights when you went in or when you won at bingo, and everybody used to go until they got a complete set. It was saucers one night, then it was cups and plates. You'd see cartoons and the cowboys. I grew up seeing people like Humphrey Bogart. But oh God, man, I dug Tex Ritter.

—Otis Blackwell, 1990

From the first time I heard voices on the radio, I was practically hypnotized. Working in the cotton fields I heard migrant pickers singing. The blacks would be singing in one field, the Mexicans singing nearby, and us local hands singing our own stuff. It was an awesome sound, all those voices blending, and it sure taught me the blues. . . . The Grand Ole Opry was a necessity on Saturday night. In the daytime I'd listen to the Light Crust Doughboys from the Baker Hotel in Mineral Wells. Hank Thompson had a show on WACO then in Waco at noon, and I listened to it every day. I loved Lefty Frizzell, Bob Wills, Floyd Tillman, Leon Payne, Hank Williams, Bill Boyd & the Cowboy Ramblers.

—Willie Nelson, 1988

People keep asking me where the blues started, and all I can say is that when I was a boy we always was singing in the fields. Not real singing, just hollerin', but we made up our songs about things that was happening to us at the time, and I think that's where the blues started.

—Son House, 1965

Back in that time [1950s] boogie woogie was very popular. I would say that boogie woogie and rhythm and blues mixed is rock & roll. Also, back in that time, black people were singing a lot of country music. You didn't see this separation of music as you do today. I'm a country music lover. I think it's true music. It's from the heart.

—Little Richard, 1990

Until the kitchen had been cleared from supper, the table cleared of homework, Barney our police dog fed, and the wood and coal in and the ashes out, we were not allowed to turn the Philco [radio] on. We took turns sharing the punishment if Mother caught us listening without permission. The beautiful harmony of the country music that KMOK radio station [in St. Louis] played was almost irresistible. Kitty Wells, Gene Autry, and Kate Smith singing love songs were popular then, along with the piano playing of Fats Waller and old World War I songs like "My Buddy" and "Fraulein," which I suppose will never leave my memory.

—Chuck Berry, *The Autobiography*

Hank Williams was the first influence.

—Bob Dylan, *In His Own Words,* 1961

I read a biography of Hank Williams which said he used to go right up to people's faces and play them, like, "Your Cheatin' Heart" and say, "That's a good one, isn't it?" That was an inspiration for me, that you could play a song like doing a card trick.

—Elvis Costello, 1988

I listen to the radio, and I like all kinds of music, you know, but I do like to hear from people who

have been there. That's just my personal taste. Now, Hank Williams has been there.

—Leonard Cohen, 1988

I liked Hank Williams back in the '50s. Hank Williams never got played on any crossover, it was just hard country. When his songs were popular, they were sung by Jo Stafford or Tony Bennett. I'd tell people, "God, you oughta hear the guy who really sings 'em." They did and they didn't like him, but to me one was like bland mayonnaise and the other was like salsa.

—Kris Kristofferson, 1990

When she was young, my grandmother was a cook in migrant camps in Colorado and Wyoming, and she learned a lot of country and western songs. My mom would listen to "The Ernest Tubb Show" along with Mexican radio. She'd take me downtown to the Million Dollar Movie House where there'd be variety shows with Mexican singers and mariachi bands, and at the climax, the star singer would come out on stage on this huge white stallion—right on stage!—and sing into the mike. I always remembered that.

—Louie Perez, 1987

I wasn't into the blues real heavy. Back then

they were called "race records." I didn't hear many people live. The only person I really remember hearing live was the first time I ever went over to New York from Brooklyn and I saw Count Basie at the Paramount Theatre. My sister-in-law took me. That must have been in the late 1940s. That was the first time I'd ever seen New York at night, and that stage was goin' up and down. I wasn't into jazz that much, though. I was really mostly goin' to the movies or listenin' to the cowboys on the radio or listenin' to the blues, what they call rhythm and blues now. It was all called blues at that time.

—Otis Blackwell, 1990

There was a station in Memphis that had the hillbilly stuff, and one in Arkansas that had all the black music—what they used to call race records when I was growing up—like the Golden Gate Quartet, Mahalia Jackson, Sister Rosetta Thorpe. It was the black and the blues, living alongside the Mississippi River as we did, that was more of an influence on me than I'll ever really know.

—Johnny Cash, 1990

When I began to listen to boogie woogie and swing, my desire to hear anything without a beat diminished. I became a fan of Tampa Red,

Big Maceo, Lonnie Johnson, Arthur Crudup, Muddy Waters, Lil Green, Bee Boo, Rosetta Thorpe, and later, Louis Jordan, T-Bone Walker, Buddy Johnson, Nat Cole and Charles Brown, all of whom were black artists whose songs were only played by the black radio stations in East St. Louis.

Whenever [sisters] Thelma, Lucy and [brother] Henry bought any records, they favoured Duke Ellington, Count Basie and Tommy Dorsey. Dorsey's "Boogie Woogie" was what launched my determination to produce such music.

—Chuck Berry, *The Autobiography*

You have to understand that in the days when R&B music was the popular art form, it contained a sense of humour that is totally lacking in pop music today. There was a kind of whimsical, lighthearted characteristic to some of the writing. I've got a huge collection of stuff—I could play you examples of records that are really funny. They're not comedy records. They're still rhythm & blues records, but the people who are singing them sound like they're alive.

—Frank Zappa, 1980

In high school I was an absolute nerd. I grew

four inches in one year, dropped twenty pounds, and my co-ordination went. I mean, I couldn't get a chick with a hundred dollar bill in a Mexican whorehouse. So the whole thing of driving around in a car, and being one of the boys and getting laid, it just didn't happen to me. That's when I started playing music. I found in music you can create your own world.

—John Stewart, 1989

I spent a lot of time by myself, at my dance classes, or just writing in my notebook. Discovering folk music was another way of finding a place that wasn't violent or noisy or threatening as so much of New York can be. I was attracted to folk music for its simplicity, its timelessness, and a means of putting things together.

—Suzanne Vega, 1987

Glenn [Frey] and Jackson [Browne] and I wrote a lot of songs together—that's where it all started. The three of us were living together in this building in Echo Park, a real run-down apartment building. We had one car between us, but we also had guitars and pianos and lots of time on our hands. Sure, we influenced each other a lot, just because we were so different. Jackson was very Californian—he always had this edge of socialism about him.

Glenn was from the suburbs of Detroit—he was sort of into Detroit heavy metal music, midwestern rock & roll. I was from Texas and liked rockabilly music. We also read different things. Jackson read a lot of Spanish authors, Pablo Neruda and guys like that. I was reading a lot of Celtic poets, some German stuff and Jorge Luis Borges, who was my idol.

—J.D. Souther, 1980

I had those things [a woman, kids, a clean and orderly place] and then I decided to become a songwriter. I don't know what it was, something to do with money. Although I was being affirmed in certain circles, I couldn't pay the rent. . . . I had an enormous success at the beginning. That's always a trap; you think, "I can repeat that." This seems like a wonderful way to live. Everywhere you go people seem to be delighted to have you around. It seems more lively, but it wasn't. . . . I found myself mostly alone in cities that I didn't know very well, trying to find a date for dinner.

—Leonard Cohen, 1988

In 1964 I was working with a group in England called the Embers. We were going to do a record date and they didn't have any tunes, so the night before, I wrote two tunes. One of my songs was the one that was released. When my mother heard it on the radio, she ran screaming into the room where I was sleeping (as I normally did during the day), woke me up and said, "You're the George Gershwin of the '60s! Stop playing the drums, you'll make a fortune of money!"

—Brian Potter (Lambert & Potter), 1977

When you start writing, it doesn't matter where the first one comes from. You've got to start somewhere, right? So Andrew Oldham locked Mick [Jagger] and myself into a kitchen in this horrible little apartment we had. He said, "You ain't comin' out," and there was no way out. We were in the kitchen with some food and a couple of guitars, but we couldn't get to the john, so we had to come out with a song. In his own little way, that's where Andrew made his great contribution to the Stones. That was such a fart of an idea, that suddenly you're gonna lock two guys in a room, and they're going to become songwriters.

—Keith Richards, 1994

After I entered junior high school, I met the guys who became the Miracles. We sang all through high school and I used to write songs for us to sing. We got our audition with Jackie Wilson's manager. He used to come to town [Detroit]

because a young songwriter named Berry Gordy wrote material for most of his people. Berry was at the audition, and came outside afterwards and stopped us and said, "Where did you get the material that you sang?"

—Smokey Robinson, 1976

It was just a hobby. I don't know why I began writing. I don't think anybody really does know why they write. If they tried to think why, they probably wouldn't be able to. It's kind of like going to sleep. If you thought too much about going to sleep, you probably wouldn't be able to do that either.

—Jim Weatherly, 1975

I was using yesterday's records as blueprints, as all pop music is. All the good pop clichés had been written and there hadn't been any new ones for a while. I wanted to take some of the ready-made clichés that Goffin & King or Smokey Robinson would come up with and come up with my own photo-negative versions of them. Almost every song on my first album was an opposite—a diseased version of another song.

—Elvis Costello, 1988

One day I heard a record by the Penguins called

"Earth Angel," and everything changed. I told my friend Howie [Greenfield] that I heard something fantastic called rock & roll. Howie said "I don't like it. It's off-key. It just doesn't make it." But my enthusiasm won him over, and we began writing rock & roll songs.

—Neil Sedaka, 1976

Until about four years ago, I'd never even discussed writing with another songwriter. The only proper musical education I've had was eight years of classical piano lessons; I quit at eleven when the teacher slapped me for not practicing. I left high school in the tenth grade, and words like "simile" make my head spin. Everything I know, from guitar chords to orchestral scoring, I either taught myself or picked up along the way.

—Janis Ian, 1990

My first car was a white convertable Chevy Impala, and I would drive that thing down Kings Highway [Brooklyn] and hear my voice on the radio and just love it. One day I had a three-er . . . a triple. You know, you set your push buttons to the most popular radio stations. I pushed three of the buttons, and "The Diary" was on three radio stations at once!

—Neil Sedaka, 1976

In the beginning of my career, I was a protegé of a very brilliant songwriter, Frank Loesser, who won a Pulitzer Prize for "How to Succeed in Business." He also wrote "The Most Happy Fella," "Guys and Dolls," "Where's Charlie" . . . a Broadway legend. I would write a song and show it to him and he would go over it with a fine-tooth comb. If I got off the subject, if I didn't circle my subject and repeat it in a different way. . .metaphorically repeat the idea, but in another kind of image, I'd hear about it.

—Norman Gimbel, 1978

Thank God for the theory and harmony because it enables me to have total command at the piano . . . total finger facility. I know chord structures, harmony and rhythm and I don't have to fish around at the keyboard. Yet the Julliard training didn't spoil my taste for the simple structure of contemporary songs. The first time I heard "Earth Angel" I said, "Oh my God, I know there's only four chords, but it's marvelous and infectious." You must understand that I was a do-wop street singer. I started the Tokens at Abraham Lincoln High School in Brooklyn.

—Neil Sedaka, 1976

My father is a Baptist minister, and there is a special time in a Baptist Church when they pass the [collection] plate. The task falls to the musicians to fill up that time with something other than the gauche clatter of coins in the plates, so I began improvising hymns and hymn arrangements for that particular period of the service. It's probably the first creative music I ever did in my life. . . . Out of that I developed a real desire to create music and it provided me with a kind of basic understanding of chord structure and the way these things fit together.

—Jimmy Webb, 1976

I started off writing chamber music when I was fourteen, and I didn't write a rock & roll song until I was twenty-one or twenty-two. I'd always liked it, but I just never felt I could do it; so about that time I met Ray Collins [original member of the Mothers of Invention], and he could sing real good, so I started writing.

—Frank Zappa, 1980

I think if you listened to Puccini, Verdi, Bizet, that kind of stuff, you would find the roots of a lot of our music. Some of our songs could be arias. They're just set differently.

—Anna McGarrigle, 1978

I had to play Chopin, Beethoven, you know, the normal things. Just music lessons. Not really theory—I don't know what it is.

—Ray Charles, 1973

I guess you could call me a sentimentalist. I like Chopin or Sibelius. People who write softness, you know, and although Beethoven to me was quite heavy, he wrote some really touching songs, and I think that "Moonlight Sonata"—in spite of the fact that it would end up being very popular—it's something about that, man, you could just feel the pain that this man was goin' through. Somethin' had to be happenin' in that man. You know he was very, very lonesome when he wrote that.

—Ray Charles, 1973

I was a kid [fifteen]. When you're unsophisticated, and you don't have a great deal of training or a family tied into the business your expression is raw, but pure. I wasn't afraid to sing "Puppy Love" or "I'm Just a Lonely Boy." Those were just natural things that most guys felt at that age, and I just said them.

—Paul Anka, 1976

When I started to write and play, the main reason I did it was because there was a piano to play in the house. . . . I didn't go through looking in the mirror and doing the pop star pose or dreaming that I'd be making records and things like that. I just wrote songs for my own enjoyment, like a hobby.

—Joan Armatrading, 1984

I started off writing instrumentals. Words came much later.

—Neil Young, 1975

I blew a good thing. Those [early] songs all sounded the same and were very repetitious. The record executives forced me to stay with basically four chords: C, A minor, D minor, and G. It was very confining and they wouldn't let me change and only wanted certain kinds of lyrics and certain kinds of arrangements. When I put that G minor in "Breaking Up is Hard to Do," it caused a fury.

When the success stopped after five years [1964] I went to them and pleaded for the opportunity to do something else. They said, "No!"

—Neil Sedaka, 1986

The A&R [Artists and Repertoire] men used to be pretty omnipotent. They'd say, "That's a three-bar phrase, you can't have a three-bar phrase. Make it a four-bar phrase." I ruined some pretty good songs that way, because I believed them.

—Burt Bacharach

I noticed when an artist had a hit record, they would try to write another like it. I came to learn later that was known as the follow-up. My game was I used to write my own follow-ups. No one ever heard them. Then I would compare my follow-up with the one they came up with, and that served as my training ground. There were times when I was sixteen or seventeen that I might have had justification to say, "Hey, that time I wrote a better follow-up than they did," and that's when I had the first little spark that I might be able to do this professionally and make some money at it.

—Jimmy Webb, 1976

I didn't learn to play the piano until I was around nineteen or so. I had a piano that some girl had given me. It had been left out in the rain. It was frozen except for the black keys, so I learned how to play in F-sharp. I still play in F-sharp.

—Tom Waits, 1980

My aunt Clara dumped a sofa on my family—I was ten years old at the time—along with an old upright piano, which I remember had a mandolin pedal: the middle pedal turned the instrument into a kind of wrinkly sounding mandolin. And I just put my hands on the keyboard and I was hooked for life. You know what it's like to fall in love: you touch someone and that's it. From that day to this that's what my life's been about.

—Leonard Bernstein, 1990

I was given a songwriting contract when I was about twenty-one. I'd sit on a bus stop bench on Santa Monica Boulevard and feel like I was so stupid—I didn't feel like I was qualified to be a songwriter yet. I still feel as though I snuck in, that as soon as they find out, they're going to ask me to leave, but I guess I kind of grew into it—it's like I got a suit, then I grew into it.

—Tom Waits, 1980

Tim [Hardin] talks about Lenny Bruce buying him a piano and giving Tim a room in his home so Tim could write and record. He said, "That's where fifty percent of the tunes you hear off me were written."

—Phil Freeman, liner notes, *Tim Hardin: The Homecoming Concert*, 1980

Influences? Lightnin' Hopkins, Robert Frost, Bob Dylan, Edgar Allan Poe.

—Townes Van Zandt, 1990

In '65 or '66 I first ran into Townes Van Zandt and Jerry Jeff Walker. Townes was just starting to write and Jerry had been writing for a while. It was the first time I heard somebody do something that I felt like I wanted to do.

—Guy Clark, 1984

My sister was two years older than me, and she hung around with those guys who wrote songs and did a lot of civil rights stuff. I started hanging around with them and writing songs when I was fifteen. We gravitated toward Bob Dylan, Pete Seeger kind of stuff.

—Jackson Browne, 1989

I was a janitor. My first job was when they [Bob Dylan and his band] recorded *Blonde on Blonde* and I was the only songwriter allowed at the session. He would go in there and write all night long, and record in the morning, after the musicians played cards all night.

—Kris Kristofferson, 1990

People have this idea that I was a poet who decided to be a songwriter, when actually, it was the other way around: I came to poetry through music. Music was my first job when I was sixteen playing rhythm guitar in a country band. In university, I remember going to the Harvard library, and I listened to all the folk music records they had over the course of a month.

—Leonard Cohen, 1988

Back in high school I was the only kid with a leather jacket, slicked-back hair, and Banlon shirts who wrote poetry.

—Bob Seger, 1983

Most adolescents go through that period of trying to write poetry. I just never grew out of it.

—Billy Bragg, 1986

The first thing that turned me on to singing music was Odetta. I heard a record of hers in a record store. I saved the money I had made working on my daddy's truck and bought a Silvertone guitar from Sears & Roebuck. I was twelve.

—Bob Dylan, 1978

I moved to Lubbock [Texas] when I was about ten and that was when I first picked up a guitar and there was a guy down the street that showed me a few Buddy Holly songs. At that time I didn't even know Holly was from Lubbock. It was kind of like a well-kept secret, because the town is right in the Baptist belt and didn't want to have anything to do with rock & roll. Because of that atmosphere, it kind of led people to sit around back rooms and basements and play music a lot.

—Joe Ely, 1986

When I started writing those kinds of songs, there wasn't anybody doing things like that. . . . Woody Guthrie had done similar things but he hadn't really done that type of song. Besides, I had learned from Woody Guthrie and knew I could sing anything he had done. But now times had changed and things would be different. He contributed a lot to my style lyrically and dynamically but my musical background had been different, with rock & roll and rhythm & blues playing a big part earlier on. Actually, attitude had more to do with it than technical ability and that's what the folk movement lacked. In other words, I played all the folk songs with a rock & roll attitude.

—Bob Dylan, *CBS Biography*

When I started listening to records as a kid it was The Band, Bob Dylan and Creedence Clearwater Revival. I think the images were so strong that I could visualize a world that I wanted to be a part of—being with women in sleeping bags, elephants in the backyard, everybody getting stoned—I bought it all and couldn't wait to grow into that world. When I got older I realized what the songs were really about, but it was too late to turn back. Fortunately.

—Dan Zanes, 1990

I knew that when I got into folk music, it was more of a serious type of thing. The songs are filled with more despair, more sadness, more triumph, more faith in the supernatural, much deeper feelings: "My Bonnie Love is Lang A Growing," "Go Down Ye Bloody Roses," even "Jesse James" or "Down By The Willow Garden," definitely not pussy stuff. There is more real life in one line than there was in all the rock & roll themes. I needed that. Life is full of complexities and rock & roll didn't reflect that. It was just "Put on a Happy Face" and "Ride Sally Ride," there was nothing even resembling "Sixteen Snow White Horses" or "See That My Grave Is Kept Clean" in even the vaguest way. If I did anything, I brought one to the other. There was nothing serious happening in music when I started, not even the Beatles. They were singing "Love Me Do." And Marvin Gaye didn't do "What's Going on" until the '70s.

—Bob Dylan, *CBS Biography*

I was tellin' somebody that when you go to see a folk singer now, you hear somebody singin' his own songs. And the person says, "Yeah, well, you started that." And in a sense, it's true. But I never would have written a song if I didn't play all them old folk songs first. I never would have thought to write a song, you know? There's no dedication to folk music now, no appreciation of the art form.

—Bob Dylan, 1984

One day I was sitting at home and watching television—"Top of the Pops"—and on TV was Spandau Ballet and they were singing "Chant Number One" wearing frocks, and I realized this is what punk rock had made all those sacrifices for—this is why I'd thrown all my flared jeans out, and this is why I'd given all my Eagles albums away and had my hair cut really short, you know, and made holes in my body with safety pins—was just so Spandau Ballet could be on "Top of the Pops"! That was the end result of punk! And I was so angry about that that I went upstairs, and I picked up my guitar, and everything has been a blur since.

—Billy Bragg, 1986

I started making up songs about age three just for fun, like drawing pictures.

—Buffy Sainte-Marie, 1990

After I learned to play guitar, at the age of five, I thought of the songs I composed as poems with melodies. I'm not sure whether I'm a poet or a songwriter, but I do think the first poems I wrote would have turned out to be songs had I known how to set down their melodies.

—Willie Nelson, *Willie: An Autobiography*

I started writing songs myself when I was about

twelve. I started writing some poems and then made up some music to go along with them. They were love songs, sad songs. I think the death of my brother Jack, when I was twelve, had a lot to do with it. My poems were awfully sad at the time. My brother and I were very, very close.

—Johnny Cash, 1973

I wrote my first song in 1940 on a farm in Michigan, trying to write the type of songs Ernest Tubb was singing.

—Harlan Howard, 1990

I wrote my first songs when I was a little kid on the prairies as a way of playing make believe, long before the influence of TV.

—Gary Fjellgaard

In 1963, when I was twelve, I wrote "Hair of Spun Gold." To this day I don't know why.

—Janis Ian, 1990

I wrote my first song in the back seat of my mom's Studebaker when I was about four years old. It was called "I Don't Know and You Don't Care." That was all the lyrics; it was like a chant. I wrote it for the Coasters.

—Dave Alvin, 1990

I was ten when I had my first group: a kid with drumsticks who beat on a can, an accordion player and a few guitars. I made my first song, "Stay Away (From Me—I'm No Good For You)"— which was basically just that, repeated over and over, C to A minor.

—Peter Case, 1990

My first [song] was a rock & roll thing called "Baby, You're Not Leaving Me Out, Baby, I'm Leaving You Out." It was about as terrible as it sounds.

—Bruce Cockburn, 1971

Hell, I wrote my first song, called "Hula Hoop," when I was sixteen. I took it to BMI, and they told me to keep writing. Then I wrote another forty songs before I even started getting good.

—Gordon Lightfoot, 1981

In the course of Lennon and McCartney developing as writers there was obviously some sort of revelation that you could do these little things. Suddenly these bars of 2/4 started creeping in, as early as *Beatles For Sale*. It really took over around *Rubber Soul*. That was the stuff that influenced me when I was learning. It was uneven structure, and after that the rulebook went out the window. *Revolver* is the textbook on how to write really melodic pop songs that don't obey any of the normal rules.

—Elvis Costello, 1990

The first song I wrote was the first one I ever recorded. I was about thirteen years old and the song was called "Movie Magg." It was about the way things were in Lake County. You took your girl to the picture show on the back of a mule. Stupid little ol' song; I was ashamed to sing it to Sam Phillips.

—Carl Perkins, 1990

The first song I wrote was a song to Brigitte Bardot. I don't recall much of it. It had only one chord . . . it's all in the heart.

—Bob Dylan, 1978

I learned to play three chords on the guitar when I was fourteen. The first thing I did was write a song styled after Roger Miller. At the time I was going with this blonde girl named Dallas. She told me she'd heard his record "Dang Me" on the radio and that he reminded her of me. She could tell me anything—if she had told me I reminded her of Rudolph Nureyev I'd probably be a ballerina today. Anyway, I started listening to Roger Miller, and I said, "Now there's my kind of guy. If a guy as crazy as he is can get on the radio, then I can write a song too!"

—John Prine, 1978

I wrote my first song in 1965—everybody did the old ones better than me.

—Townes Van Zandt, 1990

The first time I was aware of writing a song was about 1961. It was a very simple sort of country and western thing. Nobody was writing their own songs then; it was just doing covers. . . . It was mainly because I got fed up with other people trying to dump their songs on me, just so they could get more money. I'd say, why should I do *their* songs? And so I really started writing as a reaction to that.

—Van Morrison, 1990

I wrote songs from the time I learned to play the guitar when I was about fifteen. I don't know why I did it; I didn't have any ambitions to be a professional musician, but I always wrote songs.

I remember quite distinctly certain songs occurring to me when I was still working in a day job. I just wrote them down on the train on scraps of paper in my pocket—lines snatched out of nowhere.

—Elvis Costello, 1988

I started when I went to McLean, a psychiatric hospital, in 1965. It was where I started writing seriously.

—James Taylor, 1979

At Surprise Lake Camp, Pete Seeger came up and played for us. Some of the kids played their songs for him, and they were all singing about causes, you know, whatever causes meant something to a fourteen-year-old. That was the first time that I realized that my peers could write songs. And that I could do it too, maybe, just for fun. Not thinking, "Hey, this would be my life."

—Neil Diamond, 1988

CHAPTER 3

TAPDANCE
ON A TIGHTROPE

PHILOSOPHY
OF A SONG

As Joni Mitchell says in this chapter, to be a writer you have to retain your innocence; perhaps more than that, your sense of wonder, your ability to be surprised and delighted. Most creators remain children in some sense, discovering new possibilities in the same way that a baby discovers and examines its fingers and toes. I think that's why we get so down and desperate when the ideas don't come. We become dependent on those surprises, that wonder. When it's working, it's like no feeling on earth.

—S.T.

One wants to tell a story," said novelist Carlos Fuentes, "in order not to die." The urge to tell a story in song—to sing "the news"—is as old as mankind. I think of the troubadours travelling from castle to castle with their ballads. If the song was good, they were given food and drink. If the song was ill-received, they might lose their heads. Times haven't changed all that much. The bottom line of songwriting is focused on finding one's writing voice. It's an inside job. In the words of Christ, taken from the Gnostic gospel of St. Thomas, "Everything you bring forth from within will save you; everything you do not bring forth will destroy you."

—T.R.

I'm not an entertainer; I'm a songwriter. I try to put into perspective things that are unclear.

—Jackson Browne, 1987

The biggest challenge for me is the opportunity to constantly try new things. I believe it's the writer's job to educate the audience; to bring them things they would never expect to see. It's not easy, but writing never has been.

—Stephen Sondheim

The aim of a good song is, within the context of three minutes, to provide a couple of lines that just go "bang" in the back of the cranium so that people go, "Yes, I know that feeling."

—Neil Finn (Crowded House), 1994

I am trying to do something for the future of American music, which today has no class whatsoever and is mere barbaric mouthing.

—Jerome Kern, 1920

They are really going to kill music if they keep it up, because they're not writing songs anymore. They're only writing ideas. They don't really care about repetition. They don't really care about a hook or melody. And I know the Beatles do. I mean, "Lady Madonna" was a hit song. . . . We must have more *songs*.

—Phil Spector, 1969

There's nothing that's going to take the place of the human being. They can get all the Moog synthesizers they want but nothing will take the place of the human heart.

—Johnny Cash, 1973

I think [junk culture] is all part of the water we swim in. It's part of our environment. Sometimes I get a kick out of it, a laugh out of it, but sometimes it bothers me. Sometimes I like the taste of it, though.

—David Byrne, 1988

Bob Marley said that the amount of vision, the sense of being, the pain and the joy you've experienced, they come inside you and create a centre of gravity. That's your centre—that's who you are. You have to maintain a certain sense of integrity to yourself, to your centre, in whatever you do.

—Kostas, 1994

Music is so big, man, it just takes up a lot of room. I've dedicated my life to my music so far. Every time I've let it slip and gotten somewhere else, it's showed. Music lasts a lot longer than relationships do.

—Neil Young, 1975

I have suffered economically. I have had deprivations of the spirit. I was hungry, down to my last can of mushroom gravy. I know what love of music can do—what matters to me is to make music a constant part of my life. If a day goes by without music, it's a day of oblivion.

—Van Dyke Parks, 1990

It's like the only thing that's really yours. Relationships are never yours. Property is never yours. Your body isn't even yours. Music is something that actually is. It's forever, in a way.

—Chris Cornell (Soundgarden), 1993

All I can do is just remember that William Blake wasn't even published in his lifetime, ya gotta keep creating.

—Kris Kristofferson

There's a point at which, when you're writing, you just have to admit to the fact that sometimes you really don't care if anybody listens.

—Pete Townshend, 1986

There are certain songs I've written that wouldn't have been accepted in my early Screen Gems days because they're not ever going to be hits, but I like them, and I need to write those songs too.

—Carole Bayer Sager, 1977

You tend to like a song [of yours] that nobody else likes. [It's like] your shy little kid that you have to take care of and nurse along and eventually it's gonna blossom and everybody's gonna like it and say, "Yeah, we were wrong."

—Dave Alvin, 1990

Songs are like children. Everybody's proud of theirs, you know. Good, bad or indifferent, you love your children.

—Steve Goodman, 1978

Music is ninety-nine percent of my life. I've sold out everything else. I've sold out my heart. I've sold out my head. I've sold out my body. I've sold out everything from my health to any lover I've ever had. When it's time to get on that airplane, that's it. . . I'm pushed by the music. . . . I think it's a noble profession.

—Buffy Sainte-Marie, 1974

A sunny day when I can sit down and write—that's what makes life so good. And the brain is an amazing thing. I could sit down and write nine songs right now, and I don't know what would come out. That's the wonder of it all.

—Jule Styne, 1990

Hear me, people, hear Peter Bucking-Horse cry

in the New York dawn at four-thirty. . . . We are comin', and we are rolling this big rock all the way to the top of the hill. And when we get there, the ages can always find a singer resting in its shadow away from the hot sun, making up a ballad, just as we before him.

—Peter LaFarge, 1964

The process of Creation is turning yourself into a child again, and being liberated from the restraints of civilized behaviour.

—E.Y. (Yip) Harburg, 1977

There's a child inside you, and that child has to be very, very reassured before he can come out. . . . The world wants you to pay your bills.

Michael Smith, 1992

It really terrifies me when people five to seven years younger than I am are starting to write songs about maturing and growing old. Ex-shit-stirrers believing what they're told about life ending at twenty-five. One of the directors I had at Boulder [where Biafra attended acting school] emphasized not to let the child in you die, because once you do you're going to be as stale as all those other people you hate so much. And she's right. You have to stay immature and retain a sense of humour. Otherwise, you might

as well be hooked on heroin or valium. Same difference.

—Jello Biafra, 1990

My innocence is regenerative in certain ways. By that I mean joy still comes to me, which I think is the main aspect of innocence. I think as a writer you want to hang onto that.

—Joni Mitchell, 1988

There may be three levels to me. Level one is a fairly amiable, easy-going person, level two is a bit darker and determined and perhaps a nastier piece of work, and level three is a naïve little boy. I think I can see all three at work in different areas, and we all need to allow them to come up for air, to find a place where things aren't being hidden or suppressed.

—Peter Gabriel, 1987

Songwriting for me is literally like having five people living in the same body. One day I'm an insular child-like artist, just going by emotion, the next day I'm a crass technician. The person who writes the riffs argues with the person doing the vocals. But the different personalities can work together. Sometimes my heart says, "This song needs to move," and the tactical part suggests, "Try a key change." It goes back and forth until some kind of graceful compromise is reached.

—Billy Corgan (Smashing Pumpkins)

I love writing songs. You know, I'm not really that nice a dude. I've been drunk on my ass in alleys, been in a fist fight and all that. . . . I probably caused as much trouble as I've alleviated in my life, but writing has really been a calmative for me, and has given me a great deal of pleasure.

—Hoyt Axton, 1976

Songwriting is the cheapest psychiatrist I know.

—Billy Joe Shaver, 1994

I know quite a few people whose individuality is expressed every Saturday afternoon when they go to soccer and beat up the opposite team. I don't think that's necessarily the best way to work out your territory. For me, it was always writing. Not just writing songs, but writing, period. And I think you're always very shy about it, but when you get together with a load of other guys to form a band, who equally have difficulty in expressing themselves in any other way than bashing drums and stuff like that, you become a bit less self-conscious.

—Billy Bragg, 1986

I mean, I don't know how to exactly present my own feelings, and that's why we make records instead of just talking to people, 'cause you can make records and make a separate discourse with the world apart from what you do when you're lying to your friends. You can lie to the *world* on a CD, or tell the truth sometimes.

—Stephen Malkmus (Pavement), 1993

If I could be a fuckin' fisherman, I would. If I had the capabilities of being something other than I am, I would. It's no fun being an artist. You know what it's like, writing, it's torture. I read about Van Gogh, Beethoven, any of these fuckers. If they had psychiatrists, we wouldn't have had Gauguin's great pictures.

—John Lennon, 1971

Songwriting is the way of perpetual want. Songwriters are the blessed cursed people, because if you are truly a songwriter, meaning that you hear the voices, you will never have a moment's peace in your life. You will always be wanting that next song.

—John Stewart, 1979

Writers can be so happy living inside ourselves. Wife divorces you? God, that's sad. I'm really going to miss her, but I wrote a couple of really great songs.

—Harlan Howard, 1994

To tell you the truth, I don't delve deeply into the reason why of things. The reason they feel good to me is that they are forever.

The wind calls the sailor, it waves the flag, it brings the dust, it clears the storms, it is the messenger of the universe.

—John Stewart, 1979

The art is *to do*, not to discuss. There are mysteries to life not discernible to the microscope and the telescope, and that's a good thing.

—Joe Hall, 1990

You cannot make a mistake in art, so even if you think you've made the worst mistake in the world, you just sit down, take a deep breath, and realize that you cannot make a mistake; even if you cannot fix what's happened you can tell everybody that it's exactly what you wanted.

—Stevie Nicks, 1986

Stella Adler tells young actors that "your talent lies in your voices." That's even truer for us as writers.

—Janis Ian, 1990

I think the music and lyric become farther apart the more you try to intellectualize about the song. The first thing you know, you've got something nobody gives a damn about or understands.

—Boudleaux Bryant, 1978

I don't worry so much any more about imperfections in my work. Imperfections are not a problem when you turn in a project. But the most creative thing of all is life. All the arts are shorthand manifestations of life. To me, my first act of art is how I live my life.

—Joni Mitchell, 1979

. . . Meanwhile, I am just a troubadour going down the road, learning my lessons in this life so I will know better next time. In the field of love, some say I have loved too many people at the same time. They get confused and don't understand that love is what I live on.

—Willie Nelson, *Willie: An Autobiography*

My songs are like a diary where you can look back after ten years and say what my preoccupations were.

—Sting, 1988

The question of what songs mean and what they do is sort of terrifying when you think about it. But then you begin to realize there's such a thing as taking yourself too seriously. You back off and say, "Isn't it a little pretentious of me to start wondering how I'm influencing society? Shouldn't I address myself to how well I'm doing the job of producing this piece of entertainment?"

—Warren Zevon, 1981

I think you want to keep your sense of humour—I mean, it's possible to enjoy life and to want social justice. It's important; as a matter of fact it's your duty to have fun, to enjoy life, and to maintain a robust attitude toward it.

—Jackson Browne, 1987

I want to do something that's coming from inside, and see if anybody wants to hear it. In the end what's real is real. My feeling about things is most music is bad, most films are bad, most TV is bad, most people are bad, but, hopefully you can find a little good in anything. Most music offends me deeply, I take it as a personal attack on my life.

—Iggy Pop, 1990

I believe that people are basically good. I don't think life is a sewer like some books and movies make it out to be. I know it doesn't sound like it from my work—people are always saying I'm a cynic, but I've never thought of myself as one. I have a fairly optimistic view of what people are like individually, though not in groups.

—Randy Newman, 1979

Don't go out into the world as a missionary to save it, but be a part of the world for your own sensibility. As a songwriter, I need to sing about the things that I see for my own sanity, and for my own education.

—Holly Near, 1981

I picked up a girl hitchhiking and she said, "I used to write poetry." I said, "What do you mean, 'used to'?" She said, "I used to stutter. When I stopped stuttering, I stopped writing poetry." I thought that was a great analogy.

It's a luxury to have a voice to be able to express these things. It doesn't matter if it's private: just to write it down helps. And the process of making this thing—a poem or a painting—probably prevents cancer.

—Joni Mitchell, 1985

I believe songs save lives, that it's a worthwhile thing to be doing. Not just the big songs of life, love and death, but the little ones, silly ones, blue ones, one timers, jokes, dirges, work songs, romantic numbers, dreams, painting songs, rockabilly, child songs. It's all good sharing experience, strength and hope through music.

—Peter Case, 1990

I was sort of a poetic kid. I was fascinated with the concept that when you write something down, you can come back later and it will still be there. If you hadn't written it down it would be lost. That's always been important to me.

—Bob McDill, 1977

To quote the lyrics the genius Ray Charles sang, "Sometimes I get sideways and stay up all night with a tune. . . . I like what I am doing and I sure hope it don't end too soon."

—Chuck Berry, *The Autobiography*

In a way, a part of my mind is always writing.

—Harlan Howard, 1990

You can't tell a real songwriter he isn't any good, because he knows better, and he'll keep hacking his way through show-biz hell until he proves it.

—Willie Nelson, *Willie: An Autobiography*

There's no idea that I'm trying to express; I'm trying to express feelings. I don't have a philosophy of music; I just believe that there is nothing more important than feeling, and I don't think music can express anything more than feelings.

—Galt McDermot, 1972

To me, everything is interesting, but if you start to analyze, you're wasting your time. I don't fit into any category and I don't want to. I don't recognize any master, any school of writing. I write a song, it's worth what it's worth, and maybe it helps to clear a small path in the jungle. Maybe it helps a bit.

—Felix LeClerc, 1973

The ultimate aim in writing is the most perfectly balanced song I can write—a song that's balanced in all elements. I have my own formula, or at least I think I have my own unconscious formula.

—Jane Siberry, 1984

You always have to keep stretching—to wage the daily battle against the great leveller. All you have to go on is your own self and if you just listen to what's in your head, then you'll always be different.

—Jane Siberry, 1990

I don't feel I'm in control, actually—I think being a creative person is just being a vehicle, and I just want to be a vehicle.

—Annie Lennox

The only style [of songwriting] God has blessed us with is what people seem to like, whatever that is. It's basic black with a string of pearls.

—Felice Bryant, 1978

A good song is like a well-brought-up child. It's got its own reality, tonality and toughness. It has reflections of the parent, but hopefully it's got a different personality and it's got its own way.

—Harry Chapin, 1978

I want to create something that is beyond vogue, that is classic. There's the long dollar and the short dollar. If I were to become a "hit-making" artist, I would come to a peak more rapidly, and I would decline more rapidly. The steadiness of my career has been the success of my career.

—Joni Mitchell, 1979

When Dylan sang, "You've got a lotta nerve. . . ," I thought, Hallelujah, now, the American pop song has grown up. It's wide open. Now you can write about anything that literature can write about.

—Joni Mitchell, 1985

A lot of people try to make something out of nothing. If you don't have a good song, you can go into the studio and make it appear to be good, but that stuff don't last.

—Bob Dylan, 1978

People who create things, even things which you think, "God, that's great," and then you see that the guy is irresponsible, you see that the guy isn't committed to what he's doing, doesn't stay with it, has other people turn it out for him; you realize as you get older that art without responsibility is bullshit.

—Mark Knopfler, 1987

You draw a line in your subconscious. You say, "I don't want to say that," but *really* if we were sitting having a drink, I might lean across the table and say that. I might not want to *live* by it, but I might say it, or I might *think* it. . . . You have to think about it. You have to draw your own lines there. You have to think, If this is dangerous to society, perhaps I shouldn't do it.

—Tom Petty, 1986

Since "Heroin," people have come up to me and said, "Don't you feel responsible for turning people onto drugs and glamourizing violence?" My answer to that is, that's not what I was doing. I've not been glamourizing anything. There was one arrangement we had [of "The

53

Gun"] that pushed it too far. None of us could even listen to it. The one that's on the album went far enough. The vocal is really a disturbed person talking. I didn't like being in that mode.

—Lou Reed, 1984

Let's say a really great group emerged, and say they are advocating, I don't know, killing, Satanism. And they came out with a really great album and turned a lot of people on to Satanism. There's got to be a point when you're going to say, "Look, guys, we're all for artistic freedom, but maybe we just don't want *de debbil* trampling across America at the moment." I mean, what would you do? I don't know. I think censorship's very dangerous. . . . It's not a bad thing to have watchdog groups; you just must-n't let them get too much power.

—Paul McCartney, 1986

I think music is a very powerful tool. The wrong kind of ideas, yes, they are too dangerous, but anything that is for the positiveness of people moving ahead is right on. I think that people talk about screwing all the time. That's danger-ous because young kids don't necessarily understand what it's all about, and if they do understand, they're not ready to accept the responsibility. I agree with Smokey [Robinson]'s song "Be Kind to the Growing Mind."

—Stevie Wonder, 1985

I don't want to spend my life, as Toscanini did, studying and restudying the same fifty pieces of music. It would bore me to death. I want to con-duct. I want to play the piano. I want to write for Hollywood. I want to write symphonic music. I want to keep on trying to be, in the full sense of that wonderful word, a musician.

—Leonard Bernstein, 1990

Well I tell you, you don't have to atrophy because you get older. It's, again, the belief sys-tem, right? When we were kids, thirty was death, right? I'm forty now and I feel better than before. You can atrophy your ideas of life at twenty or thirty or forty. You can become mel-lower without becoming rigid. I still believe in almost anything until it's disproved. I don't have any set answers. I'm as open as ever, but my hormones don't work the same, that's all.

—John Lennon, 1980

A kind of thread running through my work cur-rently is this idea not so much that you can rock & roll in a wheelchair, but that you can still work miracles of discovery and make things that appear to be impossible work, simply by reduc-ing your expectations and putting a value on what you already have.

—Pete Townshend, 1986

I'll do this until I stop getting letters, because if they stopped, that would mean no one is listening any more. As long as people still write to me saying, "You're great," or "Piss off back to Russia, you raving Commie," or whatever, I'll still feel of some use. The day I'm ignored is the day I'll just disappear.

—Billy Bragg, 1986

I'd like to die with my boots on. I don't see myself dying in some place where they play dominoes. It'll probably be in a little club. I'll be playing guitar, an old walking stick hung up over my amp.

—Mark Knopfler, 1985

Probably one of these days I'll be sitting around in one of my favourite bars talking with some cute little bartender or some old songwriter at the bar, and fall over backwards, and I'm outta here. And that ain't no bad way to go.

—Harlan Howard, 1994

The older you get the more specific your life becomes. You can't say, "I could be a forest ranger," or "I could be a brain surgeon," when all the while you're this songwriter living in L.A. It takes a long time to know it, to say, "Well, okay, that's what I'm gonna be," or even, "That's

who I am, now I'm going to be a good one."

Now I know what I am. I'm not a novelist. I'm not the light of my generation. I'm not the spokesman for new sensibility. I'm a songwriter living in L.A. and this is my new record.

—Leonard Cohen, 1988

When you're young, what you think and what your generation thinks is very much the same, but the older you get, the more complex your work tends to become. Then your vision becomes more private, more personal, and when that happens, it's hard to find a mass following.

—Paul Simon, 1988

I feel that as a writer I haven't even started. If you're lucky to have a couple of hits when you're young, they tend to weigh on you because they're born of innocence and honesty. Then you gather up experience and wisdom and cynicism, and it becomes much harder to use catchphrases and rhetoric and blame everybody else for what's wrong with the world or your life, and songwriting then becomes more complicated.

—Pete Townshend, 1990

You know, sometimes I think about people like T-Bone Walker, John Lee Hooker, Muddy

Waters—these people who play into their sixties. If I'm here at eighty I'll be doing the same thing. This is all I want to do—it's all I can do.

—Bob Dylan, 1986

I think I must take this opportunity of apologizing to the gentle reader for having written so very very much for such a very very long time . . . but the compulsion to make rhymes was born in me. For those sated readers of my works who wish ardently that I would stop, the future looks dark indeed.

—Noel Coward

I am a contemporary artist, not the Ghost of Christmas Past. I have continued writing songs ever since I first started and have tried to stay aware of what people are interested in hearing. I hope my songs have developed and grown. I have a need to express myself musically, and I feel I have something to contribute through my music.

—Neil Sedaka, 1976

I admire a lot of young writers, but they seem to come and go. They don't want to write anything but great songs. I want to write a few great songs, but I'd like to write a lot of good ones too. It would be terrible to have a one-year career, and then live to be eighty.

—Tom T. Hall, 1979

I really believe that you've only got so much to say. It gets to the point where you start repeating yourself, no matter who you are. You can only expose so much of your soul. Then you have to take some time for a refill.

—Sonny Throckmorton, 1980

I'm alone now and filled with lonely pain. Pain always sends me home to write.

—Peter LaFarge, 1964

Some artists (most of us go through it at one time or another) buy into the myth of the "artist as debaucher." They point to all the great artists who've been addicts as proof. They neglect to mention that those same great artists usually died early deaths, possibly depriving us and themselves of their greatest works.

—Janis Ian, 1990

You've got to watch the old emotional ups and downs. That's why people kill themselves and stuff. Writers go through it. You're in a funny state of mind when you write.

—Randy Newman, 1979

I was brought up with the belief that you take nothing for granted, and that all good fortune is a gift. Sounds austere, eh? And perhaps it is a bit, but I respected my father for his will to balance the hard times with the happy ones. When things go badly, I try to bear up and go on, but it does affect me greatly, and I guess it shows up in my music. In recent years I've written a lot about death and loss.

—Steve Winwood, 1988

I've had periods of being happier than hell and having a great time, and I pull up short and tell myself, "I've got to stop this!" So there you go— another paradox. This thing that songwriters do is really torture. You're happy, and suddenly you feel, "I shouldn't be happy. I do my best work when I'm unhappy." So then you're unhappy. I guess there just isn't any answer to it.

—Jimmy Webb, 1976

Cannibalizing your own feelings as a sole source of inspiration can inflate your ego in desperately unhealthy ways. (For instance, by always leaving you in the victim stance, or by convincing you that the only feelings worth having are tortured ones.) It can also leave you addicted to high drama...really believing that you must suffer constantly in order to create.

—Janis Ian, 1990

I can't say that I never felt bad in my life. I have and will, but I'm pretty comfortable with myself. I accept my faults, but not to the point where I accept them and don't want to correct them. As far as pity, I don't pity myself.

—Stevie Wonder, 1985

I feel things very deeply. I can get very angry, I can get sad. I don't get into self-pity—I was cured of that by going to this observation ward (when he was suicidal) and seeing people who had really deep-seated problems. I'll only give myself about thirty seconds of good self-pity, and then this button switches on and goes, "Get off it."

—Billy Joel, 1986

When you're creating something you have to feel pretty strong and confident, otherwise you wouldn't be so bold as to try to make something. If you feel miserable, you just feel like going to sleep, or crawling into a hole, or watching television. At least that's been my experience.

—David Byrne, 1985

It becomes therapy, in a sense. The more you say, the more difficult it becomes to keep tapping that source. You have to dig a little deeper each time, and eventually that introspection can get to be a drag for the listener. I mean really, who gives a shit what Kenny Loggins thinks when he eats cornflakes?

—Kenny Loggins, 1976

During some hashish reverie I was thinking to myself, "I'm really in a weird position. I earn my living by writing songs and singing songs. It's only today this could happen. If I were born a hundred years ago I wouldn't be in this country. I'd probably be in Vienna or wherever my ancestors came from—Hungary—and I wouldn't be a guitarist songwriter. . . . I would have been a tailor."

—Paul Simon, 1972

Everybody gets fucked up sooner or later. You're just pretending if you don't let your music get just as liquid as you are when you're really high.

—Neil Young, 1975

Success is the real enemy of creative talent. Some writers, hell, all they might want is a new car. Someone buys them a new car and they don't write another song. Once somebody figures they've made it, then it's all over. The hunger disappears, that one thing that makes 'em write.

Success just reaches out and grabs the one thing that makes a guy write. Suddenly people begin to look at you differently, people begin to tell you how great you are. . . . Now you dump two or three hundred thousand dollars on somebody and they ain't gonna sit up all night writing fucking songs. They're gonna go down the alley and get drunk and get some pussy. Wouldn't you? If I was a starving songwriter, I'd write songs. But if I was a rich songwriter I wouldn't bury myself in some room and write 'cause that would be like goin' through the fucking motions.

—Bobby Bare, 1980

You have to have a little success—a little taste of it—and it makes you feel that now you did it, you can do it again. Then you do it again and you *know* you can really do it. It's like breaking a psychological barrier . . . the four-minute mile.

—Bob McDill, 1977

Determination is what did it for me. My pattern of life in poverty taught me a lot. Being poor was a great college. You know you have to make a go for yourself.

—Hank Snow, 1979

Writing songs and writing songs for money are two different things.

—Don Gant (producer), 1979

I describe myself as a hack because basically I can write on any subject, but I think my songs transcend "hackism." I'm versatile, and this is my curse as well as my blessing.

—Nancy White, 1983

To me, being commercial is appealing to the masses. If you write a song that millions of people can relate to and enjoy, what in the hell is wrong with being commercial? For the guy who says he doesn't write for the masses, but only for a small segment of the audience, or writes for himself and a few musician friends, why go in and record it at all?

—Bobby Goldsboro, 1977

I don't want to be what e.e. cummings called a local hero. I don't want to nurture a small cult following—that's like fascism. I'm for the masses because that, for me, somehow legitimizes what I do.

—John Hiatt, 1990

The mob is always right. It seems to be able to sense instinctively what is good; and I believe there are darned few good songs that have not been whistled or sung by the crowd.

—Irving Berlin, 1978

In general, the best people to depend on for criticism (other than the ideal: a brilliant songwriter, extremely articulate, whose work you admire, and who happens to have loads of free time) are laymen. They are, after all, the people who'll be buying the song.

—Janis Ian, 1990

If you have a song that sells eight million records, the classic line in Nashville is, "That's a piece of shit!" Well, of course it's not. If it communicates with eight million people, it's good writing. You're not writing for critics, you're writing for people.

—Tom T. Hall, 1979

It takes a lot of ego to like everything you write, but I try to be an accurate judge of my own tunes.

—Harry Warren, 1977

Now, I've written some real turkeys, you know, but my real turkeys are not as bad as some other people's great songs, I think.

—Stephen Stills, 1979

My attitude these days is, if you write a bad song what are they gonna do, throw you in songwriter jail?

—John Hiatt, 1990

Songwriting is something you have to do a lot of to be proficient. It's like someone who wants to be a sculptor—he's got to smash his way through tons of rock to come out with something in the end that's beginning to look like what he aimed it to be.

—Dennis Lambert (Lambert & Potter), 1977

Writing songs is a profession, and requires a professional job. We are living today in a world of amateurs. Anything goes, and there is no time for sophistication. One must be well-educated to develop taste. You cannot learn to be a song-writer. You are born with a special gift to write or play, to be a creator or a performer. The creator has the right instinct about what to write, which words to use, whether they'll fit a character or not.

—Jule Styne, 1977

The great folk music and the great rock & roll you might not hear again. Like the horse and buggy. Sure, a horse and buggy is more soulful than a car but it takes longer to get where you're going and besides that, you could get killed on the road.

—Bob Dylan, *CBS Biography*

CHAPTER 4

FELLOW TRAVELLERS

IDOLS & INFLUENCES

One thing Ian and Sylvia always did was to include songs by other writers in their repertoire. We were among the first to record songs by Bob Dylan and Joni Mitchell, and certainly the first to record Gordon Lightfoot songs. Dylan wrote "Tomorrow is a Long Time" for us, and didn't record it himself until many years later. Gordon always said that he knew Peter, Paul and Mary had discovered "Early Morning Rain" through our recording of it and not his because they used minor chords in the first line that only appeared in our version of it. I've always envied Joni Mitchell's ability to write intensely personal lyrics so well that they don't make people uncomfortable. In lesser hands reaction to a song like that would be, "I don't know if I wish to know that." I find Paul Simon to be creatively neurotic, with an exquisite balance between lyric, melody and arrangement.

—S.T.

After I realized people wrote their own songs I began to follow the folk writers in the '60s. My favourites were Dylan and Ian and Sylvia. I thought Ian and Sylvia were the strongest folk group of all time. They looked good, they sounded good, they never wrote a mediocre song, but they never had the big label push. Later on, in 1986, I met Ian in New York and slipped a lyric into his guitar case about a "Navajo Rug," and he finished it. I'd written a song with one of my idols and it was a hit. Later I met Sylvia in Toronto. I was eventually able to write with both of them—two masters.

It's strange to write with someone you've grown up admiring, but I've learned a tremendous amount from both of them. The craft of writing is a lifetime job. Both these artists are still writing great songs. Writing with strong, experienced writers, I've picked up some of the "nuts and bolts" of the trade. I've also learned that these writers possess an accurate built-in "shit-detector"—an alarm that goes off when something within a song is false-hearted or doesn't work. It's a proven fact that many songwriters (and most people in general) do not possess a built-in "shit-detector."

—T.R.

Don't touch the holidays. Berlin has a lock on them [referring to "Easter Parade" and "White Christmas"].

—Oscar Hammerstein, 1978

The mob [crowd] sensed the eternal feeling in Stephen Foster's ballads. The old folks at home of whom he wrote may have been black, but the feelings that thoughts of them inspired are the same as the longings inspired by mothers and fathers of all colours.

—Irving Berlin, 1978

Hoagy [Carmichael]'s outfit was playing in Palm Beach and he met Irving Berlin. . . . The hostess asked the great man [Berlin] to play his new song, "Lady of the Evening." He did, and the young Carmichael, fascinated, endorsed the words spoken to him by George Johnson: "Hoagy, if a man that plays that feeble can write a song that good, you can write a song too."

—Mark White, *You Must Remember This*

I was delivered myself of a nifty. It was at a dinner in London, and I was asked what, in my opinion, were the chief characteristics of the American nation. I replied that the average United States citizen was perfectly epitomized in Irving Berlin's music. I remember I got this off quite glibly, just as if I'd thought of it on the spur of the moment. Of course I enlarged upon the notion, and went on to explain that both the typical Yankee and the Berlin tune had humour, originality, pace, and popularity; both were wide-awake, and both sometimes a little loud; but what might unsympathetically be mistaken for brass was really gold.

—Jerome Kern, letter to Alexander Woolcott

In short what I really want to say, my dear Woolcott, is that Irving Berlin has no place in American music. He is American music but it will be by his verse and his lovely melodies that he will live, and not in his diabolically clever trick accents.

—Jerome Kern, letter to Alexander Woolcott

My most vivid recollection of Gershwin was Christmas Eve, 1934. . . . He and composer Kay Smith burst in on us like two irrepressible Magi. When the scene was set to his satisfaction, he sat down at the piano and started to play the entire score of "Porgy and Bess," months before its Broadway premiere. That was a Christmas we shall never forget.

—Richard Rodgers

Jerry [Jerome] Kern is dead. I feel profoundly sorry; no more of those lovely, satisfying melodies. It happened that on Sunday afternoon I spent an hour playing all the old tunes of his that I could remember. This must have been just when he was dying. His is a great loss.

—Noel Coward, *The Noel Coward Diaries*

Frank Loesser was a great lyricist. He never wrote a lyric down on paper until it was finished. If he couldn't memorize a song, it simply wasn't memorable. His thoughts were clear and simple, so his songs were, and are, memorable. But some lyricists today are pedantic rhymsters.

—Jule Styne, 1977

Larry [Lorenz Hart] was a great friend. I knew him long before I knew Dick Rodgers. He was an amazing writer. I can give you an example. In *Pal Joey* we needed a second chorus for the girl who played the journalist and sang "Zip." He took a piece of brown paper and wrote down obscene endings for each line like, "Zip! Da-da-da-da-da-da-da-da fuck. Zip! Da-da-da-da-da-da-da suck," and then we went out into the lobby of the theatre, and in fifteen minutes he came back with the second chorus! "Zip! I consider Dali's paintings passé. Zip! Can they make the Metropolitan pay?," but the original was all obscene.

—Gene Kelly, *On Performing*

Johnny Mercer is a great songwriter. . . . He was a singer to begin with (and so was I) and so he knows where words should fall and when to use an open vowel instead of a closed vowel. . . . He feels things very deeply. . . . He knows how to use tender corn. . . . There's nothing wrong with good corn, believe me.

—Irving Berlin

I think the greatest lyric writer of our time is Stephen Sondheim. And I'm including Oscar Hammerstein, who was a poet, and Larry Hart, who was a brilliant wit. When you write with Sondheim, you actually feel good as a composer. He places value on the music—what kind of word fits each note. When you soar musically he soars lyrically.

—Jule Styne, 1980

[Andrew Lloyd Webber]'s tunes "take the stage," as we say in the theatre. His music makes the play happen. But I do agree that his albums deal in themes rather than character development. That seems to suit the public; they are not really listening to the words. Rodgers and Hammerstein wrote serious plays with music—but not Andrew. He's not Rodgers and Hammerstein and he's not opera. He offers wall-to-wall music and themes.

—Charles Strouse, 1990

I think Lloyd Webber is a wonderful musician but he has a lot to learn about songwriting. Make-it-fit writing is not the way. He needs to collaborate. He writes the score and leaves it for the lyric writer to do. With him, the dollar sign is the big goal. He's the only creative person I ever met like that.

—Jule Styne, 1990

Andrew Lloyd Webber, in a fit of exasperation, once asked lyricist Alan Jay Lerner, "Why do people take an instant dislike to me?" Replied Lerner, in a flash: "Because it saves time."

—*Toronto Star*, 1990

Robert [Johnson] was like a father to me. . . . He was real open with me, and he had me playing inside of six months. In fact, I learned three of his tunes inside of two weeks. . . . Robert wouldn't show me stuff but once or twice, but when he'd come back, I'd be playin' it.

I didn't go near his funeral. I guess maybe I would never have been able to play again if I had. As it was, everything I played reminded me of Robert, and whatever I tried to play, I would just come down in tears. That's what really inspired me to start writing my own material.

—Robert Lockwood, *Deep Blues* (Robert Palmer)

At the Palladium on Wabash Avenue [Chicago] we looked up and found the marquis glowing with MUDDY WATERS TONIGHT. Ralph [Burris, a friend from high school] gave me the lead as we ran upstairs to the club, knowing I sang Muddy's songs and that he was my favourite blues singer. We paid our fifty-cent admission and scrimmaged forward to the bandstand, where, in true living colour, I saw Muddy Waters.

He was playing "Mojo Working" at that moment and was closing the last set of the night. . . . I quickly told him of my admiration for his compositions, and asked him who I could see about making a record. Other fans of Muddy's were scuffling for a chance to just say "Hi" to him, yet he chose to answer my question.

Those very famous words were, "Yeah, see Leonard Chess. Yeah, Chess Records, over on 47th and Cottage."

—Chuck Berry, *The Autobiography*

I met Chuck Berry once. We played the Maryland Armory in the early '70s and we got a call from the promoter. My manager said, "Gee, you know we're going to open on a bill for Jerry Lee Lewis and Chuck Berry." I thought this was like *forget it!* I was twenty-three or twenty-four and these guys were our heroes, so we were really excited. The promoter said he's getting a band that's going to back Chuck Berry up, and we said, "No, no, don't get one of the local bands, tell him we'll back him up." . . . We were really nervous. There wasn't supposed to be an extra guitar player, so I came up to him and I said, "Gee, is it okay if we play?" and he said, "Yeah, yeah, you can play," and I said, "Well, Chuck . . . ." And he said, "What?" And I said, "What songs are we going to do?" And he said "Well, we're going to do some Chuck Berry songs." That's all he said, so we went, "Okay." . . .

Chuck Berry created great characters. Which I'm sure had to be part of him and part of what he imagined. Like he said, he was writing all of them high school songs when he was thirty-two! But he knew what it was about. His thing was fantastic—tremendous use of detail, which in my later writing particularly is something I've really tried to work on, to get better at. Because I admire his music and that unbelievable sense of detail that would bring the whole verse alive.

—Bruce Springsteen

I remember seeing Jerry Lee Lewis playing on a flatbed trailer [in Lubbock, Texas] in front of a Pontiac dealership in a dust storm when the winds were about forty miles an hour, and you couldn't see across the street, and the winds were blowing so hard that the mike stand kept blowing over but he just pounded it on out right through that dust storm and that image always sticks in my head, this wild man beating on a piano and somebody would have to bring his mike stand up every time the wind blew it over.

—Joe Ely, 1986

Bo Diddley had an incredible guitar rhythm with maracas. It was the sound of emptiness and percussion and a groove without a backbeat, and I loved it. When I listened to Bo Diddley I didn't know what he was saying, whether it was, "My pretty baby, she was a bird" or "My pretty baby, she was murdered." But it didn't make any difference. It moved me. It was powerful. And it still doesn't make any difference, if someone's singing in Zulu or in Portuguese or in the language of rap. The ear is willing to accept it when the rhythm is right.

—Paul Simon, 1990

If you want to get into the origins of rap, you can go all the way back to Africa. Rhythm and rhyme started there. You had the '40s with bebop and that was just like hip-hop, only different time and music. You had entertainers like Cab Calloway and Duke Ellington. They were the original masters of rap and hip-hop.

—2-Bigg MC, 1992

Otis Blackwell will always be remembered as an original, like Chuck Berry. They created something new. Otis invented that medium-tempo rock song that Presley picked up on, like "Don't Be Cruel" and "All Shook Up." It was Otis' invention. He's a pure soul.

—Doc Pomus, 1987

My songwriting really developed in the three years I was with Roy Orbison. He was a very big influence on me. Roy was writing more involved chord progressions and by playing in his back-up band [The Webbs], I was learning these things. He was not only a great guy to work with, but he was really instrumental in my starting to use more chords.

—Bobby Goldsboro, 1977

Down under there, Roy [Orbison] always seemed to have a knowledge that he could write something. He'd sing some of these slow songs a lot of times in the car. We'd work a lot together, and he'd ask, "What do you think about this?" I'd say, "How high can you go? You're just about through the car roof now."

—Carl Perkins, 1990

When I saw Smokey Robinson driving a Cadillac . . . that's what inspired me. And I actually ran up to him one day and asked him, "How did you get started?" and he gave me the most ridiculous answer I've ever heard: "Make your own bed, brother, because you've got to sleep in it."

—Norman Whitfield, 1991

Berry [Gordy] was a tremendous help to me as a songwriter. All the songs we sang for him that didn't make sense, he told me they didn't make sense, and why they didn't. He was very instrumental in making me grasp the idea that a song should be like a book. It should have a beginning, a middle and an end, and tell a complete story. I had a lot of songs at the time where the first verse would start off in one direction and the last verse would end up in another. I thought that if I made it all rhyme it was cool. Gordy made me understand that the rhyme had to have reason.

—Smokey Robinson, 1976

The first major influence that really excited me was the Burt Bacharach-Hal David songs, because of their interesting song and chord structure. . . . Then the *Revolver* record [by the Beatles] came out and I began to hear these two hot British songwriters. . . . I was also influenced by Holland-Dozier-Holland and all the Motown stuff.

—Jimmy Webb, 1994

Rock has had some good shots in the arm through the years, a great one with the Beatles in 1964. 'Cause when they first came out, these boys were hittin' hard at the old Sun Records sound. . . . When I met 'em, it was at the end of the tour that Chuck [Berry] and I did over there [in England] in 1964. They gave a party for me and I didn't know them. . . . They asked me to go to Abbey Road and sit there as they cut three of my songs that night. I was sittin' in a chair kinda against the wall in the studio and Ringo was sittin' beside me, and he called me Mr. Perkins. I said, "I wish you'd call me Carl, son. Mr. Perkins is my daddy." He said, "This is sure hard for me to do."

I knew something was on his mind, and I said, "Shoot, spit it out, man. What is it?" He said, "Would you care if I sang some of your songs?" "You mean you want me to write you some songs?"

He said, "Well, yes, sir, that would be fine, but I love 'Honey Don't,' and 'Matchbox.'"

I said, "Do I *care*? Shoot, no, man. I'd love it."

And he jumped up and said, "Guys, he said it was all right!" Then he sat down on the drums and "Matchbox" was the first thing they cut. They got that thing in two or three cuts.

—Carl Perkins, 1990

As I sat in prison for a no-no seed I sowed, I thought of the manner in which we lost Dr. Martin Luther King and John F. Kennedy, but I never would have dreamed that music would lose [John] Lennon's genius in the same manner.

—Chuck Berry, *The Autobiography*

To me the Beatles were the best songwriters since Gershwin.

—Leonard Bernstein, 1990

No one, be it Beatles, Dylan or Stones, have ever improved on "Whole Lotta Shakin'" (Jerry Lee Lewis) for my money.

—John Lennon, 1971

At least the first forty songs we wrote were Buddy Holly-influenced.

—Paul McCartney, 1990

I was Buddy Holly.

—John Lennon, 1990

The most important thing I learned from him [John Lennon] was to follow through—to finish what you start. If you say you're going to send someone a postcard, send a postcard. He always followed through.

—Harry Nilsson, 1981

I just dug the effects they [the Beatles] got, like echoes, the voice things, the writing, like "For the Benefit of Mr. Kite . . ." I just said, "Why can't I?" I wanted to do something else, go other places. Same thing about keys. I don't want to stay in the same key all the time.

—Stevie Wonder, 1973

I started thinking about my own emotions. I would just try to express what I felt about myself. I think it was Dylan who helped me realize that by hearing his work.

—John Lennon, 1971

Dylan once said, "I could've written 'Satisfaction,' but you couldn't have written 'Tambourine Man'" . . . It's true, but I'd like to hear Bob Dylan sing "I Can't Get No Satisfaction."

—Mick Jagger, 1968

We met Bob Dylan there [The Bitter End, New York City]. We were looking for songs, and he was writing "Lay Lady Lay" at the time. He sangs parts of it, and we weren't quite sure if he was offering it to us or not. It was one of those awestruck moments. We wound up cutting the song about fifteen years later.

—Don Everly, 1986

Phil Everly once said he wasn't sure at the time what Dylan was singing. . . . They thought he was singing "Lay Lady Lay . . . lay across my big, bad breast," and told Bob they probably couldn't get away with that . . . and he looked at them kind of funny.

—Tom Russell

We sang "Blowin' in the Wind" together. Dylan sang the first four verses, the only ones I knew, then he stopped, looked at me and said, "Now you carry on." My mind was totally blank, so I made it up. Trying to re-write "Blowin' in the Wind" on the spot is not a good idea, but he liked it, and said to me, "Aww, I make 'em up all the time too."

—Bono, 1989

I remember one time he [Dylan] stayed at the Thunderbird Motel, on the strip, for about three weeks. He had a typewriter on the balcony. He'd sit there and write a song a day. We were impressed by that. We never did it, though. It was too hard.

—Roger McGuinn, 1990

In those days I was writing obscurely, à la Dylan, never saying what you mean, but giving the impression of something, where more or less can be read into it. It's a good game. . . . Dylan got away with murder. I thought, Well, I can write this crap, too. You know, you just stick a few images together, and you call it poetry.

—John Lennon

Songwriting is like fishing in a stream; you put in your line and hope you catch something. And I don't think anyone downstream from Bob Dylan ever caught anything.

—Arlo Guthrie, 1991

If you are an artist like Bob Dylan, you got to make the crowd follow you. I can tell you that it doesn't mean anything to him that people might not like what he is doing. Him still do it. And that is the most important thing.

—Bob Marley

Ray Charles and James Brown still get me off, but they're not influences now. I don't really have any influences since I've done my own thing. But there's still some people I admire and listen to who can't be ignored. Dylan is the greatest living poet.

—Van Morrison, 1985

The nice thing about Dylan for me was he brought back poetry. We'd come from that student thing, like poetry readings in Liverpool. Hamburg was a student scene. There were kids in Hamburg who called themselves "the Exies"— the existentialists—and wore a lot of black. . . . The Beatles thing got so huge that the student thing got cut short, but Dylan re-introduced that into all our lives.

—Paul McCartney, 1993

I hope I am [influenced by other writers]. I hope that I soak in some of it. I hope that I'm as witty as Elvis Costello, as sardonic and tongue-in-cheek. I want to be as eclectic, playful, smart, and funny as They Might Be Giants. I hope I am as mysterious and disturbing as Leonard Cohen. I want my images to have the kind of feeling that Dylan's do.

—Suzanne Vega, 1990

After the first solo album, he [Paul McCartney] never referred to any Beatles' language. It's quite amazing, quite unique really. The only parallel I can think of in pop music is Richard Rodgers. He had two distinct styles, one with Hart and one with Hammerstein. It isn't just that the lyrics changed, the melody changed as well. . . . It's quite an achievement to dispense with a whole musical vocabulary and come up with another one. A musicologist would give you credit for that.

—Elvis Costello

It's his [Elvis Costello's] use of the English language—it's beautiful and also a tough language. Costello has tied them both together. . . . He's the godfather of the whole new wave. I don't think you can be a thinking writer and not have been affected by him.

—Billy Joel, 1986

Alan Jay Lerner said that genius was an overworked word when applied to lyricists, but in British rock Ray Davies is our only true and natural genius.

—Pete Townshend, 1987

I studied songwriting with Paul Simon for a while and that was an incredibly invaluable experience. There's an element of Lewis Carroll in Paul Simon that he tried to bring out in everybody, which was wonderful. If you could write a whole song in gibberish, it was great. There were times he would go pick up the guitar and say "I've been working on this idea . . . what do you think?" We were so flabbergasted that he was sharing the seeds of an idea, because we all did respect his work so.

—Melissa Manchester, 1976

Eventually all records are dated, but the song comes back. "Eleanor Rigby" was a really fine song. . . . There's the whole group of Smokey Robinson songs that mean something. There's a couple of old Steve Cropper songs that mean something.

—Paul Simon, 1972

Paul Simon said, "Say what you have to say in your own way and say it as simply and as quickly as possible, and then get the hell out of there."

—Melissa Manchester, 1976

I can't remember a single black group playing New Zealand when I was growing up. I thought the Beatles invented the blues. I'm now discovering country & western, which I used to hate. It has tremendous emotional impact. Hank Williams is songwriting in its purest form. I now subscribe to the theory that there are no bad forms of music, just bad musicians.

—Neil Finn (Crowded House), 1987

The story is always told that Hank Williams used to ride around in the back of his car just working on songs, day and night. He'd write constantly, playing the same song over and over, and keep saying "Gotta keep it simple, gotta keep it simple." It was a real deliberate effort to make things succinct and elegant and within reach.

—J.D. Souther, 1980

I just happened to pick up enough on Jimmie Rodgers and the black songs to know how to say things in a simple way; to be influenced correctly.

—Billy Joe Shaver, 1994

When I wrote "The Only Flame In Town," I was trying to write like Allen Toussaint. I was thinking, "How tough does Hank Williams ever get?" He didn't ever shy away from the matter. If you're going to be true to yourself you've got to say, "Could I say it as cool as Hank Williams did?" You have to keep reminding yourself how strong the really strong songs are.

—Elvis Costello, 1988

Music is a beautifully subversive language because it can get through anything. . . . You've only got to look at the front of the new Billboard—who's on the front? Fuckin' Beethoven and Mozart. You can't ask for better than that, boys. Imagine what they'd have done if they'd had a little DAT recorder. You wouldn't have had twenty-six overtures, you'd have had fifty-bleeding-nine.

—Keith Richards, 1994

I don't want to get too influenced by one particular thing, get locked into it. I try to learn from as many different things as I can. It's all related in some way or another; that's the interesting thing about it. . . . My tastes really haven't changed since I was fourteen. Any idols I have in music are people that are dead, and some of them have been dead for a long time! Beethoven, Mahler, Shostokovich, Sibelius. Carl Neilson is very underrated, I like him. You know, Duke Ellington, Charlie Parker, the giants.

—Joe Jackson, 1986

I went to Elliott Carter's eightieth birthday concert with the New York Philharmonic last year. Carter is the greatest living composer, in my opinion. Zubin Mehta brought him out on stage to take a birthday bow. I was standing on my feet all thrilled and excited, and I looked around and these people in their furs were just kind of patting their palms, and I thought, Jesus, this is the amount of appreciation the greatest living composer gets from the people, who I guess have subscription tickets and are waiting for Ravel's "Bolero."

—Warren Zevon, 1990

People have told me about meeting their heroes and what a disappointment it is. It has always filled me with a sense of wonder and pleasure in the generosity of other people, of artists, that never goes away. It confirmed what I had hoped,

which was that a life in fine art was exciting and adventurous and rewarding. Those first visits to [Igor] Stravinsky's house where there were books in every imaginable language on every wall, and he had paintings and drawings by his friends like Picasso and Cocteau on the walls that were incredibly exciting.

—Warren Zevon, 1990

I'm looking at people like John Prine and K.T. Oslin for inspiration. It's like a whole new world has opened up. I think of myself as a songwriter now.

—Bonnie Raitt, 1990

We were playing with Steve Goodman in Chicago and he did a song I liked that John [Prine] wrote. And he kept sayin', "You gotta see this guy!" Well, everybody always tells me that. I didn't want to go. But the last night I decided to go see him. It happened that I'd run into Paul Anka and he was doing a song of mine, so we all went over to this club, the Earl of Oldtown, to see John. Well, we sat there and heard the greatest set of songs you could imagine. . . . I mean, you never hear songs that good from an unknown! He sang "Sam Stone," "Donald & Lydia," "Paradise," "Hello In There," "Far From Me." Aw, shit! We made him do it twice! I'm real critical on words and to hear one good song after another, God, it was amazing.

> —Kris Kristofferson, *Written in My Soul*

Phil Spector taught me the importance of stance. He said we could put anything into the song as long as we kept the attitude.

> —John Prine, 1978

Tim Hardin really made a strong impression on me with his second album—the one with "Reason To Believe" on it. What affected me most was the feeling, the attitude and the mood it would create in a room when you played it. What that album did for me was to help me find a place in myself that I could touch. That's what I think inspiration is: when somebody comes along that shows you something about yourself . . . opens up a place in you that you can tap.

> —Kenny Loggins, 1976

The main thing with Joni [Mitchell] is that she's able to look at something that's happened to her, draw back and crystallize the whole situation, then write about it. She brings tears to my eyes, what more can I say? It's bloody eerie.

> —Jimmy Page, 1975

I think Joni Mitchell has *really* hit a tough spot [currently]. As her work becomes more and more on her own terms you realize that she is a bit of a Pollyanna, a romantic, and she's less afraid of allowing that to surface. She's not disguising her naïveté and simplicity and need for affection in artifice.

> —Pete Townshend, 1986

I don't re-work a song the way Joni Mitchell does. Joni is amazing. If you ever looked inside her notebook. It blows your mind the way she writes. She writes the first draft, and the second draft and the third draft, and eventually there's four or five pages that are nothing but lines. I admire her more than I can say. . . . The courage it takes to distill a song like that.

> —Jimmy Webb, 1976

I've known Joni [Mitchell] since I was eighteen. I met her in one of the coffee houses. What an incredible talent she is. She writes about her relationships so much more vividly than I do. I guess I put more of a veil over what I'm talking about.

> —Neil Young, 1975

One of the things that knocks me out about Joni Mitchell—she picks out small things like a red dirt road that she went down, and the way she says it, it comes alive and it makes you think of something you did when you were a kid. There's a lot of other ways to touch the human mind and heart.

—Jim Seals, 1979

Joni [Mitchell] and I have often had shared our thoughts on work and lovers, and on one of my visits to Los Angeles she sang for me "Jealous Lovin' Can Make You Crazy," a song about the price of freedom, and I responded by singing her my own latest song, "Houses." Up above the New York streets I had sat at my piano writing this song of mountains and meadows. I escaped into an interior place of beauty and peace. When I finished, she looked at me with that beautiful wide smile and shook her head. "Judy, after all the shit you've been through, how can you still be so romantic?" she asked.

—Judy Collins, *Follow Your Heart*

I feel Carole King really did a lot to change things [for women writers]. Before she split up with Gerry Goffin, everyone used to say it was because of him that they were having so many hits. *Tapestry* really proved that women songwriters could make it too.

—Janis Ian, 1979

One of my greatest heroes is an old guy in New York named Doc Pomus. He wrote "Save The Last Dance For Me," "Suspicion," a lot of great Elvis stuff. I think he's probably the archetypal pop songwriter.

I do love Randy Newman. He wrote my favorite love song, "Marie." It completely destroys me now. That song is elegant simplicity.

—J.D. Souther, 1980

[Roger] McGuinn is still ahead of his time. There is a quote attributed to Charlie Mingus about Charlie Parker that rings true about Roger: "If Charlie was a gangster, there would be a lot of dead saxophone players." Well, if Roger McGuinn was a gangster, there would be a lot of dead R.E.M.s and groups like that. Not that they're not good groups, but without Roger McGuinn they wouldn't exist, and he's not really given credit for his influence on modern music.

—Elvis Costello, 1989

After twenty-five years as a professional, any compliment floors Steve [Winwood], any trace of recognition surprises him, and any little thing he can learn or discover is a source of delight. From him, you get a man's wisdom as well as a boy's love of fun.

—Billy Joel, 1988

I like Randy Newman—one of the few songwriters left with anything to say.

—Bob McDill, 1990

If I write a song and it doesn't sound as good as Randy Newman, I just put it away. I mean, who wants to put a mediocre song on a record just because you wrote it?

—Bonnie Raitt, 1990

Randy Newman, for instance, drives me crazy. I've gone on record saying that. What drives me crazy about him is that he's so great, but there's something emotionally blocked there. It may be something about his nature, but he doesn't put heart into his songs. He's got a tremendous intellect and a sense of humour, but he has a detachment. That's the reason why the guy makes me so mad.

—Warren Zevon, 1981

The turning point for me was a Lou Reed gig I attended in 1979; the first rock & roll concert I ever went to, in fact. Up to then I had been writing traditional songs, but after listening to Lou's songs I discovered there were all kinds of things I could write about that I hadn't written about before, and in different styles. For example, I discovered that I didn't have to have a chorus—

or for that matter, a melody.

—Suzanne Vega, 1987

People get too famous too fast these days and it destroys them. Some guys got it down—Leonard Cohen, Paul Brady, Lou Reed, John Prine, David Allen Coe, Tom Waits—I listen more to that kind of stuff than whatever is popular at the moment. They're not just witchdoctoring up the planet, they don't set up barriers. . . . Gordon Lightfoot, every time I hear a song of his, it's like I wish it would last forever.

—Bob Dylan

Harry Partch was an innovator. He built all his own instruments and kind of took the American hobo experience and designed instruments from ideas he gathered travelling around the United States in the '30s and '40s. He used a pump organ and industrial water bottles, created enormous marimbas. He died in the early '70s.

—Tom Waits, 1988

Stan [Rogers] was a great romantic. He really touched chords. He was a master of lyrics as far as I was concerned. His subject matter was quite narrow and yet every song was a masterpiece. He could just sum up a song beautifully in one line, and with the best songs you can look at one line and say that's what it's about. I still feel really angry and annoyed that fate could not have spared him a few more years.

                                    —Eric Bogle, 1985

I remember when *Blue* was first recorded that it was the first really confession-kind of writing. It was life, nothing left to lose, let's spit it out. When it was finished I went over to a friend's house and Kris Kristofferson was there, and I [showed him the lyrics]. He said, "Joni, save something for yourself." It was hard for him to look at it. There was an odd sense of respect like it was a Diane Arbus photo book or something.

                                    —Joni Mitchell, 1985

Kris [Kristofferson] is, of course, one of the best songwriters of all time. He shows more soul when he blows his nose than the ordinary person does at his honeymoon dance. But commercial is a word Kris refuses to hear. He has written a lot of hits and some standards, but he writes what he wants and sings what he wants—even if the record labels drop him—and for my album *Picnic* he was going to do his new songs about the Sandinistas in Nicaragua and about Jesse Jackson.

                        —Willie Nelson, *Willie: An Autobiography*

Well, I tell everybody I know about Townes [Van Zandt], 'cause Townes, as I see it, influenced Mickey Newbury, who influenced Kristofferson, who in turn influenced the whole fucking world. . . . Townes might have fucked it up himself. Whereas Townes was over here laid out somewhere, there was Kristofferson. . . . Kris never did blow a publisher's appointment. Even if he was drunk and stumbling around he'd get up and throw up his guts and keep his appointments. Townes would disappear. Different people have different styles. Same way with Mickey Newbury. I love Newbury, I produced an album with him, but he's the same way. He'll get a little roll going and disappear up in Oregon.

                                    —Bobby Bare, 1980

So there we were, Billy Joe Shaver and I, throwing pennies in the Suwannee River, sipping on a jug of Mogen David blackberry wine and talking to two black men who were fishing. . . . They have a Stephen Foster memorial somewhere along there where the river is. We went to see it and damned if they didn't have his royalty statements and all. (He didn't make any money either.) I know you think I'm going to compare Billy Joe to Stephen Foster, but I'm not. I'm going to compare him to the river. His thoughts run deep and black, until he hits a riffle, and then he can smile all over the damn place. . . . Billy Joe writes the kind of lines that make you think that you and he are the only ones who understand them.

—Tom T. Hall

On a tour in 1965, I stopped in Phoenix where the hottest act in town was a kid called Waylon Jennings. I went to catch his show, and afterwards we shared a bottle of tequila and he asked my advice on his career. "Whatever you do, Waylon, stay away from Nashville," I told him. "Nashville ain't ready for you. They'll just break your heart."

Upon hearing my advice, Waylon did what any good songwriter would do. He went to Nashville.

—Willie Nelson, *Willie: An Autobiography*

The best songs for me are the Scottish ballads. They're very distilled. They're very terse with very powerful language. In one verse you get tremendous economy and imagery. That's the finest form of songwriting for me. What I hear in people like Dylan is the kind of collage of traditional music. He cuts up all those things—blues, Scottish music, Appalachian music—kind of rearranges it into more surreal form.

—Richard Thompson, 1982

It's like this painter who lives around here—he paints the area in a radius of twenty miles, bright strong pictures. He might take a barn from twenty miles away, and hook it up with a brook right next door, then with a car ten miles away, and with the sky on some certain day, and the light on the trees from another day. A person passing by will be painted alongside someone ten miles away. And in the end he'll have this composite picture of something which you can't say exists in his mind. It's not that he started off willfully painting this picture from all his experience. . . . That's more or less what I do.

—Bob Dylan, 1968

For everyone writing these days, Dylan is the benchmark. At one point you have to put your song against one of his and realize you got a long way to go. My favourite album is *Blonde On Blonde*.

—Michael Timmins (Cowboy Junkies), 1990

I don't need for Bob Dylan to become one thing or another. What he is is a constant—a constant mystery, always a surprise.

—Jackson Browne, 1987

She [Stevie Nicks] doesn't mind staying the same. It's the most undemanding thing for the listeners, but it's unbelievably demanding for the writer; however you feel about Stevie Nicks, there's no question that she is one of the most *tortured* songwriters ever. She gets into a mental state for about two or three months for a record. All she does is write! I mean, that's *all* she does!

—Pete Townshend, 1986

A lot of people think that Stevie Nicks is really nuts. She isn't. She has just found, or created for herself, a lifestyle so she can function with the right side [of her brain], and she writes all the time. She's one of the most underrated songwriters in America.

—John Stewart, 1979

I would love to write a couple of great rock songs in my life, like Chrissie Hynde did. If you write something that will transcend a long period of time and make people feel a certain way, there's really nothing like that.

—Courtney Love, 1994

Malvina Reynolds' songs are sneaky things. They slip across borders, proliferate in prisons, penetrate hard shells.

—Pete Seeger, 1978

I honestly love a lot of music—it just goes in me. That's why I get angered when people say I'm obviously influenced by somebody else. That makes me more stubborn just to do what I like, and not listen to anybody—I'm a child that way. Anyway, it's pointless and misleading to throw out a few names, so when people ask me about it, I just make vague circles in the air.

—Jane Siberry

By the time I was twenty or twenty-one, I heard Van Morrison. He was an inspiration, because his music and his lyrics and everything, to me, are just too . . . good. I don't think I've found anybody in all the years who can sort of equal him.

—Joan Armatrading, 1989

I have a letter at home from a girl who told me about her life, which was not going particularly well. She finished off by saying, "Thank you for being in my empty room when nobody else was there." Now, Smokey Robinson did that to me, and if I met him today, I would have to say exactly that to him. I'd probably not even be able to bring myself to speak to him, because he had such a powerful influence on me when I was alone and lonely.

—Billy Bragg, 1976

After Richard [Farina] died I had a dream about him. We ran into each other on the street in New

York. He was wearing a red and black sweater. We talked intensely about writing while we drove uptown in a bright yellow taxi. I told him I had finally started writing songs.

"I'm so happy for you," he said, hugging me hard. He leaped out of the taxi and vanished up the street, looking over his shoulder at me, smiling, his eyes twinkling. I miss him still.

—Judy Collins, *Follow Your Heart*

The most famous musician in Austin when I got there [1971] was Jerry Jeff Walker. Janis Joplin had sung for years at Kenneth Threadgill's place in Austin, but she'd gone to San Francisco to make her reputation. Jerry Jeff and I had some wild nights and days partying and picking in joints and people's homes around Austin. Everybody wanted Jerry Jeff to play his classic "Mr. Bojangles," but he never did like to be told what to play or when to play it. If some host asked Jerry Jeff to play "Mr. Bojangles" or anything else, he was liable to whip out his dick and piss in the potted ficus plant, and the fight would start.

—Willie Nelson, *Willie: An Autobiography*

I asked Willie Nelson when he was going to retire. He said, "All I do is play golf and play music. Which one do you want me to give up?"

—Jerry Jeff Walker, 1984

A guitar-pulling is where songwriters gather in somebody's room and fight it out for attention and approval. You might say it's like a bunch of old west gunfighters coming together to see who is best—only instead of slapping their holsters and coming up with six-guns blazing, they unsnap their guitar cases and come up singing. This would be a room full of real piranhas too. Picture a dozen novelists getting together in one room, and each in turn reads his latest chapter out loud to the others, who are all competing for the same publishers and audience. That would be a novel-pulling. You can imagine the tension in the room, scornful glares, caustic remarks—but you can also imagine the tremendous feeling of pleasure when the other writers couldn't help but break into murmurs of respect.

—Willie Nelson, *Willie: An Autobiography*

I'm very country-influenced, from quite young—Merle Haggard, Johnny Cash, George Jones, and so on. I heard those people, really, before I heard blues.

—Mick Jagger, 1994

For me, without George [Jones], there is no "country"(music). The lyrical content of the working man in his songs has always hit the bulls-eye, and touched at the heart of what is country. George Jones is also no quitter.

—Gene Simmons (Kiss), 1994

My heroes at this point in time all have lines in their faces. . . . I prefer to spend a day with Johnny Cash than a week with some up-and-coming pop star.

—Bono, 1989

Everybody I admire is either dead or real sick.

—Tom Waits

[Kurt Weill and I] were ardent readers of people like Hemingway and Fitzgerald, and we saw all the movies.

—Lotte Lenya, 1935

Minneapolis was the first big city I lived in if you want to call it that. I came out of the wilderness and just naturally fell in with the beat scene, the Bohemian, BeBop crowd. It was all pretty much connected. . . . There were always a lot of poems recited—"Into the room people come and go talking of Michaelangelo, measuring their lives in coffee spoons" . . . "What I'd like to know is what do you think of your blue-eyed boy now, Mr. Death." T.S. Eliot, e.e. cummings. It kind of woke me up.

—Bob Dylan, *CBS Autobiography*

Words paint pictures, and I'd rather leave a lot to the imagination. Music should always do that. I've been influenced by the Beat poets such as e.e. cummings. I've always had a surrealist's view of the world.

—Ric Ocasek (The Cars), 1984

There've been some instructive things, some standards that writers have given me. T.S. Eliot and Robert Lowell can get away with really complex stuff in a conversational tone. To me, Eliot is a real hard-boiled guy—he never lapses into fancy writing because he likes to live. That's a quality I admire.

—Warren Zevon, 1987

I originally read novelists, newspaper writers and columnists. You take a Buchwald, or an Irma Bombeck, William Safire, Mary McGrory. You wonder how they do it day after day. They write such interesting things and such good things and well-informed things. Writing to me is all just one big word. It's not just songwriting.

—Tom T. Hall, 1979

It's important for songwriters to read as much of anything as they can. Good novels, or good poetry, or good pulp fiction. Listen to me—I grew up on science fiction. Who am I to talk?

—Janis Ian, 1977

I just got a book of poetry, an anthology of American verse, and I found that the ones closest to the kind of music I was interested in were by the black poets and the Jewish poets, and by the uneducated folk poets who didn't use words out of dictionaries but the words that ordinary people used.

—Galt McDermot, 1972

When I was about eight or nine, for about three years I got through dozens and dozens of books, mostly fiction, but as soon as I began writing poems at school—basically as soon as I started writing songs—everything else seemed to go out the window. When I'd sit down and read a book, I'd think how I could be writing songs.

—Kate Bush, 1989

I've always envied writers like Tom Wolfe, who could write quickly. He'd write 35,000 words in a day, standing, on top of the refrigerator. Then there are the other kinds of writers, like Flaubert, who would do just a few sentences a day, or Hemingway, who would do his 500 words and then stop, even if he was in the middle of a sentence. I'm in that tradition. I have to think about every single word I write.

—Leonard Cohen, 1985

"Seven Steps To The Wall" ended up as an interpretation of the Arthur Koessler book *Darkness At Noon*, about a Soviet prisoner awaiting execution. When I had the idea for those songs, I kept seeing a room that was very bare, with a certain quality of light, and someone sitting in the middle of it. Then I read the book, and decided, "There he is! Perfect."

—Jane Siberry

These days Raymond Chandler is my favorite author. He would have made a great songwriter. I used to dig Herman Hesse but I don't think I would rush out to buy one of his records.

—Dan Zanes

Sinclair Lewis was asked one time to talk to a class of students about writing. When he got there he asked the class, "Do you people want to be writers?" and they all said yes. Then he said, "Why the hell aren't you at home writing?"

—Tom T. Hall, 1979

CHAPTER 5

"I PICK UP THE PEN AND GOD MOVES IT"

INSPIRATION AND MOTIVATION

"What is an artist?" asked Henry Miller. "He's a man who has an antenna who knows how to hook up to the currents which are in the atmosphere, in the cosmos. He merely has the facility for hooking on." Ezra Pound went a step further: "The artist is the antenna of the race." Many songwriters subscribe to that belief. Bukka White called them "sky songs"—songs that fell down from the sky. Most writers talk about the ones that just "moved through them"—of the feeling of acting as a medium or an antenna.

My experience of a "sky song" was centred around the song "Gallo del Cielo." I had written the word "cockfighting" in a notebook in 1978. It was a code word that I couldn't decipher. A year or so later I was in a garage in Mountainview, California and felt the urge to write. Within half an hour a fully realized Tex-Mex-style corrido, with seven verses, was finished and polished. It sounded like an age-worn folk tale. I never knew where it came from. I walked into the kitchen and played it for my then-wife. She said it was a great song. She had tears in her eyes. These experiences are rare.

—T.R.

Most of us have written at least one song that strikes us like lightning. You write it in twenty minutes, and you don't change a word or a note. You think to yourself, "I've finally got it figured out. This is how it's done." This euphoria lasts right up to the point when you try to write the next one. Generally I find that inspiration only provides you with the heart, the germ of the song. The rest of it you sweat blood over. I do know one thing—if it strikes you and you don't act on it, somebody else will. There is a time and a place for certain songs to happen, and you'd better be there first.

—S.T.

I pick up the pen and God moves it.

—Hank Williams, *Willie: An Autobiography*

It should be: I pick up the [computer] mouse and God moves it.

—Eddie Schwartz, 1990

The songs are there. They exist by themselves just waiting for someone to write them down. If I didn't do it, someone else would.

—Bob Dylan, 1962

I understand that when you don't hear anything, and you hear this very high frequency. That's the sound of the universe.

—Stevie Wonder, 1973

Woody Guthrie said he just picked songs out of the air. That meant they were already there and that he was tuned into them. "Changing of the Guards" might be a song that might have been there for thousands of years, sailing around in the mist, and one day I just tuned into it. Just like "Tupelo Honey" was floating around and Van Morrison came by.

—Bob Dylan, 1978

Melodies are the easiest part for me, because the air is full of melodies. I hear them all the time, around me everywhere, night and day. If I need a melody, I pluck one out of the air.

—Willie Nelson, *Willie: An Autobiography*

Ideas really flow through the air. I've seen it too many times to call it a coincidence. Creative thought must be so incredibly strong and vital that it must be like a radio transmitter. Either that or there must be some kind of flow in the air itself that we all draw from, because there's too many similarities, sometimes, in the things that people do.

—Jimmy Webb, 1976

There's a famous blues guitarist, Booker T. Washington, better known as Bukka White, who writes what he calls "sky songs." His theory is that they fall out of the sky and into his head and on to the paper. That, to me, is the most marvelous description.

—Leo Sayer, 1978

I just pull them down, and when I feel that they are there, I try to put them into something and make them and shape them into songs.

—Donovan, 1967

I'm a radio receiver. I do not know where the songs are coming from, but they are all out there, and they just come in.

—John Stewart, 1979

I don't want to sound spiritual, but I try to make an antenna out of myself, so whatever is out there can come in. It happens in different places, in hotels, in the car—when someone else is driving. I bang on things, slap on the wall, break things—whatever is in the room. There are all these things in the practical world that you deal with on a practical level, and you don't notice them as anything but what you need them to be. But when I'm writing, all these things turn into something else, and I see them differently—almost like I've taken a narcotic. Somebody once said I'm not a musician, but a tonal engineer. I like that. It's kind of clinical and primitive at the same time.

—Tom Waits, 1988

I'm the antenna. You just stick your finger in the air and you grab a bit of it. That's the way to avoid writer's block, because that's the thing that happens to people that think they actually create things. Nobody creates anything. It's there and you just fucking grab hold of it.

—Keith Richards, 1994

That's one of the reasons why, when I write an

album, I want to get it out right away. Because someone, somewhere is thinking the same things.

—Steven Tyler (Aerosmith), 1994

Bundini Brown, who used to be in Muhammad Ali's corner during his heavyweight champion years, believes powerful thoughts and sounds are always passing through us in radio waves, and what we must do is learn to listen. Bundini's classic line, "Float like a butterfly, sting like a bee," popped into his head through radio waves, he says. He recognized it as inspired advice for Ali to adopt as his philosophy in the ring. Bundini believes God is in the radio waves that our conscious minds too often choose to tune out. I agree with him about all of that, as you know by now, but for the purpose of talking about songwriting, we will stick to the part about inspiration.

—Willie Nelson, *Willie: An Autobiography*

I don't know how many times I've been in a conversation with people and looked at the whole room as if it were a play, as if I had ripped open the roof of a motel room and was looking into it. Christ! If I'm not a songwriter or a mathematician, maybe I'm an astral projectionist.

—John Prine, 1978

I can't say I've ever seen the clear light and been given a sign from the sky, but I definitely feel I've been used at times to say certain things, and I feel, re-reading these things, that it wasn't altogether me. I go back and read it, and say, "Oh . . . there's an elemental truth in this phrase that I didn't intend. . . . I didn't conceive of it." I definitely do believe in some spiritual aspect to this . . . some kind of energy.

—Jimmy Webb, 1976

There's a thing I call "the beast." It's just something that writers deal with. It's the ability to look into the darkness and not blink. At the same time, you can't get overly morose about it, because it feeds you.

—Steve Earle, 1987

All of a sudden there's a song—there in your hotel room playing your guitar—and you write it, and two or three years later it will come true. That happens a lot. Sometimes I'm almost afraid to write one because of that. The serious ones—I write them first and it happens later. It keeps you on your toes.

—Townes Van Zandt, 1981

When you're writing a song and it's working, it feels like ten or fifteen minutes, and when you look up, you see it's been three hours. It's like a state of euphoria. I'm just not there. Anybody that talks to me gets an unintelligible or stupid answer, or a bark. I dont know if it comes from the conscious or your unconscious which mixes with your conscious, or whether it's just sitting in the air and you luck into it. A universal brain: you've heard that theory.

—Janis Ian, 1977

They say creative people are always not quite there. I'm beginning to believe that. Some days it gets very, very spooky.

—Lionel Richie, 1980

What is that magic? It's a real scary process judging by the way some people look at you when they realize that you are the writer of a song that is particularly meaningful for them. It's scary too, because when you're sitting there in the process of writing that song, you go through such changes. It's almost like, when you hit that area of right, your body reacts like a pinball machine that just hit the jackpot. You all of a sudden know it's right. But what makes you so accurate that it should be right? It's a weird thing, really.

—Paul Anka, 1976

I have to separate the emotional contribution from the technical knowledge. The emotion comes from somewhere else . . . somewhere up above. Nobody can really define that.

—Neil Sedaka, 1976

It's a strange thing, writing songs. I wish I could explain what happens. Here's my analogy: you get an idea, a single idea or a seed, and that seed by some code—like a D.N.A. code—grows arms and legs, choruses and bridges, and what you do as the songwriter is you monitor that growth. Sometimes the arms and legs grow in the wrong place and you have to whift them around, but the actual process of writing is very strange and kind of magical.

—Sting, 1988

We were checking out of a hotel in West Virginia one morning, and I started singing "Get Closer." From the time we got to the airport and got on the plane to the next town, the song was already written. I had discovered it.

—Jim Seals, 1979

I once read a description by another writer that I carry around with me: "The song goes from your heart to your pen, and it must not go anywhere near your head, because if it goes anywhere near your head, then it becomes a construction. But if it goes from your heart to your pen, then it becomes a feeling." I don't even remember who said it.

—Leo Sayer, 1978

Ideas? It's like whistling. Why did I whistle that? I don't know. It just came out, right? Did it just pop into my head or was it a combination of preconceived programs or ideas? I don't know about the higher power. It happens so quickly it seems like it's coming from somewhere else. It's not, it just means you're in sync with yourself. The closer you get to it, the faster it comes out. If you start studying it or analyzing it, it goes away.

—Harry Nilsson, 1989

When I write songs, I don't think. There's no thinking process. In fact, it's a non-thinking process. It's very difficult for me to talk about it because when I write I'm not thinking about it, I'm just doing it.

—Van Morrison, 1985

You can be really creative without thinking about it. Ideally you want to get to a place in songwriting where you're not consciously writing a song; where you can just pick up an instrument and the song comes.

—Peter Buck (R.E.M.), 1994

Creating is a physical, instinctive thing. Analysis is retrospective. If you sat down and talked with your girlfriend about why you were about to go to bed, it would spoil it. Music isn't accessible to logical analysis. Most of us don't quite know what we're doing. We turn on the tap and what comes out—that comes from somewhere else. We're not the source of creative power, simply tools in the hands of forces we cannot presume to understand. Even the best gardener couldn't make a single flower.

—Robert Wyatt, 1992

This power inside, that's what makes you a singer, a poet, an author. And it will never dry up as long as you live. When you distrust it, when you don't believe in it, that's when it dries up. It is in you forever. It is you, it is your life. You can never use enough of it. There's a huge well of it. When you are lying down looking up and counting the rafters, and you can't think what to do because you are so lost in pain, that's when the subconscious comes to you and brings you what you need. When you think everything is finished and you finally let go, that's when it happens. You just have to tap it, and it will start to flow.

—S.E. Rogie, 1994

The big disappointment about being a song-writer is that you get an idea, and you think, "This is incredible! I've got to write this down," and you write it down, and then you play it the next morning and it seems really flat. But that's also partly being slightly schizophrenic. Which voice do you want to listen to? The shut-down voice or the enthusiastic voice? The enthusiastic voice is the only one that matters. The other is the voice of death. It's nowhere. You're better off writing really bad songs than living in some kind of critical orbit. That'll give you writer's block.

—Peter Case, 1992

Very often ideas come to me when I'm falling asleep—when the busy mind gets out of the way, and the intuitive, imaginative mind gets a shot at the steering wheel. My friend, writer William Gibson, told me, "It's an established phenomenon. The elves take over the workshop." That's why all writers keep a pen and paper by their beds.

—David Crosby

It's not a matter of craftsmanship. It's like being possessed; like a psychic or medium. The thing has to go down. It won't let you sleep, so you have to get up, make it into something, and then you're allowed to sleep. That's always in the middle of the bloody night when you're half-awake or tired, and your critical faculties are switched off.

—John Lennon

Sometimes things just pour out in a sensual way, and I think some of your best writing does bypass the intellect, but you have to go in there and prime the pump, and certainly you have to use it [the intellect] to double-check things, to criticize your own work. And then you have to be able to switch out.

—Joni Mitchell, 1988

I hear a catchy expression and I pass it on to my subconscious and I say, "I want a song out of this." I believe everything useful comes from there. It creates the song, passes it back to me, and says, "Hey, you, take it out. Go use it!"

—S.E. Rogie, 1994

I feel songs are gifts. I mean I think I was meant to write a certain amount of songs, and I feel that when you start slowing up that you've said all that you can say.

—Mel Tillis, 1977

I do not think the concept of writing completely

embodies my inner God. I think there's something inside of me. I'm not an atheist. I have cause to question religion because it's responsible for most of the wars and inhumanity in the world today. I believe there's one presence and it comes to people in different ways. There's a big picture out there. All my music is strangely centred on that. I'm not a religious writer but I'm aware of my connections. I believe that the good and bad things in the world, unless it's a horrible victimization of weak people, are done for a reason. Good and bad things happen to you, and as long as they don't kill or maim you, they've got to be done for a reason.

—Ray Davies, 1990

I think it comes from the will to create, and I believe songwriters get the ideas for songs from the same place that computer designers get their ideas . . . the same place that Edison got his ideas. Out of the ether, from God, whatever, primarily just from the will to create, and if that is strong and true, then you're going to create or re-create some original ideas.

—Hoyt Axton, 1976

I take today and tomorrow as it comes. I can't sing. I don't know a lick of music, but God gave me a gift somewhere along the line, and He gave me what I have to write my songs. I live the day and I love the people.

—Wilf Carter (Montana Slim), 1971

The first place those barriers [of colour] broke down was in music. I believe in God very strongly, and I think the reason I was given my musical ability is because that was His mission for me, and if I could have chosen my own mission, I wouldn't have wanted it any other way.

—Smokey Robinson, 1976

There is an "essence of hit song" that writers have. There is a little piece of something there that if you can reach that essence and tap it, the song that emerges is of such high quality that it will grab even the most jaded ears. But getting your finger on that essence and keeping in touch with it is what has been so difficult for me at any rate, and I assume for a lot of other writers too.

—Alan O'Day, 1975

The blues is only an outward voice to that inward feeling, and way back yonder, when Adam and Eve was put out of the Garden of Eden to till the earth—he began to sing a song.

—Rev. Emmett Dickinson, 1930

In blues it's what you call a felt-inward feeling—of your own self. It's not a spiritual feeling that you have. . . . It's something that happened to you and caused you to feel sorry . . . then you would compose a song to that feeling that you have. And then you would sing it. . . . You become accustomed to it through psychology that most anybody could have the same feelings as you did. It's universal, but it don't bring joy to the spirit.

—Rev. Rob. Wilkins

The blues is a natural fact.

—Brownie McGhee

Whenever I heard the song of a bird and the answering call of its mate, I could visualize the notes on a scale. This was the primitive prelude to the mature melodies now recognized as the blues. Nature was my kindergarten.

—W.C. Handy

If Tom [Tommy Johnson] was living, he'd tell you, he sold hisself to the devil. He said, "If you want to learn how to play anything you want to play and learn how to make songs yourself, you take your guitar and you go to where a road crosses that way, where a crossroad is. . . . Be sure to get there just a little 'fore twelve o'clock so you know you'll be there. You have your guitar and be playing a piece sitting there by yourself . . . a big black man will walk up there and take your guitar, and he'll tune it. And then he'll play a piece and hand it back to you. Thats the way I learned how to play anything I want."

—Rev. LeDell Johnson

Robert Johnson's singing becomes so disturbed it is almost impossible to understand the words. Johnson seemed emotionally disturbed by the image of the devil, the "Hellhound," and he used the image in at least two blues songs.

—Samuel Charters, *The Country Blues*

It was in Friar's Point [Mississippi], and this guy had a lot of people standing around him. He coulda been Robert [Johnson], they said it was Robert. I stopped and peeked over, and then I left, because he was a dangerous man. I got to see his picture a little while back, and since I've seen it, I think I really heard him.

—Muddy Waters, *Deep Blues* (Robert Palmer)

The blues derive mostly out of the Baptist churches. Because a preacher, if he's preaching gospel, he doesn't have to be making no particular sound as long as he was preaching from the bible, right? A preacher could do that until he gets warmed up and get a certain sound going.

—Baby Doo Caston

The difference between blues and spiritual songs is, you can only sing the one and not the other. . . . See, the body is the temple of the spirit of God, and it ain't but one spirit can dwell in that body at a time. That's the good spirit or the evil spirit. Blues are songs of the evil spirit.

—Rev. Robert Wilkins

If a man hurt within and he sing a church song, then he's askin' God for help. If a man sing the blues, it's more or less out of himself. He's not askin' no one for help. That's what make it a sin.

—Li'l Son Jackson

Jimmie Rodgers was a bluesman. A lot of those songs Jimmie Rodgers didn't write. He got them from the blacks he heard when he was growing up in Mississippi and when he worked as a brakeman on the railroad.

—Bill Neely, *Meeting the Blues* (Alan Govener)

I worked hard at listening to country music, but it all came together in the back of a Cadillac one night. It belonged to a friend of mine, and he had a great stereo in that Cad. An old George Jones song, "It's Been a Good Year for the Roses," came on and what I was working so hard to understand, became instantly understood. I suddenly became aware of what country music was all about.

—Bob McDill, 1977

The whole area of creation plays all kinds of tricks on the writer. It can fool him into thinking it's easier than it is; it can fool him into thinking it's harder than it is; it can fool him into thinking it's working when it's not, or not working when it is.

—Mark Knopfler, 1985

Almost anything else is easy except writing songs. The hardest part is when the inspiration dies along the way, then you spend all your time trying to recapture it. I don't write every day. I'd like to but I can't. You're talking to a total misfit. Gershwin, Bacharach—they've got songwriting down. I don't really care if I write. I can say that now, but as soon as the light changes, it'll be the thing I care about most. When I'm through performing I'll probably be writing for other people.

—Bob Dylan, 1976

Pursue your interests. If writing songs is what you want to do, then apply yourself and do it. I love to write. It's what makes me move. I'll write for the opening of a supermarket if need be. I'm writing as expertly as I know how to write. What else can I do?

—Sammy Cahn, 1976

I take great pride in my work and I not only feel competitive with all other writers, I feel competition within myself. I don't want my songs to be repetitive. I like to think I'm progressing.

—Smokey Robinson, 1976

When I first started out, the idea that soft music is female and hard music is male was in the process of being flushed down the toilet, and women were starting to write about things that had seemed perfectly natural for me to be writing about. I just never knew how else to do it. Whatever rejection I met within the business, I was not told the reason. But rejection was not going to deter me from what I was doing, because I was doing it for my own emotional existence and sanity. If you have a need to sing or write, it's part of you.

—Melissa Manchester, 1976

Writing ten melodies to get one has never been a problem for me. I've written a lot of songs because I enjoy writing. I can't think of any-

thing else I'd rather do, and it was never work for me.

—Harry Warren, 1977

Texans know no guilt—it takes a high incentive to get us to work.

—J.D. Souther, 1980

There is nothing that can quite compare with being broke and desperate to make a real writer keep working.

—Willie Nelson

I didn't have to find time to write. I had a lot of time because I wasn't workin', and I didn't have the obligation then. Shit, I was starvin'.

—Ray Charles, 1973

I love writing, but I am not a true writer. I wrote because maybe I heard an idea, or somebody said something, or I needed some material and I couldn't find none that suited me, so I sat down and wrote my own.

—Ray Charles, 1973

I don't see how anybody can write songs when they are miserable. I think that one has been done to death. I mean, maybe Leonard Cohen can do it, but I can't.

—Van Morrison, 1990

Melancholy isn't a bad word. That state of mind has been a motive for writing songs for people throughout history in different places. Writing a song is one response, a courageous response to that state of mind.

       —Leonard Cohen, 1985

In the middle of the night you'll wake up, and you think you have this bit, and you'll sing it to yourself [into a tape recorder]. Then you'll wake up in the morning and play it back, and it's [hums "Mary Had a Little Lamb"]. God, last night that sounded good, it fit right in with my nightmare.

     —Rick Neilson (Cheap Trick), 1981

No [schedule for writing]. I wrote "If I Needed You" in my sleep.

      —Townes Van Zandt, 1990

Writing a song is like doing a crossword puzzle, though you can't get too literary. It's a gift when the words come.

       —Joni Mitchell, 1980

Sometimes it's just "Whoopee!" you've got a song. That's the best way, when it just comes upon you and you've got to stop doing everything. It's wondrous. It's what makes you want to write songs.   —Robbie Robertson, 1970

The spirit doesn't move me too often, about once a month. The rest I have to dig for.

       —Bob McDill, 1977

I don't get in touch with her [the muse]. She gets in touch with me.

      —Robbie Robertson, 1991

I've learned that there are cycles of creativity. There are years when you write better than other years and you're not even responsible for it.

       —Glenn Frey, 1988

If you write every day, and finish everything, then when a great piece of inspiration comes along you'll be ready for it.

       —Don Schlitz, 1990

The writing of a song tends to take precedence over anything else I may be doing. It's easy to lose a song if you get distracted at the wrong time. That's not always bad, of course.

      —Bruce Cockburn, 1978

It's like football, in a way, because you have to get yourself in shape for it. But then, the inspired teams win, and the inspired players accomplish.

      —Tom T. Hall, 1979

My songwriting process has never changed. I never try to write. I know when it's there. I hear a bell ringing in my head and I just leave, but I don't try. Sometimes three months can go by.

—Neil Young, 1979

I see two stages of writing. First comes inspiration, all by itself like a dream. I can't fake it. It just shows up. Then comes working on the song. This part is objective. It might be fun, but it's still work. If there's a deadline, like for a film score, I go on a schedule: do it 'til it's done.

—Buffy Sainte-Marie, 1990

You actually start because there's a sound to what you want to do, or there's a passion that pulls the music along. The music slots into place behind it.

—Richard Thompson, 1994

I compose under a nervous strain. More often than otherwise, I feel as if my life depends on my accomplishing a song.

—Irving Berlin, *As Thousands Cheer—The Life of Irving Berlin*

Musical inspiration is a peculiar sort of thing. It just comes. One cannot sit down and think and think until melodies come to the mind. I am much too busy for that. . . . I just go on with the business of living until something occurs to me. It may be while I am at dinner, or on a bus, or even when I am having a bath. If I am anywhere near a piano I fly to it and play the tune with one hand. That "fixes it," as a photographer would say, and I can proceed with the rest in a more leisurely way.

—Noel Coward, *How I Write My Songs*

So I think it's not so much alcohol or drugs themselves which are the keys to creativity, but the fact that for certain individuals suffering and discomfort start you off on some new pursuit for understanding and possibly even for the different kind of pleasure release which the adrenaline rush of creativity produces. It's like a by-product of a by-product. I don't think anybody who sits and writes is absolutely contented, absolutely happy. People like that just don't write. A drug or drinking problem is just a symptom of something which is already part of their makeup.

—Pete Townshend, 1987

[In the past] I'd find myself stirring things up, stirring up the people around me. If things started to get too placid or idyllic I'd just do something to get everything stirred up. It took a lot to admit that to myself, but I think I would just get everything in a turmoil so the music would come. It's a hard thing to talk about because it's not something you're conscious of or you wouldn't do it.

—Tom Petty, 1986

I just do what I do for the people who already like it. If I pick up a few new friends along the way, then that's fine, but my obligation is to people who like what I do, not the critics or any pressure group. I do what I do first of all for my own amusement, because I enjoy it, and second of all for the audience.

—Frank Zappa, 1980

Aroma! The scent of burning oak leaves in October in Missouri. Next, an oncoming breeze loaded with the smell of mint plants, a Chinese restaurant while waiting for a table, a passing pipe-smoker using rum and maple tobacco, the uncontaminated breasts of a female companion, the brewing of coffee in the winter, the interior of a new automobile I just purchased, and although I detest the smell of liquor, somehow I'm carried asunder by the surprise of liquor on the breath of a strange lady.

—Chuck Berry, *Chuck Berry—An Autobiography*

Ideas—they're almost like a smell. I just kind of feel the images of the spirit or something. Not so much the lyric or the melody.

—Rickie Lee Jones, 1989

You walk down the street and see a bag lady talking or crying to herself, and right beside her are two businessmen saying, "See you for lunch tomorrow," and a bus goes by with somebody reading a paper. All this is going on right in front of you. That's when I think, "Fuckin' hell! Some people say they had to go away for inspiration? Shit!"

—Dave Stewart, 1988

You got to be strong and stay connected to what started it all, the inspiration behind the inspiration, to who you were when people didn't mind stepping on you. It's easy to say but the air gets thin at the top, you get light-headed, your environment changes, new people come into your life.

—Bob Dylan

CHAPTER 6

ORDER
OUT OF CHAOS

THE CRAFT OF
SONGWRITING

To my mind, there are three kinds of songwriters: those who write intricate lyrics with simple melodies (e.g., Bob Dylan), those who write glorious melodies with simple lyrics (e.g., Paul McCartney), and those who strike a balance between the two (e.g., Paul Simon). The latter of the three is what I aspire to, but don't always accomplish.

Every song has a shape, a form. You can see it when it's written down. Think of it as freedom within a framework, as a painter would. Writing the lyrics first can make the song a little inflexible and, well, wordy. We tend to fall into the same patterns over and over again. Melody is freer than lyrics. When the melody comes first it allows you to jam words up, or toss some of them away altogether to make the rest of them fit. Either way, nothing is carved in stone. It's all Silly Putty.

—S.T.

Many amateur songwriters confuse the ability to write poetry or be clever with rhyme with the essence of lyric writing. Many writers quoted below are very specific in their belief that poetry is vastly different from song lyrics. Sammy Cahn said Shakespeare would have been a lousy songwriter. Maybe—I keep thinking of those song-shark ads in the back of comic books—"Songwriters, send us your poems!" I've often thought there's a closer kinship between the painter and the songwriter than there is between the poet and the songwriter.

I think it's also important to develop that (aforementioned) "built-in shit-detector." Writers have got to trust their intuitive sense about what works and what rings true. Writers' chops and "tricks of the trade" generally take a lifetime of work to develop, and they usually lead you back in a circle to the point where you were as a six-year-old kid with that unfettered ability to make up stories and create magic.

—T.R.

To me a song is like a piece of sculpture. You hammer it from all angles until the pure thing is left in the middle. And then if it works from every angle you know you've got something.

—Suzanne Vega, 1990

For my own use, I've always just called a song a song. I didn't even hear the word "ballad" or "folk" 'til I hit New York in the snow of '41. . . . After all, every song is a song, by the folks and for the folks. I don't recall really ever writing any songs for cows, chickens, fish, monkeys, nor wild animals of any kind.

—Woody Guthrie, 1948

If no music paper were handy, he [Stephen Foster] would take whatever paper he could find, and proceed without hesitation to write. . . . These first drafts were taken out and sold to a publisher, practically without correction.

—George Cooper, 1862

Your songs and your ballads, just like every kind of job of work you'll ever do, will be just as good as the number of days and months and weeks and years that you put in a song and a ballad maker. You are always on the job.

—Woody Guthrie, 1948

You just sit down and do it. I mean, these songs don't just pop off the top of your head when you're walking down the street. You can have the thread of an idea, but you've got to sit down and write it down and work it out, and this sometimes takes a couple of days.

—Gordon Lightfoot, 1976

I try to work, or at least be in the office five days a week from nine to five. This gives some order to the chaos.

—Bob McDill, 1990

I try to write three days a week, but it is not something you can just turn off. People without the gift have a hard time understanding that you can be working furiously with your feet up and staring out the window. You can also pretend you're working while in the same position. Just about everyone would appreciate being able to do that. Writers are sure lucky!

—Peter McCann, 1990

I take pride in the speed with which I write and my dependability. If I tell you I'll have a song, I'll get it to you when I promised. Many times I've gotten jobs over men with far superior talents but who were undependable.

—Sammy Cahn, 1976

101

It's not given to all of us to be the most talented, but it is given to all of us to be disciplined and prompt.

—Buddy DeSilva (quoted by Sammy Cahn), 1976

In the old days when Tin Pan Alley was a row of brownstone houses on 28th Street, and every room had a piano with a man working out songs, I'd say most of them had talent. But the talent for work is something else again. You either have to have that, or cultivate it.

—Irving Berlin, 1978

Although songwriting requires a great deal of discipline, I've never been able to do it as a sort of regimented exercise. There are professional writers who sit down and say "Well, Tuesday morning, I've got to write a song" and they do it. I've got to have certain freedoms in my head and around me—and an environment for me to write in, and it all usually takes shape at the piano.

—Paul Anka, 1976

You have to be diligent that when you exercise discipline in your writing you don't over-discipline your work and become too slick. Otherwise, all you end up with is a marvelous example of a clump of verse with no life or blood in it. —Norman Gimbel, 1978

A lot of the discipline problem with writing, I think, stems from the educational process; the "Oh God, I've got to do my homework" syndrome. It's not really drudgery to write songs, it's actually fun, but you think it's going to be drudgery because you're used to someone cracking the whip. It's hard to get that out of your system. I was always one of those guys who put his paper off 'til the night it was due.

—Patrick Simmons, 1979

In order to write, you have to be very very rude to people . . . get them out of the way. And you have to insulate yourself from everybody and really think.

—Mel Tillis, 1977

I'd like to write more, but it's like learning tennis at thirty-nine; you have to practice and take lessons before you can get good enough to enjoy it.

—Bonnie Raitt, 1989

I have to shut myself up in a room for days at a time to get anything good done. After about three days I come out, and if I'm lucky, I've got a song. If I'm not, I've got a problem, because I just have to go back until I do get one.

—Arlo Guthrie, *Follow Your Heart* (Judy Collins)

I write songs out over and over. They have to look good to my eye—that's part of the quality check.

—Warren Zevon, 1987

I try to use a different process on each song so I don't get into a formula. Sometimes I'll write at any typewriter and then read the words into a cassette recorder. It'll sound real weird because I don't do it in a normal voice. I'll repeat a phrase several times to see which one is more interesting.

—David Byrne, 1989

It's interesting to write on instruments you don't understand. I'll pick up a saxophone or bang on a drum, anything I'm unfamiliar with. It's good for your process—kids' toys.

—Tom Waits

I love to hear drummers. I knew that Brazilian percussionists create the most dense, lush landscapes. When they come into a studio to record, they cart in three or four crates of instruments, with bird sounds, gourd sounds, bottles. It's hard to resist.

The drums were originally used for religious ceremonies, but when the Africans came to Brazil, they were forbidden to play and worship, so they synchronized their deities to various Catholic saints so they could play. The rhythms of those deities became the rhythms of specific saints.

—Paul Simon, 1990

You can get an idea in the morning sitting with your guitar and a cup of coffee. Once you've had that start, though, it takes a long time to uncover the rest of what's there. Sometimes you never get it, so you piece it together the best you can with chicken wire and Band-Aids. If you can patch it together convincingly enough, it works. Then comes the polishing.

—Leonard Cohen, 1985

I do work better in the day, because at night, you're winding down. I think it's important to begin work before you have anything important on your mind, rather than at the end of the day.

—Tom Waits, 1980

I'm primarily a night person. I think it's unnatural to be out in the daytime. People didn't start doing that until we developed the agrarian culture, and all that's helped people to do is develop a need for eyeglasses, and contract hemorrhoids.

—Harry Nilsson, 1981

I usually write lying down, so I can go to sleep easily. I write about ten minutes, and sleep for two on the average. I write on legal pads in very small writing, partly for frugality. I find it very useful to use a separate pad for each section of the song.

—Stephen Sondheim

I have to be in the proper frame of mind to write. I cannot dictate to myself that tomorrow, between two and four in the afternoon, I'm going to be free, so I'm going to write.

—Bobby Goldsboro, 1977

I ran into Lucinda Williams, and asked her if she writes all the time, and she said, "No, I write when I have to, and I do it under pressure, and I think it's going to be a disaster." And I just said, "Praise the Lord!" You know, finally, someone who does it the way I do.

—Shawn Colvin, 1993

Ellington'll end an evening show by saying, "Okay, recording session at ten in the morning." Next day, about 10:30, people start to wander in. At eleven some of the guys are lying on the floor sleeping, some are playing cards, and there's a bottle of wine. The instruments are still in their cases, and there's no sign of Duke: no telephone calls, no nothing. The engineers are terrified. At twelve, Duke shows up with no music. He looks around, says "Take a break!" and sits down at the piano in a corner by himself. He'll play a chord or two, a cluster of notes, then he'll write it down, play another chord. Twenty minutes later it's finished and he hands it to the copyist he carries with the band.

He uses a code system which doesn't mean anything to anybody but the copyist. It's impossible—scratched up, no instrument names, no clefs, no keys. Tom Whitely, the copyist, scores it. He knows exactly what Duke wants. Then they pass it out, and Duke picks up the mike, taps it to see if the guys in the booth are listening, and says, "Okay, put this one down."

—Freddie Stone, 1970

Like a lot of people who are John Lennon fans, I wondered how the hell he did some of this stuff [on work tapes], what it took to realize these concepts and ideas. . . . [He] would sit down to compose with an acoustic guitar or at the piano, a portable cassette player and mike, and his lyric sheets, if he had any. He'd just start putting to tape whatever ideas he had. If he stumbled on anything that sounded good he'd stop the tape at the end of the take and make notes on his lead sheets; just before you hear the tape clicking off, you can hear him start to rustle the paper, then the tape clicks back on, and you hear him wrestling the paper back. The next take will sound similar but it will be the next evolution. In some cases, by the time he gets to the eighth or ninth take it's a completely different song.

—Stephen Peoples, 1988

In creating tunes, Cole [Porter] was the model of tidiness and efficiency. He would insist that certain customary objects always be close at hand as he worked: sharpened pencils, disposable tissues, cigarettes, cough drops, trash baskets and an assortment of language and rhyming dictionaries, reference books, and geographical guides. . . . He kept his songs—both finished and unfinished—neatly arranged in folders and looseleaf notebooks for easy accessibility.

—Charles Schwartz, *Cole Porter: A Biography*

When I'm writing a song and it's right, I know it. I just sit there and shine and glow all by myself. . . . I just sit in the living room and write songs. And when they're coming, they really flow, and when they don't, I don't get uptight. I don't set aside time like eight hours a day or whatever. I can write in a hotel, or a parked taxi with the meter running.

—Hoyt Axton, 1976

I do some of my best writing driving around. I don't keep a pad with me. That's one of my faults. Think about the lines that got away.

—John Prine, 1975

I've always written well on the road. I think the road is for writing. I'll lock myself in a motel room with a piano, and once I get the basic idea or a fragment of melody, I can write anywhere.

—Paul Anka, 1976

The road is the only place I can get anything done. I'd say ninety-five percent of the songs I've written, I've written on the road. I write mostly on guitar but lately with my voice. I voice the melodic line just the way I hear it in my head and I find I have more freedom that way. I use the tape recorder to overdub harmonies and I hum what I hear the instruments doing, and figure it all out later on guitar.

—Jim Messina, 1976

I don't have a set format, because I'm always on the run. I'd like to go away for two months to write, but I'm not that organized as a songwriter. I usually start off with a piano, or a Casio; the chord structure comes first, and the lyrics come out of it. Sometimes I think of a good rhythmic structure for a line, and I'll write it down, putting accents underneath it in my own short-hand, to catch the phrasing, and then I'll record something on a cassette. Sometimes I'll disappear into a toilet or somewhere like that, and do the recording there. That's why I like train journeys—I'm trapped in a space, and that's how I'll occupy my time.

—Ray Davies, 1987

On the show buses, while travelling to engagements, I would pass the idle time away writing lyrics that would be put to melody during dressing-room jam sessions or lonely afternoon hotel rooms with the guitar as a guide.

—Chuck Berry

The first time I came to America I got a notebook, and half the Armed Forces album came from just jotting down things that went past the bus window.

—Elvis Costello, 1988

[Recipe for writing while jet-lagged:] Drink a lot and try not to get too much sleep.

—Ray Davies, 1990

Sometimes you've only got an airline sickbag to write on, hotel notepaper, backs of envelopes, toilet paper. I've done it on everything, you know. It's an adventure every time I do it.

—Paul McCartney, 1989

I've got thousands of titles laid away like postal savings bonds. I spend hours and hours just writing down my ideas for titles to my songs.

—Woody Guthrie, *Born to Win*

I keep a journal. I think that if every day you just get up and write about what's on the top of your mind, skim the surface, you allow what's going on in the subconscious to show up. I think the same is true of dreams. . . . You say hello to your subconscious mind. It's another source to get information about yourself.

—John Ims, 1994

I always admired those old '30s movies where they show a couple of really great, classic songwriters whipping out a song in a night, and I'd think, "Why can't I do that?"

—Rickie Lee Jones, 1989

Cole Porter, "Worker" and Cole Porter, "Playboy" were two different beings. The secret of those marvelously gay and seemingly effortless songs was a prodigious and unending industry. He worked around the clock.

—Moss Hart, *Cole Porter: A Biography* (Charles Schwartz)

I work at least twelve hours a day. I write every day of the week. On Sundays I take half a day off. . . . I like coming to an office. I'd never leave my house if I worked at home. I've had my writing room for about ten years now. It's never been cleaned. I'm either immune to every disease or I've gotten every disease from working in there.

— Diane Warren, 1994

I have trouble with the word "inspiration," because it suggests that something just hits you out of the blue and you have to kind of scramble to write it down. For me, it really is a matter of craft. It's a very rational process. I sit down at a particular time when all the other work is done, make a pot of tea, take the phone off the hook, and I make notes—reams of them.

—Brad Roberts (Crash Test Dummies), 1994

I like to begin with an idea and then fit it to a title. I then write the words and music. Often I begin near the end of a refrain, so that the song has a strong finish, and then work backwards. I also like to use the title phrase at the beginning of a refrain and repeat it at the end for a climax. Writing lyrics is like doing a crossword puzzle.

—Cole Porter, *Cole Porter—A Biography* (Charles Schwartz)

I think of an idea for a song and then I fit it to a title. Then I go to work on a melody, spotting the title at certain points in the melody. Then I write the lyric—the end first—that way it has a strong finish. I do the lyrics the way I'd do a crossword puzzle. I try to give myself a meter which will make the lyrics as easy as possible to write, but without being banal. . . . I try to pick for my rhyme words of which there is a long list with the same ending.

—David A. Jasen, *Tin Pan Alley*

I find it useful to write backwards, and I think most lyric writers probably do, too, when they have a climax, a twist, a punch, a joke. You start at the bottom of the page, you preserve your best joke for the last. The ideas should be paced in ascending order of punch.

—Stephen Sondheim

You've got to figure out where the title's going to fall in the song. A lot of times I start writing in the middle of the song and work out to the ends. If the title's going to be in the first line, then you work from the beginning to the end. If the title's in the first chorus, then you've got to work back into the first verse. There are many many ways you can lay these things out.

—Gordon Lightfoot, 1976

For me, a title is like the song's clothing. A good

title is helpful in developing what you want to say and how you're going to support what the song is about lyrically.

—Dennis Lambert, 1977

One thing that seems to be working particularly well for us is the old "coming up with the hook title first" method. I always keep a notepad at arm's length to jot down song title ideas. It makes writing so much easier if you always have a selection at your disposal. We then work on setting the title to a strong melodic hook, and the backing track becomes the support. I'm a firm believer that the chorus should always be developed first as it is the most important part, the foundation of a great song. You may have other bits and pieces ready to put into place, but too often, we've attempted to write a song verse first and gotten lost by the time we hit the chorus section. It's like trying to construct a building from the sky down.

—Lee Aaron, 1988

I usually get a phrase first that might hit me. I keep repeating it over and over, and the first thing I know, I begin to get a sort of rhythm and then a tune.

Sometimes I have a tune first, and then I start trying to fit words to it. I never use a rhyming dictionary for my lyrics. I'm too impatient to look up the words. In either case, whichever part comes first serves as a mold into which the other part must be poured.

—Irving Berlin, 1978

I do believe that the opening line of a song should be something off-the-wall, but not off-the-wall for off-the-wall's sake. "Every time I go down south, I stick my foot inside my mouth." While everybody's going "Huh?" then you go "I lovvve yoouuu!"

—John Prine, 1978

If I have an idea, everything revolves around it. If a line doesn't enhance that idea, doesn't amplify it, doesn't lead to the hook, you don't want it. . . . It can't be there.

—Bob McDill, 1977

You are more accountable as a person when you write words than you are as a composer. Your form as a composer is more abstract.

—Norman Gimbel, 1978

One of the earliest principles I adopted was to write, and then go back and cross out everything that didn't absolutely have to be there. Too many songs today are loaded with "buts" and "ands" and "justs," or extra lines that say the same thing three times over.

—Bruce Cockburn, 1981

I think it takes more talent to write music, but it takes more courage to write lyrics.

—Johnny Mercer

Johnny Mercer's work illustrates a principle stated by T.S. Eliot: that poetry can communicate before it is even understood.

—Gene Lees, 1987

When you look at the work of someone like [T.S.] Eliot, it's apparent that he would spend months writing pages and pages of stuff, stripping stuff down so that every line had that kind of intensity. Apparently Dylan Thomas was the same way. I don't care that much about the lines. It's nice every now and again to come up with a good one, but it's also quite nice to throw them away. Because it recognizes that songwriting is not poetry. It has so much else going for it: rhythm, pace, immediacy, delight, and, most of all, backdrop. You've got a backdrop both of atmosphere and, in an even more interesting sense, a backdrop of history.

—Pete Townshend

I don't think of myself as a particularly sophisticated wordsmith. I'm less concerned with expressing me, me, me, and more interested in exploring a subject from different points of view—and where better to look than to classical writers whose works resonate on so many different levels? Like Yeats, I'm interested in the pagan notion that spirituality is derived from the natural world, the Celt sense of the sacred, the holy and the spiritual, but ultimately I've let my curiosity drive me more than a mandate to serve things Celtic.

—Loreena McKennit, 1994

It's very hard to talk about music in words. Words are superfluous to the abstract power of music. We can fashion words into poetry so that they are understood the way music is understood, but they only aspire to the condition where music already exists.

Music is probably the oldest religious rite. Our ancestors used melody and rhythm to co-opt the spirit world to their purposes—to try and make sense of the universe. The first priests were probably musicians, the first prayers probably songs.

—Sting, 1994

The basic differences between lyric writing and all other forms are two principles which dictate what you have to do as a lyric writer. First, lyrics exist in time, as opposed to poetry. You can read a poem at your own speed, but on stage, as the lyrics come at you, you hear them only once; if there's a reprise, you hear them twice; if there are two reprises you hear them three times. The music is a relentless engine and it keeps the lyrics going.

—Stephen Sondheim

Journalists, for the most part, always tend to tune into a lyric. I've never wanted to print my lyrics on my LPs because lyrics are not poetry. They're part of songwriting; they're colouring, and they have to be heard at the same time as the music.

—Billy Joel, 1980

I usually feel like suppressing a chuckle when songwriters are called poets, whether it's me or somebody else they're referring to. I think they are very rarely the same thing. I think there are some song lyrics that approach the standards of poetry, and if that happens, sometimes it's very nice. Other times it's really cumbersome, not phonetically fun. You can write a line that looks great and reads great and would be dynamite in a certain kind of verse, but as you say it, it's a phonetic jungle, not fun to sing.

—J.D. Souther, 1980

That's the difference between a lyric and a poem—singability. A poem is read by the eye, transferred to the mind, and then to the emotions. A song lyric is sung to the ear, transferred to the mind and then the emotions. I think Shakespeare was one of the great word geniuses of all time, but he was a bad lyric writer. A line like "Love laughs at locksmiths" might work as prose, but you can't sing it. Those words you do not sing.

—Sammy Cahn, 1976

Remember that writing a song is not like writing a poem. Because lyrics set to music, phrasing and phonetics must be considered at all times. Certain vowel sounds just simply sing better than others—especially on longer notes and the ending of lines.

—Lee Aaron, 1988

I have to hear the music. I don't consider myself a poet. To write words alone and naked always makes me feel they read like a Hallmark card, as opposed to e.e. cummings.

—Carole Bayer Sager, 1977

When I look at [beginners'] songs, what I find missing most of the time is a sense of form. Lack of form is what fails to satisfy my aesthetic idea of what a song should be. Either they aren't concerned with form or they just don't understand it. It doesn't have to have a rigid, negative connotation. I think probably the greatest living songwriter of this decade and probably for the next couple of decades is Joni Mitchell. As free as Joni's things are, they have form—sometimes very intangible at first listening, but if you listen to the song again, you'll find she's very strict about giving her songs form.

—Jimmy Webb, 1976

We played on Hallowe'en, and all these weird purists showed up. Total fans, but every time we'd go into one of our pop songs they'd start chanting, "Don't do it! Sellout!" Girls were throwing riot-grrrl 'zines at me and stuff. I was, like, "Uh, I'm really glad you're here, girls, but check it out. I can write a bridge now."

—Courtney Love, 1994

I have a preconceived image of what a song looks like. The idea of the song becomes a picture, and then it becomes a song.

—Ray Davies, 1987

A song will write its own form.

—Jimmy Webb, 1994

I want people to listen to my words. I'd rather that my lyrics landed like an absolute sore thumb. Take the old blues songs where there's a magic sort of flow with the words, and then, all of a sudden, you get a stab in the back, which is so marvelous.

—Leo Sayer, 1978

Where [Robert] Johnson stands out the most is as a lyricist. There were bluesmen going for irony, but not really satire. He really did add—I don't want to be trite about it and call it poetry—he added a poet's touch. Johnson's more literary, in a weird kind of semiliterate way. Listen to "Dead Shrimp Blues"—"I woke up this mornin' and all my shrimps was dead and gone"—who had said that? That's Johnson talking about being impotent. Blues guys had made sexual allusions, or pitied the human condition, but they'd never taken it over to a kind of black humour and surrealism.

—Jim Dickinson, 1991

I adopted the style of making a statement, repeating the statement in the second line, and then telling in the third line why the statement

was made.　　　　　　　　　　—W.C. Handy
It's like when you cook: you have to put in all the ingredients and have to put 'em in the right order or it won't come out right.

　　　　　　　　　　　　　　　—Furry Lewis

I had sense enough to try and make 'em rhyme so they'd have hits to 'em with a meaning, some sense to 'em, you know.

　　　　　　　　　　　　　　　—Son House

If you don't rhyme it up, you don't understand nothing and you ain't getting nowhere.

　　　　　　　　　　　　　　　—Furry Lewis

I never rhyme the word "gum" with the word "fun," which may be a little prim, but I can't help it.

　　　　　　　　　　　　　—Nancy White, 1984

Anyone who could rhyme "aurora borealis" with "red and ruby chalice" is not bad. Not bad at all.

　　　　—Harry Nilsson (referring to Johnny Mercer), 1989

It's no big secret—some Egyptian songwriter back in the days of the Pharoahs was probably doing it—but I write conversationally. I try to write lyrics the same way I would say them. I wouldn't call my wife and say, "Hi, hey listen, my heart longs for you every night and every day, and I want our love to last forever, okay?" That's not believable.

　　　　　　　　　　　—Randy Goodrum, 1980

I had an ambition for a while to write songs that used ordinary conversational language instead of archetypal rock language. It was successful when people didn't really notice it.

　　　　　　　　　　　　—David Byrne, 1979

My words are more colourful than my music. I'm very much a fan of real simple, elegant melody lines. I like Brahms, things that move and have an emotional logical length. I don't like music that's frenetic. I don't listen to or play music to encourage tension. Even if the way you may turn a line creates a little tension, it's always part of this greater thing that's supposed to move and uplift.

　　　　　　　　　　　　—J.D. Souther, 1980

I think my being a woman has helped me. A woman tends to write a lyric that's more picturesque, more detailed. Instead of just saying "I feel bad," she might get really specific about just "how" she feels. This is good, because with records, you have no visual aids. You're relying on a person's imagination, and the more details you give 'em, the better it is.

　　　　　　　　　　　　—Sylvia May, 1979

Lyrics for me are the most difficult. I've got five melodies for every set of lyrics. I write some songs with my voice because it's a lot different than playing it. Ultimately the song has to be sung and some words flow better than others. I try to avoid too many hard consonants in ballads. You need more vowels and softer sounding words that sing out smoothly.

—David Gates, 1976

You can't really control what comes out, other than rejecting or accepting things and putting them into different bits of order. Its not something that you actually own. It's the lyrics that take me a long time—they're like a big process that keeps on happening 'til I've done the last lead vocal. Still then I'm playing with little bits here and there that maybe weren't quite right.

—Kate Bush, 1986

I do like going back over a lyric after leaving it alone for a couple of weeks. If there's something good there, it's like the rest of the stuff is in invisible ink. You can shake the paper and the good stuff will stick while the bad stuff falls right off.

—John Prine, 1978

The lyrics with which I am totally satisfied have yet to be written. Perhaps that is a good thing. In general, I like to look for a personal feeling or thought which can be translated into a universal theme. Something that makes me happy, or sad, or especially angry, that I can see affecting other people's lives too.

—Neil Peart (Rush), 1986

I have to sing them to write them 'cause it's all in my mind. So I write the lyrics and melody all at the same time. They're welded together.

—Roy Orbison

To me a song comes with the music, a sound or rhythm first, then I make up words as fast as I can just to hold onto the feeling, until actually the music and the lyric come almost simultaneously. A song is more primitive [than a poem]. A song usually has a rhyme and a basic meter, whereas a poem can go anywhere.

—Jim Morrison, 1969

Sometimes the group is jammin' or something, and then you might run across something really nice. And then you keep running across that, then you start shoutin' out anything that comes to your mind, you know, whatever the music turns you on to. If it's heavy music, you start singing things.

—Jimi Hendrix

When it's a rocker, I'll just turn on my little drumbeat out of my ten-dollar Casio keyboard and run that through an amplifier so I have something to tap to. That's essential. I could never write a rock & roll song just sitting there with an acoustic guitar. I'll just start hitting chords and shouting along. As soon as I get something that feels fun, I'll hunt for a title.

You have to get your gut feeling out, whatever it is. Even if you think, "Oh, I can't say that," go ahead and fucking say it. Spit it out, and if you're going to be a fool, be a fool.

—Paul Westerberg

I decide on which mixture of a tune to use and then I find it about a dozen times easier to herd my words into my tune I've already built for them.

—Woody Guthrie, 1948

I can play a song like crazy in one key and go to the next key and not even know where I'm at. If I get any better as a keyboards player it's because I'm trying to write a song and that spurs me on.

—Michael McDonald, 1979

I learned how to read music and subsequently forgot, and I'm very glad. I was told that I couldn't put certain notes after certain notes because "Beethoven never did it." Reading music is based on what everyone has done in the past, it's not based on trying anything new.

—Sinead O'Connor, 1990

Cole Porter was good at key-change surprises. You never knew what key he was in. Major, minor—some of the tunes wormed all over the place, like "Night and Day." They say he got the idea from hearing a Mohammedan priest calling in his flock near Marrakesh (you don't get that sort of lead sitting in a Tin Pan Alley office).

—Ian Whitcomb, *After the Ball*

[Irving] Berlin could neither read nor write music. He knew nothing about musical theory. It has long been known that he composed on a special piano he called his Buick—an instrument that changed keys at the push of a lever. Such instruments were common in music publishing houses early in the century. Berlin continued to use one long after they ceased to be popular, playing in what for him was always F-sharp, though the music came out in other keys.

—Gene Lees, 1990

How do I like synthesizers? Great in the theatre pit and on discs. But for composition? Fuck 'em!

—Leonard Bernstein, 1990

When I hear a beautiful piece of music it absolutely mesmerizes me. The first time I heard Ray Charles sing "Georgia on My Mind," I was in my car and had to pull over to the side of the road. If I didn't I would have just drifted away.

—Sammy Cahn, 1976

I'm more interested in melodies. I've always offended the purists. I was always trying to combine Woody Guthrie with Sinatra.

—Don McLean, 1980

It's much easier to write a good melody over simple chords, because I can really control the melody and dig deep into it when it's very simple and steady.

—Michael Stipe, 1991

I've never watched them [R.E.M.] compose, but I know their music is done by committee. There's three people composing on chord instruments. They record about forty chord sequences and then Michael Stipe comes in with his notebook, writes words for about half of them, and they throw out the rest. There's a very high casualty rate. Their strength is that it's a kind of lattice work.

—Robyn Hitchcock, 1994

The music comes first, the words sometimes seconds after, but the words don't come first, ever.

—Randy Newman, 1979

I always find the gist of the lyric contained in the melody line. Just as the chords are contained in the melody line, I find the words are in there too.

—Peggy Lee, 1991

It's definitely not the lyrics [that are most important]. I think, in terms of the end product, a good beat or a good musical sound, or a good groove, is the most important. The best way to prove it is to read some of my lyrics. We didn't write any fantastic lyrics. We wrote whatever fit the bar. A lot of the things we did with Otis [Redding] he would forget from the night before when we wrote it. He'd make up the words as he went. Not for the whole song, but he'd forget a line and just improvise one to fit it as he went.

—Steve Cropper, 1976

Normally, the music comes first. I play guitar and play piano, and all of a sudden I hit on a structure that gets me off, makes me feel good, and then I'll put the words to it, but there have been about half a dozen times that a song has just popped out of me . . . boom, like laying an egg. One time at a party, I sat down and wrote an entire song in about four minutes, and there was all this hectic, chaotic noise going on all around me.

—Hoyt Axton, 1976

Chord structure usually comes before melody, for me. The way I begin to write a song is to sit down and explore a progression that gives me a tingle somewhere. In fact, I usually have five or six of these working in my mind, even if I'm not at the piano. Sometimes I will hear one in a classical work, and it's not that I steal it, but it's that it triggers something in me, some kind of little chemical reaction . . . and I go "Hey, wait a minute, I'd like to hear that again," and when I listen to it again, it gives me some information about how certain chord progressions work.

—Jimmy Webb, 1976

When I sit down at the piano, I usually fish for a bite. What I mean by that is I try to hit on a very beautiful chord change. If I can get two or three, that's even better. Then I get a flow of a melody. I use my voice as the melody line, and I play the chords underneath. I try to turn myself on . . . to please myself.

—Neil Sedaka, 1976

If I am writing the music as well as the lyric, I sometimes try to get a vamp first, a musical atmosphere, an accompaniment, a pulse, a melody idea, but usually the tone comes from the accompanying figure, as I find the more specific the task [in writing for the musical stage], the easier. If somebody says write a song about a lady in a red dress crying at the end of a bar, that's a lot easier than somebody saying write a song about a lady who's sorry.

—Stephen Sondheim

I'm terribly afraid of melodies that wear me out a little bit when I'm working, because I feel they're going to wear the people out. I like things that I like hearing again.

—Burt Bacharach, 1980

Texture is probably the most important aspect of my songwriting. I sound like a lunatic, but I know other writers think of it the same way. The way that you see music and songs is in shapes and textures and colours. You see the shape of it, the texture of it, the colour of it. The guitar with the keyboard, the notes each one plays, goes to weave the fabric. It's like making a carpet.

—Sinead O'Connor, 1990

I'm very much a romanticist, musically. I prefer to be drawn into something by the way it makes me feel emotionally. It's not a technique that I listen for; it's content, feeling, tone. With one note, if it sounds right, you can create everything.

—Eric Clapton, 1993

I know there's a whole mythology about me about how I wrote "Up, Up and Away" in thirty minutes, and all that stuff. Well, it's basically true. I get it down very quickly, but it's been going around in my head for a few days, and working itself out.

—Jimmy Webb, 1976

I never stop writing. I have an intuition when I hear melodies, and words form in my mind. I've been doing it all my life, and I've now become more relaxed to it. I never sit down with a doubt in my mind that the words will come. I don't walk around with an idea for a song in my head. From the beginning I never had a doubt that I would be a songwriter.

—Sammy Cahn, 1976

Every time you start, you start from scratch. You have your talent, you have your excitement about your idea, and you have a certain knowledge of musical and lyrical tools, but you never know a song is a hit when you're writing it.

—Alan O'Day, 1975

It's easy for people to say about my work in retrospect, "Oh, well, that was a big hit for you." But it wasn't when I wrote it. It was just another one of a dozen songs.

—Robert Palmer, 1994

In each case I started off with nothing—just an idea and a blank sheet of paper. The effort that goes into each one [song] is equal. In fourteen years I've written maybe forty songs that counted. I've got to be fairly well-motivated to write a song.

—Eric Bogle, 1985

When I wrote "Angie Baby," I had no trouble picturing this guy being wafted into the radio literally and spiritually by the strength of Angie's beliefs. My whole purpose in the song was to make that line between sanity and insanity a little fuzzy for a while.

—Alan O'Day, 1975

I just hear things in my head. What I hear is what comes out. I'm very instantaneous, I guess. I feel something, get an idea how I want to do it, and I just do it. I have no special ways about it. Anything I do, good or bad, it's very natural. That's it.

—Ray Charles, 1973

Buddy [Holly] was a peculiar songwriter. He'd leave home in the evening, after we had our evening meal, and be gone for an hour, or two or three hours. Then he'd come back, go straight to his room, pick up his guitar and start to sing something he had been thinking about while he was out in the car by himself.

—Lawrence Holley, *Quick Fox* (John Goldrosen)

If you get an idea you just elaborate on it. If you're singing about a house, you talk about the shingles, you talk about the door, the window . . . there aren't any rules. I hate to sound flowery, but that's what I learned from Bob Dylan. He did that. He broke all the rules. His songs didn't have any bridges.

—Lucinda Williams, 1989

I guess I organize details, that's how I write a song. I take details and put them in an order and perspective. I pick the ones that are the most beautiful, even if they are really ugly. It's like the way other people do crossword puzzles or something. You like to have the last detail perfect.

—Suzanne Vega, 1987

For three or four days before I write a good song, I am like a woman with PMS. It's ridiculous. You know—just do things you are totally ashamed of, say things or hurt somebody's feelings for no reason, and not even know why you do. Then I'll write a song, maybe four or five songs, and the weight of the world is off my shoulders for six months or so. I can feel the pressure of people saying, "Write that song, Hag. Come on, give us one more." Sometimes people will go to the trouble to come up and tell me so in their own individual manner. And if there is one person that will go to that trouble, how many are out there that you never know about? The brain is incredible. How far that power extends is not certain. Those thoughts those people have—I feel the pressure of those people sometimes.

—Merle Haggard, 1990

I don't think that you can censor yourself at that stage of the creative process. If you start saying, "Well, I can't make it look attractive," you'll never finish the song. The only question you can really ask yourself is: "Am I honest? Am I bull-shitting? Am I doin' what I want to do?"

—Kris Kristofferson, 1990

Everybody has a different way of working. Picasso would hardly have used the same technique as Rembrandt, but it's still art. He'd still end up with a timeless canvas and what counts at the end of the day is "Did you get anything?" Not how you did it. Because we can all sit around and talk about it and say I did it like this and I did it like that, but I don't really think we know how we do it.

–Keith Richards

I will go for weeks sometimes without writing anything, but when I do work, I work my ass off. I will be the first to say that I don't write songs to any great degree by inspiration. I'll get an idea for a title or a chorus line or a hook line that appeals to me, and I will try to discern what rhythm is implicit in that line of lyrics and at the same time go to the piano with a possible rhythmic idea and see if any melodic ideas develop. I have pieces of these on tape scattered all over the place, and I play them back to see if they still sound good. From then on it's pure sweat.

–Alan O'Day, 1975

If I'm not really in the mood to write, I try to plant seeds. I have a big thick book of fragments and clippings. If I feel like writing but nothing seems to come out, I try to put something in the book. It's like a soup that's been cooking for four or five years. When I do feel inspired I open the thing at random, and read it, and many times that triggers an idea.

–Norman Dolph, 1978

I've had to really work my way down to the depths of depression sometimes before a song would come out. My attitude would get worse and worse, and then, when I felt I really couldn't get any lower, the song would pop out! It's an amazing experience to look back a few minutes later and realize that's happened. And there's a whole cathartic thing that goes on. Suddenly you feel better. It's like you've thrown up or something.

–Jimmy Webb, 1976

A great songwriter borrows; a genius steals.

–Dan Zanes (stolen from Jules Shear)

Steal all you want, but only from the best places. If your talent shows the source will be forgotten.

–Earl Robinson, 1990

If you're a good composer, you steal good steals! Because a composer is the sum total of his listening experience, plus the voice and jism that belong specifically to him and that make him instantly identifiable: I am Wolfgang Amadeus! I am Ludwig! Me, me Sibelius!

–Leonard Bernstein, 1990

I was on an airplane leafing through the airline magazine and came across something about

Quincy Jones, who underwent brain surgery years ago. As they were wheeling him in he looked up at the surgeon and said, "Don't steal any songs when you're in there."

–Tom Russell

I stole the melody ["I Done The Best I Could"] from Leadbelly, a friend that I'd met in New York. The melody is "Goodnight, Irene." I told Leadbelly in later years when he came to Hollywood. By that time it had been recorded by The Weavers. I loved the melody and I just took it! After so many years I can confess to my crimes.

–Tex Ritter, 1973

Each one of my blues is based on some old negro song of the south, some folk song that I heard from my mammy when I was a child—some old song that is part of the memories of my childhood and my race. I can tell you the exact song I used as the basis for any one of my blues.

–W.C. Handy

The school of thought which states that you aren't a composer if you can't write music, or haven't studied it intensively, is stupid. Great music, the symphonies, the classics—where do you think they came from? In the popular suitcase, in the tunes hummed in the streets or the fields by a farmer, a carpenter, a weaver, that's where. Great composers took a tune from the streets, or a bird cry, and made something of it.

–Felix LeClerc, 1973

Music is all tied up together! I could go through Stravinsky's *Rite of Spring* with you and point out what comes from Mussorgsky and Ravel—outright, out-fucking-rageous steals! I could show you what Beethoven took from Haydn and Mozart. But what's the point of doing that? Everyone comes from somewhere.

–Leonard Bernstein, 1990

What's obvious in those '60s records is how those people all had a desperate desire to move ahead of each other. You can hear it in the way the Beatles at one point were obviously copying the Beach Boys and in the way Lennon would copy Dylan. Though it was kind of shameless, it must have been a fantastic period to be a songwriter, and I wish it were going on now. Today, if you want to progress in your work you have to do it in your own little world.

–George Michael, 1990

The process of writing wasn't such an artistic endeavour as some of the more pompous critics would like to believe. Every record wasn't the bloody tablets of stone. In the construction it was a lot more of a hack job. But hopefully in the heart of the thing, in the good songs, was the true bit. There's a little bit of Tin Pan Alley in it. I don't have any purist tradition to lean on. Every pop musician is a thief and a magpie. I have an emotional affinity for certain styles, but none of them belong to me.

—Elvis Costello, 1987

I have never considered writing songs just as a craft. It was like if you sat down at a desk and scrambled for a pencil and couldn't find one, you'd write in lipstick. The same thing happens with musical things. If I couldn't find a rhythm, I'd borrow one and then change it.

—Elvis Costello

I never waste my time by asking or even wondering in the least whether I've heard my tune in whole or in part before. There are ten million ways of changing my tune around to make it sound like my own. I can sing a high note instead of a low note or a harmony note for a melody note or put a slow note in for several fast ones.

—Woody Guthrie, 1948

My greatest enemy is my hands. They want to go to the familiar.   —Burt Bacharach, 1977

I think a lot of writers try to avoid writing the same song over and over again, but I put booze, a blonde and a car in most of my tunes.

—Tom Waits, 1980

Willie Dixon told me, "A hit song is when a man's going crazy over a woman." That seems like good advice.

—Peter Case, 1990

It's not that I don't want to write as much now, it's just that I'm more selective in how I write and what I write about. In the early days if somebody had said "Bring me a Jack Daniels and a Coke," I would have made up a song about that in five minutes. It wouldn't have been a good song, but it would have been a complete one.

—Bobby Goldsboro, 1977

It gets harder the more I do it, but it's there. Every once in a while something will sneak out. I reject a lot of ideas. I never even finish them. I get one or two lines down on paper or even sometimes almost a finished song before I realize it's not what I think is good.

—Guy Clark, 1984

I have always believed that anyone can write a song, even a good song, but it takes a professional songwriter to continue to write good songs. It's not an accident, it's a knack.

—Irving Berlin, 1978

If you want to build a garage, you need a saw, hammer, all the tools. A thesaurus is a tool. A rhyming dictionary is a great tool; however, I don't believe that the fact that you use all of these tools eliminates the possibility that genius might strike you, or that by using them, you automatically become a craftsman.

—Boudleaux Bryant, 1978

There's two or three kids out there trying to make good music, and the rest of them sound like it's been strained through some kind of white toast or something. It all sounds just too neat and perfect, and no surprise to it at all. No story, no nothing. It's like building cars—like an assembly line. It doesn't sound like anything that came from a guitar.

—Merle Haggard, 1994

One of the important things I've learned about writing is that after you've written a song, you should put yourself in the position of a stranger walking into the room and hearing the song for the first time. The question you must be able to answer objectively is, does that stranger under-

stand what she's listening to?

—Melissa Manchester, 1976

What I would say is to use the unfriendly eye, if you can. I like to write a thing, and put it away, and wait until at least the next day and then look at it with the unfriendly eye. Generally twenty-four hours is enough to cool any passion.

—Ervin Drake, 1978

I feel if you can put a finger through a song, the song isn't finished. You can just look at a finished song and know that there isn't any more that needs to be done to it.

—Tony Macauly, 1978

It's important to begin a story by putting you somewhere, giving at least some kind of geography, rather than just stating a feeling.

—Tom Waits, 1980

I never come down on the side of commerciality when I think that the other way is better. That's not being particularly heroic, because I don't have a great sense of commerciality.

—Randy Newman, 1979

It took me a long time to learn the difference between being abstract and being unintelligible, between stick drawings and drawing. There's shadings and pastels and water colours.

—Janis Ian, 1977

You've got all the words in the world to choose from—all the musical notes. All you've got to do is edit. You don't write, you edit.

—John Prine, 1979

If I can get into it and move, if I'm tapping my foot constantly, if I'm humming along with it, if I can hear it in my head when I'm driving or listening to a ball game, if it keeps creeping back into my mind, then I know it's a contender.

—Freddie Perren, 1979

There is a built-in shit-detector in everybody's head, and I think a lot of songwriters submit to what Robert Frost called the tyranny of rhyme. There's another Robert Frost trick: If one of two rhyming lines is weak, put the weaker one first.

—Harry Chapin, 1978

I do a sort of analysis of a song more often when I don't like it. The reason is because I wonder if I'm missing something. How does this song get to be number one and sell a zillion copies when I hate it?

—Carole Bayer Sager, 1977

I find in writing songs, even before I put them on tape, I like to keep them in my head for a long time and do the mental exercise of going over and over it again. It works almost like a piece of wood on a lathe. I go over it until all the edges are smoothed off. The things I forget are usually the things that shouldn't be there anyway.

—Larry Groce, 1980

I've got tons of stuff that doesn't get done, that I don't finish because it just doesn't go anywhere. It's got to go someplace, so if you're working on a song for quite a while and it isn't going anywhere, it's better just to chuck it, or put it on file and maybe look back at it later.

—Gordon Lightfoot, 1976

The reason a song takes me a long time to write is because I am so aware that it can be a good song, so I wait until it is. I don't want to rush something out that I know deep down is not right. I wrote a song called "Once in a Lifetime Thing" that took me a year-and-a-half to write, and all I lacked for all of that time was four lines.

—Jim Weatherly, 1975

Say what you have to say and get off the soapbox.

—Felice Bryant, 1978

Craft writers will sneer at instinctive writers, saying they just "luck in." Instinctive writers will call craft writers assembly line machines, or hacks.

—Janis Ian, 1990

All my songs have been very simply stated, right from the beginning. How much clearer can you get than "Hello, Walls"?

—Willie Nelson

The best tunes are the simplest. I believe that it was Paul McCartney who said that the best songs have no more than twenty-five words in them.

—Peter McCann, 1978

Simplicity is the thing. Every line has to focus on that centre-point you're working toward. There's no throw-away lines and no symbolism. Everything is well laid out in the simplest way possible.

—Bob McDill, 1977

People's attention span these days, what with TV commercials and the like, isn't long enough for them to sit through twenty minutes of elliptical images floating past them. You really have to strike them with short, compact statements.

—Janis Ian, 1977

Lyrics go with music, and music is very rich—in my opinion, the richest form of art. It's also abstract and does strange things to your emotions, so not only do you have that going, but you also have light, costumes, scenery, characters, performers. There's a great deal to hear and get. Lyrics therefore have to be underwritten. They have to be very simple in essence. That doesn't mean you can't do convoluted lyrics, but essentially the thought is what counts, and you have to stretch it out enough so that the listener has a fair chance to get it. Many lyrics suffer from being much too packed.

—Stephen Sondheim

Before, I'd been a sketch artist, a piss artist if you like. I just made it up. I banged words into each other and I used sound and colour rather than meaning. Then, in the blues, in the Beat poets, in Langston Hughes, I found other meanings. I still haven't found my voice, but I know where I am with the words now.

—Bono, 1989

All the best songs don't feel like they've been stuck together. They flow from beginning to end.

—Geddy Lee (Rush), 1981

Invariably, with the exception of "MacArthur Park," which was fairly complex for a pop tune, my most successful songs have been the ones with very simple, insinuating melodic lines, like "Wichita Lineman" and "By the Time I Get to Phoenix"—things like that which are very easy for people to understand, so I try to address myself to that more and more. Otherwise, why not just go shut yourself in a room somewhere and write the Great American Symphony.

—Jimmy Webb, 1976

Some people say I write simple lyrics, but I like to state what I can as clearly as I can. A good lyric, to me, shouldn't be an exercise in vocabulary, but should communicate meaning and feeling with clarity. And when it marries right with the melody line, it usually feels right. Rhyme schemes and progressions are technical facets of songwriting that we're aware of, but they are subordinate to the feel and the spirit of the song.

—Nick Ashford, 1977

Most folk music is so fantastic because it's like an old wood banister. So many people have put their hands on it, smoothed it out, that there's no possibility of splinters.

—Harry Chapin, 1978

You be as honest and sincere with your subject as you can and just write whatever happened. Give the listener a break. Don't tell him what every little thing means. Maybe in a little punchline you tell him why it was important to you, but the rest of the song is his.

—Tom T. Hall, 1979

You have to draw some conclusion for the person who's listening to it, and if you don't, there's no reason to write it in the first place.

—Jimmy Webb, 1976

If you have a song with a lot of chord changes and musical activity, try to keep the words at a minimum, otherwise they cancel each other out. The whole experience gets too dense, and a lot of people don't appreciate it. Songs that have many verses usually work the best with simpler backgrounds, so that the words come to the forefront.

—Frank Zappa, 1980

I am a visual writer. I like writing songs because they are small, three-minute plays. I like to use other people's words. I see characters talking. I consider a song as a whole—words, music, singer, show. And I write for the sake of the music of the words themselves.

—Luc Plamonden, 1973

An actor's "entrance-focus-energy-exit," a painter's use of shading, an architect's attention to the space between the columns, all apply equally well to songwriting.

—Janis Ian, 1990

CHAPTER 7

ALL YOU CAN WRITE IS WHAT YOU SEE

THE ART OF LYRIC WRITING

James Joyce said that there's "the sound of words, the sound of words against words, and the sound of the space between words." Jimmy Webb likes the way words sound when they "clash together and bang up against each other." Some people dream lyrics and others find them implied in the melody. Some writers can only write from the personal angle, others can only write about other people's lives.

The point is to connect with a story—dissolving complex emotions and ideas into simple words that work with a melody; in effect, achieving the "universal." Good luck!

—T.R.

Good songwriters are vicious editors. Sometimes you have to take a good hard look at that turn of phrase you absolutely love, realize that it simply doesn't belong in the song, and get rid of it. Sometimes whole verses have to go. It's something akin to cutting off your own extremities at the time, but you'll thank yourself for it later.

I'm also a great believer in the importance of the subtext of a song; who is singing it, who are they singing it to, where are they, what is their frame of mind? It's not that any of these things have to appear directly in the song, but rather that it gives you a context within which you know what this person would or would not do or say.

—S.T.

All you can write is what you see.

—Woody Guthrie

I just like words. I like the way they clash around together and bang up against each other, especially in songs. I like striking, colourful words. I really like taking them and jamming them up together to see what happens. Then people say, "Well, what does the cake out in the rain mean?" My only response is "Why not?" It was something I did. What does "Yellow mustard custard running from a dead dog's eye" mean? John Lennon is a fantastic word painter. He clashes them around with great ferocity.

—Jimmy Webb, 1976

I have a strong background in poetry and if people don't read poetry then they probably wouldn't understand my lyrics. I want to put people in a particular mood, to use words against words. . . . If one takes the lyrics and tries to put them into their own reality, they're obviously going to miss the point. My lyrics are little word paintings, to sort of jar one.

—Ric Ocasek (The Cars), 1986

I actually believe I learned the majority of the first bunch of words in my vocabulary from listening to the lyrics of the songs that my mother would sing while doing the housework. Whatever the chore, she'd unfailingly tackle it while belting out hymn after hymn. Sometimes she'd emphasize a passage in a song and the change in her volume and expression would frighten me. It was as if she'd suddenly discovered Jesus standing in the house enjoying the song.

—Chuck Berry, *The Autobiography*

There's a world of difference between "she walked" and "she strolled," between "I miss you" and "I long for you."

—Janis Ian, 1990

Even two years ago I'd really toil over one word, like in "I Would Die For You," the line "I never kissed a sweeter mouth." It took me four hours to decide what kind of mouth I was kissing. Those little word moments come easier for me now.

—Jann Arden, 1994

English has drawbacks as a language in which to write lyrics. For one thing, it is poor in rhyme. There are only four words in English that rhyme with love. . . . In French, however, there are fifty-one rhymes that I know of for *amour*.

—Gene Lees, *Singers and the Song*

In practice we [French songwriters] end up using the same rhymes over and over again, just as you do in English. It's what comes before them that gives a lyric freshness.

—Charles Aznavour, *Singers and the Song*

You try to make your rhyming fresh, but inevitable, and you try for surprise, but not so wrenchingly that the listener loses the sense of the line. The true function of the rhyme is to point up the word that rhymes. If you don't want that word to be the most important in the line, don't rhyme it. Also, rhyme helps shape the music, it helps the listener to hear what the shape of the music is.

—Stephen Sondheim

Without the word "dream," or the concept "dream," and without the word "blue" in the emotions, I would have been really limited in the things I've written.

—Roy Orbison, 1988

As a songwriter and a creative artist, your dreams are a real reservoir of experience you can't ignore. To ignore your dreams is to ignore half your life.

—Sting, 1988

I found that I was working from my dreams, because my dreams are really vivid and visual and really violent, and often filled with people I don't know. The images stay with me a long time. A man in the street. Children doing things. Children setting themselves on fire. Or a man burning in the street.

—Suzanne Vega, 1990

I wrote a song about burnout, and ever since then, I've had a lot of social workers in my audience.

—Nancy White, 1984

I don't like to use words like "erotic" or "spiritual" to describe my songs—they tend to scare people away. What they are is just songs, and anything I could do to explain them really can't help them.

—Leonard Cohen, 1985

If such a thing as a mojo hand had've been good, you'd have had to go down to Louisiana to find one. When we were in the Delta they couldn't do nothing, I don't think. And there is no way I can shake my finger at you and make you bark like a dog, or make frogs and snakes jump out of you. Bullshit, no way. But you know, when you're writing them songs that are coming from down that way, you can't leave out something about that mojo thing, because this is what black people really believed in at that time . . . but even today when you play the old blues like me, you can't get around that. I would play "Goin' to Louisiana" every night, if I could do it.

—Muddy Waters, *Deep Blues*

There are things more insidious than violence [in songs], like hypocritical optimism.

—Warren Zevon, 1981

I was signed to a small record label and put out a single which stiffed out, and had a song recorded that became a hit by the Diamonds called "She Say Ooom Dooby Doom." It was a Top Ten record, would you believe it? Later on I followed it with "Who Put The Bomp (In the Bomp Ba Bomp Ba Bomp)" . . . and then when I learned to talk, I did all the songs that were really good with bigger words.

—Barry Mann, 1976

As for alliteration, my counterpoint teacher had a phrase: "The refuge of the destitute". . . . Anytime you hear alliteration, get suspicious. When you hear "I feel fizzy and funny and fine," *somebody* doesn't have something to say.

—Stephen Sondheim

Human nature is still human nature. . . . People got off to "Silent Night" in the old days and they're still digging it this year. Time is not an element. . . . In songs like "Sweet Little Sixteen," I change things. I used to say, "She's wearing tight little dresses and lipstick" and now I'm saying, "miniskirts and hotpants." In "Too Much Monkey Business," I change places from Okinawa to Vietnam. It's just a matter of what's contemporary and what isn't.

—Chuck Berry, 1972

Something that means nothing to you now may mean everything to you next year. These songs are not what I would call deeply personal. They're more stage-oriented, or whatever. They're like Paul Bowles. He had a collection called "She woke me up so I killed her"—a translation he did from these old Morroccan fishmonger tales. There was a like a four-page recipe for a shrunken head in there that is *thrilling.* So songs can be about anything. If you master the art of it, you can aim at anything.

—Tom Waits, 1987

Writing—you can make it come out any way you want. The character can stand up, he can sit down, he can say this. Then the music is like a screen in a movie theatre. It envelops it all.

—Lou Reed, 1989

It's like a kids' song . . . Songs find their own logic. . . . Sometimes a lyric comes to me, I try to deliberately find things that don't have a meaning at the moment. Then I write 'em down, then I think about 'em. Then I understand 'em.

—Tom Waits, 1988

Lyrics are a very connected thing. Like a newspaper, they are very much a part of the culture.

—Norman Gimbel, 1978

Successful song lyrics put forward complex ideas in very simple language.

—Sylvia Tyson, 1990

I have a separate songwriting John Lennon who wrote songs for the meat market, and I didn't consider them—the lyrics or anything—to have any depth at all. They were just a joke. Then I started being *me* in the songs, not writing them objectively, but subjectively.

—John Lennon, 1971

Since I am not a commercial songwriter (though I've had a few hits largely through the accident that I write good songs), I do not limit myself to sureshots, even if I knew how to write them. I write about anything that interests me, that moves me and that seems to move into a song.

—Malvina Reynolds, 1978

My background is working-class Scottish Calvinist. I write better when social values are there, when the songs are about something. I'm a moralist inasmuch as I want to be moral in what I do.

—Murray McLachlan, 1983

I like more economy in my writing now, maybe not something so narrow and Presbyterian as economy, but created spaces where a tiny thing stands out, making room to splash around. I like messy stuff too. A lot of what I really love I can only put into talking parts in songs, and that's not very economical, I suppose.

—Jane Siberry

I think we went in different directions. I try to use economy, where Bruce [Springsteen] can expound. I think he uses a lot of words very well. I like to use as few words as I can, because efficiency is something I like.

—Billy Joel, 1986

These days I can use less words and say what I need to quicker. Like a smart bomb.

—Henry Rollins, 1994

My new songs are clearly written; there are less obscure meanings in them. There's less trickery in the words. They're recorded and arranged in such a way as to put the voice and the song absolutely first. I just tried to talk more straight.

—Elvis Costello, 1988

I don't think songwriters listen to themselves talk. I think they sit down to write a song and they fall into rock clichés, this kind of "lyric-speak." That's what I try to avoid.

—Aimee Mann, 1993

I think most writers are just sitting in a room looking out a window trying to create something out of a hook, and trying to be clever. Hooks are important, but too much of it is like what they just finished. . . . Without the hunger or the pain, they aren't going to write or create anything. You need the chaos, you need the frustration. You need something with which to extract that which is beautiful within you.

—Kostas, 1994

Country blues lyrics are meant to be coy—make people laugh with it or at it. The whole sadness thing about country blues is white publicity bullshit.

—Nick Perls

As for humour in lyric writing, it's always better to be funny than clever—and a lot harder.

—Stephen Sondheim

Not all rap machismo should be taken entirely at face value. Like other black literary and oral traditions, rap lyrics also involve double entendre, allegory and parody. Some rap machismo can be a metaphor for pride or political bewilderment; it can be a shared joke, as it often is in 2 Live Crew's wildly hyperbolic rhymes.

—Jon Pareles, 1990

[Duke University] Professor Henry Gates traced the role of black heritage in rap and described 2 Live Crew's lyrics as an art form called 'signifying'—rhythmic teasing and cajoling, often peppered with lewd or off-colour remarks that can be meant as an insult or compliment. . . . It was the way black people *could* fight against the oppression of their slave masters . . . rapping is a contemporary form of signifying."

—*New York Times*, 1990

I see rap as reflective, and what people should be scared about is the extent to which songs reflect reality. That there is such unbelievable violence in these communities is a national tragedy, while the fact that people express themselves in terms of that goes back to the Wild West. I wouldn't worry about rap leading to violence. On the contrary, rap leads to a productive expression of alienation and oppression, and it's good that it gets channeled into creative outlets rather than drug addiction or physical violence.

—Philippe Bourgeois, 1990

With rap, there's a lot of humour in it. If you don't listen to the humour, it will scare the shit out of you. It will be like, "Oh my God, they really mean it!" An Ice-T fan can listen to the record and say, "Now he meant that . . . and he meant that . . . now he's full of shit . . . now he's talking crazy . . . he meant that." They know when I'm being serious.

—Ice-T, 1993

Everybody said, "You seem to write a lot about alienation." "Right, I do," I said. "Alienation seems to be your big theme." "That's my theme," I said. And I proceeded to write more about alienation. Actually, Dylan was writing protest, and whatever it was, everybody had a tag. They put a tag on the alienation. And it was a self-ful-filling prophecy that I wrote alienation songs. Of course, we all had feelings of alienation.

—Paul Simon, 1972

I don't write about apples and oranges and trees, and I don't write about the things of life that people can't hold on to. I write about things that will give people strength.

—Lionel Richie, 1980

George Martin had a book on guns which he had told me about . . . or I think he showed me a cover of a magazine that said "Happiness is a Warm Gun." I read it, thought it was a fantastic, insane thing to say. A warm gun means you just shot something.

—John Lennon, 1971

I put a lot of work into my lyrics. Not all my stuff is meant to be scrutinized, though. Things like "Black Dog" are blatant let's-do-it-in-the-bath type things, but they make their point just the same. People listen. Otherwise, you might as well sing the menu from the Continental Hyatt House.

—Jimmy Page, 1975

I think the way people distort their attitudes is the most fascinating thing to write about. I like finding an area of the personality that is slightly exaggerated and, if I can identify with it, to perfectly cast a person with that particular char-acter trait.

—Kate Bush, 1989

There is power in just giving the image alone without explaining it. I think there are a lot of things to write about that have a lot of mystery in them. There's a whole other area of life that doesn't have anything to do with what your mind is telling you, and I wanted to explore that a little more.

—Suzanne Vega, 1990

There's something I keep trying to put into words but I haven't quite satisfied myself that I've said it. It's getting closer, but there's a lot further to go, that's for sure.

—Jane Siberry

The word I want to say is easy to say, and yet it is the hardest word I've tried to say.

It tries to make all my feelings plain. . . .

I am trying to be a singer singing without a dictionary, and a poet not bound down with shelves of books.

—Woody Guthrie, *Born to Win*

It's a matter of just flooding the rhythm with more lyrics than you could ever use, then weeding them out and making a story of it. When you just start free-associating like that over some rhythm, you end up not really talking about nonsense, but talking about yourself. It's weird, it's cool, it's scary.

—Shawn Colvin, 1993

If I don't have an idea, I'll just start running my mouth, I'll just start making vocal sound. It's all feel. With James Brown, that "Uh!" speaks volumes to me. That's genius, that's one of the best lyrics that ever was. Just hearing that gets you up in the morning.

—Henry Rollins, 1994

It's all jumbled-up thoughts that come out, and you put yourself on that emotional plane, in that corridor, and it leads to an idea. It's like sensory plotting. You get yourself into the role, the moment. It's all based on the truth, otherwise it would be purely cosmic and have no substance. There's nothing wrong with writing cosmic thoughts, but its got to tie up mathematically. I hate math, but I love symmetry.

—Ray Davies, 1990

[In my writing] there's nothing "Christian" in the sense of going to church, but maybe my lapsed Catholicism is showing. If you're raised that way, the imagery stays with you.

—Neil Finn (Crowded House), 1987

I guess that generally I'm drawn to imagery that portrays the kind of confusion that I feel right now. I'm much more drawn to lyrics that contain that dichotomy—the yin and yang of living.

—Neil Finn (Crowded House),1989

I'm a young person. I would have had to have started this rough life pretty early to have gone through all the things I've written about in songs. They're generally from looking around, and seeing what's happening and trying to put myself in that position, which is why they come out sounding personal.

—Joan Armatrading, 1984

Your ballads will be lots better and sounds lots plainer and clearer when you stop all kinds of hiding, even hiding from your own people or from your own self.

—Woody Guthrie, *Born To Win*

Sometimes when you're found out you run for cover. You don't want to admit it. There are certain songs I'd be fearful of when I sing them, either because I associated them with some time I didn't want to consider, or because they said something so bleakly personal that even the morbidity of the song didn't do justice to the darkness of the thought behind it. . . . I wrote one good line in "The Imposter," which otherwise isn't a very good song: "When I said that I was lying, I might have been lying." The minute I wrote it, it scared the hell out of me. It's like saying black is white. A very undermining thought. Doubting the things you know is the road to madness.

—Elvis Costello, 1988

I have an idea that the popular songs of a country give a true picture of its history. When you hear the Marseillaise, you can almost see the French Revolution. Take some of those songs that were sung when I was a kid: "Two Little Girls in Blue," "Little Annie Rooney," "A Bird in a Gilded Cage." Aren't they all perfect pictures of the gaslight age? You couldn't find a better description of the city in the 1880s than "The Sidewalks of New York." Even the bicycle craze found its song, and so did the automobile. The dizzy heights that stocks reached were recorded in music, and many a song owes its life to prohibition.

—Irving Berlin, 1978

Stephen Foster touched but one chord in the gamut of human emotions, but he sounded the strain extremely well. His song is of that nostalgia of the soul which is inborn and instinctive to all humanity, a homesickness unaffected by time or space.

—H.V. Milligan

I honestly think that what I've always been trying to do is something incredibly simple, which is storytelling, completely ancient, not at all avant-garde. And the things that work the best are the simplest, the most direct stories. There is nothing new about that. —Laurie Anderson, 1989

Story songs provide ample opportunity for the lyricist who has a lot to say, but it's a challenge to write a really good story and wrap it up neatly in a three minute package. The best story songs present recognizable characters, some sort of conflict and either a resolution of the conflict, or a moral to the tale.

—Marcia DeFreu, 1976

Randy Newman's one of the best character writers. A lot of people who write songs these days think it's always got to be about *them*. That's very limiting. It's always, "Me, you, me, me"; it's always gotta be how I feel about this, and it's all very serious. But you can reveal yourself through characters. You can get out, you can say things that you wouldn't say. I used to worry about it, but now I don't think everything you sing should be your creed, should be how you live your life, or you're going to limit what you can say—you're going to intimidate yourself.

—Tom Petty, 1986

I don't interest me, writing about me. I couldn't name you any song where I was writing about me. I mean there's a whole world of people and there's no reason why a songwriter would be more limited than a short story writer or a novelist. . . . I've been trying to write something about a southern industrial worker. I've had that

idea for a long time. Stuff like that interests me, the average person, nothing startlingly dramatic. I read that they had figured out the average person in the country would be a forty-seven-year-old woman who's a machinist's wife outside of Dayton, Ohio. I wanted to do a song about her through this industrial worker character.

—Randy Newman, *In Their Own Words*

You get tired of listening to your life story. I'm pretty much a vicarious storyteller. I don't necessarily have to live the life I'm singing about.

—Pat Alger, 1990

With all the strange things that have happened around my life, I find it takes little effort to conjure a story worth somebody hearing. So far as rhyming the words, my love for poetry lays the obvious in my lap for lyrics.

—Chuck Berry, *Chuck Berry: The Autobiography*

I describe people in my songs, and the more a song is local, the better are its chances of being universal.

—Gilles Vigneault, 1976

William Faulkner wrote only about the swamp, James Jones wrote only about the war, but I didn't want to write just about dope and New York. I did my drug songs. That's it. I don't want to make that my war, my swamp, my city. I'm interested in emotions, things that happen to people.

—Lou Reed, 1989

There are certain people who are rarely used as subject matter in song or story, and I think they need to be represented. I feel they really need to have some kind of voice.

—Tom Waits, 1980

To me, there are still a lot of feminine points of view that haven't been expressed musically yet.

—Melissa Manchester, 1979

Sometimes I'd propose [lyrics] as if it happened to me, in order to hit somebody else, 'cause everything that happened to one person has at some time or other happened to someone else. If not, it will.

—Reverend Rubin Lacy, *Early Down Home Blues*

I think of my songs as having a tone that is somewhat autobiographical. I don't necessarily think of them all as being directly songs that are my own experience, but certainly there is a part of me that's in them. I'm also fond of saying that I feel free to exploit the lives of my friends and the people around me.

—Mary Chapin Carpenter, 1990

[The songs] come from real life right up to the point where they don't rhyme, and then I make the rest up.

—Huey Lewis, 1990

I've maintained all along that I write fiction. And I still believe that, but it's like John Cheever or somebody said: the best fiction reflects real life.

—John Hiatt, 1987

I'm an avid people-watcher to the point of being a harmless voyeur. I don't look under window-shades, but I do listen in shamelessly in restaurants. I see people on the streets, in airports, at train stations, and I say, "What's their story?"

—Rupert Holmes, 1980

I'm fascinated by America . . . it's so odd. It's only been here such an itty bitty time and, my God, the good and bad things it's caused all over the world.

—John Prine, 1978

CHAPTER 8

GETTING PERSONAL

SONGS OF LOVE, SEX AND LOATHING

Keith Richards said it: "Not much has changed since Adam and Eve." The trick is to tell it from your own angle—what you've felt. The English language seems to be somewhat restricted when it comes to words of love, while the French have dozens of words for love and romance. The Mexicans and Spaniards dig very deeply into their language to communicate love, torment and rejection. There are a thousand ways to howl. I'm most moved by writers who've developed their own language and distinct way of looking at love (Bob Dylan, Lucinda Williams, Dan Penn, Smokey Robinson) rather than those who pump out factory hits full of clichés. Some of us have to shed a few more layers of skin than others.

—T.R.

Until about fifteen years ago, I pretty much avoided writing songs that were directly about my personal feelings. I managed to skirt the issue by writing mainly story songs, and if the subject of love came up it was carefully masked as someone else's experience. I finally realized that if I wanted to continue to grow both as a person and as a writer, I had to stop worrying that someone might find out something about me from my songs. Then, for a while, I wrote intensely personal lyrics. I feel now that I've finally achieved some kind of balance.

—S.T.

American songs of the first half of the twentieth century gave us a vision of sexless love, rock & roll a vision of loveless sex.

—Gene Lees, *Singers & the Song*

Rock & roll isn't supposed to be legal. Rock & roll is supposed to be rebellious crap. Rock & roll is supposed to be about humping and fucking and sneaking around the parents and proclaiming your freedom, your independence. . . . I happen to think that if the authority [i.e., critics] disapproves of you, then you must be doing the right thing.

—Billy Joel, 1990

It was amazing to see. Here was this very quiet kid [Prince], but once he discovered the notion of sex as a vehicle for his writing, it was as if a door had been unlocked for him.

—Chris Moon (Minneapolis studio operator), 1988

I think that my problem is that my attitude is so sexual that it overshadows anything else. I might not be mature enough as a writer to bring it all out yet.

—Prince, 1988

I want to be the rock & roll Kurt Weill. My interest has really been in one really simple guiding light idea: take rock & roll, the pop format, and make it for adults, with subject matter for adults, written so adults like myself could listen to it.

—Lou Reed, 1984

I'd like to meet Madonna. I'd say, "Gee, you're pretty!" I seriously doubt she's a virgin, but "Like a Virgin"'s a good song.

—Brian Wilson, 1985

A poem or a song that tells about any kind of a fight will catch most every eye that can read.

A song or poem that tells about a love affair, legal or illegal, will catch most every eye and ear that can hear.

The fight can be a fight that leads up to a love affair, or your song can tell about how a love affair led up to a fight. Love affairs and fights are all tangled up like dry leaves in a spider web.

—Woody Guthrie, 1948

It's a proven fact: most people who say "I love you" don't mean it. Doctors have proved that. But love generates a lot of songs. It's not my intention to have love influence my songs any more than it influenced Chuck Berry's songs, or Woody Guthrie's, or Hank Williams'. Hank Williams' songs, they're not love songs. You're degrading them by calling them love songs. Those are songs from the tree of life.

—Bob Dylan, 1991

During the course of his train trips to and from Marion, Indiana [as a youth] in quest of higher musical knowledge [violin lessons], Cole [Porter] discovered that candy vendors sold more than sweets. They were also the purveyors of those spicy naughty books that have always been the forbidden fruit of young people. Cole soon made a point of stocking up on these books, secretly stashing them away in his violin case for reading when no one was around. Later in life Cole even maintained that his delight in the excitement and titillation of these books was eventually to find its way into his lyrics.

—Charles Schwartz, *Cole Porter: A Biography*

Cole Porter, in at least one aspect of his writing, was something of a modernist. In a prudish age of spoon-moon-June pop romanticism, the composer, who was married but homosexual, was far more candid in sexual matters than most. His headiest '30s love songs, like Joni Mitchell's confessional ballads, are suffused with the sense of someone simultaneously surrendering to and demolishing his own romantic fantasies. His double vision extended beyond sex to society at large. While his elegant diction suggested a certain snobbery, his lyrics often gently mocked the airs and pretensions of the international set.

—Stephen Holden, 1990

What happens to the *real* stories—we're talking about somebody feeling like breaking up somebody's home, about somebody knocking somebody down because they caught them coming out of a hotel room.

—Etta James, 1990

Being blue is a very glorious feeling. It's not the same as being depressed. Depression is like an illness, but being blue is a rite of passage—everyone has to go through it, especially if they're lovelorn. It seems like you're adrift on this sea; one moment you're on the crest of this wave, filled with the righteousness that only comes with being truly misunderstood, and the next, you plunge into the depths. You're just this sad fucker who's been kicked in the nuts. If you're any kind of writer, you use that as a source.

—Nick Lowe, 1994

I would like the song to be a part of life, because I've always felt like the blues was the facts of life being expressed to people that didn't understand the other fellow's condition.

—Willie Dixon

The Male of everything has more *nature* than the Female. In the bible, one man had lots of wives. One rooster had thirty hens, one bull forty cows, one tomcat's all over the neighbour-hood! Facts are facts! That would be a good song to write. But you'd lose all your contacts with women, they'd all be mad at you. You don't write songs that make people mad.

—Willie Dixon

Nobody's all heart or all soft. Things aren't either one way or another. You can say things that are madness and still be tender, or you can say "I love you" and be ferocious.

—J.D. Souther, 1980

There's so many ways of saying "I love you" or "Where the hell do I fit in?" and it's nothing arty, nothing lofty, just fucking different. I'm just try-ing to do my thing.

—Jeff Buckley, 1994

Real love is serious and funny and sad and angry, and a real love song can be a little funny. There is humour in real life. It seems to me that when you write a real love song you don't have to be yearning all the time. You can be funny and it doesn't take away from the song.

—Huey Lewis, 1988

I think it's a big challenge to write a love song that isn't all soppy. "Wonderful Tonight" has a little bit of irony in it. I didn't write it in a par-ticularly good mood. I wrote it because my wife was late getting ready to go out. I was in a foul temper about it.

—Eric Clapton, 1993

Springsteen and I say the same things, in differ-ent ways. I'll say, "I miss you darling." Bruce will say, "I miss you, motherfucker."

—Barry Manilow, 1990

[Songwriting] is about experience in general, that denominator of things. It's about relation-ships primarily—the love song is so basic, that won't ever die. It's about living with other peo-ple and waking up in the morning—and working.

—Gordon Lightfoot, 1983

Basically what people want to hear in a song is I love you, you love me; I'm O.K., you're O.K.; the leaves turn brown, they fall off the trees; the wind was blowing, it got cold, it rained, it stopped raining; you went away, my heart broke, you came back and my heart was okay. I think basically deep down that is what everybody wants to hear—it's been proven by numbers.

—Frank Zappa, 1974

The same notes and the same words have been used since the days of Beethoven and Bach, so I just try and say it in a different way and make the best of what I have to work with. . . . I write about love and life because they are always current.

—Smokey Robinson, 1991

American audiences mostly want to hear things that sound like they've heard them before. In other parts of the world that's not necessarily so.

—Buffy Sainte-Marie, *In Their Own Words*

A good mechanic could write good songs about an automobile, a good surgeon could write a fairly decent song about an appendectomy, but we have a problem here: songs about automobiles and appendectomies are not big sellers. Songs about boys and girls are the most popular songs. That's vanilla. But there's chocolate, raspberry, strawberry, pistachio, too. Songs come in a lot of other flavours, and people seem to like some of those once in a while. I seem to be stuck with pistachio. I've never been a romantic, but I survive.

—Tom T. Hall, 1979

People get down on me for not writing enough personal stuff. I do write personal, I just figure it's going to stay personal. Why waste a good song on something that's been said to the point where I'm ready to vomit?

—Jello Biafra, 1990

If love is all you think about, I am sorry for you. If you think about other things, but only write about love and other pretties, you are hopping when you could run, walking when you could fly.

—Malvina Reynolds, 1978

I could sing the blues after the man I had started wanting liked everybody but me, so I sang the blues about the way the man treated me. When I sing the blues, I am talking about myself.

—Sippie Wallace, *Meeting the Blues*

With "Call Me Names," I was actually quite surprised when people didn't see the humour in that. I was very surprised at the amount of people that thought I was saying that it was a good idea for a husband to beat up his wife. Well, all that did was prove to me they hadn't listened to the song, because in fact, it's the wife that's beating up the husband, and it's a very comic situation, because I'm talking about a great, big, fat woman with a little short man.

—Joan Armatrading, 1984

I like haunting melodies and haunting guitar lines. I love the despair, the emptiness, the feeling of love in vain.

—Bryan Adams, 1987

These days my themes are still love, mostly love, but adult love; a level of maturity, a higher level, a more refined kind of love.

—Brian Wilson, 1985

My art is now created out of joy rather than angst. I'm not inclined to mix politics and music. My job is to entertain. To write love songs about personal relationships. That's what I know about.

—Glenn Frey, 1988

I'm not much good at relationships—it's more a case of thinking about them all the time rather than doing them. The experiences that I sing about in my songs have usually been nicked from other people. I get them 'round to let them pour their hearts out, stay up all night with them and then, when they're gone, I reach under the bed for me pen and pad. I'm not joking, I've got a pen and pad under my bed! Some of them happen to me personally though. God, if all of them did I'd be dead by now.

—Billy Bragg, 1986

This is a sad world. Individuals are not totally happy. Someone may tell you, "I feel great, I feel happy, I'm fine," but you can make him cry because there's one part of him that's not satisfied, that's hurt, that's not quite fulfilled. I have found that the emotions of pain, hurt and rejection make for the greatest stories.

—Lionel Richie, 1980

Somebody—I think it was Morrissey—said, "I could never write a love song without having a get-out clause in verse three." There was something of that in a lot of my writing. There was always the unwillingness to be vulnerable.

—Elvis Costello, 1988

There's nothing wrong with love songs, but there are love songs that perpetuate something that's not good for us all to learn from, like one song I love the music to "You're My World": "You're every breath I take / If our love ceases to be / Then it's the end of my world for me." My love relationships are not like that. When they're over, I get the blues for a while, but I don't die. I have to fight with all of those songs I listened to when I was growing up in how I relate to people in romantic relationships, because we are taught dependency, we are taught heartbreak.

—Holly Near, 1981

After [grandfather] Daddy Nelson died I started writing cheating songs. I was writing songs about infidelity and betrayal at the age of seven, long before you would sing such songs in Texas. There was heartbreak in all my early songs—a lot of you-left-me-but-I-want-you-back-again.

—Willie Nelson, *Willie: An Autobiography*

A song like "Love is a Stranger" is emotionally sadomasochistic. It's not the love act, nothing so literal, but it is taken from my experience. It's about falling for people who never want you, and feeling ambivalent toward the people who do want you. I've hurt people and felt totally cold about them, but when it's happened to me, I can't take it. My best songs come from suffering because I've indulged in my pain; a very typical masochism. I'm not interested in that anymore. I respect myself now.

—Annie Lennox

The sexual experience for women is extremely different than it is for men and a lot of the time women's reasons for having sex are very different. A man can just have sex with a woman because she's beautiful; they don't have to love her or like her. Whereas women, most of the time, have to be fairly much in love with somebody. That is in itself a form of sexual abuse—the

fact that a woman is giving herself and a man is just sticking a knob into her. There aren't nice words to use to describe it. It's funny, everyone uses bad language, yet they all jump at it.

—Sinead O'Connor, 1990

Somebody had to write about vulnerability. Thinking as a poet, forgetting "pop," what was left to us? All that was left when I began to write, basically, was the internal landscape. We were coming through a psychologically exploratory period. I hadn't read Sylvia Plath, but there were women poets who had done the pioneering already, and taken a lot of flack for it. Pioneers take a lot of flack so that other people can do it. Not unlike Sting going over my turf after I took a lot of flack. It was still pretty shocking, especially in pop circles, to write about such intimate things in the song form, but that was the new territory.

—Joni Mitchell, 1988

Personal politics, to me, are intriguing; more so in fact than the politics of government and stuff like that, because the politics of government at least pretend to be right and pretend to be truthful and pretend to be honest. It's the area where politics and relationships mix that I find the most interesting to write songs about.

—Billy Bragg, 1986

I couldn't write anything personal for about forty years. I was brought up in the arm's-length school of writing, since I learned from Pete Seeger and Woody Guthrie. They wrote about the world "out there": the masses, the ideas of life. I had to go through a lot of personal pain before it would come out in my writing and I could talk about my own feelings, my own emotions.

—Arlo Guthrie, *Follow Your Heart* (Judy Collins)

I'm interested in dealing with subjects I was too frightened to deal with before, when it got to the point where I was like the Don Quixote of rock, railing at windmills, pissing and moaning. The notion of expressing vulnerability was something I couldn't deal with before. It was too close to home, maybe. I didn't want to admit I was in need of basic affection.

—Iggy Pop, 1986

I don't write purely abstract, theoretical mathematical songs, but I'm not interested in everyone knowing about my love life or my insecurities.

—Suzanne Vega, 1987

I'm still learning to say personal things in an effective way—and I see this vast ocean in front of me.

—Neil Peart (Rush)

CHAPTER 9

WE ALL WANT TO CHANGE THE WORLD

SONGS OF POLITICS AND CONSCIENCE

believe in Sting's conclusion that you have to save yourself first before you can save the world. I've always tried to approach "issue" songs by writing from one viewpoint; that of one character. The power resides in the simple view of what that character has been through. Address the human heart rather than the issue. Many people never learn that one. Buddhist Chogyam Trungpa says that if we try to solve society's problems without overcoming the confusion and aggression in our own minds, then our efforts will only contribute to those problems rather than solving them.

—T.R.

Having been part of the '60s protest-song era of Dylan, Baez and Ochs, along with a host of now-forgotten wanna-be political writers, I quickly became aware of the creative minefield a social conscience could lead you into. Two of the major problems I identified were that (1) many of those songs became as obsolete as yesterday's newspaper, and (2) quite often musical integrity was sacrificed for political integrity. In short, good protest does not necessarily make good songs.

When I have written about social issues (I leave politics alone when I write songs), I tend to go for the larger issues as reflected in the small histories—i.e., how the individual is affected. People are less intimidated if the scope is not too wide, and can identify more closely with things that are related to their own lives.

—S.T.

If you say it's subversive, it isn't subversive. It just says what it means.

—Elvis Costello, 1990

In the song, "Big Brother," I speak of history, the heritage of violence, or the negativity of being able to see what's going on with minority people. "My name is secluded; we live in a house the size of a matchbox" . . . You never know the person, and they can have so many things to say to make it better, but it's like a voice that speaks is forever silenced.

—Stevie Wonder, 1973

At it's best, [pop music] is subversive, capable of subtle interpretations of relationships and problems. Instead of beating people over the head with an idea, I think it's better to get people comfortable; then you start beating them with the message. If we're going to save the world, we have to do it from the inside.

—Sting, 1985

Save yourself first, be happy, and then you can save the world.

—Sting, 1985

Brecht got more political by the minute. . . . He came to visit us and we gave him a guest room that was quite comfortable. . . . When I came up after a few minutes he had completely transformed the room (with Chinese scroll and Red Star flag). . . . Kurt [Weill] said, "I'm not interested in composing Karl Marx; I like to write music."

—Lotte Lenya, 1979

I don't write finger-pointing songs because I think I can put the world right. I don't think I can, and I don't really care if I can or not. I just write what I feel. If other people think it has a message, it's up to them, but I'm not deliberately trying to put one across.

—Bob Dylan, *In His Own Words*

I wasn't "one of the guys" growing up. I'm sure Kurt Cobain felt like a real outcast too. So when people start talking to you about how you're some sort of "spokesman for a generation," you can't help wondering where that generation was when you were fifteen. . . . So when they tell you that you're supposed to speak for a generation, I think your response should be, basically, "Fuck you!"

—Adam Duritz (Counting Crows), 1994

There's no answers in the stuff I write. I question things like everybody else. The most I can do as a "rock guy" is maybe let people know we feel the same things they do.

—Louie Perez, 1987

The problem with protest stuff like "Society's Child" is that I was singing to people who felt the same way I did. I wasn't changing anybody, or making any difference to the people.

—Janis Ian, *The Top Ten*

I suddenly realized you don't exist by yourself, you can't just withdraw. You have to exist in the world and you do have an effect. I guess I learned that with "Luka." That song had an impact on people. Maybe it didn't change the situation—I can't say it wiped out child abuse in America—but it had an impact. I wrote the song, I put it on the record, it went out and I felt it come back to me. I guess I feel that in order to keep growing, I have to become more involved and not do the isolationist thing.

—Suzanne Vega, 1990

I don't want to come to the tea party and bore everybody with my slides, but once in a while you have a feeling about something and you want to talk about it. Basically Creedence [Clearwater Revival] was a rock & roll band, but somewhere along the way, just before "Suzie Q,"

I started to realize I could write another kind of song. I could say something with a little depth. A song like "Who'll Stop The Rain," for instance.

—John Fogerty, 1985

When I got to playing in clubs I'd be hanging out late at night with other singers and they'd want protest songs. The kind of songs they were writing were for everybody to slap themselves on the back. It wasn't songs that would change anybody's mind or explain anything to anybody.

—John Prine, *Written In My Soul*

I don't think any given song is going to change the world. You make a song because it's there to be made, not really to convince people of things.

—Bruce Cockburn, 1986

I used to be a crusader to educate other people in music. Invariably, someone would say, "That's not very commercial." "Well," I'd say, "I don't care because I believe the public has the capacity to understand that." . . . I don't know how I feel about that today.

—Jimmy Webb, 1976

When you sing with the intention of changing something and it doesn't change, your inward voice becomes tired. I had to take some distance and admit to myself that things were changing very slowly.

—Gilles Vigneault, 1976

I'm a songwriter. That's what I do. I write songs. I'm not a politician, I'm not the leader of a women's group. The time I've got is to write songs, and if you can't be involved in anything else and really follow it through, then you're doing a disservice to people and shouldn't get involved. I don't want to.

—Joan Armatrading, 1984

I'm not a political songwriter. I write some political songs, but I live in a country at the moment that's very political, and part of my job is to reflect the society that I come from. I can't divorce politics from life, I'm afraid. . . . I think politics are far too important to be left just to politicians.

—Billy Bragg, 1986

I write songs about whatever I have any strong feelings about. If you work that way, it's inevitable that at some point it's going to be political. Politics is just about people in society; and the way societies relate to each other. It's not a conscious decision to make political statements.

—Joe Jackson, 1986

I hate to be told what to think or how to act, so I try not to do that to other people. But at the same time, I feel that I should say something. There's an advice song on the [*Strange Angels*] record called "Ramon." It says, "when this happens, do that"—that was kind of hard for me to write. I barely know how to run my own life and who am I to tell anyone else what to do? And then I thought, "Well, hang on. There's a couple of things I know something about, and I want to try to say them real simply."

—Laurie Anderson, 1990

You've really got to be careful with message songs because if they are too earnest they look really schmaltzy.

—Bonnie Raitt, 1990

A patriotic song is an emotion and you must not embarrass an audience with it, for they'll hate your guts. It has to be right, and the time for it has to be right.

—Irving Berlin, 1978

[Pop] music is not supposed to be nationalistic. It started out as American music and I'm proud of that. I am a patriot. Don't get me wrong; I'm proud that music is America's most redeeming culture, but what bothers me is that artists are supposed to lead, and it seems to me that a lot of people are putting "America" in their songs just because they think it's going to make it sell. That bothers me. If our artists are following the public, my God, we're in terrible trouble.

—Huey Lewis, 1986

I think Ruben Blades is really incredible. He talks about subjects that have political implications, and he speaks about it completely from a human point of view. He portrays the life of a policeman—maybe a member of a death squad—waking up and talking to his wife and kissing his kids goodbye as he leaves to go arrest someone.

—Jackson Browne, 1987

I remember when protest songwriting was really big. Phil Ochs came to town, Tim Hardin was around, Patrick Sky, Buffy Sainte-Marie; but there never was any such thing [as a protest movement]. It was like the term "beatnik" or "hippie." These were terms made up by magazine people who were invisible, who liked to put a label on something to cheapen it. Then it could be controlled better by other people who were also invisible. Nobody ever said, "Well, here's another protest song I'm going to sing." . . . The guy who was best at that was Peter LaFarge. He was a champion rodeo cowboy and sometime

back he'd also been a boxer. He had a lot of his bones broken. I think he'd also been shot up in Korea. Anyway, he wrote "Ira Hayes," "Iron Mountain," "Johnny Half-Breed," "White Girl," and about a hundred other things. There was one about Custer, "the general, he don't ride well anymore." We were pretty tight for a while. We had the same girlfriend.

—Bob Dylan, *CBS Biography*

The first music I heard that I really went crazy for was Bob Dylan's. Songs like "Talkin' World War III Blues" or "Blowin' In The Wind." Those songs are political, and it was a time when the civil rights movement was in full sail. It was 1963-64. The early '60s was when I started playing the guitar. Of course, I heard Woody Guthrie and Pete Seeger too, and the Staples [Singers], and Sonny Terry and Brownie McGhee. A lot of blues artists. But Bob Dylan, Bob Dylan, Bob Dylan.

—Jackson Browne, 1987

People say the '60s were a wash, but my experiences then were tremendously valuable to me. A war was stopped and we learned that powerful political figures could be taken down by young voices. Unfortunately, the young voices that came later had nothing left to say. When your leaders are being assassinated, and there's a war going on, there's a lot to work with. Now people at Woodstock [in 1994] are asking themselves, What are we here for? The mud? There's so much anger and frustration in many young musicians today, and it's aimed at themselves. What are they hungry for? For something to happen.

—Robbie Robertson, 1994

I've always had this very Scroogie point of view. When people demonstrate against nuclear weapons, I think, "These people think that if they eliminate nuclear weapons, they eliminate death." It promotes something like "eternal peace." But they're not going to live forever; maybe I think, basically, that nothing really changes. I'm not attached to that opinion, though. I don't even care if it's true. When you're banging your head against the dirty carpet of the Royalton Hotel trying to find a rhyme for "orange," you don't care about these things.

—Leonard Cohen, 1988

I tend to get more inspired when I come across something I haven't come across before. When I was in Germany recently, I was jogging alongside the river, thinking about how, not all that long ago, cities nearby were being bombed, and people we thought we hated were being killed, but now we're all very friendly. There just seems to be no absolute truth about conflict. I'm intrigued by the patterns of history and the types of things that humankind keeps repeating.

—Amy Ray

My family is Quaker, and I spent every summer on the east coast with councillors from Swarthmore and all of the colleges that were in the peace movement, civil rights and the folk music revival. I always wanted to be part of that culture—Joan Baez and peace marches—and not the quasi beach-bunny/Goldwater aspect of L.A. which was running rampant.

—Bonnie Raitt, 1989

If you want to get political, you ought to go as far out as you can.

—Bob Dylan, 1986

It's more fun to write songs about political issues than, "I love you baby, suck my weenie, buy my record and then hit the road, and sing the boo-hoo, it's so bad to be on the road" songs. That shit drives me nuts!

—Jello Biafra, 1990

These types of ["obscene" and "violent"] lyrics

are just hyperbole and overstatement. Politicians and professional wrestlers use those devices all the time.

—Mojo Nixon, 1991

I'm a nigger. That's why I call and use the word "nigger" 'cause I think it represents the black man who will not co-operate.

—Ice-T, 1990

It wasn't like we were actually seeking controversy, but in order to get some people to listen to you, you've got to slap them in the head sometimes. If they're asleep, you've got to wake them up.

—Chuck-D (Public Enemy), 1990

Skillings: Whether it's political or not depends on your point of view. As a young black man, I can write a song about not being able to hail a cab in New York and that's not political, that's just reality. Or if I write about drug dealers taking over the block. . . .
Glover: We don't set out to write socially conscious songs. We just write about what's around us—what we see.

—Muzz Skillings and Corey Glover (Living Colour), 1990

When I started making music, I decided to take what I knew about rap, which was a hell of a lot,

and what I knew about some of the situations that kept black people down, which I knew more about than some other rappers, and put them together.

—Chuck-D (Public Enemy), 1990

What's the appeal of rap? Different artists feeling free to sing, to express themselves about limitations.

—Stevie Wonder, 1988

There are issues that I will write about. Some of them still surprise people. I think the whole situation with crime has gotten out of hand. The whole situation with joblessness has gotten out of hand. Also, the situation of illiteracy has gotten out of hand.

—Stevie Wonder, 1985

I think there is a mistake in the view of some of that material now. "Riot in Cell Block No. 9" wasn't a ghetto song. It was inspired by the "Gangbusters" radio drama. Those voices just happened to be black. But they could have been white actors on radio, saying "Pass the dynamite, because the fuse is lit." People have said, "These are protest songs, early prophesies of the burning of Watts." Bullshit. These are cartoons. We used to write cartoons.

—Jerry Leiber, 1990

There's an argument about pop music that it means nothing, it's just a set of words that rhyme, just a beat you can dance to—which is fine, but there's room for songs that mean something too.

—Sting, 1988

There's more political content in songs than there used to be. The fact of Tracy Chapman having a hit around the world is an amazing breakthrough, to get politics to that level of kids. I doubt people of Elvis' age in the hinterlands are going to be changed much by any of this.

—Jackson Browne, 1989

It's just time for people to grow up, and to me the place that has grown up the most is music, with all its different cultures and colours.

—Stevie Wonder, 1988

I'm heartened by the fact that there's such great political music out. A baby songwriter like myself, it's a goal of mine to get better and let a little of that come through more. I'm not saying that defensively; I don't have a need to make an overtly political song, but there are some things I relate to on a personal level: a lot of women who are divorced, alcoholic, their kids are turning on them and they don't understand. There aren't a whole lot of movements for them to join. I'm saying there's a certain line where there is no difference in our lives between a personal and political quest.

—Bonnie Raitt, 1989

Our songs brought about an attack of conscience over our national identity, and this brought about the need to be politically involved. More and more, those who wanted to make a living had to take a position, and show exactly where they stood. I myself am first and foremost a Quebecois. As a result I am all for a Quebec for Quebeckers, and that means *Québec libre*.

—Claude Gauthier, 1970

When you're playing political music to young people in America—in Texas—you can't go onstage and suggest that the Soviet Union is not such a bad place after all to a load of Texans . . . You know the North American audience is the great challenge to anybody working in the English language—to come over here [from England] and to put our ideas up against the blandness of American radio.

Anybody who accuses me of preaching to the converted all the time should come over here and see some of the gigs we do in the States and realize that there are a lot of unconverted people out there.

—Billy Bragg, 1986

If you don't take risks, you might as well give up.
—Joe Jackson, 1986

Let's face it, the majority of the country is always the poorer class. These are the guys who are brainwashed into thinking this is what you should have, and they go along with it. But then some jackass like Stompin' Tom comes along and throws a monkey wrench into the whole machinery and says, "Look, that's not the way it is. The way it is is the way you want it. We ain't going by what somebody from a university or college or from government says. Whatever they say, take it with a grain of salt. Meantime, we've got some songs here, and we're going to sing them the way you like them." And, you know, that tears them apart. They know I've done these jobs. I've lived with them. There's not one guy from the working class can come up to me and say "Look here, Tom, you're full of crap."

—Stompin' Tom Connors, 1971

I know what being a commercial fisherman is. I did it. Most of my life was poor. Most of my life

I had weird jobs. But there's also a thing called imagination, which is what writers have. We should be able to use pronouns any which way we want to get a narrative across. I don't like getting up on a soapbox, being one of those social/political-message guys. I think the best way to do it is to tell a story about a human being, not about an issue.

—Billy Joel, 1990

"Hey, guitar man!" One old boy seen me and Ruth walk up from the side of the store. "Could you turn loose of that purty gal this mornin' long enough to sing us a little song?"

I said I reckoned as how I could.

"Play us something about all of us standin' 'round here waitin' to go to work!"

So I flipped a few strings to see if the box was in tune, and I smiled a little at Ruth watching me; and sang "Pastures of Plenty."

They just kept quiet 'til I got done. Then every single person seemed like they took a deep breath, and started to say something, maybe; but I heard a screen door slam behind me, and when I looked around I saw Ruth's old dad walk out into the little porch, and the orchard boss walked out with him. The boss carried a piece of paper in his hand, and he waved it in the air, meaning for all of us to get quiet.

"Quiet, everybody. Listen.... won't bother to

read all of this order. . . .

"Dear Sirs: Due to cold weather of the past 30 days, the apricot crop will not be ripe enough to be suitable for canning. There will be a 10-day waiting period to allow the fruit to mature. Pickers may stand by and await orders, as the weather may take a warm change and ripen the fruit sooner. Usual credit slips may be obtained by making the proper arrangements at the company store. . . . Anybody want to ask any questions?"

I believe this was the quietest crowd I was ever in.

—Woody Guthrie, Bound for Glory

CHAPTER 10

MARRIAGES OF CONVENIENCE

COLLABORATIONS

In all the years Ian and I worked together, we wrote maybe three or four songs together. Ian would always write a set of lyrics and hand them to me for a melody. When I have written with Shirley Eikhard, she generally gives me a completed melody and either a chorus or a lyric outline. My other collaborative efforts have been sit-down bash-it-out head-banging sessions, and I actually warned one less experienced writer that if he didn't learn to stick up for his ideas I'd steamroll him for sure.

Tom Russell and I have worked in all the aforementioned ways, although I've only managed to get him to write one melody for all the sets of lyrics I've shown him. I hope I'm wearing him down so he'll work on the others.

—S.T.

As regards the writing and publishing split, I generally insist on fifty-fifty, unless it is very clear that either the melody or the lyrics were complete when I started working on the song, and the other half of it is a collaboration, in which case it's a fifty/fifty split on that part of the song which I worked on. I feel it's clean and simple, and that the song would not exist in that form if I had not contributed to it.

Co-writing presents difficulties. Sometimes it's magic; sometimes it's like two people trying to paint a picture with one brush. I've found it useful, when I'm blocked on a song or I want to stretch my boundaries, to write with someone with a different orientation. Many writers I've worked with are stronger melodically than I am. They stretch the melody and take the song to a different realm. I've written with Dave Alvin and Peter Case, who come from a rock background; Katy Moffatt and Sylvia Tyson, who are very melodic; Bob Neuwirth (whose first rule is, "Just blurt it out, I won't be self-conscious if you won't"), and a few Nashville writers who keep their ears tuned to current radio standards. All of these people have helped me stretch my composing skills and my melodic sense.

—T.R.

The only collaborator Cole Porter ever had was William Shakespeare [*Taming of the Shrew/Kiss Me Kate*]. . . .

I remember cabling Cole Porter [during World War II] to ask his permission to rewrite "Let's Do It." He gave it generously. "Let's Do It" was not only a great song as he originally wrote it but it happens to have a rhyming scheme which can be utilized indefinitely without destroying the basic metre. I wrote special refrains for the Navy, the Army, the Air Force, hospital nurses, CWIC receptions, et cetera.

—Noel Coward

Collaboration is not an art. It's a job. Some people call it a marriage. Well, marriage isn't an art either; it's an expression of the desires and loves and wills of two people. In collaboration, two people come together for a goal, and calling that an art is ludicrous. The creation is the art, not the collaboration. The collaboration is the means of reaching that goal.

—Gary William Friedman, 1977

The whole trick of a song is that it should seem like it wasn't written. It should seem not that two people wrote it, or three people, but that it came out of one mind.

—Hal David, 1991

It's very hard to write with the same person [Barry Mann] for as long as we've been writing together. As you know, most writing teams don't last, much less marriages. It's hard to live with the same person and keep the creative spark going.

—Cynthia Weil, 1976

When Boudleaux [Bryant] makes up his mind that something is not any good, it's like sending a woman out to a party when she feels she doesn't look good. She feels bad, therefore she acts bad. If he doesn't like something, it's very difficult. . . . And I'm somebody he likes very much. So another collaborator? He's not going to fight that battle with anybody else if he doesn't have to go home to them at night.

—Felice Bryant, 1978

It's like a blind date. It's just kind of trial and error where some people compliment each other, and others don't.

—Vince Gill, 1994

Our relationship [with Dave Stewart, Eurythmics] ranges from really intense battles to very close friends, when we know we'll never be able to work with anyone else. All the songs we've written have been in circumstances when we've been just about to split up, but something comes together again, and each time it's stronger than before.

—Annie Lennox

[Annie Lennox and I] will really get tense. We meet like strangers over a new song, and we'll argue like hell! We're very protective when we're playing each other new songs, but we can always work anything else out of our system by working with other people.

—Dave Stewart

Mann: We fight a lot.
Weil: We go through good and bad work cycles. We went through a cycle where Barry just didn't like the way I was writing for a while, and there was nothing I could do about it, so I started writing to please him instead of to please me.
Mann: I had my problems too. I was trying to expand the scope of my writing and everything was becoming more abstract. I went through a period of denying what came to me so easily. It's done with such ease I figured there must be something wrong with it.

—Cynthia Weil and Barry Mann, 1986

If we were both like me, we'd have a thousand unfinished songs. If we were both like Annie

162

[Lennox], we'd probably have one single every two years.

—Dave Stewart, *Sweet Dreams: The Definitive Biography*

Songwriting is my business. When you work, your feelings about the person you work with do not affect the work itself; you just do a good job. In fact, it's better if you don't socialize. Then you can be more openly objective about each other's work.

—Jule Styne, 1977

When you work with someone, you have a relationship with working with them, which is different than the people you might go out with, hang out with. It's a different relationship because there's an end to it.

—Mick Jagger, 1994

If anyone's offended, I tell 'em I wrote the music, not the words. Don't shoot me, I'm only the piano player.

—Elton John, 1988

In one afternoon I acquired a career, a partner, a best friend—and a source of permanent irritation.

—Richard Rodgers (referring to Lorenz Hart), *Tin Pan Alley*

When you get two people together, they shouldn't just agree with each other, there should be some tension and a little disagreement, and out of that good ideas come.

—Elvis Costello, 1989

Stoller: We started fighting the moment we met. We fought about words, we fought about music, we fought about everything.
Leiber: One thing we never fought about was chicks. Because I got the good lookin' ones.

—Mike Stoller and Jerry Leiber, 1990

Often we'd sit down with nothing to go on. He'd start playing, and I'd start shouting. There was some kind of balance in our metabolisms.

—Mike Stoller (referring to Jerry Leiber), *You Must Remember This*

Songs never take us three or four days to write. If it takes that long, we're heading in the wrong direction. We might struggle through a whole day on a song with the lyrics taking us five or six intense hours, never budging from the piano. It's like a fistfight. We're determined to beat the song into shape because we know it's there, we just haven't found it yet.

—Dennis Lambert (Lambert & Potter), 1977

Working with a collaborator you must learn to be political. If you have something to say about his melody, you have to find a nice way of saying it. You can't go around saying you like things if you don't like them. And so you don't react immediately if you don't like something. You say, "I'd like to hear it again." There are so many ways you can do it.

—Hal David, 1974

Some guys, if you don't rhyme, the blood runs out of their heads and they go white with shock.

—Norman Gimbel, 1978

I'll tell you the facts of life. In the theatre you need someone to talk to. You can't sit by yourself in a room and write. You gotta get along.

—Jule Styne, 1990

I don't like writing alone. I don't trust myself. You don't have to have the conversation with yourself, "Is this good enough?"

—Glenn Frey, 1984

When I met Kyr Fleming in 1986, I casually mentioned that I'd always hoped to write another "Jesse," and had never been able to. Three months later, we wrote "Some People's Lives," probably the finest song I've ever been involved with. It would never have come about on my own; the magic was that Kyr and I were writing together at that particular moment in time.

—Janis Ian, 1990

When we started the Beatles, John [Lennon] and I sat down and wrote about fifty songs, out of which I think "Love Me Do" is the only one that got published. The songs weren't very good because we were trying to find *the next new sound.* The minute we stopped trying to find that new beat the newspapers started saying it was us.

—Paul McCartney, 1980

The good thing about working with John is that he didn't like to hang about too much. Didn't like to be bored, which is always a good instinct.

—Paul McCartney, 1989

[Paul McCartney and I] always wrote separately, but we wrote together because we enjoyed it a lot sometimes, and also because we would say, well, you're going to make an album, get together and knock off a few songs, just like a job.

—John Lennon, 1971

I know I've lost my edge. I like edgy stuff, actually—I was the one who decided in "Norwegian Wood" that the house should burn down, not that it's any big deal. But I do need a kind of outside injection, stimulation, and it's not there anymore.

—Paul McCartney, 1985

It was Paul [McCartney] who asked *me* to write with *him*. I tell you, I was so afraid that we might look at each other and not have any inspiration that, as an insurance, I took two songs along in my pocket when I went to his studio. I had started to work on them and he helped me to finish them; and by that time we were relaxed enough to write brand new songs.

—Elvis Costello, 1989

When I started doing some writing with Elvis [Costello], we originally said, "Well, look, let's not tell anyone we're working together, because if it doesn't work, we're going to look like idiots."

How we started writing together was that, rather than just going in the deep end, he played me a couple of songs he'd been having trouble finishing, and said, "Tell me what's wrong with these." And then, "Back On My Feet" was one where in *my* case, I wasn't totally happy with my lyrics, though I'd pretty much written it. So

I fixed up his two songs, he fixed up this one of mine, and we were off and running. The next song we wrote from scratch, which was better yet!

—Paul McCartney, 1988

[Paul McCartney]'s very logical about songwriting, and really pays attention to the details, so it's like having somebody correct your work all the time. Paul is very precise.

—Elvis Costello, 1989

It's an interesting footnote to music history that along an early English tour, Dylan would visit the home of John Lennon and the two would pen a song together. "I don't remember what it was, though," said Dylan. "We played some stuff into a tape recorder but I don't know what happened to it. I can remember playing it and the recorder was on. I don't remember anything about the song."

Lennon would later comment on their relationship. "I've grown up enough to communicate with him. . . . Both of us were always uptight, you know, and of course I wouldn't know whether he was uptight because I was so uptight, and then when he wasn't uptight, I was—all that bit. But we just sat it out because we just liked being together."

—Bob Dylan, *CBS Biography*

[Bob Dylan and I] were both shy. He had been out of commission socially since his accident [1966]. I was nervous in his house, and he was as well. We fidgeted about for two days and only relaxed when we started playing some guitars. The song "I'd Have You Anytime" was an accident. I was just saying, "Hey man, how do you write all these words?" Which people probably said to him all the time. I kept thinking he would come pouring out with all these lyrics! Meantime, he was saying "How do you get all them chords." . . . He's fantastic, you know. There's not a lot of people in the world who I see from a historical point of view. Five hundred years from now, looking back in history, I think he will still be the man. Bob, he just takes the cake.

—George Harrison, 1987

When I'm working with either Phil [Cody] or Howie [Greenfield], there's a definite interplay which I just love. At one point Howie and I decided to split. We'd been writing together for so long, I felt things were getting a little stale. He came to my apartment and told me he had a present for me. I looked around and didn't see any present and Howie explained that his present was a title, "Our Last Song Together." I said, "Oh, my God," and realized that I had a tune that would work well with that title. We completed the song, and then we cried. I'm a big crier.

—Neil Sedaka, 1976

I heard he [Charlie Mingus] wanted to see me. He had written six melodies for me to set words to. By then Charlie was paralyzed. He sang them into a tape recorder, and a piano player friend of his fleshed them out into a voiced piece of music. The tape presented to me was a piano with a metronome. The tape nearly drove me crazy. I took it out to the beach at Malibu and the second day I woke up in bed with my foot ticking back and forth under the covers to the rhythm of this metronome. . . . There weren't many conflicts between us. Maybe because I was a woman. He liked women. He was such a flirt.

—Joni Mitchell, 1979

The two men [Bertold Brecht and Kurt Weill] wrote and re-wrote furiously night and day with hurried swims between, I recall Brecht wading out, trousers rolled up, cap on head, cigar in mouth.

—Lotte Lenya, *Kurt Weill: An Illustrated Biography*

Working with Wilson Pickett was what really got the ball rolling. One afternoon him and Jerry Wexler flew in [to Memphis] and we hung out in a hotel room. Jerry went off to do business and Wilson and me wrote songs. It was about nine or ten o'clock and Jerry and Jim Stewart [of STAX Records] came by to see how we were doin' and they brought us a bottle of scotch. We had already written "In The Midnight Hour" and they said, "That's pretty good. We'd better leave you alone," and they split. Before the night was over, we wrote "Don't Fight It." Both tunes turned out to be pretty good. . . . I'm glad I had the chance to work with the STAX group in its formative period and on through their big years. I look at myself as fortunate because those cats really had it together. That's where the inspiration came from, and I wish I had it today. Sitting in a room with a Wilson Pickett or an Otis Redding, the songs just came like crazy. Otis was the kind of guy that when he was out on the road, he'd come back to Memphis and have ten or fifteen ideas for different songs—little bits and pieces of things, and we'd work on whichever ones felt most comfortable to us on a given night.

—Steve Cropper, 1976

One day during the mid-'60s, David Porter said to me, "Ike, I'm a lyric man and you're a music man. Let's hook up," and after fifteen or twenty duds we began to find our niche. We were teased a lot in our early days. We had our little attaché case, and David had this old raggedy car. That damned car would break down every two or three blocks, and guys on the corners would tease us: "Hey hit-makers, how many songs y'all write today?"

—Isaac Hayes, 1994

When I was writing "Joy To The World" I walked around for four months with the chorus in my head and I kept trying to fit the other pieces to it. Well, I'm in the studio with David Jackson, who co-wrote that song with me, and he was playing piano for me and helping me cut a demo on another song. We were paying twenty-five dollars an hour and we still had about eight bucks worth of time left and and he said, "Hey let's not waste the eight bucks, man, let's do something." We just leaned over on the Leslie speaker and wrote all the verses of "Joy To The World" in five minutes.

—Hoyt Axton, 1976

When I was working with Burton Lane for the animated film *Heidi*, I said, "Every day we will meet from two to four. We will not talk about how to write a song. We will not discuss songs we have written. We will write a song!"

—Sammy Cahn, 1977

I am very undisciplined. Most of the writers I've worked with have been disciplined. Arthur Laurents, James Goldman, George Furth, Hugh Wheeler always met deadlines. They work steady hours and they get up at a certain time in the morning and knock off at five. I have to have somebody pushing me constantly to get it in by Tuesday, and then Monday night I start work.

—Stephen Sondheim

The way Bill [Rice] might say it is that he understands a particular line but he has to work at understanding it, and that is the weakness. A line has to have a certain amount of simplicity to have an immediate impact. So we work it out to where we both agree on it.

—Jerry Foster, 1976

When I wrote with Ira Gershwin we were working on a film called *Barclays of Broadway*, and I felt the music should sound a little more sophisticated than ordinary popular music. To successfully write songs you have to think of cadence where the rhymes are going to fall. When a composer collaborates with a lyricist I think the composer is in control. The way I write, I know I'm in control.

When I worked with Johnny Mercer he'd just sit in a room with you and stare silently. You had to sit at the piano and play the tune four or five times until he got familiar with it. He'd just sit there, then after three or four hours, he'd get up, get paper and pencil, and write out the whole lyric in a matter of minutes. He was amazing.

—Harry Warren, 1977

Writing with Kostas is like playing chess against a computer. His brain works so fast it's difficult to keep up with him. It's like playing Tetris. You're going to lose.

—Pete Anderson, 1994

Simpson: I write the music and Nick writes the lyrics, but he contributes to the melody and I to the lyrics. One thing we don't do is try to make it happen. We keep it always relaxed, and it feels good like that. When we maintain that approach we can expect something to happen, and it always feels new.
Ashford: The creative atmosphere has to be right, but you can't schedule your creativity.
Simpson: But if there's a really strong creative pull from either one of us it will pull the other one.

—Nick Ashford and Valerie Simpson, 1977

In a good collaboration, this is what I look for: intelligent objectivity, openness to new ideas and ideologies, facility with language—words should come easily. The lyricist must be both poetically and musically aware of style.

—Gary William Friedman

With the Eagles, everybody brought things to [Don] Henley. He was the lyrical genius, the English literature major who could help us put these stories together.

—Glenn Frey, 1984

I think that I do everything that it is possible to do in terms of writing songs. Sometimes Keith [Richards] and I would sit with two guitars and just play. He would have a lick that would counter what I was playing, and if he would come up with a certain riff, I would counter that. Sometimes I wouldn't play guitar at all; I would just sit there and clap hands and make up top lines. Sometimes I would get a drum groove going and sing to it, or else I played keyboards and just had a bass drum going. Then again, I might have a lyric idea to start with, and then I would come up with the melody, and on other occasions they'd come up at the same time. I wouldn't get stuck in one way of doing it. You get different things happening that way.

—Mick Jagger, 1989

[Bernie Taupin and I] have never actually written anything together. Never sat down to work in one place. I think I'd kill him. Having done his own records, Bernie is much more musical now. He has his own ideas and wants to get more involved with the music. In the future we may even collaborate a little more. It must be frustrating for him to see me take his lyrics, go off with them and come up with a song, but he never complains. This year will make twenty-one years we've been together. We know each other backwards and forwards.

—Elton John, 1988

When I work with a collaborator, there's always a pattern.
1. We talk about the concept of a song.
2. There's some lyrical input—a title, a first line, sometimes more.
3. I work alone and get a model melody which I play for the lyricist.
4. Then he sets his words to my tune.
5. We work together to polish.

—Gary William Friedman, 1977

People said, "How do you write your stuff? Who does the words? Who writes the music?" We'd [the Beatles] say, "No, man! The minute we discover a formula we're gonna junk it," because the last thing you need is to be trapped inside a formula of your own making. It's not only bad to be trapped, but you set the trap.

—Paul McCartney, 1990

The added dimension of Dennis [Lambert] being a great singer really helps our songwriting. We're writing songs to be sung, and it's important to be conscious of how a song is going to flow and feel, and how the lines we choose to write lie on the notes.

—Brian Potter, 1977

In terms of popular songwriting, Barry [Mann] told me what to listen to. He'd tell me to listen to the Everly Brothers. I had never heard of people like that. He was my mentor, and did his best to try to keep my writing commercial and not get carried away with the sophistication [of show tunes].

—Cynthia Weil, 1976

Unfortunately, we all have a tendency to resort to familiar doctrines usually without even realizing: using the same rhyming patterns, structuring the same style of melodies using a lot of the same chords. Collaborating with outside writers is something that many artists are very

stubborn about doing, but I personally feel it's one of the best ways to break old habits and learn new and different methods of composition.

—Lee Aaron, 1988

Different people push you and move you in different ways. It's fun and therapeutic as well. Getting together with a songwriter can be better than going to a shrink.

—Peter Case, 1990

Co-writing has very often been an unsatisfying experience for me. On occasion it has felt like I have written songs myself while the "co-author" just merely happened to be in the same room. But if they had not been in the same room would I have written the song? God only knows . . . assuming, of course, there is a God. Apparently He co-authored the Bible, but I don't think even He was in the room when some of it was written.

—Ian Thomas, 1991

I've written things with people, some of which I liked and others I think are total travesties. Collaborating is trying to make a piece of music and getting someone else to come up with the ideas. What's the fun of that? If I'm trying to put together a piece of music, I don't want to go to someone else and say, "Hey, invent something for me here." Then someone else is doing it. I'm not doing it.

— Alex Chilton, 1994

One day Biff Rose walked into my office, hysterically funny, played eight of his songs and just broke me up. So I signed the songs, gave him whatever monies I did, and he went off to buy a piano.

The next day my secretary says there's a guy named Paul Williams to see me. He's got a Levi's jacket and bow tie on, blond hair down to his shoulders, and glasses. He must have been all of four-foot-three. He's got a big grin on his face and he says, "I wrote half those songs, where's my money?"

I was real pissed at first, but the guy was so charming that we discussed it and we both got pissed off at Biff. So I squared with Paul, gave him the bucks. I really dig his music.

—Chuck Kaye, 1978

CHAPTER 11

BLOOD
FROM A STONE

WRITER'S BLOCK

S.E. Rogie says that when you distrust the power, that's when it dries up. It has to do with believing in yourself. I've found that my driest spells were personal transition periods when I was burnt out on music. Solutions? Some writers play golf, or go for a drive. Others pick up a different instrument. I usually work on some sort of writing every day, and I try to pick up the guitar or pound the piano and sing at least one song so the tools don't rust. When you're searching for the trigger, anything goes; a double espresso, a bottle of wine, an exhortation to the muse, prayer, long walks, hot baths, old journals and notebooks, new tunings on the guitar . . . banging against the wall with your head and heart.

—T.R.

I've always found that there's nothing like a deadline to break down the stone wall of writer's block. I'm basically lazy. In some sense I'm always writing—that is, there's always something simmering away on the back burner—but unless I feel that urgency, the process can take months. If no deadline exists, I'll create one. I'll book a studio to record an album when I have only eight or nine out of twelve songs. I've never found I have to apologize for anything I've written under pressure. Try it.

—S.T.

There are times when the river just won't be rushed.

—Janis Ian, 1990

Sometimes the well runs dry and you have to wait until it fills up again before you have anything to say.

—Roger Miller, *Willie: An Autobiography*

When it's raining you can't find enough things to catch it in. When it's not you can stand out in the middle of the street in a dress and a funny hat and nothing's gonna make it rain. . . . I go through periods, or spells, when I'm more receptive.

—Tom Waits

The ancient Mayans depended on visions to guide their daily lives. When the visions wouldn't come, they would mutilate themselves in slow, painful ways, usually involving sexual organs. Sounds like a bunch of songwriters to me.

—Hugh Moffatt, 1990

If you have an idea and you don't see it through to the end, or to what it thinks the end is, and you stop it, you won't get any ideas for a long time. You will be punished for snubbing it.

—Leo Kotke, 1994

Made a little progress musically today, but my mind and hands feel heavy. It will pass soon, I hope. I know nothing so dreary as the feeling that you can't make the sounds or write the words that your whole creative being is yearning for.

—Noel Coward, *The Noel Coward Diaries* (1945)

I think every songwriter goes through this feeling that "Wow, maybe I'm finished. . . . Maybe that's the last song I'm ever gonna write," and then all of a sudden, you've written another one. It's like "Hey, I'm still here," and it's a good feeling.

—Jimmy Webb, 1976

People talk about drying up. I personally won't let myself believe in that. If you can keep your ideas and emotions fresh when you sit down to write, there's no worry. Should anything like that ever occur, I've got books just stacked back with songs and ideas ready to reach in.

—Jim Weatherly, 1975

Don't get so attached to your songs, and keep a lot of them going. That way, none of them will drive you crazy, and when somebody says, "I don't like that one," you can say, "Fine, I've got all these other ones I'm working on." I've got nothing but half-written songs all over my life. It's the only way to do it. It's also the only way to keep from getting writer's block. I think, if you're a real songwriter, you've got a ton of songs all over the place.

—Don Henry, 1993

I rarely have writer's block because I give voice to my life process by journalizing.

—Chuck Pyle, 1990

Sometimes it helps to "lower my standards" and just write a song that's a little bit fuzzy or muddled—silly, prententious or whatever—who am I to judge? Besides, if it's really dumb it could be a big hit record.

—Peter Case, 1990

I think the biggest problem with any creative writing is getting that critic off your shoulder.

—Patty Larkin, 1993

Don't let the critic become bigger than the creator.

—Randy Newman, 1988

The trouble with being around for a long time is that people think that when you change you're not being authentic. I've never been afraid of

drying up as a writer, because I like music and I will always like music. Tomorrow there may be a new kind of music born, and if I like it, it will come into my music, so that's not a problem.

—Joni Mitchell, 1985

If you look at the different arts, a sculptor, a novelist, a poet, a painter—they take a whole lifetime. There are certain times that are very prolific, and other times when they're planting seeds.

—Laura Nyro, 1989

Laura Nyro made a choice that has tempted me on many occasions—to lead an ordinary life. She married a carpenter and turned her back on it all, which is brave and tough in its own way. Many, many times as a writer, I've come to a day where I say, "None of this has any meaning."

—Joni Mitchell, 1979

The process is never-ending. It doesn't stop after you have a hit. In fact it gets worse because you think you're never going to write another one. At least in the beginning you think the first hit has got to come some day, but you're not that sure about the second.

—Cynthia Weil, 1976

I think the only time I got really concerned was back in 1966. I had stopped selling the amount of records I was accustomed to, and I came as close as I could to being really distraught. I began to question if it was all over for me as a writer.

Something I dearly loved—having a streak of hits—had suddenly stopped happening. It wasn't working, and I had some heavy thinking to do. I was still performing, but I was living on my past; and I was concerned.

Then I wrote "My Way," and all that changed. I realized that I was going to be mature a whole lot longer than I was a teenager, and that song gave me a more mature identification.

—Paul Anka, 1976

Creative people are a little closer to some kind of subconscious source than most people, and when we unblock, it starts flowing out. But you don't know why that happens, or how to make it happen. Everybody has their own little procedures they go through, and can tell you their little tricks. There were times I would listen to a certain writer until that turned me off. Or I'd listen to the radio/don't listen to the radio. Wear my shoes/don't wear my shoes. Write in the living room/write in the den. It never comes out the same way twice, and that's why I think we're all nuts. —Cynthia Weil, 1976

Go eat and play golf. I guess the right solution is to write when it rains. You don't have any of that distraction.

—Vince Gill, 1994

I think that thought flow is very important when you're writing songs. And if, in fact, your thought flow has stopped—which is basically what writer's block is—then you should do something that has nothing to do with song-writing.

—Smokey Robinson, 1978

I finally make myself sit down. About five minutes into it I'll say, "Well, this isn't so bad." For every five times you sit down with your hands on the keyboard, one of those times you're going to do it, but there's nothing more frustrating than those other four times when you finally slam the lid down and say, "I can't write anymore," and you go beat up your dog, or something.

—Michael McDonald, 1979

If I'm blocked it's good to do an inventory on paper of the things on my mind, feelings, problems, et cetera. Is there something I really need to say to someone that I'm holding back? This is a block. I need to get it out.

—Peter Case, 1990

Take a vacation—go diving, but don't forget your guitar.

—Steven Stills, 1979

Different guitars I own have different songs in them. I'll do that when I'm stuck. I'll get out a different guitar or one I haven't played in a while and find something fresh in it.

—Steve Earle, 1990

For writer's block I listen to recorded Shakespeare, because he handled so many subjects so well. If you can come away from *Romeo and Juliet* without a song idea, get help.

—Peter McCann, 1990

I read a lot of Shakespeare. I go rent Shakespeare videos. I sit in front of the TV with a Shakespeare book and read along. I do a really good *Richard III.*

—Dave Alvin, 1990

I think all songwriters are bananas. We don't know where it comes from. You can learn a certain amount of craft. At this point we can write a professional song. Either it's good, it's bad, or it's medium, but it's professional. Where the great ones come from, you don't know, and you never know where the next one is going to come

from and when. When you're on a hot streak, you're on a hot streak, and when you're in a slump, you're in a slump.

—Cynthia Weil, 1976

I hadn't written in two years, since I wrote "Luka," because so much had happened in my life that it took a while to find the rhythm of writing again and get my confidence back. My career had gotten in the way of my work. I was trying to write, and I couldn't come up with anything, and I felt horribly impotent. The more I would try to write, the more I would feel like I was just doing nothing.

—Suzanne Vega, 1987

Unlike some of my peers, I haven't hit a writer's block. When I hit a block, I just paint, which is an old crop rotation trick.

—Joni Mitchell, 1995

CHAPTER 12

USE A #2 LEAD PENCIL WITH A GOOD ERASER

SOUND ADVICE

About six months ago, I started walking in the mornings, four to five miles. I see people out walking their dogs or running with earphones on, and I think they're crazy. Why would anyone want to fill their head with external stuff when they have this opportunity to be alone with their uninterrupted thoughts? Writing inside your head without any of the tools or the distractions not only turns your mind loose, but makes you the ultimate editor. You simply forget all the boring bits and retain the good stuff. If it's not memorable, it doesn't stick. I highly recommend this method. I've written four keepers this way, and I'm also a lot more fit. You should also try driving long distances without the radio on, especially when you're blocked.

—S.T.

I was walking around a pasture in Alberta one time, trying to solve the lyrical puzzle of a song about a guy leaving a woman. As usual, I was overwriting the scene—too many images, too much information. Ian Tyson leaned his head out of the writing cabin and yelled, "You don't have to be Leo Tolstoy, goddammit! Just keep it simple and get out." Keep it simple, say it, get out. Write from the heart. Develop your own writing voice. Quick pieces of advice that take a lifetime to sink in. Leonard Cohen has said that if you work a song long enough it will yield. I ran into him at party in Toronto once, and repeated that to him. He said, "Yes, the problem is, it could take ten years. . . . It could take a lifetime." He shook his head in frustration.

—T.R.

—Look at newspapers for your storyline
—Acquaint yourself with the style in vogue
—Avoid slang
—Know the copyright laws

> —Chas. K. Harris, *How To Write A Popular Song* (1900)

1. Carry a notebook all the time.
2. Don't edit yourself while you're writing down an idea.
3. Transfer ideas into spiral notebooks. Number the pages; date the books.
4. Allow unfinished similar works to borrow ideas from each other as in "See page 39, Nov. 1989 book."
5. If a song wakes you up at night, make some note of it, tape it, write it down.

> —Buffy Sainte-Marie, 1990

Bob Seger once told me you can never say the title of your song too much.

> —Glenn Frey, 1984

It's easy to be simple and be bad, but to be simple and be good is very difficult.

> —Hal David

There is no formula for writing songs. If a song is true for you, it will be true for others.

> —Willie Nelson

Try to find the courage to follow your bliss, as Joseph Campbell would say.

> —Steve Young, 1990

Stay open, stay lean.

> —Janis Ian, 1990

You don't want anything between you and the song. A couple of acoustic guitars and a battery-operated blaster should be all that's required. Pre-production is where the details and the arrangements will be addressed.

> —Tim Thorney, 1994

The best piece of advice I ever got on songwriting was when I was thirteen years old and I wrote a song for Big Joe Turner in my head. I finally got up the guts to sing it to Big Joe. I, this little white kid, went up to him and said, "Big Joe, I got a song for ya." Big Joe asked for me to sing it. But I couldn't remember it. I was goin' "Oh, my God," and Big Joe said, "Son, if you can't remember it, it was no good to begin with."

> —Dave Alvin, 1990

I learned a lot from Hanns Eisler, the great German anti-fascist composer who warned me gently, "The workers don't carry around a piano, so keep your music singable."

> —Earl Robinson, 1990

It's self-defeating for a songwriter to ignore or mask pain. It's sort of the fuel that all this runs on in the first place.

—Steve Earle, 1990

There's an old cliché about writing about what you know. I tend to believe that. I have to hit myself over the head with a hammer that says this. I can't write a song that'll appeal to a thirteen-year-old kid. You'll go crazy trying.

—Dave Alvin, 1990

It's important to light a fire under yourself. It's hard to feel familiar and comfortable with the uncomfortable and unfamiliar, but I think it's important, so that you feel that you're carving new wood and throwing a rock through the window now and then.

—Tom Waits

Be quiet, listen closely, observe what's going on. Inside and outside is a reflection. Breathe deeply. Do not be occupied with hope and fear of the hustle and bustle of everyday life. Write it all down; throw it all away; then start over again!

—Peter Rowan, 1990

Some new writers think being clever is what it's all about. Cleverness isn't what you're trying to do. You're trying to say something that's real. You've only got so many lines, and if you waste them on cleverness you'll probably miss the rest of it.

—Sonny Throckmorton, 1980

The less chords, the better. Wouldn't a one-chord hit song be fantastic?

—Harlan Howard, 1990

Get a guitar and blow everything else off—love, family, security, comfort, money, safety, future, respect, peace of mind. You'll be rockin' and rollin' soon.

—Townes Van Zandt, 1990

Use a No. 2 lead pencil with a good eraser.

—Randy Goodrum, 1980

I use soft lead pencils, very soft. Supposedly that makes the writing easier on your wrist, but what it really does is allow you to sharpen it every five minutes. I do lots of re-copying—that's like pencil sharpening. I get a quatrain that's almost right, so I tear off the sheet and start at the top on a clean one with my nice little quatrain which I know isn't right, but this makes me feel I've accomplished something.

—Stephen Sondheim

Write in your underwear at your kitchen table. You'll always write good songs.

—Dave Alvin, 1990

Do not be trite. Do not be redundant. Do not be afraid to be adventurous—and don't forget the art part.

—Stephen Stills, 1979

Don't be afraid to dream, feel, explore, write down what's real to you. Don't be afraid to be original.

—Buffy Sainte-Marie, 1990

Invest in real estate, and don't buy yachts.

—Harry Nilsson, 1981

First, don't compromise. That is, unless you write fifteen-minute songs about the war. Second, try to keep your publishing.

—Stephen Bishop, 1979

I always feel that all of nothing is still nothing. And working through an established publisher is a good place to start.

—Valerie Simpson, 1977

One thing I should mention which is so important yet so often neglected is publishing. Always negotiate splits amongst the involved writers upon completion of the song. It avoids so much complication if you do it before Mr. X flies home to New York, so you're not trying to recall who wrote what three months down the road.

—Lee Aaron, 1988

When Sidney [Goldstein, publisher] criticized my lyrics back in 1970 it was like an arrow going through my heart and I could hardly stand it, but I realized he was right, and for one of the first times in my life I tried to stop trying to reinvent the wheel, and take a little direction.

—Alan O'Day, 1975

First, respect the masters—the Tin Pan Alley guys who really invented popular songwriting. Second, take criticism—you can take it unwillingly, but you have to take it nonetheless. Third, concentrate on finding your own voice.

—Pat Alger, 1993

Everybody goes through rejection. Take it seriously, but don't take it personally. And just keep at it, because no one really knows their ass from a hole in the ground about hit songs. I took "Daydream Believer" to four groups before the Monkees recorded it and sold five million copies. So if someone doesn't hear it, it doesn't mean that it is not there.

—John Stewart, 1979

Remember that when you get discouraged, "Over The Rainbow" was nearly left out of *The Wizard of Oz* because the front office and powers-that-be thought it was too maudlin, and could never be a hit.

—Janis Ian, 1990

Trust your instincts. If doors slam, go around them. When walls loom, learn to dig under. Don't let anyone squash you, or treat you like a child.

—Janis Ian, 1990

It always amuses me when young writers come in to show me their catalogue and I ask how many songs they've got. "Oh, six or seven," they say. What they really need is fifty. Then, just maybe, they've got something.

—Gordon Lightfoot, 1981

When I meet young songwriters in town [Nashville] for, say, six months, they're feeling their way. And when I see them again a year-and-a-half later and they still haven't had a record out, they believe if they could get just one cut, they'd be okay. I say, "Well, you'd be okay for about a month." There's rarely been one song that made a songwriter's career.

—Pat Alger, 1980

I run into intelligent and sensitive people at parties who want to show me a song they've written. It's unbelievable how their concept of a song has nothing to do with what they are personally—just accepted clichés of songwriting. It's as if, once they've got a pencil in hand, these people are afraid to reveal themselves, naked and vulnerable. Or perhaps they feel if they didn't use accepted modes they'd fail. I tell writers to set things down as they feel them.

—Sheldon Harnick, 1977

Unless one feels driven to compose and at the same time has all the instincts of a Mississippi riverboat gambler, he should never seek songwriting as a profession. Unless you know in your heart that you're great, feel in your bones that you're lucky, and think in your soul that God just might let you get away with it, pick something more certain, like chasing the white whale, or eradicating the common house fly.

—Boudleaux Bryant, 1978

TIPS FOR GUERRILLA MUSICIANS AND SONGWRITERS

1. Absorb all the media-generated "information" you can.
2. Ignore all the media-generated "information" you've absorbed.

3. Live a goddamned life, and show it.
4. Hone your craft relentlessly.
5. Do not avoid, bypass or obliterate your musical idiosyncracies; these oddities are likely keys to your most personal expressions. Amplify them, distort them, delay them, turn up the reverb.
6. Grow your own musical idiom. Feed it with the pre-existing idioms that you love most.
7. Do your damnedest to skate your psyche neatly around, or smack-dab into, folks who listen exclusively to this or that "kind of music."
8. Are you primarily seeking fame? Do the musical community a favour, and become a Hollywood celebrity instead.
9. Subscribe only to myths of your own devising.
10. Forget the "music industry" whenever you can. It's a whole goddamn planetload of frightened mothers out there.
11. Remember your first magical immersion in music? Revel in that human animal innocence, and bring that to the gig.
12. Listen.

—David Torn, 1994

I'd advise all you songwriters out there, if you're getting into it for the *business*, go home and get a job digging ditches or something. Get a life. You'll learn a lot more, and you won't write a lot of rotten poetry.

—Butch Hancock, 1994

If it doesn't burn in your soul, if it doesn't demand to be voiced, if you can live without it, then please do. You'll save yourself a lot of heartache, and the rest of us a lot of time.

—Janis Ian, 1990

You want to be a good writer? You spend an hour a day writing, and at the end of the year, you'll have 365 hours of experience.

—Burl Ives to Mel Tillis, 1977

John [Lennon] gave me some good advice. He said that once you start to write a song, try to finish it, because if you come back to it later you might be in a different state of mind.

—George Harrison, 1979

Once you've finished your first verse and chorus, the lyric becomes even more important. You've reached the Dreaded Second Verse. It's no time to get lazy. That second verse might make the difference between a minor hit and one that stays charted for three months.

—Janis Ian, 1990

We are really in a rut with the three-minute song. You know where it's going to go. If you're trying to get your message across sometimes it's wise to say, "Why don't we stop here and have a moment of silence, then go in a completely different direction?"

—Jimmy Webb, 1994

Too early on, if your nose is in the paper with your eyes all scrunched up going, "Let's see, that doesn't rhyme," or "That's a false rhyme," then you're really doing what Quincy Jones called "strangling the baby in the crib." You have to be more open.

—Jimmy Webb, 1994

Beware of over-using a metaphor. Some concepts are just too small to carry an entire song.

—Janis Ian, 1990

You shouldn't ignore the traditional. You have to know what's gone on before in order to write a song.

—Bruce Cockburn, 1971

I would suggest reading every great play you ever admired, and pretend it was a vehicle for a musical and write songs for it.

—Fred Ebb, 1977

If you're going to write songs and you really want to be a songwriter, write the whole thing. Write the words and the music. It's important to take English literature and absorb as much poetry as you can. It's very important to study the work of other songwriters even if it means nothing more than sitting and listening to ten or twelve albums every day, or listening to the radio all the time. I would stress most importantly a good musical knowledge, because it's very hard to decide, all of a sudden, that you want to be a songwriter, go out and buy an old guitar and start trying to pick up a few chords. You're putting yourself at a disadvantage, because heaven help you if you're successful and suddenly find yourself in the music business, you won't have time to go back and learn those things.

—Jimmy Webb, 1976

You can analyze other writer's structures, listen to them tell you how and when they "do it," but I have found all of this information virtually useless. Unless I listen to myself, I will have only other people's ideas. Sometimes even when I listen to myself other people's ideas appear. Very often those who are telling writers what to do are non-creative types who think that writing songs couldn't possibly be all that different from law or accounting, and sadly, sometimes they're right. But one should always learn to listen to and respect the inner voice.

—Ian Thomas, 1991

When I first came to Hollywood [1932] I couldn't even make a decent lead sheet, but that left me at the mercy of the arrangers. Those guys were trying to change my harmony all the time. I used to tell them, "I don't want you to change it. Do it the way I wrote it." So it was in self-defense that I began to make my own piano copies. Then I used to turn it over to the arranger and say, "This is it! If you want it, take it the way it is."

—Harry Warren, 1977

Obviously, not all of what a person is, feels, thinks, is worthy of putting in a song. You don't have to display your asshole any more than you have to limit yourself to only heroic roles. I guess the best of it would be to chronicle as much as possible the heroic parts of your thinking as well as your frailties, so you give a balanced picture. That's what makes a good pact in any art form, otherwise it becomes a caricature.

—Joni Mitchell, 1985

I had a great seventh grade English teacher who told me it was important to write in my own blood.

—Joni Mitchell, 1985

You have to believe in the songs. You can write about anything as long as it's true for you. U2 writes about politics and Prince writes about sex. The two things are real for them. The song either rings true or it doesn't ring true. A false love song is as false as a false tune about apartheid.

—Huey Lewis, 1988

Pay no attention to the man behind the curtain and write about what you know.

—Greg Trooper

My advice is worth nada. My wife says, "When Vince gives advice, thousands flee."

—Vince Gill, 1994

CHAPTER 13

MADE TO ORDER

WRITING FOR HIRE

The whole idea of writing for anyone else is foreign to me. I write for myself. The few covers I've gotten have been totally out of the blue. It's not that I'm against the idea, I simply can't do it. I do have tremendous admiration for those writers who are successful at it, who can tailor a song to the abilities and persona of a great singer. I'm not a great singer either. Oh, well.

—S.T.

Otis Blackwell came over to my place in the early '80s and told me stories of writing some of the early rock classics in the '50s on Broadway—"Don't Be Cruel," "Return to Sender," "Fever." He told me the Coke bottle story about "All Shook Up" and how he was influenced by comic books and cowboy singer Tex Ritter. He talked about Elvis and the deals the Colonel made—putting Elvis' name on some of Otis' songs.

Some time after that, I walked out onto the street in Brooklyn. I was thinking about Tin Pan Alley and those early writers who wrote for hire. I heard some familiar music. In front of this candy store there was this little toy horse for kids that played "Oh Susanna" by Stephen Foster over and over. A few seconds later an ice cream truck passed by playing Scott Joplin's "Maple Leaf Rag."

Both Foster and Joplin died broke and dissolute. I don't think they ever collected any royalties. Their songs and legacy are entrenched in the culture—ice cream trucks and toy ponies and elevators. I thought of Otis Blackwell, Stephen Foster, Scott Joplin—pioneers of writing for hire, some of them dying in the trenches.

—T.R.

Why were the railroad flats around 28th and Broadway called "Tin Pan Alley"? [Note: By the '20s the Alley shifted uptown as far as 42nd and Broadway.] Monroe Rosenfield wrote a series of comic articles about the new business for the *New York Herald* and thought up the collective title "Tin Pan Alley." The publishing houses were clustered on top of each other. Every window was open. Almost every room had an upright piano playing. The babel of different embryonic tunes all being played at once in the song factory must have struck Rosenfield as reminiscent of tin pans being clashed.

—Ian Whitcomb, *After the Ball*

Harry Von Tilzer was one of the first to open his business on 28th Street in New York in 1902. He was, unknowingly, virtually starting what was to become popular as "Tin Pan Alley." It is alleged that the phrase "tin pan music" was coined in his offices.

—Mark White, *You Must Remember This*

Monroe "Rosie" Rosenfield—what a card and what a chronicler. He stole tunes mercilessly and he sub-contracted song ideas, one time getting an advance from a publisher and actually hiring some poor devil to write the thing.

—Ian Whitcomb, *After the Ball*

Stephen Foster was the first American song-writer to receive royalties. Irving Berlin, after he'd become rich and famous in the 1910s, had a nicely framed picture of Foster hanging in his office. But Foster otherwise appears to have been a bit namby-pamby. One moment he does-n't want his name on "Old Folks At Home" (because he's ashamed of the minstrel show stigma), next moment (when it's a hit) he wants his name printed in boldface. Ed Christy, the minstrel who'd plugged the song into popular-ity, called him a "vacillating skunk."

—Ian Whitcomb, *After the Ball*

[Stephen Foster's tunes] are only skin-deep, hummed and whistled without musical emotion. They persecute and hunt the morbidly sensitive nerves of musical persons so that they too hum and whistle them involuntarily, hating them even while they do.

—*Dwights Journal of Music*, 1852

The day of the rough coon song is over. Styles in songs change as quickly as ladies' millinery.

—Chas K. Harris, *How to Write a Popular Song*, 1900

A fatal calling was songwriting! In the "Bohemian Years" many were the writers who ended tragically. . . . [Stephen Foster] drank heav-ily. Broke and alone, he moved into a room in New York's Bowery. One day he fell over a wash basin. Somebody took him to Bellevue Hospital where he died in 1864.

—Ian Whitcomb, *After the Ball*

The '20s were a bad time for less flexible older writers, the specialists in story ballads. Monroe Rosenfield threw himself out a window (but recovered and limped ever after). Arthur Camb, writer of "A Bird In A Gilded Cage," was reduced to hawking his water colours to sympathetic publishers. Richard Gerard became a *New York Post* clerk and, in 1927, was still carrying a card stating that he was author of the world famous song "Sweet Adeline."

—Ian Whitcomb, *After the Ball*

Any song he [Al Jolson] sang became a hit, so pluggers beat a path to his door. He was the first performer to insist upon being "cut in" on the writing credit to a song. It is known that he never wrote anything in his life, yet shared authorship of some of the greatest songs in the Alley!

—David A. Jasen, *Tin Pan Alley*

Ralph Butler [old-time English song-plugger] kept his life in an attaché case which was forever flying open, scattering inland revenue forms, lyrics, false teeth and sandwiches. . . . America was the enemy as he saw it; he called her pop songs "lugubrious lamentations of a dissappointed lover." Once he'd got the required cash advance on royalties, he'd scamper off to his mysterious farm deep in the country where he would read Anatole France or Voltaire and write songs about animals.

–Ian Whitcomb, *After the Ball*

There he was, Edgar Leslie, sipping his boullion at lunch. The man who was one of Irving Berlin's first collaborators, who wrote the words to "For Me And My Gal," "Among My Souvenirs." He told me his favourite writers were Gilbert and Sullivan. What about Shakespeare? "The guy doesn't bother me." When, after lunch, I played him my recording of his "Tain't No Sin to Take Off Your Skin (And Dance Around Your Bones)," he said, "A guy takes time writing clever lyrics to a good tune, and what do you rock boys do? You murder it!" Johnny Marks ("Rudolph the Red-Nosed Reindeer"), whose office we were in, led me away quietly.

–Ian Whitcomb, *After the Ball*

Irving Caesar sang while George Gershwin played their song ["You-oo Just You"] for Fred Belcher, hoping they might make twenty-five dollars for their effort. After the demonstration, Belcher said, "Well, boys, how about 250 dollars?" Caesar and Gershwin looked at each other speechless. Seeing them hesitate, Belcher then said, "Tell ya what, boys, I'll pay you 500 dollars instead."

.–David A. Jasen, *Tin Pan Alley*

Early rock & roll songs weren't all written by hillbillies. A lot of them were really crafted. All the Leiber & Stoller things rhyme really well, they never accommodate a three-syllable word rhyming with a two-syllable word. They never add extra bars or extra beats. Everything's exact. And that was true for the whole tradition of songwriting from the '30s, except where it was done obviously for effect, like Cole Porter's.

–Elvis Costello, 1990

Back then it was all about independent publishing and the open-door policy. Everybody had a piano in their room. You'd go in and sit down and play and they could tell you if they didn't like it. Today you've got to have a tape. You want to be a songwriter now, you've got to start off with almost half a million [dollars]. In my time, all you had to do was go to a corner store, get a pad and pencil, and go to work.

–Otis Blackwell, 1987

When I met Colonel Parker he offered to introduce me to Elvis. That's when we auditioned "Return to Sender." But I was doing a session with Mahalia Jackson. I think that I was a little more scared than anything else, as I look back on it.

—Otis Blackwell, 1987

When we were writing for Elvis there was a staff up there and they would give us titles, especially to his movies. He had a movie called *Roustabout*, and Leiber & Stoller got their song "Roustabout" in it. We did a "Roustabout" that he recorded but never came out because [because of] the Leiber & Stoller "Roustabout."

—Otis Blackwell, 1987

Back then ASCAP [the music publishing company] didn't consider what we were writing as music. You know, like people are saying now about the rap stuff. That's why BMI was formed, because writers like us were not accepted. It wasn't considered the music the good stations were playing. The kind of blues we were writing had a different feel. Big stations wouldn't play it, like the race thing. ASCAP would not accept writers like us. It was a lot of ASCAP writers who formed BMI.

—Otis Blackwell, 1987

You got it . . . he's tellin' the truth. ASCAP only liked those old-time songwriters. The reality is this: you know you read about Tin Pan Alley and the Brill Building songwriters? The real Brill Building songwriters were those old guys who wrote all the show tunes. The people they later called Brill Building songwriters, the early rock & roll writers, they were never in the Brill building. It's really funny to me. Neil Sedaka and Carole King, they weren't in the Brill, they were at 1650 Broadway. The real hipsters know that, but historically everything gets fucked up. Rodgers and Hart, Rodgers and Hammerstein, Jerome Kern . . . those are the Tin Pan Alley writers. The people that came later were looked down upon.

—Doc Pomus, 1987

Not only are most of the BMI songs junk, but in many cases they are obscene junk pretty much on the level with dirty comic magazines. It is the current climate on radio and TV which makes Elvis Presley and his animal posturing possible. When ASCAP's songwriters were permitted to be heard, Al Jolson, Nora Bayes and Eddie Cantor were all big song salesmen. Today it is a set of untalented twitchers and twisters whose appeal is largely to the zoot-suiter and the juvenile delinquent.

—Billy Rose, to the Anti-Trust Subcommittee House
Judiciary Committee, 1956

I think the words to country songs are very earthy like the blues. They're not as dressed up and the people are very honest and say, "Look, I miss you, darlin', so I went out and got drunk in this bar." That's the way you say it. Where in Tin Pan Alley they would say, "Oh I missed you, darling, so I went to this restaurant and I sat down and I had dinner for one." That's cleaned up now, you see? But country and the blues tells it like it is.

—Ray Charles, 1973

It was insane. Cynthia [Weil] and I would be in this tiny cubicle, about the size of a closet, with just a piano and a chair. No windows or anything. We'd go in every morning and we'd write songs all day. In the next room Carole [King] and Gerry [Goffin] would be doing the same thing. Sometimes when we all got to banging on our pianos you couldn't tell who was playing what.

—Barry Mann, *You Must Remember This*

That's why those Brill Building guys were such an exciting period. They were in a building where the walls were thin and they could hear music come in from different rooms. They were being influenced just by being there. There are still rooms like that in Manhattan where you can rehearse: you rent a room for eight bucks an hour, a little room the size of a bathroom with a piano in it. And if you just sit there quietly you can hear everything from Schoenberg to *Sugar Babies*. It's exciting.

—Tom Waits, 1988

I took a little office of my own above Birdland. It wasn't really an office; it was a storeroom I sublet from a printer. I paid, like, forty dollars a month. I put in a chair, a desk, a phone, an old piano. I lived in that room for a year—for the first time working without some specification about what I could write. I wrote some of the best songs I had written up to that point.

—Neil Diamond, 1988

Nobody wrote with a guitar in New York. They were all piano writers there. So when I walked in with a guitar, I was like a hayseed, despite the fact that I was from Brooklyn. I had some staff jobs, but they didn't end happily. Actually, I was fired from all of them, which is a pretty good record.

—Neil Diamond, 1988

If I offered one of my songs to another singer, they'd say, "If it's not good enough for him, who needs it?" so I decided there would be two Paul Ankas [performer and writer].

—Paul Anka, *You Must Remember This*

While I was at Aldon Music, they [Don Kirschner and Al Nevins] had Neil Sedaka, Howie Greenfield, Jock Keller, Carole King and Gerry Goffin. I had bumped into Carole King when I was bringing demos around before I met her at Aldon. She used to bring all her material around too. She was fifteen, and I saw this confident little broad I couldn't believe. She thought everything she wrote was great. And she was right, by the way. Ninety percent of it was.

—Barry Mann, 1976

When I started writing with Tony Wine, I'd run into Don Kirschner in the hallway of the Brill Building and he'd say, "Are you listening to the radio? Are you listening to what's a hit?"

—Carole Bayer Sager, 1977

Simpson: We'd go to all the publishers on Broadway, knock on the door and say to whoever was there, "You've got to hear this—this is a great tune" and we'd sit down at the piano and perform our songs.
Ashford: We had a lot of fun, but it's not too great when you're doing that. Whether you sold your songs or not could very well have determined if you ate that weekend!
Simpson: If we sold a song, we'd treat ourselves to a liberal piece of strawberry shortcake at Howard Johnson's on Broadway & 45th Street.

If we sold two songs we'd have a double. That was the measure of one's success, and it made it all so simple.

—Nick Ashford and Valerie Simpson, 1977

I earned money by writing special material for cabaret singers who did covers of hit songs, old show tunes or obscure album cuts. The bulk of them had no noticeable conscience, and the songs I wrote reflected it.

—Allee Willis, 1978

The "for hire" label carries some interesting baggage. Some artists are offended by any terminology that involves money. This could be why so many "artistes" get ripped off by people who are ever so eager to take care of those disgusting areas. And then, of course, we scream rape. If songs were children we parents might be more concerned for their well-being. As soon as someone listens to your work you have been hired in a sense, if only for a brief moment. I have no problem with the concept of writing for money as I have this annoying little habit called "eating."

—Ian Thomas, 1991

Ashford: In the beginning [at Motown] they didn't give us specific writing assignments, but just let us write what we felt were hit songs. It took a while to get that first record because there were a lot of great writers there.

Simpson: It was really exhilarating. You'd go by one of the music rooms and stick your ears up to the door, and what you'd hear was usually great. Then you'd go back to your room and try to figure out how to make what you were working on that much better.

Ashford: They had meetings where they would play the records that had been completed and it really would turn you on. The first one we had was "Ain't No Mountain High Enough" by Marvin & Tammy.

—Nick Ashford and Valerie Simpson, 1977

A lot of people have asked me what comes first, the music or the lyric. In my case, more often than not, it's the phone call.

—Tim Thorney, 1994

Writing for hire is like getting paid for sticking your head in a lion's mouth to count his teeth. Actually it's a challenge that can spark your creativity, but at some point you wonder what you're really "saying" with all the quantity if you're a performer of your songs as well.

—Peter Rowan, 1990

[Writing for hire] is excellent training—something every writer needs. It teaches you not to be a fool.

—Janis Ian, 1990

It's very difficult, but challenging, to write for a market other than one's own heart. To write a song for a movie feels a little bit like being an actress. You pretend to be someone else, and then be true to that point of view.

—Buffy Sainte-Marie, 1990

Writing for a marketplace must work for those who have the same sensibilities as the people who buy in that marketplace—the more common, the more successful. You figure it out.

—Katy Moffatt, 1990

Writing "by the yard" or combining hooks with three other writers is profitable but not very satisfying to the artist. I strongly recommend a writer search themselves deeply on this one. A bad decision could poison your enthusiasm for years.

—Chuck Pyle, 1990

I've always loved the idea of having an assignment—being a Brill Building writer, a staff writer, being told, "Write a song by noon about this subject." Since I wasn't a staff writer, I asked my girlfriend, before she went to work each morning, to write me an assignment on a piece of paper. I couldn't watch a baseball game, hang out at the park or call my friends until I got the assignment done.

—Steve Wynn, 1990

There's two major differences today. One, there's not that kind of fun anymore. We were out for one thing, to make a record. Nobody cared who got what percentage, as long as we were making a great song or a great record. The difference today is it's all business people taking over the whole thing. When you go to a BMI dinner you don't see any writers or singers. It's all business people and representatives.

—Doc Pomus, 1987

Symbolically, Tin Pan Alley died on April 12, 1954 when Bill Haley and his Comets recorded Max Freedman and Jimmy DeKnight's "Rock Around the Clock."

—David A. Jasen, *Tin Pan Alley*

David Susskind says to me, "What's it like on Tin Pan Alley?" I said, "Where the fuck is Tin Pan Alley?" I mean, you tell me where it is, and I'll go.

—Phil Spector, 1969

CHAPTER 14

LET'S MAKE
A DEAL

SONG

PLUGGING

don't believe I've ever personally placed a song of mine. When "You Were On My Mind" was done by We Five, they got it from an Ian and Sylvia album. I didn't even know they had recorded it until I heard it on the radio. I've had at least six people tell me they were responsible for Crystal Gayle recording "River Road," and I know for a fact that she first heard me sing it at a benefit concert and later asked Ian for a tape of it. Kitty Wells' recording of "Trucker's Café" was a really nice thank-you from Jerry Bradley for Ian and Sylvia recording an album at Bradley's Barn in Nashville. Nana Mouskouri got "Yesterday's Dreams" through my then-manager who was in partnership with her then North American booking agent.

I don't really have what it takes to go out and actively promote my songs to anyone except through live performance, and I've never had a publisher who did it either. It would be nice.

—S.T.

My best "song plug" experience came at a low point in my career in 1980. I'd quit the business for a while in New York City and drove a cab. One morning at 3 a.m. I was out in Queens, and I picked up Robert Hunter, who writes lyrics for the Grateful Dead. I told him I was a songwriter, and he came back with, "Yeah, sure buddy, sing me one of your songs." I started singing him my cockfighting song "Gallo del Cielo." He wanted to hear it again and again, and it's a seven-minute song. We were running up the meter.

He asked me to drive back to my house and get him a tape of the song. He loved it. He said he was going to give it to the New Riders of the Purple Sage. I was honoured. I dropped him off, never expecting to hear from him again. He came back to town a month later and invited me to his concert. He had a big following of "Dead Heads." He started talking to the audience about this great song he'd heard from a cab driver in Queens. Then, he called me out of the crowd, handed me his guitar and walked off stage. I hadn't performed in a year. I looked out at a thousand silent, reverent faces. I sang "Gallo" and three other songs. It went well. I was suddenly jerked back into the music business.

—T.R.

Go home and live with the guy until he publishes your song.

    —Hank Cochran, *Willie: An Autobiography*

I was plugging songs for Shapiro and Bernstein and I had a song I had written called "I Love My Baby" that I thought was good. I went to Elliot Shapiro and said to him, "I can't make these theatres anymore . . . It's degrading and demeaning. These stage-doormen always treat you like some kind of broken-down dog." So Elliot said "OK, we'll put you on as a staff writer." So that's how I started to write songs professionally. I was paid the flat sum of fifty dollars a week which I had to try and earn by writing songs.

    —Harry Warren, 1977

In 1957 I was doing P.R. for Colonel Tom Parker, who was managing Hank Snow, but had taken over Elvis Presley. So the Colonel and Hank were coming to a parting of the ways and I was asked to finish promoting a tour for Hank in the Pacific Northwest. I stopped at a radio station in Vancouver, Washington. This young kid who interviewed me was very shy and clean-shaven. His jeans were worn and patched. He had a butch haircut. I thought he was a local boy. He told me he played every record of mine on the air, and I thought, this kid is all right. Then he

said he read every story he could find that I wrote in magazines. That blew my mind! He said he'd written some little songs that I'd never heard of. He didn't know if he had a chance to be a top songwriter, but did I have time to listen to one of his songs? He looked poor from hunger and so sweet. He was shy, but when he looked at me he looked directly at me with those eyes that show straight into his soul.

    I said, "Son, I've got a plane to catch, but I'll take time to hear your music."

    In the lobby of the radio station, this young Willie Nelson turned on a little tape player. The first song he played was "Family Bible." It took about four bars before my chin hit the proverbial floor.

    —Mae Axton, *Willie: An Autobiography*

Let's say Burl Ives was coming to Nashville to hear some new songs and asked Hank [Cochran] to get six or seven writers together for a guitar pulling. . . .

    Hank didn't care anything about Burl recording my songs or Kris [Kristofferson]'s songs, but being a good song plugger and a professional, he would call a few of his writer friends together and say, "Burl wants to hear your songs." . . . We'd pick our best songs and start singing them to him. Burl would sit there and listen to all of us sing and Hank would wait. After we had sung every song we knew, they would all be running together in Burl's mind. About the time all the songs sounded the same and he was thoroughly confused, Hank would sing his own songs. Hank's songs would be the last ones Burl remembered when he went into the studio.

—Willie Nelson, *Willie: An Autobiography*

I offered Ray Price a piece of the song "I'm Tired" if he would take it to Nashville and record it. He was singing it backstage at the Opry and Webb Pierce heard it and said, "Hey, I like that kind of song." Ray had a song on the charts for over a year at the time, and couldn't put my song out just then, so he gave it to Webb, who needed a hit. I heard it on the radio one night, and I liked to died. I didn't know Webb had cut it, and I said to myself, "That don't sound like Ray Price."

—Mel Tillis, 1977

He [Kris Kristofferson] was working at Columbia studios in Nashville. He had a pocketful of songs but no place to stay so he got a job as a janitor in the recording studio . . . I used to see him there working as a backup engineer or cleaning up something. And he had songs back then, and

they always just knocked me out. June [Carter] always loved his songs. He'd slip her the tapes to give to me so the people around the studio wouldn't see him do it. He was still trying to eat, so he didn't want to get fired.

—Johnny Cash, 1973

Andrew Oldham brought Paul [McCartney] and John [Lennon] down to the rehearsal. They said they had this tune ("I Wanna Hold Your Hand"). They were really hustlers. I mean, the way they used to hustle tunes was great: "Hey, Mick, we've got this great song." So they played it and we thought it sounded pretty commercial, which is what we were looking for, so we did it like Elmore James or something.

—Mick Jagger, 1968

Usually I know the people very well who want to record my songs, and I don't need somebody running across town with a satchel full of my material. Something is lost in the translation with that method. What I do is sit down with these people and play for them, and get a real gut level reaction from them right on the spot.

—Jimmy Webb, 1976

Nobody really plugs songs for you. I've found you've really got to get the cuts yourself. Those are the ones that work. My covers have come from friends and from writing with the artists themselves.

—Katy Moffatt, 1994

Most song covers come from exploiting the song yourself, [through] your own records and touring—making the song accessible. But there's still song plugging going on in Nashville. That's the other side of the fence.

—Greg Trooper, 1994

You have to be kind of pushy without being a pest—sort of an adorable pest. Go to every little function, workshop, meeting, writer's night you can go to. You have to become part of the wheel, and find a place to wedge yourself in. Be visible until people start saying, "Who is that guy?" The songwriters who stick out are the ones who make it work. Persistence may be the only thing that makes the difference.

—Don Henry, 1993

I got a part as an actor in the film *The Longest Day*. During the shooting I asked the producer, Darryl Zanuck, who was doing the music for the film, and he answered, "Nobody. I don't want any music. It's a very important picture about a very important time in this country and I don't want any themes in there cluttering it up!" I seized the opportunity and said, "I agree with you, but I have an idea and I don't even want a commitment. I'll write it out and put it on tape and send it to you. No commitment. If you like it, fine!" So I put it down on tape and sent it to him in France, and I got a wire back: "Very interested. Loved the theme. Let's make a deal."

—Paul Anka, 1976

Don't be content to play your songs for your friends, because they'll love them anyway. Visit publishers. Play your material for them and get feedback, because they're the ones who have to show songs to producers and artists. Either become acquainted enough with electronics to turn out your own demos, or make sure you have access to friends who can help you. Demos are critical. Learning how to under-produce a demo so that you're not insulting anybody by handing them an imitation record, but at the same time, put in arrangements ideas that can be picked up on by a producer.

—Alan O'Day, 1975

CHAPTER 15

EVEN A DOG CAN SHAKE HANDS

BAD BUSINESS DEALS

Allen Ginsberg once travelled to see the venerable old poet and physician William Carlos Williams in New Jersey. Ginsberg asked Dr. Williams a question about the meaning of life, based on what the older poet might have learned in his seventy-odd years. Dr. Williams stared out the window for minutes, his hands folded in a contemplative position. Finally he turned sagely toward Ginsberg and pointed back toward the window.

"You know," he said, "there's a lot of assholes out there."

I think of Otis Blackwell's old stories about Elvis and the Colonel and their publishing deals. I recall that Willie Nelson actually sold a couple of early songs outright ("Family Bible"), and his name was taken off them forever.

Early in your career you never know what a bad move can cost you. I've only lost publishing on a few songs, but they were key songs. Down the line I've learned that when you lose your publishing or copyright it basically means you're going to have to hunt your money down and demand it. You, or your lawyer, had better be well armed. William Carlos Williams had it right.

—T.R.

All the publishing shares on to "You Were On My Mind" finally reverted to me a couple of years ago after twenty-eight years. I'd have had it back two years earlier if they had registered it when I wrote it. It was standard practice back then not to register a song until it was actually recorded. I wouldn't have it back now if I hadn't given them written notice that I wanted it. The publisher was under no obligation to tell me it was due, and could have automatically renewed his control of the copyright if I hadn't caught it. That is still standard practice as far as I know. As W.C. Fields once said, "Those were the good old days. I hope they never come back."

Now, of course, you can make any deal you want, at any percentage you can negotiate, for whatever length of time, for only one song if you want to instead of having to commit your whole catalogue for the lifetime of your unborn children. That's if you have a bit of a track record. Otherwise, you're just as open to being hung out to dry as I was.

Most of the writers I talk to now are much more savvy about the business end of the business than I was, but there are always those who feel their job is only to create, and that taking care of business is a drain on their creative energy. They certainly have a point, but there are people standing in line waiting to take advantage of them. As Albert Grossman warned me early on, there are people out there who feel that much taller if they can stand on somebody else's back.

—S.T.

There's no damned business like show business. You had to smile to keep from throwing up.

—Billie Holliday, *Jazz Anecdotes* (Bill Crow)

Now you ask which comes first, the words or the music? I'll tell you which—the money!

—Sammy Cahn, *You Must Remember This*

Some people think that if you've got money behind you, you can do whatever you want, but money doesn't guarantee anything. Sometimes it's the worst thing for you—it can shackle you and bind you into keeping your mouth shut. I have trouble keeping my mouth shut.

—Andrew Cash, 1988

Without the business part of it, there would be no popular music, only folk music.

—Ian Whitcomb, *After the Ball*

I do not discuss the price of things, or which car I drive or how much money I make.

—Hank Snow, 1975

Like Kinky Friedman always says, "No sell out too small."

—Townes Van Zandt, 1990

You have to be savvy about [the business], or somebody else who is will wear you for a tie. They'll pick their teeth with you. They'll chew you like a chicken bone, and when all the meat's gone they'll throw you over the fence. That happens every day.

—Tom Waits, 1988

Songwriters might write cynical, world-wise lyrics, and constantly talk about money, but most of us are downright naive when it comes to business.

—Willie Nelson, *Willie: An Autobiography*

Artists don't think like accountants. We think like artists. We're supposed to represent the other side. We're knuckleheads when it comes to business. Money isn't why I did what I've done with my life. I did what I did because it made me happy, but I'm tired of getting it all taken away from me by other people who haven't earned it.

—Billy Joel, 1990

I didn't know people owned songs. I thought they lived in the air, but you're Fagen, and your songs are like little children that go out and steal for you every night. I had the necessary nightmare of business interruption through difficult deceptive alliances with characters I no longer associate with.

—Tom Waits, 1988

There are a number of lawsuits where my copyrights are in question. For better or for worse, your songs are your kids. Then somebody comes along and tells you they're not your kids anymore. The bank is going to take your kid. And I don't know how many mortgages there are on my copyrights these days. There are a lot of things involved in this lawsuit. Forget about the lawyers. I'd rather be the same stupid dickhead I was and not have learned the lesson.

—Billy Joel, 1990

The worst deal I ever signed was signing my publishing over to my manager who also owned the record company I was with. I was no longer a free creative spirit. Everything I created was owned by someone else. It was suffocating. If only I'd taken the time to look under his desk, I would have seen the goat's hooves in his penny-loafers. . . . Try asking your manager to get you an advance from the company when he is the company.

—Ian Thomas, 1991

Those [lawyer] guys can really get you if you don't watch 'em. When we did *Damn the Torpedos* just blocks of my time was all legal stuff, day in, day out. You can get pretty mad about it 'cause you wrote those songs, dammit! I wrote the fuckin' song and this guy sittin' across the courtroom is gettin' a million dollars for it, and I live in a little shithole, and I can't fix the brakes on my car!

—Tom Petty, 1987

I sold a song called "Right Now" to Shelter Publishing for 100 dollars. I went down to pick up the cheque and while I was inside my car broke down—jumped the timing chain or something. Getting it fixed cost way more than 100 bucks.

—Peter Case, 1990

Even a dog can shake hands.

—Warren Zevon

I'm surrounded by sharks. I made money. When you make money, even if you're frugal, even if you don't smoke it or stick it up your nose, there are 101 ways they can take your marbles.

—Joni Mitchell, 1988

What I am saying to all you songwriters is to get yourself a good Jewish lawyer before you sign anything, no matter how much the [publishing or record] companies say they love you.

—Willie Nelson, *Willie: An Autobiography*

Negotiating your own deals without the assistance of a qualified lawyer is like doing brain surgery on yourself.

—Peter McCann, 1990

I'm assuming anyone who writes for hire loves it. Why else would one choose such a masochistic business?

—Dee Moeller, 1990

Dear Sir:
. . . I will wish to establish my name as the best Ethiopian songwriter. But I am not encouraged in undertaking this as long as "The Old Folks at Home" stares me in the face with another's name on it . . . I will, if you wish, willingly refund you the money which you paid me on that song . . . I find I cannot write at all unless I write for public approbation and get credit for what I write.

—Stephen C. Foster, letter to E.P. Christy, May 25, 1852

I fully agree with you about the record companies wanting unpublished songs so they will only have to pay 1/2 cent per side (on 78s). . . . In fact, that is the reason I am not recording for Columbia any more. Art Satherly didn't want me to get any of my songs published, and he would not let me pick my songs to record. . . . He has eight masters of my best songs, and now his only reason for not releasing them is that they are too popular [i.e., would cost him too much in publishing royalties—S.T.]. He doesn't want a good song or a good songwriter. He wants ignorant hillbillies that can't play a tune right, and of all things he wants them to write their own songs [i.e., unpublished].

—Shelley Lee Alley, letter to
R.B. Gilmore of Southern Music, 1941 *(Travellin' Blues)*

I really feel I was cheated out of some monies due me in payment for my creativity. The kids today seem much more aware of what's coming to them, and I hear it's possible to make a fortune from just one song.

—Harry Warren, 1977

In the early '60s I'd been in New York about a week. Chas Daniels of the Highwaymen told me that their group, who were coming off a hit record, "Michael Row The Boat Ashore," wanted to record "Universal Soldier." I mentioned this to Elmer Gordon, who offered to "do me a favour" by publishing it. He gave me one dollar. Ten years later I bought my song back for $25,000. Donovan, who'd heard me sing it in concert, usually got credit for writing it.

—Buffy Sainte-Marie, 1990

I suppose I can say it right quick—he [Alan Freed] grabbed a third of the writing of "Maybellene" in lieu of my rookieness. He got the money solely for doing us some favours in those days. He actually didn't sit down with me at all and write anything.

—Chuck Berry, 1972

I was about the same age as Alan [Freed], and though I didn't participate in his dressing-room drinking parties, I was always invited because he liked the interest I took in him and the stories he told.

Back then it was in no way popular for a black person to be invited to an all-white get-together, so I hung around for the experience and information I could get about the business.

There, at one of the loose-speaking drinking gatherings, a bit of information was exposed that induced Alan to tell me that he intended to give me back the one-third writer's credit rip-off from Chess' false registration of "Maybellene." This was a promise that lingered on through his death and probated estate. It was some time in the later '70s that I finally got litigation going that brought me rightful full ownership of the copyright.

—Chuck Berry, *The Autobiography*

Deals? I remember a story I once heard. A guy by the name of Joe Meyer, who was a great old songwriter, was in the subway one day and he bumped into Al Jolson. He told Jolson, "Wait 'til you hear the song you and I wrote today!" That was typical. . . . If you knew you were guaranteed an enormous income, you didn't really object to putting a singer's name on your song.

—Doc Pomus, 1987

[Elvis Presley's] name was put on some of the songs. . . . It was put to me that that's what they wanted. Not so much Elvis. If I'd have known Elvis personally it might not have happened. It's more or less what the Colonel [Tom Parker] wanted. They put the proposition to you. . . . If you were smart enough not to take it then you'd know how to get the songs across [i.e., covered] without it happening.

—Otis Blackwell, 1987

In 1956 I was blackmailed into giving up half of two songs to get them recorded. It still bothers me.

—Harlan Howard, 1990

I knew the Colonel, and he didn't want me to get near Presley. The Colonel was a hustler—a different kind of hustler. See, the Colonel was smart. He made himself partners with all these publishers and record people and they couldn't expose him. Those guys knew all the sharp turns.

—Doc Pomus, 1987

They [Tommy Durden and Mae Boren Axton] presented the song ("Heartbreak Hotel") to Elvis in his hotel room. He liked it right away but then the Colonel stepped in and said Elvis wanted a third of the writer's credit, which I think is kind of cheap, you know.

—Hoyt Axton, *The Top Ten*

My publishing company dealt with theirs [Elvis Presley's]. I was a little bitter at first, but I was new at it. I was going for any kind of a deal. Now, recently we've come to a little better agreement over the songs. I mean, if Elvis hadn't had a child, I might have gone after it a little more. But finding out after his death that a lot was left to Lisa. . . . I said, man, I wouldn't want to be taking anything from a little girl. I mean if she wasn't in the picture I might have struck out real hard to get my shit back, to get what I could get. But we came to a good agreement.

—Otis Blackwell, 1987

Rhythm and blues to me meant "rip off and bullshit" [referring to selling his entire song catalogue]. You'll sell the shirt off your back if you're tryin' to feed your kids. You'll do it to keep from goin' out and blowin' some sucker up, turnin' into a criminal.

—Bo Diddley, 1987

I didn't write "Ready Teddy." They brought me the words and I made up the melody, and at the time I didn't have sense enough to claim much money, because I really made them hits. But now I've learned; you know, you pay a whole lot of big dues, but I still didn't cheat anybody. I was cheated, but I didn't cheat anybody, so I let that man sleep at night at his house and let his conscience be his guide while he's resting. I didn't get the money, but I still have the freedom.

—Little Richard, 1970

Not having none, then all of a sudden having a bundle [of money] and being told you're gonna be having this damn near forever—until you learn the business you really think that's going to happen. And then I had a real serious problem with alcohol for a while. I don't drink anything but water and soda now.

—Otis Blackwell, 1987

"Night Life" had been turned down by D Records and the Pappy Dailey people [of Pasadena, California, in the late 1950s] for not being a country song, even though I owed D Records some songs. I know "Night Life" was good. I sold it to [Paul] Buskirk for enough money to go into the studio and record it. Pappy Dailey heard what I was doing, and threatened to sue me, but I didn't care. I just changed my name. The record we put out was "Night Life" by Paul Buskirk, performed by Hugh Nelson and Paul Buskirk and the Little Men.

It's now one of the most recorded songs in history. It's been performed by more than seventy artists from country and blues and jazz and pop all the way to opera singers. It's sold more than thirty million records. All I got out of it was $150. But so what? At the time I needed the money. Suppose I'd been stubborn and waited and maybe never sold it at all? The fact that both songs ("Family Bible" on the B-side) became hits encouraged me to think I could write a lot more songs that were just as good.

—Willie Nelson, *Willie: An Autobiography*

Everybody tried to give me this bullshit that "Bo Diddley" is public domain . . . and they say you can't copyright a beat. But "Bo Diddley" is not just a beat; it's a melody and a rhythm pattern.

The same as "Harlem Nocturne" or anything else. So what is this bullshit everybody tries to tell me?

—Bo Diddley, 1987

When John [Lennon] and I came down from Liverpool we didn't know anything about songs, didn't know what a copyright was, and no one was about to explain it to us either. They saw us coming. There were big, big grins on their faces when these guys who were good writers turned up and said, "I don't know, doesn't everyone own songs?" They said, "Yes, step this way. Come into my parlour, said the spider to the fly."

We were very naïve, and I think it was fair enough to take advantage of that since young writers will do anything to get published, but after you've made millions, and after, let's say a decent period of three years, I think it would be nice if you could go back to them and say, "This is a slave deal. Let's change it."

John and I ended up with the same deal that we had in the beginning, which was that the publisher automatically took the copyright, so we never saw anything.

—Paul McCartney, 1988

So these people who think they own the rights [to Beatles' recordings and songs] never had anything to do with the promotion of them or the writing of them, but obtained them because of all this devious stuff that happened in the past.

EMI and Capitol think they own all our songs on record and, according to contracts maybe they do. But they have a contract to put out our records and promote our records—they don't have a contract saying, "We can sell you to shoe manufacturers or we can sell you to sausage manufacturers," and if we don't do anything about it, every Beatles' song in the whole world is going to be a commercial.

—George Harrison, 1987

That's one of the reasons Billy Gaff [his manager] and I parted company. He couldn't understand why I wouldn't let some ketchup company use "Hurts so Good." It was for a hot sauce. I didn't write the song for that reason. However good or bad the song was, it was entertaining; but it wasn't written for ketchup to pour out to.

—John Cougar Mellencamp, 1986

Generally I don't like [using the songs in commercials], particularly with the Beatles stuff. When twenty more years have passed, maybe we'll move into the realm where it's OK to do it.

That's a little bit why I feel it's not so bad with Buddy [Holly—McCartney holds the copyrights on Buddy Holly's songs]. There may be people out there who say you shouldn't do it with Buddy. I've done it once or twice with [his songs] but I don't really like doing it, I must admit. One thing I can't do with Buddy is ask him. One thing they can do with us [the Beatles] is ask us, since there are still three of us alive. That'd be a good move, to say, "Do you fancy being in a car ad?" and we'd say, "No."

—Paul McCartney, 1988

We had a very legitimate complaint and that was settled out of court, very handsomely, I might add. The movie company wanted my song, "I Want a New Drug." The ethical question was: Who paid Ray Parker Jr. to write "Ghostbusters" which was an obvious rip-off of our song? Depositions were taken, it's a long long story, but there are people in Hollywood who think they can buy any damned thing. Well, they can't, damn it. It wasn't for sale!

—Huey Lewis, 1986

I'm not sure [what the worst business deal I've made is]. I never read any of the contracts.

—Townes Van Zandt, 1990

212

I don't own my own publishing. It's a very accounting kind of job, and you start having to collect money . . . it's a whole industry in itself. I'd just as soon give somebody fifty percent and let them do all the paperwork and just send me my share. I want to spend time making music; I don't want to spend time collecting money.

—J.J. Cale, 1994

Right now I've got the Internal Revenue Service still after me for the '70s—the crazy times; once, we ran up $90,000 in two months on an American Express card. We're still settling that. They shouldn't have given me that piece of plastic. . . . We never even left North America, didn't even go to Mexico. We had no one keeping any books or any records or anything.

—Jerry Jeff Walker, 1984

For years we didn't know how to read our statements and we didn't know enough to hire our own lawyers to negotiate our contracts. The record companies and the middle men would tell us, "You don't need a lawyer. You're a good old country boy and I'm a good old country boy. We're just good plain honest folks. Be nice to us. You know we won't screw you. Hell, we're a big happy family here. Sign this contract and let's go have a beer, pal."

Waylon [Jennings] to this day says when somebody calls him "pal," it makes him paranoid.

—Willie Nelson, *Willie: An Autobiography*

I thought Leonard [Chess] was the best man in the business. He did a lot for me, putting out that first record and everything, and we had a good relationship with one another. I didn't sign no contract with him. It was just, "I belong to the Chess family."

—Muddy Waters, *Deep Blues*

The royalty statement [from a manager or producer or record label] charged the artist for everything in sight. Stuff you thought you were getting free—telephone calls, bar tab, room service, postage stamps—they charged you for all of it. You'd get your statement and be excited and open it to see how much money you had made, and find out you owed the record company $50,000. Instead of being semi-rich, you'd suddenly have to scramble for money to pay your income tax.

—Willie Nelson, *Willie: An Autobiography*

We had something like twenty, twenty-five songs we'd done over the last couple years, ready to put on the album. Then these [CBS record] executives came on out to the house in Redding to talk to me about it and play some songs for me—which just happened to be Tree Publishing songs, which CBS Records owns—and I said, "OK, I'll put a couple of the songs you want on the album." That's the trade I made. "Your experience is in the line of marketing," I told 'em, "and now you're gettin' into creative work." They maybe spot-listened to two, three songs for the album, and they came up with their opinion on matters. They always seemed to get the upper hand somehow. . . . They aren't even old enough to understand what I'm talking about. They don't understand the value of preserving talent. What they're interested in is a fast record sale, and promotions, and gettin' the wives to the Virgin Islands.

—Merle Haggard, 1990

It's always been part of the challenge to squeak by. Part of the deal in making art in North America is that you've got to deal with the money folks and the marketing folks.

—John Hiatt, 1990

Who do you gotta know to get *out* of this business?

—George Jones

CHAPTER 16

SEND IN THE CLOWNS

SONGS AS PERFORMED BY WRITERS AND OTHER ARTISTS

There's something quite special about a song sung by its creator. Even if the voice is flawed, that understanding of the lyric and the passion that went into its creation is always intrinsic in the performance. No matter how many times people tell me what a terrible singer they think some songwriter is, I always reply, "It doesn't matter. It's not about vocal technique."

I perform because I write. My ego is wrapped up in the songs, not in myself as a stage personality. As Tom says, you become instantly aware of how good (or bad) a song is when you perform it for an audience, and you tend not to try the ones you're not sure of until you find a couple of sympathetic peers to use as guinea pigs. If their eyes glaze over and their smiles become fixed, you know you're in trouble.

I don't recommend you sing songs for your family. The first time I sang "You Were On My Mind" for my mother, she smiled and tapped her foot, and when it was over she said, "Well, it's very nice dear, but it was your sister who used to run away all the time." Funny how your parents can turn you into a five-year-old.

I've never been thrilled with the way other people do my songs. I'm pleased that they want to, but when a song is conceived one way and performed another it's always a bit of a shock; however, I'm hoping to be pleasantly surprised any day now.

—S.T.

erforming a song for the first time in front of an audience is like test marketing a new movie. You count all the walk-outs. You want to see if the reaction balances with your own gut-level feeling about the song. You learn very soon what works and what doesn't. There are a variety of songs I've written or co-written that I don't feel capable of ever performing because the feel or melodic range is beyond me. Other songs find their own form through performance. Peter Case once told me that he aims his singing at the one person in the audience who seems bored or indifferent, and tries to convince them.

—T.R.

When I go around from place to place, even out of the country, people out there know through B.B. King that the blues is alive and well.

                              —B.B. King, 1990

The big step, obviously, is getting onstage, but once you get onstage, you find out whether you can express anything, whether you are any good at writing songs.

                             —Billy Bragg, 1986

I started singing because I always tried to get other people to sing my songs and it never sounded right. I ended up doing it myself out of sheer desperation.

                           —Joe Jackson, 1986

There's something at the back of your mind that says, "I'm not giving you a hundred percent. I'm not giving *anybody* a hundred percent. I'm gonna give you this much, and this much is going to have to do. I'm good at what I do. I can afford to give you this much and still be as good as, if not better than, the guy over across the street. I'm not gonna give it all—I'm not Judy Garland, who's gonna die onstage in front of a thousand clowns." If we've learned anything, we should have learned that.

                           —Bob Dylan, 1986

I hate to think of it as a craft. It's something that I love to do, but it is a job, and we work very hard to write a song and make it work. You must sing the song with great affection and feeling. It takes the men who write the lyrics a long time. Just believe in their words, do them simply and honestly. That's how a singer should interpret a song.

                   —Richard Whiting, *You Must Remember This*

It's also the job of the lyric writer to consider the singer's problems. To be careful of consonants. Some very odd things happen when you string words together with music because actors can't play with rhythm an awful lot.

                          —Stephen Sondheim

The bottom line with all the songs, whether the audience is giggling over a song about dog shit, or having a few yucks about a song that's very serious, or just sitting there dealing with a song that's very serious, is as long as it's affecting them in one way or another, I think it's working. That's how I see my job.

                      —Loudon Wainwright, 1989

If the price of fame is that you have to be isolated from the people you write for, then that's too fucking high a price to pay.

                      —Bruce Springsteen, 1985

During the months of preparation, the piece [of musical theatre] itself has a way of becoming something of a person to me—not always a nice person, perhaps, but at least someone that I've grown fond of. The minute it's exposed to its first audience, however, I feel that it's no longer mine. It belongs to the performers. And I become just another $8.50 customer.

—Cole Porter, *Cole Porter: A Biography*

I genuinely started playing solo just to take everything back to basics and to build on it. That was the the bottom line—let's just see if these songs work.

—Billy Bragg, 1986

The hard thing is to write a song for yourself, knowing you've got to sing it. Sometimes I have a hard time singing my own stuff.

—George Harrison, 1987

For me it's always emotional: can I live with this song? I'm going to have to get onstage and be this song. I'm going to have to represent this point of view, this idea. And if it doesn't work for me, I can't do it. I can't act, you know? So there has to be something authentic about it.

—Jerry Garcia, 1993

I know what it's like to stand at the microphone in the studio and try to sing a song I wrote in my bedroom three months ago with the same conviction and emotion that I felt at the time I wrote it. I know that there's a problem. When I wrote it in my bedroom it was perfect. It was complete. It was real. And now I've got to involve this guitar player and this drummer and this bass player in this process, and I'm going to sing you this song, and if you play one damned note before I finish this song and you know what this song is about, I'm going to go for your throat.

—T-Bone Burnett, 1987

It's as hard to write a simple pop song as it is to write something topical. But the fact that the songs are more personal means that I can sing them with more passion, because they are more real to me.

—Bryan Adams, 1987

A few years ago I went through a period when I found myself trying to imitate Johnny Cash. I was just tired of everything, going through the motions.

—Johnny Cash, 1990

There are some songs I don't care to sing anymore, but that's probably because I'm not eighteen anymore.

—Jackson Browne, 1987

The person who wrote those songs that were on the first album was a frustrated little fuck-up. . . . Even now, when I do a great gig—everybody applauding what you do and patting you on the back, you get some great reviews, and everybody's happy with the show—I still have to go home or back to the hotel or wherever and admit to myself that despite it all, I'm still a frustrated little fuck-up.

—Elvis Costello

My basic fundamental reason for performing has always been to test material. I consider myself a songwriter. Always have, always will.

—Hoyt Axton, 1976

Simpson: When we released our first album, we had done little performing. My standard answer to that was that I really didn't like to perform, but the real reason was out of fear, you know? *Ashford:* I think I will always write, and consider myself primarily a writer. I think performing helps me in the sense that it allows us to relate to the people we're writing for. When you write, you're cut off from the world. But there's always something I feel I want to say that I can accomplish through my writing that I can't accomplish through performance. Once the applause is over, the experience is ended, but writing is a continuous flow through my life. In fact, I think of living and writing as one thing.

—Nick Ashford and Valerie Simpson, 1977

I'm extremely shy about performing, which is probably the reason I like to write and record much more than I do to perform. To perform, I almost have to assume another identity. I have to almost play a part and get psyched up to walk onstage. Otherwise I couldn't do it.

—Van Morrison, 1985

If somebody had played me "Hello, Dolly!" before it became a hit, I would have turned it down. I thought it was just a plain song, and that there was nothing to it. But then I didn't have any idea "You'll Never Know" was going to be a hit either. The first inkling I had that maybe we had something was at a party one night when the producer of the film "Hello, Frisco" for which the song was written asked us to sing it. Mack Gordon, who wrote the lyrics, was a hell of a song demonstrator and after he sang the song, the people loved it.

—Harry Warren, 1977

I think half the kick of writing songs for me has been to do live demos of my material. Sometimes it's been awkward like singing "Be My

220

Love" to Mario Lanza and trying not to make all the high notes sound too bad, but singing "Call Me Irresponsible" to Fred Astaire was a high point. I sang my heart out.

—Sammy Cahn, 1976

In terms of performing, that's a big help to me. With me, it's all one ball of wax—I write songs and I go out and perform them. I make records and I publish my own material. I probably have as much autonomy as anyone in the music business because I also produce or co-produce my own albums.

—Hoyt Axton, 1976

I think the best way I ever came up with to explain what I am is that I'm a songwriter with a record deal. I have four jobs: I'm a performer, I'm a recording artist, I'm a politician, and I'm a writer. I work very hard at the other three jobs so I can do the one.

—Clint Black, 1994

It was only after the release of the first album that I realized songs which had sounded good in the studio were really flat and boring when presented to a live audience. I realized I had to road-test the songs which meant I had to work on being a better performer. I was terrible at the beginning.

—Bryan Adams, 1985

You're up there with your guitar and voice and you will see, unbelievably swiftly, the weaknesses of your own material.

—Nick Lowe, 1994

To me, every one of my records is like an ongoing autobiography. I can't write the same book every time. There are artists who can. . . . My trip is to express what's on my mind. I don't expect people to listen to my music all the time—sometimes it's too intense.

—Neil Young, 1975

Each song had a kind of shopping list of ideas that I wanted to be used. I'd work until each part was in place, adding more layering, and then stop. At any stage you can compare what you have to earlier tapes, and you try to stop at a point when things are still getting better, before they get worse.

—Kate Bush, 1985

Sometimes now I'll get a verse done and then I think "Yes, but is this good enough to be on a Kate and Anna McGarrigle album?"

—Kate McGarrigle, 1978

I write rock songs all different ways. If it's a song me and the guys are having some laughs with, I'll cook it up on the spot. If the song's simple enough, we'll just go ahead and try it out on stage as soon as it's written. Then I'll perfect it later.

—Frank Zappa, 1980

I don't write songs on an acoustic guitar in the kitchen, and then go and perform them with a sound system. I write them with the sound system and I think "performance." I have no desire to intellectualize. My only interest is in direct communication. I want people to "get it" immediately.

—Luka Bloom, 1994

My music is nearly always played the way it is written. There are a few great performing artists who understand phrasing. If Streisand and/or Sinatra feels that a slight change emphasizes the emotion of that interpretation, I allow the change.

—Jule Styne, 1977

I have one [cover] in particular which has always knocked me out which is "Desperados Waiting for a Train" done by Slim Pickens. He read it as a poem with the music in the background and it's just breathtaking.

—Guy Clark, 1984

I lose all critical objectivity in a case like that.

Whenever I hear someone wants to sing one of my songs, I'm really touched, deeply touched.

—Leonard Cohen, 1985

One day I was in an elevator with piped-in music and I'm listening to this song, and I said to myself, "God, that sounds familiar." As I reached my floor it hit me—it was "Tracks of My Tears." It was one of those upright forthright downright unrecognizable versions—you know, just strings and French horns—but I feel flattered on any version of my songs that I hear. I think it's a tremendous compliment to a writer to have artists record their songs.

—Smokey Robinson, 1976

Foster: You know what is still a thrill? When you get a song recorded by somebody who you always wanted to hear cut one of yours.
Rice: I remember our first Kitty Wells cut. We sent her a letter of thanks. Now, when I was back home, Kitty Wells was the queen of country music. There was just no competition. You just did not jump in there with Miss Kitty.
Foster: It's that way too with Tex Ritter. When he cut our stuff, we used to go down and see him on Saturday afternoon. And when Patti Page did our stuff it blew my mind. I had idolized her since I was a kid!

—Jerry Foster and Bill Rice, 1976

222

No one has quite the bond with me as far as singing my songs goes that Linda [Ronstadt] does, just because of our past. It's a very special, deep kind of relationship between us that now is a musical relationship exclusively, but she sings the songs with a lot of love. She'll change the tense in my songs—she usually makes a one-word mistake in every song that no amount of coaching will get her to reverse, but it's still always real satisfying.

—J.D. Souther, 1980

My audience in the U.S. was made much larger by Linda Ronstadt, who did my songs even though I didn't much care for her interpretations. In fact, I've been really rude about them. In retrospect, it did open other people's ears.

—Elvis Costello, 1989

I will always be very much a writer, but the singer side of me wants to sing other songs.

—Kim Carnes, 1981

Always sing other people's stuff. Otherwise you end up getting real selfish. You get stuck in your own world, and your perspective is crooked.

—John Prine, 1978

Writers are so important. I think a lot of our artists [at Motown] could have been more suc-cessful if they had had other writers besides Hol-land-Dozier-Holland, because they would have found their identity—and that's what everybody needs.

—Stevie Wonder, 1973

I guess I could have retired modestly at the age of thirty off of royalties from songs like "Crazy." I might have had to live on a houseboat, but I would have had enough money coming in to provide me with potted meat sandwiches for the rest of my life, but I enjoyed playing music too much to consider retiring to the life of a writer. If I had quit playing professionally I would have been out every night sitting in with somebody anyhow. Working the road kept me organized. If I have to be somewhere tomorrow, I won't fuck up too bad today. It's when I have too much time on my hands that I really get in trouble.

—Willie Nelson, *Willie: An Autobiography*

I know that what I do is looked on as a "prod-uct," but I can't just look at it that way. The music has to give you the chills or tickle your funnybone.

—Cyndi Lauper, 1988

You can be a product, and let people tell you how to dress and what to sing for a while, but you have to live with yourself; so if you think you've got something to offer, stick to your guns and stay the course.

—Lionel Cartwright, 1990

Some of the songs are very cold and sinister, about elements I've experienced, and the way I perform them is sometimes a bit robotic. . . . People might not know how to take me, but at the end of the show I come out as a human person behind it all, which I find interesting. It's a mixture of the coldness and the human nature.

—Annie Lennox

I write in a different way for different characters, maybe like a novelist writes. I'll sing through a character, and it might not necessarily be my philosophy.

—Ray Davies, 1986

You see, I don't want to be up there on the stage being me. I don't think I'm that interesting. What I want to do is be the person that's in the song. If I can be the character in the song, then suddenly there's all this strength and energy in me which I wouldn't normally have, whereas if it was just me, I don't think I could walk on stage with confidence.

—Kate Bush, 1989

I remember thinking at some point that it was a

very different person who got up and sang these songs than the person who wrote them, and I don't feel that way now. It's real difficult for me to write on the road and I would literally have to come off the road for a year before I could remember how you write a song, because the person who wrote a really introspective song was not the same one who could get up there and perform. At one point there was a murder that took place. The writer who had been writing these songs assassinated the one that had been standing there smiling and singing these things and taking credit for it.

—Jackson Browne, 1989

I feel embarrassed by saying this, but I'd like to be recognized more as a songwriter. I don't pay attention to polls and charts. But I thumb through them once in a while and see, like, Eddie Vedder is nominated number one songwriter in some magazine and I'm not even listed.

—Kurt Cobain, 1993

I'm not going to present a picture of myself to people which is false, you know, this deeply aware social, caring person which I am, but not all the time, you know. In my best moments I am. Other times I'm just a hopeless Scottish drunk, and some of my songs reflect that as well.

—Eric Bogle, 1985

I don't believe you should live hard, die young, and leave a good-looking corpse. On the other hand when you're in the public eye at any level, people are interested in your personal life. Whenever you talk to a lot of different people, I find that rather than tell the truth, you'd be better off making something up, because if you don't, they will.

—Tom Waits, 1980

If, somehow, I could walk around invisible when I'm not on stage. . . .

—Tracy Chapman, 1988

After I got over the initial terror of being up there with just me and a guitar, I really started to enjoy it, because I started doing a lot of things I would never do with a band, simply because the songs are more focussed on the lyrics as opposed to the beat or the instrumentation.

—Joe Ely, 1986

I can evoke a response in three people who are standing around a piano, but that isn't the measure of a song. There is a magic between the person who creates a song, and the people who listen to it, that isn't present after it's filtered through another artist. That's why the whole phenomenon of the singer/songwriter came about. It wasn't a fad. —Jimmy Webb, 1976

It's funny, but people still attach a lot of mystery to Bob. I mean, Dylan's just a guy like anybody else, except he's a guy who has something to say, and he has a personality that makes it his own. There's not many people who can walk into a room of 20,000, stare at them, and get their attention. That's not an easy trick.

—Tom Petty, 1986

I opened a show for George Hamilton IV in Canada about twenty years ago, and a critic wrote, "Where on earth did they dig up this freak Willie Nelson, who can't sing, and is an illiterate songwriter?"

Maybe I wasn't as sure of my singing twenty years ago as I became later when my voice grew stronger, but being called an "illiterate songwriter" pissed me off profoundly.

—Willie Nelson, *Willie: An Autobiography*

You must never let the audience know that you are brighter than they are. When people are drinking in a cabaret, not intimidated by a proscenium, they don't want to think about what the lyric is saying. And you are actually asking us to listen to rhyme and meter and to the ideas behind the lines! And some of us are too drunk to bother!

—Noel Coward to Lena Horne

So many of those numbers [*Three Penny Opera*] are informed by what Brecht called the *Verfremdungseffekt*—the "alienation effect." You don't try to enlist the audience's sympathy, you just do your thing straight out, as if to say, "This is a play. You've paid to watch us, this is what we hope to say, if you don't like it, go home."

—Leonard Bernstein, 1990

An audience doesn't listen to each new song with lyric sheets in front of them. They will hear every line only once, and they have to "get it" immediately before the next line is upon them. You can't stop to elaborate on your text, or provide Cliff Notes, or send your characters offstage while the audience ponders your deeper meaning.

—Janis Ian, 1990

I'm not a politician, I'm a singer. My first function is to entertain. My second function is to maybe give you a little information; I'm not sure it's my responsibility to give you answers.

—Sting, 1988

You can't fool a crowd for long, whether it's a concert for 100,000 or a honky-tonk with 300. People will pick up your vibrations and take their business elsewhere. When you open your heart to an audience, you share your deepest feelings with them. They want to find love in your heart. They don't want to see that it is nothing but a bank vault.

—Willie Nelson, *Willie: An Autobiography*

There's no way you can shock them. How can you shock people who are so totally numb that they just put up with anything? That's my perception of the American way of life. Americans are so used to seeing the worst atrocities on television that none of it is real to them anymore. They can sit and watch the most heinous acts being perpetrated all over the world, and when that little film clip is over it's not really part of their life anymore, except as cocktail conversation. You can't shock these people, and why should you? They seem blissfully happy, so why bother them?

—Frank Zappa, 1980

When people know the songs too well, I feel uncomfortable. With "Mimi On The Beach," you sometimes get the impression that they're just tracing the song along with you instead of really listening to it.

—Jane Siberry, 1985

I was talking to Peter Gabriel on the phone two

years ago. I'm a great admirer of his. I was telling him I wanted to move more onstage. I wasn't expecting any advice and I wasn't sure what he would say. He was very quiet for a minute and then he said, "The thing you have to do is take your idiosyncracies and blow them up, make them bigger." And that's all he said.

I thought about it and I was so happy and relieved, having just come off the road. You feel this pressure to iron out all your idiosyncracies so that you are acceptable to everyone and so that everyone will like you. In order to be liked by that many people [you feel] you have to become flat, you have to iron out your character and all the weirdnesses in it.

—Suzanne Vega, 1990

I don't think a good beat precludes there being meaning in a song. If anything, there is more appeal in having rhythmic music with good lyrics. Right now, I'd rather be doing music that makes my seat move, and also affects my brain.

—Bruce Cockburn, 1983

For years I thought, "Well, I'm an artist. I'm not an entertainer," but I've finally come to the conclusion that if you sing songs to people, then you're an entertainer whether you like it or not.

—Steve Winwood, 1988

CHAPTER 17

CHICKEN SOUP AND THE MEANING OF LIFE

ONE-LINERS

There's a one-liner from Plato that I like: "He who approaches the temple of the muses without inspiration, in the belief that craftsmanship alone suffices, will remain a bungler and his presumptuous poetry will be obscured by the songs of the maniacs."

—T.R.

... and then there's the one I saw in the newspaper recently about an English gymnast who moved to the United States to escape a stalker. Over a six-year period he had written her 5,916 letters and 519 songs. In court he denied he was obsessed with her. "I admit I wrote the songs," he told the judge, "but they were good songs."

—S.T.

I don't have the answers. Somebody asked me, "What is the meaning of life?" Well, it's chicken soup, isn't it? What do I know?

—Joan Armatrading, 1984

It isn't music that makes people, it's people that make music.

—Irving Berlin, 1941

I don't really care if I'm broke or not because I can walk down the street and get me a goddamn hamburger with a song.

—Merle Haggard, 1994

The German poet Rilke said, "Good art is born of necessity."

—John Hiatt, 1990

Strange how potent cheap music is.

—Noel Coward, *Private Lives*

If a person keeps living he'll run into himself.

—Carl Perkins, 1990

You know, you plant wheat one year and maybe flax the next. I don't like to repeat myself too much.

—Joni Mitchell, 1985

Writers are a cruel lot, aren't they? They just raid life.

—Joni Mitchell, 1988

I'm such a slut. I couldn't write my wife a love poem without putting a melody to it.

—Harlan Howard, 1994

I wish I could be who I was before I was me.

—Screamin' Jay Hawkins, *Nowhere to Run*

The blues ain't nothin' but a poor man's heart disease.

—Early Blues/Alabama, *The Country Blues*

I was always afraid that if I lost the stomach problem, I wouldn't be creative. Who knows?

—Kurt Cobain, 1993

One of my favorite sayings is "Pain is inevitable, but misery is optional."

—John Hiatt, 1990

Ragtime is the best heart-raiser and worry-banisher I know. Someday I'm going to write a syncopated grand opera.

—Irving Berlin, *After the Ball*

One guy said I was "the Irving Berlin of narcissistic alienation." I kind of liked that—the Irving Berlin part, anyway.

—Billy Joel, 1990

Listen kid, never hate a song that has sold a half-million copies.

—Irving Berlin to Cole Porter, *Cole Porter: A Biography*

I don't think the urge to be timeless permeates the pop-tune marketplace. The urge to be rich permeates the pop-tune marketplace.

—Frank Zappa, 1993

Nothing is as bad as I think it is.

—Ray Davies, 1981

As someone once put it, "I have seen the future of rock & roll, and I want my money back."

—Glenn Frey, 1988

Here today, gone later on today.

—David Lee Roth, 1989

I must play to work, and I must work to play.

—Cole Porter, *Cole Porter: A Biography*

No real writer is ever bored, except by himself.

—Janis Ian, 1990

I have spent my life escaping boredom, not because I am bored, but because I don't want to be.

—Cole Porter, *Cole Porter: A Biography*

I've always tried to go against the rules. Rules drive me around the pole. I could never get on with Cole Porter.

—Leo Sayer, 1978

Like Phil Everly says about this job: At least there's no heavy lifting.

—Tom Petty, 1987

I'm different. It's allowed.

—David Byrne, 1988

For all you know I'm a bad junkie with a spit-shine on my shoes.

—Joni Mitchell, 1985

I don't like straight lines. The problem is that most instruments are square and music is always round.

—Tom Waits, 1988

If a song is good you can play it softly, and the world will hear it anyway.

—Sammy Fain, 1981

To me, pop songs are the folk music of high-tech countries.

—David Byrne, 1987

Dylan opens up worlds. He's the Picasso of pop!

—Bono, 1989

My sense of humour is probably some form of genetic deformity. I can't help it.

—Frank Zappa, 1980

[Upon hearing a fellow songwriter state that songwriting wasn't a big deal compared to brain surgery] Songwriting *is* brain surgery!

—Katy Moffatt, 1993

To be a songwriter in Nashville you need the heart of a poet, and the hide of a rhino.

—Bob Morrison, 1987

You will find out most of the things that are worthwhile by yourself, I think. I'm not even sure about that—it's a definite maybe.

—Ray Stevens, 1979

For me, there's no right and there is no left. There's truth and there's untruth. There's honesty and there's hypocrisy.

—Bob Dylan, 1986

The papers are full of the atomic bomb which is going to revolutionize everything and blow us all to buggery. Not a bad idea.

—Noel Coward, 1945

If there's still a human race 500 years from now, we [songwriters] will be one of the reasons why.

—Pete Seeger, 1991

Truth is a lofty word to use regarding a song, but I think that when the notes are right on a song, you approach the truth.

—Charles Fox, 1979

My talent, if I have one, is to be part of the times.

—Irving Berlin, 1978

I've clawed my way to the middle and this is about as far as I'm going to get.

—Nancy White, 1985

I plan to become an institution before they put me in one.

—Gordon Lightfoot, 1970

I want to create music that's like meat. Music that is juicy, rare and sensual.

—Frank Dervieux, 1972

If I knew where the good songs come from, I'd go there more often.

—Leonard Cohen, 1993

The secret of a great melody is a secret.

—Dave Brubeck, 1993

When I see we're shy of sentimental ballads, I sit down and write one.

—Irving Berlin, *After the Ball*

There's a song for every sin out there.

—Lou Reed, 1984

There's only one song in the world, and Adam and Eve wrote it. The rest of them's variations.

—Keith Richards, 1994

I wrote a happy song once. Now what the fuck was it called?

—Sting, 1984

It's good to know who hates you, and it's good to be hated by the right people.

—Stevie Wonder, 1988

I'm dirt-road country looking for easy street.

—Buddy Cannon, 1990

What I do for a living is to get people feeling good. —Willie Nelson, *Willie: An Autobiography*

Don't compromise yourself, you're all you've got.

—Janis Joplin, *Follow Your Heart: An Autobiography*
(Judy Collins)

I'm Canada's voice of liberal guilt.

—Nancy White, 1984

Life is what happens to you while you're busy making other plans.

—John Lennon

As soon as you start talking about mystique, you have none.

—Neil Young, 1979

I hold to moderation in all things, including moderation.

—Ray Davies, 1987

Marcel Marceau gets more airplay than I do.

—Tom Waits, 1980

Love has nothing to do with money. Until the end.

—Glenn Frey, 1988

I care not who writes a nation's laws, if I may write its songs.

—Anonymous

INDEX

2–Bigg MC 67
2 Live Crew 133

Aaron, Lee 108, 110, 170, 182
Adams, Bryan 24, 145, 219, 221
Aldon Music 194
Alger, Pat 137, 182–183
Alley, Shelley Lee 6, 208
Allison, Jerry 11
Alvin, Dave 41, 47, 177, 180–182
Anderson, Eric 3
Anderson, Laurie 136, 152
Anderson, Pete 168
Anka, Paul 11, 17, 36, 73, 88, 102, 105, 176, 193, 202
Arden, Jann 129
Armatrading, Joan 36, 79, 136, 144, 152, 230
Armstrong, Louis 6
ASCAP 192
Ashford, Nick 125, 168, 194–195, 220
Asso, Raymond 5
Astaire, Fred 221
Autry, Gene 31
Axton, Hoyt 13, 18, 49, 91, 105, 116, 167, 210, 220
Axton, Mae 200, 210
Aznavour, Charles 130

Bacharach, Burt 30, 37, 68, 93, 116, 121
Baez, Joan 149, 154
Band, the 39

Bare, Bobby 58, 77
Basie, Count 32
Bayes, Nora 192
Beach Boys, the 120
Beatles, the 15–16, 40–41, 46, 68–69, 71, 120, 211–212
Bechet, Sidney 6
Bee Boo 32
Belcher, Fred 191
Bennett, Tony 31
Berlin, Irving 5, 29, 59, 63, 65, 96, 102, 108, 114, 122, 136, 152, 190–191, 230–231, 233
Bernstein, Leonard 37, 54, 114, 119–120, 226
Berry, Bill 22
Berry, Chuck 7, 31–32, 52, 66–69, 97, 106, 129, 131, 137, 209
Biafra, Jello 48, 144, 154
Big Maceo 32
Bishop, Stephen 182
Black, Clint 221
Blackwell, Otis 8, 30, 32, 67, 188–189, 191–192, 204, 210
Blades, Ruben 153
Bloom, Luka 222
BMI 41, 192
Bogle, Eric 14, 77, 117, 224
Bono 70, 81, 124, 232
Bourgeois, Philippe 134
Boyd, Bill and the Cowboy Ramblers 30
Bradley, Jerry 198
Brady, Paul 76
Bragg, Billy 39–40, 49, 55, 79, 145–146, 152, 157, 218–219

Brill Building songwriters 192–193
Brecht, Bertold 166, 226
Brooks, Garth 20
Brown, Charles 32
Brown, James 9, 70, 135
Brown, Lew 4
Browne, Jackson 18, 33, 38, 46, 51, 153, 156,
   219, 224
Brubeck, Dave 233
Bruce, Lenny 38
Bryant, Boudleaux 50, 122, 162, 183
Bryant, Felice 53, 123, 162
Buck, Peter 89
Buckley, Jeff 143
Burnett, Ernie 4
Burnett, T-Bone 219
Bush, Kate 82, 134, 221, 224
Buskirk, Paul 210
Butler, Ralph 190
Byrne, David 22, 46, 57, 103, 112,
   231–232

Caesar, Irving 191
Cahn, Sammy 28, 94, 101, 110, 115, 117,
   167, 206, 221
Cale, J.J. 213
Calloway, Cab 67
Camb, Arthur 190
Cannon, Buddy 233
Cantor, Eddie 192
Capitol Records 212
Carmichael, Hoagy 63
Carnes, Kim 223
Carpenter, Mary Chapin 138
Carter, Elliot 73
Carter, June 201
Carter, Wilf 91
Cartwright, Lionel 24, 224
Case, Peter 41, 52, 90, 121, 170, 175–176,
   207, 217
Cash, Andrew 206

Cash, Johnny 10, 32, 41, 46, 80–81, 201,
   219
Caston, Baby Doo 93
CBS Records 213–214
Cecil, William
Chandler, Melanie 5
Chapin, Harry 53, 123, 125
Chapman, Tracy 225
Charles, Ray 20, 36, 52, 70, 94, 115, 117,
   193
Charters, Samuel
Chess, Leonard 66, 213
Chess Records 66, 209
Christy, Ed 190
Chuck-D 155
Chilton, Alex 171
Clapton, Eric 117, 143
Clark, Dick 10
Clark, Guy 18–19, 38, 121, 222
Cobain, Kurt 18, 150, 224, 230
Cochran, Hank 200
Cockburn, Bruce 25, 41, 95, 109, 151, 185,
   227
Cody, Phil 166
Coe, David Allen 76
Cohen, Leonard 13, 31, 33, 38, 55, 76, 82, 95,
   130, 154, 222, 233
Cole, Nat King 32
Collins, Judy 13, 29, 75
Collins, Ray 36
Colubia Records
Colvin, Shawn 104, 135
Connors, Stompin' Tom 15, 29, 157
Coolidge, Calvin
Cooper, George 101
Corgan, Billy 49
Cornell, Chris 47
Costello, Elvis 31, 34, 41, 71–72, 75, 106, 121,
   133, 136, 145, 150, 163, 165, 191, 220, 222
Coward, Noel 5, 28, 56, 64, 96, 161, 174, 225,
   230, 232
Creedence Clearwater Revival 39, 151

Cropper, Steve 115, 167
Crosby, Bing 29
Crosby, David 89
Crudup, Arthur 32
Curtis, Sonny 11

D Records 211
Dailey, Pappy 211
Daniels, Chas 208
Danny and the Juniors 10
Danoff, Bill and Taffy 19
Davies, Ray 71, 91, 106, 111, 135, 224, 231, 233
Dawes, Charles Gates 4
David, Hal 68, 161, 164, 180
DeFreu, Marcia 137
DeKnight, Jimmy 195
Denver, John 19
Dervieux, Frank 232
DeSilva, Buddy 4, 102
Diamond, Neil 43, 193
Diamonds, the 131
Dickinson, Jim 111
Dickinson, Rev. Emmett 91
Diddley, Bo 67, 210–211
Dion 11
Dixon, Willie 6, 121, 142–143
Dolph, Norman 119
Donovan 86, 208
Dorsey, Tommy 32
Drake, Ervin 122
Durden, Tommy 210
Duritz, Adam 150
Dylan, Bob 3, 12, 28, 38–40, 42, 53, 56, 60, 62, 69–71, 76, 78, 81, 85, 93, 97, 99, 118, 120, 134, 140–141, 149–150, 153–154, 165–166, 218, 225, 232

Eagles, the 21, 40, 169
Earle, Steve 87, 177, 181
Ebb, Fred 185
Eikhard, Shirley 160

Ellington, Duke 32, 67, 73, 104
Ely, Joe 39, 67, 225
EMI Records 212
Eurythmics 162–163
Everly, Don 11, 69
Everly, Phil 70
Everly Brothers 15, 69

Fain, Sammy 231
Farina, Richard 79
Finn, Neil 46, 72, 135
Fjellgaard, Gary 41
Fleming, Kyr 164
Fogerty, John 151
Foster, Jerry 168, 222
Foster, Stephen 29, 77, 101, 136, 188–190, 208
Fox, Charles 232
Frantz, Chris 22
Freed, Alan 209
Freedman, Max 195
Freeman, Phil 38
Frey, Glenn 33, 95, 145, 164, 169, 180, 231, 233
Friedman, Gary William 161, 169
Frizzell, Lefty 29–30
Furth, George 168

Gabriel, Peter 48, 226
Gaff, Billy 212
Gant, Don 58
Garcia, Jerry 219
Gates, David 113
Gauthier, Claude 156
Gaye, Marvin 40
Gayle, Crystal 198
Gerard, Richard 190
Gershwin, George 34, 93, 191
Gershwin, Ira 168
Gilbert and Sullivan 27, 191
Gilbert and Theroux 4, 12, 19
Gill, Vince 162, 176, 186

Gimbel, Norman 18, 35, 102, 108, 132, 164
Ginsberg, Allen 204
Glover, Corey 155
Goffin, Gerry 12, 34, 75, 193–194
Golden Gate Quartet 32
Goldman, James 168
Goldsboro, Bobby 20, 59, 104, 121
Goldstein, Sidney 182
Goodman, Steve 47, 73
Goodrum, Randy 112, 181
Gordon, Elmer 208
Gordon, Mack 220
Gordy, Berry 34, 68
Grateful Dead 198
Greenfield, Howie 166, 194
Groce, Larry 123
Grossman, Albert 13, 205
Guthrie, Arlo 70, 102, 147
Guthrie, Woody 28, 39, 85, 101, 106, 114–115, 121, 129, 135–136, 141, 147, 153, 158

Haggard, Merle 80, 118, 122, 214, 230
Haley, Bill 2, 195
Hall, Joe 50
Hall, Tom T. 56, 59, 77, 81–82, 95, 125, 144
Hamilton IV, George 225
Hammerstein, Oscar 63
Hancock, Butch 184
Handy, W.C. 92, 111, 120
Harburg, E.Y. (Yip) 48
Hardin, Tim 38, 74
Harnick, Sheldon 183
Harris, Chas. K. 180
Harrison, George 16, 166, 184, 211, 219
Hart, Lorenz 64, 163
Hart, Moss 106
Hatfield, Juliana 24
Hawkins, Screamin' Jay 230
Hawkins Singers, Edwin 16

Hayes, Isaac 10, 167
Henderson, Ray 4
Hendrix, Jimi 24, 113
Henley, Don 169
Henry, Don 175, 202
Hiatt, John 59, 138, 214, 230
Highwaymen, the 208
Hitchcock, Robyn 115
Holden, Stephen 142
Holland, Dozier and Holland 68, 223
Holley, Lawrence 118
Holliday, Billie 206
Holly, Buddy 11, 15, 39, 69, 212
Holmes, Rupert 138
Hooker, John Lee 55
Hopkins, Lightnin' 38
Horne, Lena 225
House, Son 30, 112
Howard, Harlan 41, 49, 52, 55, 181, 209, 230
Howe, Bones 14
Hunter, Robert 198
Hynde, Chrissie 79

Ian and Sylvia 62, 198
Ian, Janis 17, 35, 41, 50, 56–57, 59, 75, 81, 88, 123–124, 126, 151, 164, 174, 180, 183–185, 195, 226, 230
Ice–T 134, 155
Iglesias, Julio 21
Ims, John 106
Ives, Burl 184, 200

Jackson, David 167
Jackson, Joe 72, 152, 157
Jackson, L'il Son 93
Jackson, Mahalia 32, 192
Jagger, Mick 34, 69, 163, 169, 201
James, Elmore 201
James, Etta 142
Jasen, David A. 107, 190–191, 195
Jennings, Waylon 78, 213

Joel, Billy 24, 57, 71, 75, 110, 132, 141, 157, 206–207, 231
John, Elton 163, 169
John, Little Willie 8
Johnson, Buddy 32
Johnson, George 63
Johnson, Rev. LeDell 92
Johnson, Lonnie 32
Johnson, Robert 65, 92, 111
Johnson, Tommy 92
Jolson, Al 4, 190, 192, 209
Jones, George 80, 93, 214
Jones, Jimmy 8
Jones, Quincy 120, 185
Jones, Rickie Lee 97, 106
Joplin, Janis 80, 233
Joplin, Scott 188–189
Jordan, Louis 32

Kaye, Chuck 171
Keller, Jock 194
Kelly, Gene 64
Kern, Jerome 46, 64, 192
King, B.B. 218
King, Ben E. 30
King, Carole 12, 34, 75, 192–194
Kingston Trio 14
Kirschner, Don 194
Knopfler, Mark 22, 53, 55, 93
Kostas 46, 133, 168
Kotke, Leo 174
Kristofferson, Kris 31, 38, 47, 74, 77, 118, 200–201

Lacy, Rev. Rubin 138
LaFarge, Peter 48, 56, 153
Lambert, Dennis 59, 108, 163, 170
Lane, Burton 167
Lanza, Mario 221
Larkin, Patty 175
Lauper, Cyndi 23, 223
Laurents, Arthur 168

Leadbelly 120
LeClerc, Felix 52, 120
Lee, Geddy 124
Lee, Peggy 8, 115
Lees, Gene 5, 109, 114, 129, 141
Leiber, Jerry 9, 155, 163, 191–192
Lennon, John 15–16, 41, 49, 54, 69–70, 90, 120, 132, 134, 164–165, 184, 201, 211, 233
Lennon, Julian 16
Lennox, Annie 52, 146, 162–163, 224
Lenya, Lotte 81, 150, 166
Lerner, Alan Jay 65, 71
Leslie, Edgar 191
Lewis, Furry 112
Lewis, Huey 24, 138, 143, 153, 186, 212
Lewis, Jerry Lee 66, 69
Light Crust Doughboys 30
Lightfoot, Gordon 14, 41, 62, 76, 101, 107, 123, 143, 183, 232
Lil Green 32
Little Eva 12
Little Richard 9, 30, 210
Lockwood, Robert 65
Loesser, Frank 35, 64
Loggins, Kenny 57, 74
Love, Courtney 79, 111
Lowe, Nick 142, 221

Macauly, Tony 122
Madonna 141
Malkmus, Steve 49
Manchester, Melissa 71–72, 94, 122, 138
Manilow, Barry 17, 143
Mann, Aimee 133
Mann, Barry 131, 162, 170, 193–194
Marks, Johnny 191
Marley, Bob 46, 70
Martin, George 134
Marvin and Tammy 195
May, Sylvia 112
Mayer, L.B. 5

McCann, Peter 101, 124, 177, 208
McCartney, Paul 15–16, 41, 54, 69, 71, 99, 106, 164–165, 170, 201, 211–212
McDermot, Galt 52, 82
McDill, Bob 19–20, 52, 58, 76, 93, 95, 101, 108, 124
McDonald, Michael 114, 176
McGarrigle, Anna 36
McGarrigle, Kate 29, 221
McGhee, Brownie 92, 153
McGuinn, Roger 70, 75
McGuire, Barry 13
McKennit, Loreena 109
McLachlan, Murray 132
McLean, Don 115
Mellencamp, John Cougar 23, 212
Mercer, Johnny 18, 65, 109, 112, 168
Messina, Jim 105
Meyer, Joe 209
Michael, George 120
Miller, Roger 42, 174
Milligan, H.V. 136
Mingus, Charles 75, 166
Miracles, the 34
Mitchell, Joni 45, 48, 50–51, 53, 62, 74–75, 77, 90, 95, 166, 175, 177, 186, 230–231
Moeller, Dee 208
Moffatt, Hugh 174
Moffatt, Katy 195, 202, 232
Monkees, the 182
Moon, Chris 141
Morrisey 145
Morrison, Bob 232
Morrison, Jim 113
Morrison, Van 42, 70, 79, 89, 94, 220
Mothers of Invention 36
Motown Records 223
Mouskouri, Nana 198

Near, Holly 51, 145
Neely, Bill 93

Neilson, Carl 73
Neilson, Rick 95
Nelson, Hugh 210
Nelson, Willie 21, 40, 50, 52, 77–78, 80, 86–87, 94, 124, 146, 180, 200–201, 204, 206–207, 211, 213, 223, 225–226, 233
Newbury, Mickey 77
Newman, Randy 21, 51, 56, 75–76, 115, 122, 137, 175
Newton, John 4
Neuwirth, Bob 161
Nevins, Al 194
New Riders of the Purple Sage 199
Nicks, Stevie 50, 78–79
Nilsson, Harry 69, 89, 103, 112, 182
Nixon, Mojo 155
Nyro, Laura 175

Ocasek, Ric 81, 129
Ochs, Phil 3, 149, 153
O'Connor, Sinead 114, 116, 146
O'Day, Alan 91, 117, 119, 182, 202
Oldham, Andrew 34, 201
Oliver, King 6
Orbison, Roy 11, 67, 113, 130
Oslin, K.T. 73
Owens, Buck 28

Page, Jimmy 74, 134
Palmer, Robert 117
Pareles, Jon 133
Parker, Charlie 73, 75
Parker, Colonel Tom 192, 200, 204, 209–210
Parker Jr., Ray 212
Parks, Van Dyke 47
Partch, Harry 76
Paxton, Tom 3
Payne, Leon
Peart, Neil 113, 147
Penguins, the 34
Penn, Dan 140
Peoples, Stephen 105

Perez, Louie 31, 151
Perkins, Carl 10, 41, 67–68, 230
Perls, Nick 133
Perren, Freddie 123
Peter, Paul and Mary 12, 62
Petty, Tom 53, 97, 137, 207, 225, 231
Piaf, Edith 5
Pickens, Slim 222
Pickett, Wilson 166–167
Pitney, Gene 30
Plamonden, Luc 125
Pomus, Doc 67, 75, 195, 209–210
Pop, Iggy 51, 147
Porter, Cole 5, 29, 105–107, 142, 161, 191, 219, 231
Porter, David 10, 167
Potter, Brian 34, 163, 170
Presley, Elvis 8, 29, 188, 192, 200, 204, 209–210
Price, Ray 201
Pierce, Webb 201
Prince 141, 186
Prine, John 42, 73–74, 76, 87, 105, 108, 113, 123, 138, 151, 223
Pyle, Chuck 175, 195

Raitt, Bonnie 73, 76, 102, 152, 154, 156
Ramsey, Ken 13
Ray, Amy 154
RCA Records 28–29
Redding, Otis 115, 167
Reed, Lou 54, 76, 131, 138, 141, 233
R.E.M. 22, 75, 115
Reynolds, Malvina 79, 132, 143
Rice, Bill 168, 222
Richards, Keith 34, 72, 86, 119, 140, 169, 233
Richie, Lionel 88, 134, 145
Ritter, Tex 30, 120, 222
Robbins, Marty 13
Roberts, Brad 20, 107
Robertson, Robbie 95, 154

Robinson, Bill 19
Robinson, Earl 119, 180
Robinson, Smokey 11, 34, 54, 67–68, 72, 79, 91, 94, 140, 144, 176, 222
Rodgers and Hammerstein 65, 71, 192
Rodgers and Hart 29, 71, 163, 192
Rodgers, Jimmie 6, 72, 93
Rogers, Richard 64, 71, 163
Rogers, Stan 76
Rogie, S.E. 89–90, 173
Rolling Stones 34, 69
Rollins, Henry 132, 135
Ronstadt, Linda 21, 222
Rose, Biff 171
Rose, Billy 192
Rosenfield, Monroe 189–190
Roth, David Lee 231
Rowan, Peter 181, 195
Russell, Tom 70, 120, 160

Sainte-Marie, Buffy 3, 40, 47, 96, 144, 153, 180, 195, 208
Sager, Carole Bayer 47, 110, 123, 194
Sam and Dave 10
Satherly, Art 208
Sayer, Leo 86, 89, 111, 231
Schlitz, Don 21, 95
Schwartz, Charles 105, 142
Schwartz, Eddie 85
Seals, Jim 75, 88
Sedaka, Neil 30, 35, 37, 56, 88, 116, 166, 192, 194
Seeger, Pete 38, 43, 79, 147, 153, 232
Seger, Bob 38
Shapiro, Elliot 200
Sharp, Dee Dee 12
Shaver, Billy Joe 49, 72, 77
Siberry, Jane 52, 79, 82, 132, 135, 226
Sigman, Carl 4
Simmons, Gene 81
Simmons, Patrick 102
Simon, Paul 55, 58, 62, 67, 71–72, 99, 103, 134

Simone, Nina 15
Simpson, Valerie 168, 182, 194–195, 220
Sinatra, Frank 10, 29, 115, 222
Skillings, Muzz 155
Sky, Patrick 153
Sloan, P.F. 12
Slim, Sunnyland 6
Smith, Kate 31
Smith, Kay 64
Smith, Michael 48
Snow, Hank 29, 58, 200, 206
Sondheim, Stephen 46, 104, 107, 110, 116, 124, 130–131, 133, 168, 181, 218
Souther, J.D. 21, 33, 72, 75, 94, 110, 112, 143, 223
Spandau Ballet 40
Spector, Phil 46, 74, 195
Springsteen, Bruce 23, 66, 132, 218
Stafford, Jo 31
STAX Records 167
Steinfels, Peter 4
Stevens, Ray 232
Stewart, Dave 97, 162–163
Stewart, John 33, 49–50, 79, 86, 182
Stewart, Jim 167
Stills, Stephen 59, 177, 182
Sting 22, 50, 88, 109, 130, 149–150, 156, 226, 233
Stipe, Michael 22, 115
Stoller, Mike 163, 191–192
Stone, Freddie 104
Stravinsky, Igor 73, 120
Streisand, Barbara 222
Strouse, Charles 65
Styne, Jule 47, 60, 64–65, 163–164, 222
Sun Records 68
Susskind, David 195

Talking Heads 22
Tampa Red 32
Taupin, Bernie 169
Taylor, James 42

Terry, Sonny 153
Thomas, Ian 170, 186, 194, 207
Thompson, Hank 30
Thompson, Richard 78, 96
Thorney, Tim 180, 195
Thornton, Big Mama 8
Thorpe, Sister Rosetta 32
Throckmorton, Sonny 56, 181
Tillis, Mel 18, 90, 102, 184, 201
Tillman, Floyd 30
Timmins, Michael 78
Tin Pan Alley 102, 114, 121, 182, 188–190, 192–193, 195
Torn, David 184
Toussaint, Allen 72
Townshend, Pete 47, 54, 71, 74, 79, 96, 109
Trooper, Greg 186, 202
Tubb, Ernest 29, 31
Turner, Big Joe 180
Tyler, Steven 87
Tyson, Ian 13, 179
Tyson, Sylvia 132

U2 186

Vallance, Jim 24
Van Zandt, Townes 38, 42, 77, 87, 95, 181, 206, 212
Vedder, Eddie 224
Vega, Suzanne 23, 33, 71, 76, 101, 118, 130, 135, 147, 151, 177, 227
Vigneault, Gilles 137, 152
Von Tilzer, Harry 189

Wainwright, Loudon 218
Waits, Tom 21, 37–38, 76, 81, 86, 103, 121–122, 131–132, 138, 174, 181, 193, 206, 225, 230, 233
Walker, Jerry Jeff 19, 80, 213
Walker, T–Bone 32, 55
Wallace, Sippie 6, 144

Waller, Fats 31
Warren, Diane 107
Warren, Harry 59, 94, 168, 186, 200, 208, 220
Washington, Booker T. 86
Waters, Muddy 6, 32, 55, 66, 92, 131, 213
We Five 198
Weatherly, Jim 34, 123, 174
Weavers, the 120
Webb, Jimmy 14, 30, 36–37, 57, 68, 74, 86–87, 111, 116–117, 119, 125, 129, 151, 174, 185, 201, 225
Webber, Andrew Lloyd 65
Weil, Cynthia 162, 170, 175–177, 193
Weill, Kurt 81, 141, 150, 166
Wells, Kitty 31, 198, 222
Westerburg, Paul 114
Wexler, Jerry 166
Whitcomb, Ian 4, 114, 189–191, 206
Wheeler, Hugh 168
White, Bukka 84, 86
White, Mark 63
White, Nancy 58, 112, 130, 232–233
Whitfield, Norman 68
Whiting, Richard 218
Wilkins, Rev. Rob 92–93
Williams, Hank 28, 30–31, 72, 85
Williams, Kim 20
Williams, Lucinda 118, 140
Williams, Paul 171
Willis, Allee 194
Wills, Bob 30
Wilson, Brian 141, 145
Wilson, Jackie 34
Wine, Tony 194
Winwood, Steve 57, 75, 227
Wonder, Stevie 54, 57, 69, 85, 150, 155–156, 223, 233
Woolcott, Alexander 64
Wyatt, Robert 89
Wynn, Steve 195

Young, Neil 37, 46, 58, 74, 96, 221, 233
Young, Steve 180

Zanes, Dan 39, 82, 119
Zanuck, Darryl 202
Zappa, Frank 32, 36, 97, 125, 143, 222, 226, 231–232
Zevon, Warren 51, 73, 76, 81, 103, 131, 207

ABOUT THE AUTHORS

Sylvia Tyson was part of the landmark folk and country duo Ian and Sylvia who recorded thirteen albums from the early sixties to the mid-seventies. She then embarked on a successful solo career and has recorded seven solo albums. She has headed up her own record label and publishing company, and has had a parallel career as a host, producer, researcher and writer for both radio and television. She has been a songwriter since 1962. She is active in several music industry associations, and in 1992 was inducted into the Canadian Music Hall of Fame. Her most recent project is an album with three other female singer/songwriters called Quartette. On March 1st, Sylvia received the Order of Canada.

Tom Russell has recorded eight albums of original material and co-produced records by Katy Moffatt, Barrence Whitfield, and Sylvia Tyson, as well as a current tribute to Merle Haggard. His songs have been recorded by Johnny Cash, Suzy Boggus, Ian Tyson, Dave Alvin, Jerry Jeff Walker, and Nanci Griffith. He received the 1993 ASCAP country award for "Outbound Plane," among the most performed songs of 1992. He is completing his first novel.